ARROWSMITH'S
DICTIONARY
OF
BRISTOL.

EDITED BY

HENRY J. SPEAR & J. W. ARROWSMITH.

Bristol:
J. W. ARROWSMITH, PUBLISHER, QUAY STREET.
1884.
All rights reserved.

This scarce antiquarian book is included in our special *Legacy Reprint Series*. In the interest of creating a more extensive selection of rare historical book reprints, we have chosen to reproduce this title even though it may possibly have occasional imperfections such as missing and blurred pages, missing text, poor pictures, markings, dark backgrounds and other reproduction issues beyond our control. Because this work is culturally important, we have made it available as a part of our commitment to protecting, preserving and promoting the world's literature. Thank you for your understanding.

PREFACE.

No apology is needed for the publication of a *Dictionary of Bristol*. Nothing of the kind has been attempted before, and the editors trust it will prove acceptable to the general public. It is not to be assumed that the information contained in the Dictionary is entirely original, but at least an immense amount of labour has been gone through to obtain that which will be found herein. All the histories of Bristol, from Barrett and Seyer down to Nicholls and Taylor *(Bristol: Past and Present)*, have been gone through, and for modern municipal affairs the city and contemporary records have been consulted.

Special articles have been supplied by the following gentlemen, and the thanks of the editors and the public are due to them: LEONARD BRUTON; C. H. COOTE, Map Department, British Museum, *Cor. Mem. New Eng. Hist. and General Soc., Boston U.S.A.*; J. W. CUNDALL; F. J. FARGUS; WM. GEORGE; A. E. HUDD; E. J. SHELLARD; Professor W. J. SOLLAS, M.A.; J. TAYLOR; J. W. WHITE.

The editors also desire to express their indebtedness to the various officials of the Corporation, also to the representatives of numerous Associations for their valuable assistance in the compilation of the work.

August, 1884.

ARROWSMITH'S
Dictionary of Bristol.

BRISTOL is situated in north latitude 51° 27′ 6·3″ and west longitude 2° 35′ 28·6″. The city lies on low ground, in a somewhat triangular basin formed by the valleys of the rivers Avon and Frome; the latter a small tributary from the north east, which flows through the picturesque little valley of Glen Frome, and not to be confounded with the larger stream passing by the town of that name. Where the Avon debouches from the Conham gorge, it spreads into a broad valley which it has lined with alluvial deposits. On this low land much of the old city is situated, viz., the parts round Temple street, Marsh street, Queen square and Canons' marsh, while High street and Redcliff hill stand on solid ground superior to the alluvial plain; part of the latter is so little above the level of high tide—though the city is seven miles by water from the mouth of the river—that at spring tide the waters have been found to overflow and fill the cellars of the houses which line the river in the Hotwells and Quays. The river Avon which here divides the counties of Gloucester and Somerset, also separates the city into two portions. The artificial bed or New Cut is excavated in the new red sandstone, which is not left uncovered along the natural course of the river, *i.e.*, the existing Floating Harbour.

But the population have long ago, in great measure, ceased to confine their dwellings to the low ground, and extending gradually up the hills, now crown all the heights with their houses, so that the Clifton Union district contains twice as many inhabitants as Bristol.

These hills are more or less broad table-lands, and we may speak of them as the north-western, the eastern plateaus, and southern ridge. The steep acclivities on the north, which we ascend in leaving Bristol, are seen to be the edge of a large plateau of palæozoic rocks structurally, though these are sometimes masked by later rocks, such as lias, lying upon them in discordant stratification; the inclines of Granby and Clifton hill (237 feet), Brandon hill (259 feet high), are descents from this high ground towards the Hotwells. Again, the end of this upland plateau extends eastward from here by Park street along Kingsdown parade (220 feet), from whose abrupt slopes the city, with its fine church towers, may be overlooked to great advantage. The whole of this ridge so far consists of the hard siliceous beds of the millstone grit,—dipping at a high angle with the rest of the palæozoic beds,—and these same grits also face the edge of the plateau on the Leigh down side of the river. To this plateau belongs Durdham down (312 feet), which is intersected by the Avon gorge, and that in so picturesque a fashion that Clifton must always be famous for its river scenery. The high land on the Leigh side is to all intents and purposes one and the same table-land with Durdham down, for the Clifton gorge has little to do with the structure of the country,—its formation is entirely subsequent to the upraising of the anticlinal arch of old red and carboniferous rocks which either continuously or in a series of echelons runs through the district from Clevedon to Tortworth. The renowned Avon gorge is but a notch in the ridge, a mark indeed of the tooth of time, but a small matter compared to the lengthened processes by which the old palæozoic rocks were raised in dome-shaped ridges, and were then cut down some 5,000 feet lower by the inexorable plane of denuding agents, till the shorn-off edges of the uplifted strata were left as the level table of Durdham down. The height of the Observatory hill, Clifton, is 315 feet, and that of Ashton Tump 270 feet.

To the south of the town extend the swelling slopes of Knowle and Totterdown, which extend round Dundry hill in a belt of intermediate height, and which has for its *raison d'être* the existence of nearly horizontal beds of lias limestones below, harder and more capable of resisting denuding forces than the clays which have been cut back at the intermediate base of Dundry hill. The summit of this hill is 769 feet above mean sea level; the solid jurassic beds which crown the ridge are in the same way the cause of the existence of this high ground, which bounds the horizon for a considerable sweep on the south.

On the east of the city we have irregular high land, with an average height perhaps of 180 feet. It extends from the river Frome on the north-east to the cliffs which bound the river Avon by Conham and Brislington: it consists for the most part of coal measures, and contains the sites of numerous coalpits. It is the hard sandstones (pennant) of the coal-period which are cut through by the Avon in the picturesque windings of the river by Conham.—E. B. TAWNEY, F.G.S., *Bristol and its Environs*.

Bristol's crowded thoroughfares teeming with life and activity; its busy marts of commerce, extensive manufactories, handsome public buildings and streets; civic, educational, commercial, scientific, religious and philanthropic institutions; its rapid increase in population, both in the city and environs, sanitary improvements, extension of docks and railways, erection of new and the restoration of old churches; its magnificent suburbs, public recreation grounds and palatial residences of merchants, manufacturers, traders and others, together with other memorable instances, all point to the fact that the city and port of Bristol has made rapid strides and is fully alive to the competition of modern times, and that it still retains its ancient prestige as one of the most important centres of the kingdom.

Agricultural Shows.

The first visit of the BATH AND WEST OF ENGLAND took place on June 13th to 17th, 1864, on Durdham Down; 33,800 persons paid for entrance, and the sum of £3,050 was taken for admission. The society's second visit to Bristol was on June 8th, 1874, on Durdham Down, but not upon the same site as in 1864. The money taken at the gates was £8,313, being nearly £1,800 more than had been taken at any previous exhibition; 110,120 paid for entrance.

The first visit of the ROYAL was on July 12th, 1842. The exhibition was held at the back of the Victoria Rooms; the ploughing, &c., at Sneyd Park. A splendid banquet was given at Merchants' Hall to H.R.H. the Duke of Cambridge and other distinguished visitors by the Mayor, G. W. Franklyn. The society visited Bristol a second time on July 9th, 1878, on which occasion H.R.H. the Prince of Wales honoured the city and the society by his presence. The total attendance was 123,051.

Aldermen.
The first election of Aldermen was made under the provisions of the "Municipal Reform Act," 1835 (*see* that heading, also "Municipal Elections" and

"Wards"), when sixteen gentlemen were elected as Aldermen (eldermen) at the first Town Council meeting under that Act, on 30th December, 1835. This election secured the preponderance of the Conservatives in the Council which they have ever since retained. Eight retire every three years, and the election to fill their places is made by the Town Council, but the eight retiring are disqualified from voting for their successors. Any gentleman refusing to serve as Alderman is liable to a fine of £50, in accordance with a by-law passed September 2nd, 1836, but may be remitted, and this is confirmed by the Municipal Corporations Act, 1882, sec. 34.

Analyst, City, appointed by the Town Council under the Adulteration of Food Act. His duties are to examine and test samples of food and drinks as to purity or otherwise, and the fees he receives from such are handed over to the City Treasurer. The Analyst's yearly allowance for laboratory and expenses connected therewith is £50. The appointment is held by F. W. Stoddart, and the laboratory is in the Freemasons' Hall, Park street.

Anchor Society. (See "Colston Societies.")

Ancient Bristol. William Worcestre describes the city as being fenced with massive walls, 8 feet in height, and at parts 6 feet in breadth. These had in their circuit no less than 25 strong embattled towers, and on a raised mound at the part most open to attack was erected a noble castle (see "Castle of Bristol"), fortified by outworks and bulwarks, and also by a massive keep. The original cruciform arrangement of the city is still indicated by the rectangular intersection of the four central streets, viz., Broad street, High street, Wine street and Corn street, which have continued from mediæval days to be the principal business thoroughfares.

Though the boundary walls no longer exist, yet the ancient gateway with its portcullis grooves at the lower end of Broad street is a typical feature of the old city that maintains its original position. From St. John's Gate the wall passed along Bell lane westward of St. Giles' Gate, which stood at the bottom of Small street; then winding through St. Leonard's lane to the gate of the same name at the bottom of Corn street, it coursed along St. Nicholas street in a line with the church, the chancel of which stood upon St. Nicholas' Gate, at the bottom of High street; it then went towards St. Peter's Church, nearly parallel with the river, and connected itself with the old gate in Narrow Wine street, opposite Chequer lane; then westward till it reached the site of the fourth house in Wine street, whence it diverted in a northerly direction to the Pithay, where was another gate; its course then was along Tower lane, and finally the wall swept along the right hand of St. John's lane to St. John's gateway. In addition to the foregoing, there was an external line of wall subsequently erected to enclose a greater area; of this latter the exact course has never been clearly made out, but for the most part it followed the banks of the Frome. From the Frome Gate the outer wall ran straight along the Quay westward to a strong tower opposite the Drawbridge; then changing its course it proceeded to Marsh Gate, at the end of Marsh street, and on by King street to the Avon, where it terminated. In the reverse direction it left the Frome Gate and joined a tower, partially incorporated with a modern wall in the Police Station in Bridewell street; then boldly sweeping round towards the present Union street, it finally joined Newgate and the Castle. Within this encircling of walls were to be found ancient churches (18 in Leland's time, 1540), monasteries, friaries, religious hospitals, and other buildings.

Almshouses.—The following is a list of Almshouses and the extra benefits attached. Almshouses marked thus, * are under the administration of the Charity Trustees.

ALMSHOUSES.	SITUATION.	FOUNDERS.	DATE OF FOUNDA-TION.	NO. OF INMATES. Male Female	Allowance per week, unless otherwise stated.	SPECIAL CONDITIONS, &c.
All Saints'	All Saints' st.	Stephen Gnowsall	1350	... 8	5/3 and extras	
*Barnstaple's or Trinity	Old Market st.	John Barnstaple	1402	13 47	7/-	Above 50 years of age
Ditto	ditto	Isabella Barnstaple		... 24	6/- and extras	
*Bengough's	Horfield road	H. Bengough	1818	5(a)15	7/-	(a) Five married couples
Blanchard's	Milk street	Miss E. Blanchard	1722	... 5	4/-	Baptist persuasion
Burton's	Long row	John Burton	1450	... 16	5/- and extras	
Clifton	Clifton hill	T. W. Hill		12		
Colston's	St. Michael's hill	Edward Colston	1691	12 16	7/- and coals	The elder brother 10/-. Prayers in the Chapel twice daily
*Foster's	Colston street	John Foster	1483	12 12	7/-	Four women elected by mayoress
Fry's	Colston parade	...		... 8	3/-	Single women
Merchant Seamen's	Great King st.	...	1696	19 12	6/- and extras	The elder brother 10/-. There are various other benefactions and out-pensioners receive 7/- per week
Merchant Tailors'	Merchant st.	Charter of Richard II.	1399	... ...	6/-	Nine apartments for tailors, widows or daughters of tailors

ALMSHOUSES.	SITUATION.	FOUNDERS.	DATE OF FOUNDATION.	NO. OF INMATES Male / Female	Allowance per week, unless otherwise stated.	SPECIAL CONDITIONS, &c.
Redcliff ...	Redcliff hill	Canynges	...	14	1/6	Some receive 2/-
Redcliff Poorhouse	Commercial rd.	...	...	11	3 have 2/3 fortnightly 8 ,, 2/-	
Ridley's ...	Milk street	Miss Ridley	1739	5 5	9/- fortnightly	Bachelors and spinsters
Spencer's ...	Lewin's mead	...	1493	16	2/6	From St. Peter's Hospital
St. James' Poorhouse	Whitson street	...	...	... 12	4/-	
St. John the Baptist	St. John's steep	Robert Strange	1490	... 7	3/5 and extras	
St. Nicholas ...	Great King st.	...	1652	... 16	Gifts and a weekly sum	From St. Peter's Hospital
St. Raphael's ...	Cumberland rd.	...	...	6 ...	Coals and allowance	Seamen
Stevens' ...	Old Market st.	Alderman Stevens	1679	16	5/-	Widows and daughters of Freemen
Ditto ...	Temple street	ditto	...	... 12	5/-	
Unitarian ...	Stokes' croft	...	1726	... 12	12/11 (per month)	
White's ...	Temple street	Thos. White, D.D.	1613	32	7/- and extras	

Arcades.

THE UPPER ARCADE extends from St. James' Barton to the Horsefair, and on the opposite side of this thoroughfare the LOWER ARCADE extends to Broadmead. These arcades were commenced in May, 1824, and opened in June, 1825, by three spirited individuals for the accommodation of the inhabitants of St. Paul's and Kingsdown, as affording a better communication with the centre of the city. Both of the arcades are covered in with glass roofs, shops being on either hand, occupied chiefly by second-hand dealers, especially in old literature. Ingress and egress to each arcade is obtained by flights of stone steps.

Archæological Society,

The Bristol & Gloucestershire originated with John Taylor, of the Bristol Museum and Library. The inaugural meeting was held on April 22nd, 1876, at the Bristol Museum and Library, under the presidency of the Lord-Lieutenant of the County, the Earl of Ducie. Gloucestershire had long been wanting in archæological organisation. Nature itself, indeed, may be said to have prepared her both by structure and position for the theatre of those historic energies and events of which a rich antiquity is the vestige. Occupying the lower courses of the largest river system and river valley in Great Britain, she has always commanded, whether for war or commerce, the ports and maritime passes of the West. Occupying, too, the considerable heights that fortify the opposite sides of this river valley, she commands what is perhaps at once both physically and historically the chief border land of the island—a border land which, having the Welsh mountain fastnesses on the one side, and the Midland hills on the other, has formed a natural battle-ground for all the competing races and most of the contending parties in the development of our country. The objects of the society are as follow :— (1) To collect and classify original and existing information on the antiquities of this district, and to thus accumulate materials for an improved county history. (2) To establish a library and museum for the preservation and study of these and other objects of antiquarian value. (3) To promote, by meetings, publications, &c., such an interest throughout the district in the monuments of its past history as shall tend to counteract their present liability to inconsiderate and needless destruction. The terms of admission are :—As life members, for a composition of £5 15s. 6d. (entrance fee 10s. 6d., life payment £5 5s.); as annual members, for a payment of £1 1s. (entrance fee 10s. 6d., annual payment 10s. 6d.) Application for election to be made to the General Secretary, Rev. Wm. Bazeley, Matson, Gloucester.

Architecture. *(See* "Street Architecture.")

Architects' Society.

After a lapse of 17 years, this society, which at one time had great influence in the West of England, is now in progress of reorganisation. W. J. Jones, Prince street, hon. sec.

Artillery Volunteer Corps. *(See* "Volunteers.")

Ashley Down

was in ancient time called the manor of Asseley, and was granted by charter to the monks of St. James' Priory by William of Gloucester in 1170. This and other charters relating to the priory are still preserved in the Museum and Library.

Assembly Rooms,

Prince street, once a fashionable concert hall, now used as a warehouse. The front is built with freestone, and consists of a rustic basement, which supports four double columns of the Corinthian order, over which is a pediment. In front are inscribed the words *Curas cithara tollit* ("music is a specific for care"), which is only suggestive of the sweet memories of its past experience.

Assize Courts, Small st., built upon the site of Colston's house, in the Perpendicular Gothic style, erected in 1870. Within its walls are held the Courts of Assize and Quarter Sessions, the Tolzey and County Courts. The Incorporated Law Society and the Bristol Incorporated Chamber of Commerce and Shipping also occupy portions of the building. Some of the most interesting relics of ancient domestic architecture in the city are preserved and enshrined here. In the witnesses' waiting-room is a fine 17th century freestone chimneypiece, preserved from a room, now destroyed, in which Joanna Southcott used to preach. In the Law Library are remains of the 12th century: they consist of some clustered piers with cushion capitals of a grand Norman hall, divided by two ranges of arches. The roof is of panelled oak; it was once the private chapel of the building wherein Charles I. and his two sons were entertained in 1643 by Edward Colston. A finely carved chimneypiece in the Renaissance style has been refixed in the adjoining room. The Chamber of Commerce board-room contains the handsome stone mullioned windows in the three stages of the Tudor period, panelled ceiling and Perpendicular Gothic chimneypiece.

Athenæum, Corn street. The institution was begun in 1844, at the Assembly Rooms, Prince st. The present building was opened in October, 1854, by a company of shareholders, at a cost of £6,500. Lord John Russell delivered the inaugural address. The institution is an expansion of the Mechanics' Institute and the Church Book Association. It is entered by corridors from Corn street and St. Nicholas street, and contains on the ground floor a spacious reading-room, lecture-room, library, ladies' room, secretary's office, &c. In the vestibule is an ornamental iron staircase which leads to the committee and class-rooms and offices. A stranger can be introduced by a subscriber. The provision of London, local and provincial papers, also magazines, serials, &c., is liberal. The library contains 14,000 volumes, and is constantly augmented by the newest works. Annual day subscription, 27/-; evening, 13/6. Secretary, Mr. Robert C. W. Ross.

Athletics. Clubs for the practice of varied sports exist in great numbers, and mention is made of the principal ones under their alphabetical headings.

Autographs. In the Council House are several autograph letters of acceptance of the freedom of the city (*see* "Freedom of the City") from Sir Thomas Lawrence, Lord Nelson, Lord Rodney, Lord Hood, the Duke of Wellington, and others. Also, the original articles of the surrender of the city to Prince Rupert, in July, 1643.

Avon. This river is sometimes called the Lower Avon, to distinguish it from the Upper, or Warwickshire. It rises in the hilly district of North Wiltshire, not far from Wotton Basset; but various springs are assigned for its origin, as well as that of the Thames, from whose numerous sources it is not far distant. Emerging from the hills, it makes a compass to fall into the vale which leads from Christian Malford to Chippenham, after which its windings are numerous and sharp as it advances through the county of Wilts, bordering upon that of Somerset, and for some space divides the two counties. Its course is at first southward, and it makes a long compass by the west towards the north, and then to the west, at last encircling the city of Bath on two sides, from whence it pursues nearly the same direction with frequent meanders to Bristol. It then inclines to the north-west, and eventually reaches the Bristol Channel at Kingroad.

Avonmouth Dock. (*See* "Docks.")

Banks. Bristol possesses very good banking accommodation, and most of the establishments having been specially built for the purpose, the internal arrangements are all that can be desired. The first bank in Bristol was opened, in 1750, by Messrs. Elton, Lloyd, Miller, Knox and Hale, at the premises now occupied by Messrs. Osborne, Ward, Vassall and Co., Broad street, and at that time there was no other banking-house out of London, except one kept by a Jew at Derby. On December 20th, 1825, Messrs. Browne, Cavenagh, Browne and Bayly, Bullion Bank, Corn street, suspended payment. The Branch of the Bank of England (which first commenced business here on the site of the Bank Hotel, Bridge street, in 1827) adjoins the Guildhall, Broad street. It is in the Grecian style, with Doric pillars, surmounted by a handsome pediment. The London and South Western Bank, upon the site of St. Werburgh's Church, is an elaborate building; it is only partially completed in consequence of a dispute with the Commercial Rooms' authorities. The Bristol and West of England Bank Limited commenced business on February 1st, 1879. It stands on the site of the once famous Bush Tavern. The present structure is elaborately ornamented in the Venetian Renaissance style. The lower story is Doric, and the upper Ionic. Emblematic sculptures of the towns in which the original company had branches adorn its front. The carved keystones represent the rivers Avon, Severn, Taff and Usk, and the Bristol Channel. The practical art of the moneyer is represented in groups of boys, life size, personating die-sinking, coining, bank-note printing, &c., and commercial relations with the four quarters of the globe. The interior is fireproof, well lit, commodious and lofty; its cellarage is perfect, and it is said to be perfection itself for banking purposes. The old company, named the West of England and South Wales District Bank, opened these premises on the 2nd February, 1857, and on the 9th December, 1878, closed with liabilities which amounted to upwards of £3,200,000. This stoppage caused a panic throughout the West of England and South Wales. Within a short space the new company was formed on a smaller scale, and is in a very prosperous condition. Portions of the premises not required by the bank are let off to insurance companies, &c.

The following is a list of Bristol banks and their London agents:—

BRISTOL AND WEST OF ENGLAND BANK LIMITED, Corn street. General managers, J. Dester and G. J. Pickin. Branches: Haberfield Crescent, North street, 19 West street and 88 Redcliff street. Draw on Union Bank, London.

BRISTOL BRANCH BANK OF ENGLAND, Broad street. Agent, F. Howard; Sub-Agent, Walter Nisbet.

BRISTOL COMMERCIAL UNION BANK, Quay street.

CAPITAL AND COUNTIES BANK LIMITED, 6 Victoria street (about removing to premises in Clare street). Manager, J. E. Mills. Branch at Southampton Parade, Redland. Draw on Head Office, Threadneedle street, London.

CHEQUE BANK LIMITED. Agent, T. Thatcher, 44 College Green.

LONDON AND SOUTH WESTERN BANK LIMITED, Corn street. Manager, F. L. Jermyn. Draw on Head Office, 7 Fenchurch street, London.

MILES, CAVE, BAILLIE AND CO., Corn street. Manager, H. F. Price. Branch at Mall, Clifton. Draw on Prescott, Cave and Co., and Barnetts, Hoares and Co., London.

NATIONAL PROVINCIAL BANK OF ENGLAND LIMITED, 36 Corn street. Manager, A. C. Smith. Draw on Head Office, London.

STUCKEY'S BANKING COMPANY, Corn street. Managers, W. G. Coles, J. C. Aiken and Alfred Deedes. Branches: Royal Promenade, Queen's road, and 181 Whiteladies' road, Redland. Draw on Robarts, Lubbock and Co., London.

WILTS AND DORSET BANKING COMPANY, Corn street. Manager, W. T. Mavius. Branch: Regent street, Clifton. Draw on London and Westminster Bank.

All the foregoing are open from 10 a.m. to 3 p.m., except on Saturdays, when they close at 1 p.m.

BRISTOL SAVINGS BANK, St. Stephen's Avenue. Established 1812. Secretary, C. H. J. Vining. Open daily from 10 a.m. to 3 p.m., and on Saturdays from 7 to 8 p.m. Sums as low as one shilling may be deposited. As showing the popularity of the institution, it may be mentioned that on Nov. 30th, 1882, there were 13,561 depositors, from whom, during the year, there had been received £99,025.

PENNY SAVINGS BANK. Established in 1859. Open from 7 to 9 on Monday evenings, at the Guildhall, Broad street. In 1882 there were 17,072 depositors, and the amount received was £1,506 15s. Actuary, F. W. Waite, 47 Nicholas street.

There are also Penny Banks connected with Sunday Schools and Missions throughout the city.

POST OFFICE SAVINGS BANKS, at Head Office (Small street), Clifton, Temple Gate, North street, Redcliff, Ashley road, Cheltenham road, Bedminster, Cotham, Hotwells, Horfield, Lawrence Hill, Queen's road, Redland, Stapleton road, Totterdown, West street, Newfoundland street, Woodwell Crescent and Park street.

Baptist College, Stokes' Croft, an institution for educating young men for the ministry in connection with the Baptist denomination. It was commenced in 1679, when Mr. Terrill, by deed, devised a large portion of his estates for the maintenance of "a holy learned man well skilled in the tongues—viz., Greek and Hebrew, one who doth own and practise the truth of believers' baptism." He was to devote three half-days in the week to the instruction of "some young men, not exceeding twelve, who were members of any baptised congregation in or about Bristol for two years at the most." The bequest did not come into operation until the year 1720. The Rev. Bernard Foskett was tutor, and the first student was Thomas Rogers, of the Pithay Chapel. In 1770 the Bristol Education Society was formed through the exertions of Dr. Caleb Evans, as an additional aid to Mr. Terrill's bequest, with which it continues united. During the early part of the present century it became well known as the Baptist Academy. There are some choice treasures amongst the stores of its library, many fine editions of the Bible, some of them of great age, the chief being the only perfect copy of Tyndale's translation of the New Testament (1526), and a miniature on ivory of Oliver Cromwell, for which the Empress Catherine of Russia offered 500 guineas. This college has been very successful, many of the most eminent scholars and preachers of the Baptist persuasion having been trained therein. The course of study is four years. The number of students averages about 25. Dr. F. W. Gotch, D.D., one of the revisers of the New Testament, was the principal for many years.

Baptist Mills comprises a large and increasing district. There are two reasons assigned from which it derives its name. In 1651 a doubt arose as to the scriptural validity of infant baptism, it being argued that as John the Baptist baptised in

Jordan, so the true Gospel example was fluvial immersion; many, therefore, in the Frome renewed their baptism—a circumstance that gained the name of "Baptist Mills" to one passage of that river. There is also a tradition that some French cambric weavers came over to England about 1743 and settled at this place, the word "baptist" being derived from *baptiste*, meaning "cambric."

Barracks. These are situated in the parish of Horfield, two miles from Stokes' Croft, on the great North road. The foundation stone was laid on June 3rd, 1845, by the Right Worshipful Deputy Provincial Grand Master and the Freemasons of Bristol, by permission of Her Majesty's Board of Ordnance. The ceremony was an imposing one; the mayor, sheriffs, corporation, and the local military authorities being in attendance, headed by the band of the 75th Regiment. The barracks are occupied as a depôt, having accommodation for 350 infantry and 112 horses. Adjoining the barracks is the Garrison Church, opened in 1857. During the past two years the barracks have been enlarged.

Barristers. Practising in the city are eleven in number.

Baths and Washhouses. The Corporation of the city have erected two sets of baths and washhouses—one on the Broad Weir, opened August 12th, 1850, and the second in the Mayor's Paddock, New Cut, opened May 1st, 1870. The charges for use of the baths, which may be had hot, cold, shower or swimming, range from sixpence to one penny. Open from 7 a.m. to 8.30 p.m. (Sundays excepted), and on Fridays and Saturdays to 9.30 p.m. At the Broad Weir is a laundry, at which, for the nominal charge of one penny per hour, each woman is provided with a place to herself, hot and cold water, a house in which to dry the clothes, and conveniences for ironing. There are also the following swimming baths: Rennison's, Picton street; Popham's, Kingsdown; and Victoria, Oakfield Place, Clifton. There are Turkish baths in College street and the Royal Promenade, Clifton. There are also baths in Zion Row, Clifton, and in College Green.

Beating the "Bounds" is generally done every ten years. It is an ancient custom, and was instituted for the purpose of inspecting the boundaries of the city. This is done by the Mayor and officials. The boundaries were first beaten, according to the new Boundary Act, on September 27th and 28th, 1841. It has also been done on the following subsequent dates:— October 14th and 15th, 1852; August 10th and 11th, 1863; August 20th, 1863 (water boundary to the Flat Holms); September 8th, 1863 (river boundaries to Hanham Mills), and in the autumn of 1874.

Bedminster is a large parish on the south side of Bristol, with which it is connected by two bridges, and forms a considerable portion of the borough of Bristol. The manor of Bedminster was the property of the Crown, but was granted by William Rufus, with the greater part of the hundred and other possessions, to Robert Fitz-Hamon, whom he created Earl of Gloucester. From him it came into the possession of Robert Fitzhardinge, son of the governor of Bristol. In 1416 it passed, by marriage, to Richard Beauchamp, Earl of Warwick, and again by marriage to the Duke of Buckingham. It reverted to the Crown in the reign of Henry VIII. Henry Bourchier, Earl of Essex, subsequently possessed it, from whom it passed to the Nevills, and was sold by them to the Smyths of Ashton Court. The parish is in the county of Somerset, and is the only one in the county not included in the diocese of Bath and Wells, but belonging to Gloucester. It contains a number of compact houses, and some of its streets will bear comparison with any of the east suburbs of London, as Spitalfields and Bethnal Green, in density of population. The population of this district, according to the census of 1861, was 19,924; in 1871, 28,123; and in 1881, 44,747.

Bells and Bell-ringing

have from time immemorial proved to be a prominent feature in the history of Bristol. Amongst the old wardens' accounts may be mentioned the following:—"St. James': In 1572, payd for lycher at to (2) times to lycher the bells, 11d. In 1585, payd to the ringers for the ringing the hold yeare corful, 2/-. In 1586, paid to the ringers when the Earl of Pembroke came to the city, 1/-. In 1638, paid to the ringers the 17th November, being Queen Elizabeth's coronation day, 1/–," which is repeated on to 1642. "In 1641, to the ringers at the retourne of the King from Scotland, 10/4. In 1665, paid to the ringers when my Lord Bishop came, 2/6." The principal churches with peals of bells are those of St. Mary Redcliff, St. James', All Saints', St. Nicholas', Christ Church, St. Michael's, St. Peter's, St. Stephen's, St. Matthew's, and St. Andrew's, Clifton. (*See* also " Ringers.")

Benefit Societies.

BRISTOL, WEST OF ENGLAND AND SOUTH WALES NEWSPAPER PRESS FUND. Established 15 years, for the relief of reporters in necessitous circumstances. The only fund of the kind in the kingdom. The members of the fund, together with their friends, hold an annual dinner, which is looked forward to as the most enjoyable of the year. W. Grogan, of the *Bristol Mercury and Post*, is the president; T. Bradford, *Bristol Times and Mirror*, hon. sec.

CALEDONIAN BENEVOLENT. For the relief of unfortunate, but deserving, Scotchmen. Established in 1820. During the year 1882 it gave assistance to 280 poor mechanics, &c., and 38 Scotch families and three poor persons are annuitants. The society meets on Friday evenings, at eight o'clock, at Mr. Stevens' office, Nicholas street. Treasurer, John M'Cartney, Redcliff hill.

CAMBRIAN SOCIETY. Established for the purpose of promoting friendly intercourse among the Welsh residents in Bristol and for general benevolent purposes. The annual dinner is held on St. David's Day. Treasurer, W. Thomas, 9 John street.

DRUIDS, ANCIENT ORDER OF. There are 25 lodges in the Bristol and West of England district, representing 1,206 members. The Provincial Arch Conclave meet the first Monday in each month, at the Full Moon, Broad street.

FORESTERS, ANCIENT ORDER OF. The Bristol United District consists of 99 courts, comprising 10,320 members. Over £13,200 was distributed in this district during the year 1881. The registered office is 48 Castle street, where the District Secretary may be seen Mondays, Wednesdays and Fridays, from 7 to 9 p.m., and Thursdays 1 to 2 p.m.

FREE GARDENERS, ANCIENT ORDER OF, SCOTTISH UNITY, have seven lodges in the city, including the Provincial Grand Lodge; the latter meets quarterly at the Athenæum, Corn street, on the last Mondays in January, April, July and October, at eight o'clock p.m.

ODDFELLOWS, INDEPENDENT ORDER OF, MANCHESTER UNITY. District offices, Rupert street. The number of lodges returned in the Bristol district is 29, and the number of members 2944. The provincial corresponding secretary is Thos. Adams, Bridge street Hall.

PAWNBROKERS' ASSISTANTS' BENEVOLENT SOCIETY meets at The George, Narrow Wine street.

SHEPHERDS, LOYAL ORDER OF ANCIENT. The Bristol District branch numbers over 7,000, and the worth of the district, exclusive of widow and orphan and juvenile funds, is £30,000. The District house of the society is the Cat and Wheel, Castle Green.

Benevolent Institution, The, has been established 13 years. Every candidate must have resided or carried on business or profession for seven consecutive years within the municipal boundary of Bristol, and during that period have occupied, as owner or tenant, a dwelling-house rated for the relief of the poor at not less than £25 per annum, or unfurnished rooms of the same value; or a house and business premises together, rated to the relief of the poor at not less than £40, or unfurnished business or offices of equal value; or individually have rented room and steam power of the annual value of £100 and upwards; or rented room and machinery of the annual value of £100 and upwards, irrespective of poor rates; or be the widow of a person who was so qualified, and have attained the age of 55 years, in which case she is entitled to add her late husband's residence or occupation to her own, in order to make the required term of seven years: this rule has since been extended to unmarried daughters (who have attained the age of 60 years and have been left dependent on their own efforts) of parents so qualified. The amount of each annuity is at the discretion of the committee, but in the case of males it does not exceed £24 per annum, or females £18 per annum, unless the applicant (or, in case of a widow or daughter, her deceased husband or parent) has been a member of the institution for five consecutive years, in which case the annuity may be to a male £30, and to a female £22 per annum. An annual subscription of one guinea constitutes membership, and a donation of ten guineas at one time life membership, and for every additional subscription of one guinea, or donation from a life member of ten guineas, the voting power is increased *pro rata*. Attached to the institution is a Ladies' Association, which enables every lady, whether a subscriber to the institution or otherwise, who secures new subscriptions, to the amount of five guineas and upwards, to secure the privilege of a vote for every five guineas so obtained, such privilege to continue as long as the said five guineas be kept up. Privileges of a corresponding value are allowed for all donations of ten guineas and upwards obtained in like manner. Every such donation entitles the lady gaining it to a vote for the year in which it is given, and whenever the donations so obtained reach in the aggregate to 30 guineas she is entitled to a vote for life at every election. There are now 56 annuitants upon the funds. E. T. Collins, 39 Broad street, secretary.

Benevolent Society for Ladies, 2, Portland street, Clifton. It is instituted for the purpose of assisting ladies in necessitous circumstances. This is done in a variety of ways, but the most general is by disposing of needle and other work, useful and fancy, either at the institution or at a special sale held annually, which affords an opportunity to ladies of reduced or limited incomes of helping themselves. The society admits 50 members, some of whom are invalids. The last report is a very encouraging one, and mentions, among other things, that by rearing poultry and keeping bees the funds of the society have been augmented. An executive committee of four ladies superintends the rules, orders, &c., whereby a good and truly benevolent work is being accomplished. Secretary, Miss Walker, 4 Buckingham Villas.

Bibles, Old. In All Saints' Church, Corn street, is a copy of Matthew's edition of Tyndale and Coverdale, blotted and raddled by Papal authority, 1534. In this edi-

BIB   DICTIONARY OF BRISTOL.   BIS

tion the 5th verse of the 91st Psalm reads—

"So that thou shalt not nede to be afrayed for any bugges by night, etc."

The Free Library in King street contains a vellum bible of the 13th century. (*See* "Baptist College" for the copy of Tyndale's translation of New Testament.)

Bible Society. The Bristol Auxiliary is at 6 Park street. Subscribers may obtain Bibles and Testaments on low terms of the society.

Bicycling. The majority of the country roads around Bristol are favourable for this sport, and contests frequently take place.

BRISTOL CLUB. Head-quarters, The Swan, Bridge street; number of members, 116; established August, 1876. The club is open to amateurs only. Uniform, grey knickerbocker suit, stockings, special jockey cap and club badge. Racing colours, black and yellow. Captain, Fred. Brock, Temple Gate.

CLIFTON CLUB. Formed in February, 1876. This is the oldest club in the city, and is open to amateurs only. Head-quarters, Queen's Hotel, Clifton. Uniform, grey suit, round cap with monogram C.B.C. Number of members, 40. G. Ashmead, Glenthorn, Alma Vale, Clifton, hon. sec. As the tricycle is now coming so much into use, users of this means of locomotion are admitted as members to the club, and a separate detachment is being formed for their convenience at the runs.

CYCLING CLUB. Formed in Jan., 1883, having its head-quarters at the Grand Hotel; also includes tricyclists amongst its (30) members. S. Young, Florence House, Coronation road, hon. sec.

JOCKEY CLUB. Head-quarters, The Angel, Redcliff street; number of members, about 30. Uniform, grey suit, with jockey cap.

WEST GLOUCESTERSHIRE CLUB. Uniform, blue, gold monogram in cap. J. W. Bartlett, 26 Apsley road, Clifton, hon. sec.

Most of the bicyclists of Bristol are members of the Bicycle Union, founded in 1878. Its main objects are to secure a fair and equitable administration of justice as regards the rights of bicyclists on the public roads, to examine the question of bicycle racing in general, to frame definitions and recommend rules, and to arrange for annual race meetings at which the Amateur Championship shall be decided. The present membership in the Local Centre is 442, and they annually promote a large Bicycle Meet, which is held at the Clifton Zoological Gardens.

Bishopric of Bristol. The first bishop was Paul Bush, who was consecrated in 1542, and including him and the present the city has had 46 bishops, the four last being united with the see of Gloucester, which took place on the 17th of October, 1836. Dean Elliott and the Chapter, in pursuance of the *congé d'élire*, elected Dr. Charles John Ellicott to the bishopric of the united sees in 1863. Value of see, £5,000. Chancellor, C. J. Monk, M.P.

Bishop's College and Bristol College. The former was opened August 17th, 1840, temporarily in a house in Bellevue, Clifton, until the building at the top of Park street, and adjoining that of the Blind Asylum, was purchased by the Bishop of Gloucester and Bristol (Dr. Monk), and conveyed to the college on the security of mortgage. This structure was originally erected for the Red Maids' School, but was never occupied for that purpose, the boys of the college being the first inmates. The late Duke of Beaufort and the Bishop were the patrons. This college was emphatically a Church of England school, and was started in opposition to the BRISTOL COLLEGE, which was opened on the 17th January, 1831, in the house formerly occupied by Mr. Matthew Wright, in Park Row, which has

13

since been razed for the construction of Perry Road. The college just ran out ten years, and closed at Christmas, 1841. During its existence it did good work, and turned out boys who afterwards distinguished themselves as men in various departments. The college was largely, but not wholly, in the hands of Liberals and Dissenters.

Bishopston, an ecclesiastical district, is formed out of the parishes of Stapleton, Horfield and Montpelier. Of late years it has been very extensively built upon.

Blanket. To Bristol belongs the honour of having first made this necessary article of domestic use. *Baker's Chronicle* records that in "1340, soon after the revival of the trade in England, a citizen of Bristol, named Thomas Blanket, and several other inhabitants of this city, set up looms in their own houses for weaving those woollen cloths from him called blankets." In the reigns of Henry II. and Richard I. the woollen trade in England was carried on with a fair amount of success, but afterwards appears to have been lost, the English people purchasing their cloth from foreigners, principally Flemings. At that time English wool was superior to most, and, in order to revive the industry, it was enacted that no English wool should be exported, and that none except the King, Queen, and privileged persons should wear cloths made beyond the sea. It was no doubt in consequence of these regulations that Thomas Blanket (baillie in Bristol in 1342) and others set up looms in their houses. On this account they were favoured by the King, for when the authorities—instigated thereto by other trades, particularly the weavers—levied a rate on them for setting up machines, &c., he wrote a letter relieving them from the burden.

Blanket Loan Society. Established in 1855. It performs a very useful work during the winter months amongst the poor of Clifton and Hotwells. Depôt-keeper, R. Whitehead, 9 Meridian Vale, Clifton.

Blind Institutions.

BLIND ASYLUM, or School of Industry for the Blind, stands at the top of Park street; established in 1793. The building is in the Tudor Gothic style, and was erected in 1836. It measures 1a. 2r. 13p., and cost £1,850. A spacious lecture-hall is attached to the building. About 60 inmates of both sexes, from all parts of England, here find a comfortable home, and are taught a number of trades. The work of the inmates is principally basket-making and rug-weaving, and is much sought after on account of its neatness and ingenuity. Its support is derived from the sale of work, from subscriptions, donations and legacies. The institution is open free to the public on Mondays, Wednesdays and Thursdays, from 11 to 12 a.m., and from 2 to 4 p.m. On Mondays, at 3 p.m., the inmates give a concert of sacred music. A new wing was added in January, 1883. Its elevation harmonises with the old portion of the structure, and is 48 feet long, 23 feet wide, and 24 feet high; it is used as the sale and music instruction room.

BRISTOL AND CLIFTON ASSOCIATION FOR THE HOME-TEACHING OF THE BLIND, in Park Row. In connection with the home-teaching branch of the society the blind are visited in their own homes, and taught to read the raised type, of which there is a large lending library belonging to the institution, books being circulated amongst the blind by three teachers. In the industrial branch women and girls are taught knitting and chair caning, and paid weekly according to the amount of work done.

Board of Trade. Local offices, 32 Prince street. Open 10 a.m. to 4 p.m.; Saturdays, 10 a.m. to 2 p.m. The members of the Local Marine Board are twelve in number, including the Secretary.

The board is appointed under the provisions of the Merchant Shipping Acts, its duty being to take cognisance of infringements of those Acts. The officers are:—One superintendent and deputy of the Mercantile Marine. The superintendent for the transfer of Lascars for the port of Bristol is appointed by the Secretary of State for India. One examiner in navigation and seamanship for the Bristol Channel ports; one examiner of engineers for the Bristol Channel district; inspector of ships' lights and fog signals; and emigration officer and surveyor. Board meetings are held on the first Thursday in each month. Examinations in navigation and seamanship, second Tuesday in the month; and for engineers, fourth Tuesday in each month. Secretary, James Inskip.

Book of Wills, The Great, preserved in the Council House, supplies several instances of bequests to the various parishes. It dates from 1382 to 1554; two register-books, from 1594 to 1633, and 1633 to 1674. The Great Red Book contains chiefly ordinances, &c., of the dates of the reigns of Henry VI. and Edward IV. The Little Red Book is of earlier date, from 1344 to 1574. The Mayor's Audit Book, 1532. The Great White Book of Records, 1496 to 1590, and many minute-books of the meetings of the Corporation, admissions of freemen and expenditure, are preserved in the Council House.

Borough (or Bower) Walls, Clifton. Overlooking the Avon, these existed a few years since in their original state. A Belgic British camp formerly existed here; it was triangular in form, and protected on two of its sides by the natural acclivities of its elevated situation. (*See* "Sea Walls.")

Boundaries of the City. The boundary of the city within its ancient limits comprised 755 acres. In 5 and 6 William IV. (1835) the Municipal Corporations Reform Act was passed, by which the city was extended, to include within its boundaries the adjoining parish of Clifton, the out-parishes of St. James and St. Paul and St. Philip and Jacob, with portions of the parishes of Bedminster and Wesbury-on-Trym, by which the area, included in the city, was increased to 4,879 acres, with a circuit of about 15 miles. The water boundaries of the city are the river Avon (high water mark), from Hanham Mills to Kingroad, and the Bristol Channel to the Holms, and up the Severn as far as Aust Cliffs, in a straight line from the Denny. The foregoing, for magisterial jurisdiction, are considered in the city and county of Bristol, in the parish of St. Stephen's, that being formerly the nearest parish church adjacent to the river.

Boys' Homes. (*See* "Homes.")

Brandon Hill, approachable from Park street or Hotwell road, is the property of the Corporation of the city of Bristol. It was one of the chief defences of the city during the sieges of 1643-4, and many of the pits, forts, and trenches may be readily traced. It is 259 feet in perpendicular height and 25 acres in extent. From the summit the grandest panoramic view of the city and surrounding neighbourhood is obtained, and here on August 19th, 1857, were planted two 36-pounder Russian guns captured in the Crimean war; here, too, once stood a Gothic hermitage, the first inhabitant of which was Lucy de Newchurch, whose disappointment with the world induced her to importune the Bishop of Worcester to allow her to seclude herself and become an anchoress. The hill is pleasantly laid out with winding walks, seats, &c. Tradition asserts that Queen Elizabeth conferred the privilege on the Bristol washerwomen, that the right of drying their clothes on the

Hotwells' side of the hill should be reserved to them for ever.

Brass Pillars. Four in number, in front of the Exchange, Corn street. They were used by the merchants in lieu of tables for making payments, writing letters, etc., and from their form were sometimes called "nails," which is said to have given rise to the phrase "to pay down on the nail." One at least was removed from the Tolzey before the Council house in 1771, the others probably came from the colonnade under All Saints' Church on the opposite side of the street. The first (nearest to Wine street) stood in the old Tolzey in 1550 and is much worn by time and use. The second pillar is inscribed in Latin on its face, and in Roman capitals—

"THEY HAVE RELATED THAT WHICH IS UNWORTHY OF NOTE · WHAT IS WORTHY OF PRAISE THEY HAVE OMITTED · NO MAN LIVES TO HIMSELF · "

Between this inscription appears a very large Roman letter P, extending its entire depth, and under it—

"HILARLIDATORE D . . . CLI DEVS"

In a circle surrounding the above, in the same character, is—

"THIS POST IS THE GIFT OF MASTER ROBERT KITCHIN · MERCHANT · SOMETIME MAIOR AND ALDERMAN OF THIS CITY WHO DEC · 5 · SEPTEMB · 1594 · "

Round the upper edge or rim of the pedestal is inscribed—

"HIS EXECVTORS WERE FOWER OF HIS SERRVANTS · IOHN BARKER · MATHEW HAVILAND · ABELL KITCHIN · ALDERMEN OF THIS CITY · AND IOHN ROWBOROW SHERIFF · 1630 · "

Encircling the face of the third pillar is—

"PRAIS THE LORD O MY SOVLE AND FORGET NOT ALL HIS BENEFITS HE SAVED MY LIFE FROM DESTRVCTION AND TO HIS MERCY AND LOVING KINDNESS · PRAISE · "

And round the rim, or upper edge, beneath is—

" + THOMAS HOBSON OF BRISTOL MADE ME ANNO 1625 · NICHOLAS CRISP OF LONDON GAVE ME · TO THIS HONORABLE CITTY IN REMEMBRANCE OF GODS MERCY IN ANNO DOMINI · 1625 · N C · "

Inscribed round the face of the fourth pillar is—

"AD · 1631 · THIS IS THE GIFT OF MR GEORGE WHITE OF BRISTOL MERCHAUNT BROTHER VNTO DOCTOR THOMAS WHITE A FAMOVS BENEFACTOR TO THIS CITIE · "

And upon the rim beneath is—

"THE CHVRCH OF THE LIVINGE GOD IS THE PILLAR AND GROVND OF THE TRVETH SO WAS THE WORKE OF THE PILLARS FINISHED · "

Bridewell, in Bridewell street, dates from 1507. This building was burned by the rioters in 1831, and afterwards reconstructed; but not being in compliance with the Prisons' Act, 1865, was condemned. It is now partially pulled down, and a handsome wing of Messrs. H. H. and S. Budgett and Co., wholesale grocers, occupies a portion of its site.

Bridges.

BATH BRIDGE (or Hill's Bridge), leading from Temple Meads to Knowle and Bath roads. On March 20th, 1855, the first erection was knocked down by the *John*, a screw barge of 180 tons, when two lives were lost. A new structure of wrought iron, containing nine girders, each 107 feet long and 17 feet above high water, replaced the old one, at a cost of £5,700.

BEDMINSTER (or Harford's) BRIDGE, which connects Redcliff hill with Bedminster. The foundations of this iron bridge were laid by John Scandrett Harford in 1805, and it was opened for carriages July 15th, 1807. As these pages are passing through the press a new and improved structure is being erected.

BRISTOL BRIDGE, connecting High street with Victoria and Redcliff streets. It is more than probable that a bridge over the Avon, on or near the site of the present structure, was erected in the 12th century, but the earliest record of one is in the reign of Henry III., in 1247, when a four-arched stone structure was constructed, flanked on either side with houses, which were let at the highest rents in the city, many of the wealthiest tradesmen living there; in the centre of the bridge was a chapel. This bridge becoming too small for the increased traffic, it was resolved, in 1760-1, to erect a larger structure; this was opened in September, 1768, and cost £49,000. In 1784, the bridge was widened to 60 feet. During September, 1793, serious riots occurred on account of the non-cessation of toll on this bridge. In 1873 it was again widened and improved.

DOCK BRIDGES. Several bridges span the entrance locks to Cumberland and Bathurst Basins, and many of them are worked by hydraulic machinery. (*See* "Docks.")

DRAWBRIDGE, The, connecting Clare street with St. Augustine's Parade, was built in 1714. It consisted of two arches, and cost £1,066. Up to this date all traffic between Bristol and Clifton had been carried on *viâ* Christmas street, Frome Bridge and St. Augustine's Back, or Host and Trenchard streets. It was rebuilt in 1755, and was widened in 1796. In 1827 a new bridge was erected at a cost of £1,930, weighing 120 tons, the carriage-way being 18 feet, and two footpaths each 5 feet wide. In 1868 a new and greatly improved structure, capable of being opened and closed within a minute, weighing 130 tons and of greater width, was erected. The bridge is opened, when necessary, twice each day.

GREEN'S BRIDGE connects Canons' Marsh with St. Augustine's; at present a very dilapidated structure, and only 9 feet wide. The Corporation are about erecting a new one, or filling in the graving dock which is adjoining it, and thus making an improved thoroughfare.

PRINCE STREET BRIDGE. This bridge was erected by the old Bristol Dock company, in 1809, over the site of an ancient ferry (called the Gib ferry), owned by the Dean and Chapter, and leased by them to the late Sidenham Teast. On the completion of the bridge, the Dean and Chapter retained the ownership of the foot tolls, and the Dock company collected the horse and carriage tolls. The Great Western Railway company purchased the foot tolls at the time of the construction of the Harbour railway, and continued their collection until 1878, when they sold the right to the Corporation for £15,000. The present structure was then erected by the Corporation at a cost of £8,000, and opened, free of toll, on the 27th January, 1879, by the chairman of the Bristol Docks committee.

STONE BRIDGE, or St. Giles', is situated at the head of the Quay and the Floating Harbour, and is mentioned as early as 1314. The present bridge was commenced April 16th, 1754, and cost £1,825 14s.

ST. PHILIP'S BRIDGE, connecting Counterslip with St. Philip's, was opened September 27th, 1841. It was built at a cost of £11,000, but, with the approaches, cost nearly £20,000. It was freed from toll in 1875, the city having acquired it of the St. Philip's Bridge company under the St. Philip's Bridge Transfer Act of that year, and the Sanitary Authority paid to the company a bonus of £2,000 for the property. It has recently been reconstructed on an improved principle.

SUSPENSION BRIDGE, Clifton. In the year 1753 Alderman Vick left £1,000 as a nucleus for the purpose of building a bridge across the Avon from Clifton Down; he estimated the cost at £10,000, and in 1830 the estate had accumulated to about £8,000. In 1831 Lady Elton turned the first sod on the Clifton side, but the Bristol riots intervened and stopped the works. The Marquis of Northampton, in August, 1836, laid the foundation stone of the buttress on the Somerset side of the river, and donations and subscriptions were collected to carry on the work which had been designed by I. K. Brunel. Several ineffectual attempts to complete the bridge were made; but, in 1861, the Clifton Suspension Bridge company was formed, and under the superintendence of Messrs. John Hawkshaw, F.R.S., and W. H. Barlow, F.R.S., the contractors, Messrs. Cochrane and Co., completed the present structure. It is a curious fact that the chains which had been originally manufactured for this bridge had been sold for the construction of Hungerford Suspension Bridge, London, but were now re-purchased for the one for which they were originally made. Amidst great rejoicing the bridge was opened on December 8th, 1864. The height of the bridge from high water is 245 feet; the span of the chains from saddle to saddle is 702 feet 3 inches; the span between the abutments is 627 feet; and its weight is 1,500 tons. There are 4,200 links, of 24 feet in length and 7 inches in width, in the chains; these sweep gracefully through two pillars, 86 feet high, on each side of the river at a height of 73 feet; they are then carried more abruptly on the land side to the surface, and are securely anchored 70 feet within the solid rock; 400 bolts, 4⅝ inches in diameter and 25 inches in length, fasten the links together, and the bridge is attached to the chains by rods of iron, 1⅝ inches in diameter, which are placed 8 feet apart, and which vary in length from 3 feet to 65 feet. The handrail is of oak, and the carriage road of Baltic timber braced together, covered with a plank floor laid transversely. The abutment on the Leigh Woods' side, which commences at a height of 130 feet, is carried up 110 feet to the floor of the bridge, and with the pillar cost £13,971. Due precautions were taken to allow of the expansion and contraction of the metal, and the bridge was tested under a load of 500 tons of stone, with a result that satisfactorily proved it to be the strongest suspension bridge in the world, as well as the handsomest. Its total cost has been somewhat over £100,000.

Bristol Bargain. This term is simply the purchase of an annuity to be paid for a set number of years. In a pamphlet entitled *Usury Explained, or Conscience Quieted in the case of putting out Money at Interest* (1695), the writer affirms the "Bristol Bargain" to be "just and commendable." "The bargain," he continues, "as proposed to me some twenty years ago, is this:—Five hundred pounds, then running at six per cent., was given for an annuity of a hundred pounds to be paid yearly, the space of seven years." He defends this from being thought usury, because "it contains the requisite equality between the price and what is bought, so that it is guilty of no injustice; it is not purely for lending, so that it is free from usury."

Bristol Board, a stiff drawing paper, originally manufactured at Bristol.

Bristol College. (*See* "Bishop's College.")

Bristol Diamonds. In the "Magnesian Conglomerate," a formation referred by some of the most distinguished geologists to what is termed the "New Red Period," occur frequently at Clifton, Wells, Clevedon, &c., the so-called "Bristol diamonds," which are hollow quartz globes, or earthstones, the crystals being enclosed and pointing inwards. At one time the Clifton rocks were an English Golconda for these now unprized and neglected gems, which were used for cheap jewellery. Many satirical allusions are to be found in the old poets, in their reflections upon contemporary follies and fashions, to these additions to personal finery. Thus Bishop Hall, in his *Satires* (1597, Book III., Sat. 4), has the following reference to the foppery of his day:—

Nor can good Myson wear on his left hand
A signet ring of Bristol diamond,
But he must cut his glove to show his pride,
That his trim jewel may be better spy'd ;
And, that men might some burgess him repute,
With satin sleeves hath grac'd his sackcloth suit.

Also, *Wit Restor'd* (1658) :—

Oh you that should in choosing of your own
Know a true diamond from a Bristowe stone.

Again. *Hudibras Redivivus*, Vol. II., p. 3, 1707 :—

The cap the stalking hero wore
Was set with Bristowe gems before.

Mention is made of "above 2,000" of these brilliants being supplied by Sir John Young, of Bristol, to Secretary Cecil, in the time of James I., to decorate the royal palace, he having been "entreated," he says, when at London, "by Mr. Blagrove, to help the same to some of the precious stones of St. Vincent's Rock near Bristol, to help finish a device in the great chamber of Theobald's." In 1655 we find John Evelyn searching for diamonds among the precipices of St. Vincent, which he called a "horrid Alp," and "equal to anything of that nature I have seen in the most confragous cataracts of the Alps." Queen Catharine of Braganza was at the Clifton Wells on July 11th, 1677, but probably she had too many real diamonds to search for false. The Rev. William Goldwyn, master of the Bristol Grammar School in 1712, in his description of Bristol in a poem of that date, does not forget to magnify the local gems. Here he says :—

In clustering brightness lie,
Like constellations studded in the sky,
Some glistening stones which careful Nature locks
Within the cabinet of the firmest rocks,
Whose brilliant sparks, when lapidaries fine,
With Eastern pearls in second beauty shine.

Specimens of Bristol diamonds may always be purchased from open air dealers on Clifton down, or at shops in the neighbourhood.

Bristol Hoax. *The Bristol Hoax; or, The Merchant's Wedding; being a History of the Adventures of Mr. Woolley in search of a Wife with £47,000*, is the title of a scarce local novel based upon facts in the biography of its hero, a well-known timber merchant of the city named. An adventuress, in the guise of a lady with a large fortune, won the heart, together with the hand of Woolley, who, as *The Times* in a leader on the hoax satirically remarked, "went out wool gathering and came back shorn," for he found, when too late, that his deceitful wife was no lady and that she had not a penny. The following citation of a presumed letter of the amorous timber merchant will supply some idea of the book named, and show it to be a work of no high art :—

Believe me, most beautiful and idolized of beings, that a whole timber yard in flames could not equal the conflagration you have lit up in my heart. I am charmed with the good sense with which your tastes have been formed, and cannot but agree with you that the best chance one of your dearly prized sex possesses from matrimonial happiness is when she fixes her affection upon one of maturer years. I am just at that age when the true heart may be relied upon. My constitution has all the soundness of oak, the solidity of boxwood, and the enduring quality of the best Honduras mahogany. There are only two things which could affect me—the cold edge of your indifference, or the sharpened points of your anger. The first would plane me into shavings, and the second reduce me into sawdust.

Bristol Long Range Club. Established for the promotion of rifle shooting at long ranges. Practice ground at Avonmouth, where shooting up to 1,000 yards takes place during the summer. It may be mentioned that Sergeant Lane, who won the Queen's prize at Wimbledon in 1867, and Drum-Major Hutchinson, who won the silver medal in 1868, were both members of this club, and it is interesting to state that W. E. Metford, C.E., one of the earliest members of the club, is the inventor of the best rifle made for long range shooting. J. W. Arrowsmith, 99 Whiteladies' road, Clifton, hon. sec.

Bristol Milk, sherry sack, once given by Bristol people to visitors and friends. "Though as many elephants are fed," says old Fuller, "as cows grazed within the walls of this city, yet great plenty of this metaphorical milk, whereby Xeres, or sherry sack, is intended. Some will have it called milk, because (whereas nurses give new-born babes in some places pap, in others water and sugar) such wine is the first moisture given infants in this city. It is also the entertainment, of course, which the courteous Bristolians present to all strangers when first visiting their city." Macaulay speaks of it as a "rich beverage made of the best Spanish wine, and celebrated over the whole kingdom as Bristol Milk."

Bristol Tokens. In 1811 so great was the deficiency of specie that it was almost impossible to obtain change in silver for a guinea, which would then readily fetch 26s. Bank notes for £1 formed the chief circulating medium. Shopkeepers gave a premium of one shilling in the pound to obtain silver from those who had hoarded it. To counteract this evil, several Bristol tradesmen issued, with the tacit consent of the Government, sundry silver and copper tokens, which were available for the purchase of small articles and the payment of wages. The shilling tokens were worth intrinsically eightpence, and the sixpenny fourpence; some copper tokens had been issued during the scarcity of coin in 1793-5. The vendors bound themselves to take them in payment at their nominal value when presented.

Building Societies. The following is a list of the principal incorporated building societies in Bristol, and is compiled from the last official return, being for the year ended December 31st, 1881:—

ATLAS (OF BRISTOL) PERMANENT. Members, 312; receipts, £45,480; liabilities to shareholders, £29,876; of these, £18,056 are preferential shares; to others, £18,992; unappropriated profit, £1,809; assets, on mortgage, £49,825; and other securities, £852. W. H. Phillips, secretary, 1 Small street.

BRISTOL AND CLIFTON PERMANENT. Members, 645; receipts, £28,681; liabilities to shareholders, £24,061; to others, £61,745; unappropriated profit, £4,917; assets, on mortgage, £89,136; and other securities, £1,587. T. S. Smith, secretary, St. Stephen's chambers, Baldwin street.

BRISTOL CROWN. Members, 19; receipts, £13,449; liabilities to shareholders, £4,043; of these, £2,298 were preferential shares paid-up; to others, £7,902; unappropriated profit, £211; assets, on mortgage, £12,156. E. Thomas, secretary, 11 Small street.

BRISTOL AND DISTRICT BALLOT AND SALE (formerly 192nd Starr-Bowkett). Members, 290; receipts, £1,447; liabilities to shareholders, £4,401; unappropriated profit, £63; assets, on mortgage, £3,686; and other securities, £778. J. Norman, secretary, Nicholas street.

BRISTOL AND DISTRICT PERMANENT ECONOMIC. Members, 905; receipts, £40,956; liabilities to shareholders, £46,094; of these, £12,347 are preferential; to others, £24,810; unappropriated profit, £5,511; assets, on mortgage, £74,907: and other securities, £1,508. John Watling, secretary, Shannon court, Corn street.

BRISTOL AND SOMERSET PERMANENT. Members, 107; receipts, £8,062; liabilities to shareholders, £6,864; to others, £11,454; unappropriated profit, £605; assets, on mortgage, £18,894; and other securities, £29. Milne and Co., secretaries, St. Stephen's avenue.

BRISTOL AND WEST GLOUCESTERSHIRE PERMANENT. Number of members not stated; receipts, £35,274; liabilities to shareholders, £29,679; to others, £37,951; unappropriated profit, £3,703; assets, on mortgage, £70,868; and other securities, £465.

Young and White, secretaries, 22 Clare street.

BRISTOL EQUITABLE PERMANENT. Members, 313; receipts, £15,435; liabilities to shareholders, £13,515; to others, £16,724; unappropriated profit, £1,929; assets, on mortgage, £32,158; and other securities, &c., £10. S. Hare, sec., 44 High street.

BRISTOL GENERAL PERMANENT. Members, 174; receipts, £15,284; liabilities to shareholders, £9,197; to others, £20,977; unappropriated profit, £2,598; assets, on mortgage, £32,597; and other securities, £193. F. W. Tricks, sec., 12 Bridge street.

BRISTOL SUN. Members, 3; receipts, £23; liabilities, £175; fully paid-up assets on mortgage, £136; and other securities, £41. W. H. C. Salmon, sec., St. Stephen street.

BRISTOL, WEST OF ENGLAND AND SOUTH WALES. Members, 1,875; receipts during the last financial year, £152,677; liabilities to shareholders, £114,625; to depositors and other creditors, £109,793; of these, £56,090 are preferential shares. The balance of unappropriated profit was £20,745; assets, balance due on mortgage, £194,748, and £42,415 invested in other securities and cash. C. J. Lowe, secretary, St. Stephen street.

CITY AND COUNTY OF BRISTOL PERMANENT. Members, 20; receipts not stated; liabilities to shareholders, £2,531; to others, £610; unappropriated profit, £74; assets, on mortgage, £3,035; and other securities, £180. Baker and Langworthy, secretaries, Bank chambers, Corn street.

COSMOPOLITAN PERMANENT. Members, 161; receipts, £1,237; liabilities to shareholders, £488; to others, £740; assets, on mortgage, £1,157; and other securities, £45. C. Gardiner, sec., 14 John street.

FOURTH BRISTOL PERMANENT. Members, 572; receipts, £23,930; liabilities to shareholders, £40,979; to others, £5,622; unappropriated profit, £1,950; assets, on mortgage, £47,404; and other securities, £1,147. Alfred Hiley, secretary, 55 Nicholas street.

GRESHAM BRISTOL PERMANENT. Members, 79; receipts, £6,310; liabilities to shareholders, £4,477; to others, £8,407; assets, on mortgage, £12,659; and other securities, £228. A. J. E. Williams, sec., Exchange.

GUARDIAN PERMANENT. Number of members not stated; receipts, £30,678; liabilities to shareholders, £52,185; to others, £35,138; unappropriated profit, £2,577; assets, on mortgage, £89,440; and other securities, £460. W. Kent, secretary, 17 Small street.

LION. Members, 58; receipts, £703; liabilities to shareholders, £1,240; to others, £4,642; unappropriated profit, £663; assets, on mortgage, £6,319; and other securities, £226. E. W. Barnes, secretary, Shannon court.

NEW BRISTOL AND DISTRICT PERMANENT ECONOMIC. Members, 509; receipts, £13,850; liabilities to shareholders, £22,474; to others, £8,627; unappropriated profit, £1,464; assets on mortgage, £31,948; other securities, £617; of the shares, £9,190 are preferential. John Watling, secretary, Shannon court, Corn street.

PHŒNIX (BRISTOL) PERMANENT. Number of members not stated; receipts, £7,541; liabilities to shareholders, £5,601; of these, £2,277 were preferential shares; to others, £10,676; unappropriated profit, £15; assets, on mortgage, £16,175; and other securities, £117. E. J. Richards, secretary, 29 Corn street.

QUEEN (BRISTOL) PERMANENT. Members, 104; receipts, £4,806; liabilities to shareholders, £1,911; to others, £9,883; unappropriated profit, £335; assets, on mortgage, £12,076; and other securities, £53. W. H. Tricks, sec., 49 Broad street.

ROYAL BRISTOL PERMANENT. Members, 110; receipts, £6,396; liabilities to shareholders, £6,625; to others, £10,138; assets, on mortgage, £16,542; and other securities, £26. C. Ware, secretary, Shannon court, Corn street.

SECOND BRISTOL AND DISTRICT STARR-BOWKETT. Members,

354; receipts, £1,062; liabilities to shareholders, £2,548; unappropriated profit, £22; assets, on mortgage, £2,305; and other securities, £265. C. Gardiner, sec., 14 John street.

SECOND UNION. Members, 372; receipts, £15,195; liabilities to shareholders, £7,594; to others, £28,235; unappropriated profit, £1,359; assets, on mortgage, £36,785; and other securities, £403. S. Joyce, secretary, 24 Bridge street.

SHAREHOLDERS' HAND-IN-HAND. Members, 887; receipts, £40,686; liabilities to shareholders, £30,603; to others, £69,161; unappropriated profit, £1,011; assets, on mortgage, £99,710; and other securities, £1,065. A. Gill, secretary, 4 Colston street.

STANDARD PERMANENT. Members, 282; receipts, £15,236; liabilities to shareholders, £28,358; to others, £9,198; unappropriated profit, £1,240; assets, on mortgage, £38,766; and other securities, £30; £17,640 of the shares are preferential. F. W. Waite, secretary, 47 Nicholas street.

UNIVERSAL (OF BRISTOL). Members, 134; receipts, £5,249; liabilities to shareholders, £9,939; to others, £2,272; unappropriated profit, £41; assets, on mortgage, £12,839. and other securities, £113. E. H. Davies, secretary, 6 Exchange, West.

VICTORIA OF BRISTOL. Members, 115; receipts, £6,010; liabilities to shareholders, £3,279; to others, £3,867; unappropriated profit, £243; assets, on mortgage, £6,826; and other securities, £563. H. Anstey, secretary, John street.

Bull-baiting. The love of this brutal sport lingered in Bristol as late as 1822. The bull-ring was the open space in which the Church of St. Jude now stands. The inhabitants of that locality bore the name of "bull paunchers," and the euphonious appellation still adheres to one of its lanes.

Burgess. The term burgess, or burgher, implies that such persons were freemen (see "Freedom of the city"), deriving their right from inheritance, servitude, &c.

Cabmen's Rests. These were commenced in Bristol through the instrumentality of the late Henry Taylor, ex-Mayor. The following is a list of stations and date of erection. Those marked with an asterisk (*) are in connection with the United Telephone company's subscribers:—

	ERECTED.
*Blackboy hill, St. John's school	1875
*Bristol Bridge	1875
Caledonia place, Mall	1877
Cheltenham road, Stokes' croft	1878
Clifton down, Suspension Bdge.	1876
ditto near Christ Church	1877
Clifton road, Clifton Church...	1876
College green	1877
Joint Railway station (2) 1877 & 1881	
Old Market street	1875
Redcliff hill	1876
St. Augustine's parade, Butts	1878
*St. Augustine's parade, Drawbridge	1874
St. James' barton, the Barton	1875
Triangle	1875
West street, St. Philip's Church	1876
*Whiteladies' road, Clifton down station	1877

Cab Regulations and Fares.

HIRING.—The hiring shall be by distance or by time, as the hirer may express at the commencement of the hiring, but unless so expressed to be by time shall be taken to be by distance. If the hiring be by distance the driver shall not be compelled to drive more than eight miles, and the distance shall be computed from the stand or place where the carriage shall be engaged or hired. If the hiring be by time the driver shall not be compelled to drive for more than two hours, but subject to these regulations the driver shall drive at a reasonable pace; if the hiring be by distance not less than the rate of six miles an hour, and if by time not less than the rate of four miles an hour, and he shall be obliged to

CAB DICTIONARY OF BRISTOL. CAB

drive by the shortest, most convenient and practicable route to any place enclosed in a circle of which the centre is the front door of the Exchange, in the city of Bristol, and of which the circumference is described by a radius of four miles in length.

FARES BY DISTANCE.—The fares shall be as follows when the hiring is by distance:—For a carriage drawn by one horse—

	s.	d.
If the distance does not exceed one mile	1	0
If the distance exceeds one mile—for the first mile	1	0
And for each succeeding half-mile or any part thereof	0	6

For a carriage drawn by more than one horse—

	s.	d.
If the distance does not exceed one mile	1	6
If the distance exceeds one mile—for the first mile	1	6
And for each succeeding half-mile or any part thereof	0	9

FARES BY TIME.—When the hiring is by time:—For a carriage drawn by one horse—

	s.	d.
If the time does not exceed one hour	2	6
If the time exceeds one hour—for the first hour	2	6
And for each succeeding quarter of an hour or part of a quarter of an hour after the first hour	0	6

For a carriage drawn by more than one horse—

	s.	d.
If the time does not exceed one hour	4	0
If the time exceeds one hour—for the first hour	4	0
And for each succeeding quarter of an hour or part of a quarter of an hour after the first hour	0	9

DISPUTES AS TO DISTANCE.—In case any dispute shall arise between the hirer and the driver as to the distance for which the driver shall be entitled to charge, and either party shall be desirous of having the ground measured, and shall deposit with the Justices' Clerk the sum of 5/- on account of the expenses of measurement, then and in such case the distance shall be measured under the direction of two Justices, and in case such distance shall be found to be as great a distance as that for which the driver has charged, the cost and expenses of the measurement shall be paid by the hirer; but in case the distance shall be found to be less than the distance for which the driver has charged, then the cost and expenses of the measurement shall be paid by the driver.

DOUBLE FARES AT NIGHT.—The driver shall be entitled to double the above fares for so much of any hiring, whether by distance or time, as may be performed between the hours of twelve o'clock at night and six o'clock in the morning.

EXTRA PAYMENTS FOR LUGGAGE AND MORE THAN TWO PASSENGERS.—The driver shall be entitled, in addition to the fare for the hiring, whether by distance or time, to an extra payment of 2d. for every package of luggage carried outside, and to an extra payment of 6d. for every passenger above two, carried together at any time during the hiring. Provided that two children under ten years of age (except infants in arms, for whom there shall be no extra payment) shall count for one passenger, and for one such child the driver shall be entitled to an extra payment of 3d.

EXTRA PAYMENTS FOR WAITING.—If the hiring is by distance, the carriage may be detained for a period not exceeding ten minutes without extra payment; but if the period of detention exceeds ten minutes, the driver shall be entitled, in addition to the fare, to an extra payment of 6d. for each quarter of an hour, or fractional part of a quarter of an hour, during which he may be detained beyond such ten minutes, whether in one or several stoppages.

DRIVERS NOT TO DEMAND MORE THAN FARE.—No driver shall charge or ask for more than the fare and any extra payments to which he may be entitled under these by-laws.

TABLE OF DISTANCES FROM CAB STANDS.—The distances between the places hereinafter named do not exceed the distances specified. A distance of less than half a mile is reckoned as half a mile.

TO	Bedcliff Hill.	Welsh Back.	St. James' Churchyard.	St. Augustine's Back.	Victoria Rooms.	Durdham Down.	College Road.	Richmond Terrace.	Cumberland Basin.	Old Market St.	Trinity Road and Clarence Place.
	Mls	Mls	Mils.	Mils.	Mls	Mls	Mls	Mils.	Mils.	Mls	Mils.
All Saints Church, Clifton	2	1½	1½	1½	1	1	1	1	2	2	2½
Ashley Down Orphan Asylum	2½	2½	1½	2	2½	2½	3	3	3½	2	2
Ashley Hill Railway Station	3	2½	2	2½	3	3	3½	3	3½	2½	2
Ashton Road, "Coach and Horses"	2½	3	3½	3	3	3½	3	2½	3½	3	3½
Ditto "Ashton Lodge"	3½	3½	4	4	4	4	3½	3½	4½	4	4½
Ditto Bedminster Union House ..	5½	6	6	6	6	6½	6	5½	6½	6	6½
Barrow Road, "The Reservoir"	5	5½	6	5½	6½	7½	7	6½	6½	6	6½
Bath Road, "The Three Lamps"	1	1	1½	1½	2	3	3	2½	2½	1½	1½
Bathurst Basin	1	1	1	1	1½	2½	2	1½	1½	1½	1½
Bedminster Bridge	1	1	1	1	1½	2½	2½	2	1½	1	1½
Bishport Road, "Telegraph Inn"	2	3	2½	2½	3	4	4	3½	3	2½	3
Ditto The Church	3	3½	4	3½	4	5	5	4½	4	3½	4
Ditto Dundry School	4½	5	5½	5	6	7	6½	6	6	5½	5½
Brislington Road, Kensington Place	2	2	2½	2½	3	4	4	3½	3½	2	2½
Ditto West Town Lane	3	3	3	3	4	5	4½	4	4	3	3½
Ditto Keynsham, "Lamb & Lark"	5½	5½	6	5½	6	7	7	6½	6½	5½	6
Bristol Bridge	1	—	1	1	1	2	2	1½	2	1	1
Bristol Railway Station	1	1	1½	1	2	3	2½	2½	2½	1	1½
Cambridge Park, Redland	2½	2½	2	2½	1½	1	1½	2	2½	2½	2½
Cattle Market	1	1	1½	1	2	3	2½	2	2	1	1½
Central Police Station	1	1	1	1	1	2	1½	1½	2	1	1
Christ Church, Clifton	2	1½	1½	1½	1	1½	1	1	2	2	2½
Clifton Church	2	1½	1½	1	1	1½	1	—	1½	2	2
Clifton College	2½	2	2	1½	1	1	1	1	1½	2½	2½
Clifton Down Station	2	2	1½	1½	1	1	1	1	2	2	2½
Clifton Police Station	1½	1	1½	1	1	1½	1½	1	1	1½	2
Clifton Station, Port and Pier Railway ..	2½	2	2½	2	2	1½	1	1½	1	2½	3
Colston Hall	1	1	1	1	1	2	1½	1½	1½	1	1½
Cumberland Basin	2	1	2	1½	1½	2	1½	2	—	2	2½
Drill Hall, Park Street	1½	1	1	1	1	1½	1½	1	1½	1½	1½
Exchange	1	1	1	1	1	2	2	1½	2	1	1
Failand Road, Longwood House	4½	5	5	5	4	4½	4	4	5	5½	6
Fishponds Road, Clifton Exten. Ry. Viaduct	3	2½	2½	3	3	3½	4	3½	4	2	1½
Ditto Police Station	4	3½	3½	4	4½	4½	5	4½	5	3	3
Ditto Overn Hill	5	4½	4½	5	5	5½	6	5½	6	4	3½
Ditto Staple Hill	5½	5	5	5½	5½	6	6½	6	6½	4½	4
Gas Works, Canons' Marsh	1½	1	1½	1	1	2	2	1½	1	1½	2
Hanham Road, Whiteshill	4	3½	3½	3½	4½	5½	5	4½	5	3	2½
Hanham Road, Stone Hill	5½	5	5	5	6	6½	6½	6	6½	4½	4
Highbury Chapel	2	1½	1½	1½	1	1	1½	1	2	2	2½
Horfield Road, "Royal Oak Inn"	3½	3	2½	3	3	2½	3½	3	4	2½	3
Ditto The Barracks	3½	3	3	3½	3	3	4	3½	4½	3	3½
Ditto Filton Church	5	4½	4	4½	4½	4½	5	4½	6	4½	4½
King Square	1½	1	1	1	1	2	2	1½	2	1	1
Lawford's Gate	1½	1	1	1½	2	2½	3	2½	2½	1	1
Lawrence Hill Railway Station	2	1½	1½	1½	2½	3½	3	2½	3	1	1
Leigh Road, Ashton Court Lodge	3½	2½	2½	2½	1½	2	1½	1½	2½	3	3½
Ditto "The George Inn"	4	3½	3½	3½	2½	3	2½	2½	3½	4	4½
Ditto Ham Green	5½	5	5	4½	4	4½	4	4	5	5½	6
Mansion House	2½	2	2	2	1	1	1	1	1½	2½	3
Merchants' Hall	1	1	1	1	1	2	2	1½	1½	1	1½
Midland Road Railway Station	1	1	1	1	2	3	2½	2	2½	1	1
Montpelier Station	2	1½	1	1½	2	1½	2	2	3	1½	1½
Portland Square	1½	1	1	1	1½	2	2½	2	2½	1	1
Queen Square	1	1	1	1	1½	2½	2	1½	2	1	1½
Redland Green	2½	2	2	2½	1½	1	1½	1½	2½	2	2
Royal Hotel	1	1	1	1	1	1½	1½	1	1½	1	1½

TABLE OF DISTANCES FROM CAB STANDS (*Continued*).

TO	Redcliff Hill.	Welsh Back.	St. James' Churchyard.	St. Augustine's Back.	Victoria Rooms.	Durdham Down.	College Road.	Richmond Terrace.	Cumberland Basin.	Old Market St.	Trinity Road and Clarence Place.
	Mls	Mls	Mils.	Mils.	Mls	Mls	Mls	Mls.	Mils.	Mls	Mls.
St. George's Rd., "George and Dragon Inn"	2½	2½	2½	2½	3½	4	4	3½	4	2	1½
Ditto Rose Cottage	3½	3	3	3½	4	5	5	4½	4½	3	2½
Ditto Kingswood Church ..	4½	4	4½	4	5	6	6	5½	6	4	3½
St. James's Barton	1	1	—	1	1	2½	2	1½	2	1	1
St. John's Church, Whiteladies' Road.. ..	2½	2	2	1½	1	1	1	1½	2	2½	2½
St. Matthew's Church, Kingsdown	2	1½	1	1	1	1½	1½	1½	2½	1½	1½
Stapleton Road Station	2½	2	1½	2	2½	3	3	3	3½	1½	1
Stapleton Road, Clifton Exten. Ry. Viaduct	3	2½	2	2½	3	3½	3½	3½	4	2	1½
Ditto Stoke House Lodge	4	3½	3½	3½	4	4½	5	4½	5	3	2½
Ditto to Frenchay	5	4½	4½	4½	5	5½	6	5½	6	4	3½
Stoke Road, Spring Fort	3	2½	2½	2½	2	1	1½	2	2½	3	3
Ditto Trym Bridge	4½	4	4	4	3	2	3	3	4	4½	4½
Ditto "Kingsweston Inn"	5	4½	5	4½	4	3	3½	4	4½	5	5½
Stoke's Croft, Junction Cheltenham Road ..	1½	1	1	1	1½	1½	2	2	2½	1	1
Theatre, King-street	1	1	1	1	1	2	2	1	2	1	1
Ditto Park Row	1½	1	1	1	1	1½	1½	1	2	1½	1½
Victoria Rooms	1½	1	1	1	—	1	1	1	1½	1½	2
Wells Road, "Talbot Inn," Knowle	2	2	2½	2	3	4	3½	3	3½	2	2½
Ditto Manor House, Whitchurch ..	3½	3½	4	3½	4½	5½	5	4½	5	3½	4
Ditto Whitchurch Church	4	4	4½	4	5	6	5½	5	5½	4	4½
Westbury Road, Road to Henleaze	3½	3	2½	3	2	1	2	2½	3	3	3½
Ditto "White Lion Inn," Westbury	4½	4	3½	3½	3	2	2½	3	4	4	4
Ditto "Salutation Inn," Henbury	5½	5	4½	4½	4	3	3½	4	4½	4½	5

TABLE OF DISTANCES FROM RAILWAY STATIONS.—The distances between the places hereinafter named do not exceed the distances specified. A distance of less than half a mile is reckoned as half a mile.

TO	Temple Meads.	Ashley Hill.	Clifton Down.	Clifton Port and Pier Railway.	Lawrence Hill.	Midland Road.	Montpelier.	Stapleton Road.
	Mils	Mils.	Mils.	Mils.	Mils.	Mils.	Mils.	Mils.
All Saints Church, Clifton	2½	3	1	1½	3	2½	2	3
Ashley Down Orphan Asylum	3	1	2½	4	2	2	1½	1½
Ashley Hill Railway Station	3	—	3	4	2½	2½	1½	2
Ashton Road, "Coach and Horses"	3	5	3	3	4	3½	4	4½
Ditto "Ashton Lodge"	4	6	4	4	5	4	5	5½
Ditto Bedminster Union	6	8	6	6	7	6½	7	7½
Barrow Road, "The Reservoir"	5½	8	7	7	6½	6	6½	7
Bath Road, "The Three Lamps"	1	3	2½	3	2	1½	2	2½
Bathurst Basin	1	3	2	2	2	1½	2	2½
Bedminster Bridge	1	3	2½	2	2	1½	2	2½
Bishport Road, "Telegraph Inn"	2½	4½	3½	3½	3½	2½	3½	4
Ditto The Church	3½	5½	5	5	4½	4	4½	5
Ditto Dundry School	5	7	6½	6½	6	5½	6	6½
Brislington Road, Kensington Place	2	4	3½	4	3	2½	3	3½
Ditto West Town Lane	2½	5	4½	4½	4	3	4	4½
Ditto Keynsham, "Lamb & Lark"	5	7½	7	7	6½	5½	6½	6½
Bristol Bridge	1	2½	2	2	1½	1	1½	2
Bristol Railway Station	—	3	2½	3	2	1½	2	2½
Cambridge Park, Redland	3	2½	1	2	3	2½	1½	2½
Cattle Market	1	3	2½	3	2	1	2	2½
Central Police Station	1½	2	1½	2	1½	1	1	2

TABLE OF DISTANCES FROM RAILWAY STATIONS (*Continued*).

TO	Temple Meads.	Ashley Hill.	Clifton Down.	Clifton Port and Pier Railway.	Lawrence Hill.	Midland Road.	Montpelier.	Stapleton Road.
	Mils.	Mils.	Mils.	Mils.	Mils.	Mils.	Mils.	Mils.
Christ Church, Clifton	2½	3	1	1½	3	2½	2	3
Clifton Church	2	3	1	1½	2½	2	2	3
Clifton College	2½	3½	1	1	3	2½	2	3
Clifton Down Station	2½	3	—	1½	3	2½	1½	2½
Clifton Police Station	2	3	1	1½	2½	2	2	2½
Clifton Station, Port and Pier Railway	3	4	1½	—	3½	3	3	3½
Colston Hall	1½	2½	1½	2	1½	1	1½	2
Cumberland Basin	2½	3½	2½	1	3	2½	2½	3
Drill Hall, Park Street	2	2½	1	2	2	2	1½	2½
Exchange	1	2½	1½	2	1½	1	1½	2
Failand Road, Longwood House	5½	6½	4½	4½	6½	5½	5½	6½
Fishponds Road, Clifton Exten. Ry. Viaduct	3	2½	3	4½	2	2½	2	1
Ditto Police Station	4	3½	4½	5½	3	3½	3½	2
Ditto Overn Hill	5	4½	5½	6½	4	4½	4½	3
Ditto Staple Hill	5½	5	6	7	4½	5	4½	3½
Gas Works, Canons' Marsh	2	3	1½	1½	2½	2	2	2½
Hanham Road, Whiteshill	4	4½	5	5½	2	3	4	3½
Hanham Road, Stone Hill	5	6	6½	7	3½	4½	5½	5
Highbury Chapel	2½	3	1	2	2½	2	1	2
Horfield Road, "Royal Oak Inn"	3½	1	3	4	3½	3	2	3
Ditto The Barracks	4	1½	3	4½	4	3½	2½	3½
Ditto Filton Church	5	3	4½	5½	5	4½	3½	5
King Square	1½	2	1½	2½	1½	1	1	1½
Lawford's Gate	1½	2	2	3	1	1	1½	1
Lawrence Hill Railway Station	2	2½	3	3½	—	1	2	1½
Leigh Road, Ashton Court Lodge	4	4	2	2	4	4	3	4
Ditto "The George Inn"	5	5	3	3	5	5	4	5
Ditto Ham Green	6	6½	4	4½	6	6½	5½	6½
Mansion House	3	3½	1	1	3	2½	2½	3½
Merchants' Hall	1½	3	1½	2	2	1	1½	2
Midland Road Station	1½	2½	2½	3	1	—	1½	1½
Montpelier Station	2	1½	1½	3	2	1½	—	1½
Portland Square	1½	1½	2	2½	1	1	1	1½
Queen Square	1½	3	1½	2	1½	1	1½	2
Redland Green	3	2½	1	2	2½	2½	1½	2½
Royal Hotel	1½	2½	1½	1½	2	1½	1½	2
St. George's Rd., "George and Dragon Inn"	3	3½	4	4½	1	1½	2½	2½
Ditto Rose Cottage	3½	4	4½	5	2	2½	3½	3½
Ditto Kingswood Church	4½	5	5½	6	3	3½	4½	4½
St. James's Barton	1½	2	1½	2½	1½	1	1	1½
St. John's Church, Whiteladies' Road	2½	2½	1	1½	3	2½	1½	2½
St. Matthew's Church, Kingsdown	2	2	1	2½	2	1½	1	2½
Stapleton Road Station	2½	2	2½	3½	1½	1½	1½	—
Stapleton Road, Clifton Exten. Ry. Viaduct	3	2½	3	4	2	2	2	1
Ditto Stoke House Lodge	4	3½	4	5½	3	3½	3	2
Ditto to Frenchay	5	4½	5	6½	4	4½	4	3
Stoke Road, Spring Fort	3½	3½	1½	2	3½	3	2	3
Ditto Trym Bridge	5	4½	2½	3½	5	4½	3½	4½
Ditto "Kingsweston Inn"	5½	5½	3½	4	5½	5½	4	5
Stoke's Croft, Junction Cheltenham Road	2	1½	1½	2½	1½	1	1	1½
Theatre, King-street	1	2½	1½	2	1½	1	1½	2
Ditto Park Row	1½	2½	1	2	2	1½	1½	2
Victoria Rooms	2	2½	1	2	2½	2	2	2½
Wells Road, "Talbot Inn," Knowle	1½	4	3½	4	3	2½	3	3½
Ditto Manor House, Whitchurch	3	5½	5	5½	4½	4	4½	5
Ditto Whitchurch Church	3½	6	5½	6	5	4½	5	5½
Westbury Road, Road to Henleaze	4	3½	1½	2½	3½	3½	2	3½
Ditto "White Lion Inn," Westbury	4½	4½	2½	3½	4½	4	3	4½
Ditto "Salutation Inn," Henbury	5½	5½	3½	4	5½	5	4	5

Caer Brito. An ancient British name given to Bristol, signifying the painted or embellished city. Possibly the name was given to the city in the 6th century.

Caer Odor. Supposed to be one of the names given to Bristol by the ancient Britons, as under such name an inhabited place corresponding in situation to Bristol is mentioned in old Welsh chronicles.

Cambridge Higher and Local Examinations. The latter take place each year in the month of December. Bristol has been a centre since this system of local examinations was first established. The average number of junior candidates that enter yearly is about 70, and the senior students about 15. In December, 1882, there were 101 male and 101 female candidates. Prizes are given for first class honours and to those who have distinguished themselves in any special subject. A scholarship of £10, tenable for two years, is also presented by the Charity Trustees to any boy from Queen Elizabeth's Hospital who has taken a first class at this examination. It is intended ultimately to open this scholarship to all candidates. The examinations were opened to girls in 1865. The average number of senior candidates is about 60, and juniors about 70. A gold medal is given to each girl gaining first class, and a silver medal to each gaining second class honours. The Rev. R. W. Southby, 4 Royal park, Clifton, is the hon. secretary. The Council of University College have kindly allowed one of their rooms to be used for the purpose of forming classes, in which instruction is given by clergymen of the Church of England and Dissenting ministers on religious knowledge, founded on selected portions of the Bible and other books. These classes are not confined to candidates for the Cambridge Examination, and are explanatory in their nature. Fee, for each course of lectures, 2/6. The nearest centre for the Higher Cambridge Examination is Cheltenham. Several Bristol ladies have presented themselves and passed well, and others have done so at the women's examination of the London University held in London. The local arrangements for women are under the management of a committee of ladies, of which the hon. sec. is Mrs. Killigrew Wait, St. Vincent's Hall, Clifton park.

Canadian Home for Little Girls. (*See* "Homes.")

Canals. Prior to the introduction of railways a large traffic was carried by canals, but from various circumstances many of these have fallen into comparative disuse; in consequence of the continuous increase in the traffic of the country canals are regaining their position.

CANAL BOATS, or FLY BOATS, leave Bristol and Bath daily; also to and from Bradford, Trowbridge, Devizes, Pewsey, Marlborough, Hungerford, Newbury, &c. Owners, Gerrish and Co., Limited, Redcliff street.

THE MIDLAND, WESTERN AND METROPOLITAN CANAL CARRYING COMPANY LIMITED has been formed for the carriage of merchandise between the ports of Bristol and London and the Western and Midland counties. Secretary, H. White, 22 Clare street.

THE SEVERN AND CANAL CARRYING COMPANY, Bull wharf, Redcliff street, are general carriers by water between Bristol and the following towns:— Sharpness, Frampton-on-Severn, Gloucester, Newent, Upton-on-Severn, Worcester, Stourport, Bewdley, Coalbrookdale, Ironbridge, Stourbridge, Kidderminster, Birmingham, Oldbury, Wolverhampton, Dudley, Tipton, West Bromwich, Brierley hill, Bilston, and the Midland district generally. The company collect and deliver in most of the above-named places.

Canynges. (*See* "Monuments.")

Carriers. The following is a list of carriers to and from Bristol :—

DESTINATION.	DEPARTS FROM.	TIME OF DEPARTURE.	CARRIERS.
Almondsbury	Full Moon, North-street	Tues, Thur, Sat, 5 a.	Brown
Ditto	Ditto ditto	Tues, Thurs, Sat, 4 0 a.	Williams
Alveston	Ditto ditto	Wed, Sat, 5 a.	Beaver
Ashton	Talbot, Bath-street	Daily, 12 noon and 5 a.	Brown
Ditto	Ditto	Daily, 4 a.	Porter
Ditto	Old Fox, Redcliff-street	Daily, 12 noon and 5 a.	Vickery
Aust	Full Moon, North-street	Tues, Thur, Sat, 4 30 a.	Collins
Backwell	Talbot, Bath-street	Daily, 4 a.	Porter
Badminton	White Hart, Old Market-st.	Tus, Thu, Sat	Eyles
Banwell	Three Queens, Thomas-street.	Mon, Thur, 3 30 a.	Wride
Berrington	Three Kings, Thomas-street.	Friday, 4 a.	Wookey
Ditto	White Hart, ditto	Fri, 3 a.	Derrick
Bishop Sutton	Wheat Sheaf, ditto	Tues, Thur, Sat, 4 a.	Gibbs
Ditto	Three Queens, Thomas-street	Tus, Thur, Sat, 4 a.	Elms
Bitton	Castle and Ball, Lr Castle-st.	Daily, 4 0 a.	F. Wilton
Blagden	Hope & Anchor, Redcliff-hill.	Mon, Thur, Sat, 4 a.	Carpenter
Ditto	Old Fox, Redcliff-street	Tues, Fri, 3 a.	Filer
Bourton	Talbot, Bath-street	Daily, 4 a.	Porter
Brockley	Ditto	Daily, 4 a.	Porter
Cheddar	Three Queens, Thomas-street	Tues, Fri, 12 noon	Wall
Chew Magna	Ditto ditto	Tues, Thur, Sat, 4 a.	Hazard
Ditto	Wheat Sheaf, Thomas-street.	Tues, Thurs, Sat, 4 a.	Buzzard
Chew Stoke	Ditto ditto	Mon, Thur, Sat, 4 a.	Horler
Chipping Sodbury	White Hart, Old Market-st.	Tues, Thur, Sat, 3 30 a.	Eyles
Ditto	Castle and Ball, Lr. Castle-st.	Tues, Thur, Sat, 5 a.	Jones
Ditto	White Horse, Barrs-street	Friday, 10 m.	Frewin
Churchill	Wheat Sheaf, Thomas-street.	Wed, Sat, 8 0 a.	Thatcher
Cleeve	Talbot, Bath-street	Daily, 4 a.	Porter
Clevedon	Three Kings, Thomas-street.	Daily, 4 a.	Broad
Ditto	Three Queens, Thomas-street	Tues, Thur, Sat.	Coles
Coalpit Heath	Castle and Ball, Lr Castle-st.	Daily, 4 30 a.	Jones
Congresbury	Bear Yard, Thomas-street	Tues, Thur, Sat, 4 a.	Crew
Cromhall, Iron Acton	Castle and Ball, Lr Castle-st.	Tues, Thur, Sat, 4 a.	Gabb
Downend	White Hart, Old Market-st	Daily, 4 30 a.	Turvey
Ditto	Castle and Ball, Lr Castle-st.	Daily, 10 30 m., 2 & 5 a.	Davis
Dyrham	White Hart, Old Market-st.	Mon, Wed, Fri, 4 30 a.	Carter
East Harptree	Hope & Anchor, Redcliff-hill	Mon, Thu, Sat, 4 a.	Millard
Ditto	Old Fox, Redcliff-street	Mon, Thur, Sat, 4 a.	Weaver
Falfield	White Horse, Barrs-street	Wed, 3 a.	Malpass
Ditto	Ditto ditto	Sat, 6 a.	Hock
Frenchay	White Hart, Old Market-st.	Daily, 4 30 a.	Gilby
Ditto	Castle and Ball, Lr Castle-st.	Daily, 4 & 4 30 a.	Pearce
Frampton Cotterell	White Hart, Old Market-st.	Daily, 4 30 a.	Gilby
Ditto	Castle and Ball, Lr Castle-st.	Daily, 4 & 4 30 a.	Pearce
Hambrook	Ditto ditto	Daily, 4 & 4 30 a.	Pearce
Hanham	White Hart, Old Market-st.	Daily, 4 30 a.	Wilton
Hawkesbury	Ditto ditto	Wednesday, 4 a.	Thompson
Henbury	Parcel Office, High-street	Daily, 11 0 m., 4 a.	Farr
Ditto	Hatchet Inn, Frogmore st.	Daily, 4 0 a.	Else
High Littleton, Formborough	} Three Kings, Thomas-street.	Tues, Thur, Sat, 3 a.	Brooks
Hinton	White Hart, Old Market-st.	Mon, Wed, Fri, 4 30 a.	Carter
Iron Acton	Ditto ditto	Mon, Fri, 4 30 a.	Holloway
Ditto	White Horse, Barrs-street	Wed, Sat, 1 a.	Mainton
Iron Acton & Cromh'll	Ditto ditto	Friday, 3 a.	Jesse Edge
Keynsham	Talbot Hotel, Bath-street	Daily, 4 a.	Ford
Ditto	Three Queens, Thomas-street.	Daily, 4 30 a.	Keates
Kingswood	White Hart, Old Market-st.	Daily, 4 30 a.	Cooper
Ditto	Castle and Ball, Lr Castle-st.	Daily, 1 a., 6 a.	Jefferies
Littledon	Full Moon, North-street	Tues, Thur, Sat, 4 30 a.	Stafford
Litton	Wheat Sheaf, Thomas-street.	Fri, 3 a.	Middle
Malmesbury	Bear Yard, ditto	Tues, Fri, 1 a.	Evans
Mangotsfield	White Hart, Old Market-st.	Mon, Wed, Fri, 4 30 a.	Carter
Marshfield	Ditto ditto	Thursday, 4 30 a.	Billett
Ditto	Castle and Ball, Lr. Castle-st.	Tues, Thurs, 4 30 a.	Rice
Mells	Wheat Sheaf, Thomas-street.	Tues, Fri, 2 a.	Butler
Nailsea	Three Queens, Thomas-street	Daily, except Wed., 4 a.	Shepstone

LIST OF CARRIERS TO AND FROM BRISTOL (Continued).

DESTINATION.	DEPARTS FROM.	TIME OF DEPARTURE.	CARRIERS.
Newport (Glo.)	Full Moon, North-street	Friday, 2 30 a.	Summers
Oldbury	Ditto ditto	Mon, Th, Sa, 4 a.	Riddle
Olveston	Ditto ditto	Tues, Thurs, Sat, 4 30 a.	Whitfield
Ditto	Ditto ditto	Mon, Fri, 4 a.	Oakhill
Pensford	Three Kings, Thomas-street	Tues, Thurs, Sat. 4 a.	Dowling
Pill	Old Fox, Redcliff-street	Tues, Thurs, Sat, 3.30 a.	Weaver
Portishead	Hope & Anchor, Redcliff-hill	Tues, Fri, 4 a.	Brown
Ditto	Three Queens, Thomas-street.	Tues, Thurs, Sat, 4 a.	J. Brown
Pucklechurch	White Hart, Old Market-st	Mon, Wed, Fri, 4 30 a.	Carter
Redwick	Full Moon, North-street	Tues, Fri, 12 noon	Bishop
Ditto	Ditto ditto	Friday, 3 a.	Brittan
St. George's	Castle and Ball, Lr Castle-st.	Daily, 6 a.	Wilton
Shirehampton	Parcel Office, High-street	Daily, 11 0 m, 4 a.	Farr
Ditto	Hatchet Inn, Frogmore-street	Daily 4 a.	Else
Shurston	Bear Yard, Thomas-street	Tues, Fri, 1 a.	Evans
Stapleton	White Hart, Old Market-st.	Daily, 4 30 a.	Gilby
Ditto	Castle and Ball, Lr Castle-st.	Daily, 4 & 4 30 a.	Pearce
Staple Hill	White Hart, Old Market st.	Mon, Wed, Fri, 4 30 a.	Carter
Stone	Full Moon, North-street	Thursday, 2 30 a.	Fowler
Thornbury	White Horse, Barrs-street	Mon, Wed, Th, Fri, Sat, 4 a.	Bayliss
Ditto	Full Moon, North Street	Mon. Thur, Sat, 5 a.	Riddle
Timsbury	Wheat Sheaf, Thomas-street.	Mon, Thur, 4 a.	Hutton
Two Mile Hill	Castle and Ball, Lr Castle-st	Daily 1 a., 6 a.	Jefferies
Ubley	Hope & Anchor, Redcliff-hill.	Tues, Fri, 4 a.	Payne
Upton	White Hart, Old Market-st.	Wednesday, 4 30 a.	Thompson
Warmley	White Hart, Old Market-st.	Daily, 4 30 a.	Cooper
Wells	Bear Yard, Thomas-street	Tues, Fri, 1 a.	Scudamore
Westbury	Parcel Office, High-street	Daily 11 0 m. 4 a.	Farr
Ditto	Hatchet Inn, Frogmore st.	Daily, 4 0 a.	Else
West Town	Talbot Hotel, Bath-street	Daily, 4 a.	Porter
Westerleigh	White Hart, Old Market-st.	Mon. Wed, Sat, 4 30 a.	Battin
Ditto	Ditto ditto	Tue, Thu, Sat, 4 30 a.	Bailey
Wickwar	Ditto ditto	Friday, 4 a.	Pitt
Winscombe	Three Kings, Thomas-street.	Tues, Sat, 1 a.	Hemmons
Winterbourne	White Hart. Old Market-st	Daily, 4 30 a.	Gilby
Ditto	Castle and Ball. Lr. Castle-st.	Daily, 4 & 4 30 a.	Pearce
Wootton-under-Edge	Midland Inn, Batch	Mon, Fri, 4.30 a.	Gabb
Wrington	Talbot Hotel, Bath-street	Daily, 4 a.	Porter
Ditto	Three Queens, Thomas-street.	Wed, Sat. 4 a.	Player
West Harptree	Hope & Anchor, Redcliff-hill.	Mon, Thur, Sat, 4 a.	Horler
Yate	Castle and Ball, Lr. Castle-st.	Tues, Wed. 5 a.	Jones
Ditto	White Hart, Old Market-st.	Tue, Thur, Sat, 4 30 a.	Eyles
Yatton	Wheat Sheaf, Thomas-street.	Daily, 4 a.	White
Ditto	Bear Yard, ditto	Mon, Wed, Thur, Sat, 4 a.	Crew

Castle of Bristol. The date of the foundation of the castle is open to conjecture; it was destroyed by command of Oliver Cromwell, and at the present time the entrance to the banqueting hall in Tower street, and a few arches, &c., in cellars are all that can be verified. The walls ran round from Peter street by the Castle Ditch, crossing Old Market street, down Tower hill, and then bent round, intersecting Queen street just where the opening of the deep dark moat is still to be seen. Its area was six acres, or thereabouts. Its great tower stood just within Castle street from the west, partly on the site of the street and partly upon its left. It measured 60 feet by 45 feet, and the thickness of the walls at its base was 25 feet. In appearance and impregnability against the weapons of that age, it ranked only second to the White Tower of London. For the exhaustive but interesting history in connection with the castle, the reader is referred to *Bristol: Past and Present.*

Cemeteries. The burial grounds in the city were ordered to be closed wholly or in part in the month of January, 1854. The Bristol

General Cemetery, at Arno's vale, on the Bath road (there is also an entrance on the Wells road, called the High Grove), contains 27a. 3r. 30p. The first report of the Company, issued in August, 1841, stated the cost of the land, roads, building, &c., as £13,340. There are two chapels. One side of the cemetery was consecrated in 1840. It is a beautiful spot, most carefully conserved and admirably managed. Amongst the great variety of monuments here we may notice at least three : Robert Hall's, Rev. J. Pratt's and Rajah Rammohun Roy's, all on the right between the gate and the chapel. The office of the Company is in Liverpool chambers, Corn street, open from 10 till 5, except Saturdays, when the office is closed at 1.

The following are the charges, exclusive of the Clergy's Mortuary Fee, where payable:—

	Charge for the grave.	Interment fee.
An interment in catacombs under chapel	£10 0 0	£5 5 0
In the Cemetery, a brick grave in perpetuity, masonry included	10 0 0	3 3 0
A private grave, not bricked, but also in perpetuity, 7 feet by 3	3 0 0	*1 11 6
A similar grave, 6¼ ft. by 2¾, including stone	2 0 0	*1 1 0
A common interment	0 12 6	*No fee on 1st interment afterward.

No mourning favours are expected at the Cemetery. The Cemetery is open to the public, free of charge, from Eight o'clock in the morning until sunset; but on Sundays it is closed until Two o'clock p.m, except for funerals.

Close by is the Roman Catholic Cemetery, and on the opposite side of the road is the cemetery of Redcliff parish, which was acquired by that parish as compensation for the disturbance of the remains in Redcliff churchyard during the construction of the Harbour Railway.

In Sheen lane, near the Malago, Bedminster, is a small cemetery, which pertains to Bedminster parish church.

In Stapleton is Greenbank Cemetery, belonging to St. Philip's parish. A church and chapel are placed on the summit of the hill, divided by a piazza. The whole cost, including purchase of land, was below £12,000. It was consecrated 14th April, 1871. It comprises nearly 20 acres. The ground is laid out with winding walks, each having a name to denote it, bearing tablets, viz., Oak tree avenue, Laurustinus avenue, Arbutus avenue, Cypress avenue, Laurel avenue and Cedar avenue, so that it prevents the ordinary difficulty of identifying graves. There are about 4,000 trees and shrubs. Samuel Baber, clerk and registrar, 71 Stapleton road.

The Unitarians have a cemetery in Brunswick square, the Society of Friends one in Rosemary street, and the Jews one in Rose street, Temple, but these are rarely used.

Census. (*See* "Population.")

Chamber of Commerce

and Shipping (incorporated) is a voluntary institution, originally founded in 1823 by the merchants, traders and manufacturers of the city, who found the trade and commerce of the city and port very prejudicially affected by the high local charges on ships and goods. During the operation of the Free Port Association it was suspended; but in 1853 it was resuscitated, and has continued from that time to the present to take part in all questions, whether local or imperial, calculated to influence the commercial prosperity of the city or nation. For the work the chamber has accomplished reference must be made to its reports, published annually. The following are the objects of the chamber:—The promotion of the trade and commerce, the shipping and manufactures, of the city and port of Bristol, and of the home, colonial and foreign trade of the United Kingdom generally; the collection and dissemination of statistical and other information relating to trade, commerce, shipping and manufactures; the promoting, supporting or opposing, legislative or other measures affecting the aforesaid interests. The chamber became incorporated in the year 1874. Since 1860 it has been an active member of the Association of Chambers of Commerce of the United Kingdom, which association was entertained at their autumnal gathering in Bristol in September, 1876, and was attended by over one hundred delegates from all parts of the United Kingdom. The annual meeting of the chamber is held in April each year, in the hall of the Society of Merchant Venturers, who have been for over thirty years liberal supporters to the chamber. The annual subscriptions are two guineas and one guinea. The subscribing members are nearly 300, and the council of the chamber consists of 24 members, including a president and two vice-presidents. The ordinary meetings of the council are held on the fourth Wednesday in each month, at the offices of the chamber, in the Guildhall (Assize Courts' building), Small street. Mr. Leonard Bruton is the secretary, and he has held that position since the resuscitation of the chamber in 1853.

Channel, Bristol,

an arm of the Atlantic, entering between St. Ann's Head on the north and Land's End on the south, extending in a south-western direction, bounded on the north by South Wales and on the south by Somerset, Devon and Cornwall. At its eastern extremity it terminates in the estuary of the Severn (*see* "Severn"), besides which river it receives the Parret, Tawe, Torridge, Taff and Towy. The island of Lundy, with its lighthouse, is in the mouth of the Channel. The Channel contains Milford Haven, Carmarthen Bay and Swansea Bay on the north, and Barnstaple, Porlock and Bridgwater Bays on the south. Tides flow rapidly upward and unite with the Severn (*see* "Tides").

Chapel of the Three Kings of Cologne,

situated at the top of Christmas Steps, adjoining Foster's Almshouse, was founded in 1504 by John Foster, mayor in 1481, in honour of God and the three Kings of Cologne, viz., the three wise men of the East. The first allusion to these pious monarchs is in Psalm lxxii. 10, 11. The first particular account is to be found in Venerable Bede, who tells us that Melchior was the King of Nubia and Arabia; he was old and had grey hair, with a long beard, and offered gold to Christ in acknowledgment of his sovereignty. Gasper, the second of the Magi, was the King of Tarsas and Egypt. He was young and had no beard; he offered frankincense to the Lord's divinity. Balthazar, the third King (of Godolie and Seba), was of dark complexion and had a large beard; he offered myrrh to our Saviour's humanity. In their old age these Kings were baptised by St. Thomas. After death their bodies underwent various removals by pious devotees, their permanent resting-place being now the Cathedral of Cologne. By an ordination of Foster's will, a priest was required to say mass daily in this chapel during 12 years ensuing upon the founder's death, for his soul and the souls of his relations. The rector of St. Michael's Church is the chaplain. At the eastern end of this chapel are two rows of sedilia, or seats recessed in the wall, six on each side, said to be for the twelve Apostles. Over the cavities adjoining the chapel is the following inscription, which, together with the seats, was restored in 1882:—

THIS STREETE WAS STEPPERED DONE & FINISHED, SEPTEMBER, 1669. THE RIGHT Worpfl. THOMAS STEVENS, ESQR. THEN MAYOR, HVMPHRY LITTLE, AND RICHARD HART, SHERRIFFES. THE RIGHT WORPFL. ROBERT YEAMANS, KNT. & BARRONET, MAYOR ELECT, CHARLES POWELL AND EDWARD HORNE, SHERRIFFES ELECT OF THIS CITTY. BY AND AT THE COST OF IONATHAN BLACKWELL, ESQR. FORMERLY SHERRIFFE OF THIS CITTY, AND AFTERWARDS ALDERMAN OF THE CITTY of LONDON, & BY YE SAID SIR ROBERT YEAMANS, WHEN MAYOR AND ALDERMAN OF THIS CITTY, NAMED, QVEENE STREETE.

Chapels. A short description of a few of the leading chapels is here given. For the times of services, ministers, &c., see the tabulated statement of all the chapels in Bristol.

Baptist.

BROADMEAD. The original structure was built in 1671, but the present was erected about the beginning of the 18th century. The chapel is indelibly associated with Nonconformist religious life in Bristol, and many eloquent men have occupied its pulpit. It was enlarged in 1764, in 1799, in 1872, and in 1881 it was remodelled and greatly improved.

BUCKINGHAM (Richmond terrace, Clifton), a fine chaste Gothic structure, with rose window. Opened 2nd June, 1847; it cost £6,000. In point of architecture it is one of the finest Nonconformist places of worship in the city.

CITY ROAD was opened on the 11th September, 1861, the first discourse being preached by the Rev. C. H. Spurgeon. The cost, including schoolroom, &c., was £5,000. The congregation formerly worshipped in the Pithay Chapel, the oldest in the city (built 1650, rebuilt 1719), now converted into a portion of Messrs. Fry's factory.

COUNTERSLIP, Victoria street, is an ornate structure of recent date. The congregation that worship here formerly were at Counterslip, Bath st.

OLD KING STREET, erected in 1815 by the congregation from the Pithay, was opened 2nd April, 1817, by the Rev. Isaac Birt. The style is Debased Grecian.

TYNDALE, Whiteladies' road. Cruciform in plan, with vestibule, open porches, large baptistry under the east end, minister's, deacons' and ladies' vestries, a gallery at the west end, a stone staircase in the tower, which is only partially completed. The building is of Pennant stone, with freestone dressing, in the Second Pointed style. The windows throughout have been thoughtfully designed, and are unusually good specimens of modern construction. The chapel was opened 30th September, 1868, by the Hon. and Rev. Baptist Noel. In 1880 commodious lecture and class rooms were added eastward, the design being in accord with the main building. In December, 1882, three of the apex windows were filled in with stained glass, the gift of E. S. Robinson. The cost of chapel, lecture-hall, &c., has been about £13,000.

Calvinistic.

NEWFOUNDLAND STREET was adopted about the year 1809 by a section of the congregation of the Tabernacle, where they considered Calvinism was insufficiently set forth. The first preacher was the extraordinary William Huntingdon, S.S. (i.e., "Sinner Saved").

WELSH METHODISTS, Broadmead. The foundation stone was laid 1739. It is asserted that this chapel is the first John Wesley built in Bristol.

Congregational.

ARLEY, Cheltenham road, top of Stokes' croft, the foundation stone of which was laid by R. Ash, 22nd May, 1845, is in the Italian style of architecture, cruciform shape. The first sermon delivered within it was on the 20th June, 1855, by the Rev. J. Angell James.

BRUNSWICK, Brunswick square. The foundation stone was laid 25th

June, 1834, and opened 6th May following, by the Rev. Dr. Raffles preaching in the morning and Dr. Fletcher in the evening. The style of building is Grecian. The first marriage in a Dissenting chapel in Bristol was celebrated here on July 31st, 1837.

CASTLE GREEN. The present chapel succeeds one that was erected in the 18th century, rebuilt in 1815, and opened on 22nd November that year. The Rev. J. Angell James preached in the morning, and the Rev. William Jay in the evening. The dimensions are 76 feet in length and 53 feet in breadth. Edward Irving on one occasion preached within the walls of this chapel.

CLIFTON DOWN, a very handsome building. Its groined tympanum bears three sculptures in bass relief —Christ on the mount, St. John in the desert, and St. Paul at Athens; the interior is simple and chaste. The tower, when finished, will terminate in an open turret carried on four flying buttresses, light and airy, like the celebrated tower of Saint Nicholas in Newcastle-on-Tyne. The style is Early Decorated. This chapel —the original of which is one of the oldest in the city—was erected for the congregation that formerly worshipped in Bridge street, and was opened on the 13th November, 1868.

DAVID THOMAS MEMORIAL, Bishopston, was opened March 30th, 1881. It commands a very prominent position, especially its tower, which occupies the north-west angle, and commencing with a stoutly buttressed and square base, gradually diminishes in easy stages, until the spire, 125 feet high, of an octagonal form, is reached, and at this point the buttress is crowned with pinnacles.

HIGHBURY, Cotham New road, was opened for public worship 7th July, 1843, free of debt, by the Rev. W. Jay in the morning and Rev. J. Parsons in the evening. It is erected on the site where in 1556-7, during the reign of Queen Mary, five persons suffered martyrdom by being burned at the stake. A tablet is placed in the chapel recording the event. This was also the site of the gallows in a later age. The tower of the chapel is 75 feet high; transepts and lecture-rooms were added in 1863. The whole effect of the chapel in its mantling of ivy is picturesque. The first pastor was the Rev. David Thomas, which office he held till his death, Nov. 7th, 1875, and his son has now succeeded him.

HOPE, Granby hill, Hotwells, was built by Lady Glenorchy and Lady Henrietta Hope, and opened in 1786.

LODGE STREET was erected in 1831 to accommodate the congregation of Lady Huntingdon's Chapel in St. Augustine's place. Its cost was £4,500. The roof forms a nave and side aisles without pillars.

REDLAND PARK was opened on September 4th, 1861. Its style is Early English, and it has a square spire covered with slates. The structure consists of a nave, two aisles, and a north and south transept.

RUSSELL TOWN, built in the Perpendicular style, of Pennant stone, with Bath stone dressing. It has a nave, north and south aisles and semi-octagonal apse, with large stained-glass windows. The cost of the structure was £3,400, defrayed by William Sommerville, of Bitton, and the site was given by Christopher Godwin. The memorial stone was laid by the Mayor, E. S. Robinson, 10th June, 1867, and the chapel opened by the Rev. David Thomas, 2nd April, 1868.

STAPLETON ROAD. The memorial stone was laid by H. O. Wills, on 8th March, 1871, and opened on the 22nd March in the same year. The architecture is in the Italian order, and consists of blue Pennant stone with freestone dressings. Its cost was £2,350. Attached are several large class-rooms and a school.

TABERNACLE, Penn street. Opened in 1752, by George Whitefield. In 1771 the Rev. Rowland Hill began his preaching in this chapel. The first Sunday school in Bristol was commenced here.

ZION, Bedminster, erected at the sole expense of Mr. John Hare, at a cost of £4,000. It was opened 15th June, 1830, by the Rev. Dr. Chalmers, of Glasgow.

The Society of Friends.

This society was established in this city by one Dennis Hollister, in 1653. The present meeting-house in Rosemary street, on the site of the Old Dominican Friary, is the second on the same site; the latter being built in 1747 at a cost of £1,830, the earlier house having cost £655. "John Clark, of Bridgwater, who was well versed in architecture, used to say that the interior of this house would have been a perfect specimen of the style—the Roman Doric—if the bases of the pillars had been square instead of octagonal; and it appears from the minute of the Building Committee, which directs the cutting off of the corners, that they were originally square."

Jews' Synagogue.

JEWS' SYNAGOGUE, Park row, in the Moresque style, was opened on Sept. 8th, 1871. The cost of the site and building was upwards of £4,000. The Jews formerly met in Temple street, nearly opposite Temple Church gates; but the building was demolished in the recent street improvements of that locality.

Presbyterian.

The first anniversary of this body was held in Bristol at the Broadmead Rooms, May 18th, 1856, and the only church of this connection in the city is on St. James' parade; it is a neat Gothic building, with an elegant spire. Opened on Sept. 8th, 1859, by Dr. Macfarlane, of Glasgow.

Roman Catholic.

HOLY CROSS, Victoria street, was opened in 1874. The services now held here were formerly held in Bedminster.

ST. MARY, Quay, in the Grecian style, built originally for the Irvingites in 1840, at an expense of £15,000, was purchased by the Roman Catholics for £5,000 in 1843. It was dedicated by Bishop Baines (its title being changed to St. Mary's) on 5th July the same year. It was the last public labour of that prelate, for he was dead the next morning. In 1871 it was purchased by the Society of Jesus.

ST. NICHOLAS, Pennywell road, opened 21st September, 1850.

THE HOLY APOSTLES, or THE PRO-CATHEDRAL, Clifton. This church was opened 21st Sept., 1848. The church became a pro-cathedral, such title being given to express that it was only to be in the place of a cathedral until such time when the latter could be built and consecrated. It lays claim to have been the first church in which the confessionals were publicly erected and the stations of the cross put up since the time of Queen Mary, and is the only place in this part of England where the ritual and services of the Catholic Church are fully carried out.

Unitarian.

LEWIN'S MEAD. This chapel stands on the site of the Franciscan Monastery. The present capacious structure was erected prior to 1790. It has three aisles and three galleries. The first chapel is inferred to have been erected in 1693, being founded by John Weeks.

OAKFIELD ROAD, opened Dec. 8th, 1864. The building consists of a nave, 72 feet by 28; aisle, 72 feet by 13; chancel, 19 feet by 21; organ chamber and singers' gallery, and minister's and deacons' vestries. The nave is separated from the aisle by an arcade of five arches, supported on polished granite shafts from Aberdeen. The whole of the seats are formed on the most modern principle, with cut bench ends. The chancel seats have carved bench ends, with poppy heads. The roof is supported upon corbels, with

Devonshire marble shafts and carved capitals and bases, and between the spandrils are panels filled in with Devonshire marble. The east window is filled with stained glass representing the last supper, by O'Connor, of London. The style of the exterior is that of the 14th century, and the materials used are native stone from the Pembroke road quarries. The cost, including the land, was about £6,000, and it was opened by the Rev. James Martineau.

United Methodist Free Church.

HEBRON, Victoria road, Bedminster. Founded in 1853 and opened in 1854. Its cost, including burial ground, was £2,500.

MILK STREET was opened in February, 1854, by the Rev. W. Spencer Edwards, and re-opened on October 27th, 1861. Its architecture is of the Italian order.

Wesleyan.

GRENVILLE, near the Cumberland Basin, Hotwells, was built at the expense of Thomas Whippie, who, though a member of the Church of England, had wide sympathy with all Evangelical bodies. Opened in 1839.

EBENEZER, Old King street, was erected in 1795, and renovated and improved in 1869.

OLD MARKET STREET was opened in 1817, when sermons were preached by the Revs. Richard Watson, Jabez Bunting and Robert Newton. The chapel was improved and new class-rooms erected in 1865.

PORTLAND STREET was opened on 26th August, 1792, by Samuel Bradburn, whose text was Acts xxxiii. 22, the subject being—"Methodism set forth and defended." The building was erected principally through the instrumentality of Lieut. Webb, of the 48th Regiment Foot, who frequently preached in it in his regimentals. He died in 1796 and was buried there, and to his memory a neat monument is placed on the eastern side of the chapel. In 1871 the building was enlarged.

TRINITY, Whiteladies' road, Clifton, was erected in 1866, and opened Nov. 1st in that year, when the Rev. W. Shaw preached in the morning and the Rev. W. M. Punshon in the evening. It is a handsome building in the Decorated style, and has a neat spire.

VICTORIA, Whiteladies' road, in elegant Decorated Gothic style, was erected in 1863. The plan is a parallelogram, 86 feet by 39 feet. The height from the base to the top of the cross in front is 68 feet. The exterior, which is of freestone, is interspersed with bands of Clevedon yellow magnesian limestone and of Williton red sandstone. The deeply recessed doorway of the porch is of elaborate workmanship, as also are the three windows above it. The interior is not divided by piers and arches, the roof being in one span, supported by framed trusses with collar beams and arched ribs. These ribs rest on banded freestone shafts, with carved capitals. It is lighted on either side by six two-light windows, with plate tracery heads, and by three windows in the western end of similar character, but larger and more elaborately treated; also by a circular window in the gable of the east end of richly stained glass. The pulpit and reading desk are of oak, inlaid with mahogany; the seating is also of oak. There is a gallery. The cost of the site was £1,025, and of the chapel £5,350. Underneath the chapel is a large room running the entire length and breadth, 14 feet high, used for meetings. The foundation stone was laid by James Budgett, on April 22nd, 1862, and the chapel opened by the Rev. F. A. West on June 29th, 1863.

WESLEY, Baptist Mills. Opened in 1837. It is built on the spot where the Rev. J. Wesley preached his first sermon in the open air, April 2nd, 1739, his text being—"The spirit of the Lord is upon me." The stone on which he then stood has been used as the foundation stone of the present building.

CHA   DICTIONARY OF BRISTOL.   CHA

Chapel.	Situation.	Sunday Services A.M.	Sunday Services P.M.	Week-day Services.	Pastor.
BAPTIST—					
Broadmead	Broadmead	11.0	6.30	Tuesday, 7.30	Rev. E. G. Gange.
Buckingham	Buckingham pl., Clifton	11.0	6.30	Tuesday, 7.30	Rev. J. Penny.
City road	Stokes' Croft	11.0	6.30	Tuesday, 7.0	Rev. W. J. Mayers.
Cotham grove	Cotham	11.0	6.30		Rev. G. P. Gould, M.A.
Counterslip	Victoria street	11.0	6.30	Tuesday, 7.0	
Old King street	Old King street	11.0	6.30	Tuesday, 7.30	Rev. G. D. Evans.
Philip street	Bedminster	10.45	6.30	Tu. & Th., 7.30	Rev. J. J. Ellis.
Providence	Grosvenor rd., St. Paul's	10.30	8.0	Thursday, 7.30	
Thrissell street	Easton road	10.30	6.0	Tu. & Th., 7.0	Rev. C. Griffiths.
Tyndale	Whiteladies' road	11.0	6.30	Tuesday, 7.30	Rev. R. Glover.
Upper Maudlin street	Upper Maudlin street	10.30	6.30	Mo.&Wed. 7.30	Supply
West street	Bedminster	10.30	6.30		
BIBLE CHRISTIAN—					
Gladstone street	Stapleton road	11.0	6.30	Thursday, 7.30	Rev. J. Gifford.
Redcliff crescent	New Cut	11.0	6.30	Wednes., 7.30	Rev. Alex. Trengrove.
Mission hall	St. Philip's marsh	11.0	6.30		
BRISTOL CITY MISSION, CHAPELS OF THE—*					MISSIONARY.
Sergeant street		—	6.30	M., 7.30, Th., 7.0	Mr. H. Kingdon.
Great Ann street		10.45†	6.30	M.,Th.&S.,7.30	Mr. S. Jordan.
York street		—		Wednes., 7.30	Mr. A. Wiltshire.
Salmon street				Services conducted by friends from Highbury.
John street		10.45	6.30	Wednes., 7.30	Mr. Owen Butler.
Barton hill		11.0	6.30	Wednes., 7.30	Mr. H. Webb.
Cumberland street		11.0	6.30	Tu. & Th., 7.30	Mr. J. H. Bell.
Owen street		11.0	6.30	Wednes., 7.30	Mr. J. Rees.
Wells street	Near Lodge street			Wednes., 7.30	

* Hon. Secs.:—C. Townsend, Avenue house, Cotham park ; L. Waterman, The Shrubbery, Redland. Treasurer:—W. Mack, 88 Park street. † Service at 2.30 p.m.

36

Chapel.	Situation.	Sunday Services. A.M.	Sunday Services. P.M.	Week-day Services.		Pastor.
CATHOLIC APOSTOLIC CHURCH—						
Upper Berkeley place	Clifton	10.0	5.0	M., & Th., W. & Th.,	5.0 A.M. 6.0 9.30	Mr. S. Handcock, Sec.
CHRISTADELPHIAN—						
Oddfellows Hall	Rupert street	11.0	6.30	Wednes.,	8.0	
CHRISTIAN BRETHREN—						
Clifton Bethesda	Alma road	10.45	6.30	Wednes.,	7.0	Mr. G. Muller,
Great George street	Park street	10.45	6.30	Monday,	7.0	Mr. G. F. Bergin,
Stokes' Croft	Stokes' Croft	10.45	6.30	Thursday,	7.0	Mr. James Wright, and Supplies.
Gospel hall	Totterdown	10.45	6.30	Wednes.,	7.15	
Midland road	St. Philip's	10.45	6.30*	Tu. & W.,	7.30	Mr. W. J. Morgan.
CONGREGATIONAL—						
Anvil street	St. Philip's	10.45	6.30	Tu. & Th.,	7.15	Rev. B. G. Archer.
Arley	Cheltenham road	11.0	6.30	Tuesday,	7.30	Rev. J. Comper Gray.
Bethel	Windmill hill					
Brick Street Mission (connected with Stapleton road)				Wednes.,	8.0	
Bridge street	Barton hill		6.30	Tuesday,	7.30	
Brunswick	Brunswick square	11.0	6.30	Tuesday,	7.30	Rev. Alex. Wilson, B.A.
Castle green	Castle green	10.45	6.30	Tuesday,	7.30	Rev. E. S. Bayliffe, B.A.
Christ Church	Sneyd park	10.45	6.30			Rev. J. P. Allen, M.A.
Clifton down	Clifton park down	11.0	6.30			Rev. Arthur Hall
David Thomas Memorial Ch.	Bishopston	11.0	6.30*	Tuesday,	7.30	Rev. W. Clarkson, B.A.
Gideon	Newfoundland street	11.0	6.30			
Highbury	Cotham	11.0	6.30	Tuesday,	7.30	Rev. H. A. Thomas, M.A.
Hope	Granby hill, Clifton	11.0	6.30	Tuesday,	7.0	Rev. F. W. Browne.
Kingsland	Dings, St. Philip's	11.0	6.30	Tuesday,	7.0	Rev. W. Mobram.
Lodge street	Lodge street	11.0	6.30	Tuesday,	7.0	
Lower Castle street (Welsh)	Lower Castle street	11.0	6.15	Wednes.,	7.0	Rev. W. H. Skinner.

* Third Sunday in month, at 3 p.m., service for the young.

CHA — DICTIONARY OF BRISTOL. — CHA

Chapel.	SITUATION.	SUNDAY SERVICES. A.M.	SUNDAY SERVICES. P.M.	WEEK-DAY SERVICES.	PASTOR.
CONGREGATIONAL, *continued*—					
Pembroke	Oakfield road, Clifton	11.0	6.30	Tuesday, 7.30	Rev. L. H. Byrnes, B.A.
Redland park	Whiteladies' road	11.0	6.30	Tu. & Fri., 7.30	Rev. Urijah R. Thomas.
Russell Town	Lawrence hill	11.0	6.30	Tuesday, 7.0	Rev. W. Lance.
Sergeant street	Bedminster	11.0	6.30		
Stapleton road	Stapleton road	10.45	6.30	Tu. & Th., 7.15	
Tabernacle	Penn street	10.45	6.30	Tu. & Th., 7.15	Mr. — Betts.
Wycliff	Guinea street	10.45	6.30	Tu. & Th., 7.0	Rev. S. W. McAll.
Whitfield Memorial	Ashley road	10.45	6.30	Tuesday, 7.30	Rev. George Wood, B.A.
Zion	Bedminster bridge	11.0	6.30	Tuesday, 7.0	
FRIENDS, THE—					
Rosemary street	Rosemary street	10.30	6.30	Thursday, 7.0†	Mr. W. Hobson, *Supt.*
New street	St. Jude's	10.45	6.30*	W. & Fri., 7.30	
JEWS' SYNAGOGUE	Park row	Fri., sunset		Sat., 8.30 a.m., 2.0 p.m., and half an hour after sunset.	Rev. David Fay. Rev. A. H. Eisenberg.
METHODIST, PRIMITIVE—					
Eastville	Eastville	10.45	6.30	Wednes., 7.30	Rev. C. Stockdale.
Mission hall	Mina road	10.45	6.30	Thursday, 7.30	
Bedminster down	Bedminster	11.0	6.0	Tuesday, 7.0	
Essex street	Bedminster	11.0	6.0	Thursday, 7.0	
Totterdown	Anjer's road	11.0	6.30	Wednes., 7.30	Rev. T. T. Shields.
Barton hill	Somers town	10.45	6.30	Wednes., 7.30	
Mount Tabor	Newfoundland road	11.0	6.30	Thursday, 7.30	
Rose green	Rose green	—	2.30 6.0	Thursday, 7.0	
Ebenezer	Orchard street, Batch	10.45	6.30	Wednes., 7.30	Rev. J. Butcher.
Fishponds	Fishponds	10.45	6.0	Tuesday, 7.0	Rev. T. J. Watson.
Salisbury street	St. George's	11.0	6.0	Thursday, 7.30	
Whitehall	St. George's	11.0	6.15	Tuesday, 7.30	

* Extra service at 2.45 p.m. † Service on Wednesdays at 10.30 a.m.

Chapel.	SITUATION.	SUNDAY SERVICES. A.M. P.M.	WEEK-DAY SERVICES. P.M.	PASTOR.
METHODIST FREE CHURCHES, UNITED—				
Bristol North Circuit:				
Milk street	Milk street	10.30 6.30	Tuesday, 7.0	
Horfield	Horfield road	10.30 6.30	Tuesday, 7.0	Rev. Wm. Motley Hunter,
Durdham down	Blackboy hill	10.30 6.0	Thursday, 7.0	Rev. G. Thompson.
Westbury	Westbury-on-Trym	10.30 6.0	Wednes., 7.0	
Tyler's Fields	St. Philip's	11.0 6.0		
St. George's road	St. George's road	11.0 6.30	Wednes. 7.0	
Country chapels: Redwick, Compton, Patchway, Pilning, Olveston and Littleton.				
Bristol South Circuit:				
Hebron	Bedminster	10.30 6.0	Tuesday, 7.0	
Portwall lane	Portwall lane	10.30 6.30	Wednes., 7.0	Rev. W. H. Beekin,
Spring place	Pyle hill	10.30 6.0	Wednes., 7.0	Rev. Wm. R. Tungate.
Ashton Gate	Bedminster	10.45 6.0		
Oxford street	Totterdown	10.45 6.30		
Country chapels: Keynsham, West Town, Nailsea, Claverham and Chew Magna.				
Bristol East Circuit:				
Trinity road	Newtown	10.30 6.30	Wednes., 7.0	Rev. J. Elsom,
Baptist mills	Baptist mills	10.30 6.0		Rev. H. R. Wilkinson.
Russell town	Russell town	10.30 6.0		
Eastville	Eastville	10.30 6.0		
Easton Home Mission	Easton	10.30 6.0		Rev. J. H. Birkett.
Country chapels: Winterbourne, Watley's End, Frampton and Kendleshire.				
Bristol West Circuit:				
Redland grove		11.0 6.30	Tuesday, 7.30	
METHODIST, WESLEYAN—*King Street Circuit:*				
Ebenezer	Old King street	11.0 6.30	Tu. & Fri., 7.30	Rev. W. Nicholson,
Cotham	Redland road	11.0 6.30	W. & Sat., 7.30	Rev. J. R. Gregory,
Country chapels: Ashley down and Filton				Mr. W. R. Williams,
				Mr. W. E. Sellers.

39

Chapel.

METHODIST, WESLEYAN, continued—

	SITUATION.	SUNDAY SERVICES. A.M. P.M.	WEEK-DAY SERVICES. P.M.	PASTOR.
Portland Street Circuit:				
Portland street	Kingsdown	11.0 6.30*	W., 7.15, F., 7.15	Rev. G. Bowden,
Old Market street	Old Market street	10.45 6.30	W. & Fri., 7.30	Rev. W. Hawken,
St. Philip's marsh	St. Philip's	11.0 6.30	Tuesday, 7.30	Rev. W. Wood,
Country chapel: Bedwick	...	...	...	Mr. E. Tovey,
				Mr. W. Way,
				Mr. W. D. Williams,
				Mr. S. Atkinson.
Langton Street Circuit:				
Langton street	Langton street	10.30 6.30	W. & Fri., 7.15	Rev. S. Cox,
Bedminster	Bedminster	10.45 6.0	Th. & Sat., 7.30	Rev. J. Spensley,
Knowle	Knowle	11.0 6.30	M. & W., 7.30	Rev. T. B. Harrowell,
Rose street	Rose street	— 6.0		Mr. J. Philp,
Country chapels: Keynsham, Chew Stoke, Pensford, Stanton Drew, Nailsea, Downside, Brislington, Burnett, Greenbank road, Upper Knowle and Chewton Keynsham				Mr. W. C. Bourne, Mr. P. Prescott.
Clifton Circuit:				
Victoria	Whiteladies' road	11.0 6.30	W., 7, F., 8.0	Rev. W. J. Tweddle,
Grenville	Cumberland basin	11.0 6.30	Tu., 7, F., 7.30	Rev. M. G. Pearse,
Trinity	Whiteladies' road	11.0 6.30	W. & Fri., 7.30	Rev. G. T. Keeble,
Wesley	Durdham down	11.0 6.30		Mr. J. Wolfendale,
Country chapels: Pill, Failand, Westbury-upon-Trym, Lawrence-Weston, Shirehampton and Avonmouth				Mr. W. Woolmer.
Wesley Circuit:				
Wesley	Baptist mills	10.30 6.30	Tu. 7, F., 7.30	Rev. W. R. Jones,
Country chapels: Redfield, Crew's Hole and Bloy street				Mr. J. C. Stanfield

PLYMOUTH BRETHREN—

Orchard street	St. Augustine's	10.30 6.30		
Hampton road	Hampton road	10.30 6.30		
Windmill hill	Bedminster	10.30 6.30		
Stapleton road	Stapleton road	10.30 6.30		
Victoria street	Clifton	11.0 —		

* Extra service at 8.0 p.m.

Chapel.	SITUATION.	SUNDAY SERVICES. A.M.	SUNDAY SERVICES. P.M.	WEEK-DAY SERVICES. P.M.	PASTOR.
PRESBYTERIAN—					
St. James's parade	St. James's	11.0	6.30	Thursday, 7.30	Rev. A. F. Forrest.
					PRIEST.
ROMAN CATHOLIC—					
Church of the Apostles	Park place, Clifton	7.0 8.0 11.0	3.0 6.30 —	Holydays, 7.0, 8.0, 11.0 a.m.; 6.30 p.m.	Hon. Rt. Rev. Clifford, D.D. Rev. Canon J. J. Clarke, D.D. Rev. Arthur Russell. Rev. Thomas Hill
St. Mary's	St. Augustine's Bank	7.30 8.30 9.30	2.30 6.30 —	...	Hon. Rev. W. I. Clifford. Rev. Ignatius Grant. Rev. Wm. Strickland, S.J.
St. Nicholas	Pennywell road	11.0 8.0 11.0	— 3.0 6.30	...	Rev. Canon Coxon, M.R. Rev. Joseph O'Grady.
Holy Cross	Victoria street	8.30 11.0	6.30	...	Mons. E. English, D.D.

Monastery.—Franciscan Friars, Minors, St. Catherine's, Park place, Clifton.
Convents.—"Our Lady of Mercy," Dighton street; Arno's court, Brislington; Little Sisters of the Poor, Cotham park; Monastery of the Visitation, Westbury-on-Trym; Clifton Wood Convent; Dames de la Mere de Dieu, Manilla hall, Clifton.

SALVATION ARMY—					
Stations: Circus, York street, St. Paul's; West street, Bedminster; Horton street, St. Phillip's; Salem chapel, Colston street; Eastville; Lawrence hill. Services every evening, 7.30.; Sunday, 7.0, 10.30 a.m.; 3.0, 6.0 p.m.					
SEAMEN'S MISSION ROOM—(formerly Floating chapel)	Quay	11.0	2.30 6.30	...	Mr. Simon Short.
					PASTOR.
UNITARIAN—					
Lewin's Mead	Lewin's Mead	11.0	6.30	...	Rev. A. N. Blatchford, B.A.
Ditto Domestic Mission	Lower Montague street	—	6.30	Wednes., 8.0	Rev. W. Matthews.
Oakfield road	Oakfield road	11.0	6.30	...	
UNITED BRETHREN (MORAVIANS)—					
Upper Maudlin street	Upper Maudlin street	11.0	6.30	Wednes., 7.30	Rev. T. Orr.
UNITED FRIENDS' PREACHING ROOM	Great gardens				

Chapter House of the Cathedral.

Chapter houses received the same rite of consecration as the churches to which they were attached; they were honoured with the interment of patrons, abbots, and other great persons; in them elections were made of heads of monasteries, and from them all processions commenced after such elections. The chapter house, with its vestibule, exhibits some most interesting Norman work of advanced or transition date. The arches of the vestibule spring from clustered columns with cushioned capitals, and are studded with nail-head ornaments. The chapter room is greatly enriched with zigzag trellis and other mouldings on the wall, arcades and groined ribs of the vaulting. The room is now of only two bays.

Charity Organisation,

or Mendicity Society, 19 College green, assists the helpless and unveils the roguery of the professed mendicant. During the year 1882 553 cases of mendicity came under its notice. Of these, when examined by the society's officers, 43 could not be found owing to the false addresses given by the parties; 102 turned out to be not requiring relief; 138 were totally undeserving; and 182 were cases for ordinary poor law relief, or otherwise ineligible. These figures account for more than five-sixths of the total. As for the few deserving applicants, nearly all were assisted, directly or indirectly, by the society, some receiving grants and others being found employment. The institution is very slenderly supported, and the committee state that unless they receive a larger measure of support the society must cease to exist. The statement will be tidings of great joy to the worthless class who prey upon the almsgiver, but it may be hoped that the good sense of the truly benevolent only requires to be appealed to in order to prevent such a result. The society has two enquiry clerks, for the purpose of ascertaining whether applicants are fit and proper persons to have charity dispensed to them. Keynon Stow, hon. secretary; Henry J. Howse, assistant secretary.

Charity Trustees.

The administration of the Bristol charities was originally in the hands of the Corporation, but by the Municipal Corporations Act, 1836, the management was removed from the Corporation and vested in a body composed of 21 trustees. The net annual income of the charities dispensed may be roughly stated at £27,000. In 1852 the Lord Chancellor decided against the claim of the trustees to nominate and choose persons to fill vacancies in their body and himself appointed nine gentlemen. The offices were formerly in Queen square, but they are temporarily at Lucas Hall, Baldwin street. F. W. Newton, secretary. The Board meet every Friday, at 10.30 a.m.; the Finance Committee, nine in number, every Thursday after the first Monday in the month, at 2 p.m.; the Estates Committee, eight in number, and the Almshouse Committee, six in number. There are seven Christmas Gift Committees, viz., one each for St. Mary Redcliff and St. Thomas, Temple, St. Michael and St. Augustine, Central, St. James, St. Paul, Castle Precincts and St. Philip.

There are three governing bodies, viz.:—

Grammar School Governors, who meet the second Friday in March, June, September and December at 11.30 a.m. The School Committee consists of eleven members.

Queen Elizabeth's Hospital Governors meet the second Friday in January, April, July and October, at 11.30 a.m. The School Committee, of eleven members, meet on the first Tuesday in each month at noon, as follows:—March, June, September and December, at the Hospital; otherwise at the office.

The *Red Maids' School* Governors meet the second Friday in February, May, August and November, at 11.30 a.m. The School Committee, consisting of four ladies and seven gentlemen, meet at the School on the third Wednesday in each month, at 3 p.m.

A Finance Committee of nine members serve the three governing bodies, who meet the Thursday after the first Monday in each month, at 2 p.m.

The following is a list of LOAN MONEYS and CHARITIES (*see also* "Almshouses") :—

Loan Moneys.

Sir Thomas White, John Heydon, Robert Thorn, Robert Aldworth, George White, John Whitson, Thomas Jones, Robert Kitchen, Robert Rogers, John Dunster, Robert Redwood, Francis James, John Doughty and Thomas Pearce Allison each left sums of money to be loaned. These moneys are all consolidated and are lent in sums not exceeding £500 or less than £50 to any merchant, trader, manufacturer, or mechanic residing and trading in Bristol, free burgesses having the preference, on the joint security of the borrower and two or more sureties, for a term not exceeding six years. All sums under £100 are free of interest; from £100 to £300, at 1 per cent. per annum; from £300 to £500, at 2 per cent. per annum. Young men commencing business are preferred. Dr. Thomas White's Loan Fund is in sums of £30, free of interest, within the enlarged boundaries of the city. The loans are obtained on petition, upon the bond of the borrower and two or more sureties. Under a scheme of the Endowed Schools' Commissioners, of the 13th May, 1875, one moiety of the funds was added to the endowment of the Grammar School. The present Loan Fund amounts to £3,400, added to which £1,000 is invested as a sinking fund for making good occasional losses.

Charities.

BONVILLE'S. Five recipients of £21, 17 of £10 10s., and 53 of £5 5s., all poor housekeepers in Bristol, not recipients of alms, and able to attend some place of divine worship twice every Sunday; also 50 poor lodgers in the city of Bristol, viz., 15 of £10, and 35 of £5 5s.

CHESTER'S, THOMAS. £8 is distributed in gifts of 10/- each to 7 inmates of St. John's Almshouse, and 5/- to 18 poor parishioners of St. John's.

COX'S, EDWARD. £10, which is given away in sums of 10/- or £1, to persons in the parishes of St. Philip's, St. James', or Redcliff.

ELTON'S, ABRAHAM. Ten poor persons of All Saints', 4/- each.

FULLER'S, FRANCIS. £12, distributed in sums of 10/- at the discretion of the individual members of the Charity Trustees, to the poor of St. Philip and Jacob Within.

GIST'S. Three men, £20 12s., and three females, £18; must be over 50 years, natives of Bristol, without an income of £20 a year.

HABERFIELD'S, LADY. 30/- each to 10 poor married women, whose husbands are living, not receiving parish relief.

HARRINGTON'S, GEORGE. 54 free burgesses and housekeepers of the ancient city, 10/- each, on the nomination of the churchwardens of the several parishes.

HOLBYN'S, THOMAS. Nine poor people in St. Thomas' parish, 10/- each.

JACKSON'S, JOSEPH. 4/- to 44 housekeepers, being freemen or widows of freemen, recommended by the overseers and churchwardens.

KITCHEN'S. £27, in gifts of 10/- each, amongst the poor of the several parishes of the city. Grants of £3 at Lady-day and £3 at Michaelmas to the Alderman's poor kindred, and grants not exceeding £5 are bestowed on distressed citizens.

LUDLOW'S, ELIZABETH. £30 amongst 5 poor widows and widowed daughters of free burgesses, residing within the limits of the ancient city. The gratuity is not as a rule given two years following to the same person.

LUDLOW'S, HANNAH. 18 widows and single women above 50 years of age, £30.

MERLOTT'S. 47 blind persons, £10 each. The petitioners are divided into four classes: the first, persons who have attained 80 years; the second, those of 70 and under 80 years; the third, those of 60 and under 70 years; the fourth, those of 50 and under 60 years.

PELOQUIN'S, MARY ANN. The interest of £5,200 amongst 38 poor women, freemen, or widows or daughters of freemen, housekeepers in the ancient city, £6 6s. each; this gift can only be obtained once in three years by the same person. The interest of £2,500 amongst 52 poor lying-in women, wives of freemen, 30/- each; these gifts are in the nomination of the mayoress for the time being. The interest of £1,000 amongst 20 poor widows and single women and 10 poor men; nominated by the minister and churchwardens of St. Stephen's.

SLOPER'S, CHARLES. Bibles amounting to £15 for distribution amongst the poor in the ancient city.

THURSTON'S, ANN. Nine gifts of £1 each to women in childbed, being the wives of freemen, without distinction of residence; nominated by the mayor or mayoress.

WHITE'S. Four poor maidens, who have lived at least 5 years in one place, or have been for a like period steadily engaged in the pursuit of some trade or other calling, upon their marriage, £10 each; also 4 men and 4 women, £35 each; candidates must be 50 years of age and unable to work, and not in receipt of parochial relief within 12 months next preceding the time of election.

WHITSON'S, ALDERMAN. £1 to poor lying-in women residing within the boundaries of the ancient city; also £1 to 104 poor men, being householders, residing within the ancient city; and further, 52 poor widows, resident in the ancient city, 10/- each.

The following charities are not under the administration of the Charity Trustees :—

BIRKIN'S, ABRAHAM. Testator was a Bristolian, a soapmaker by trade, who made his will 18th Nov., 1668. After payment of certain specific gifts of small aggregate amount, the residue of the income of the charity is appropriated (under a scheme approved by the Charity Commissioners, 25th March, 1875) in bursaries or scholarships of £4 per annum and upwards, granted to children in public elementary schools in the parishes of St. Mary-le-port, St. James, Temple, St Philip and Jacob, St. Nicholas and St. Paul, and their district parishes, and in assisting such children in obtaining technical education. Trustees, the senior churchwardens of the parishes participating and ten elected trustees; secretary, James R. Bramble, 2 Bristol chambers, Nicholas street.

COLE'S, MRS. ALICE. The trustees of this charity hold an annual examination for scholarships in the month of May. The scholarships are of the value of not more than £10 each, and are assigned to the most meritorious candidates, being poor boys, resident in the city of Bristol and scholars in any parochial or other elementary school there, who shall be elected by the said trustees for proficiency and good conduct. An additional scholarship of £5 a year, tenable for two years, is awarded on certain conditions to the boy who does best of all the candidates at the examination. The trustees also award scholarships to boys in Certified Industrial and Ragged Schools, for which a separate examination is arranged. The trustees invite the masters, trustees, or managers of any school of the above description desirous of sending boys for examination to apply in writing, in October, for the conditions and subjects of examination to J. Curtis, Secretary, Exchange buildings, Bristol.

LANGTON'S, MRS. JOHN, for the benefit of poor widows whose husbands were free burgesses of the city, amounting to £2. Applications to be made at the office of Osborne, Ward, Vassall & Co., giving the certificates of age and marriage of the applicants, the burial of the husband and copy of his freedom, on a day named by advertisement, which appears in the local newspapers about the middle of January. Forms of petition to be had on application.

REYNOLDS', RICHARD. Managed by nine trustees. Was founded by Richard Reynolds in 1809, during his lifetime, for the benefit of certain charitable institutions in Bristol whilst they shall be supported by voluntary contributions, and shall not invest any annual income except legacies, the net income being applicable to any one or more of them in such portions as the trustees shall determine upon, or to be distributed by the trustees themselves amongst the objects of these institutions, or any of them, at the discretion of the trustees. J. S. Fry, chairman.

Charters. The Bristol archives are rich in ancient parchment lore, some of its charters being unique specimens of an early age, and many of them in a good state of preservation, amongst which may be mentioned, as the most interesting, that given by John when Earl Moretoñ (1185); that of 1373, which made Bristol a county of itself; the charter granted by Charles II., on June 2nd, 1684 (costing £554 13s. 6d.), which enacted "that the city be incorporated by the name of the mayor, burgesses and commonalty of the city of Bristol, having the same legal privileges as heretofore, to have a common seal," &c.; and on July 24th, 1710, Queen Anne granted a new and the last charter to the city, wherein she confirmed all former privileges.

Chatterton, Thomas, the second son of Thomas and Sarah Chatterton, was born at Bristol on the 20th of November, 1752. He was a posthumous child, his father having died three months before his birth. On the 1st of the following January he was baptised at St. Mary Redcliff, the register of the same church having already received the entries of the baptism of a brother and a sister of the future poet. The early education of the latter was acquired under Mr. Thomas Love, at the Free School, Pile street, of which humble institution his father had been the previous master. The boy is said to have made but slow progress in learning, a fact which seems hardly to agree with the precocity of his poetical genius, the rapid development of which has led some critics to assume that the maturity of his intellectual power had been reached at the time of his premature death. This we believe to be an unqualified inference, but we need not here delay to discuss the question. An early consciousness of his own mental capacity seems to be reflected in some quaint lines uttered by one of the persons of his imagination:—

In all his harmless gambols and child's play
I kenned a purpled light of wisdom's ray;
He sat down learning with the wastle cake
As wise as any of the aldermen;
He'd wit enough to make a mayor at ten.

Attached to the Pile street school, which yet flourishes nearly opposite the northern side of Redcliff Church, is the schoolmaster's house, where Mrs. Chatterton was living at the time of her poetic son's birth, but which she quitted soon after for a dwelling on Redcliff hill, opposite the western end of the same edifice. Chatterton's boyhood was thus spent beneath the shadow of that magnificent fane whose influences inspired his imagination and mediævalised his spirit. It is remarkable that in an age when Gothic architecture was no more appreciated than was the young poet himself, and was treated by so-called people of taste with as much neglect and contempt as were the *Rowley Poems* of Chatterton's creation by the readers of the day, that a boy of humble parentage and inferior culture should be able to perceive the inexhaustible interest and understand the majesty of this, in his own phrase, "wonder of mansyons." Its fretted walls and columned aisles, its effigied tombs and quaint brasses, with the ancient atmosphere of the fabric, were the spell that wrought upon the boy's impressionable temperament; and though no monk had ever been associated with its services, we need hardly wonder that some cowled and visionary Rowley should appear between the living and the dead to rehearse in poetry to a poet the romantic images of his mediæval fancy. But we have somewhat anticipated the course of the boy's biography. At the age of eight years he became a scholar in Colston's Blue Coat School, a charitable foundation somewhat upon the plan of Christ's Hospital, London. The gabled building that for more than a century served for school purposes has been removed, and Colston Hall stands on its site, the school itself being transferred to Stapleton. Curiously enough, William Howitt speaks of the school in Pile street as no longer existing, but of that on St. Augustine's back as not only standing, but likely to stand, the fact being that the former, and not the latter, has been preserved. Before passing to Colston's school the boy had taken to studious habits, his passion for reading having been apparently awakened by what his biographers have described as an "ancient black letter Bible," but that would appear to have been rather a family *History of the Bible*. At least such a volume, that unquestionably belonged to the Chatterton household, has recently come to light, having been discovered by John Taylor, of the Bristol Museum and Library, at the shop of a curiosity dealer in Maudlin street, and is now in possession of William George, Park street. It contains the original entries of the birth and baptism of each of Thomas and Sarah Chatterton's children, including those of the poet. The book has been much thumbed, some of the illustrative pictures having been rudely coloured with ochre, probably by the boy-poet himself. From the time he began to read he grew thoughtful and reserved. His pocket money went for the purchase or borrowing of books, and on Sundays or holidays "he was either wandering solitarily in the fields, sitting beside the tomb of Canynges in the church, or was shut up in a little room at his mother's, attending to no meal times, and only issuing out when he did appear begrimed with ochre, charcoal and black lead." The meaning of his behaviour and condition was not at first clear, and was only explained when the character of the *Rowley Poems* came to be investigated. As little regarded in general as the church itself were the materials of its history by those in charge of the structure. There were contained in certain chests, one of which, called Canynges' coffer, was originally secured with six locks, but which in young Rowley's time was thought worthy of no lock at all, for except certain deeds that affected ecclesiastical property a multitude of documents were allowed to be scattered and misused. Some of these caught the attention of young Chatterton, the result being to suggest the fabrication of the *Rowley Poems*, by using the old parchment as writing material. In his 14th year Chatterton became apprenticed to an attorney named Lambert, a proud and insolent man, with no more poetry in his nature than was to be found in the title deeds of property executed for his clients, of whom he had very few. Here the boy's life was one of degradation and insult, having after twelve hours' work in the office (dinner hour only excepted) to sleep with the footboy and to undergo many like indignities. Lambert's office was in Corn street, at a house yet standing opposite the Exchange. It was from this place that he addressed some letters to Dodsley, the publisher, and to the Hon. Horace Walpole, which strongly affected the destiny of the writer. He had once affirmed to a friend that "it was very easy for a person who had studied antiquity, with the aid of a few books which he could name, to copy the style of the ancient poets so exactly, that the most skilful observer should not be able to detect him; no," said he, "not Mr. Walpole himself." In conformity with this opinion, the young poet wrote (December 21st, 1768) to Mr. Dodsley, bookseller, of Pall Mall, to acquaint him that he could "procure copies of several ancient poems, and an interlude, perhaps the oldest dramatic piece extant, 'written by one Rowley, a priest of Bristol, who lived in the reigns of Henry VI. and Edward IV.'" Any reply to this offer was to be directed to "D. B., to be left with Mr. Thomas Chatterton, Redcliffe hill, Bristol." No reply, however, appears to have come, and in less than two months later Mr. Dodsley was addressed with particulars concerning the tragedy of Ælla, an ancient piece with which his correspondent professed to have met in the hands of a person who would not part with its possession for less than a guinea. To tempt the remittance of this poor sum the tragedy was described as "perfect, the plot clear, the language spirited, and the songs (interspersed in it) as flowing, poetical and elegantly simple," and as extending to about a thousand lines. A specimen extract of the tragedy was included in the letter, but it is generally thought that no answer was deigned from Mr. Dodsley. It seems pitiable that in an age when such commonplace versifiers as Blackmore, Yalden, Garth and Sprat, whose sepulchres remain to this day in that extensive cemetery, Chalmer's *British Poets*, should have been thought worthy of a hearing, that poetry of such force of imagination and fulness of picturesque description and incident as the tragedy of Ælla, with its idyllic love scenes and homeric rush and tumult of battle should be offered and refused at less than one farthing a line. Chatterton's failure with Dodsley was followed by an appeal to the Hon. Horace Walpole, then engaged on his *Anecdotes of British Painters*. The attorney's clerk offered to furnish that noble writer with an account of some eminent painters who had flourished in old time at Bristol, at the same time mentioning the discovery of some old poems, enclosing also a specimen of the latter on the death of Richard I. Walpole, unacquainted with the lowly condition of his correspondent, and charmed with the style of the letter and the offer of such acceptable particulars, gave the politest welcome to his communication. He thinks himself "singularly obliged," and gives him a thousand thanks for his very curious and kind letter. "What you have sent," he declares, "is valuable and full of information; but instead of correcting you, sir, you are far more able to correct me, and I shall be happy to lay up any notices you will be so good as to extract for my *Anecdotes* and send me at your leisure; and I flatter myself, sir, from the humanity and politeness you have already shown me, that you will give me leave to consult you." Chatterton, thus encouraged, furnished Walpole with a *Historie of Peyncters yn Englande, bie Thomas Rowley;* and at the same time imparted the history of his own life, pathetically observing that he was the son of a poor widow, who supported him with great difficulty, that he was apprentice to an attorney, but had a taste and turn for elegant studies, and expressed a wish that Mr. Walpole would assist him with his interest in emerging out of so dull a profession by procuring him

47

some place in which he could pursue his natural bent. To Walpole's selfish, cold and unimpassioned nature an appeal like this would be as ineffectual as supplication to a heathen god cut in alabaster; except, indeed, that the wrong sentiment was roused —contempt instead of compassion. His aristocratic feeling revolted at his unintentional submission to the son of a poor widow, and, to conclude the contaminating correspondence, he wrote to Chatterton, expressing himself to be a man of no interest, and advised him to labour at his business profession; and "when," says he, "you have made a fortune, you may unbend yourself with the studies consonant to your inclination." In reply to this freezing counsel, Chatterton confessed himself not able to dispute with a person of Mr. Walpole's literary character, and adds:—"Though I am but sixteen years of age, I have lived long enough to see that poverty attends literature. I am obliged to you, sir, for your advice, and will go beyond it, by destroying all my useless lumber of literature and never using my pen again but in the law." Receiving no immediate answer to this expression of his resolution, and the Rowley papers being still in Mr. Walpole's possession, the poor poet again wrote both to assert their genuineness and to request their return, as he had no other copy. This further letter is dated from Corn street, April 14th, 1769. On July 24th Chatterton again wrote to complain that no notice had been taken of his request of the former date, and the terse and forcible style of his reproachful address showed the author of *Otranto* that though his humble correspondent might have the soul of an ancient monk, he had also the feelings of a modern gentleman:—

Sir,—I cannot reconcile your behaviour to me with the notions I once entertained of you. I think myself injured, Sir; and did not you know my circumstances, you would not dare to treat me thus. I have sent twice for a copy of the MS.; no answer from you. An explanation, or excuse for your silence, would oblige,
THOMAS CHATTERTON.

Mr. Walpole had just returned from France when this letter was delivered. He thought it "singularly impertinent," and collecting both manuscripts and letters of its writer, he returned the whole in a blank cover. Having taken the opinion of some literary friends, the documents were concluded to be "forgeries"; and said Mr. Walpole, "All of the house of forgery are relations." This was a liberal admission, for it included the author of *The Castle of Otranto* himself, which fiction had been palmed upon the world as being the work of an ancient hand, in the same manner as were the *Rowley Poems*, and in the same sense might have been called a forgery. To call Chatterton's fictions forgeries is an abuse of language. There is, perhaps, as much moral as legal difference between forging cheques on the Bank of England and fathering poems upon a mediæval monk who existed but in the poet's imagination. The poems were a fiction, and the monk, their imputed author, was a part of the fiction. The value of a counterfeit bank note is nothing, and is intended to defraud; but the literary value of the poems as works of fancy remains the same, whether written by a living author or by one long dead. If the *Rowley Poems* are to be condemned as forgeries, *The Castle of Otranto* and *The Waverley Novels* must come under the same condemnation. Why, then, Chatterton should be the scapegoat, and Walpole and Scott be blameless, can only be explained on the principle, *quod licet Jovi non licet bovi*. The contemptuous treatment of Walpole reduced Chatterton to misanthropy and despair. Turned out of doors by his master, whose hard temperament was in no sympathy with the gloomy mood of his clerk, he removed as a literary adventurer to London. Four months struggling for existence there found him penniless and starving, when, to save the slowness of this painful exit from life, he hastened his fate by poison. His untimely death was, perhaps, the most melancholy waste of genius in the literary annals of England. Who could estimate the prospective issues of a mind that could produce such marvellous poems as did Chatterton, whose career closed before he had completed his 18th year? What could we have known of the intellectual capabilities of Shakespeare, Milton, Dryden, Pope, or Byron, had we only what they had written previous to this age to predict from? That the full growth of his imagination was unrealised, that his exuberant but uncultured fancy would have flourished and ripened with his years, the study of what he has produced affords full evidence, the very crudeness of his compositions being part of the evidence. To conclude, St. Mary Redcliff is not more the masterpiece of Bristol architecture than is Chatterton the highest representative of the personal genius of that place; and Redcliff is not more superior to parish churches in general than is the boy poet proudly eminent above all but the greater poets of England. Redcliff may hardly vie with our noblest cathedrals, nor would Chatterton come into equality with our mightiest poets, who stand as the solemn cathedrals of literature. But the Chaucers, Shakespeares and Miltons are few, and the Shelleys and Byrons not many, and had these all died at the age of Chatterton they would have been still fewer, or none at all.

Chess Association. (See "Clubs.")

Cholera Visitations.
In the year 1832 this dire epidemic visited Bristol. The first case occurred on July 11th, in Harford's Court, near the Stone Bridge. The ravages of the disease were most deadly: up to the 9th of August 73 deaths had occurred in the city. A piece of ground near the Cattle Market was set apart as a place for the burial of the victims. On the 11th the plague was virulent in St. Peter's Hospital, where 600 paupers were crowded, 58 girls sleeping in 10 beds and 70 boys in 18 beds. On the 12th the curate of Temple interred 31 persons, victims in that locality. A cholera hospital was erected on the New Cut, strenuous efforts were made to prevent the spread of the contagion, good food was supplied to the poor, and by the beginning of October the blue, or Indian-form of the disease, had disappeared. The visitation cost the city in direct expenses over £2,738. In 1866 the disease again broke out at six different places; these, by infection, increased to 26, but only 29 deaths occurred from this last visitation.

Christian Knowledge.
The society for promoting this object has its depository on the Park street Viaduct. Rev. J. G. Alford, hon. sec.

Christianity Amongst the Jews.
The Bristol Auxiliary for the promotion of this object have annual sermons preached at many of the city and suburban churches in aid of the society. Rev. D. E. M. Simmonds, hon. sec.

Christmas Steps,
formerly called Queen street, was no doubt a public way leading from the city to Horfield road; but in 1669 Jonathan Blackwell, vintner, erected the steps at his own expense. The sedilia or recessed seats at the top are said to have been erected by the inmates of St. Bartholomew's Hospital (at the bottom of the steps), and were occupied by them as places for levying alms and the sale of relics, scriptural MSS., &c., on the passers-by. After the abolition of monasteries, the almsmen of the Three Kings of Cologne often sat there to receive contributions. (See "Chapel of the Three Kings of Cologne.")

Church Aid Society.

Instituted 1869. The society assists in a variety of ways, sometimes by erecting a church, or providing a stipend, or portion of one, for a missionary curate. Its object is not to create any new machinery of its own, it does not endeavour to put aside existing organisations; but simply assists clergymen in the performance of their parochial work. During its existence 25 parishes have received assistance, and the clergy have thus been able not only to minister more widely and more efficiently to large and increasing populations, but also to bestow a fuller and more individual care on those who are living in neglect of divine ordinances. During the year 1882 the grants made or renewed were 31 in number, 17 parishes being benefited thereby, in addition to several grants of £10 each for rent of mission-rooms in the parishes of St. Clement's, St. Gabriel's, St. Mark's (Easton) and St. Matthias', and three grants towards the stipend of mission curates in St. Philip's and Bedminster parishes. President, the Right Rev. the Lord Bishop; hon. secretaries, Rev. W. S. Bruce and W. Wilberforce Jose, 16 Apsley road.

Church Association

(Branch of the London Association), Royal Insurance Buildings, Corn street. Hon. secretaries, Rev. James Ormiston, M.A., James Inskip and E. W. Bird.

Churches.

ALL SAINTS', Clifton, is one of our finest modern churches. Its foundation stone was laid on 4th November, 1864, and it was consecrated by the Bishop of Gloucester and Bristol June 8th, 1868. Its cost has been about £40,000, chiefly collected from the voluntary offerings of the congregation. The length of the building is 178 feet, of which the nave is 112 feet, and the width of the latter 56 feet. The barrel roof is elaborately diapered and figured, while the pillars and arches are diversified with natural polychromy obtained by the use of three stones—cream-coloured, warm brown and light blue. The nave, with transept and chancel, is simple but grand; the dwarfed massive columns give great effect to the unusually lofty clerestory windows, which are in the Geometrical style. These windows—ten in number—are filled with stained glass, representing the whole life of our Saviour, from His baptism to His ascension, and also the descent of the Holy Ghost at Pentecost, with two series of types from the Old Testament under each incident in the life, by means of which the chief saints of the Old Testament are introduced. In the small lancet windows are figures of saints of the British Isles, both men and women, and in the circles over these lancets are symbolical representations of the fruits of the Holy Ghost. The west window represents the creation and fall of man, and cost £1,000. The east window—said to be Hardman's finest work—represents the great gathering of the saints in glory around the Divine Redeemer, and cost £700. The north and south chancel windows represent types of the glory of Heaven, the whole series thus representing the great work of Redemption. The reredos (by Redfern) and the font are sumptuously carved, the former representing the testimony of the saints to the divinity of Christ. In the centre panel our Lord is seated upon His throne; an angel sits on the open sepulchre beneath; on the right are the Virgin, SS. Peter and Paul, Mary Magdalene and King David, and on the left Isaiah, Saints John the Baptist, Jerome and Augustine from Canterbury. The seating of the church is rush-bottomed chairs, males sit one side of church and females the other. The service is of the highest ritual, and the choral services are magnificently rendered.

ALL SAINTS' (otherwise Al-Hallowen) stands nearly opposite the Council-house, Corn street. Of the great antiquity of the original building (1066) there can be no doubt. The date of the present structure was most probably immediately after the fire in 1466. The tower is remarkable for the cupola, ball and cross that surmount it; this was begun in 1716 and finished in 1721, at a cost of £589, raised by voluntary subscription, towards which Edward Colston gave £250. Lofty and elegant piers, with well-proportioned arches, divide the interior into three aisles of equal width, with the centre considerably larger than the sides. Except four Norman piers, the interior is in the Perpendicular style. The compartments of the pulpit are most elaborately carved with a crown, angels' heads, trumpets, &c.; the pulpit was probably erected about 1603. The altarpiece, "The Salutation of the Virgin," painted by Simmons, has been replaced by a handsome reredos. The exterior of this sacred pile is barely discernible, from the buildings by which it is hemmed in and which are built against it, particularly on the northern side. The monuments are numerous and interesting, that to the memory of Edward Colston (by Rysbrach) being the chief. (See "Monuments.") Every Sunday a nosegay of such flowers as the season affords is placed on this monument, money having been left for the purpose. Probably no parish church in England could present a more interesting series of historic documents than All Saints'. In 1883 the church was reseated with modern low-backed seats and other internal improvements were made.

BLIND ASYLUM CHURCH, Queen's road, a graceful specimen of Early English, was built in 1832. The inmates of the Blind Asylum attend here; it is open also to the general public.

CATHEDRAL (Church of Holy Trinity). The abbey of St. Augustine Black Canons, the church of which now forms the Cathedral, was founded in 1142 by Robert Fitzhardinge, a burgess of Bristol and progenitor of the noble family of Berkeley. The church was consecrated on Easter-day, 1148, in the presence of the Bishops of Worcester, Exeter, Llandaff and St. Asaph. The following is a tabulated statement of the measurements of the various parts:—

	Length. ft. in.	Width. ft. in.	Height. ft. in.
The entire building	174 0	68 0	56 0
Choir	100 0	34 0	56 0
Ante-Choir	43 0	34 0	56 0
Aisles (exclusive of the Chapels)	58 0	17 0	56 0
Choir and Aisles	—	68 0	56 0
Transept from N. to S.	117 0	—	56 0
Elder Lady Chapel	52 0	19 0	26 4
Chapel of the Virgin	17 8	20 0	22 4
Newton Chapel	23 4	18 0	40 8
Chapter Room	42 6	25 9	30 0
Tower	—	—	127 0
Cloisters	108 6	9 5	—
New Nave	120 0	68 0	56 0

The general effect of the interior is that of breadth rather than height, but there is, nevertheless, a fine sense of proportion in the relations of the parts. Its chief speciality is the uniform height of the vaulting, the central and two side aisles, though different in construction, being at their highest points exactly at the same elevation from the ground, a peculiarity, it is said, not to be elsewhere observed. Amongst the styles of architecture to be found in the Cathedral are Early English, Early Decorated, Norman Decorated and Perpendicular. The windows are magnificent, especially the great east, representing a stem of Jesse, and the richly-hued glass is among the best in England. The north porch is a monument to the liberality of its donor, W. K. Wait. It is sumptuously enriched with groining and bosses, arcades, tabernacles and effigies. Four of the principal niches were, in March, 1876, filled with "four Latin doctors," St. Gregory, St. Ambrose, St. Jerome and St. Augustine. This caused a perfect irruption in the city, and on 6th

April that year the condemned figures were removed to East Heaterton church, Yorkshire; the vacant niches have since been filled by images of the four Evangelists—Saints Matthew, Mark, Luke and John. Over the new nave are to be erected two western towers, to be called the Bishop Butler and Edward Colston towers. (See "Monuments.") The Cathedral underwent an extensive restoration in 1861, at a cost of £12,000. After an interruption of four centuries this beautiful cathedral once more possesses a nave, it being for that period the only one in the kingdom deficient of that important architectural member. This addition was opened by the Lord Bishop of the Diocese, October 23rd, 1877, who selected for his text Eph. ii. 21. The richly intoned service is judged to be now one of the most effectively developed in England, the choral staff being well sustained by the habitual presence of the clerical body; and the edifice may claim to rank among our national cathedrals. There have been 46 Bishops of Bristol, the first being Paul Bush, consecrated in 1542, and the present, Dr. Charles James Ellicott, who was consecrated in 1863. The number of deans has been 30, the first being William Snow, installed in 1542, and the present, the Very Rev. Gilbert Elliot, D.D., who was installed in 1850. The value of the deanery is £1,500 per annum. There are four senior canons, value £700 each; twelve honorary canons and three minor, £150; a precentor and sacrist, two minor canons, nine lay clerks and eighteen chorister boys.

CHRIST CHURCH, at the angle formed by the junction of Wine street and Broad street, was originally dedicated to the Holy Trinity. Its present site occupies that of an old church pulled down, on account of its ruinous condition, in 1787. The building thus destroyed—probably the third or fourth from the foundation of the church, somewhere about 1000—was a low edifice with a tower and spire. The present structure was opened for divine worship in 1790. It is built of freestone, nominally in the Grecian style, and is divided into three aisles by Corinthian pillars, the proportions being symmetrical and chaste. The chancel is adorned with a stained-glass window representing Moses and St. John, and at the west end is an organ gallery. Nearly the whole of the old-fashioned interior arrangements, including high-back seats and dingy fittings, were removed in January, 1883. The old wooden sashes have given place to several stone windows filled with stained glass. A fine stone reredos takes the place of the former wooden one, and a centre-light of the new window at its rear delineates the Ascension. The internal decoration of the roof has a good effect, and care has been taken to harmonise it with other parts of the building. The chancel floors are laid with Minton tiles, and separating the chancel from the nave is a low open screen of marble and freestone with brass and iron gates. The choir stalls, &c., are handsomely carved, and the choir has been entirely reseated. The cost of the restoration was about £1,500. The tower contains a peal of ten bells. Its spire is 160 feet high, and beneath the church is a spacious crypt. (See "Monuments.")

CHRIST CHURCH, Clifton down, is an elegant and commodious structure in the Early English or the Pointed style, and effectively situated. It is cruciform, with an aspidal chancel and north and south transept. The ceiling is open and appropriately decorated. The body of the church was erected in 1844 at a cost of £10,000, in addition to £500 for the site. The tower and spire at the south-west angle of the aisle were not completed till 1859, the outlay being £2,400. Its consecration took place on the 8th of October, 1844, by the Bishop of

Gloucester and Bristol (Dr. Monk). The church was brought into prominence a few years ago by the great sacramental case of Henry Jenkins *versus* Rev. F. S. Cook.

EMMANUEL, Clifton (parish church), in the 13th century style, comprises nave, north and south aisles and transepts, aspidal chancel with lateral chapels, a western narthex porch and tower, which serves as a north porch. The tower is 108 feet high. The church is built of local stone of two tints, quarried on the site, with Bath stone dressings and relieving lines of red sandstone. Internally it is 123 feet in length, 61 feet in width and 60 feet in height. The foundation stone was laid on October 23rd, 1865, and on January 7th, 1869, it was consecrated by the Bishop of Gloucester and Bristol.

EMMANUEL, St. Philip's (district church), built in the Early Decorated style of Hanham stone, with freestone dressing and floored with Bridgwater tiles. It has a nave 87 feet long by 28 feet wide and height 51 feet, two aisles 87 feet by 12 feet and height 44 feet, aspidal chancel 18 feet by 23 feet and 42 feet high, and south porch. The principals of the roof are supported on carved corbels, representing natural foliage. The pulpit is octagonal, carved with diaper panels and shafts of Devonshire marble. The font corresponds in style, being supported by five shafts in Devonshire marble. The foundation stone was laid 21st August, 1860, and on the 9th December, 1862, Bishop Thompson consecrated the church. The cost, exclusive of site, was £3,000.

GUTHRIE MEMORIAL CHAPEL, adjoining the Clifton College on the east. It is a clever architectural gem in Early Decorated style. At its west end is a magnificent rose window, 18 feet in diameter, which is perhaps the principal feature of the chapel, arranged in twelve circular lights in the outer part for images of the Apostles (the wheel is therefore called an Apostle window), and a large circle in the centre for a representation of Christ, with small intervening spaces for angels. The chapel was erected at the sole expense of the widow of the late Canon Guthrie, who died in July, 1865, as a token of affectionate remembrance, and the tower was added by the College Company to the memory of the same reverend gentleman, whose warm interest in the institution they thus desired to perpetuate. The corner stone was laid by Mrs. Guthrie on December 19th, 1865, and the edifice consecrated by the Bishop of the Diocese in 1867. The nave is 75 feet long, 33 feet wide, and is divided into six bays by arched principals on carved stone corbels.

HOLY NATIVITY, Knowle, is a chapel-of-ease to Bedminster. The building is in the Byzantine style. The usual nave arcade is so arranged that the pillars are only at a short distance from the side walls. The chancel apse is semi-circular and surmounted by a dome roof 30 feet in diameter. The foundation stone was laid by the Mayor in 1870, but in consequence of certain rites and ceremonies not having been complied with, the church was not consecrated till June 4th, 1883, when the ceremony was performed by Bishop Ellicott.

HOLY TRINITY, Hotwell road, parish church, built in the Tuscan order, presents a bold and effective frontage. It cost £10,000, of which £6,000 was provided by Thomas Whippie, who also built Grenville chapel. The church was consecrated by the Bishop of Llandaff, 10th November, 1830. The chief front is facing the south. The large niche (frequently seen in continental churches) is of great beauty. The pediment is surmounted by a cupola of light and elegant construction, and above the niche is a dove. The interior dimensions are 84 feet by 60 feet, and it forms—by the arrangement of the pillars supporting the roof and galleries—a nave and transept in the figure of a cross.

The height of the church to the centre of the dome is 40 feet.

HOLY TRINITY (parish church of St. Philip and Jacob Without), at the end of West street. The foundation stone was laid September 23rd, 1829, and the church was consecrated and opened on February 17th, 1832. It is in the Gothic style, with two turrets to correspond at the west end. The interior is commodious, measuring 67 feet in width, and the whole area from east to west is 114 feet, and consists of a nave and two side aisles, divided by four lateral arches, supported by clustered columns. Spacious galleries are formed on three sides of the building. The ceiling is flat, ribbed and interspersed with Gothic blocks and enrichments. Over the communion table is a large and handsome-coloured window.

ORPHAN ASYLUM CHURCH, Hook's Mills, Ashley hill, was built in 1827. The inmates of Hook's Mills' Orphanage attend here.

REDLAND GREEN EPISCOPAL CHAPEL is one of the purest specimens of Palladian architecture in the kingdom, and has gained considerable admiration for correctness of proportion. It was built and endowed at the expense of Mr. Cossin in 1740, who also built Redland court. Its altar-piece represents the embalmment of Christ—a copy of one by Annibale Caracci, the original of which was burnt at Moscow. The interior carving is well worthy of notice for its great beauty of execution. In consequence of some dispute, not satisfactorily explained, divine service was suspended for several years. It was consecrated as a chapel-of-ease to Westbury, 12th November, 1790, by the Bishop of Bristol. The chapel was restored in 1860 at a cost of about £700, chiefly collected from friends of the incumbent, the richer parishioners being opposed to the project.

ST. ANDREW (Clifton parish church). The foundation stone was laid in June, 1819, and the church was consecrated by the Bishop of Bristol on the 12th of August 1822. It is 120 feet long, 75 feet wide and 39 feet high. The crypt is 7½ feet high, and has graves formed under the whole of the floor 8 feet deep. The whole building is in the style of Debased Gothic. There are three galleries, with two stone staircases leading from the entrance lobbies; in these are placed most of the monumental tablets of the old church that stood here in the time of Henry II.

ST. ANDREW, Montpelier, is Early English in style, and cost £2,428. It was consecrated by the Bishop of the Diocese (Dr. Monk) 31st January, 1845. Its plan is cruciform. The tower is at the west end, and is 60 feet high. The communion table is of carved oak, and is a model of one in Cologne Cathedral. In 1878 it was enlarged by lengthening the chancel, and by the erection of an organ chamber and new vestries, which cost more than £1,100. The new portions were consecrated by Bishop Ellicott, October 11th, 1878.

ST. ANDREW-THE-LESS, Hotwells. The corner stone was laid in August, 1872, and the church consecrated by the Lord Bishop of the Diocese 24th Sept., 1873. Its style of architecture is 13th century Early Decorated, and consists of nave, three bays, with side aisles and chancel, with bays opening into a *quasi* transept on the north and organ and choir chapel with vestry on the south. The whole width of the chancel is a finely designed screen. The entrance to the building is by a porch beneath the tower, with bell chamber surmounted by a campanile. An edifice known as Dowry Episcopal Chapel formerly stood here; it was erected in 1744 for the benefit of visitors to the hot springs, but was never consecrated, and after Easter-day, 1872, was finally closed to give place to the present pleasing structure. In 1784 the ground at the back of the chapel was consecrated as a cemetery, and the last interment was in March, 1855. The old monuments belonging to the original chapel are well arranged in the existing building.

ST. AUGUSTINE-THE-LESS, College green, was founded by the abbots of St. Augustine's Monastery. It is mentioned in Gaunt's deeds in 1240. The existing edifice dates from about the year 1480. It has several times been restored, the last time being in 1877. The church is a plain fabric, characterised rather by neatness than by elegance. It has three long aisles. The chancel is spacious and the ceiling richly ornamented. The upper part of the windows on each side of the altar contains fragments of ancient stained glass, and in the mutilated remains may be traced portions of the arms of Abbots Newland and Elliott. There are a number of mural monuments. (*See* "Monuments.") The tower was built at the cost of the parishioners, and the edifice is in the Third or Perpendicular style.

ST. BARNABAS, Ashley road, built by Church Building Association, aided by private subscriptions, cost upwards of £2,200; consecrated by the Bishop of the Diocese (Dr. Monk) 12th September, 1843. The erection is in cruciform shape, with a steeple rising over the west entrance. The chancel, which is more than usually commodious, is formed by the head of the cross in the east end. The church is built on stone vaulting about seven feet high, intended originally as a crypt for burials; only one body was interred before burials there were prohibited. The church underwent repairs in 1882.

ST. BARTHOLOMEW'S, Union street, with an entrance in Little St. James' Back. Cost of site, £1,400; cost of church, £2,200. Internal length, 106 feet; width, 30 feet, and height, 46 feet. It was consecrated by the Bishop of Gloucester and Bristol, 22nd January, 1861. It contains a stained glass window in the church to the memory of Sir H. M. Lawrence, Bart. The church underwent renovation in 1882. It is the parish church of the ecclesiastical parish of St. Bartholomew, which was formed in 1861 by separating from the parish of St. James all that portion lying south of the northern side of the Horsefair.

ST. CLEMENT'S, Newfoundland road, is in the Early English style, with clerestoried nave, chancel, north and south aisles, octagonal bell turret 65 feet high, with a spirelet. The foundation stone was laid 24th May, 1854, and the church opened in the following year.

ST. GABRIEL'S, Upper Easton. The foundation stone was laid in 1868, and the church was consecrated on the 14th March, 1870. It is a brick structure in the 13th century style; cruciform in shape, with chancel, nave and transepts. The south-east corner is surmounted by a small tower with spire. In length the church is 84 feet, and the breadth from north to south, 60 feet. The cost of building and furniture was £4,400, which was defrayed solely by voluntary contributions. The church forms a district cut off from Holy Trinity and St. Philip's.

ST. GEORGE'S, Great George street, Park street, is remarkable for the great ascent of steps and porch by which it is approached, which has a very imposing and commanding effect. Its style is Roman Doric, from the design of Sir R. Smirke. The portico of the church is very handsome. It was built in 1823 at a cost of £7,000. The church having been built without any chancel, a choir of white marble, with *ambones* for pulpit and lectern, was, in 1871, constructed in the body of the church, after the model of Basilican churches of the 8th and 9th centuries. It was originally built as a chapel-of-ease to St. Augustine-the-Less, but it has subsequently been made parochial.

ST. JAMES' CHAPEL-OF-EASE, or the Hensman Jubilee Memorial Church, Clifton, was consecrated by the Bishop of Gloucester and Bristol (Dr. Thompson) on 23rd December, 1862. Its style is Decorated. Length of nave, 83 feet; width, 33 feet; height, 57 feet. The late Rev. John Hensman was 55 years incumbent of Clifton, and in his 50th year of service this church was built to commemorate his long connection with the adjoining parish church.

ST. JAMES' originally belonged to a Benedictine priory, dedicated to the Virgin Mary and St. James the Apostle. It was built and consecrated in 1130, and the tower added in 1374. It is recorded that Robert, Earl of Gloucester, when building the Castle, set aside every tenth stone to be employed in the original structure of the church. It consists of a nave, 84 feet in length, 31 feet in height, and 29 feet 9 inches between the massive piers which support five arches, each 12 feet 6 inches, diameter of the piers 9 feet 9 inches, and the clear distance from pier to pier 12 feet 4 inches, and which divide the north and south aisles from the nave. The nave and north aisle are parts of the old church, and the fine old Norman pillars and arches stand out in their original stateliness, and the handsome oak roof imparts an air of grandeur to it. The west front affords a fine specimen of Norman architecture, the upper stage of which shows an original arcade of intersecting arches, three of which are pierced for circular-headed windows, and above is a small but exquisite wheel window of the same date; both the windows and the arcade are enriched with zigzag moulding. The south aisle, which to enlarge the church was rebuilt at the beginning of the 17th century, is of Debased Perpendicular style; it has a range of square-headed windows of four lights each, cinque foiled, with mullions that have simple mouldings. The eastern end is a modern reproduction of the Norman style, and consists of three circular-headed windows with chevron mouldings; beneath are two series of stone arcades. The north aisle consists of Purbeck marble. This portion is of recent date, being only consecrated 26th October, 1864, and it presents a singular contrast, being quite at variance with the general character of the church. The tower is a heavy square unornamented one of the 15th century, not standing at the western end, but at the eastern. But few of its original features remain, it having undergone much alteration in the last century. It is crowned by a pyramidal pinnacle at the south-west corner; the smaller pinnacles at the other angles have been removed, and urns and a balustrade substituted. (*See* "Monuments.")

ST. JAMES-THE-LESS, a chapel-of-ease to St. James, situated in Upper Maudlin street, adjoining the Penitentiary, the inmates of which have the gallery of this church apportioned for their exclusive use. The church was consecrated by the Bishop of the Diocese 30th November, 1867.

ST. JOHN THE BAPTIST, Bedminster, is erected on the site of a church dating from 1003. The old parish church was pulled down in 1853. It was destitute of any architectural features, and so small as to be totally inadequate for so populous a parish. The plan of the present edifice comprises a nave, north and south aisles, chancel, transepts, western tower and north porch. The interior dimensions are 151 feet in length by 54 feet in width and 58 feet in height. The tower is 100 feet, and is intended to be surmounted with a stone spire. The stone reredos occupies the entire length of the chancel, and is 15 feet high. In the main panels are sculptured in bright relief the subjects of the Nativity, the Crucifixion and the Ascension, separated by canopied niches containing statues of the four Evangelists. At the time of its erection considerable excitement was created, this being the first instance in modern times of the introduction of sculpture on so large a scale into a parish church. This was the first parish church in Bristol to introduce a surpliced choir.

ST. JOHN THE BAPTIST, Broad street, is one of the smallest churches in Bristol, consisting of one nave and chancel, divided by a pointed arch. It has no window either at its eastern or western end. The walls on either side are pierced by nine perpendicular windows. An ancient ornamented hour-glass stands upon an iron bracket in the vestry. It was formerly attached to the pulpit, to regulate the time for the delivery of the sermon. Near this is a mutilated figure, with a crown upon its head, but whom it represents is not known. The roof is of open timber-work of 15th century date. At the east end of the chancel is a wall, in which are two Tudor doors, which was built about 1570 to form a vestry. The tower, built about the close of the 14th century, stands upon an archway which contained a gate of the old city; the channel, in which the portcullis used to traverse, may still be seen. Two arches were formed in 1828 for foot-passengers on either side of the gateway. The western arch, on the right side entering from Quay street, exhibits on a corbel at the spring of the arch a warrior's head and on the left a bishop's, both carved on freestone. On the inner side are the ciphers G.R. and C.B., denoting that the church is protected by the royal and civic, by the military and ecclesiastical authorities of the State. The eastern arch is also ornamented with corbels, and the *tout-ensemble* of the three arches has a light and graceful appearance. On the south side of the tower are, quaintly carved, two venerable figures intended to represent the brothers Brennus and Belinus, said to have been the original founders of the city. The church was founded by Walter Frampton, three times Mayor, who died and was buried here in 1357. (See " Monuments.")

ST. JOHN THE EVANGELIST, Whiteladies' road, consecrated by the Bishop of Gloucester and Bristol April 27th, 1841. Its style is Gothic, and its interior arrangements are simple and elegant. The church was enlarged in 1864 by having a transept east and west added. Thirty years ago the present Archbishop of Canterbury (Dr. Benson) preached his first sermon after ordination as a deacon at this church.

ST. JUDE'S, Poyntz Pool, is a district church in the out-parish of St. Philip and Jacob. Its style is that of Decorated or Middle Pointed of the 14th century, and consists of nave, 65 feet by 28 feet 6 inches, and chancel, 26 feet 5 inches by 23 feet 6 inches, with a tower at west end, 82 feet high, surmounted by pierced battlement with pinnacles at the corners. The foundation stone was laid 7th August, 1848, and the church was consecrated and opened June, 1849. It cost £2,500.

ST. LUKE'S, Barton hill, was opened 19th September, 1843; cost £2,700. The church is situated near the Cotton works, and is for the purpose of providing religious instruction to the *employés* and the large population in the immediate neighbourhood. It resembles in style the churches of the 13th century, in which more detail and ornament are dispensed with than in any other style. The tower rises about 100 feet from the ground. The interior of the church is 100 feet long by 46 feet broad.

ST. LUKE'S, Bedminster, on the south side of the New Cut, was erected in 1859, and consecrated by the Bishop of Gloucester and Bristol 23rd January, 1861. It is in the Decorated style, and has a nave and apsidal chancel 134 feet in length, and the nave and aisles 62 feet 6 inches. The tower terminates the west end of the north aisle. Externally the chief feature is the treatment of the aisle windows, which are of four-lights with geometrical tracery set in lofty gables. The original design was a lofty stone tower rising from an octagonal belfry, but for want of funds the tower is incompletely finished. The cost of the church was about £7,000.

ST. MARK'S, Lower Easton, is in the Early Norman style, with a circular apse and a tower on the north side, and consists of a nave and chancel. It was opened May 18th, 1848. The pulpit is of Painswick stone. The ground was given by Sir Richard Colt Hore, whose arms are placed in the centre of the stained-glass window immediately over the western entrance of the church. This district church is taken out of the parishes of St. George and Stapleton.

ST. MARK'S (or the Mayor's Chapel), in College green. It is observable that this edifice is not built as churches commonly are, east and west, but rather nearer to the north and south, one reason assigned being that it was to point to the place of residence of the joint founders and their ancestors (Berkeley castle), and another, that it should point towards the lands with which it was endowed. The church was formerly called Gaunt's church, in connection with the Bons Hommes hospital, after which it was granted to the French Protestant refugees, and in 1721 it was fitted up for the use of the Mayor and Corporation. In 1820 the chapel was partially repaired and a superb stained window added, and on 31st October, 1830, after it had been completely "repaired and beautified," it was re-opened for divine worship. The general effect of the interior is very impressive. The emblazoned roof, rich fretwork stalls of dark oak, the sombre illumination derived from the traceried windows glowing with images of saints and martyrs, fill the mind with awe and devotion. The building is of mixed architecture. On the north and south sides is a range of grotesque corbels of Early English character, and some of the windows are of the same style, but somewhat advanced. The great west window is a combination of the Decorated and Perpendicular styles; the head is a wheel of twelve spokes, which, together with the tracery, is modern, but a reproduction of the old work. In the outer south aisle or chapel is a remarkable stained window, in pontificals of Archbishop Becket. In the side aisle is a pure Decorated window, enriched with ball flower ornament. Some of the glass of the church is dated 1543. In the centre of the exquisitely beautiful altarpiece of Late Perpendicular niches and tabernacles is placed a highly-finished painting of the dead Christ surrounded by His sorrowing disciples. The pulpit and the throne for the Mayor—the first of Painswick stone and the latter of oak—are in a style of workmanship of a very superior cast. The canopies over the stall erected for the members of the Town Council and officers of the Corporation are very chastely conceived, the decorations being of vine foliage, tracery and tabernacle work, the carving being exquisite. Under the canopies the niches are decorated with ogee mouldings and embossed cornices. The original Old English ceiling remains, its bosses, spandrils, mouldings, corbels, spandril-bosses and demi-angels are all in high preservation. The tower was finished in 1489, and is 86 feet in height. The length of the body of the church, which is undivided by columns, is about 123 feet, and breadth 24½ feet. (*See* "Monuments.")

ST. MARY-LE-PORT, St. Mary-le-port street, is dedicated to our Lady of the Port, there having been formerly an open approach from the river to the south side of the sacred building; hence the appropriateness of the dedication. The earlier fabric on the same spot is believed to have been founded by William, Earl of Gloucester, son of the great Robert, "for he is expressly said about 1170 to have granted and confirmed this church to the priory of Keynsham, for the sustentation of the canons there." The present building consists of two aisles of unequal breadth, the clustered columns dividing which are of Perpendicular date, assignable to the 15th century. The roof has been more than once renovated, and at present shows a concave ceiling with some attempt at ornament. In the south wall of the chancel is a flight of steps, now leading to the pulpit, but formerly to the rood-loft. The tower is of the florid style, like the interior, and is 72 feet in height to the base of the pinnacles. The windows in the upper part of the tower, the panelled parapet and corner turret are among the best details of the church and deserve notice. The old church records have been kept in the form of a separate book for each year, and contain many quaint and interesting entries that illustrate current events and customs as well as the individual life of the church. The earliest dates back to the time of Queen Mary, 1551. The church possesses a large eagle lectern weighing 692 lbs., which formerly belonged to the Cathedral, being a gift in 1683. The most recent restoration was in 1877, and cost £2,150, and on this occasion a new font was added to the church. In the north wall have been discovered and opened to view the mullions and tracery of the windows which had been blocked up three centuries ago by the houses outside.

ST. MARY REDCLIFF is allowed to be the finest parish church in England, and is

"The pryde of Bristowe and the Westerne Londe."

It is dedicated to the Virgin Mary, and is built on a red sandy-rock or cliff, from which it derives its name. Popular tradition ascribes this magnificent erection first to Simon Burton; then to William Canynges, the elder, six times Mayor of Bristol; and lastly to William Canynges, his grandson, who was five times Mayor. As usual, tradition has a modicum of truth with regard to each, but archæology and history have of late years considerably varied the proportions that have been assigned to the so-named founders. For instance, Robert de Berkeley granted a conduit to the church of Redcliff in 1207; hence it is proved to demonstration that there was a church here at least 50 years before Burton was born. We know also that it was Early English in style, and that only the inner vestibule to the north porch and a few fragments remain of that building. Simon Burton, when Mayor, probably laid the foundation stone of the exquisitely beautiful north porch. But before his day, and between the years 1232 and 1287 indulgences were granted to all persons who made a pilgrimage to the church of St. Mary Redcliff or aided in its erection; a ten days' indulgence from purgatory was granted by the Archbishop of Cashel in the year that William of Bristol was Lord Mayor of Dublin (then a sort of colony to Bristol) "to all who should pray at the grave of Helen de Wedmore, whose body is buried in the churchyard of St. Mary Redcliff." Hugh le France, on the day before the exaltation of the holy cross, 1337, left "a tenement in Redcliff street, and a messuage, with cartileges, crofts, &c., in Steven street, to provide a chantry chapel in the church of the Blessed Virgin Mary of Redclyve, for the good of my soul," &c., &c. That year John Botiler, Thomas de Uphill and Geoffrey Feltere were guardians of the works; this was 25 years before the name of Canynges occurs in our municipal annals. During his sextuple mayoralty, William Canynges, assisted by the voluntary contributions of the affluent, carried on the work, the lower part of the body of the church from the cross aisle downwards, and the whole of the south transept, with its grand windows and plain exterior, are of this date, being in the Decorated style. It is therefore to be assumed that the work was continuous also during the 56 years that elapsed ere another William Canynges sat in the civic chair. This Canynges, who ended life as Dean of Westbury, finished "the covering and glazing of the church," repairing the steeple which was destroyed by tempest in 1445, between his first and second mayoralty. The south porch to this day bears marks of the fall, and so does the south aisle of the nave. The later work is in the Perpendicular style. The church is cruciform, with its massive tower in the north-west angle; it has north and south porches to its nave and aisles, a chancel with aisles, a Lady chapel at the eastern extremity, two chantry chapels outside the north aisle, with divers priest-rooms in different parts of the building. Its length to the end of the nave is 240 feet; of the transept, 117 feet; breadth of ditto and aisles, 44 feet; breadth of nave and aisles, 59 feet; height of aisles, 25 feet; height of nave, transept and chancel, 54 feet 9 inches; the height of the open-worked parapet of the tower is 120 feet; total height from the ground to the weathercock, 285 feet. The exterior north porch, restored through the munificence of Alderman Proctor, at a cost of £2,500, with its elaborately elegant doorway, is without a parallel; the sculptural mouldings are bold and beautiful. "Twelve distinct varieties of groining exist in this church, but that in the vaulting of the transepts is the most remarkable for its lightness, richness, and beauty of construction;" the bosses display an amazing fertility of invention, they are 1,220 in number, yet it is said that no two are alike. The old font stands close by the south-west pier near the west door; the second, of small marble, is in the Lady chapel; whilst that which is in present use, adorned with alabaster figures and inscriptions, stands at the west end of the church. Hogarth painted some altar-pieces for this church, Simmons, a Bristol painter of repute, filling in the subsidiary niches. These pictures have been appropriately removed to the Fine Arts Academy, and their place is supplied by an exquisite reredos by G. Godwin, F.S.A. This reredos is of Caen stone, with four small shafts of red marble, and a Greek cross and circle of mosaic work in the central gablet by Salviati; the capitals of the column and the ornamentation is from nature. The capstone of the new spire was laid on May 10th, 1872, by the Mayor and Mayoress, Mr. and Mrs. Proctor Baker. The cost of the spire was £5,500. Over 30 years has been occupied in the successful restoration of the church, during which period upwards of £40,000 has been expended on the work.

ST. MARY THE VIRGIN, Tyndall's park, is of Geometrical 14th century Pointed style, built of local red sandstone, unplastered inside. The dressings and other wrought stone work is of Doulting stone. The chancel is 36 feet high to the plate-line. West of the chancel and transepts the church consists of a nave, 84 feet 6 inches long and 26 feet wide, with side aisles of the same length and 12 feet wide, with arcades of four arches, 20 feet span on each side. The nave has a clerestory, lighted with four three-light windows on each side. The nave is 40 feet high to the plate, spanned by a tie-beam roof. The aisles are 16 feet high to the plate, and lighted by two-light windows on the north and south sides, and three-light windows on the west. Arches open from the aisles to the transept. The choir is 39 feet by 24 feet. North and south of the choir are transepts, 21 feet 6 inches by 18 feet, between which there are arcades springing from clustered shafts. The outer order of the arches rise and form one large arch, the spandrils of which are carved. The south wall has a triple sedilia and a piscina. The chancel arch springs from clustered polished granite respond shafts, and is 23 feet 6 inches wide and rises to the height of 35 feet from the nave floor. Above the doorway there is a large wheel window of 12 lights, 15 feet diameter. The west door is approached by a flight of wide steps. Externally the walls of the church are boldly buttressed. The roofs are tiled. The foundation stone was laid 23rd November, 1870, and the church was consecrated 30th June, 1874, being then only partially built. About £9,700 has already been expended on the church.

ST. MATTHIAS-ON-THE-WEIR, opened and consecrated in November, 1851. This district was formed out of the parishes of St. Philip and Jacob and St. Peter. The church is built in the Decorated Gothic style of ecclesiastical architecture. In plan it is a lofty nave, spacious chancel, north and south aisles, the south porch and western tower opening to the nave. The east window is filled with stained glass of five-lights, the centre filled with the figure of the Saviour, and the four side-lights on either side with figures of the patron saints of the several parishes from which the district is formed, all under elegant canopies. The west window is also filled with stained glass. The floors of the passages are formed of black and red tiles, those at the east end of the chancel being richly figured. The dressings generally of the edifice are of Coombe Down stone, the general face of the walls being of Stapleton stone. The foundations had to be cut to a great depth through an ancient ropewalk, which was very treacherous. This was the first of the Peel district churches erected in this city. The cost was under £3,000.

ST. MATTHEW'S, Kingsdown, was consecrated by Bishop Ryder, of Lichfield and Coventry, in April, 1835. It consists of a nave, which is lofty and lit by clerestory windows, and two side aisles with a handsome east window; galleries all round, except at the communion table. Its peal of eight bells, presented by John Bangley, is particularly fine.

ST. MICHAEL THE ARCHANGEL.—The first notice of this church occurs in 1174; it was one of the fees of William, Earl of Gloucester. The present church was founded in July, 1775, and opened for divine worship 22nd June, 1777, by the Rev. Mr. Wilkins, who took for his text Psalm cxxxii. 3-5. The building is a nondescript style, being a combination of Grecian and Gothic. The tower is about 90 feet high, and is surmounted with four pinnacles. There are no monuments of public interest, but two or three curious epitaphs in the church and churchyard.

ST. NATHANAEL'S, Lower Redland road. The style is Early Pointed, and consists of nave, north and south aisles, apsidal chancel with organ chamber on the north side and vestries for the clergy and the choir on the south. Width of nave and aisle, 57 feet; length from chancel to western extremity, 80 feet; floor to apex of roof, 51 feet. The chancel is 34 feet long, 21 feet wide and 37 feet high. The nave is divided from the aisles on either side by six arches of bold design with carved caps; it is lighted by two-light windows on either side facing six bays, and by clerestory windows. The west window is 20 feet high and 12 feet wide and is divided into mullions of five-lights, and is of good design in geometric pattern. The pulpit is a circular-fronted one of Skellet stone, divided into four panels, pillars of polished Devonshire marble supporting the arches. Each panel contains the sculptured head of one of the evangelists, finely executed. The church was opened and consecrated on the 18th of February, 1875.

ST. NICHOLAS, High street. The present structure was finished in 1769, at a cost of £6,000. Above the tower rises a spire of 205 feet from the ground. The original church was founded probably in 1030, and stood upon the town wall. The present crypt is of peculiar interest; it has heavy and massive columns, richly moulded and ornamented arches, and quaint and ever-varying decorations of its bosses at the intersections. The heads of Edwards II. and III. and of Queen Philippa, wife of Edward III., are pointed as being among the busts in the arched ceiling of the crypt. The church contains several monuments (*See* "Monuments.") The ancient chancel stood across High street, forming one of the city gates, under which gate John Wesley nearly lost his life through a carriage accident. The old altar before the Reformation was in this chancel, and was approached by a magnificent ascent of 23 steps of alternately black and white marble. Some small portions of the marble still remain, and are relaid in the new paving. In cutting the new vestry windows it was found that many carved fragments of the old stonework are also built into the walls of the present church, while a fine keystone of the old groining was discovered under the floor, and has been placed in the crypt. Though not an architectural church, the extensive alterations carried out in 1882-83 have made it as handsome internally as any in the city; the western gallery and the old vestry have been removed, and a chancel formed with a freestone screen. The organ has been removed to the east end, the seating arrangements are slightly altered, and other work done which has much improved the church, the total cost of which was about £1,800.

ST. PAUL'S, Bedminster, was consecrated by the Bishop of Bath and Wells, 24th October, 1831. In 1879 it was renovated and improved by a new gallery front, pulpit and choir stalls, &c.; and again, in 1881, further improvements were made, consequent on the large congregation attending the church.

ST. PAUL'S CHURCH, Clifton, in its earlier form was partially destroyed by fire 16th December, 1867. It was re-built and re-consecrated by the Bishop of Gloucester and Bristol, 29th September, 1868. Its style is Early Decorated, and its plan is a nave and chancel with side aisles. The height of the tower and spire is 105 feet. There are some stained-glass windows in the church. The western porch has a sculptured representation of St. Paul preaching at Athens.

ST. PAUL'S, Portland square. This parish was taken out of that of St. James for the accommodation of the inhabitants of the district. The church was opened on St. Paul's Day, in 1794. No sacred edifice perhaps in England has suffered more ridicule than this building for incongruous and anomalous composition of parts. It is stated that the production of so original a fabric was occasioned by the employment of two rival architects, who were severally favoured by two disagreeing churchwardens, and by a mutual concession that certain features should be combined in one, the present architectural solecism being effected. The altar-piece of the church is a representation of St. Paul preaching at Athens, executed by Edward Bird, R.A.

ST. PETER'S, Clifton wood, was consecrated on the 26th September, 1882, by the Bishop of Gloucester and Bristol. The building is of Early Gothic type, constructed of Pennant stone, bunch faced, in random range work, the Draycott stone archings to the windows and doors, and the Bath freestone dressings, being a happy contrast. The nave measures 83 feet 2 inches by 39 feet 7 inches. The aisle on the south side, 65 feet 8 inches by 13 feet 8 inches, and the aisle on the north side measures 81 feet 2 inches by 13 feet 8 inches. On the south-east side is a chapel which utilises a portion of the site, and affords greater accommodation; in size it is 22 feet by 13 feet 6 inches. Opposite this, on the north side, is the organ chamber, which is about equal in dimensions with the chapel. Both these are divided from the nave aisles by freestone arches, with moulded cusps and bosses and sanded

Mansfield octagon piers. Owing to the loftiness of the church, scope is given for bold arches and pillars of Mansfield stone. At the west end is a small gallery, the stone front of which is divided into cusped panels and supported by columns of octagon Mansfield stone. The chancel arch is a fine one, the design being attractive. On the north side of the aisle is the pulpit, octagonal in shape; the body is of rouge royal marble, plain, the top and base being of red Mansfield stone. In the centre of the most prominent panel is an elegant cross of Sienna marble. In the centre of the south chapel stands the font of Calne stone, supported by green marble shafts resting on a step of rouge royal marble. The clerestory contains on the north ten windows and on the south eight, and the aisles have windows of a similar character. In the chancel are seven lancet windows; at the west end are five and a small but pleasing rose window above. The central window of the chancel contains a representation of the Good Shepherd, and below this, Christ's charge to St. Peter. In the central north window in the chapel or baptistry is a representation of our Lord being baptised by St. John, surmounted by canopy work. The general windows contain rolled cathedral glass, varied in design, the tints being excellently blended and very chaste in effect, with foliated work above the springing. The roof is very handsome, trefoil in shape, and is constructed with pitch pine, ornamentally treated, unvarnished; the chancel is the same, springing from a corbel course. The aisle ceilings are open ribbed work. The choir seats in the chancel are of oak, massive in character, with end carved with incidents in the life of St. Peter. The communion table, with trefoil panels in front, and stalls, are also of oak. The church is still unfinished, inasmuch as the tower at the south-west end is lacking, being only now carried to about 30 feet.

ST. PETER'S, Peter street (city), is confidently stated to have been founded before the Norman conquest; little, however, is known of its origin. It was repaired in 1749, in 1795, and in 1870. The only portion that remains of the early fabric is probably the tower, erected in the 12th century, which is a massive structure of Norman workmanship, the walls of the belfry being said to be more than six feet in thickness. The height of the tower without the pinnacles, which are a later addition, is 79 feet. The church has three aisles, the north and south being 96 feet long, the middle 111, the height about 36 feet, and the width of the whole body is 54 feet. The pillars dividing the nave from the aisle consist of small clustered columns with filleted capitals of Perpendicular date. In the south aisle the windows are of the same style and of good design; those in the north aisle have been renewed with much loss in effect. Both the roof of the nave and the aisles is divided into squares by ribs springing from corbel heads, and are likewise of Perpendicular date. (*See* "Monuments.")

ST. PHILIP AND JACOB (or James) was primarily a chapel of some Benedictines. It is mentioned as early as 1174, as then being one of the fees of William, Earl of Gloucester. The tower, except the upper stage, which is Debased Perpendicular, is a beautiful piece of Early English, having two collateral lancet windows, with bold mouldings on each of the four sides. A deeply-recessed, boldly-cut arch of the same (13th century) date opens from the base of the tower into the church; a corresponding arch divides the north aisle of the chancel from the nave aisle. The nave is separated from the aisles by three arches of exceedingly broad span, which are sustained by massive pillars having no capital or base, the moulding springing direct from the ground and round the soffit of each arch. The roof is of timber, with carved bosses; it is an excellent specimen of the time of Richard II. (1390), and until the recent restoration of the church the roof was concealed by a plaster ceiling. Some interesting corbels which supported the old roofs of the aisles still jut from the walls. (*See* "Monuments.")

ST. RAPHAEL'S, Cumberland road, built and endowed for decayed sailors belonging to the port of Bristol. It was erected, in 1859, at the expense of the Rev. R. H. W. Miles, rector of Bingham, Notts, as a memorial church, together with the adjoining vestibuled modern almshouses, the total cost being about £10,000. The building is picturesque, being of Decorated Gothic, with a prettily designed bell turret. In consequence of the high ritual of the Rev. A. H. Ward, the Bishop has withdrawn his license for the use of the church, which is unconsecrated.

ST. SAVIOUR'S, Woolcot park (formerly an iron church, removed from Tyndall's park in 1875) was consecrated by the Bishop of Gloucester and Bristol, on the 30th of May, 1882. Its style is Early French Gothic of a massive type, and consists of a nave, north and south aisles, organ chamber, clergy and choir vestries on the north side, and the south a transept. The width of the nave with north aisle, but exclusive of the south aisle yet to be built, is 41 feet, and the length 93 feet; from the floor to the apex of roof the height is 58 feet; chancel 38 feet long by 25 feet wide and 52 feet high, having on the south side an aumbyre or locker. The nave is divided from the aisles on either side by six arches and columns with capitals. The chancel arch is 20 feet wide and 38 feet high to the point of the arch. The nave and aisle roofs are open timbered with plaster between the rafters, and the chancel and organ chamber roofs are boarded, with moulded ribs dividing them into bays and panels. The whole of the roof timbers are left without stain or varnish upon them, with the hope (at no distant date) of their being stencilled with colour. The nave is lighted by two-light windows in the aisle walls, and by three-light windows in the clerestory. The west window of the nave and the east window of the chancel are large, and, though somewhat severe in treatment, are handsome and thoroughly characteristic of the period of work adopted. The church is paved throughout with tiles. The pulpit is octagonal in form and divided into panels, with columns of polished Devonshire marble supporting carved capitals at the angles, Irish green and other marbles being used for inlays. The centre panel contains the subject of the "Sermon on the Mount," and the other panels emblematical foliage. The steps to the sacrarium are of polished Devonshire marble. At the exterior west end, springing from a gable, is a lofty bell turret, with a canopied niche at the apex containing a figure of our Lord as the Good Shepherd. This is a striking feature of the church, and its treatment alone is sufficient evidence of the beauty and grace of the building and the general harmony that prevails. The contract for the erection was £4,100.

ST. SILAS, St. Philip's marsh. The foundation stone was laid in 1866, and the church was consecrated by the Bishop of Gloucester and Bristol 2nd October, 1867. The edifice is in the First Pointed style, and was rebuilt in 1872.

ST. SIMON'S, Baptist Mills; foundation stone was laid 18th June, 1846; church consecrated by the Bishop of Gloucester and Bristol (Dr. Monk) 22nd December, 1847. It is in the Decorated style of the 14th century, with a tower and broach spire 120 feet high. The interior consists of a nave 80 feet long, and north aisle and porch, with a chancel 30 feet deep; the exterior is built of lias stone with freestone dressings.

ST. STEPHEN'S. The original church was probably built early in the 13th century, and dedicated to

St. Stephen, the proto-martyr. It is mentioned in deeds as early as 1304, when it belonged to the Abbots of Glastonbury (who were its patrons till the Dissolution), by whom and the parishioners it was rebuilt about the year 1645. By will dated 25th May, 1398, John Wyell gave to the church "one ring, in which was set a stone, part of the very pillar to which Christ was bound at the scourging, to be kept among the relics for ever." The interior is in the Florid or Perpendicular style. It consists of three aisles, divided by slender columns composed of clustered shafts, with capitals embellished with demi-angels holding unfolded scrolls, surrounded by a fillet or band. The arches are pointed, supporting a range of modern clerestory windows. The ceiling of the centre aisle is of oak, divided into square, bold panels, by deep moulded ribs, with rosettes at the intersections. The great east window has recently been restored, and the incongruous oak Grecian altar-piece that formerly stood here has given place to an elaborately carved reredos, erected by the Society of St. Stephen's Ringers in 1876, who have also restored other portions of this magnificent church. The stained-glass window at the west end was inserted at the expense of the Society of Merchant Venturers. The pulpit is of mahogany, richly carved and decorated with cherub heads. The roof of the south porch is filled with elaborate fan tracery, and there is some florid embellishment to the exterior. The tower was erected by the sole munificence of John Shipward, a wealthy merchant, who was mayor in 1455. It is 133 feet in height without the pinnacles, and is generally allowed to be one of the handsomest parish towers in England. It has the appearance of a Gothic version of the old Italian Campanile, and ascends from stage to stage with increasing profusion of florid decoration, and finally crowned with a diadem of latticed battlements and pinnacles. Three of the pinnacles were blown down by a great wind that swept over the city in 1703, but these were rebuilt and the damage done at the same time to the church and tower repaired at the expense of the inhabitants. Falling again into decay in 1822, the turrets were removed, but have been reconstructed in pursuance of a partial restoration of the church. In the church formerly existed seven chantries with endowments for saying masses for the souls of their founders. (*See* "Monuments.")

ST. THOMAS THE APOSTLE, Thomas street. The only portion of the ancient structure remaining is the mutilated tower, which has been shorn of turrets and battlements. The roof of the belfry internally shows some ribs and bosses of the Early English style, but externally the buttresses and windows are of the Perpendicular period. The old church is said to have been conspicuous for beauty, and to have ranked second to St. Mary Redcliff for spaciousness and elegance. The existing building was completed in 1793, and opened on St. Thomas' Day in that year, having occupied four years in erection. Of its style it is no very bad example, there being no heterogeneous mixture of Gothic and the so-called classical modes, though the arrangement is typically that usual to the former style. It consists of three aisles, the columns dividing which are square in section and have plain moulded capitals, from which spring semi-circular arches. The ribs of the ceiling rest on carved cherubs, with a dove at the points of intersection. The nave has a barrel roof, the ceilings of the side aisles being flat. Over the Grecian altar-piece, which is flanked on either side by a life-size statue carved in mahogany, is a large picture of the incredulity of St. Thomas, which has been much admired ; it was painted by the late John King, of London. Several chantries were founded in the earlier church, one being for the soul of Richard II. Some members of the Canynges' family were interred within the earlier building. The walls are much encrusted with sepulchral memorials, but none of the inscriptions call for particular mention. The church has been recently restored at a cost of £3,500, and was re-opened on 17th April, 1880. A new rose window has been placed in the chancel, and the whole of the lights taken out and replaced by cathedral glass, and the pillars and walls have been highly decorated in the Byzantine style.

ST. WERBURGH'S, Baptist Mills, formerly stood in Corn street, on the site of the London and South-Western Bank, but is now removed and successfully reproduced in this eastern outlying district of the city. Werburgh was a Saxon saint, the daughter of Wulferus, King of Mercia. The original church is said to have been founded in 1190, but being very old and much decayed was rebuilt in 1760, with a curtailment of the chancel end. During the first 200 years of its existence the church was without a tower, this important feature being added in 1385; and, though it has undergone repairs and been removed to its present location, it is substantially the same as when erected. The whole of the structure is in the Perpendicular style. The tower is of four stages, richly executed, of fine proportions, and with its open battlements and turrets presents a good specimen of Somersetshire type. The interior of the church is lofty and spacious, and divided into three aisles by fluted pillars, supporting obtusely-pointed arches, on which rests the roof. George Whitefield and John Wesley both preached in the old church. (*See* "Monuments.")

SEAMEN'S MISSION CHAPEL, Prince street, was opened by the Bishop of Bristol and Gloucester on the 10th February, 1880. The building is in the Venetian style of architecture. The decorations and the interior arrangements are exceedingly chaste, so much so that it is considered one of the prettiest of its kind in England. The chapel occupies the upper portion of the edifice, and the Seamen's Institute the lower (*see* "Institutes"). W. F. Lavington, at his own cost of £4,500, undertook the erection of this building. The chapel will accommodate 300.

TEMPLE (otherwise the Holy Cross) was founded in the reign of Stephen by the Knights Templars, an order instituted in 1118, wearing a white habit with a red cross on the left shoulder. It is evident from its long aisles, large windows, lofty ceiling, slender pillars and spacious area that the present church has been erected since that period, yet there is no data to determine when or by whom it was rebuilt. The oldest portion of the existing fabric is the chancel, which belongs to the Decorated period of the 14th century. The remainder of the church, including the pillars of the nave and the north and south ranges of windows, is of the Perpendicular style of the 15th century. Over the chancel arch is a window with modern stained glass. The roof of the nave is pointed and divided into squares by oak ribs, with bosses at the intersections. The north aisle of the chancel is known as the Weavers' chapel, from the Guild of Weavers having anciently adopted it for their special oratory. In the chancel a candelabrum, representing with enrichments a mail-clad knight thrusting his spear into a dragon, is an exquisitely-designed piece of 15th century work. Some remains of ancient coloured glass still occupy several windows of the chancel and Weavers' chapel. The dimensions of the chancel are: Length from east to west, 159 feet; width, 59 feet; height of middle aisle, 50 feet; height of tower, 114 feet. The church has recently undergone a most judicious restoration. The tower, as far as the trefoil band (about two-thirds upwards) probably belongs to the year 1397, at which date a hermit named Reginald Taylor, residing at the chapel of St. Brendon on Brandon hill, bequeathed money towards its erection. Another authority says the tower was built anew in 1460, but it is likely this assertion applies only to the upper stage, or that above the ornamental band referred to. The interval occurring between these distinct erections is fairly attributable to the foundations of the earlier story having sunk while the work was in progress, thus causing the remarkable inclination, which overhangs the base as much as 5 feet. (See "Monuments.")

Churches and Chapels existing.

The following list is taken from *Western Daily Press*, October 30th, 1881:—

Denominations.	No. of Churches and Chapels.
Baptist	18
Bedminster White Ribbon Temperance Army	4
Bible Christians	3
Catholic Apostolic	1
Chapels of the City Mission	9
Christadelphians	1
Christian Brethren	10
Church of England	67
Colston Hall Lecture—Afternoon	1
Congregational	26
English and Foreign Seamen's Bethel	1
Her Majesty's Prison	1
Jews' Synagogue	1
Presbyterian	1
Primitive Methodist	9
Red, White & Blue Temperance Army	1
Roman Catholic	4
Salvation Army	6
Seamen's Bethel, late Floating Chapel	1
Seamen's Institute	1
Strict Baptists	1
Swedenborgian	1
The Friends	3
Unitarian	2
United Brethren (Moravians)	2
United Methodist Free Church	16
Welsh Calvinistic Methodist	1
Wesleyan Methodist	16

Total number of Places of Worship 209

In the Saturday issue of *Bristol Mercury and Post* will be found a list of preachers at most places of worship on the succeeding day.

Churches Destroyed.

The following is a list of destroyed churches and chapels which have never been rebuilt, numbering 14:—

ST. EWEN'S, which stood on the site of the Council-house, in Corn street, had its chancel end in Broad street. From the east window of this destroyed church Edward IV. witnessed the procession that conducted Sir Baldwin Fulford to execution. The parish is now amalgamated with that of Christ Church.

ST. GILES' stood at the bottom of Small street. Barrett says it was pulled down in 1319.

ST. LAURENCE stood on the west side of St. John's. It was incorporated with the latter in 1580.

ST. LEONARD'S, whose arch and tower formed the western termination of Old Corn street, stood in a line with the entrance to Baldwin street. It was pulled down in 1766, and the parish consolidated with St. Nicholas.

CHAPEL OF THE HOLY VIRGIN, Bristol Bridge. This chapel had a tower 108 feet high, on each side four large windows of three lights, also an east window of stained glass.

CHAPEL OF ST. JOHN THE BAPTIST, belonging to St. Nicholas Church, in Spicer's Hall, on the Welsh back. A 14th century exterior doorway, together with an interesting roof within of the same date, yet exist in the relics of the above hall.

ST. BRENDON'S CHAPEL, on the summit of Brandon hill.

ST. CATHERINE'S CHAPEL, Brightbow, Bedminster.

ST. CLEMENT'S CHAPEL, on the site of the Merchant Venturers' Hall, King street.

ST. GEORGE'S CHAPEL, on the north side of the Old Guildhall, Broad street. The handsome Gothic east window was upon its demolition re-erected at The Grove, Brislington.

ST. JORDAN'S CHAPEL, College green.

ST. MARTIN'S CHAPEL, in the outer or first ward of the Castle.

ST. SPRITE'S CHAPEL, in Redcliff churchyard.

ST. VINCENT'S CHAPEL, now the Giant's cave, St. Vincent's rocks.

CHU   DICTIONARY OF BRISTOL.   CHU

Church.	Situation.	App. Sun.	Week-day Services.	Vicar, Rector, or Incumbent.	Patron and Value of Living.
*†All Saints	Pembroke road	3 30	Daily 8 m., 5 a.	Rev. R. W. Randall, M.A., V.	Trustees .. £498
All Saints	Corn street	..	M., Tu., St.-d. 11 m., Th. 7.30 a.	Rev. Clement D. Strong	D. and C. of Bristol. £154
Blind Asylum Chapel	Queen's road	3 30	Daily 10 m., 4 a.	Rev. A. Medland, Chaplain (¶)	
The Cathedral	College green	..	St.-d. 12 m., W. 8 a.	Rev. E. P. Cole, R.	T. Cole .. £435
Christ Church & St. Ewen	Broad street	3 15	W. 11.30 m., Th. 12 m.	Rev. Horace Meyer, V.	Simeon Trustees .. £385
Christ Church	Clifton park	..		Rev. T. W. Harvey, C. in char.	
Clifton College Miss. Room	Newfoundland road	..			
Emmanuel	Guthrie road	3 30†	W., 5 a., F., St.-d. 11 m.	Rev. T. G. Luckock, M.A., V.	Simeon Trustees .. £550
Emmanuel or Unity	Dings, St. Philip's	..	Tu. 7.30 a.	Rev. R. Cornall, M.A., V.	Trustees .. £370
*Holy Nativity, The	Knowle	3 30	Daily 7.30 m., 6.30 a. W., F. 12 m.	Rev. Hon. F. H. Tracy, V.	
Holy Trinity	Hotwells	3 15	F. 7.30 a.	Rev. C. H. Wallace, M.A., V.	Simeon Trustees .. £325
Holy Trinity, par. church of St. Philip and Jacob Without	West street	3 0	W. 7.30 a., F. 11 m., H.-d. 7.30 a.	Rev. H. A. Hall, A.K.C., V.	Trustees .. £340
Holy Trinity, par. church	Horfield	3 30†	W., F. 10 m., other days 7.30 m. in sum. 8 m. in win. W. 7.30 a., F. 5 a. 9 30 Sunday morning	Rev. F. Bingham, M.A., R.	Bishop of Glos. and Br. £800
Orphan Asylum Chapel	Hook's mills	..		Rev. J. Fox, M.A., Chaplain	Trustees .. £52
Redland Green Chapel	Redland	3 30	W., F. 11 m., W. 7.30 a.	Rev. W. Cartwright, M.A.	
St. Andrew	Clifton hill	3 15	W., 8 a., F. 11.0 m.	Rev. A. L. T. Greaves, M.A., V.	Simeon Trustees .. £750
St. Andrew	Montpelier	3 0†	Th. 7.30 a.	Rev. W. P. Steele, B.A., V.	Bishop of Glos. and Br. £300
St. Andrew the Less	Dowry square	..	W., 7 a.	Rev. P. Hathaway, M.A., V.	See St. Andrew's, Clifton.
St. Augustine	College green	3 30	W., F. 11 m.	Rev. T. C. Price, M.A., V.	D. and C. of Bristol. £420
St. Barnabas	Ashley road	..	W., H.-d. 8 a.	Rev. E. A. Fuller, M.A., V.	Bishop of Glos. and Br. £300
St. Bartholomew	Union street	..	W., 7.30 a.	Rev. C. W. Hickson, M.A., V.	Trustees .. £287
St. Clement	Newfoundland street	3 0	W., F. 10 m., Th. 7.30 a.	Rev. J. Wadeworth, V.	Trustees .. £320
St. Gabriel	Easton	3 0		Rev. J. Thompson, B.A., V.	Vicar Holy Trinity .. £200
St. George	{Great George st., Park street}	3 30†	F., H.-d. 8 a.	Rev. F. A. Lefroy, V.	D. and C. of Bristol. £420
St. James, chapel of ease	Victoria Square	..	W. 11.30 m.	Rev. A. L. T. Greaves, M.A.	See St. Andrew's, Clifton.
St. James	Horsefair	3 0	T. 7.30 a., F. 5 a., dy. 8.45 m.	Rev. J. Hart-Davies, M.A., V.	Trustees .. £464
St. James the Less	Upper Maudlin st.	..	W. 7.30 a.	Rev. J. Hart-Davies, M.A., V.	
St. John	Bedminster	3 15	Daily 7.30 m., 7 a.	Rev. A. C. C. Anstey, M.A., V.	Bishop of Glos. and Br. £450
St. John the Baptist	Broad street	..	T. 7 a., certain H.-d. 7 a.	Rev. W. S. Bruce, M.A., R.	Trustees .. £198

Service commences at all Churches at 11 a.m. and 6.30 p.m. except those marked * 10.30 a.m. and † 7 p.m. ‡ First Sunday in the month. § Last Sunday in the month. ¶ For details see Cathedral history. H.-d.—Holy days. St.-d.—Saints' days. V.—Vicar. R.—Rector. C.—Curate. D. and C.—Dean and Chapter. Most of the Parish Churches have Glebe Houses attached to the living.

DICTIONARY OF BRISTOL.

Church.	Situation.	Sun. Ser. a.m.	Week-day Services.	Vicar, Rector, or Incumbent.	Patron and Value of Living.
St. John the Evangelist	Apsley road, Clifton	3 30	F. 11 m., 7 a.	Rev. H. G. Walsh, M.A., V.	Bishop of Glos. and Br. ...£340
St. Jude	Poyntzpool	3 45	.. ..	Rev. Wm. Kerry, V.	Crown and Bishop alt. ...£300
St. Luke	Barton hill	..	W. 7.30 a.	Rev. Sidney Pike, M.A.	V. of St. Philip & Jacob..£300
St. Luke	Bedminster	..	Th. 7 a.	Rev. D. A. Doudney, D.D., V.	Trustees £400
" Mission hall	William street	..	.. ..		
St. Mark (Mayor's chapel)	College green	3 0	W.7.30a., H.-d.10m.7.30a.	Rev. J. H. Bright.	Mayor for the time being..£100
St. Mark	Easton	3 30½	W. 7 a.	Rev. T. H. Barnett, V.	Bishop of Glos. and Br. ...£235
St. Mary-le-port	Mary-le-port street	3 0½	Daily 8 m., 5 a., H.-d.	Rev. James Ormiston, R.	Trustees £230
St. Mary Redcliff	Redcliff hill	3 30	8, 11 m., 7.30 a.	Rev. C. E. Cornish, M.A., V.	Bishop of Glos. and Br. ...£420
St. Mary	Barnard's place, New Cut	3 0	Tu. and W. 8 a.	Rev. D. M. Claxton, M.A., C. in charge	
St. Mary the Virgin	Tyndall's park	3 15	St.-d., W., F. 11 m.	Rev. W. F. Bryant, V.	T. T. Walton £480
St. Mathias	Broad weir	3 0	M., Th. 7 a., other d. 8 a.	Rev. J. P. Myles, M.A., V.	Crown and Bishop alt. ...£300
St. Matthew	Kingsdown	..	W. 7 a.	Rev. W. B. Doherty, V.	Trustees £445
St. Michael	St. Michael's hill	..	W. 7.30 a.	Rev. N. Heywood, M.A., R.	Trustees £330
St. Michael	Two Mile hill, St. George's	..	Daily 8.30 m., 7.30 a.	Rev. J. T. Baylee, M.A., V.	Trustees £330
St. Michael and All Angels	Bishopston, Horfield	3 0†	W. 7.30 a., Th. 7 a.	Rev. G. W. Bence, M.A., V.	Bishop of Glos. and Br. ...£300
St. Nathaniel	Redland road	..	.. ..	Rev. N. Cornford, M.A., V.	Trustees £172
St. Nicholas with St. Leonard	Bristol Bridge	3 0	F. 7.30 a., H.-d. noon	Rev. J. G. Alford, M.A., V.	D. and C. of Bristol.. ..£300
St. Paul	Clifton	3 30	Daily 8 m., 5 a.	Rev. F. V. Mather	Simeon Trustees ..£400
St. Paul	Coronation road	3 0	D'y. 8a., Th., St.-d. 7.30a.	Rev. C. J. Atherton, M.A., V.	Bishop of Glos. and Br. ...£400
St. Paul	Portland square	..	W. 7 a.	Rev. James Davidson, V.	Trustees £400
St. Peter	Clifton wood	3 15	Th. 8 a.	Rev. John Rooker, M.A.	Simeon Trustees ..£300
St. Peter	Peter street	..	W. 7.30 a.	Rev. W. T. Hollins, M.A., R.	Bishop of Glos. and Br. ...£380
St. Peter	Bishopsworth	..	F. 7 a.	Rev. R. Molesworth, V.	Trustees £300
St. Philip and Jacob	Old Market street	..	W. 7.30 a.	Rev. G. B. James, A.K.C., R.	Bishop of Glos. and Br. ...£400
St. Saviour	Woolcott park	3 45	W., F. 10 m., 7.30 a.	Rev. C. W. Prideaux, M.A., V.	
St. Silas	St. Philip's marsh	3 0†	W. 7.30 a.	Rev. W. Saunders, P.	Trustees £628
St. Simon	Baptist mills	..	Daily 7.45 m., W. 7.30 a.	Rev. N. Y. Birkmyre, M.A., P.	Crown and Bishop alt. ...£264
St. Stephen	Clare street	4 0§	St.-d., F. 12 noon	Rev. F. Wayet, M.A., R.	Lord Chancellor £292
The Temple, or Holy Cross	Temple street	3 30†	W. 7 a., F. 11 m.	Rev. W. Huddleline, V.	Five Trustees £325
St. Thomas	Thomas street	..	W. F., St.-d. 7.30 a.	Rev. C. S. Taylor, M.A., V.	Bishop of Glos. and Br. ...£300
St. Werburgh	Mina road	..	W. 7.30 a.	Rev. J. Fox, R.	Lord Chancellor £140

Service commences at all Churches at 11 a.m. and 6.30 p.m. except those marked * 10.30 a.m. and †7 p.m.
† First Sunday in the month. ‡ Last Sunday in the month.
St.-d.—Saints' days. V.—Vicar. R.—Rector. C.—Curate. D. and C.—Dean and Chapter.
H.-d.—Holy days. Most of the Parish Churches have Globe Houses attached to the living.

Church Extension in Bristol.

A commission was appointed in 1881, by the Bishop of the Diocese, to enquire into the spiritual needs of the poor districts of the city. From time to time an informal statement has been made of the work done, and since the last, held on June 10th, 1882, meetings have been continued at the Council-house, and much progress has been made. Four applications for the formation of new parishes have been forwarded to the Ecclesiastical Commissioners—two for the relief of Bedminster, one for the relief of Holy Trinity, St. Philip's, and one for the relief of St. Barnabas. In all these cases the boundaries of the new parishes have been carefully traced, maps prepared and sent to the commissioners, and provision made for endowment. Towards the endowment of these new parishes the Church Extension Fund is pledged to the following grants:—

In Bedminster, for St. Francis, Ashton gate	£3,000
In Bedminster, for Holy Nativity, Knowle	1,500
Holy Trinity, St. Philip's, for St. Lawrence, Lawrence hill	3,000
St. Barnabas, for St. Agnes, Newfoundland road	3,000
Total for endowments	£10,500

These grants will in all four cases be met by grants from the Ecclesiastical Commissioners. The other grants made or promised are as follow:— In St. Mark's, Easton, £500 towards the completion of the mission chapel (used also as a school) has been paid; the chapel was opened for service on the 27th September, 1882. In St. Luke's, Barton hill, for a new church and mission-room, on a site already secured, £3,000. The local committee intend to build the mission-room at once, and the church as soon as the congregation is formed. In Holy Trinity, St. Philip's, £1,000 for the purchase of a site for the new church of St. Lawrence. In St. Andrew's, Montpelier, £450 for the purchase of a site for the new church. £485 have been granted for the purchase of a site for the church of St. Agnes. The grants out of the capital fund to which the Bishop's Commissioners have thus pledged themselves amount, therefore, to £15,500, viz.: Endowment, £10,500; church building, £3,000; church sites, £1,450; mission chapel, £500. Within a few months further grants will be needed for building other churches. The total sum promised amounts to about £27,000, out of £47,000 asked for. On Windmill hill, Bedminster, the site is being conveyed to the Ecclesiastical Commissioners; for the church to be built thereon a grant will ere long be needed. Mission chapels are under consideration for Pyle hill, Bedminster, and for Pennywell road, Holy Trinity, St. Philip's. Further subscriptions are also needed for the "Mission Curates' Stipends' Fund." Thus far only £211 per annum have been promised; and of this £160 have been already granted—£70 to the Pennywell road Mission, and £90 to the Two-Mile hill Mission. There are other applications equally pressing that cannot be met without further subscriptions. When the public understand that the work is going rapidly forward, and that the money is paid out as fast as it comes in in relief of our most necessitous parishes, more subscriptions will, it is hoped, come forward. The chairman is G. W. Edwards, and the secretary the Rev. J. G. Alford, St. Nicholas' vicarage.

Church of England Association.

Objects: The maintenance of the principles of the Protestant Church of England, and to counteract the efforts now being made to pervert her teaching on essential points in the Christian faith, or to assimilate her services to those of the Church of Rome, and further, to encourage concerted action for the advancement and progress of spiritual religion. Honorary secretaries, Rev. T. H. Clarke,

M.A., James Inskip and E. W. Bird, Royal Insurance buildings, Corn st.

Church of England Temperance Society. This branch is established for the purpose of promoting the formation of Parochial Temperance Societies in the various parishes within the Deanery of Bristol, and as a means of communication between such societies and its members generally when united action is considered desirable. Numerous Parochial Societies have been formed and are in active operation. The central committee is composed of several clergy and delegated representatives of each parochial affiliated association. The objects of the society are—(1) The promotion of habits of temperance. (2) The reformation of the intemperate. (3) The removal of the causes which lead to intemperance. Hon. secs., Rev. G. B. James, and F. Sturge, St. Stephen's avenue.

Church Pastoral Aid Society, Bristol and Clifton Auxiliary, established in 1836. President, Right Rev. Bishop Anderson; hon. secretaries, Revs. E. P. Hathaway and G. B. James, and W. W. Jose. Annual meetings held in the Victoria Rooms. Sermons are preached and collections made at some churches annually in aid of the society, which is, strictly speaking, a Home Missionary Society.

Church Schoolmasters' and Mistresses' Benevolent Institution. The Bristol Local Board has been established 14 years. Out of 111 such boards in England, Bristol was the fourth established. Its object is to afford relief to necessitous members and to orphans of deceased members. Local secretary, H. J. Walker, Victoria street Schools.

City Arms. The arms of Bristol are gules, on a mount, on the sinister side vert a castle argent (silver), issuant therefrom on waves argent and azure, a ship Or (gold). The crest upon the helm is a wreath of gold and gules, issuant out of the clouds two arms saltire charnew, the hand on the dexter side holding a serpent, that on the sinister side a pair of balances—gold. Supporters, two unicorns sejant rampant, gold maned and horned and clayed sables, mantled gold and silver. Motto, "*Virtute et Industria.*" Granted 1569.

City Mission Society. To communicate religious knowledge to the poor inhabitants of Bristol and its vicinity, especially to those who are living in the entire neglect of religion, by the employment of paid and gratuitous agents, to be engaged in visiting the poor and afflicted, preaching the Gospel, circulating the scriptures and religious tracts, and the establishment of schools. Treasurer, W. Mack, 38 Park street; secretaries, Charles Townsend, Avenue House, Cotham park, and Lewis Waterman, Rupert street; tract depository, H. Pike, 2 Union street. (*See* "Chapels.")

Civic High Cross, The, is first mentioned in the city annals in the year 1247, and is described as being the place where the Market was kept. It was re-erected in 1373, and within its niches were placed statues of the several kings, John, Henry III. and Edward III., to which was afterwards added that of Edward IV. Standing at the intersection of the four principal streets, High street, Wine street, Broad street and Corn street, the spot it there occupied, though of no visible significance, is suggestive of many memories, some of them tragical. Close to the carved imagery of the cross were hanged, drawn and quartered, in 1320, Sir Henry Womington and Sir Henry Mountford, two of the barons whom Edward II. pursued and sacrificed in his fight for life. Here, too, were beheaded, at the outcry of the populace, Scrocp, Earl of Wiltshire, Sir John Bushey and Sir Henry Green, steadfast adherents of Richard II. Bolingbroke, with his great northern army, having surrounded the town and taken both city and castle, one of the terms of the capitulation of the latter was that these three courtiers should be delivered into his hands. In Shakespeare's "Richard II." (Act III., Scene 1) there is a scene relating to the tragic event referred to at this spot:—

(*Enter* Bolingbroke, York, Northumberland, Percy, Willoughby, Ross; officers behind, with Bushey and Green prisoners.)

Bolingbroke: Bring forth these men.
Bushey and Green, I will not vex your souls
(Since presently your souls must part your bodies)
With too much urging your pernicious lives,
For 'twere no charity; yet, to wash your blood
From off my hands, here, in the view of men,
I will unfold some causes of your deaths.
You have misled a prince, a royal king,
A happy gentleman in blood and lineaments,
By you unhappy'd and disfigur'd clean.
You have, in manner, with your sinful hours,
Made a divorce betwixt his queen and him,
Broke the possession of a royal bed,
And stain'd the beauty of a fair queen's cheeks
With tears drawn from her eyes by your foul wrongs.
Myself—a prince, by fortune of my birth,
Near to the king in blood; and near in love,
Till you did make him misinterpret me,
Have stoop'd my neck under your injuries
And sigh'd my English breath in foreign clouds,
Eating the bitter bread of banishment;
While you have fed upon my signories,
Dispark'd my parks, and fell'd my forest woods;
From mine own windows torn my household coat,
Raz'd out my impress, leaving me no sign—
Save men's opinions and my living blood—
To show the world I am a gentleman.
This, and much more, much more than twice all this,
Condemns you to the death: see them delivered over
To execution and the hand of death.

Bushey: More welcome is the stroke of death to me
Than Bolingbroke to England. Lords, farewell!

Green: My comfort is—that Heaven will take our souls,
And plague injustice with the pains of hell.

Bolingbroke: My Lord Northumberland, see them dispatch'd.

(*Exeunt Northumberland and others with prisoners.*)

The Duke of Lancaster sent the heads in a white basket to London with a letter, which was read before all the commonalty of London:—

I, Henry, Duke of Hereford and Earl of Derby, commend myself to all the people of London, high and low. My good friends, I send you my salutation, and I acquaint you that I have come over to take my rightful inheritance. I beg of you to know if you will be on my side or not, and I care not which, for I have people enough to fight all the world for one day, thank God. But take in good part the present I send you.

The disheartening effect of the intelligence of the fate of these men upon the weak and terror-stricken King has been notably portrayed by the same supreme poet:—

Aumale: Is Bushey, Green, and the Earl of Wiltshire dead?
Scroop: Yes, all of them at Bristol lost their heads.
King Richard: No matter where. Of comfort no man speak.
Let's talk of graves—of worms—and epitaphs;
Make dust our paper, and with rainy eyes
Write sorrow on the bosom of the earth.
. . . . . .
Our lands, our lives, and all are Bolingbroke's.

Within recent years an attempt was made to revive the earldom of Wilts in the person of a descendant of the Lord Scroop here executed, whose attainder involved the forfeiture of the family title, including the right to wear a kingly crown in the Isle of Man. Another noble victim to the same lost cause was Lord Spenser, who met a like fate at this spot, "weeping and lamenting his sad life." Brighter scenes were the reception at the High Cross of Henry VII. (1490) and of Queen Elizabeth (1574). In relation to the former personage, here "was a pageant full of maiden children, richly beseen, and Prudentia had the speech as ensueth:—

"Most noble Prynce, our sovereign Liege Lord,
To this poore Town of Bristow that is youre,
Ye be heartely welcom, God to record,"

with many other lines of equally inspired character. The phrase, "poore Town of Bristow," the King seems to have interpreted in its poetical sense rather than as prosaic fact. Anyhow, he ordained that every man worth £20 should pay him 20/-, "for the which tax there arose great grief among the Commons." Moreover, his Majesty having come to Bristol and made the exaction by the advice of Morton, Archbishop of Canterbury, the apprentices arose and "made a bishop" in effigy, and went about the town singing this hymn following:—

"He that can his paternoster, his ave and his crede,
Pray for the Bishoppe of Caunterbury that evill may him spede."

But as soon as the Mayor understood thereof he caused 24 of the eldest of them to be taken and carried into Newgate, and shortly after they were "grievously whipped and punished." With regard to Queen Bess, here on a stage stood Fame, "an excellent boy,", who, having repeated some verses hardly up to the mark of his name, "flung up a great garland to the rejoicing of all beholders." In the year 1574 the High Cross was painted and gilded at the expense of £66 13s. 8d., in preparation for the visit of Queen Elizabeth to the city, which occurred on August 14th. In 1633 it was again repaired and heightened, and there were added also figures of Henry VI., Queen Elizabeth, James I. and Charles I. It was also curiously painted, gilded and surrounded by iron rails and steps, and when the markets were held in High street these served for seats. The additions were at the expense of the Chamber of the city, and cost £207. Its height from the ground was 40 feet. Col. Fiennes, who became Governor of Bristol in 1642, came in his coach on Saturday, March 4th, being chief market day, to the High Cross, attended by a troop of horse, to see that the proclamation of the King, respecting the navy, was publicly burnt. At the High Cross, also, James Naylor, the Quaker, whose religious frenzy led him to personate the Second Person of the Holy Trinity, was, with his deluded followers, laid hold of by the authorities. In accordance with the gentle spirit of the times (1656), he was condemned by the House of Commons to be whipped through the streets of London, receiving thus 310 lashes, one on crossing each gutter. Then, in the pillory, his tongue was bored by a hot iron and his forehead branded. Afterwards he was flogged through Bristol and finally imprisoned. After enduring three years' confinement he was discharged, when he, at Bristol, made an effecting and convincing recantation in a meeting of his friends. The Cross, in 1697, was again fresh painted and gilded in a costly manner, and continued a dignified ornament to the city till the year 1733, when a timorous silversmith, who lived opposite to it, declared that his house and life were endangered by its tottering and threatening to fall in a very high wind. It was consequently taken down, and for some time lay in fragments in the Guildhall; but by the interest of some private citizens it was by-and-bye again brought to light and re-erected in College green. Here it contracted the animosity of Mr. Champion, of Bristol china celebrity, who might have better employed himself in reproducing its light and elegant design on his porcelain than in procuring its removal; but this he effected, and for five years it lay neglected in a corner of the Cathedral. About the year 1768 Cutts Barton was appointed as Dean of Bristol, and he covenanted for some pieces of silver or gold to sell the cross to his friend Henry Hoare, of Stourhead, in whose grounds it now stands. It still retains its statuary of royal persons, and these, with its rich tabernacle work, venerable appearance and historical associations, make it a monument of remarkable interest, and as such its removal is a disgraceful loss to Bristol. The foundation stone of the cross in College green was laid on the 8th of August, 1850, with full Masonic rites, by the Mayor, J. K. Haberfield. The architect was C. Norton; the ground was given by the Dean and Chapter. The centre supporting column is of an octagonal shape, and beneath the arches from which spring the groining are eight shields, which are intended to be charged with the arms of the monarchs destined to adorn the niches of the superstructure. It has a statue of Edward III. in one of its niches.

Clergy Society, founded in 1692, for the relief of necessitous clergymen and their widows and children. Sermons and special collections are made annually at some of the churches in behalf of the society. Hon. secretaries, Rev. T. G. Luckock, The Avenue, Clifton, and W. H. Clark, 28 Broad street.

Clerical Education Society, established 1795, for educating young men belonging to the Church of England for the ministry. Secretary, Rev. N. Heywood.

Clifton. On leaving the busy wharves of Bristol the prospect of the Avon opens like a romantic vision. The wrinkled, creviced and moss-grown precipices on the one hand, where the symmetrical rows and crescents of handsome houses are piled story upon story like the Hanging Gardens of Old Babylon, and on the other hand the long, serpentine range of lofty woods, broken into combes and valleys of the richest luxuriance and beauty (though unfortunately these woods are being now much mutilated for quarrying purposes), make together a composition that scarcely requires improvement from fancy, and Walter Savage Landor agreed with Robert Southey in pronouncing the scene to be of its kind unsurpassed in Europe. It is a real triumph of art that the catenary bridge which has been thrown across the chasm, instead of impairing the scenery, emphatically adds, with its rainbow-like curve, to the effect of the natural view. Clifton, staring like an eagle from her throne of rocks, is now balanced by a second Clifton on the Somerset side of the gorge, which promises to spread into that county as does the original into Gloucestershire. The defensive earthwork, or, as it is commonly called, "camp," on the Observatory hill, together with the corresponding works on the opposite side of the Avon, are considered by antiquaries to have been thrown up by the Belgic-British before the Roman conquest of the country; and in viewing them we cannot but recall the long-past day when the wolfskin-clad Briton anxiously watched the imperial galleys coming up the yellow stream beneath, quickly to drive him and his young barbarians from their sylvan home. These works are respectively known by the names of Clifton, Bower Walls' and Stokeleigh camps, the first being on the southern summit of the picturesque glen called Nightingale valley, and the second on the opposite point of the same ravine. We are told by Tacitus that Ostorius Scapula (who succeeded Aulus Plautius in the government of Britain about A.D. 50), in order to keep in subjection the conquered territories and to repel the irruptions of the tribes beyond, established a chain of fortresses between the Avon and Severn. Upon usurpation by the Romans, the camps on the Avon were made to form part of a system of military defences that stretched from Clifton 40 miles N.E. to Bredon hill, in Worcestershire. Like the flying torch from Ida to Lemnos, which finally told the watchman on the palace roof of Argos that Troy had fallen, a sudden attack could be signalled by fires from Clifton to Blaize hill and Deorham, or Sodbury, and onward, till assistance came to the beleaguered post. Bower Walls' camp has been almost obliterated to provide materials for the modern builder, the great quantity of lime in the structure being converted into mortar, and the stone pounded into gravel for roadmaking. Happily, the interesting earthwork on the opposite side of Nightingale valley is as yet untouched, and it is to be hoped that the educated intelligence of the modern hill-tribes of the district will be sufficient to ensure its protection. How so lace-like a fabric as the Suspension Bridge appears from 250 feet beneath could be woven in upper air is a problem that many who did not witness the gradual process of its construction are unable to explain, unless they imagine it was done, as has been sagaciously suggested, in balloons. The descent of the manor of Clifton has for the first time been made clear by A. S. Ellis, in a paper of much research in the Bristol and Gloucestershire Archæological Society for 1878-9, Part I. The first record appears in *Domesday*, where it is said that Lewin, the Provost of Bristou, had held the manor of Clistone (Clifton) under King Edward, but that Robert Fitz-Ralph was tenant of the same manor under the Conqueror. The inhabitants were three serfs, six villanes and six bordars, none of whom had liberty to remove beyond the manor. Of these three classes the *servi*, or serfs, were the lowest; they were servile labourers, and, with their children, belonged to the land, like trees or cattle. The villanes were the original farm-servants of the Roman villa; the bordars were tenants of cottages *(bords)*. Of the descent of the manor of Clifton till it reached (1544) the hands of Sir Ralph Sadleir at the dissolution of monasteries, it having then belonged to the college of Westbury-on-Trym, information will be found in A. S. Ellis's paper. For more than two centuries the manor and manorial rights have been, at least, partially in the hands of the Merchant Venturers of Bristol, who purchased the same from Sir Ralph Sadleir's descendants.

Clifton College Company Limited, The, was formed on the 13th September, 1860, with a capital of £10,000. The magnificent site now occupied by the college, consisting of about 15 acres, was purchased. The Council expended £100 in prizes for a suitable design, and that of C. Hansom was approved. In about a year the schoolroom (which will accommodate 800) and class-rooms, together with the head master's house, were completed. These buildings, with the subsequent additions and the chapel (*see* "Guthrie Memorial Chapel"), form a quadrangle facing the close. The college was opened on September 30th, 1862, by the Rev. John Percival, Fellow of Queen's College, Oxford, as head master, and with 69 boys who had attended the preliminary school. Subsequently a preparatory and junior school have been attached, and the boarding arrangements extended; several large boarding-houses, a residence for the bachelor masters, a new wing to the college building, a physical science school with chemical laboratory, a library, a museum, additional class and lecture-rooms, swimming baths, ten fives courts, &c., have been added in order to meet the growing requirements. Between £90,000 and £100,000 have been expended in establishing the college, of which sum about £13,000 were contributed by private benefactions from members of the Council, masters, parents of boys, and other friends. On the 16th March, 1877, her Majesty signed the royal charter of the college, and its governing body consists of the original shareholders and life governors of £50. The governors are each entitled to have one boy in the college on his nomination. The original governors have a right to nominate someone to replace them in lifetime, or to succeed them after death. The Council have the power to nominate boys to the college subject to such annual charge as they think fit, and they, under this right, charge £5 per annum. The college is a public school open to all boys without distinction of class; this is a slight alteration from the original constitution, which restricted the boys to sons of gentlemen. The religious teaching is in accordance with the teaching of the Church of England, but no boy is compelled to attend services to which his parents conscientiously object. The college now consists of 650 boys, its fullest complement, under the head mastership of the Rev. James M. Wilson, late Fellow of St. John's College, Cambridge, who was appointed in 1878 on the retirement of Dr. Percival, elevated to the presidency of Trinity College, Oxford. Music and the fine arts are cultivated assiduously. All boys have their places in the varied sports, and the result has been that the college has excelled in athletics. Though the building of the quadrangle is as yet incomplete, the college is without doubt one of the most important in England, and is a credit to the ancient city of Bristol. Honours have been obtained by the college in the open scholarships and exhibitions at Oxford and Cambridge; admissions to the Royal Military Academy, Woolwich; to the Royal Indian College, Cooper's Hill; to the Royal Military College, Sandhurst; to the Indian Civil Service; to the Foreign Office and other minor distinctions.

Clifton Conference.
Annual conferences of Christians of all denominations are held in October at the Victoria Rooms, Clifton. Convener, Rev. James Ormiston, rector, St. Mary-le-port, 14 Arlington villas, Clifton.

Clifton Friendly Society,
formed for the purpose of aiding those who aid themselves, by receiving cash deposits. Attendance given at the Infants' school, Merchant place, Hotwells, the first Wednesday in each month at 7 o'clock. There is also a Redcliff branch at 8 Cathay, the first Monday in each month, and a St. Philip's branch at the Hannah More schoolroom on the second Monday in each month. Clerk, A. G. Lucas, 23 Clare street.

Climate.
The climate of Bristol is mild, and the hygrometric state of the atmosphere is generally high; in winter it is not subject to extreme colds, nor in summer to extreme heats. The air in the lower parts of the city is soft and relaxing rather than bracing; but, as the city lies on so many different levels and so many different soils, no general description will apply to the whole. The lower parts are situated on alluvial overlying the new red sandstone, but the newer and more elevated parts are on the new red sandstone and millstone grit and other allied formations. The elevation above sea level varies considerably; the lower parts are but a few feet above high water level, whilst the upper parts of Clifton are 315 feet above. The air on the higher levels is very pure and bracing, and readily shows the presence of ozone on the application of the proper test, and is exceedingly well adapted for invalids, who can here choose the climate most suitable to their constitutions. Those who require a soft, mild atmosphere have for their selection the lower and sheltered slopes, and those who require highly ozonised and bracing air, fresh from the Atlantic and Bristol Channel, can get all they desire on Clifton and Durdham downs. (*See* "Sanitary.")

Clubs.
BRISTOL AND CLIFTON CHESS ASSOCIATION. This club meets three days a week at the Imperial Hotel, Whiteladies' road, Clifton, from 3 until 11 p.m. It numbers among its members some of the strongest and most accomplished players, and can boast of a past history such as few existing clubs possess. Some 35 or 40 years ago it gave such an impetus to the game by the skill and reputation of some of its players that several clubs were started in the provinces, and now there is scarcely a town of any importance that does not contain a chess club. In the year 1859 the club was reorganised under the presidency of the well-known and distinguished player, Captain H. A. Kennedy. The meetings were then held at the Athenæum, Corn street, but so many of the members living in Clifton and the neighbourhood, it was determined to make an effort to find suitable rooms somewhere at Clifton; and the committee were fortunate in securing a good room with all the necessary requirements at the Fine Arts Academy, where the club flourished for some few years, until the Academy committee

requiring more room, the club had to look out for fresh quarters, and were compelled to take temporary rooms at the Volunteer Club; but these not being considered well adapted for such a purpose, arrangements were made with the Imperial Hotel Company, where the club enjoys all the comfort and convenience necessary for its successful working. There are upwards of 80 members. Subscription, 15s. per annum for gentlemen, and 7s. 6d. for ladies. E. J. Taylor, hon. sec.

BRISTOL CATHOLIC WORKMAN'S CLUB, 22 Host street (opposite Colston hall), established November 4th, 1862. Its object is to promote union and cordiality amongst Catholic working men, and to aid the work of the Temperance Crusade by providing means of innocent amusement, recreation and self-improvement. Any Catholic of good character and above the age of 16 is eligible for admission. Every member on admission pays 1s., and a weekly subscription of 1d. The library contains 700 volumes, and the London and local daily papers are taken, and there are games of various kinds. At present there are about 700 members. The club is open from 7 to 10 o'clock. Rev. Wm. Strickland, S.J., president; John O'Leary, secretary.

BRISTOL CLUB, in Old Market street, was founded in November, 1880, by John Lysaght. The club is for the convenience, comfort and enjoyment of the working classes, and everything is done to contribute to their social improvement. It consists of well-lighted and commodious rooms, viz.: A large dining-room, 32 feet square, where well-cooked meals can be procured at very low prices; a comfortable room, well furnished and heated, for smoking and conversation; an excellent room for reading the principal daily and weekly papers, as well as a variety of books upon all subjects; spacious rooms for billiards, bagatelle and skittles, and a concert hall. There is no admission fee, and the present annual subscription is 2s. 6d. G. F. Cox, steward and secretary.

CLIFTON CLUB, The Mall, Clifton, stands on the site of Long's Royal Hotel and Clifton Assembly-rooms. It was originally started, in 1856, by several gentlemen who felt the want of a first-class club. The shares were of the value of £50 each (afterwards increased to £60 each). Ladies were admitted as members, and at its formation several availed themselves of its privileges; but, although up to 1882 the rule admitting them had not been repealed, after the first year or two it was used only by gentlemen. The subscription was £3 3s. per annum to non-shareholders and £1 1s. to shareholders. In 1882 the club was reconstituted and formed into a Limited Liability Company, who purchased the premises of the old company. The committee incurred a great outlay in the alterations and improvements to the premises, and the club will now hold its own with any for compactness and comfort. On entering a straight flight of stone stairs faces; these communicate with a good-sized hall, with tiled floor and wood panelled ceiling. Here there is a fireplace, handsomely carved in teak wood. The card-room occupies the first floor level of three houses in Waterloo street, at the back of the club premises; it possesses two well-carved and moulded fireplaces in oak, and its bay windows are fitted with cathedral glass in leaded lights. The subscription is £4 4s. per annum to non-shareholders and £2 2s. to shareholders. C. W. Wasbrough, secretary.

ST. AGNES WORKMEN'S CLUB AND LIBRARY, Newfoundland road. The objects are to promote social intercourse and opportunities for mutual improvement and amusement, and the means for attaining these objects are a club room, a lending and reference library, reading room, and games of various kinds. The club is open in the morning from 8 to 10 as a reading room only, and in the evening from 6 to 10.30; Saturdays, from 3 to 11 o'clock. The entrance fee is 6d., and the subscription 4s. per annum. Annual subscriptions of 10s. and upwards, or a donation of £5 and upwards, entitle a person to honorary membership with all the rights of ordinary members. The following games are permitted:— Chess, billiards, bagatelle, draughts and dominoes, subject to special rules framed for the purpose. No gambling whatever is allowed, nor any intoxicating drinks sold on the premises. Frank E. R. Davey, president; T. J. Jayne, secretary.

VICTORIA CLUB, Queen's road, top of Park street. The handsome buildings which are occupied by this club were originally built for the Red Maids' school; they were never used for this purpose, but were purchased on behalf of the Bishop's college, 1840. When the Volunteer movement sprang into existence, the whole of the buildings were purchased and a large drill hall built in the rear for the use of the Rifle Volunteers, for whose use also the greater portion of the ground-floor was reserved. The upper portion was used as a club restricted to volunteers, and upon this basis was successfully carried on for several years. About 1874 it was opened as an ordinary club, and as such has since been carried on, with a change of name from the "Volunteer" to the "Victoria" club. There are about 150 members. Subscription, £3 3s. per annum. J. W. Hickman, hon. sec.

Cocoa and Coffee Taverns, &c.
This movement was commenced by a committee building a comfortable room for the navvies at Lovers' walk during the construction of the Clifton Extension railway. In 43 weeks the total consumption there had been 8,927 gallons. The next step was to open a shed at the Black Rock end of the tunnel of that railway, which in 25 weeks had furnished 2,052 gallons; these, on the completion of the railway, were closed, and a cocoa room opened on the Grove, where has been sold over 700 gallons per week. The timber merchants on the Sea banks have provided a cocoa shed for the accommodation of their men; and in the Goods sheds and yards at the Railway station the men are supplied with refreshing beverages.

THE ALBION, in connection with Messrs. C. Hill and Sons, is in Cumberland road.

THE BRISTOL COFFEE PUBLIC HOUSE COMPANY LIMITED have "The Clarence," 12 Lawrence hill. W. Price, manager.

THE BRISTOL TAVERN AND CLUB COMPANY LIMITED have houses at the following places:—Bedminster, High street, Nicholas street, Nelson street, Redcliff street, Philip street, and near The Mall, Clifton. G. F. Barnett, secretary.

THE CASTLE COFFEE PALACE is at 48 Castle street.

THE COLSTON, 52 Broad quay. A. H. Lamb, manager.

THE VICTORIA COMPANY have two houses, one at 4 High street and the other at 27 St. Augustine's parade.

There are over 100 other coffee taverns of a miscellaneous character in the city; the above, as a rule, belong to public companies, and are conducted on first-class principles.

College Green,
a fine open area covered with grass and intersected with gravel walks. Two rows of lime trees surround the green, with walks and seats between them, and afford a pleasant promenade. It has eminently been a preaching place. St. Austin here declared the glad tidings with which he was commissioned from Rome, and St. Jordan here displayed his zeal in the same direction. In the year 1709 the green was railed in and the walks laid out with young trees. The rails were then of wood, and therefore of a more rustic appearance than the

present iron ones. It covers 4a. 0r. 2p. Some of the trees are of recent date, except those near the western steps. One tree, termed the Abbot's tree, from a seat at its root having been a favourite resort of Abbot Elliott, is said to bud first in the year of any there. The picture presented in this green is singularly effective, the Cathedral, St. Augustine's Church, the Mayor's Chapel, the High Cross, the Norman gateway of the Abbey, the Hotel and the handsome shops on one side, the tree-shaded walks and the noble but acclivitous Park street in the background, combine to form a tableau of which any city might be proud. (For a description of the above places see their respective headings.)

College of Preceptors.

Local examinations take place at Christmas annually. The examination of the boys in the Bristol centre usually takes place at the University college, the girls at the Colston hall, and in the Clifton centre at the Memorial hall, with a separate examination at Mr. Biggs' school, Redland park. In December, 1882, of the whole number of 212 Bristol candidates, 14 were entered for first class, of whom 8 passed; 82 for second class, 50 passed; 115 for third class, 79 passed; while 31 obtained certificates of a lower grade than that for which they entered. Thus it will be seen that of the 212 candidates examined, 168 passed, or 79 per cent.

Collieries.

Bristol has long been celebrated for its coal-fields. The whole of the seams of this district are good, and run from about 5 feet to 22 inches. In some instances the works spread out underground to a distance of 2 miles from the shaft, and the deepest pit is about 300 fathoms. The following is a list of pits:—Ashton vale, Bitton, Golden valley, Coalpit heath, Bedminster, Easton, Hanham, Whitehall, Kingswood, North and South Parkfield, Nailsea, Rangeworthy and Warmley. The average output from the above is 13,000 to 14,000 tons per week, and the hands employed are somewhere about 3,500. At Coalpit heath, the horses employed walk up to and step by pairs into the cage, to be drawn to bank when the shift is over; but in the Kingswood and other collieries there are some 60 who, having once descended, never again see the light of day, unless there should happen to be a strike. On June 20th, 1851, 50 colliers were buried alive in the Bedminster coalpit; after being in the pit 40 hours they were all, by great exertions, brought alive to the surface.

Colonial and Continental Church Society.

The Bristol and Clifton auxiliary of this association has been established 40 years. Its object is to convey the Gospel to Englishmen, whether travelling on the Continent or living in the Colonies. There is also a Ladies' association in connection with the society. E. Markby, association secretary, 13 Beaconsfield road, Clifton.

Colston Commemoration Societies.

In commemoration of Edward Colston the bells of St. Mary Redcliff ring a muffled peal at midnight on the 12th November in each year, and many other of the city church-bells in turn till dawn of day, and so continue throughout the 13th. The following societies assemble annually on that date to celebrate the anniversary:—

ANCHOR SOCIETY (Liberal). The 113th anniversary was celebrated in 1882 by a dinner in the evening, when the collection amounted to £1,011. The funds of the society have for some years past been applied in granting annuities of £13 a year (5s. weekly) to deserving, aged and necessitous persons, and there are now on the books 43 annuitants. The committee, thinking they would do honour to the memory of Edward Colston, and at the same time confer a benefit on the city, by the appropriation of part of the society's funds to the maintenance of a professorship at the Bristol University college, as recognising the fact that Edward Colston took no less interest in the great cause of education than in work of a purely charitable nature, have made a grant of £300 annually to the University. E. G. Clarke, Albion chambers, Small street, hon. sec.

COLSTON FRATERNAL ASSOCIATION, established in 1853, assists those who were once inmates of Colston's school. The supporters of the association dine annually. A. Beacham, 12 John street, hon sec.

DOLPHIN SOCIETY (Conservative), established in 1749. The members of this society attend, in the morning, divine service at St. Mary Redcliff church, accompanied by the boys from Colston and Temple schools, with the apprentices; after service each apprentice is presented with 3s. 6d., and each schoolboy with 1s. The members dine together in the evening. In 1882 the collection on the anniversary-day amounted to £1,619. A large portion of the funds is devoted to annuities to aged and deserving persons. There are now 60 annuitants of £10 each and 60 apprentices on the books, and upwards of 1,400 indigent persons have been relieved since the last anniversary. Subscribers may recommend fit objects of charity for relief by the committee to the extent of 10s. for each guinea subscribed, in sums of not less than 5s. each. The committee also receive recommendations, signed by five subscribers, for apprenticing poor boys, and for the election of annuitants of £10 each. Subscribers not recommending a person for a money gift are entitled to a double number of votes at the election of annuitants for each guinea subscribed. A. J. Paul, 29 Corn street, hon. sec.

GRATEFUL SOCIETY (neutral). The 124th anniversary took place in 1882. As is the custom of this society, the members attend morning service at All Saints' church, and in the evening dine together. On the anniversary celebrated the above-named year, £1,007 was collected. The bounty of this ancient society during the year 1882 relieved upwards of 900 poor and deserving married women in childbirth. An alteration, long contemplated, has been carried into effect, by granting annuities to persons of not less than 65 years of age, instead of apprentice fees to boys, which, under the altered condition of capital and labour, this society has now found to be rarely required. The number of additional annuitants (£10 per annum) elected in 1882 was six. John Harvey, Denmark street, hon. sec.

Colston Hall, in Colston street, upon the site of the Carmelite friary, afterwards known as the Great house (*see* "Great house") and then as Colston school, and ultimately purchased by the Colston Hall Company, who, at a cost of £45,000, built and opened this magnificent building on the 20th September, 1867. It contains, besides a large hall (which will accommodate 2,250 persons in the body and galleries, and 400 additional in the balconies and orchestra, or 6,000 standing), 146 feet long, 80 feet wide and 70 feet high, two other halls, one with sitting accommodation for 700, the other on the ground floor for 400. The organ in the great hall is by Willis, of London; it has 4 manuals and 60 draw-stops, is blown by 3 hydraulic engines, and cost over £3,000, and was constructed in 1870. The building, which was erected by spirited citizens to supply a great want, rather than as a speculation, has cost upwards of £50,000. Four medallions of well-beloved citizen shareholders, who will not soon be forgotten in Bristol, Conrad Finzel, George Thomas, Henry Overton Wills and Robert Charleton, have been placed in the spandrils over the arches of the great hall.

Commercial Rooms, Corn street, are the daily rendezvous of merchants and others for the discussion of commercial, imperial and local events. Many local schemes are given birth to in these rooms, and not a few civic secrets are revealed here. All the London and local daily newspapers, and a number of provincial dailies, in addition to the weekly, monthly and quarterly journals, are taken in. Telegrams giving the state of the markets in various parts of the kingdom and other news, also Stock Exchange prices, &c., are posted at intervals during the day. Local shipping intelligence is received by private wire from Shirehampton. In addition to the large room, which is 69 feet long, 40 feet wide and 45 feet high from floor to dome, there are also a library, consultation and writing rooms, &c. The building was designed by C. A. Busby, and opened 30th September, 1810. The front of the building consists of a beautiful Grecian Ionic portico, supporting a pediment. The *bas-relief*, which is by Bubb, represents Britannia, Neptune and Minerva receiving tribute from the four quarters of the globe, whilst symbolical figures of commerce, navigation and the city of Bristol adorn its summit. This commodious structure belongs to a body of shareholders, and was erected by creating 710 shares at £25 each. Proprietors pay £2 and non-proprietors £2 10s. per annum. The rooms are opened week days from 8 a.m. to 9 p.m., and on Sundays from 8 a.m. to 2.30 p.m. E. Short, manager.

Common Lodging Houses. Bristol is well provided with these establishments. There are a few at the Hotwells, at Bedminster, and in the Pithay, but in St. Philip's the bulk are to be found. In Gloucester lane, Lamb street and Great Ann street the curious observer may, if it please him, obtain an insight into the private life of some of those individuals whose importunities force the knowledge of their existence upon the public, but upon whose doings, beyond the present moment, scarcely a thought is bestowed. Here may occasionally be seen the professional beggar, whose petitions have succeeded in extracting enough copper coin from the pockets of the charitable to set him up for the rest of the evening, contentedly eating a savoury supper of meat and potatoes, while the man who was singing duets with his wife in the street a short time before, finds time to recruit exhausted nature with a huge pile of hot buttered toast and a jug of tea, his partner meantime toasting a red herring before the fire to serve as a second course. Here also is seen to advantage the gentleman who hangs around street corners and solicits a copper to "help a poor man willing to work, but unable to obtain employment," and who, having appeased the cravings of the inner man, calmly smokes a contemplative pipe while he meditates upon the sympathetic character of mankind. It is not to be expected that the accommodation provided by the proprietors is anything of a very high-class order. The price paid precludes any consideration of that kind, and the lodgers must be satisfied with what is offered them. In most of the houses the general living room is a large apartment at the back of the premises, a sort of half-kitchen, with generally a stone or brick floor thickly strewn with sawdust. The chief desideratum is a good fire and plenty of it, and whatever other complaints may be alleged by the lodgers against their landlords, that of providing insufficient firing cannot be made. A huge boiler holding some gallons stands upon one of the hobs, and from it is drawn the hot water required for making tea, &c., while at the fire cooking of all sorts of provisions goes on throughout the evening, giving off odours which appear to be highly appreciated.

The furniture is of a very rough and ready kind, and chiefly consists of forms and long trestle tables, the tops of the latter scored with lines for playing that exciting game, "shove halfpenny." In some cases a few rough attempts have been made at introducing artistic effects in the shape of a few almanacks and theatrical bills on the walls, and in one house, painted on a board, there is a roughly-written parody of a set of rules for the guidance of visitors; the poet, with a laudable desire to elicit a proper amount of sympathy with the unfortunate and the veneration due to old age, concludes one of his verses with the following choice lines:—

"Don't torment the fools that's here.
Or make the aged curse and swear."

The sleeping accommodation is not so good as that which is offered in the sitting-rooms, but as the charge which is made is very small—ranging from twopence a night for half a bed, to fourpence and fivepence for the luxury of a whole one—complaints are not often made. In most of the rooms there are four bedsteads, generally of the old four-post pattern, with a bed and covering lying upon it. Each bed holds two lodgers, so that there are often eight, and when there are more than four beds, ten and twelve, persons sleeping in one small room. But in cold weather this is looked upon as an advantage rather than a disadvantage, whatever might be the opinion of a sanitary officer upon the subject. In two or three instances the glass is entirely gone from the window-frames, and the cold night air flows uninterruptedly into the room—a free and easy kind of ventilation which, however desirable in the dog-days, must prove somewhat unpleasant in December. The facilities for washing are very limited, and in many instances beyond the tap in the yard there is no other accommodation, but as some of the lodgers look upon soap and water as a superfluity the landlord is not often troubled in this respect. To the credit of the majority of the lodging-house keepers, it must be said that they evidently do their best to keep their premises as clean as circumstances will permit, and preserve a certain amount of order. Proper provision for the separation of the sexes they are compelled to make, in accordance with the supervision of the Sanitary authorities; and in each case the houses are licensed to receive a certain number of lodgers, although this regulation is not always strictly adhered to. The placing of the common lodging-houses under inspection has been extremely useful, but whether the regulations are in all respects complied with is a matter worthy of investigation.

Conduits. Many of the conduits given by the old monks, who helped to mould the life of Bristol in the 13th and 14th centuries still flow. All Hallows, in All Saints' lane, is from a spring on the north side of Maudlin street, opposite the Moravian Chapel. Redcliff hill and St. Thomas' lane are supplied from a fine spring on Knowle hill. The Quay pipe, at the eastern end of the Tontine Warehouses, flows from two springs not far from Ashley road Railway Station. Under the north side of St. John's Church is an old conduit; the water is from a spring on Brandon hill. Jacob's well, near Brandon hill, is very ancient; it probably dates back to the time when the Jews buried their dead on the slope of Brandon hill. It rises in Clifton hill, facing the Police Station.

Congregational Theological Institute, 1 and 2 Upper Byron place. The students of this Institute during 1882 preached 1,088 times, either in the city pulpit or in the village chapel, in addition to 380 services in connection with the Bristol Itinerant society, and 58 temperance meetings and Bands of Hope held at 14 different places within and around the city.

Consuls in Bristol.

Austria—C. Hill, Albion dock.
Belgium—M. Whitwill, Grove.
Brazil—Vice-Consul, T. F. Pearse, 36 Queen square.
Denmark—E. Branth, 11 and 12 King street.
France—M.Cates,18 Queen square.
German Empire—P. D. Alexander, Quay.
Greece—Vice-Consul, M. Whitwill, Grove.
Honduras and Uruguay—P. D. Alexander, Quay.
Italy—Consular Agent, F. Perlasca, 31 Queen square.
Liberia—W. K. Wait, Welsh Back.
Netherlands — Vice-Consul, A. Aberson, 6 Charlotte street, Queen square.
Peru—J. M. Bessone, 8 Queen square.
Portugal—Consul General for Bristol and the Channel, José Maria Eça de Queiroz; Secretary, Jno. Doggett, 33 Queen square.
Republic of Chili—William Smith, Corn street.
Republic of St. Domingo—J. M. Bessone, 8 Queen square.
Russia—P. D. Alexander, Quay.
Spain—Charles T. Bennett, 61 Queen square.
Sweden and Norway—E. Branth, 11 and 12 King street.
Turkey—J. M. Bessone, 8 Queen square.
United States of America—Lorin A. Lathrop, 51 Queen square; Vice-Consul, R. H. Symes, Victoria street.

Convents.

ARNO'S VALE. "The Good Shepherd" community (Notre Dame de la Charité, a filiation from the mother house of Angers), established 22nd July, 1851. The nuns have under their charge a Reformatory school for girls and a Penitentiary.

CLIFTON WOOD. A small French community of nuns called the "Sisters of the Finding of Jesus in the Temple," who settled here in 1868. Their principal work is to visit and nurse the sick, especially of the upper classes, at their own homes, the charges for which support the convent. They offer, also, a home in the convent to ladies of limited means.

COTHAM PARK. St. Joseph's Home, a French community, established about 1861, called the "Little Sisters of the Poor," who take charge of the old, poor and infirm—about 100 old men and women, and 14 Sisters, who beg from door to door in support of the Home. They possess about three acres of land, an extensive building with a convenient chapel, opened in 1876, the whole costing about £7,000. Formerly the work of this convent was carried on in Park row. The dress of the Sisters is similar to that worn by most nuns.

DAMES DE LA MERE DE DIEU, Manilla hall, Clifton. A French community of ladies, established in Clifton 1881, who, in addition to the choir office, undertake a school for young ladies of the upper classes.

DIGHTON STREET, ST. JAMES'. A large range of buildings and school for children, dedicated to "Our Lady of Mercy." The nuns entirely manage an orphanage of 60 children, taken from workhouses, and teach in the Poor schools and in Trenchard street. They also manage a crèche for infants. The sick in the Hospital, the Infirmary and at their homes, are also visited.

MONASTERY OF THE VISITATION, Westbury-on-Trym. A community of enclosed choir nuns, following the rule of St. Francis of Sales. They have built and entirely support a Poor school on their grounds, containing about 20 children.

Cook's Folly, over Durdham down, near Sea walls, is an ivy-clad tower, now incorporated in a castellated villa. The legend runs that a gipsy foretold Goodman Cook that his unborn son would not survive his 21st birthday, but die from the attack of some silent, secret foe. To avoid the catastrophe the father built this tower, and immured his son therein on his 20th natal day. Huge were the walls, massive the locks, and strong the bars that guarded the old man's treasure, his only son. Round rolled the year without incident, the dawn of the last day found the youth hearty and well; singing like a bird at the near prospect of escape from his wearisome cage, he hauls up his last faggot of sticks to cook therewith his parting dinner and cheer the sombre night with a flickering flame. The father bids him good-night with a joyous heart, and is early astir on the coming morn. But what means this hushed silence? No answer comes to his noisy knocking! Scale the walls! Break in the door! Fifty golden guineas to the man who gets in first! Alas! all too soon are the old man's fears and the gipsy's prediction verified. There on the threshold of maturity lies all that is left of his son—a pallid corpse. A viper from the faggot had bitten him, and his destiny was fulfilled.

Coopers' Hall, King street, is a very noble freestone building; the front stands on a low rustic basement and is ornamented with four columns, with Corinthian capitals that support an attic story and lofty pediment, on which are the arms of the now defunct Coopers' company. In 1856 it was used as a Dissenting place of worship; it is now a warehouse.

Corn Market. (*See* "Markets.")

Council. The Council consists of 16 Aldermen (*see* "Aldermen") and 48 Town Councillors, who are elected for a term of three years, agreeably with the provisions of the Municipal Corporations Act of 1882. Any gentleman elected to the office of Town Councillor and refusing to serve is liable to a fine of £50. The meetings of the Council are presided over by the Mayor. The city is divided into thirteen wards, three of which (Bristol, Clifton and Redcliff) return six members each, and ten (Bedminster East, Bedminster West, District, St. James, St. Paul, St. Augustine, St. Michael, St. Philip and Jacob North, St. Philip and Jacob South, and Westbury) return three each. For the purposes of regulating the working of the city, committees—of which the Mayor is a member—are appointed, the following being a list:—Finance, Watch, Baths and Washhouses', Parliamentary Bills', Docks', Visitors of the Lunatic Asylum, Cattle Market, Contagious Diseases' (Animals), By-Laws', Libraries', Improvement, Clifton and Durdham Downs', and Sanitary. These committees are appointed annually, after the municipal elections in November. All, with the exception of the Sanitary Committee, sit with closed doors. The quarterly meetings of the Council are held on the second Tuesday in February, May and August, and the 9th November; special meetings on the 1st January and in March, June and September. The following are the principal committees:—

DOCKS' COMMITTEE.—The city docks were originally constructed out of the rivers Avon and Frome by a private company of citizens, under an Act of Parliament passed in the year 1803; but by the Docks' Transfer Act, 1848 (*see* "Docks"), were transferred to the city, and then became the property of the citizens, together with all their liabilities, for a rent charge since redeemed by the Corporation. The last meeting of the company was held at the offices in Broad street on May 2nd, 1882. The present Docks' Committee meet every Monday at the Docks Office, 19 Queen square, at one o'clock.

SANITARY AUTHORITY.—By the Town Council adopting, in 1851, the Health of Towns' Act, they became a Board of Health, or Sanitary Authority, and by a subsequent statute they had vested in them the powers relating to the construction, maintenance, lighting and cleansing the streets, and the construction and maintenance of sewers; also the powers of a Nuisance Authority for the prevention or abatement of nuisances within the city, the proper supply of water, and generally as to all matters relating to the health of the inhabitants. The Council deputed the carrying out of these powers to a committee of their body, subject to confirmation by the Council. The ordinary expenses for sanitary purposes, as well as the sums required to repay by annual instalments the monies, with interest, borrowed by the Authority for street improvements, and for the exercise of the various powers conferred by Acts of Parliament as a Board of Health, are defrayed by rates levied by the Town Council as a Sanitary Authority twice in each year. (See "Rates.") The committee meet every Thursday.

STREET IMPROVEMENT COMMITTEE is a committee appointed by the Sanitary Authority. In 1865 the Town Council adopted the Local Government Act of 1858, and a committee was chosen to exercise the powers conferred by the several Acts of Parliament for the improvement of old and the construction of new streets and roads, all their proceedings being subject to the confirmation of the Town Council at their meetings, the powers to take properties, otherwise than by agreement, being obtained by special Acts of Parliament.

WATCH COMMITTEE have the management of police affairs. It was first appointed on the 2nd February, 1836, and they produced a scheme for an efficient police force, the estimated cost being about £9,000 per annum. (See "Police.")

ELECTION OF MAYOR.—About the time of election of the Mayor in each year a few leading members of the party enjoying most power in the Council, and to whom the *soubriquet* of the "Warwick Committee" (from the last Earl of Warwick, who had the power of throning and dethroning kings, is given, meet for the purpose of choosing the Mayor for the ensuing year; as the *soubriquet* indicates they may elect whom they will.

CIVIC CUSTOM.—On Whit Sunday the Mayor and Corporation attend service at St. Mary Redcliff Church in full civic costume, when the church is decorated and strewed with rushes and flowers. The custom dates back to 1494, when William Mede, who had been three times Mayor, gave a tenement to the Corporation, the rent of which was to pay for an annual sermon on the feast of Pentecost, before the Mayor and Commonalty of Bristol and other devout people who might repair thither. For this the preacher was entitled to 6s. 8d., and the Mayor was enjoined to invite him to his table and give him a good dinner, for which the giver was allowed 3s. 4d. The residue was for strewing the church with flowers and rushes, ringing the bells, &c. The dinner has fallen into disuse, but the other items of the injunction are still regarded.

INCOME AND EXPENDITURE.—This is managed by the Finance Committee. The income is principally from rents of city properties, tolls of markets, dues on goods and ships, fines in police-courts, payments from Government towards police expenses and interest on monies in Consols, the deficiency being made up by a borough rate, which is apportioned and assessed by the Council on the several districts, and is collected by the "Incorporation of the Poor" (*see* "Incorporation of the Poor," *also* "Rates") and the overseers of the five parishes or districts of the enlarged city boundaries, and paid over by them to the City Treasurer.

OFFICIALS.—*Sword Bearer.* This official is the only individual who is allowed to remain covered before Royalty. The cap he wears and the sword he bears symbolise inflexible

justice, and the Mayor's right and readiness to maintain the cause of the burgesses whenever necessary. He acts as the private secretary of the Mayor for the time being, and accompanies his Worship, bearing the sword on all civic occasions.—
Treasurer. This office was created in 1499 under the title of Chamberlain, but since the passing of the Act 5 and 6 William IV. (9th September, 1835) the name of Treasurer has been adopted.

PLATE.—It was decided, February 15th, 1836, that the City Treasurer should have the charge of the plate, and that the Mayor should have the use of it when desired. The decorative and other plate preserved in the Council-house consists of a rose water ewer and salver, weighing 7 lbs. 6 oz. 10 dwts., the gift of Robert Kitchen, Alderman. An elegant double gilt silver grace cup, weighing 30 oz., presented by Alderman Bird. A richly chased Monteith and collar of silver, weighing 266 oz. 11 dwts; in 1821 this handsome ornament, being offered for sale at public auction by the descendants of Captain Pitts (to whom it was presented by the Society of Merchant Venturers), was purchased by the Corporation for £148 16s. A pair of massive silver gilt tankards, weighing 152 oz. 8 dwts., presented by Recorder Dodridge in 1658. In 1683 four silver badges and chains were purchased by the Corporation to be worn by the city waits; these weigh 28 oz. 13 dwts. In 1745 the water bailiff had an oar enriched with silver ornament bought for his badge of office; it is so loaded with metal that its weight cannot be correctly ascertained, probably the weight in silver is about 36 oz. At the same time a silver badge and chain were purchased for the deputy water bailiff. The year 1709 was prolific in gifts. G. Smyther, an Alderman of London, presented to the city a silver punch bowl, weighing 105 oz. 17 dwts. Mrs. Mary Boucher presented a silver tankard of the weight of 52 oz. 10 dwts. Mrs. Searchfield gave four handsome silver candlesticks, a snuffers and stand, of the weight of 100 oz. 10 dwts.; and Mrs. James gave a silver salver of 35 oz. 9 dwts. In 1722 eight maces of silver were purchased by the Corporation for the use of the officers in civic processions; these are in the usual 17th century style of art, and weigh 208 oz. Alderman Peloquin, of London, gave, in 1770, a silver candlestick with branches, that weighs 99 oz. 7 dwts. The insignia of the City Exchange keeper and the city bellman are of wood, silver mounted, the weight of metal being about 48 oz.; date, 1715; two silver trumpets of the same date, weighing 54 oz. 12 dwts. The gold chain of office worn by the Mayor is elaborate in ornament and peculiarly handsome; it weighs 26 oz. 4 dwts., and was purchased by the Corporation, in 1828, at a cost of £285. The small mace borne by the city treasurer as the insignia of his office is of the 17th century work and is copper gilt. The sacramental service in use at the Mayor's Chapel consists of a paten, two chalices and two dishes of silver, weighing 129 oz. 1 dwt., and was the gift of Thomas Champion, Mayor and Alderman of the city. In June, 1851, a magnificent silver dessert service was presented to Sir John Kerle Haberfield, Knt., on the completion of the sixth year of his mayoralty; in 1871 his widow, Lady Haberfield, presented the service to the Corporation; it consists of nine pieces—a centre ornament, with emblematic figures of Justice, Generosity and Commerce; two high fruit stands for corner dishes; two fruit baskets, with sportive boy figures; four corner dishes, with figures emblematic of the seasons; the total cost was £580. A silver salver, the gift of J. M. Kempster, for many years Councillor for the ward of Clifton, completes the list of the plate.

PORTRAITS.—Among the portraits in the Council-house, which is the

COU   DICTIONARY OF BRISTOL.   COU

municipal portrait gallery, may be enumerated that of Lord Burleigh (died 1598), which cost £3; King Charles I., by Jansen, and the Earl of Pembroke (life-size), by Vandyck. Of this latter there is the following note under the year 1627:—"Paid the picture-maker for drawing the Earl of Pembroke, £3 13s. 4d." The family are stated to have offered to purchase this picture by giving as many sovereigns as would cover its surface. To this the worthy Chamberlain, it is said, replied:—"Put them edgeways, and then we will begin to think about it." William and Mary, for which Chevalier Moor was paid, in 1681, £13 8s.; Queen Anne cost £24 15s.; Georges I. and II. and Queen Caroline; the great Burke; the Duke of Portland, by Sir Thomas Lawrence—this, with the frame, cost £149; George III., by E. Bird, R.A. Other, and principally local, portraits are:—Thomas White, Mayor in 1529; Robert and Nicholas Thorne; Sir Thomas White; Robert Cecil, Earl of Salisbury, who died in 1612; Robert Kitchen; Alderman Whitson; George Harrington, Mayor in 1617; Charles, Earl of Dorset (1691); Edward Colston; Sir Michael Foster; Lord Clare, by Gainsborough; Henry Gibbs; Aldermen Lane and Noble. A painting of James II., by Kneller, was discovered in a singular way. Being dirty, it was sent to be cleaned. The artist discovered another face underneath; obtaining leave he carefully removed the surface daub and discovered this valuable painting. The fact of James' portrait having been painted over may be accounted for by his extreme unpopularity at the time of the revolution. There are also a number of portraits of Mayors of recent date.

SALARIES OF CITY OFFICIALS:—

	£	s.	d.
Recorder and Steward of Tolzey Court	500	0	0
Town Clerk	800	0	0
Clerks in Town Clerk's Office	745	0	0
City Treasurer	500	0	0
Clerks in Treasurer's Office	250	0	0
Magistrates' Clerk	850	0	0
Clerks in Magistrates' Office	570	0	0
Chief Constable	650	0	0
Surgeon of Police	150	0	0
Dock Officials—			
Secretary and Clerks	1,409	0	0
Law Clerk	200	0	0
Engineer and Assistants	1,256	0	0
Dockmaster and Deputy	600	0	0
Water Bailiff and Deputy	600	0	0
Traffic Manager	200	0	0
Lockmen's Wages	1,761	0	0
Haven Master	450	0	0
Sanitary Authority—			
Clerk	700	0	0
Three Assistant Clerks	806	0	0
Accountant	300	0	0
Assistant Accountant	52	0	0
Rates' Clerk	148	0	0
Surveyor	800	0	0
Four Assistant Surveyors	702	1	4
Two Clerks' Surveyor and Copying Clerk	309	0	0
Medical Officer	500	0	0
Medical Officer's Assistant Clerk	13	0	0
Collector of Rents	109	4	0
City Surveyor—			
City Surveyor	750	0	0
Two Consulting Surveyors	300	0	0
Assistant Surveyor	250	0	0
Surveyor's Assistant	120	0	0
Clerk to Surveyor	120	0	0
Three Inspectors	450	0	0
City Librarian	350	0	0
Gas Inspector	250	0	0
Inspector under Cattle Plague Act	226	7	0
Inspector of Weights and Measures	215	13	8
City Analyst	100	0	0
Sword Bearer	100	0	0
Land Steward	60	0	0
Housekeeper at Council-house	100	0	0
Drawbridge Keeper and Assistants	101	16	0
Exchange and St. Nicholas' Market Beadle	109	4	0
St. James' Market Constable	36	8	0
Clerk to Haymarket	100	0	0
Bellman	4	0	0

Council-house, in Corn street, contains the Council chamber, the City Treasurer's and the Town Clerk's offices, the Mayor's parlour and committee-rooms. On the left were the magistrates' and police offices, now transferred to Bridewell street. The building is from a design by Sir Robert Smirke, R.A., and was erected in 1827 at a cost of £14,600. It is surmounted by a beautiful statue of Justice without her scales, with the city arms on one side and the royal arms on the other, sculptured on a panel in relief, from the chisel of E. H. Baily, R.A., who was a native of Bristol. The main staircase is very handsome, the steps being inlaid with brass devices and coloured enamel. The Council chamber is also chastely decorated, and should be visited for the sake of the interesting portraits of national and local celebrities (*see* "Council"), also a number of autograph letters (*see* "Autographs"). This is the third Council-house that has been erected. On the present site stood St. Ewen's Church. In a niche between the windows of the Council chamber of the old Council-house was a statue of Charles II., which the Duchess of Cleveland pronounced on her visit to the place to be more like a clumsy porter placed there to keep the entrance than a crowned monarch. A Council-house of more modern style was erected in 1704 on the site of the old one, and the statue was then placed against the Guildhall, within the precincts of which building it is still preserved.

County Court.

The County Court of Gloucestershire, holden at Bristol, was opened at the Guildhall on the 15th of March, 1847. Previous to 1846 there were the Courts of Conscience and Request; but on the passing of the County Courts' Act, in August that year, these were abolished. The court, for sums under £2, was originally in Tailors' Court, Broad street, and above £2 at 38 Broad street. Since the Act has been in operation there have been six judges, the present one being W. J. Metcalfe, Q.C., and Messrs. E. and E. A. Harley are the present registrars. Besides these there are a deputy-registrar and two high bailiffs. The number of cases coming before the court annually is about 18,000, and the court sits about 120 days a year. The office hours are from ten to four, except Saturdays, when it is closed at one o'clock. The registrars' and high bailiffs' offices are at St. Werburgh's Chambers, Small street, and the court sits in the Assize Courts.

County of Bristol.

So highly did Bristol rank as a port in the 14th century that at the siege of Calais (1347) Edward III. was provided by her burghers with 23 ships and 608 men, London itself being required to send more than these numbers only by two ships and 54 men. This naval patriotism did not go unrewarded, for it gained to the town the distinguished charter that made it a county in itself, dated 8th August, 1373. Among the privileges in this grant were included the return of two representatives to Parliament, and the empowering of the Mayor and Sheriff to elect successively from time to time 40 of the better and more honest men of the town as a Council to rate and levy taxes, &c.

Crafts' Guilds.

In 1849 the following 26 guilds existed in this city: Butchers, bakers, brewers, barbers, bowers, carpenters, cardmakers, corneesers (corn dealers), cutlers, dyers, farriers, fletchers (arrowmakers), hoopers, lockyers, masons, skinners, smiths, shermen, tailors, tuckers, tanners, tylers, weavers, waxmakers, whitawers and wiredrawers. The weavers', tuckers' and tailors' guilds were the largest, but are now all extinct; the Society of Merchant Venturers being the only guild in existence (*see* "Merchant Venturers' Society").

Cricket.

In no city of the Midlands or West of England is the national game of cricket more played or the love of it greater than in Bristol, and there are few more pleasing sights than that presented on a fine Saturday afternoon on Durdham down, nearly every available yard of which is taken up by various cricket clubs. Without by any means professing to give the names of the whole of the clubs in Bristol, it will be well to mention a few of the leading ones.

GLOUCESTERSHIRE COUNTY CRICKET CLUB naturally takes the first place as being amongst the counties playing in first class matches, and Bristol may well feel proud at the number of her citizens who help to sustain the reputation of the county. Most of the home matches are, by permission of the Council, played upon the grounds of the Clifton College, and as a rule are well attended, more especially if the match being played is a popular one. The affairs of the club are managed by a committee chosen by the members. The recognised "champion" of cricket, Dr. W. G. Grace, is captain of the club. Dr. E. M. Grace, Thornbury, than whom there are few better players, is the secretary. The subscription (10/- for single ticket, or 21/- for family ticket) admits to all the matches played in the county.

BEDMINSTER C.C. was established in 1847, and played then upon the very ground they now occupy at the Home field, Elm Tree farm, although in the interim they have used as their playground other fields in the neighbourhood. The ground is upwards of six acres in extent, and a considerable amount has been spent in developing and making it what it undoubtedly is—one of the finest in the city. It is more than probable that the club will again have to change its ground, and that it will have a local habitation in the people's park, presented to the city by Sir Greville Smyth, Bart. There is a lawn tennis club in connection. The members number 197. Subscription to the whole, 17/6 per annum; to cricket club only, 12/6 per annum; to lawn tennis, 10/6 per annum. T. J. Knight, St. Paul's Schools, Dean lane, Bedminster, and E. H. Cook, Trade School, Nelson street, hon. secs.

CLIFTON C.C. This club has obtained the privilege to rail round a portion of Durdham Down, so as to keep the ground in good condition; it possesses a strong first eleven.

There are 133 members. Subscription, 21/- per annum. H. C. Vernon, King's hill villa, Cotham, hon. sec.

KNOLE PARK. This is the oldest cricket club connected with Bristol. Although not actually in the city boundaries, most of the members of the club belong to the city. The ground is situated at Knole park, and to those who are privileged to play in the matches which are annually held there the hospitality shown by the present proprietor of the ground (S. V. Hare) is a thing not to be forgotten. The original club was started between 1830 and 1840, but after the death of Colonel Masters (about 1868) it ceased. In 1871 the club was re-started, and now numbers amongst its members (about 60) some of the best players in the county. Subscription, 21/- per annum. R. Fenton Miles, Old Bank, Bristol, hon. sec.

ATALANTA C.C. Formed in September, 1882; play on the Downs; number of members, 23; subscription, 2d. weekly, with an entrance fee of 2/6. Thomas Joseph Rigg, Mount Pleasant terrace, Bedminster, secretary.

AVONMORE C.C. Formed in 1880; play on the Downs; number of members, 30; subscription, 5/-, with entrance fee of 2/6. W. Warner, 1 West Mall, Clifton, secretary.

BAKER, BAKER AND CO.'S C.C. Started in 1864; play on the Downs; near the Zoological gardens; number of members, 60. G. T. Pimm, 50 Wine street, secretary.

BARTON HILL C.C. Formed in July, 1879; play on Durdham down; number of members, 14; subscription, 3/. James Henley, 7 Alfred street, St. Philip's, secretary.

BOHEMIAN C.C. Formed in Jan., 1883, by the amalgamation of two older clubs, the Clifton Colts' and West Park; play on the Downs; number of members, 43; subscription, 7/6. Walter J. Kidner, 1 Dean street, Portland square, secretary.

BRISLINGTON C.C. Formed in 1868; play at Brislington; number of members, 40; subscription, 3/-. Walter Coleman, Brislington, sec.

BRUNSWICK C.C. Formed in 1873; play on Durdham down; number of members, 20; subscription, 3/-. Wallace J. Luke, 6 Clarence street, Newtown, St. Philip's, secretary.

CAMBRIDGE C.C. Formed in 1880 as the Cotham Park C.C., and altered to present title in 1882; play on the Downs; number of members, 16; subscription, 2/6. Henry J. Keats, 2 Cambridge terrace, Bishopston, sec.

CLIFTON ALLIANCE C.C. Formed in April, 1878; play on the Downs; number of members, 33; subscription, 5/-. W. A. Chandler, Fern villa, Oakfield grove, Clifton, sec.

CLIFTON PARAGON C.C. Formed in 1879; play on the Downs; number of members, 50; subscription, 5/-. Harry J. Fuidge, 1 Berkeley place, Clifton, secretary.

CLIFTON PARK C.C. Formed in 1883; play on the Durdham downs; number of members, 15; subscription, 5/-. T. A. Jenks, Hill Field villa, Granby hill, Clifton, secretary.

CLIFTON VICTORIA C.C. Formed in 1872; play on the Durdham downs; number of members, about 50; subscription (for active members), 5/-. J. H. T. Brown, 21 Meridian place, Clifton, secretary.

COMMERCIAL C.C. Formed June, 1879; play on the Durdham downs; number of members, 25; subscription, 5/-. G. H. Eaves, 19 Edward street, St. Philip's, secretary.

CUTLER'S HALL C.C. Formed in 1865; play on Durdham down; number of members, 50; subscription, 3/-. G. W. Adams, 25 Goodhind street, Stapleton road, secretary.

DAY STAR C.C. Formed in March, 1883; play on Durdham downs; number of members, 16; subscription, 2/6. W. S. Gurd, Laura villa, Raglan road, Bishopston, secretary.

FRENCHAY C.C. Formed in 1846; play on Frenchay common; number of members, 40; subscription, active members, 2/6; honorary, 10/-. S. Piper, National School, Frenchay, Secretary.

GLOBE C.C. Formed in 1877; play usually on Durdham downs; number of members, about 30; subscription, 6d. each month, and an entrance fee 2/6. Francis Llewellyn, 20 Montague street, secretary.

GRENVILLE C.C. Formed in 1879; play on Durdham down; number of members, 20; subscription, 6d. per month, with entrance fee of 2/6. W. Cook, 208 Hotwell road, secretary.

KALEIDOSCOPE. Formed in 1881; play at Bedminster and Knowle; number of members, 60; subscription, 4/-. T. H. Knight, Angel hotel, Redcliff street, secretary.

KEYNSHAM C.C. Formed in 1879; play at Keynsham; number of members, 40; subscription, 4/-. Henry Chard, Eglon house, Keynsham, sec.

OLD SNEED PARK C.C. Formed in 1872; play at Sneed park; number of members, 80; subscription, 21/-. Charles Strachan, Wick house, Durdham down, secretary.

R. CLARKE AND CO.'S C.C. Formed in 1882; play on the Downs; number of members, 23; subscription, 6d. per month, with entrance fee of 2/6. A. J. Vowles, Elthelbert house, Park row, secretary.

REDFIELD C.C. Formed in 1875; play on Durdham down; number of members, 23; subscription, 6/-. W. Henry Haskins, "Fire Engine," St. George's, secretary.

RIGHT AGAINST MIGHT C.C. (Jones and Co.) Formed in 1863; play on the Durdham downs; number of members, 95. W. D. Johns, 60 Wine street, secretary.

ROCKLEAZE C.C. Formed in 1868; number of members, 30; subscription, 10/6. S. H. Herapath, Broad weir, sec.

SCHOOLMASTERS' C.C. Formed in 1853; play at Egerton road, Bishopston; number of members, 80; subscription, 10/6. Thomas B. John, 97 Richmond road, Montpelier, sec.

SOUTHMEAD C.C. Formed March, 1882; play on the Downs, close to Clifton ground; number of members, 26; subscription, 7/6. Frank W. Lucy, 5 Melville road, Hampton road, Redland, secretary.

STAR OF HOPE C.C. Formed in November, 1877; play on the Downs; number of members, 30; subscription, 5/-. Thomas Poole, Fern cottage, Walton st., Stapleton rd., sec.

ST. GEORGE'S C.C. Formed in 1871; play for practice at Vicarage field; matches at Two-Mile hill; number of members, 65; subscription, 5/-. Edwin Rees, Summer hill, St. George's, secretary.

ST. JAMES' TEMPERANCE C.C. Formed in May, 1882; play principally on the Downs; subscription, 5/-, with an entrance fee of 1/-. Joseph C. Matthews, 32 Horfield road, St. Michael's, secretary.

ST. MARK'S C.C. Formed in 1882; play on Purdown; number of members, 25; subscription, 5/-. Fredk. L. Evans, Barton Regis Union, Eastville, secretary.

ST. MICHAEL'S C.C. Formed in April, 1879; play on the Durdham downs; number of members, 38; subscription, 5/-. W. H. Gawler, Laura cottage, Hampton road, Redland, secretary.

ST. PAUL'S (Bedminster) C.C. Formed in 1880; play on the Durdham downs; number of members, 16; subscription, 2/6. Fredk. Wm. Yates, 13 Southfield place, Bedminster, secretary.

THE CASTLE C.C. Formed in 1879; play on Durdham down; number of members, 17; subscription, 4/-. Charles Lansdown, 18 Richmond street, Barton hill, secretary.

WESTBURY-ON-TRYM C.C. Formed in March, 1858; play at Westbury-on-Trym; number of members, about 30; subscription, 5/-. H. Kerslake, Eastfield terrace, Westbury-on-Trym, secretary.

YOUNG MEN'S CHRISTIAN ASSOCIATION C.C. Formed in 1877; play on Durdham down; number of members, about 40; subscription, 5/- to subscribers to the association, 7/6 to non-subscribers. F. C. Poole, 16 Perry street, Stapleton road, sec.

Cruelty to Animals' Society has been in existence 38 years. Its objects are:—The circulation of suitable publications gratuitously or by cheap sale, particularly among persons entrusted with cattle, such as drovers, cab drivers, carters, &c.; the introductions into schools of books calculated to impress on youth the duty of humanity towards the inferior animals; frequent appeals to the people through the press, awakening more general attention to a subject so interesting, though too much neglected; the periodical delivery of discourses from the pulpit; to encourage and aid any parties witnessing acts of cruelty in the prosecution of offenders; the employment of officers to render all needful assistance to check the commission of offences and to prosecute cases of flagrant cruelty. Anyone who sees an act of cruelty can, upon giving his or her name and address to any police officer who may be at hand, require him to take the offender into custody. If no constable be available, an exact account of all material facts that can be proved, the nature of the act of cruelty complained of, the time when, and place where, committed, names and addresses of any witnesses, what facts each can speak to, the name and address of the offender, number or badge of driver, name or number on vehicle, and what was said at the time, should be forthwith sent to the secretary. During 1882, 240 cases of cruelty, real or alleged, were investigated by the society's two inspectors, and proceedings taken in 105 cases. The society is managed by a committee of 17 gentlemen, and is supported by voluntary subscriptions and donations. In connection with the society is a ladies' association, which, whilst working in harmony with the former, has its distinct sphere of labour (by means of lectures, publications, meetings and otherwise), to teach the humane and intelligent treatment of animals. Hon. secretary and treasurer to the ladies' branch, Miss Marriott, Woodburnhouse, Cotham park. Francis Sturge, secretary, St. Stephen's avenue.

Cumberland Basin.
(See "Docks.")

Curfew. The custom of covering up all fires and extinguishing all lights in the city at sunset, and in the winter at 8 or 9 o'clock, at the ringing of the curfew bell, "*couvre feu*," was introduced by William I.; and from the towers of St. Mary Redcliff and St. Nicholas churches it has continued to boom out its warning every night down to the present time. It is a curious survival of the Norman age.

Custom House, Queen Square. The foundation stone of the present Custom House was laid November 22nd, 1834, on the site of the former building, which was destroyed during the memorable riots of 1831. The Government allowed £6,700 towards the cost of rebuilding, which was carried out under the direction of Sydney Smirke. The officers are:—A collector, who is also receiver of wreck, and substitute for the Marshal of the High Court of Admiralty. In Long-room: Chief clerk, five first-class clerks, seven second-class clerks, three second-grade clerks, three copyists, and a messenger. The out-door branch consists of two surveyors, six first-class examining officers, 20 second-class examining officers, and 64 outdoor officers and boatmen.

Deaf and Dumb Institution, Tyndall's Park. This institution was established in 1841, and formerly occupied premises in Park row, but in August, 1874, removed to the commodious and handsome building, in the Domestic Gothic style, at the entrance to Tyndall's park. There are at present about 40 children in the school, most of whom belong to the poorer class, the contributions of £15 a year, required toward the expenses of board and maintenance, being in many cases paid by Boards of Guardians. For children in better circumstances the charge is £25 per annum, and for private pupils, £50 per annum. The committee have discretionary power of admitting pupils at a reduced rate of payment, and in extreme cases, should the funds permit, of receiving them gratuitously. Children are eligible between the ages of 7 and 12, and are at present elected by the committee, though in case there should be more candidates than there are vacancies in the institution, the election would be by poll; annual subscribers of one guinea and upward, and life governors (who have given donations to the funds of ten guineas or upward), having votes. The school is open to the inspection of visitors on Tuesdays, from 10 a.m. to 12.30 p.m., and from 2 to 4 p.m. There are vacations at Midsummer and Christmas. The system of instruction is that known as the "Combined," both the sign and the oral methods being employed. The head master is W. Barnes Smith; the hon. sec., Alfred E. Hudd, 94 Pembroke road, Clifton.

Deaths. (See "Registers.")

Debating Societies.

The oldest recognised society in Bristol was the Athenæum Debating class, which was instituted in 1855 and existed until the

PARLIAMENTARY DEBATING SOCIETY was started in the winter of 1880. It is established as a medium for Parliamentary debate and for the purpose of discussing political and social topics according to the rules and forms of the House of Commons, as far as may be practicable. The society consists of members subscribing not less than 5s. per session, payable in advance. The present number of members is 400, who meet every Wednesday evening during the winter months at the Athenæum, Corn street. Sam Lang, "Speaker"; George Pearson, "Clerk of the House."

The University college and many of the churches and chapels of the city and district have Debating societies in connection with their respective denominations.

LAW STUDENTS' SOCIETY meet at the Queen's hotel every alternate Tuesday. The present number of members is 68. The objects of the society are the promotion of the general interests of law students and of the legal profession, the acquisition of information upon subjects connected with the study and practice of the law, the cultivation of the art of speaking, and the establishment and carrying on of suitable law lectures. The society occasionally offer prizes for the best essay on a given subject. G. E. Weare, chairman of committee; H. Holman Gregory and P. W. P. Britton, hon. secretaries.

Denny, a small, uninhabited island of carboniferous limestone, nearly in the centre of the Channel north of Portishead, and in a line which would appear to connect the calcareous chains of Somersetshire and Monmouthshire.

Diocesan Visiting Society, established for extending, under the direction of the parochial clergy, additional means of relief to the poor throughout the city and adjoining neighbourhood. The central committee meet quarterly. A. F. Woodward, Treasurer; R. Taylor, Secretary.

Discharged Prisoners' Aid Society. During the year 1882 the men's cases referred to the society were treated as follows—

	Prisoners.	Convicts.
Sent to sea	7	3
Sent abroad	3	0
Sent to friends (not abroad)	14	16
Provided with work	37	9
Provided with tools, clothing, &c., only	4	0
Temporarily assisted with railway fare, food, or otherwise	42	1
Declined	2	5
Received gratuity only	38	0
	147	34

	Prisoners.	Convicts.
Re-convicted before the close of year	12	3
The society has also acted as agent of other societies in the cases of	9	0

The cases of women remitted to the society were as follow:—

	Prisoners.
Placed in homes	14
Placed in service	9
Provided with materials for employment	4
Sent to friends	17
Temporarily assisted only	19
No assistance given	10
Given gratuity only	19
Convicted before end of year	2
	94

D. Macpherson, hon. secretary, 19 College green.

Dispensaries. (See "Hospitals.")

Docks.

AVONMOUTH DOCK, or more properly speaking, the Bristol Port and Channel Dock, was commenced on August 26th, 1868. It is situated about six miles from the city on the Gloucestershire side, at the junction of the Avon with the Severn, and less than a mile from the fine anchorage at Kingroad. It is connected with Bristol by the railway of the Port and Pier and the Clifton Extension lines. Vessels of the largest class can be accommodated. The approach to the lock forms a tidal basin of 350 yards in length by an average width of 70 yards; it has a depth at high water equinoctial spring tides of 44 feet 6 inches and of 40 feet at ordinary spring tides. Its position is in a direct line with the fairway of the channel leading to Kingroad. The lock is 454 feet in length and 70 feet in width, the depth of water over the cills at high water of equinoctial spring tides is 42 feet, at ordinary spring tides 38 feet, and at ordinary neap tides 27 feet. These depths, together with the safe and easy approach, afford to vessels of heavy draught advantages that cannot be obtained at many other ports. The dock is 1,400 feet in length and 500 feet in width, giving an available water area of 16 acres, and the depth of water constantly maintained is not less than 26 feet. The total length of the quay wall is 3,200 feet, exclusive of 500 feet of slope for unloading timber cargoes. The appliances for discharging vessels are very complete. There are several powerful hydraulic pedestal quay cranes and four spacious warehouses, 200 feet by 60 feet. The land reserved for extension of the dock works is 50 acres. On Saturday, February 24th, 1877, the dock was formally declared opened by the Worshipful the Mayor, Alderman George William Edwards, who with a large party of invited guests sailed on board the *Juno* steamship from Cumberland basin to the dock. An immense assembly lined the banks of the river to Avonmouth, the shipping of the harbour was gaily decorated, the church bells rang merry peals, and there were other abundant proofs that the event was regarded as one of the utmost importance to all Bristolians. The following is an account of the foreign and coastwise tonnage entering Avonmouth dock since its opening, as taken from the Chamber of Commerce Reports:—1877, 40,006; 1878, 80,268; 1879, 194,525; 1880, 244,170; 1881, 244,938; 1882, 238,384.

BATHURST BASIN is named after one of the Parliamentary representatives of Bristol at the time of the completion of the basin. It was constructed on the site of a pond belonging to Treen Mills, exchanged by the Abbot of St. Augustine with the Corporation.

BRISTOL DOCKS, known as the Floating Harbour, are two and a half miles long, and have an area of about 130 acres, of which about 55 are available for large vessels, and are connected on one side by the Harbour Junction Railway with the Great Western Railway system. The old channel of the river Avon and a branch of the river Frome were converted into the Harbour, and a new channel made for the Avon known as the Cut. (*See* "Port Improvements.") The Harbour is entered by two half-tide basins—Cumberland Basin, having an area of about four acres and locks 54 and 55 feet wide; and Bathurst Basin, having an area of about two acres and locks 36 feet wide. There is also a single lock at Totterdown for barges and small craft bound inland.

CUMBERLAND BASIN, so called in compliment to the King of Hanover. The old entrance lock to the Floating Harbour was opened in 1809. When first designed these works were considered of a bold character and in advance of those of most then existing ports. Since the introduction of an increased size of vessels, however, and especially long steamers, the angle of juncture of the old locks with the river was found to be both awkward and dangerous. To remedy this, as well as give increased facilities for admitting a larger class of vessels, a new entrance lock was opened from the river to Cumberland Basin on July 19th, 1873, the whole of the work being designed and carried out under the personal superintendence of the late able engineer of the Bristol Docks, Thomas Howard, C.E.

Gates. In the junction lock are a pair of tide gates to exclude the high tides from flowing into the harbour, as the level of equinoctial spring tides occasionally rises six or seven feet above the level of the float. The large lock gates built for this work are two pairs of timber and three pairs of wrought iron—the latter are of somewhat peculiar construction, the whole of the wrought iron ribs and skin being subject only to a compressive strain, so that they resist the pressure of water on the principle of an arch, whereby a considerable saving of material, both as regards weight and cost, is obtained. The gates turn upon large solid gun metal balls, working in cups accurately fitting the bottom of the heel post, and have proved to work easily and to be perfectly tight under extreme pressure such as a continuous body of water from the basin to Hanham mills.

Hydraulic. The gates, as well as the large sluice valves and the machines for opening the bridge and the capstans at the pier heads for the use of vessels, are all worked by hydraulic pressure, or in case of need by hand. The hydraulic power may be described as generated and conveyed in the following manner:— In the engine-house, built on the north side of the junction lock, are a pair of steam engines, 44-horse power, each of which works a ram or pump, which forces water into the bottom of a large vertical cylinder, and, according as this needs replenishing, the engine, by a self-acting process, works vigorously or slowly. Within this cylinder works a ram of 17 inches diameter, having forced on its head a load of some 80 tons. The water therefore which is forced in by the pumps underneath this ram is subject to a pressure of from 700 to 800 lbs. per square inch, and is carried from the accumular cylinder in pipes, which have been proved up to 2,000 lbs. to the square inch, to all parts of the works where it may be required, no matter how distant. In use at any particular work this water acts upon small gun-metal pistons in cylinders (as steam in a steam-engine cylinder) which set in motion the gear of the particular machine acted upon. All these machines are placed in chambers neatly sunk below the level of the ground, the waste pressure-water as used running away into the lock. In this way the hydraulic capstans, which readily haul the heaviest vessels, are worked, a small two-cylinder engine being placed beneath them. The means for setting at work this effective motive power is so simple that a child can put it in action. The water having been turned on by an ordinary tap and key levers used, in a few seconds the gate begins to move or the sluice is raised. The gain in time by this machinery is very great. The branch lock gates took a quarter of an hour to open or shut, those in the new locks can be shut or opened in a minute and a half. As one result of this speedy and effective working combined with the improved entrance lock it may be mentioned that vessels, instead of having to wait a long time in the basin, can go at once into the Floating harbour, and thus save several hours which were formerly wasted; while vessels can be admitted to the basin from the main channel at any state of the tide that will enable them to get to the lock gate.

Landings. At the end of this is an inclined plane 212 feet long, used as a landing place either for cattle or passengers. Below this again is placed a floating iron pontoon landing-stage for passengers, 205 feet long, rising and falling with the tide, and which is connected with the shore by a movable iron bridge, suspended at the top to a timber jetty on a level with the roadway. On the back of this jetty and closing it in are built neat waiting-rooms for the accommodation of steam-boat passengers.

Locks. The dimensions of the new locks are as follow :— the junction lock between the River Avon and Cumberland Basin is 350 feet long and 62 feet wide, having the upper sill 23 feet 6 inches and the lower sill 26 feet below the float level. The junction lock in use up to the time of the completion of the new works was only 182 feet long by 45 feet wide. The entrance lock between the basin and the river is of the same dimensions as the new junction lock, having its upper sill 29 feet 4 inches and its lower sill 30 feet 4 inches below float level.

Masonry. The whole of the works are of the most substantial character. Those portions exposed to the

DICTIONARY OF BRISTOL.

greatest wear and tear, such as the sills, the hollow groins, the scouring sluices and the coping, are of finegrained Cornish granite. Most of the lock walls are of hard mountain limestone, excavated from the river. The scouring culverts are of a hard quality brickwork, set in Portland cement. The bottom of the lock chambers is lined with a thick invert of hard brickwork. The foundations for the lock sills and gates are carried down to the solid red-sandstone which underlies the general foundation of both locks. As it was found there was much water in the ground round these extensive works and strong springs in the gravel the engineer made provision for removing the upward pressure by forming in several places through the inverts at the bottom of the locks self-acting relief valves, which open when the upward pressure is great and close against the tide. The total cost of these works was about £315,000.

Quay Wall. Below the entrance lock is a fine quay wall, the construction of which was one of the most difficult parts of the work, as it is built on the mud bank of the river, and the foundation had to be laid in some places 53 feet below the surface.

Sluices. The sluices for filling the locks and for scouring purposes are a great improvement upon the old plan; they have been designed so as to be independent of the lock gates, and are built in the solid masonry of the lock walls, so that the mud and silt is carried out behind the gates instead of being drawn up against the sills during scouring or the ordinary operation or filling the locks. At the lower end of each lock these sluice ways are designed and built with numerous mouths, so as to spread out the effluent water in a sort of fan shape over the area to be scoured instead of allowing it to be discharged in a heavy stream, the effect of which is generally to tear up a deep channel and leave the adjacent bed of the river to silt up. Not only are these sluices most effective for scouring purposes by reason of their being placed below the sill of the gate, but they are so also because they enable the water on either side of the gates to be equalised more speedily than before. The sluices let out from between the gates of the entrance lock one million gallons of water per minute, and the void thus caused is re-supplied from the basin in about the same time. When the sluices are open they cause a regular whirlpool above them, and as the water rushes through the open passages the noise as heard from the relief valves above is like that of distant thunder.

GRAVING DOCKS. The graving docks connected with the Floating harbour are:—The Society of Merchant Venturers' dock, occupied by G. K. Stothert and Co.; dimensions, 310 feet long and 55 feet wide; the Wapping Dock Company's dock, 320 feet long and 48 feet wide; Charles Hill and Son's Albion dock, 522 feet long and 43 feet wide. There are also two smaller docks known as Albert dock and Green's dock, and a patent slipway.

PORTISHEAD DOCK, on the Somersetshire side, is said to be the best, most easily accessible and sheltered harbour in the Bristol Channel, having an entrance from Kingroad, with excellent anchorage at any state of tide. Vessels can enter or leave in any weather, and steamers can enter direct from the deep fairway of the Channel without the assistance of tugs. The entrance is to the north-east looking up the Severn and sheltered from every wind excepting those from E.N.E. A considerable number of ocean steam and sailing ships of large dimensions, including the largest cargo of corn ever shipped from the port of New York, have used the dock, and the captains are very unanimous in expressing their satisfaction with its access, shelter, and accommodation generally. Steamers can lock out of Portishead Dock and

DOC   DICTIONARY OF BRISTOL.   **DOC**

into Newport or Cardiff docks on the same tide. Rails along pier and dock quays in connection with all parts of the kingdom, viâ Bristol, without break of gauge, and railway wagons are loaded under cover direct from the ship. The three sheds are very spacious and convenient, each 450 feet long, 75 feet wide and 20 feet high to the eaves. The dock is formed out of a natural harbour, called formerly the "Pill." The lock is 583 by 66 feet wide and the floating dock 1,800 feet long and 500 feet wide, with a depth of 24 feet. There are two timber ponds, one five acres and another six acres. The sills are six feet above low water, ordinary spring tides affording a depth at high water of 34 feet, and 25 feet at neaps. The works were commenced in 1871, immediately after the passing of the Act. At special meetings of the Town Council held in June and July, 1872, the Town Council of Bristol resolved by 33 votes to 22 not to contribute to the Avonmouth Docks, and by 36 votes to 19 to subscribe £100,000 to the capital of the Portishead Docks undertaking—so that the Corporation of Bristol are the principal shareholders. Water was let into the dock May 3rd, 1879, and the *Lyn* was the first vessel that entered. The dock was opened in 1880, and during the eight months ending 31st December of that year 56 vessels, of 51,824 tons and carrying 84,080 tons of cargo, entered the dock, and during the year 1881 63 vessels, carrying 55,855 tons, and in the year 1882 56 vessels, carrying 60,124 tons.

DOCK STATISTICS (taken from the Reports of the Bristol Chamber of Commerce). The tonnage of vessels arriving at the City docks from foreign parts and coastwise for years ending 31st December, 1875 to 1882, are as follows:—1875, 993,043; 1876, 1,060,424; 1877, 1,020,762; 1878, 1,014,701; 1879, 944,304; 1880, 932,748; 1881, 866,113; 1882, 920,528. The complete returns for the Port of Bristol (foreign and coastwise)—including Avonmouth and Portishead—added together are as follow:—From 1877 to 1882: 1877, 1,060,768; 1878, 1,094,969; 1879, 1,138,829; 1880, 1,228,542; 1881, 1,166,606; 1882, 1,219,036.

The dues on shipping and goods are:—

	Total amount received on each year ending December 31st.		
	1880.	1881.	1882.
Town Dues	£7,010	£3,904	£4,316
Water Bailiffs' Fees	1,258	1,162	1,134
Mayor's Dues	1,330	1,049	1,267
Wharfage	4,766	3,125	3,418
Moorage	1,450	1,152	1,323
Anchorage	358	291	304
Dock Dues—Ships	23,065	19,595	21,090
" Goods	12,632	9,847	8,251
Totals	£51,864	£40,125	£41,103

The Avonmouth and Portishead Docks both contribute a portion of their dues to the City Docks. The following has been paid from each dock from 1878 to 1882:—

	1878.	1879.	1880.	1881.	1882.
Avonmouth	£375	£585	£943	£530	£581
Portishead	77	79	544	369	115
Totals	£452	£664	£1487	£899	£696

DOCKS TRANSFER ACT. The Act received the Royal assent on the 30th June, 1848. Its objects were to release the port from the hands of a company by transferring all its rights and property to the city, and to reduce the dues. The principal reductions which were proposed to be made immediately after the passing of the Act were rendered compulsory by the intervention of the Board of Trade during its passage through Parliament; and the Act (sec. 57) provides for the surplus of ordinary income over ordinary expenditure being applied in every future year to the further reduction of the dock dues. This Act was obtained through the instrumentality of the Free Port Association, of which the late Robert Bright was president and Leonard Bruton secretary; and to the passing of this statute must be attributed the success which has attended the trade of the port. The City seal was affixed to the Docks Transfer Deed

26th August, 1848. The alterations made in the dues may be briefly stated as follow:—The dock tonnage dues on ships arriving from foreign ports were reduced from 3s. and 2s. to 1s., and from 1s. to 6d. per ton; those on vessels from Ireland from 8d. to 4d. per ton; those on vessels coming coastwise from 6d. to 4d. per ton; and the dock dues on about 530 out of about 600 articles in the dock schedule were abolished. The wharfage dues on all goods exported, and on home goods exported from Ireland or coastwise were extinguished, and those on foreign goods were reduced to a maximum of 6d. per ton. These alterations left all outward-bound vessels and goods for export free from all port charges. The town dues on 300 out of 325 articles in the schedule were reduced to a nominal rate of 1d. per 100 tons, and thus only 25 articles of foreign produce were left subject to town dues. In 1851 the dock rate on sugar was reduced from 3s. to 1s. 6d. per ton, and on tea, coffee and cocoa, about 50 per cent. From the 1st February, 1856, the 530 articles struck out of the dock schedule in 1848 were re-inserted, and the tonnage rates on vessels and the dock dues on goods were raised generally, the total additions being equal to about 20 per cent. on the amount then collected. The plea for this proceeding was that the trade of the port had fallen off, in common with that of other ports, in consequence of the war with Russia. In 1861 the dues were again reduced to the same level as in 1848-9 and 1851, with the exception that the 530 articles on which dues were re-imposed in 1856 were retained in the Dock Dues Schedule. In 1863 the dock dues on foreign goods, imported coastwise, were abolished by the town council. The effect of the Docks Transfer Act upon the Port will be seen from the following:—In 1847 the foreign and coastwise tonnage amounted to 546,753 tons, and in 1877 it was 1,020,762 tons, and the amount of dock dues rose from £28,784 in 1847 to £40,003 in 1877, notwithstanding the reductions.

Dolphin Society. (See "Colston Societies.")

Dorcas Societies.
There are several in connection with various places of worship. That established in connection with Bridge street Chapel being the first, was named "The Bristol Dorcas Society."

Downs.
CLIFTON AND DURDHAM. The former contains 230 acres and the latter 440 acres, and both were secured to the citizens as places of recreation for ever, under the Clifton and Durdham Downs Act, which received the Royal assent, May 17th, 1861. The amount paid by the Corporation to the Lords of the Manor of Henbury and Westbury-on-Trym on behalf of Durdham down was £15,000.

Clifton down is unlike Durdham down, though adjacent to it; the ground being undulating is more agreeable for promenade; the scenery of the locality is rife with the romantic associations which belong to the wild and picturesque in nature, the perpendicular precipices with suspending trees shooting their branches over the brink, the beetling rocks, the narrow gullies, the unvarying sound of birds, wheeling and eddying about their lofty homes, the shrill whistle of the recurrent steamers and trains echoing amongst the rocks, all combine to form a picture, that seen and felt, though but once, must nevertheless haunt the imagination and furnish a theme for thought for many years.

Durdham down is about 300 feet above the level of Bristol, and is admirably suited for sports, such as cricket, football, &c., a portion of it is reserved to the members of the Clifton Cricket Club. The greater portion of this down is an open plateau of grass. It is intersected with pleasant drives. From the Sea walls a profusion of objects bursts upon the view in all their interesting variety of wood and dale. river and rock, mansion and hill. Through the exertions of C. J. Thomas, a new road was constructed extending from the Westbury road to the Sea walls and thence to Clifton down, and is a great boon to the public.

Dramatic Clubs.

AMATEUR DRAMATIC SOCIETY. The performances of this society are in aid of charitable and philanthropic objects. President, Henry Irving; Vice-president, T. Bate. Meetings held at Imperial hotel.

BRISTOL AMATEUR OPERATIC SOCIETY has been established two years. Conductor, Richelieu Jones.

BRISTOL HISTRIONIC CLUB, established in 1862 for giving performances in aid of charitable and patriotic purposes partly. Since its formation it has raised about £4,000. Meetings at the Grand hotel, Broad street. President, J. Warley; secretary, G. F. Chubb, 87 City road.

MEDICAL DRAMATIC CLUB give occasional performances. Admission is by invitation card, and during the entertainment a collection is generally made on behalf of some deserving object. Hon. Secretary at the Medical School, Bristol.

Drinking Fountains.

There are over 20 fountains in different parts of the city.

ALDERMAN PROCTOR'S, Clifton down, near the Promenade, is the prettiest designed fountain in Bristol; it has the following inscription engraved at its base on a white marble slab in black letters:— "Erected by Alderman Thomas Proctor, of Bristol, to record the liberal gift of certain rights on Clifton down made to the citizens by the Society of Merchant Venturers under the provisions of the Clifton and Durdham Down Acts of Parliament, 1861, whereby the enjoyment of these downs is preserved to the citizens of Bristol for ever." The fountain also bears the arms of the city, of the Society of Merchant Venturers and of Alderman Proctor, each bearing their respective ensignia. Erected in 1872.

BATH STREET. Erected in 1860.

BEDMINSTER BRIDGE. Erected 1861.

BRANDON HILL. Erected in 1882.

CLIFTON DOWN, Gloucester row.

DURDHAM DOWN, near St. John's schools; the gift of T. W. Hill, Clifton park; erected 1863.

DURDHAM DOWN, near the reservoir. Erected by the Bath and West of England Agricultural Society in commemoration of their show in 1874.

HAMPTON ROAD, near Highbury chapel. Erected by S. and A. Tanner as a thank offering, November, 1882. Psalm cxiv. 7, 8.

HAYMARKET, St. James' churchyard. Text, Rev. xxi. 6.

HIGH STREET. Erected by some iron merchants of this city, November, 1859; text from John iv. 13, 14.

HOTWELLS. A cavity is cut in the rocks, and an ornamental iron structure erected, from which the water of the famous Hotwell spring is now procured. (*See* "Hotwells.") Inscribed on a board is the following:—"This spring belongs to the Society of Merchant Venturers, is opened to the use of the public. Any person is free to drink of the water of this spring and to carry it away in jugs or bottles without payment." In order to prevent injury the corporation have appointed an attendant to take charge of the pump and spring. Such attendant may sell minerals, &c., and charge one halfpenny to any person requiring from time to time the use of a glass for drinking the water.

JACOB'S WELLS. Opened on September 7th, 1883; presented by the Ladies' Association for Prevention of Cruelty to Animals. It consists of a fountain, 14 feet long, for cattle and horses, an under trough for sheep and dogs, and a fountain at one end for the use of pedestrians.

LOWER BERKELEY PLACE, near

the City school. Erected A.D. MDCCCLIX. St. John iv. 13, 14.

NEAR CLIFTON PARISH CHURCH. Text, Prov. xiv. 27.

NEPTUNE, Victoria Street. The figure of Neptune was presented by a patriotic plumber, in commemoration of defeat of the Spanish Armada.

NICHOLAS STREET. Erected by John Payne Budgett, 1859.

OLD KING STREET. MDCCCLIX.

OLD MARKET STREET. 1859.

PRINCE STREET. City fountain, 1859.

QUAY, bottom of Clare street. Erected by the Bristol Young Men's Total Abstinence Society, 1861. Wills Brothers, sculptors. Cast by the Coalbrookdale Co. Text, Psalm cv. 41.

ST. AUGUSTINE'S PARADE. Presented by a native of this parish. Text, Rev. xiv. 7.

ST. PHILIP'S BRIDGE, St. Philip's. City fountain, 1859.

TRIANGLE, Queen's road. The gift of Robert Lang. Cast by the Coalbrookdale Co. Wills Brothers, sculptors, London, 1859.

TRINITY ROAD, St. Philips.

WELSH BACK. City fountain, 1859.

Dunball, a small island opposite Avonmouth. Its formation is comparatively recent, as it does not appear in the old charts. Between the island and the mainland was the old north channel, or entrance to the river Avon, but now silted up, and the present entrance is through the Swash channel.

Dun Cow, the rib in St. Mary Redcliff church, on the left hand of the western entrance. It is a rib of the cow whale, which was placed in the church in 1497, and is supposed to have been presented by Sebastian Cabot to the Corporation as a trophy of his enterprise in discovering Newfoundland.

Early Closing Association. Established in 1869 for reducing, within reasonable limits, the hours of assistants throughout the city and suburbs. President, Lewis Fry, M.P.; secretary, Henry Anstey, 13 John street.

Ecclesiastical Court, The, grants marriage licenses for the City and Deanery of Bristol, and for the Deaneries of Malmesbury and Cricklade, Wilts. Licenses required on day of application, attendance must be made before twelve o'clock. The Chancellor is the Worshipful Charles J. Monk, M.A., M.P., and there are four Surrogates for the Bristol District. Diocesan registry, 28 Broad street; W. Hurle Clarke, registrar.

Education. (*See* "Schools.")

Electric Lighting. The Great Western Electric Light and Power Company Limited was established in 1882, the Brush system being principally adopted. In 1883 the Sanitary Authority prohibited the company erecting wires overhead except upon condition of their removal at forty-eight hours' notice. A trial of street lighting with six Brush arc lamps for one month, commencing 17th January, 1881, was made by the Anglo-American Brush Company; this cost the city £163 11s. 6d. On June 10th, 1879, a buoy at Prince street bridge was lighted by electricity.

Engineer Volunteer Corps. (*See* "Volunteers.")

English Church Union. Formed in 1859 for the united loyal defence of the doctrine and discipline of the Church of England. It has nothing to do with political parties, nor are its members pledged to one side or the other on any of the minor questions about which churchmen may agree or differ. Those only who are communicants of the Church of England, or of churches in communion with her, may be elected and enrolled in the English Church Union. Terms of subscription — members, 10s.; associates, 2s. 6d.;

workingmen and women, 1s. or 6d.; life members, a donation of £10. President of the Bristol District Union, Henry Marshall, M.D.; offices, Green and Penny, Park street viaduct.

Entomology. (*See* "Natural History.")

Exchange, Corn street, the foundation stone of which was laid March 10th, 1740, and the building opened for public use on September 27th, 1743, is a greatly admired piece of architecture by Wood. The north or street front is of the Corinthian order, and consists of three horizontal divisions, the first or lower section being rusticated; the second or middle section comprises four central pillars supporting a carved pediment, flanked on either side by pilasters and pierced with windows, and the final or upper portion is an entablature supporting a balustrade. The interior is a fine quadrangle with colonnades, which within the past few years has been much enriched, and is now covered with a glass roof. The cost of the building was £50,000. The Corn market has, since November, 1811, met here every Thursday. The whole structure extends 148 feet in length from north to south, and 110 feet in breadth from east to west. In March, 1822, the clock dial was placed in the front. Arranged round the Exchange, under the piazza, are the stalls of the corn factors. (*See* "Markets" and "Fairs.")

Exports. The exports of Bristol, alphabetically arranged, are chiefly—Alkali and chemicals, coal and culm, arms, barrels, beer, boots and shoes, brass articles, bricks, candles, soap, copper, cotton goods, currants, distilled products, earthen and stone ware, floorcloth, furniture, glass bottles, glue, gunpowder, galvanized iron, hardware, iron (pig, bar, rail and hoop), lead, lime, machinery, Manchester goods, manures (artificial), oils and colours, paper, railway engines, carriages and wagons, rope, salt, steam engines and boilers, steel bars, rails, solder, sugar, tar, tiles and firebricks, tinplates, tobacco, vinegar, vitriol, and British goods generally. (*See* "Manufactures and Trades.")

Fairs.

COLT FAIR. An annual Colt Fair is held in the Cattle market usually in July.

LEATHER FAIRS are held in the Corn Exchange (*see* "Exchange") on the second Wednesdays in March and September. At one time, it is said, more tanned leather was sold during these fairs than at any other place in the kingdom.

LIVE STOCK FAIRS are held biannually on the first Thursdays in March and September in the Cattle market (*see* "Markets"), and a large number of cattle are usually brought in from the surrounding country neighbourhoods on those occasions.

WOOL FAIRS, the second Wednesdays in March and September. These fairs are usually well attended by dealers and fellmongers from the North and Midland counties.

Fairs were formerly held annually in the Great gardens, parish of Temple, commencing on the first of March, and in St. James' churchyard on the 1st of September; both these lasted ten days, and were usually attended by the manufacturers of the Midland and Northern counties, with woollens, cutlery, earthenware, &c. Both fairs were abolished on the 16th July, 1838. (*See* "Markets.")

Fauna. (*See* "Natural History.")

Feeder, The, is a waterway cut from the Avon to the Floating harbour to assist in supplying (or feeding) the latter with water.

Female Strangers' Lodging House, 98 Victoria street, established under the auspices of the Young Women's Christian Association (*see* "Young Women's

Christian Association"). In connection with this is an employment agency.

Ferries. In the Floating harbour there are five ferries, viz.: (1) from Redcliff backs to the Welsh back; (2) from Guinea street to Welsh back (Grove); (3) from the Broad quay to the Butts (St. Augustine's); (4) from the Canons' marsh (Gas works) to Wapping; (5) from Hotwell road to Wapping (the Timber yards). Three ferries work the passage of the New Cut between Bathurst basin and Hotwells, viz.: (1) from the City gaol, Cumberland road, to St. Paul's church, Coronation road; (2) Vauxhall, from Timber yards, Cumberland road, to Avon Clift tannery, Coronation road; (3) from Cumberland slip to the Clifton Bridge railway station (Rownham). This ferry is open all night. There is also a ferry from Shirehampton across to Pill.

Fine Arts Academy, Whiteladies' road. This academy was, in 1844, founded by the munificence of Mrs. Sharples, a widow lady residing at the Hotwells. Hearing that efforts were being made to establish an exhibition of pictures, she generously came forward with a donation of £2,000 for that purpose, and, assisted by some of the most eminent of the citizens, established the society. At her death, in 1849, she bequeathed to the society about £3,000. The present building was completed in 1858, and cost, exclusive of ground rent, £5,000. The style of architecture is the Italian order. The principal façade is approached by wide flights of balustraded steps parallel to it, and consists of two stages, the lower having a central colonnade forming the entrance, flanked on either side by wings with niches containing statues and pilasters supporting an entablature and balustrading; the upper stage, extending only over the centre, has five segmental recesses containing sculptures, and crowning the parapet above is a group of figures. The sculpture is by the late John Thomas, who also presented the statue of Flaxman, which occupies one of the niches. In 1877 additional rooms were added costing £600. The academy contains a collection of pictures by Mr., Mrs. and Miss Sharples, amongst which will be found portraits of General Washington and many eminent Americans, and several pictures of particular interest to Bristol, notably the trial of Colonel Brereton, the races on Durdham down, and the ball-room at Clifton, all containing portraits of Bristol celebrities of the time; a gallery of pictures by the Rev. J. Eagles, the "Sketcher" of *Blackwood*; a collection of pictures by Bristol artists, presented by Robert Lang; the three large Scriptural pictures by the celebrated William Hogarth, from St. Mary Redcliff, presented by Thomas Proctor and the Vestry; the Nineveh marbles, presented by Sir Henry Rawlinson, &c., &c. An exhibition of modern pictures is held annually, opening in March. The academy is open free of charge for the purpose of study, from the antique and living model, to all who intend following the profession of an artist and are able to pass the required examination in drawing. During the annual exhibition of pictures a small charge is made; at other times visitors may obtain permission to view the academy upon application to the secretary. In the autumn there is usually held a loan exhibition, to view which there is no charge; in the year 1882 over 11,000 persons attended this exhibition. R. F. Miles, hon. secretary; J. Woodberry, assistant secretary. (*See* "School of Art.")

Fire Brigade. The first brigade was established in the city in 1677, when every member of the Common Council was ordained to keep six buckets of leather in his house to be in readiness against fire, or forfeit 20s. Nor were the citizens who eschewed municipal honours to escape, as the Mayor and Aldermen were to appoint other substantial citizens, who were required to do the same or pay 10s. For many years the fire brigades of the city were maintained by six Insurance companies, viz., the Sun, Norwich Union, West of England, Royal, Imperial, and the Liverpool and London and Globe, each supporting an officer and six men, who were paid by the hour for the services on the occasion of a fire; but in consequence of several destructive fires in 1876 the Watch Committee directed their attention to the arrangements for extinguishing fires, and at a meeting of the Town Council on May 8th, 1877, it was resolved to establish a Municipal Fire Brigade, which led to the disbandment of the insurance office brigades, with the exception of the Imperial, in Nelson street, which still exists. The present brigade, under the management of the Watch Committee, consists of a superintendent and 12 constables, who are especially cognizant of the working of the engines and other machinery, the management of the water supply, &c.; and the rest of the police force are trained to act at fires in aid of the firemen. The apparatus of the city brigade is most complete, consisting of a fine steam engine, &c., which is kept at the head office at the Central Police station, capable of delivering 300 gallons of water per minute to a height of 150 feet through a ⅞-inch nozzle. The depôts for the ordinary appliances, such as fire escapes, fire buckets, hand pumps, &c., are at the Police stations at Bedminster, St. Philip's and Clifton. In January, 1883, the chairmen's rest opposite Christ church, Clifton park, was fitted up as a depôt. A constable is on duty day and night, so that in case of an alarm of fire he is enabled to instantly communicate with the Central station by telephone. The cost of the City Fire Brigade for the year ending 31st March, 1882, was £1,489 3s. 11d.

Fires, Great.

Messrs. Stock and Fry's sugar house, Lewin's mead, April 2nd, 1813; it was insured for £12,600.

Mr. Rees, bookseller, High street (near All Saints' church), December 14th, 1819.

Messrs. Dowell's, Wine street, March 7th, 1820.

Mr. Oxley's, Wine street, December 15th, 1826. Mrs. Oxley and four children were burnt to death.

"William IV." tavern, Temple street, March 5th, 1837; four lives lost.

Messrs. Hill and Stock's sugar refinery, Old Market street, May 11th, 1854; estimated loss, £20,000.

The Porto Novo, an African trading ship, destroyed whilst unloading at Redcliff wharf, January 15th, 1859.

Messrs. Fuidge, Fripp and Co.'s sugar refinery, Stone bridge, April 30th, 1859; loss of £80,000.

The Sea Belle, in Floating harbour; she was ultimately scuttled after burning 12 hours, Dec. 17th, 1859.

Messrs. Perry's coach factory, Stokes croft, January 6th, 1860.

Messrs. Hurndall, Hellier and Wills, colour works, Castle green, May 3rd, 1861; a workman burnt to death.

Messrs. John Hare and Co., oil and colour works, Temple meads, 9th June, 1865.

Bathurst flour mills, adjoining the General Hospital, March 23rd, 1867.

St. Paul's church, Clifton, 1867.

Messrs. Llewellins and James, Castle green, March, 1875; damage, £10,000 to £12,000.

Messrs. Hudden's tobacco warehouse, early part of 1875.

Messrs. Clutterbuck and Griffin's premises, Christmas street, May 24th, 1876; damage estimated at £30,000.

Mr. Skinner's, in Castle street, August 16th, 1876, wherein he lost his life in trying to save two of his children, who perished with him.

St. George's church, Kingswood, December 22nd, 1878.

Messrs. Vicary's Malago tannery, February, 1880.

Messrs. C. T. Jefferies and Sons, wholesale stationery and printing, October 9th, 1881; damage, £30,000.

Messrs. Perry's warehouses, petroleum stores, Temple backs, November 30th, 1881; burning for many days.

Messrs. Baker and Sons, Redcliff backs, millers, October 8th, 1882; damage, £24,000.

Fishing.

THE AVON AND TRIBUTARIES ANGLING ASSOCIATION. Formed in 1865, under the presidency of Major Allen, then one of the members for the county of Somerset. It is managed by a committee of 25 members. The annual subscription is £1 1s. The waters rented by the association comprise the Frome from Freshford to Farleigh, the Midford brook from Midford bridge to its mouth, and a considerable portion of the Avon in the neighbourhood of Limpley Stoke and Freshford. The association, through the kindness of J. F. Hayward, have a breeding establishment at Waterhouse, and have turned many thousands of trout into their water. E. W. Villiers, 26 Bath street, hon. sec.

THE CITY OF BRISTOL ANGLING ASSOCIATION. No fishing is permitted except fair rod and line angling. Members using night lines, bank lines, trimmer, a casting or other net, save only a landing net, on the Association waters, are expelled. Subscription, fourpence per month; entrance fee, one shilling. Committee meetings are held on the second Monday in each month at Moreton house, Pack Horse lane.

Floods.

At a meeting of the Bristol Sanitary Authority on November 2nd, 1882, Dr. Davies presented a long report condemning 74 houses in the Baptist Mills' district as being a nuisance and injurious to health in consequence of the floods. In numberless cases the bricks were made from soft red clay, and the mortar was only mud. These materials absorbed the sewage, with its saline constituents. The floods were the highest known since 1806. On November 16th 88 additional houses were condemned. Several test cases were brought before the magistrates, but were dismissed. The Mayor (Joseph D. Weston) raised a fund for the sufferers by the floods, and in three or four weeks the sum of £5,400 was collected.

FLOOD POSTS.—The low-lying districts, after heavy rains, are subject to floods, and more especially at Baptist Mills. In the autumn of 1882 the floods were unusually high, to mark which 40 ornamental iron posts were erected with an inscription on each, setting forth the flood level in October that year. As the height of these floods varied in different parts of the city, the height of the pillars corresponds to the flood level. The posts are placed near Ashley road bridge, in the district of Botany bay, in Sevier street, Mina road and the streets branching off from that thoroughfare, in Stapleton road, near the Black Swan inn, at the Malt house and the city boundary, in Pennywell road, Newfoundland road, and in Merchant street at the entrance to the Friars; and in Bedminster district, in Catherine mead street, Mill lane, Harford street, Paul street, Doveton street, Bartley street, Hillgrove street and Sergeant street.

Flora.

The vicinity of Bristol is especially interesting to the botanist, as there are few districts in the kingdom so rich in plants. The natural features of the country and the varied conditions of its surface are both favourable to the production of a large and interesting flora, and did alp, bog and seacoast occur we should probably possess a very much larger one than we now do. These are mainly all the additions necessary to render this small district a *typical* portion of Great Britain. However, there are present such varieties of configuration and strata as are required by a large number of British plants, and in consequence we have growing within ten miles of the Exchange nearly a thousand species of flowering plants and ferns; the mosses, lichens and fungi being proportionately abundant. Such a field should afford great encouragement to the botanical student, being quite accessible to a good walker, and possessing every advantage and facility for field-work. The rocks and quarries on the banks of the Avon below Bristol will yield most of the limestone species; here and in the extensive woods of Leigh are to be found many of our best plants. Leigh wood is the great hunting ground for mosses; more than 200 species have been gathered there. Several very rare musci also, including *Grimmia orbicularis* and *Tortula Hornschuchiana*, are to be found on the Gloucestershire side of the Avon. It is on this bank of the river that the famed St. Vincent's rocks are situate, the home of very many of our rarest phanerogams, the Bristol rock-cress (*Arabis stricta*, Huds.) included. The alluvial flats extending from Avonmouth to the Passages, with their intersecting ditches of brackish water, contain most of the paludals and saltmarsh plants, with many algæ; and to the shore of the Bristol Channel we are indebted for all the maritime vegetation we can claim. Elsewhere, good botanizing can be done in Glen Frome, at Failand, Brislington and Stockwood, Filton meads, and on the dry and dusty coal measures of St. George's, Kingswood. Ferns are scarce, and receding farther from the city since their cultivation became a fashion. If the ruthless uprooting and transference to death in a garden continue, we may bye-and-by have only a few fronds of bracken left. To the deficiency of arable land may be attributed the absence of many agrarian weeds common in some other localities. We have, however, the consolatory thought that the cultivation of the soil is not likely to be so extended in the future as to alter the features of the flora to such a great degree as has occurred in the highly cultivated and more exclusively arable portions of the kingdom. In many spots around Bristol the nature of the ground absolutely forbids cultivation, whilst in others its natural character is such that it is most profitable to the owners to allow it to remain in its original state, either as woodland or for grazing ground. During the last half-century the action of the plough has not reduced the number of our plants; more dangerous by far has been the advance of bricks and mortar in the rapid expansion of this great city. However, we believe that up to the present time no single species ever recorded as native in our area has become extinct. Perhaps amid them all the most precarious existence is eked out by *Thalictrum minus* on Durdham down. Known by Sole in the last century to exist in small quantity, this rare plant is now represented at Bristol by two specimens only, and these are very much at the mercy of the scrambling Hotwells boys, whose heedless feet will some day be the cause of their decease. The *Arabis stricta*, already mentioned, is the only essentially local plant pertaining to Bristol. Being found sparingly on the bank of the Avon opposite St. Vincent's rocks, it can be claimed by Somerset as well as by Gloucester, but its whole area is extremely small. A detailed account of every Bristol plant is published by the Bristol Naturalists' Society in their *Flora of the Bristol Coalfields*. The rarer species of the district are enumerated in the following list; those marked with an asterisk grow on St. Vincent's rocks.

*Clematis Vitalba
Thalictrum minus
Ranunculus circinnatus
R. Drouetii
Diplotaxis tenuifolia

*D. muralis
*Hutchinsia petraea
Lepidium ruderale
Helleborus viridis
H. fœtidus
Aquilegia vulgaris

FLO DICTIONARY OF BRISTOL. **FRE**

Cardamine impatiens
*Arabis stricta
*Barbarea praecox
Lepidium Draba
*Cerastium pumilum
*Hypericum montanum
Tilia parvifolia
Ulex Gallii
Trifolium maritimum
T. hybridum
Lathyrus Nissolia
Poterium muricatum
*Pyrus Aria
P. torminalis
Epilobium roseum
E. lanceolatum
Sedum dasyphyllum
*S. rupestre
*Petroselinum sativum
*Trinia vulgaris
Bupleurum tenuissimum
*Foeniculum vulgare
Euphorbia platyphylla
Polygonatum officinale
Asparagus hortensis
Colchicum autumnale
*Carex digitata
*C. humilis
*Bromus madritensis
*Geranium sanguineum
*G. rotundifolium
*Hippocrepis comosa
*Potentilla verna
Rubus imbricatus
*R. leucostachys
R. villicaulis
R. rudis
*R. Radula
*Rosa micrantha
*R. stylosa
*Rubia peregrina
*Veronica hybrida
*Orobanche Hederæ
Rumex sanguineus
*R. pulcher
Daphne Laureola
Ruppia rostellata
Ornithogalum pyrenaicum
*Allium sphaerocephalum
A. oleraceum
Setaria viridis
Gastridium lendigerum
Polypogon monspeliensis

Football. As with cricket in the summer, so with football in the winter, the Durdham down is covered with competing clubs. Not only on the Down do football clubs play, but there are many fields surrounding the city in which clubs have the right to practice, in this respect having an advantage over cricket clubs. The principal clubs are here indicated:—

GLOUCESTER COUNTY FOOTBALL CLUB. Formed about 1877; play at Gloucester; subscription, 2/6. J. F. Brown, Gloucester, hon. sec.

BRISTOL UNIVERSITY COLLEGE F.C. Formed in 1880; number of members, 35; play on the Downs; subscription, 10/6. A. F. Stoddart, Grafton lodge, Sneyd park, hon. sec.

CLIFTON F.C. Formed in 1872; number of members, 150; subscription, 10/6. E. Leonard, 9 Apsley road, hon. sec.

MEDICAL F.C. Formed in 1875; number of members, 50; play at Westbury fields; subscription, 5/-. E. H. Meaden, Medical school, Tyndall's park, hon. sec.

REDLAND PARK F.C. Formed in 1877; number of members, 45; play on Durdham down; subscription, 7/6, with entrance fee of 2/6. E. J. Kiddle, 24 Fernbank road, Redland, hon. sec.

Freedom of the City. Previous to the passing of the Municipal Corporation Reform Act, 1835, the burgesses acquired their freedom either by birth, marriage, apprenticeship or purchase. This appears to have been declared by the by-law passed in 1606. A penalty of £100 was therein imposed on the Mayor and Chamberlain for admitting in any other way.

1st. Freedom by birth implied that the person must be born within the city, and that his birth must have taken place after his father became free. All the sons born under such circumstances were entitled to the freedom.

2nd. Freedom by marriage was acquired by marrying the daughter or widow of a freeman. A freeman's daughter in order to confer the right of freedom on her husband must have been born within the city after her father became free.

3rd. The apprenticeship which confers a right to the freedom must be seven years to a freeman carrying on business within the city.

4th. The freedom of the city might be purchased by paying a fine to the Corporation, which fine varies from 12 guineas to 100 guineas, according to the station of the applicant and to the benefit he is likely to derive from the freedom.

Occasionally the freedom was conferred as a gift, but only on persons of distinction not connected with Bristol. Now, under the provisions of the Municipal Corporation Reform Act, 1835, no freedom is acquired either by gift or purchase; but those who enjoyed the privileges previous to the passing of the Act still retain them.

Freemasonry. In Bristol the highest degrees of Masonry have been worked from time immemorial, and the Freemasons are a numerous and influential body; the Freemasons of America claim descent from the lodges of Bristol.

FREEMASONS' HALL. At the bottom of Park street stands this hall, which was erected by the Philosophical Institution for the advancement of Science, Literature and Arts, and formerly occupied by them. It is a Grecian design by Sir R. Cockerell, and was commenced in the year 1820. The freize under the portico is from the chisel of the late E. H. Baily, R.A., and represents the Arts, Science and Literature, introduced by Appollo and Minerva to Bristol, who, seated on the Avon, receives them under her protection and dispenses to them rewards, whilst Plenty unveils herself to Peace, as under the dominion of their happy influence. The ceiling of the staircase is enriched by paintings by E. Bird, R.A. The building was purchased by the Freemasons for £5,960 for the purpose of lodge meetings and the transaction of the general business of the craft. It is considered the finest provincial hall in England, and was opened 2nd February, 1872; it is highly decorated, has an organ, and the carpet cost £200.

LODGES. The following is a list of the local lodges, days of meeting, &c. :—

Provincial Grand Master, The Earl of Limerick; Deputy P.G.M., W. A. F. Powell.

The Royal Clarence Lodge, No. 68, meets the second Monday in every month.

The Beaufort Lodge, No. 103, meets the first Tuesday in every month.

The Royal Sussex Lodge of Hospitality, No. 187, meets the second and fifth Wednesday in every month. The fifth Wednesday is a Masters' night.

The Moira Lodge of Honour, No. 326, meets the first Wednesday in every month.

The Colston Lodge, No. 610, meets the third Wednesday in every month.

The Jerusalem Lodge, No. 686, meets the second Tuesday in February, April, October and December.

Canynges Lodge, No. 1388, meets the first Saturday in every month.

St. Vincent Lodge, No. 1404, meets the fourth Thursday in every month.

The Canynges Lodge, Mark Masters, meets the third Thursday in March, June, September and December.

The Clarence Chapter, No. 68, meets the second Saturday in January, March, May, July, September and November.

The Beaufort Chapter, No. 103, meets the fourth Tuesday in every month.

The Royal Arch Chapter of Charity, No. 9, attached to the Royal Sussex Lodge of Hospitality, meets the first Thursday in every month.

The conclave of the Masonic Knights, of the Royal Order of the Nine Elect; the Scotch Knights of Kilwinning; Knights of East Sword and Eagle; the Exalted Religious and Military Order of Knights Templars of Jerusalem, Palestine, Rhodes and Malta; Knights of Rosæ Crucis; meet annually, or as often as ordered by the several Commanders.

A General Lodge of Instruction of the Province is held in the Masonic hall, Park street, every Friday evening, at seven o'clock.

No brother is allowed to visit the Bristol lodges without a Grand Lodge certificate, nor relieved without it.

A Committee of Charity for the relief of worthy but indigent brothers and their widows, assembles at the hall on the evening of their several lodge nights, at a quarter before seven, where all personal applications must be made, and petitions presented for aid. *No application must be made at the private dwellings of individual members, as no money is ever given.*

Friend in Need Society. Instituted in 1788 for

relieving sick and distressed persons at their own homes. Society's depôt, 29 St. Michael's hill.

Frome, The, rises at Dodington and Rangeworthy, not far from Tetbury, Gloucestershire, and running through Acton, Hambrook, and by Frenchay to Stoke, meets a spring from the Duchess of Beaufort's park, thence to Stapleton, through Baptist mills, enters Bristol, emptying itself into the Floating harbour at the Stone bridge. Its course through the city is now arched over. Before the present Quay was formed and built in 1247, the Frome ran from Frome bridge, through the site of the present Baldwin street, beneath the city walls, and emptied itself into the Avon under St. Nicholas church.

Gaols.

LAWFORD'S GATE PRISON is the Gloucestershire (county) one for the western division. It is erected on the plan of the philanthropist John Howard, and is situated near Gloucester lane, Easton road. Lawford's gate means the Lord's gate (*Hlaford*).

NEW GAOL, Horfield. Just prior to the Government taking entire control of gaols, the city purchased the old Pleasure Grounds, Horfield, and commenced building the massive boundary wall for the new gaol, and in February, 1883, the Home Secretary appointed the new prison at Horfield "to be a prison, under the Prisons' Act 1865 and 1877, for all classes of prisoners from the city and county of Bristol." The present block is intended for male prisoners, but until the premises are extended some twenty-four of the cells are temporarily divided off for the accommodation of female inmates. The boundary wall was commenced and about two-thirds completed by the Bristol Corporation, but they were relieved of the burden of the undertaking by the passing of the Prisons' Bill, and building operations ceased, thereby causing a long delay in the work. This wall, now entire, is 20 feet high and 2 feet 6 inches thick on the ground level, and though less substantial at the top, buttresses of greater thickness are continued to the coping of the wall. The cells are 160 in number, and there are a few larger rooms necessary for the working of such an institution. They are arranged in four stories, down the centre running a corridor, open to the roof, which is about 60 feet high. The upper stories are approached by iron stairs, and the passages in front of each row of rooms are supported on iron girders. Each cell is 13 feet long, 7 feet wide, and 10 feet high, and is provided with a substantial double window near the ceiling, so arranged that there is no iron projection to which a prisoner might tie anything. A similar precaution has been taken in the signalling apparatus, by which a prisoner may call one of the warders to his cell. Electric bells have been erected, and the pressing of a button in the cell will not only ring for the warder, but, by moving an indicator outside, inform him of the number of the apartment to which he is to go. The floors are of wood and the walls of firm Shortwood bricks, closely laid, and cemented with the best machine-made mortar, which will defy all attempts to remove it. At a lower level than the ground-floor cells a large space is set apart for the boilers to feed the hot-water apparatus, and the arrangements are excellent for the discharge of the warm air into the various cells. The boiler-house stands to the left of the entrance, and is 16 feet 6 inches wide and 33 feet long. The cell doors are of wood, lined on the inside with iron. Between the fourth story and the roof are placed large tanks, which have a supply of water in case of an emergency, and there are two hydrants for use in case of fire. A considerable portion of the roof is of glass, and the light is ample, and one advantage of the arrangement of the cells is that a warder standing on the end passage of the third story will command a view of all the cells. On the south side of the block there has been erected a temporary cooking, bathing and washing house. The cells to be erected hereafter will be built at right angles to the first structure, and at the upper end of the ground; but the ground is of such extent that it is not likely the whole of it will be utilised for some time to come. Outside the boundary gate are officers', waiting, and other rooms, in the fitting up of which every modern improvement has been introduced. This remark applies to the whole of the work, which certainly is of the best quality. It is believed that when the gaol is completed it will be one of the finest in the country. Rd. Axford, governor.

The following is the estimated staff of Bristol prison for the year ending March 31st, 1884:—Governor, fourth class, £300 to £400 a year; chaplain, fourth class, £150 to £200; Roman Catholic priest, £25, but ranging up to £300, according to the number of prisoners; medical officer, fifth class, £150; two second class clerks, £80 to £130; chief warder, second class, £100 to £120; seven warders and other officers of corresponding rank, £70 to £75; and seven assistant warders, &c., £60 to £65; one female warder, £55 to £70; and three assistant female warders, £45 to £50. The *maximum* salary is reached by fixed increments at stated intervals. The assumed daily average number of prisoners is 160. The probable expenditure upon Bristol prison to December 31st last is estimated at £9,650, and £6,000 for 1883–4.

The OLD GAOL, on the New Cut, was built in 1820 at a cost of £60,000; but not being in strict compliance with the Prisons' Act of 1865, which requires each cell to measure 13 feet by 7 feet, and to be 10 feet in height, was condemned and closed early in 1883. (*See* "Bridewell.")

Gas Works. In the year 1811 John Breillat, a dyer in Broadmead, lighted his shop with gas made from coal and manufactured on his own premises. Subsequently he lighted one of the public thoroughfares for a time at his own expense, to show the feasibility of the use of gas. On St. George's Day, 1816, the Bristol Coal Gas Company commenced building their works on Temple backs, and began lighting in 1817. The city was lit up in 1818, J. Breillat being the first engineer. The company was incorporated on March 23rd, 1819. This was the second company formed in England. In 1823 the Oil Gas Company was established in Limekiln lane, and in the following year an Act was passed "for lighting the city with oil gas." These two companies amalgamated in 1853, under the title of the Bristol United Gas Light Company. Their works are situated in Avon street, St. Philip's, erected in 1816, Canons' Marsh in 1824, and Stapleton road in 1881. The offices of the company are at Canons' Marsh. The quantity of gas supplied nightly by the company during the winter months exceeds 5,000,000 feet. The price is 2/8 (and 2/6 per 1,000 feet for large consumption), and the illuminating power is equal to 17 candles. The cost of supplying the streets of Bristol with gas for the year ending 21st December, 1882, was £12,159 1s. 6d., exclusive of the cost of lighting, extinguishing, painting and repairs, which amounted to £3,507 9s. 4d; this, together with the cost of lamps, lamp pillars, &c., is paid by the Sanitary Authority out of the General District Rates.

Geology. Bristol is the headquarters of a district which, in the interest and variety of its geological structure, is nowhere surpassed. Within a radius of five miles a complete series of rocks, from the upper part of the old red sandstone to the top of the coal measures, and from the new red sandstone to the inferior oolite, is directly accessible to study in numerous quarries and railway cuttings, and the fine cliffs of the Avon gorge. Within 20 miles (at Tortworth) the whole Silurian series from the May hill to the Ludlow occurs; and within 30 miles, at Maiden Bradley, the chalk and upper greensand. Nor are igneous rocks unrepresented. At Damory and Weston-super-Mare different kinds of basalt occur, and pitchstone porphyry is found in the Mendips. No wonder that the labours of the early fathers of geology have rendered this classic ground. The high ground to the north and north-west of the city, including the Downs, Leigh wood, and the outlying Brandon hill, is a table-land about 200 to 300 feet above the sea level, consisting of the primary strata; carboniferous limestone and millstone grit, which dip for the most part to the south-east. From Tyndall's park to the Zoological gardens, and thence to Redland and Cotham, the upturned and denuded edges of these strata are covered by a nearly horizontal sheet of new red sandstone and conglomerate, over which, in places as at Cotham and Redland green, a capping of lower lias rests conformably. This rock also forms the soil of the St. Andrew's estate and Ashley down. On the east the table-land descends rapidly to the low ground (20 to 30 feet above the sea level), on which the city stands, and the primary rocks, in this place consisting of the lower coal measures, are buried everywhere out of sight by thick sheets of new red sandstone, over which, in the vicinity of the rivers Avon and Frome, are spread wide patches of alluvium. The table-land acquired its main features at a very ancient date. At the close of the primary, and before the commencement of the secondary period, the carboniferous rocks, of which it chiefly consists, were rolled into a dome-like fold or anticlinal, by which they were at the same time elevated above the sea level and acquired their present dip and strike. If the anticlinal rose to its full height unshorn of its fair proportions by denuding agents, it must have attained an altitude of about 10,000 feet above the sea level. Subsequent to its elevation it was worn level with the sea by the wasting action of rivers and the sea, and the "stump" which remained, now in part forming the Downs, was covered first by the new red deposits, next by the lias and oolites, and finally by the chalk and upper greensand. The cretaceous rocks have long since been denuded away, leaving only a few scattered flints behind in Leigh woods. The oolites, too, have vanished. The inferior oolite still, however, persists so near as Dundry hill, while the lias and new red sandstone have been but very partially removed. The Silurian rocks, which form the picturesque district of Tortworth, consist of Upper Llandovery, Wenlock and Ludlow beds, very poor in limestone, and broken through in places by eruptive masses of dolerite. The old red sandstone, of which the upper part alone is exposed, forms the ground about Sneyd park and Stoke Bishop, on the south-east side of the axis of the anticlinal which has determined the structure of this district. It is repeated on the north-west side of the axis at the Powder Mills. From Sneyd park the old red sandstone is continued across the river, and then extends several miles westward. It is clearly exposed in the railway cuttings on both banks of the river, as beds of red sandstone, shale and conglomerate; on the left bank a band of cornstone (nodular limestone) occurs. No fossils are found here, but a few fish scales (*Holoptychius*) occur in the neighbourhood of Portishead, where the old red sandstone is again met with, and whence it extends in a narrow band to Clevedon. The carboniferous limestone, succeeding the old red sandstone conformably, encloses it in a broad lozenge-shaped band, which extends in a N.N.E. direction from Penpole hill, through Kingsweston hill and Blaize castle to Henbury hill; it then bends sharply round, first to the south, past Westbury, and then to the south-west, over Durdham and Clifton downs, whence it continues across the river through Leigh wood, Leigh down, and away west to Cadbury camp and Clevedon, where it meets the fourth side of the lozenge, which extends from Clevedon to Portishead. The millstone grit, of which Brandon hill is composed, forms the greater part of Old Clifton; thus The Paragon, Windsor terrace, Lower crescent, Clifton hill, part of Queen's road and Richmond hill are all built upon it. It also forms the district of St. Michael's hill, Park street, part of Park row and Tyndall's park, Perry road, Colston street and St. Augustine's parade. From Clifton it extends across the river, fringing the limestone in a series of patches as far as Shepston and Ashton Watering. It is on one of these patches that Ashton Tump stands. Marine fossils are not uncommon, and drifted plants sometimes occur; remains of *Stigmaria* were discovered when excavating in Tyndall's park, by the side of Park row. The cliffs of the Avon gorge afford a continuous section across the mountain limestone and its junction with the old red sandstone and millstone grit. A strike fault extends across the gorge, from the gulley next below the Nightingale valley to the Downs on the opposite side of the river. It has had no influence on the formation of the gorge. The coal measures lie in four basins, all more or less concealed by newer deposits, around the anticlinal of the Downs. Two are on the west, of which the southern is the Nailsea basin; the northern, wholly concealed beneath the Severn and its alluvium, is unworked. The two on the east are conterminous along a line from Bristol to Wick, and they form together the Bristol coal-field, the western margin of which extends concealed by newer rocks beneath the city. The lower coal measures may be studied at Fishponds, Easton, Bedminster and Ashton vale, the upper series at Brislington, Parkfield and Radstock. The Pennant grit, or so-called middle measures, is almost unproductive of coal, but much used for building and paving purposes. It is well shown along the banks of the Avon at Hanham, and on the banks of the Frome from Stapleton to Frampton Cotterell. The new red sandstone series is exposed over a larger surface of ground than any other rock in the district. Everywhere covering up the older rocks unconformably, it has been bared itself by denudation of the later formed deposits, which would otherwise have concealed it from view. At its base where it rests on the older rocks it is always conglomeratic. A good instance of this may be seen on the side of the road which leads from the Downs to the Clifton station; a section unparalleled extends along the cliffs from Clevedon to Portishead; nearer home a section may be seen on the New Cut. Reptilian remains were found some years ago in a dyke of new red conglomerate near Lower Belgrave road, Durdham down. Much of the new red series is dolomitic. Many minerals are found in the deposit, such as quartz, in separate crystals known locally as "Bristol diamonds," and in hollow geodes called potato stones; it also forms fine agates. Galena, barytes and malachite are not uncommon. The Rhœtic series, which always lies between the new red series (Keuper marls) and the lias, is to be seen near the road leading from the Clifton station to the Downs, and it occurs in a dyke near the Suspension bridge. It is, however, best displayed in the Aust cliffs, long rendered famous to geologists by the bone bed, in which remains of fish are abundant, the most interesting being the teeth of *Ceratodus*, now known to be represented by the living *Baramunda* of the Queensland rivers. The other fish remains are some of them *remainée* from the carboniferous limestone. The landscape, or Cotham marble, is one of the beds of the Rhœtic series. The lias occurs in small patches over parts of the city and suburbs, and spreads in two extensive sheets north and south of it. The northern, or Filton sheet, covers the north-western margin of the coalfield; the southern, or Bedminster sheet, rises into Bedminster down, and forms the extensive base of Dundry hill. The inferior oolite forms the capping of Dundry hill in a series of beds 40 to 50 feet thick, which represent the upper and lower rag-stones. They are very full of fossils, and a visit to the quarries will generally be well repaid. In common with all the secondary rocks which occur within the coalfield, this series is remarkably attenuated when compared with its representatives at a distance. Dundry hill is 768 feet high, and is composed as follows:— Inferior oolite, 41 to 80 feet; Midford sands, 2 feet; lias, 450 feet; Rhœtic beds, 30 feet; new red marl and sandstone (resting on coal measures), 170 feet; total, 683 feet. A cave opened by quarrying on the Durdham downs yielded remains of bears, elephants, hyenas and other animals, as well as the bones of oxen, which had evidently been well gnawed. The alluvial deposits in this district have not hitherto yielded remains of extinct animals. From the gravel pits at Bath, however, bones of elephants, rhinoceros and other animals have been obtained. The late W. Sanders, F.R.S., after many years' labour, constructed, single-handed, a map of the whole district on the scale of four inches to the mile. This still remains a standard work. The geological survey maps are on the scale of one inch to the mile. For further information the reader may be referred to the following works:—*Buckland and Conybeare*: Obs. on the S.W. Coal District of England. Trans. Geól. Soc., Ser. 2, vol. I., p. 210. *Moore, C.:* On Abnormal Conditions of Secondary Deposits. *Quart. Jour. Geol. Soc.*, xxiii., p. 449. *Stoddart, W. W.:* Various Papers in the Proc. Brist. Nat. Soc. Report of the Commissioners appointed to inquire into the several matters relating to Coal in the United Kingdom, 1871. *Tawney and Stoddart:* Bristol and its Environs, 1875. *Anstie, John:* The Coalfields of Gloucestershire and Somersetshire and their Resources, 1873. *H. B. Woodward:* Geology of East Somersetshire and the Bristol Coalfields. (Mem. Geol. Survey, 1876.) *W. J. Sollas:* Proc. Geol. Assn., 1880, *Geol. Mag.*, 1881.

Ghyston's Cave, or "Fox Hole," St. Vincent's rocks, is 90 feet from the summit of the rock, access to which is obtained from the Observatory (*see* "Observatory"). The cave overlooks the gorge of the Avon, and commands an extensive view. A flight of steps leads to a roughly hewn tunnel of deep slope, which brings to a second flight of steps that terminates in the eastern end of the cavern. This passage, which took two years to excavate, was opened in 1837. It is presumed that this cave was a hermitage called St. Vincent's chapel, in proof of which, on removing an accumulation of earth and weeds from the surface of the cave, a large glazed tile, such as was used in paving the choirs of ancient churches, an antique key numerous fragments of pottery, the mouldings of which, though simple, are in some instances extremely good, insomuch as to induce a belief that they are of Roman origin. Lying over the above was a portion of a mullion of a small Gothic window, or probably of a tabernacle or shrine. The whole of these relics were embedded under a large flat stone.

Girls' Homes. (*See* "Homes.")

Gloucester and Bristol Diocesan Association, for the rural deanery of Bristol. E. A. Harvey, treasurer; Rev. H. H. Price, secretary.

Gloucestershire Society, The, is one of the oldest in the city, dating as far back as 1657. Its objects are to afford pecuniary relief to poor married lying-in women, natives or wives of natives of the county of Gloucester, and residing in such county or within the ancient limits of the city of Bristol; also to provide funds for apprenticing poor boys, natives and sons of natives of the same county. It would appear, also, from a history of the society published about 30 years ago, that one of its objects was the Restoration of Charles II. and the support of the Reformed Church. There is annually a "feast" in connection with the society, at which "Gaarge Ridler's Oven" is sung, and without which the "feast" would not be complete. The following explanation of the meaning of the song, taken from a book supplied by the secretary of the society, may not be uninteresting:—"It is now generally understood that the words of this song have a hidden meaning, which was only known to the members of the Gloucestershire Society, whose foundation dates from the year 1657. This was three years before the Restoration of Charles II., and when the people were growing weary of the rule of Oliver Cromwell. The society consisted of Loyalists, whose object in combining was to be prepared to aid in the Restoration of the Ancient Constitution of the Kingdom whenever a favourable opportunity presented itself. The Cavalier or Royalist Party were supported by the Roman Catholics of the old and influential families of the kingdom, and some of the Dissenters, who were disgusted with the treatment they received from Cromwell, occasionally lent them a kind of passive aid. Taking these considerations as the key note to his song, attempts have been made to discover the meaning which was attached to its leading words."

"The Stwons that built George Ridler's oven,
And thaay keum from Bleakeney's Quar;
And George he wur a Jolly old Mon,
And his Yead it graw'd above his Yare.

"One thing of George Ridler I must commend,
And that wur vor a notable theng;
He meud his Braags avore he died,
Wi' any dree Brothers his Zons should zeng.

"There's Dick the Treble and John the Mean,
(Let every Mon zing in his auwn Pleace);
And George he wur the Elder Brother,
And therevoore he would zing the Beass.

"Mine Hostess's Mold (and her Neaum t'wur Nell),
A pretty Wench, and I lov'd her well;
I lov'd her well, good Reauzon why,
Becase zshe lov'd my Dog and I.

"My Dog has gotten zitch a Trick,
To visit Molds when thauy be zick;
When thauy be zick and like to die.
O thether gwoes my Dog and I.

"My dog is good to catch a Hen,
A Duck or Goose is vood vor Men;
And where good Company I spy,
O thether gwoes my Dog and I.

"My Mwother told I when I wur young,
If I did vollow the Strong Beer Pwoot,
That Drenk would pruv my auverdrow,
And meauk me wear a thread-bare Cwoat.

"When I have dree zixpences under my Thumb,
O then I be welcome wherever I come;
But when I have none, O then I pass by,
'Tis Poverty pearts good Company.

"If I should die, as it may hap,
My Greauve shall be under the good Yeal Tap;
In voulded Earmes there wool us lie,
Cheek by Jowl my Dog and I."

The last annual report states that during the year 185 married women had been assisted from the funds with 21/- each at child-birth, and five boys had been apprenticed at an aggregate cost of £244 5s. J. Adamson-Coram, John street, secretary.

Greenwich Time was first adopted in Bristol September 14th, 1852. The clocks of the following institutions and offices are in direct communication with the electric current from Greenwich:—The Cathedral, the Commercial rooms, Messrs. Langford's, College green, Messrs. Burman's, Wine street, Messrs. Wills, Redcliff street, and Messrs. Chamberlain and Pole, Broadmead.

Guardians, Board of. (See "Incorporation of the Poor.")

Guildhall, Broad street, is built in the Tudor style. In niches are statues of Victoria, Edward III., Charles II., Foster Dunning (recorder), Colston and Whitson (all by Thomas). The foundation stone of the present building was laid by the mayor, James Gibbs, with great Masonic ceremony, on October 30th, 1843. It was opened for public business in 1846. The building is 117 feet long and 45 feet high, the tower in the centre being 28 feet higher than the general elevation. The building is now connected with the Assize courts, Small street, by two covered avenues (see "Assize Courts"). The criminal cases at Assizes and Sessions are held in the building. The old Bankruptcy court is converted into the School Board offices, and the Penny Savings bank is opened in the building every Monday evening. The site the present structure occupies is that of the old Guildhall, the earliest mention of which is in 1313, when it became the centre of a furious outbreak of the citizens against the military of the Castle, consequent on the appointment of certain officers by Edward II. to control the privileges of the burgesses. In 1685 Judge Jefferies opened his commission here for alleged conspiracy in the Monmouth rebellion. Histrionic actors, under the protection of certain noblemen, were hired by the magistrates to herein exhibit their professional talents before the townspeople. The first mention of such exhibition is in 1532, and in lack of a distinctive theatre in Bristol plays continued to be acted in the Guildhall for many years. Between Michaelmas, 1577 and 1578 the Earl of Leicester's players performed before the Mayor and Aldermen, the play being *Myngs*. Shortly after this Lord Berkeley's, Lord Charles Howard's and Lord Sheffield's, and the Earl of Sussex's, or the Lord Chamberlain's respective companies acted here before the same civic dignitaries. The last of these companies is that to which Shakespeare became attached about the year 1587, and during the interval between this date and 1603, when he is believed to have retired from the stage, it seems more than probable that he may have performed with his company at the Guildhall in Bristol. It is certain that in pursuance of their license to act in any "town hall," &c., throughout the kingdom, the Lord Chamberlain's servants did occasionally visit Bristol, and the following extract from the city records will show that they were able to draw a crowded audience :—

1576. August.—Item pd. for two ryngs of jren to be set vpon the howces of thonside of the Yeldhall dore to rere the dore from the grownd and for mending the cramp of jren wch shuthyth the barr wch cramp was stretched wth the press of people at the play of my Lord Chambleyn's surts in the Yeldhall before Mr. Mayer and thaldermen, vjd.

It has also been recently ascertained by Halliwell that Shakespeare's company of actors visited Bristol in the summer of 1597. In 1593 the once famous actor and friend of Shakespeare, Edward Alleyne, played with the company of Lord Strange at Bristol, no doubt at the Guildhall. George Peele, the dramatist, seems also to have been here about this time, and in his *Merrie and Conceited Jests* he boasts of a discreditable trick which he played the credulous Mayor and citizens. It appears that this dissipated poet found himself without means to redeem his horse from the inn stable by the payment of his host's bill. It happened that some players had just arrived in town, and were staying at the same inn with Peele. The latter thereupon went to the Mayor, and described himself to be a "scholler and a gentleman," asserting that he had a play named *The Knight of the Rodes*, which he was willing to perform at Bristol if the Mayor and Corporation would attend. The Mayor, though unable to grace the performance by his presence, granted the use of the Guildhall, and gave the poet "an angel" towards expenses. Peele thereupon hired the players and proclaimed the play; but when the audience was gathered and expecting the performance, he having pocketed the money (40/-) received at the doors, put on one of the player's silk robes, and, "after the trumpet had sounded thrice," came before the company, recited the prologue, and promised to send the actors, but instead he roguishly deserted both the unsuspecting players and the spectators, and regaining his horse departed towards London. The prologue was this:—

"A trifling joy, a jest of no account, pardie
The knight, perhaps you thinke to be I.
Thinke on so still; for why you know
that thought is free,
Sit still awhile, Ile send the actors to yee."

In the old Guildhall was the chapel of St. George, founded by Richard Spicer, a famous merchant and burgess of the town about the time of Edward III. or Richard II., and belonging to the chapel was a most dignified fraternity of merchants and mariners of Bristol. The windows of the Nisi Prius court are filled with stained glass, bearing the coats of arms of the following civic officials: 1st, Daines Barrington, recorder, 1764; 2nd, John Dunning, recorder, 1766; 3rd, Burke; 4th, Sir Vicary Gibbs, recorder, 1794; 5th, Sir Robert Giffard, recorder, 1818; 6th, Sir John Copley, recorder, 1826; 7th, Sir Charles Wetherell, recorder, 1827; 8th, Crowder; 9th, Sir Alexander Cockburn, 1854; 10th, Kinglake, recorder, 1827; 11th, Robert Fitzhardinge (Lord Berkeley), benefactor, 1168; 12th, William Canynges, benefactor; 13th, Edward Colston, benefactor; 14th, Whitson, 1627; 15th, Carr, benefactor; 16th, Rev. Dr. White, benefactor; 17th, arms of the See of Bristol; 18th, arms of the Society of Merchant Venturers; 19th, Duke of Beaufort, lord steward; 20th, Earl Ducie, lord lieutenant; 21st, Francis Adams, mayor, 1869; 22nd, Robert Phippen, sheriff, 1869; 23rd, W. K. Wait, mayor, 1870; 24th, Thomas Proctor, high sheriff, 1870; 25th, William De Coleford, 1344. In the rear of the building is a statue of Charles II. in royal robes, with a globe in one hand and, until recently, a sceptre in the other, in a good bold attitude, and apparently well executed, though defaced by time and weather.

Gully, The, a picturesque ravine leading from Durdham down to the Avon. In 1882 the Downs' Committee, at some £25 expense, raised through the instrumentality of R. G. Barnes, caused a pathway to be constructed here, which opens to the pedestrian pleasant walks by the river-side to Sneyd park and Sea mills and to the Hotwells.

Gymnastics.

A first-class Gymnasium is held at the Rooms of the Young Men's Christian Association, St. James' square, open to members of the institution. There is also a Gymnasium at the Rifle Drill hall, top of Park street.

BRISTOL AND CLIFTON ATHLETIC CLUB. Most of the runs of this club take place at the Stapleton Bridge grounds, but frequent runs during the winter months are made to the surrounding country districts. Subscription, including club badge, 6/-; number of members, about 50. Headquarters, The Swan, Bridge street. G. A. Gay, captain.

HORFIELD ATHLETIC CLUB, formed in 1882. The club house is the Volunteer tavern, Horfield, from which runs take place every Wednesday evening. The club's challenge cup is run for once a month; distance, 300 yards. Number of members, 35; subscription, 2/6 per annum. R. W. Keats, 164 Gloucester road, hon. sec.

PICKWICK CLUB. Meets at the Gymnasium, top of Park street, every Monday evening, from 7.30 to 10 o'clock; from October to March inclusive. The season consists of two quarters. The subscription is 5s. per quarter, with an entrance fee of 1s. At present there are about 40 members. W. A. Barr, hon. sec.

Halls, Public.—

NAME.	SITUATION.	Accommodation (seated).	RATES.[*]	SECRETARY.
ALBERT HALL	Hotwells	300	10/- for two hours; 5/- per hour afterwards. Municipal meetings, £2/-. Parliamentary £2.	Joseph Bryant, 11 Freeland place, Hotwells.
ALEXANDRA HALL	Merchant's rd., Clifton	500	£3 3s. Lectures ... £5 5s. Theatricals.	E. Harrison, Alexandra hall, Clifton.
ATHENÆUM	Corn street	600	£2 10s. Special arrangements for the week, month, &c.	R. W. Ross, Athenæum.
BEDMINSTER TEMPERANCE HALL	Bedminster	400	As per arrangement	D. Emmett. G.Chapple,Paul st., Southville
BLIND ASYLUM MUSIC ROOM	Queen's road	600	ditto.	The Lady Superintendent, Queen's road.
COLSTON HALL	Colston street—			
Large Hall		2656	Morning, £10 10s. Evening, £12 12s.	
Lesser Hall		700	Morning, £4 4s. Evening, £5 5s.	H. L. Riseley, Corn street.
Arch Room		300	Morning, £1 1s. Evening, £2 2s.	
Cloak Rooms		—	10/6 each	
Director's Room		—	10/6	
GOSPEL HALL (for preaching only)	St. Nicholas road, St. Paul's	700		C. E. Gittins, Ashley road.
HAMILTON'S PUBLIC ROOMS	53 Park street—			
No. 1		300	As per arrangement	R. W. Hamilton, 53 Park st.
No. 2		60		
No. 3		50		

* As a rule the prices include gas for a certain length of time. In some cases there is a slight charge for attendant.

Halls, Public (*Continued*)—

NAME.	SITUATION.	Accommodation (seated).	RATES.[*]	SECRETARY.
Jewell's Rooms	Stokes Croft	300	£1 1s.	J. Jewell, 17 Stokes Croft.
Morley Hall	Bedminster	580	As per arrangement	A. Chivers, Oswald cottage, Clifton view, Bedminster.
Museum and Library	Queen's road—			
Lecture Theatre		420	9.0 a.m. to 6.0 p.m., £3. 6.0 p.m. to 11.0 " £3 10s. 9.0 a.m to 11.0 " £5.	S. H. Swayne, P. R. Sleeman. } Hon. Secs.
Council Room (for committee or other meetings)		—	£1 1s.	
Ante-Room (for sectional or class meetings)		—	10/6	
Oddfellows' Hall	Rupert street	300	As per arrangement	R. Brown, All Saints' street.
Redland Rooms	Lower Redland road	100	As per arrangement	A. Hunt, Bolton villa, Waverley road, Redland.
Rifle Drill Hall	Queen's road	3500	£6 without seats £10 10s. with seats	C. A. Peters, Shannon court, Corn street.
Vestry Hall of St. Philip and Jacob Without	Pennywell road	800	As per arrangement	Thos. D. Jarrett, Vestry clerk, Pennywell rd., St. Philip's.
Victoria Rooms	Whiteladies' rd., Clifton—			
Large Room		1500		Wm. Roué, at the Rooms; or 165 Whiteladies' road, Redland.
Do. Ground Floor only		1400	As per arrangement	
Small Room		400		
A Smaller Room		150		

[*] As a rule the prices include gas for a certain length of time. In some cases there is a slight charge for attendant.

Harriers.

STAPLETON HARRIERS. Formed in 1882; number of members, 20; place of meeting, Eastville restaurant, near Tram terminus; subscription, 4/-. F. Brokenbrow, 2 Chaplin road, Easton, hon. sec.

STANLEY HARRIERS. Formed in 1879; number of members, 15; place of meeting, Temperance restaurant, near Stapleton church; subscription, 4/-. J. A. Browning, 9 Stuart street, Stapleton road, hon. sec.

Harvest Festivals.

It has now become the fashion in most of the city and suburban churches to hold thanksgiving services for the ingathering of the harvest each year. Many of the churches are elaborately decorated with the fruits of the earth for the occasion, and the services are made as musical as possible, generally accompanied by an anthem. These thanksgivings take place in the autumn, and are usually held on a week-day evening.

Health of Bristol. (See "Sanitary.")

Highway Boards.

The District Highway Boards are as follow:—Ashton, Axbridge, Clutton, Keynsham, Lawford's gate, Oldland, Sodbury, Stapleton, St. George and Thornbury.

Hockey.

This game was introduced, with proper rules, about ten years ago by the Bristol Hockey Club, which plays on Durdham Down, and numbers 50 members. Dr. Gibbs, Children's Hospital, hon. sec. There are also a few other hockey clubs in Bristol.

Holms, The,

two islands off Weston-super-Mare in the Bristol Channel, one called the Flat Holm, the other the Steep Holm. The former has a lighthouse on it 70 feet high, a battery with seven guns and a farmhouse, and the latter is famous as having been the residence of Gildas, the ancient British historian. The Steep Holm was, in April, 1834, sold to C. K. K. Tynte by the Corporation of Bristol. These islands mark the western boundary of the city of Bristol's water jurisdiction.

Homes and Creches.

BOYS' HOMES. There are two in Bristol. The first was established in St. James' back by the late Mary Carpenter, and the second, viz., the Mary Carpenter Memorial Boys' Home, at 4 Broad Plain, St. Philip's. The latter is partly endowed with money, the result of a memorial fund raised to the memory of Mary Carpenter. The objects of the Homes are as follow:—To provide comfortable homes for working boys, who have either no homes at all, or only those where the moral influence is decidedly bad. Each boy pays 1/- per week, and for this he is provided with a good bed, a comfortable room with fire and light, and a bath. If a boy be quite destitute, or out of work, he is not therefore refused admission or turned adrift, but—at the discretion of the committee—is maintained at the expense of the institution until he can obtain employment. His food is nicely prepared and served by the matron in charge, and his health and comfort are promoted in every possible way. No boy is admitted against the expressed wishes of his parents or guardians, unless it is an extreme case of ill-usage or bad associations, sufficient to warrant legal protection being sought if necessary. S. T. Jey, 3 Cotham grove, is hon. sec. for the St. James' back Home, and J. W. Arrowsmith, 99 Whiteladies' road, of the Mary Carpenter Memorial Boys' Home.

BRISTOL FEMALE PENITENTIARY, or Magdalen house, Upper Maudlin street. This institution was established June 24th, 1801, when it was opened for the reception and reclaiming of females who had strayed from the paths of virtue. The inmates are employed in washing, needlework, &c., till they are fit to be placed in situations or restored to their friends, and the institution greatly depends upon a constant supply of work. Adjoining the institution is the church of St. James-the-Less, to which there is private access, and the females occupy the gallery, unseen by the general public, every Sunday. Rev. W. S. Bruce and B. Kendall, hon. secs.

BRISTOL FEMALE REFUGE SOCIETY, Marlborough house, Marlborough hill. For 67 years this society has offered a way of escape to fallen women. Since its commencement many hundreds of women have been admitted to the home, where they are instructed in household work and either in laundry or needle work; and then, after having been provided with a respectable outfit, have either been restored to their friends or placed in suitable situations. The institution is mainly supported by voluntary subscriptions. Mrs. W. S. Capper and Mrs. Cousins, hon. secs.

BRISTOL HOME SOCIETY, 35 Montague hill, provides accommodation for females requiring temporary refuge. To servants especially who have been obliged to leave their situations through illness the home confers a great boon while they are recruiting their strength after sickness. Subscriptions voluntary. The terms are:—For best bedrooms, 2/- per week; first floor bedrooms, 1/6 per week; upper rooms, 1/- per week. Rev. C. R. Lilly, M.A., hon. sec.

BRISTOL TEMPORARY HOME, Southwell house, Southwell street, Kingsdown, established in 1865 for young women who have strayed from the paths of virtue. During the year 1882 92 girls were received in the home. Needlework is principally performed by the inmates. The home is chiefly sustained by voluntary contributions. Mrs. S. Thomas and Mrs. Wakefield, hon. secs.

CANADIAN HOME FOR LITTLE GIRLS, 9 Bishop street, St. Paul's, has for its object the reclamation of poor unfriended children, by giving them a fair start in life and securing suitable homes in Canada, where the society's supervision is exercised till each child has attained an age when by its training and the healthy influences by which it has been surrounded it possesses the opportunity of becoming a useful member of society. President, Mrs. Beddoe; secretary, Miss Pease.

EMIGRATION HOME FOR GIRLS, 9 Bishop street, St. Paul's, established in 1881 for the purpose of collecting and training neglected girls under 13 years of age for emigration to Canada, under the care of Miss Macpherson. Mrs. Beddoe, president; Mrs. Groggan, treasurer.

FEMALE PREVENTIVE MISSION HOME, Royal fort, St. Michael's hill. The object is to hold out a helping hand to girls of the poorest class and enable them to earn their living as domestic servants. The means are:—Two free registry offices, where young girls are provided with situations, and where such as have no suitable home may lodge when out of place, under the care of a matron. A home where 40 girls are trained for domestic service. They are usually kept a few months only, but are carefully watched over and regularly visited in their situations by an agent of the society, who receives their wages, and helps them by sympathy and kind advice. A stock of ready-made clothing is kept at the registry offices, which they may purchase at cost price. Girls in Bristol and the immediate neighbourhood are admitted free, and no subscriber's recommendation is required. Applicants are expected to attend a class held every afternoon at the home for sewing, reading, &c., when the case of each is investigated, and, if suitable, she is admitted to the home when a vacancy occurs. Girls are admitted from the age of 12 to 16; a few are received at the age of 11 on payment of 3/- per week; girls from a distance at 3/6 per week. During the year 1882 108 girls were received into the home. The free registry offices are at 3 Camden place,

St. Michael's hill, and at 2 Stapleton road. Miss Savill, the Home, Royal fort, sec.; Miss Catherine Sturge, 13 Cotham gardens, treasurer.

GUARDIAN HOUSE, Upper Maudlin street, founded 11th April, 1833. The number of young people who have passed through the house since its establishment is 427, there being now 38 inmates. Laundry and needle work are principally taught, and religious and secular knowledge is carefully attended to. The main object of the institution is to inculcate morality amongst females between the ages of 12 and 18, who, having no home, or none that is safe for them, need a shelter, where they may be maintained, preserved from danger and qualified to become good and useful servants, while it is hoped that instruction of far higher importance may prove a stay to their future steps. The house is supported by voluntary subscriptions and donations, and by the proceeds resulting from washing and needlework. The institution is open to inspection on Thursdays, except the first in the month, from 11 to 1 o'clock. Miss Seifferth, 5 Berkeley crescent, sec.

HOME FOR CRIPPLED CHILDREN, Clifton wood. The object of the home is to furnish to poor crippled children—who, being unable to go to school, grow up without receiving any adequate education, and without any means of procuring their own livelihood in after life—an education, and at the same time the advantage of good food, nursing, and fresh, pure air, with skilful medical supervision. Since the establishment of the home, in 1876, 58 children have been admitted. In the present home there is ample accommodation for 25 children at one time. The boys are kept in the home till they are 12 years old, at which age they are eligible for admission to the Kensington home for boys, where they can be kept for three years and taught a trade, and many of their patrons have availed themselves of the opportunity thus afforded to complete their benevolent efforts on their behalf. The girls can be retained in the home till they are 14 years of age, by which time they have acquired some knowledge of household duties, and are old enough to be apprenticed to dressmaking or other light employment. The home is supported by voluntary subscriptions and donations. C. J. Collins Prichard, Corn street, hon. treasurer; J. Bridger, 13 Lansdown place, hon. sec.

INDUSTRIAL HOME FOR DESTITUTE GIRLS, 11 Dowry parade, Hotwells, established April 18th, 1852, with six inmates, in James' place, Hotwells, afterwards removed to the present address. Its object is that of rescuing destitute children from the evil influences to which they might be exposed. It is conducted on the principles of the Church of England, and is capable of containing 24 children, the age of admission being from 6 to 12 years. The children are fed, clothed, educated and taught household work and washing for the payment of £10 yearly. When fit for service they are placed out by the committee, and are looked after from time to time. The number of children admitted since the opening of the home is 165; there are now 23 in the house. The committee of management consists of eight ladies and three lady visitors. Miss Douglas, 5 Gloucester row, hon. sec.

LAUNDRY HOME, THE, opened by a council of ladies in order to provide safe and comfortable lodgings for well-conducted young women working at the steam laundry at Westbury-on-Trym. These ladies often meet with young women more fitted for laundry work than domestic service, but whom they would hesitate to send to a public laundry if they had to find lodgings for themselves among strangers. A cottage has been taken and furnished, and the plan has proved a decided success. Contributions are needed to establish the lodgings on a scale which will render them self-supporting. Twelve more beds and bedding, with a few more articles of furniture, would enable the council of ladies to take a second cottage and accommodate about 20 young women, each paying 1/6 for lodgings and providing her own food, the washing being done at home by a lodger, each paying for her own. Each new lodger has her food provided from the funds for the first week, that she may begin free from debt. Coal and lamp oil are the only other expenses to be met by the funds. Miss Marriott, Oldbury house, St. Michael's hill, secretary.

LONGMAN MEMORIAL HOME, Fair lawn, 4 Clifton wood, for reclaiming fallen females. Plain washing, stocking knitting and needlework are done by the inmates. A few extra girls are admitted for short periods on payment of 5/- per week, if suitable in other respects. The inmates are expected to remain at least one year before being passed out to other employment. They are allowed to see their friends on the first Saturdays in March, June, September and December, at the home, between 2 and 4 p.m. The home is opened to general visitors on the first Friday in each month. Application for admission to be made to Mrs. May, Park house, Cotham.

MARY CARPENTER MEMORIAL WORKING WOMEN'S HOME, 10 Bishop street, Portland square, was founded for the reception of respectable young women and girls engaged in daily employment who are without homes or are strangers in the city. For the payment of 1/- or 1/6 per week they obtain comfortable sleeping accommodation, together with the use of sitting-room and kitchen. Each inmate provides her own food. As similar homes are being opened in other towns, it is hoped that soon young women going from town to town in search of employment may take introductions from one home to another, and thus be enabled to find a lodging. Miss Burt, 5 Miles' road, Clifton, hon. sec.

PARK ROW ASYLUM, for hopeful discharged female prisoners and hopeful destitute girls not prosecuted. The asylum has been established 32 years. No penitentiary case is admissible. No cases of pickpockets are admissible. No candidate can be admitted who has been in prison more than once. Candidates must be furnished with certificates of good health and good conduct during the time of imprisonment, signed by the authorities of gaols. Candidates are to be sent direct from the gaol to the asylum. No candidate admissible under 14 years. Donations and subscriptions are expected when a candidate is admitted from the gaols of other counties. A printed paper of queries will be sent to any visiting justice, chaplain or governor of gaols, on application for the admission of a candidate, which should be made at least a fortnight before the discharge of a prisoner desired to be admitted, and signed by the governor of the gaol. Hopeful destitute girls, well recommended, are also admitted. The asylum is open to the public every Thursday, from 10 to 4 o'clock. All letters concerning candidates must be directed to the Lady Secretary, Park row Asylum, and will be laid before the committee.

SAILORS' HOME, The Grove, Queen square, established 4th January, 1853, for providing accommodation for seamen of all nations while on shore, and for the relief of shipwrecked and destitute mariners. Partly self-supporting, assisted by voluntary contributions from shipping and private subscriptions. The home contains spacious dining, reading, recreation and smoking rooms and separate sleeping apartments. James Ford, King street, hon. sec.; M. Bryan, superintendent.

ST. JOHN'S HOUSE OF MERCY, Church road, Bedminster, designed to rescue fallen women and train them for domestic service. The House is conducted on Church of England principles.

WIDOWS' HOME, 4 Granville place, Alfred hill. Established about 14 years ago on behalf of widows over 60 years of age who have no means of support. There are 12 inmates. Elliott Armstrong, Winchester house, Durdham down, hon. sec.

YOUNG WOMEN'S CHRISTIAN ASSOCIATION AND HOME has been in existence for nearly thirty years. Its objects are to unite together, for mutual help, sympathy and instruction in spiritual things, young women of all classes. The association is divided into branches, as follows:—

No. 1 Bristol Branch, in Queen's road, was established 22 years ago to provide a comfortable and christian home for young women engaged in tuition or in homes of business, and to supply a place of resort on Sunday and week-day evenings for the large number of young women who reside in the city. Bible classes are held on Sunday afternoons at 3 o'clock, and on Friday evenings at 8.15. There is a library at this branch.

No. 1 Clifton Branch, at 5 Kensington place, Clifton. Ladies meet once a month in the afternoon for Bible study and once a month for prayer. There is a branch in connection with Emmanuel church; also two other Bible readings in Redland. In winter there is a meeting for governesses, at which they spend a pleasant social evening.

No. 2 Clifton Branch is composed chiefly of members who are or have been connected with the different Bible classes. A Bible class is held every Tuesday evening, and a monthly meeting for members of the prayer union only. Classes or lectures on cooking, nursing, cutting out, &c., are given at intervals.

There are also the Temple branch, St. Gabriel's branch, and others with monthly and quarterly meetings. The number of members is about 500.

YOUNG WORKWOMEN'S CHRISTIAN INSTITUTE, 14 King square, opened in 1875, is believed to be the first of its kind started in England. Girls are admitted from the age of 15 to 25: the home will accommodate 17, and the payment is 1/- or 1/6 per week. Miss Gibbs, 22 Kingsdown parade, hon. sec.

There is also a home in connection with the Young Men's Christian Association, St. James' square (see "Young Men's Christian Association").

There are Convalescent Homes at Weston-super-Mare, Portishead and Shirehampton. These institutions are useful adjuncts to the Bristol hospitals and to invalids resident in the city.

Creches.

ELIZABETH PROCTOR CRECHE, fronting the Broad plain, but ordinarily entered from Tucker's court, Bread street, owes its name to the lady who subscribed very liberally to set it on foot. Mark Whitwill took a leading part in its foundation in October, 1872. Situated in such a densely populated district, one would have expected the nursery to be the largest in the city, but though this is not so, there have been since its formation 30,000 admissions to it. It was fitted up for 24, and while as many as 26 have been admitted in one day, the average number is nearer 12 or 14. Twopence per day is the charge, and no reduction is made in the case of more than one coming from the same family. The home is suitably arranged for its young inmates. Games and toys are provided, and the cleanliness and feeding of the children thoroughly attended to. Some of those taken charge of by the matron are but a fortnight old. Open week days from 8.30 a.m. till 6 p.m., except Saturdays, when it is closed at 2 o'clock. If a child is not fetched by 6.30 the rules provide for the infliction of a fine of one penny, and if not called for for more than a quarter of an hour afterwards the fine is sixpence. There are also penalties for cases where a child is brought which is suffering from infectious disease. The institution is fortunate in never having had left uncalled for a single child, and it has worked from the first smoothly and with very few accidents. Mark Whitwill, hon. treasurer; Mrs. W. S. Capper, hon. sec.

HOTWELLS' CRECHE, at 4 Dowry parade, Hotwells, was opened in January, 1880, in connection with St. Andrew's-the-Less. The records for 1882 show that the total admissions were 2,234. The children are taken care of from 8 o'clock in the morning, and are admitted between the ages of one month and four years. The majority leave at three years. Twopence per day is charged for each child, and they are well cared for. Like several other similar institutions, the management has been once imposed on by a mother who departed and left no trace; her child was cared for, for more than a week, and was then sent to its parochial lodgings at Eastville. A special feature about this home is that orphans are received in it at a charge of £10 per annum, to be trained as servants. Five are undergoing training at the present, and ladies interested in the work superintend their education. Miss Schacht, president; Mrs. Benson, hon. treasurer; Miss Benson, hon. secretary.

NURSERY FOR HOMELESS INFANTS, 13 Southwell street, opened on 20th September, 1882, for the purpose of sheltering and saving infants, mostly, but not exclusively, the children of unmarried mothers, who have been in good service, and in other respects than this have conducted themselves respectably. The mission agencies fail to help some of the most promising cases, because there is no home for the infants. The rules of the nursery are framed to prevent its being any encouragement to sin, and the committee invite ladies to visit and judge its effects. The nursery costs less to maintain than most other institutions; 3/6 per week is paid for each child, excepting those whose mothers give their services in return for board, lodging and occasional clothing for themselves and their offspring. Five or six of these mothers are needed to keep the house and clothing clean and wholesome and take proper care of so many helpless children, all but four being unable to walk. In nine months from the time of opening 30 children and 16 mothers have been admitted, and at Midsummer, 1883, the home contained 18 children and 6 mothers. It is intended to train the girls to be useful in the house in the departments for which they are fitted, and then place them out in service. Boys of five or six will be boarded out in good country homes for 3/6 per week. Subscriptions received by Miss Marriott, Oldbury house, St. Michael's hill.

REDLAND CRECHE was opened at the British Workman, Blackboy hill, 11 years ago, from which place it was removed to Sutherland terrace, and from thence to Worrall road, close to the quarry. The number of children fluctuates greatly. On some days it is not more than eight or nine, and on others increases to 17 or 18. It is not open on Saturdays, but on the other five week days children are received between the ages of one month and five years. It is very seldom the age is over three, however. The charge is 3d. per day for one child, 5d. for two, and 7d. for three from the same family. The work is quite an unsectarian one. Rev. U. R. Thomas, president; Mrs. Temple, hon. supt.

ST. JAMES' CRECHE, 2 West street, Whitsun street, St. James', was opened in February, 1873, chiefly through the exertions of Miss Westcott. It was there carried on for seven years. Three years ago the head-quarters were removed to spacious premises, 12 Duke street, King square, and here the work has been most successfully continued. The rules provide that no child over four years of age, or coming from an infected family, or suffering from any contagious disease, can be admitted. The children of married persons only are received. All children must be brought properly clothed and clean. Threepence a day is paid for each child. When there are two of the same family 4d. is charged, and when three are brought 5d. The nursery is open on week days only, from 7 a.m. to 7 p.m. All children are required to be called for before the latter hour, or a fine of one penny per hour is incurred. Mothers may visit the nursery twice daily to nurse their infants. The greater part of the mothers are widows, but in some cases children are admitted when the mother is ill, and consequently unable to look after her young ones. The mothers' payments cover the expenses of food and incidental expenses to within about £1 a year, and the balance of rent, taxes and wages has to be provided by the liberality of friends. The extent of the work may be seen from the annual admissions for several years past. In 1877 the number was 2,275; in 1878, 2,622; in 1879, 3,737; in 1880, 4,763; in 1881, 3,400; and in 1882, 3,667. In the case of those who attend regularly, and especially those who have done so from a very early age, the improvement in condition is most marked, and it is reported that several delicate babies have become comparatively strong under the careful nursing and generous diet they have received. Visitors are invited to inspect the creche between 11 a.m. and 4 p.m. Miss Tritton, lady supt.; Mrs. May, Park house, Cotham park, hon. sec.

St. Jude's Creche, which is in connection with St. Jude's church, was set on foot in November, 1882, and has its head-quarters at the St. Jude's mission-house. The daily attendance averages 15 or 16, and as many as 22 have been admitted in one day. The mothers are charged 3d. per child, and any ages are admitted under three. The institution is open every week day. Mrs. Openshaw, treasurer and general manager; Mrs. Kerry and Mrs. Ryland, lady superintendents.

St. Raphael's Creche, Bedminster, was the first in Bristol, being established in 1867, close to Redcliff church. After a year or two it was removed to Belmont place, then to premises near Philip street chapel, and finally to Percy street. About 30 children can be accommodated each day, and the number of attendances, which seems to average between 7,000 and 8,000 per annum, shows the value that is attached to the work by the poor of Bedminster. Children are received, without distinction, between the ages of three months and three years. At the age of three years they are admissible to the elementary schools. They may be brought by their mothers at any time after seven in the morning, and left till seven at night. A penny per day has to be paid for each child. The children receive three good meals per day, and the very young more than that. The penny does not cover the cost of the food alone, so that no complaint can be made that good value is not received for the payment. A great variety of toys are provided, and in eating, playing and sleeping the juveniles pass their time. Cradles are fitted up for the infants, and little bunks for those of older growth. No attempt is made to teach anything religious or secular, and one unfamiliar with the *modus operandi* can but feel that those engaged must have plenty to do in keeping something like order in their large family. Anyone who knows how lively a few "two-year-olds" can make a house will appreciate the work that the creche does. The management is in charge of a sister from the St. Raphael's House of Charity, and she has several servants under her, the attention of one of whom is occupied in preparing the food. On the arrival of a child at the nursery it is, as a rule, washed or given a bath, and is then put in a pinafore, its outer clothing being placed in a pigeon hole till it leaves. The same mothers make use of the institution day after day, and their cases become known to the superintendent of the home. The creche is conducted most economically, but has to depend on friends for the greater part of its income. Recently there has been a considerable outlay in improving the sanitary arrangements, and a deficiency in the funds makes its own appeal. The question naturally arises, Does a mother ever "forget" to call for her child? Only on one occasion in the 16 years' existence of the institution has a child been left on the hands of the authorities; in that case, the mother, a stranger, imposed on a fresh sister, and the infant had to be placed in the workhouse. The honorary medical attendants are Drs. Swayne and Marshall, E. C. Board, A. Carr and T. O. Mayor; E. A. Harley, treasurer and hon. sec.

BOARD SCHOOL NURSERIES. Many of the School Board schools have babies' rooms, where three and four year olds are looked after and amused; occasionally even younger children than this are admitted, but not as a rule. No provision is made in these rooms for feeding the children, and the great feature of a creche, relieving the mother for the whole day of the responsibility, is therefore not touched on.

Horticultural Shows.

The first of which any record is made was held on July 2nd, 1836, at Mr. Miller's, Durdham down. In after years horticultural shows were held half-yearly at the Clifton Zoological gardens, but through want of support had to be given up, the last being held in 1878. In 1863 another society was formed for the purpose of a winter and spring show. The exhibitions were formerly held at the Rifle Drill hall, but latterly have taken place in the Victoria rooms. The winter exhibition is principally for chrysanthemums and fruit, and the spring for flowers. It cannot be said, from the number of floral exhibitions held in Bristol, there is such a great love of flowers as the gardens and windows of Clifton and the city would indicate.

Hospitals.

BRISTOL AND CLIFTON DISPENSARY for the cure of ulcers and other chronic diseases of the legs, 4 Dowry parade, Hotwells, has been established nine years, during which time more than 2,000 cases have been treated. The number of new cases in 1882 was 196, of which 150 were discharged cured. The days of attendance are Mondays and Thursdays from 10 to 12 a.m., and Wednesdays and Saturdays from 6 to 8 p.m., when tickets can be obtained at 3d. each. Subscribers of £1 are entitled to recommend two poor patients annually, and for every additional 10/- subscribed one patient. The medical officers are:—One consulting physician, one consulting surgeon, one physician and two lady dressers. Miss Blew, 36 Cornwallis crescent, hon. sec.

BRISTOL DISPENSARY, Castle green, stands on the site of the northern ballium of Bristol castle, and was established in 1775. It ministers medically to the indigent sick and lying-in women at their own dwellings. The total number of sick patients treated from the commencement of the institution to the end of 1882 was 325,718; midwifery patients, 40,269; and children born, 40,486. The talented staff consists of four honorary surgeons, opthalmic surgeon, six resident medical officers, a dispenser and three midwives. A subscription of one guinea per annum entitles the subscriber to six free tickets and two additional tickets which may be used on payment of 5/- each. Edward Stock, Queen square, secretary.

BRISTOL EYE DISPENSARY, 17 Orchard street, was opened in Frogmore street in 1812 by the late John Bishop Estlin, F.L.S., who himself defrayed its expenses for a year or two, but since that time it has been supported by voluntary contributions, and nearly 2,000 patients are seen annually. The days of attendance are Sundays at 9 and Wednesdays at 1 o'clock. Out-patients are admitted free without note, and in-patients also if their cases require operation. The number of patients since the commencement of the institution amounts to more than 114,000, and the expenses have been kept at so low a figure that, including both in and out-patients, the average cost of each is about 1/-. Surgeons, Messrs. A. and A. W. Prichard; collector, Z. Jones, 19 College green.

BRISTOL FEMALE MISERICORDIA SOCIETY, for the relief of the sick and married women in childbirth. Some time during the last ten years of the 18th century (the date cannot be fixed) several ladies undertook the visiting of sick women. Relief was at first sent from their own kitchens, but as the work extended more regular aid was required, and a kitchen was established in Philadelphia street. Though time and circumstances have induced slight changes in the outward form and working of the society, it has remained essentially the same. During 1882, 481 were relieved with money, to 91 of whom clothing was also given. Street beggars are inadmissible, and persons residing in public-houses or beershops are not admitted. No case in Clifton, Barton hill, or beyond Bedminster bridge can be admitted. Occupants of almshouses are also inadmissible. Every subscriber of one guinea is entitled to three recommendations, one only of which can be applied to a lying-in case. Every subscriber of half-a-guinea is entitled to one sick case only. No subscriber can have more than one sick case on the list at one time. The same individual, unless under very special circumstances, cannot be put on the list twice within one year. No woman at her first confinement can be admitted, and recommendations should be sent in before the woman's confinement.

Fourteen ladies of the committee voluntarily engage themselves as visitors. A parish, or part of a parish, is apportioned to each, and they render to the charity most essential service by attending weekly to the cases within the prescribed limits. All recommendations must be sent to 4 Cave street, Portland square, where the committee meet each Tuesday at 11 a.m. Mrs. E. Strickland, treasurer; Mrs. C. Townsend, Avenue house, Cotham park, secretary.

BRISTOL GENERAL HOSPITAL was erected by public subscription. It is located on the eastern side of the Floating harbour, near Bathurst basin, having its main entrance in Guinea street, one wing facing the New cut and the other in front of Bathurst basin. The hospital was founded in 1832 and rebuilt in 1858. It is in the Italian style of architecture, of blue lias with Bath stone dressings, and forms three sides of a quadrangle, with a lofty octagonal tower at the south-west angle, surmounted by a cupola. The total original cost of this noble institution was about £25,000. Joseph Eaton and George Thomas were the chief contributors. The number of patients averages about 15,000 per annum. The hospital contains every convenience that modern science can devise for the comfort of the sick and the assistance of the staff. There are beds for over 150 patients. The basement of the building contains the kitchens, stores, laundry and washhouse, and on the ground floor are the apartments of the resident officers, committee-rooms, museum and library. The north portion, for out-patients, contains waiting and consulting rooms and a dispensary. The medical staff comprises three honorary and consulting surgeons, an honorary and consulting physician, three physicians, four surgeons, physician accoucheur, house surgeon, assistant house surgeon, physician's assistant and dispenser. The number of patients admitted into the house in 1882 was 1,245, and out-patients 14,779. These figures are somewhat smaller than usual, owing to the closing of the institution for repairs during a portion of the year. The chaplain is the Rev. C. W. Hickson, and the secretary Lieut. Henry Fox, R.N.

BRISTOL MEDICAL MISSIONARY SOCIETY, 7 Redcross street. Open free of charge or fee of any kind to all poor persons on Monday, Wednesday and Friday, at 10.30 a.m. to 4 p.m. The society is supported entirely by voluntary contributions. The staff consists of a consulting physician, consulting surgeon and a lady superintendent. A. W. Cruikshank, hon. sec. and treasurer.

BRISTOL PROVIDENT MEDICAL AID SOCIETY, for supplying medical attendance and advice to the working classes. The society is self-supporting. Dispensaries situated at 26 Woodwell crescent, Hotwells; 29 Morton street, St. George's; 16 Upper York street, Stokes croft; 4 Lombard street, Bedminster; Finsbury house, St. Mark's road, Easton; and Cathay, Redcliff hill.

CHILDREN'S HOSPITAL, Royal fort, St. Michael's hill, founded in 1865, chiefly through the exertions of Mark Whitwill, is famous for having been the first medical institution in the kingdom that appointed a lady doctor to minister to the diseases of women and children. Patients during the year 1882:—In-patients, 405, of whom 330 were cured and relieved; 11 deaths. Out-patients: Women, 787, with a total of 8,783 attendances; children, 2,086, with a total of 15,231 attendances. The special features of the hospital are as follow:—No admission note is required; the in-patient department (for children) is perfectly free. No interest, not even a note of recommendation is required; enough that a child be sick and poor it will be admitted, provided there be a vacant bed, and that the medical officers consider the case a suitable one for the hospital. The out-patient department is nearly self-supporting, and is open to women and children, women paying 1/6 on admission and 3d. on each subsequent visit, children paying 6d. on admission and 1½d. on each subsequent visit. There are two beds for women who may need special surgical treatment; payment required, 8/- per week. Visitors are admitted to view the hospital on every Monday, Tuesday, Thursday, Friday and Saturday, between 2 and 4 p.m., but not on Wednesday or Sunday, which are reserved exclusively for the parents and friends of the children. The institution is supported by subscriptions and donations.

The new building is in the late Perpendicular style of architecture, and is constructed on the pavilion system, affording light and air on three sides of the wards. When completed the hospital will include five wards, with ten beds in each, for children from two to twelve years of age; two rooms for isolating special cases that may require to be kept unusually quiet; one room with steam apparatus for the treatment of croup; two wards, with four beds in each, for women; one ward in which babies requiring surgical operations may be received under care of their mothers; a play-room for convalescents, and suitable accommodation for matron, nurses, &c. In another part of the ground is a small building which contains three wards, with three beds in each, for infectious cases and those of a contagious nature. Altogether there will be 70 beds. The five main wards measure 30 feet by 20 feet. All the internal arrangements are in accordance with the most modern ideas of hospital arrangements and on the most approved principles of sanitary science. The cost of the building exceeded £11,500, exclusive of £2,500 spent on its site. The position of the hospital at the summit of St. Michael's hill is magnificent, being open and airy, a warm, sunny aspect, and commands splendid views. President and treasurer, Mark Whitwill; secretary, E. T. Collins, 39 Broad st.

CLIFTON DISPENSARY, Dowry square. The patients of this institution must be such persons as have no other means of obtaining medical assistance at the time of admission, but those who may be compelled subsequently to their admission to receive parochial relief may, at the discretion of the medical officer in attendance, be continued on the register. No person who has not been previously resident in the parish of Clifton during three months, except in cases of urgent necessity, nor any domestic servant, actually resident under his or her employer's roof, is admissible as a patient. No woman is admissible as a midwifery patient on her first confinement, except under peculiar circumstances, nor one whose children have not all been vaccinated or had the smallpox. Subscribers and donors of one guinea receive four sick notes and one midwifery note, or six sick notes; subscribers and donors of half-a-guinea, three sick notes. Each sick note is available for six weeks. A midwifery note may be exchanged for two sick notes. Additional tickets may be obtained at the Dispensary at 4/- for each sick note and 10/- for each midwifery note. Notes issued in one year are available till 31st March of the following year. During 1882 the medical registers show that 2,480 were received during that year, of which 2,327 were either cured or relieved. The medical staff consists of a consulting accoucheur, two physicians, two surgeons, a resident medical officer, a dispenser and two midwives. The management of the institution is vested in the hands of a ladies' and gentlemen's committee. There is a Redland branch of the institution at 1 Apsley road. Rev. R. W. Southby, secretary.

DISPENSARY FOR OUTDOOR TREATMENT OF WOMEN AND CHILDREN, St. George's road, Hotwells (opposite Victoria buildings), is supported partially by voluntary subscriptions. The medical staff consists of one lady honorary visiting physician, and a consulting physician and surgeon. Admission Wednesdays and Saturdays, from '11.30 till 12.30. The fees are as follow :—For women : Entrance, 1/-; subsequent attendance, 6d. For children : Entrance, 6d.; subsequent attendance, 3d.

DISPENSARY FOR THE CURE OF DEAFNESS, 5 Lower Berkeley place, Clifton, established 1851. It is self-supporting. Open on Sundays from 9 to 10.30 a.m., and on Thursdays from 9.30 to 11 a.m. The surgeon is Dr. Metford.

DISPENSARY FOR THE TREATMENT OF DISEASES OF WOMEN AND CHILDREN, Olivet place, Redland. Established in 1860.

EYE HOSPITAL, situated in Lower Maudlin street, does much good efficiently and unostentatiously. It was established in 1810. Externally it presents no feature of interest; in fact it is one of a row of well-built houses, which evidently served as a quiet and comfortable house of our well-to-do merchants some seventy or eighty years ago. The patients' waiting-room contains an old Chinese fresco, which adorns the space over the mantelpiece. The hospital is open for patients Tuesdays, Thursdays and Saturdays, from 11.30 to 1 o'clock. Since the foundation 92,134 patients have been admitted. During the year 1882 the number of cases amounted to 9,546 out-patients and 108 in-patients. The subscription is one guinea per annum. Dr. R. T. H. Bartley, who died in July, 1882, devoted thirty years of his life to this institution. Drs. R. H. Dew and F. Richardson Cross are the present oculists. In-patients are admitted on the recommendation of a subscriber; or payment of 8/- a week, without a note of recommendation, will admit a patient provided the case is one for the house. Out-door patients are received without any recommendation, provided they come under the denomination of poor persons. J. Adamson-Coram, sec.

HOMŒOPATHIC DISPENSARY, Brunswick square, for the relief of the poor. Open daily. Supported by voluntary subscriptions. J. F. Birtill, 17 Somerset street, Kingsdown, hon. sec.

HOSPITAL FOR DISEASES OF THE TEETH, 9 Unity street, College green. Established in 1860.

INFIRMARY, BRISTOL ROYAL, Charity Universal, situated in Marlborough street, was founded in 1735. It is one of the earliest asylums in the kingdom for the relief of the suffering, and the first attempt (out of London) to support such an institution by voluntary contributions. John Elbridge, deputy-comptroller of Customs in 1734, was one of its chief founders; he devoted to its establishment the last two years of his life, and at his death left it £5,000. Altogether Mr. Elbridge bequeathed £58,000 to public charities in Bristol. This amount had nearly fallen to his next of kin, for he kept his will by him for years unsigned, through a very common superstition "that signing one's will will accelerate one's death." In the committee-room at the Infirmary is a tablet beneath a portrait of this estimable man which bears the following inscription:—
"John Elbridge, esquire, was among the first who engaged in this charity. As soon as the society was formed he was chosen treasurer, and cheerfully undertook the care of the building and of providing furniture of all kinds for the house and apothecary's shop necessary for the first opening. He gave a constant and unwearied attention to this work, which he effected entirely at his own expense in the year 1737. In the next year he erected a new ward for 12 patients, which he furnished with beds and all other accommodations likewise at his own expense. Besides three most seasonable benefactions which may be estimated at £1,500 at least, he by his will bequeathed to the use of the society £5,000. He died on 22nd February, 1738, treasurer of this society. His epitaph was written by Dr. Shibbear, who in 1740 published a pamphlet on the Bristol waters. The Infirmary was opened on December 13th, 1737; the ground on which it was built was called Jobbin's leaze, or leas." The present building was begun on June 2nd, 1781, and the east wing in 1788. In 1793 further additions were made to the body of the structure, and the west wing was commenced in 1805. Two new wards were added in 1868 at the sole cost of W. T. Hill, besides which considerable increased room was obtained by raising the roof, &c. Two hundred and forty-four in-patients can now be accommodated; the average annual number exceeds 3,000, besides about 20,000 out-patients. Elbridge built a school in Fort lane near to his house, which in his lifetime he endowed with the sum of £3,000, for the clothing once a year of 24 girls and instructing them in reading, writing, cyphering, and sewing. The master of this school by sending a note signed "Elbridge" can obtain at any hour immediate admission for any sick or wounded scholar. In 1850 Her Majesty graciously ordered the affix "Royal" to its title. In 1876 this noble charity was rendered still more useful by a thorough reorganisation of its sanitary arrangements at a cost of about £20,000. The surgical museum of the Infirmary was founded by Richd. Smith, who was senior surgeon from 1796 until his decease, January 24th, 1843. Its collection of calculi is said to be second to none in value and interest, but the most prominent objects of this dismal chamber are the skeletons of murderers. One of these is that of John Horwood, a youth of 18, who was the first criminal hanged at Bristol "New Drop," April 13th, 1821, for the murder in a fit of jealousy of his sweetheart, Eliza Balsum, at Hanham, by hurling a stone at her. A subscription of two guineas entitles the subscriber to recommend two in-patients for admission to the house and six out-

patients. A donor of 30 guineas is entitled to the privileges of a two-guinea annual subscription for life. The patients admitted during 1882 were:—In-patients, 3,064; out-patients, 25,869; total, 28,933. In 1881 the numbers were: In-patients, 2,863; out-patients, 30,478; total, 33,341. Increase in number of in-patients, 201; decrease in number of out-patients, 4,609. Average daily number of in-patients, 1882, 234·07; ditto, 1881, 230·03. Average stay in the house, 1882, 25·27 days; ditto, 1881, 31·03 days. Total expenditure, 1882, £11,908 6s. 5d.; deduct cost of 25,869 out-patients at 1/3, £1,616 16s. 3d.; cost of 3,064 in-patients, £10,292. Cost of each in-patient, £3 7s. 2d.; cost of each occupied bed, £43 19s. 8d.; but without deducting the out-patients the cost of each occupied bed was £50 17s. 9d. Attached to this noble institution is a prettily designed Episcopalian chapel for the accommodation of the "movable" patients. Services are conducted on Sundays morning and evening, as in ordinary places of divine worship. There are three honorary and consulting physicians, four physicians, two consulting surgeons, five surgeons, a medical superintendent, house physician, house surgeon, surgeon to out-patient department and dispenser. The chaplain is the Rev. Octavius M. Grindon, and the secretary W. Trenerry.

LYING-IN INSTITUTION. Office, 44 College green. Established 1819.

OLD PARK LOCK HOSPITAL, for the treatment of women only, Old Park hill, St. Michael's. During the year 1882 the number of patients admitted was 48. The primary object of this institution is to relieve suffering and to restore health to the sick, but it also realises another most hopeful work in reclaiming the fallen to virtuous and happy lives. The institution is supported by voluntary contributions. There is also a Samaritan fund in connection with the hospital. Miss Hands and Miss Gertrude Thomas, hon. secs.

SMALLPOX AND FEVER HOSPITAL, St. Philip's marsh, under the control of the Sanitary Authority. It is a small structure capable of accommodating 20 patients. Opened in June, 1871, at a cost of £250.

Hospital Sunday, when special sermons and collections are made at the respective churches and chapels in the city on behalf of the Royal Infirmary and General Hospital, takes place on the second Sunday in each year.

Hotels. The hotel accommodation in Bristol and Clifton is surpassed by no other town in England. Appended are the names of the principal hotels:—

CLIFTON DOWN HOTEL COMPANY LIMITED. This hotel, which was opened in 1864, stands on the site of the celebrated Bath hotel, and is very favourably situated for visitors to Clifton. It commands fine views of the Leigh woods, the Downs and the Suspension bridge. Wilberforce Tribe, Albion chambers, secretary.

GRAND HOTEL (City Hotel Company Limited) stands upon the sites of the White Lion and White Hart hotels, and was erected in 1869. It is one of the largest and most central hotels in the city, is eminently a commercial one, and is also admirably adapted for large dinners. The Anchor and other large societies have held their dinners here for several years past. The telephone is in use at the hotel. John Curtis, Exchange buildings, secretary.

IMPERIAL (North Clifton Hotel Company Limited), Whiteladies' road, opened in 1878, is a large and well-managed hotel. One idea of its projection was the accommodation it would offer to merchants and others using Avonmouth dock, but as the railway companies do not at present run through the tunnel from Clifton down station it is very little used for that purpose. Daniel Jenkins, Alma vale, secretary.

MONTAGUE HOTEL, THE, Kingsdown parade, is very old and one of the most cosy in the city. The Grateful Society hold their annual dinner here, as do also the Society of St. Stephen's Ringers. It is a well-known house for turtle soup. Mrs. Ward, proprietress.

QUEEN'S HOTEL, Queen's road, Clifton, is one of the earliest hotels of the large and modern description in Bristol. Miss Nunney, proprietress.

ROYAL HOTEL COMPANY LIMITED, College green, opened in 1868, is centrally situated and contains a large number of bedrooms. The principal hall is 62 feet long, 32 feet wide and 40 feet high. The telephone is in use at the hotel. Chas. Ware, Shannon court, secretary.

ROYAL TALBOT HOTEL, at the junction of Bath and Victoria streets, is a commercial hotel much frequented. The telephone is in use at the hotel. James Reynolds, proprietor.

ST. VINCENT ROCKS' HOTEL, Sion hill, Clifton, gives a splendid view of the gorge of the Avon and Suspension bridge. The judges of assize when on circuit at Bristol usually stay at this hotel.

There are also the following:— The Full Moon, North street; The George, Victoria street; The Greyhound, Broadmead; The Grosvenor, Victoria street; The Rummer, High street; The Saracen's Head, Temple gate (see "Inns, Old").

There are about ten good temperance hotels in Bristol.

Hotwells, The, seems to have been celebrated as far back as 1480, at which date it is noticed by William Wyrcestre. This tepid medicinal spring used formerly to issue, at low water, from the rocks on the right bank of the Avon, near St. Vincent's rocks. By the widening of the navigable channel of the river which has been effected in recent years, the site of the spring is now nearly in the middle of the bed. In order, however, to retain and preserve the use of the water, great care was taken in carrying out the river alterations to enclose the spring in a solid chamber of masonry, with a proper self-acting outlet valve, and from this chamber the water is drawn through a solid block tin pipe by the pump under the rock arch at the back of the roadway. The natural gush of this spring is at the rate of 60 gallons per minute. The water, fresh from the spring, is about the temperature of 76° Farenheit, and appears perfectly pellucid, sparkling and abounding with air bubbles, and can be best drunk in perfection at the spring itself. The contents of an imperial gallon, as analysed by W. Herapath in 1843, are as follow:—

	CUBIC INCHES.
Carbonic Acid Gas	8·75
Nitrogen Gas	6·56
SOLID MATTER.	GRAINS.
Chloride of Magnesium	2·180
Nitrate of Magnesia	2·909
Chloride of Sodium	5·891
Sulphate of Soda	3·017
Sulphate of Magnesia	1·267
Carbonate of Lime	17·700
Carbonate of Magnesia	·660
Carbonate of Iron	·103
Bitumen	·150
Sulphate of Lime	9·868
Silicia	·270
	44·015

A circumstance worthy of remark happened at the Hotwells on the 1st of November, 1755, when, without any apparent cause, the water suddenly became very red, and so extremely turbid that it could not be drank. Many conjectures were formed to account for this phenomenon. A gentlemen present desired the company particularly to notice the day, because he was firmly of opinion that it was the effect of a violent concussion somewhere at that time, of which probably they might soon hear. His opinion was shortly after confirmed by accounts of the dreadful catastrophe at Lisbon, which city was nearly destroyed by an earthquake on the same day. It was a long while before the water of the Hotwells recovered its wonted purity. Tradition attributes the original discovery of the medicinal properties of the water to sailors, who had contracted scurvy from long voyages, and found themselves benefited by drinking freely and washing in the water, whose fresh stream was likely to attract their notice when navigating the river. Some public spirited persons made a reservoir of brickwork, paved at the bottom, for the greater convenience of frequenters, and till the beginning of the 17th century no further attention appears to have been bestowed upon it. In 1695 the old Hotwell house was built by some enterprising citizens, under a lease from the Merchant Venturers of the port, and they erected pumps and baths, which, however, were approachable only by foot passengers, and being close to the river, the only access to St. Vincent's rocks was through the house. It was at the Hotwells, under the auspices of Dr. Beddoes, that the young Davy (afterwards Sir Humphrey) made his *début* as a philosopher; and here, also, the famous Ann Yearsley, milkwoman and poetess, who was in a great measure indebted to Hannah More for her success, invested her earnings in a circulating library, which ended in failure. Here lived Bishops Ken and Butler, Coombe (Doctor Syntax), Doddridge, Cowper, Lady Hasketh (who lies buried in the Cathedral), Sarah Duchess of Marlborough, Danby and Turner, each of whom in their way have conferred celebrity upon the Hotwells.

Humane Society. Its objects are to save and rescue life in cases of drowning, for which awards are made. The following is a list of the stations of the society where hooks, drags, &c., are kept :—

Bathurst basin watch-house*
Bathurst wharf landing steps
Bridge, near the Cotton works
Bristol bridge
Broad quay transit shed
Bull inn, St. George's, Gloucestershire
Coomassie shed, Wapping
Crow, Crow lane, Welsh back
Drawbridge, Quay
Engine house, bottom of Guinea street
Full Moon, St. Philip's
Gas House ferry, Canons' marsh
George and Dragon, Bedminster bridge
Great Western Steam Packet, Limekiln dock
Hit or Miss tavern, Crew's hole
Hotwells' new landing stage*
King George tavern, Canons' marsh
Netham watch-house*
Old Fox, Baptist mills
Plough, Bath bridge
Police boat, Floating harbour
Prince's wharf transit shed, Wapping
Railings, opposite Whitehouse street, New cut, Bedminster
Railings, opposite St. Luke's church, New cut, Bedminster
Railings, opposite Baths and Washhouses, New cut
Railway inn, Stapleton road
Redcliff back ferry slip
Red Lion, Pill
Rising Sun tavern, St. Philip's
Robinson's warehouse, Bathurst wharf
Stone bridge, head of the Quay
The Butts, Blackbirds' inn
The Grove ferry slip
Toll gate, near the Cattle market
Wall near F. C. Box, blockmaker, Narrow quay
Water Police station, Prince street bridge*
Welsh back transit shed
White Lion inn, Quay head

Life Buoys are placed at the following stations :—

Bathurst basin, lower lock
    " upper " (engine-house)
Cattle market lock
Gas works ferry, south side
    " " north "
Netham lock
Prince street bridge
    " Water Police
Quay head
Stapleton road, Railway inn

With a view of encouraging swimming amongst boys attending the elementary schools, this society annually offers prizes. The first contest was held at Popham's baths, Kingsdown, on the 23rd September, 1882. The local society also offers annually a silver medal to the public schools for the competitor who exhibits the greatest proficiency in three modes of saving life. Clifton college had the honour of receiving the first medal in 1882. During the year 1882 43 cases of rescue from drowning were brought under the notice of the committee, and the efforts used to save life in every case were successful. One of the cases occurred in the Mill stream, Mina road, two in the Frome, one in the Avon, two at Pill, two at Bedmin-

* Cork life belts at stations.

ster, and the remainder in the Floating harbour. Of the 43 cases 29 were children, two of persons in a state of intoxication, three of attempted suicide, and the remainder the result of accident or bathing. The total number of cases since the formation of the society amounts to 3,052. During the year 1882 the sum of £31 6s. 6d. was distributed in rewards amongst 46 applicants for their efforts in saving life. The society has been established 76 years. A. Talbot, Richmond hill, hon. sec.

Hungroad, a portion of the river Avon, just within the mouth, where craft formerly remained (or hanged on—hence its name) until the tide had flowed sufficiently to enable them to pass up the river to the city. Many of the huge rings and chains are still to be seen on the Somersetshire side of the river. Here the Bristol privateers, the terror of Spanish Dons, used to moor, and the West Indiamen to lighten their cargoes.

Hunting. The principal packs of the neighbourhood are those of Lord Fitzhardinge, Berkeley castle, consisting of 62½ couples, and, in the season, meeting four days per week, and the Duke of Beaufort, Badminton, consisting of 75 couples and meeting five days per week. The meets are announced in the local newspapers.

Imports. The following comprise the principal imports, with their values, to the port of Bristol for the year ending 31st Dec., 1882:

	Value.
Animals	£52,453
Bacon	160,840
Beef—Salted	10,316
Butter and Butterine	33,417
Cheese	244,713
Corn—Wheat	1,874,258
Barley	1,024,227
Oats	29,073
Peas	45,458
Maize or Indian Corn	292,467
Buckwheat	5,357
Wheatmeal or Flour	205,184
Currants	39,315
Fish—Cured or Salted	22,038
Fruit—Apples, Raw	£4,883
Nuts, used as Fruit	22,080
Oranges and Lemons	43,887
Glass—Window	22,431
Plate	12,206
Manufactures, unenumerated	4,088
Hams	9,469
Hides—Wet	239,816
Iron, Manufactures of, unenumerated	27,288
Lard	81,791
Lead, Ore of	10,018
Leather—Dressed	4,048
Undressed	45,901
Manures—Phosphate of Lime and Rock	14,165
Meat—preserved otherwise than by Salting	84,504
Nitre, Cubic	37,760
Oils—Fish, Train	35,285
Animal	5,094
Olive	55,508
Palm	70,207
Seed	19,654
Turpentine	123,719
Unenumerated	1,450
Oil Seed Cake	134,820
Onions—Raw	9,561
Painters' Colours—Unenumerated	11,433
Petroleum	167,681
Pork—Salted	14,282
Potatoes	21,239
Pyrites—of Iron or Copper	33,618
Raisins	41,274
Rosin	54,665
Seeds—Clover and Grass	5,499
Cotton	72,232
Flax or Linseed	97,892
Unenumerated, other sorts	17,754
Spirits—Brandy	53,956
Rum	15,501
Stones—Rough or Hewn	13,442
Sugar—Refined in Lump & Loaves	187,982
Other Sorts, including Candy	41,374
" Unrefined, Beetroot	299,112
" " Cane and other Sorts	566,085
" Glucose	18,088
Tallow and Stearine	69,079
Tobacco—Unmanufactured	25,263
Manufactured	11,825
Valonia	84,696
Wine—Red	72,584
White	58,566
Wood—Hewn, Fir	26,452
" " Oak	28,386

The totals of the articles imported as published by the Chamber of Commerce for 1882 are as follow:—

Duty Free Articles	£7,523,724
Dutiable ditto	326,440
	£7,850,164

Incorporation of the Poor, The, was constituted in 1696

by the election of four ratepayers from each of the twelve aldermanic wards; these were called Guardians of the Poor, and were chosen for four years, half of their number to go out of office every second year. The Mayor and the twelve Aldermen were also members of the court, together with any Honorary Guardians who might be elected by the court from those who had given contributions of £100 or upwards to the Poor fund. A subsequent Act (1714) increased the number by constituting the two churchwardens of each parish members of the court; but in 1718 this was repealed, so far as related to junior churchwardens, and only the seniors were retained. Honorary guardianship was also discontinued in the beginning of the present century. The present constitution of the court consists of the Mayor for the time being, 12 members of the Town Council elected annually, 48 elected Guardians, the 17 senior churchwardens and the senior overseer of the Castle precincts, the Incorporation being thus composed of 79 members, except when some of them are chosen in more than one capacity, which is frequently done. This body is the Board of Guardians of the Poor for the 18 parishes, and by Vic. 1, cap. 86, exercise the power of overseers within those limits, and levy and collect all the local rates of the district, except the Sanitary rate. (See "Rates.") The offices of the Incorporation are in

ST. PETER'S HOSPITAL, adjacent to the church of St. Peter, with exquisite gabled frontage and profuse arabesque enrichments. It is a strikingly picturesque mansion. The earlier building, of which the eastern portion of the present structure is a part, is identical with that inhabited by Thomas Norton, who was reputed the most skilful alchemist of his time. The mansion passed from the Nortons in 1580 to the Newton family of Barr's court. In 1602 it was the property of Robert Chambers, and in 1607 it was purchased by Robert Aldworth, a merchant, who reconstructed the chief part, including the ornate frontage (except the east end) still standing. In 1634 the mansion came into the possession of Thomas Elbridge. In 1666 it became a sugar refinery, being the first in Bristol, and in 1682 Henry Willowbergh, and in 1689 Edward Colston and his partners, afterwards Gallop and Co., carried on a refinery. In the time of William III. (1695) a mint was established here, which ceased to work after the coinage of £40,000,000. In 1698 it was converted into a workhouse for the poor. The fine timber roof of the hall—which appears to have extended completely across the building, and which is now hidden by the Jacobian ceiling—of the court-room proves that the main structure, walls and roof, are those of the original building. The court-room, with its elaborate mantelpiece and decorations, the oak panelled screen, and the river entrance with its quaint Scriptural designs of the three children in the fiery furnace, Faith, the whale ejecting Jonah, and Eve with the fig-leaf apron, are, as appears by the date outside (1612), the work of Robert Aldworth, to whom also must be ascribed the pargetted front with its handsome barge-boards and colossal caryatides, some portions of which are probably restorations in the style of the earlier building. The lower part of the mantelpiece is of earlier date, probably about 1450; the arms are those of James I. A new glass-stained window was placed in the Board-room in 1882. The patron saint occupies the central panel, and is surrounded by the Royal, Beaufort and Berkeley arms, together with those of the city, the Incorporation of the Poor and past governors of that body, the names and mottoes of the latter also appearing.

Industrial Dwellings.

Through the instrumentality of Miss Sussanna Winkworth, Messrs. Wm. Killigrew Wait, Lewis Fry, George

Wills, Wm. Henry Budgett, Charles Hill, William Mills Baker and F. Gilmore Barnett, a company was formed in December, 1874, for securing better house accommodation for the working classes, on the "flat" system, in the vicinity of Jacob's Wells. The capital of the company now consists of £18,400, subscribed in shares, and £2,500 borrowed on mortgage. Land was secured from the Society of Merchant Venturers at a yearly rental, and operations commenced in raising that handsome pile of three-floor model dwellings now known as Jacob's Wells' and Brandon buildings, the former with 80 and the latter with 51 houses, which cost something like £20,000. Since the premises have been opened they have let fairly well, at rentals ranging from 6/6 for four rooms to 1/3 for a single apartment per week. The sanitary arrangements of the dwellings are most complete, being well supplied with water, washhouses, &c., whilst overcrowding is stringently avoided; and a commendable principle, conducive to good health, is that each front door opens on to a balcony which is *outside* the main building. One interesting feature in connection with the dwellings is that ladies collect the weekly rents, through which they possess a moral influence over the respective tenants, having a most beneficial tendency. The company have secured land adjoining the present buildings for the purpose of extending their operations when an opportunity presents itself. Solicitor and secretary to the company, F. Gilmore Barnett, 13 John street.

The premises now occupied by Messrs. Brightman Brothers, Lewin's mead west, were formerly "model lodging-houses." There are some model lodging-houses in St. George's road, just to the east of Jacob's Wells. These were originally started by those who built the Lewin's mead west houses. The scheme failed to pay, and the houses were sold.

Inns, Old. Of the few interesting historic "bits of Old Bristol," the following are still in existence:—

THE ANGEL, Redcliff street. The front has recently been rebuilt. There is a tradition that when Hogarth visited this city relative to the painting executed by him for the chancel of St. Mary Redcliff church he noticed, while passing through Redcliff street, the figure of an angel, that served as the sign of the inn; and on being told that it was painted by one Simmons, of Bristol, replied, "Then they need not have sent for me."

THE CAT AND WHEEL (Catherine Wheel), at the entrance to Castle green, is a quaint-looking hostelry of the 17th century date.

THE KING DAVID, St. Michael's hill, is incorporated with a few of the remains of the nunnery of St. Mary Magdalen. These are of the Perpendicular period, and consist of a winding staircase and two or three doorways.

THE LAMB INN, West street, is a hostelry bearing date 1651. At this inn the fanatic James Naylor slept on his ill-starred visit to Bristol on October 24th, 1656.

THE LAMB, Broadmead, founded in 1643.

THE LLANDOGER, King street, built in 1664.

THE MERMAID, Lewin's mead, was infected with the plague in 1655. It was rebuilt in 1883.

THE RUMMER, High street. As early as 1241 it was called the "Greene Lattis."

THE SARACEN'S HEAD, Temple gate, well accords in designation with the period of the Crusades, when the Knights of the Temple won many such a ghastly trophy from their Paynim enemy. It is one of the hostelries "that was confirmed and authorised" in Bristol in the third year of James I. (1606), but since that time has undergone external change.

THE STAR INN, Cock and Bottle

lane, Castle street, stands upon the site of the Norman keep of the Castle. Daniel Defoe frequented this house.

THE SWAN INN, at the south-east angle of Maryleport street. To this hostelry is a good ornamental barge board of the 15th century; other portions of the structure are of Tudor date.

THE THREE KINGS, Thomas street, licensed in 1606.

THE THREE QUEENS, Thomas street, established about 1640.

Irish League. A local branch of the National League usually meet on Sunday evenings, at the Coach and Horses inn, Broadmead, for the discussion of subjects affecting Irish legislation.

Irish Trade. A large trade is carried on between this port and Ireland, there being several steamers that ply to and fro regularly with passengers and cargoes. (*See* "Steamships.")

Itinerant Societies.

THE BRISTOL SOCIETY, established in 1811, sends laymen gratuitously as preachers into the country towns and villages within a radius of 13 miles of the city. During the year 1882, fifty services were held in 18 out-stations to congregations numbering in the aggregate 1,500 adults. The number of preachers regularly or occasionally engaged is 56, and more than 1,200 children are taught by 140 teachers. The churches number upwards of 500 members, and 83 members were admitted during 1882. About 800 families are weekly supplied with tracts. In many of the stations vigorous Bands of Hope and temperance organisations exist, and in some stations day schools are sustained in connection with the society, and in others night schools are conducted.

THE BAPTIST SOCIETY, connected with the Baptist denomination, is established for the purpose of promoting Sunday schools, preaching the Gospel and distributing religious tracts in the villages contiguous to Bristol. The society is supported by subscriptions and donations. C. Merrick and G. Bradbeer, hon. secs.

Jacob's Wells. Amongst the inhabitants of Bristol during the early and middle ages there must have been a number of those interesting people the Jews, who settled in this locality as early as the reign of William the Conqueror. At Jacob's Wells were baths, which it is believed originally belonged to that sect, and close by was the Jews' acre, or burial ground, on which now stands Queen Elizabeth's hospital. The Theatre formerly stood in Jacob's Wells; the situation was under Clifton hill, immediately outside the city boundary, and just above the site of St. Peter's church. On play nights the gravelled walks of Brandon hill were crowded to watch the entrance of playgoers, whilst from a field behind the theatre, separated from the courtyard by a hedge and low wall, curious people stood for hours in the evening to catch a glimpse of the actors as they passed from one side of the stage to enter on the other.

Kingroad, situated at the mouth of the Avon, is celebrated for its safe anchorage for vessels. It does not appear to have undergone any material change than is shown in the survey made in 1772, except that at the present time it is rather deeper, but considerably less in width.

Kingsdown obtains its name from having belonged to the royal demesne in connection with Bristol castle. It also retains the designation Montacute, or Montague and served in old time as a place for joustings and other martial exercises. This locality was first lighted with oil gas in 1825.

Lacrosse. The Clifton Lacrosse Club was formed in 1883. There are about 60 members, who play on Durdham down. The rules of the club are the same as those of the South of England Association. Subscription, 10/6 per annum. G. Mosely, hon. sec.

Lawford's Gate, at the end of West street, was one of the entrances to the city; it was removed in 1768. At this entrance Henry VII. was received. A gaol now stands on its site. (*See* "Gaols.")

Law Library, Guildhall, Small street. This library formerly belonged to a society called the Bristol Law Library Society, and was founded on the 16th October, 1818. It was incorporated on the 10th February, 1871, with the Bristol Incorporated Law Society. Membership and subscription, solicitors practising in Bristol, £3 13s. 6d., or a contribution of £5 5s. and an annual subscription of £2 12s. 6d. Barristers resident at Bristol may use the library on payment of an annual subscription of £3 3s., or an entrance fee of £5 5s. and a subsequent annual subscription of £2 2s. The Judges of the Superior courts, the Recorder of Bristol and members of the Bar are entitled to the free use of the library during the sittings of their respective courts. The justices of Bristol and their officials have also free access to the library, which contains over 6,000 volumes. J. J. Thomas, librarian.

Law Society, Incorporated. The Council meet the first Monday in each month at the Law Library, Guildhall, Small street. The Council consists of a president, two vice-presidents and 15 ordinary members, three of whom retire by rotation annually, a treasurer and two honorary secretaries.

Lawn Tennis. No game has sprung into prominence with greater rapidity than this, and it bids fair to take as great a hold upon athletes as cricket. It is all in favour of lawn tennis that as few as two can play, whereas in cricket at least eleven each side must be secured for a match, added to which in lawn tennis there is the charm of including ladies in the game. There are numberless private courts in Bristol and Clifton; but of clubs and public courts the following is a list:—

CLIFTON CLUB. Ground, Beaufort road, Clifton; three courts turf, two courts asphalt; members. Lacy Sweet, Pembroke road, Clifton, hon. sec.

CLIFTON WANDERERS' CLUB. Ground, Trelawney place, Cotham; three courts, turf; 100 members. Robert Field, Stuckey's Banking Company, Bristol, hon. sec.

ELMDALE CLUB. Ground, Elmdale road, Lower Cotham Park; one court, asphalt; 20 members. W. Smith, Grovelands, Meridian road, Lower Cotham Park, hon. sec.

The following are public courts:—
VICTORIA ROOMS, CLIFTON. Two courts, asphalt; charge, 6d. per hour per player.
ZOOLOGICAL GARDENS, CLIFTON. Seven courts, turf; charge, 6d. per hour per player.

Lawrence Hill derives its name from a roadside hospital for lepers, dedicated to St. Lawrence.

Lawyers. (*See* "Solicitors.")

Lectures for the People Sunday Afternoons. These lectures are delivered in the Colston hall every Sunday afternoon at three o'clock, with a slight break during the summer months, and are usually well attended. The movement was originated by the congregation at Broadmead (Baptist) chapel; now the services are conducted upon much broader principles. Many of the clergymen of the Established Church and ministers of other denominations take an active part in these services; the result has been a pronounced success. The aim of the lecturers is to give attractive titles to their addresses, so as to make them as popular as possible and within the comprehension of all, and to reach those who do not as a rule attend a place of worship. The talented organist of the Colston Hall Company (G. Riseley) accompanies the hymns and gives a sacred recital on the organ at each service.

Leigh Woods. These sylvan shades cover the cliffs and ravines of the Somersetshire shore of the Avon. From the city the woods can be approached viâ the Suspension bridge and Rownham hill. Nearly underneath the bridge is an entrance to the wood called Nightingale valley (a most sequestered spot), a winding incline leading to the summit of the plateau.

Liberation Society. The Bristol branch of the Anti-State Church Association was formed on May 2nd, 1848, when the late Thos. Waterman was elected treasurer and the late Rev. W. J. Cross secretary. This society was afterwards called "The Society for the Liberation of Religion from State Patronage and Control." The objects of the society are :—The abrogation of all laws which inflict disability or confer privileges on ecclesiastical grounds ; the discontinuance of all payments from the Consolidated fund and Parliamentary grants and compulsory exactions for religious purposes. The society is supported by annual subscriptions or donations of various amounts. Contributors of not less than 10/- a year receive the society's journal, *The Liberator*. Thomas Garner Grundy is the local agent, and he was one of the original promoters of the society. Offices, 76 Colston street.

Libraries.

The CITY FREE LIBRARY, in King street, is the oldest free library in the kingdom, having been founded in 1613. It contains a large number of volumes, many of them being valuable editions of the 15th and 16th centuries, some good MSS., especially a vellum Bible of the 13th century. The chimney-piece is one of Grinling Gibbons' *chefs d'œuvre*. The airy lightness of the flowers and foliage, and the naturalness of the plumage of the birds, carved out of solid oak, are marvellous specimens of the artist's skill. The chimney-piece is valued at upwards of £1,000.

At a public meeting held in the Colston hall on May 13th, 1874, the Mayor (C. J. Thomas) in the chair, the Free Library Act was adopted for Bristol.

The BEDMINSTER, East street, Bedminster, opened on September 29th, 1877, contains over 7,000 volumes.

The CENTRAL, King street, opened October 9th, 1876, contains 28,000 volumes.

The ST. JAMES', King square, opened March 24th, 1877, contains over 10,500 volumes.

The ST. PHILIP'S, Trinity road, was opened July 8th, 1876, and contains over 8,000 volumes.

Each library has news and magazine rooms, and the Central a reference library, and all are open daily (Sundays excepted) from 9 a.m. to 10 p.m.

In 1882 the number of visits paid to the libraries was 1,539,267 adults and 132,816 youths. Before the free lending movement was adopted the average number of persons who attended the library was nine per day.

In addition to the above, there are also large libraries connected with the following institutions:—Museum and Library, Queen's road ; Athenæum, Corn street ; Young Men's Christian Association, St. James' square ; and the Incorporated Law Society, Small street.

Licensed Houses. The number of houses licensed for the sale of intoxicating liquors in the city and county of Bristol, as presented to the magistrates at the Brewster Sessions 1883, was 444 public-houses, 511 beerhouses licensed to sell on the premises, 184 beerhouses licensed to sell off the premises, 75 beerhouses and 7 refreshment houses having also wine licenses.

50 grocers' licenses, making a total of 1,280 houses licensed for the sale of intoxicating liquors, being a decrease of 70 in comparison with the previous year. In January, 1881, a public-house census was taken between 7 and 11 p.m., with the following results of those seen to enter public-houses: Men, 54,074; women, 36,803; children, 13,145; total, 104,022.

Licensed Victuallers' Associations.

BEER AND WINE TRADE PROTECTION AND BENEVOLENT ASSOCIATION (for Bristol and the District). The 47th quarterly meeting was held on the 21st February, 1883. S. Wigens, The Bell, Kingsdown, secretary.

LAWFORD'S GATE DISTRICT LICENSED VICTUALLERS' AND BEER RETAILERS' PROTECTION SOCIETY. Founded in November, 1882. Meetings held quarterly. Daniel Sykes, Redcliff brewery, president.

LICENSED VICTUALLERS' PROTECTION ASSOCIATION AND BENEVOLENT FUND. The 31st annual meeting of this society was held 9th January, 1883, when it was reported that it was in a good position, both financially and numerically. It is established for the defence of trade interests, and for assisting widows and families of deceased publicans. C. Randall, secretary.

Lifeboat Institution,

The Royal National, is, as declared in its title and in its charter of incorporation, to afford assistance to shipwrecked persons around the coasts of the United Kingdom. It was founded in 1824. The following is a list of stations on the English coast of the Bristol Channel:—

Station.	Name of Boat.	When Stationed.
Appledore	Hope	1862
"	Mary Ann	1875
Braunton	Robert and Catherine	1881
Burnham	Cheltenham	1866
Clovelly	Graham Hughes	1881
Ilfracombe	Broadwater	1866
Lynmouth	Henry	1869
Morte Bay	Grace Woodbury	1871
Watchet	Joseph Lomes	1875
Weston-s.-Mare	William J. Holt	1882

The Bristol Histrionic Club give occasionally dramatic performances in aid of their lifeboat, the *Bristol and Clifton*, presented to the institution in 1868. Mark Whitwill is the local chairman of the society; M. Bryan, hon. sec.

Literature Society,

Pure. The number of monthly periodicals in connection with this society sold in Bristol in 1882 was 138,248, being 2,988 less than in the preceding year. Rev. Canon Girdlestone, M.A., Olveston, hon. sec.

Lloyd's Registry of British and Foreign Shipping.

The member on the committee for Bristol, nominated by the Bristol Chamber of Commerce, is J. Evans, Dunlop buildings, Baldwin street, who annually presents a valuable report to the chamber on the subject of shipping and its associations. Surveyor, H. M. Williams, Queen square.

Loan Monies. (*See* "Almshouses" and "Charity Trustees.")

Local Boards.

HORFIELD meet at the Board room, Berkeley road, Bishopston, monthly. Mark Butt, chairman.

STAPLETON meet at the Barton Regis workhouse, Eastville. The Board consists of 12 members. Chairman, John Yalland; surveyor and inspector, J. Hoddell; medical officer, Dr. Davies; clerk, F. Rawle.

ST. GEORGE'S meet at the Parochial offices, Cloud's hill, St. George's. The Board consists of 15 members. Chairman, Wm. Butler; surveyor, Wm. Cloutman; medical officer, Dr. J. A. Barton; clerk, Edwin Parry.

Locks.

In 1804 Mr. Jessop's scheme was commenced. It comprised a dam across the Avon at Totterdown, the waters of which were carried from thence through the Bedminster meadows as far as the Redcliff house, where another dam was thrown across the bend of the Avon that had flowed through the city. By this scheme the area was greatly enlarged, upwards of 80 acres being floated, and the Frome and the Avon from Totterdown lock to Rownham were made into one continuous float. The waste water was supplied by the Frome and by a feeder cut from Totterdown to Netham, where an overfall dam was thrown across the Avon in order to keep up a steady head of water. Provision was also made for land floods by a sluice between the feeder and the Avon. (See "Docks.")

Lord High Steward.

The first appointment was in 1548, when the Duke of Somerset possessed that dignity. The office has always been filled by men of high position. Of its duties and emoluments no mention is made except that it was held by Oliver Cromwell in 1551, for which it is said he received as an acknowledgment £5, with a pipe of Canary and half a tun of Gascoigne wine. His Grace the Duke of Beaufort was appointed High Steward of Bristol in 1836. He had a majority of 16 over Lord Seagrave, the Lord-Lieutenant, who was also nominated. On March 16th, 1854, Henry Somerset, eighth Duke of Beaufort, was inaugurated as the Lord High Steward. The office is purely an honorary title.

Lord's Day Observance

Society. The Bristol and Clifton branch for furthering the observance of Sunday as a day of rest for all classes of society. Lieut.-Col. Hall, 23 Hanbury road, Clifton, treasurer.

Lunatic Asylums.

BRISLINGTON HOUSE ASYLUM was founded by Dr. Edward Long Fox about the year 1806. Every care for the alleviation of the disorders of the patients and for their comfort is studied at this institution.

NORTHWOODS HOUSE, Winterbourne, situated on the old road from Bristol to Gloucester, a little beyond Frenchay, was erected by the late Dr. H. H. Fox expressly for the various forms of mental infirmity occurring to ladies and gentlemen of the upper and middle classes, and early in 1875 was purchased by Dr. R. Eager and T. G. Seymour, by whom it is now managed. The house stands in a commanding position in the centre of more than 50 acres of plantations and pleasure grounds, laid out to provide for outdoor amusement, with more than a mile of pleasure walks, in addition to which a colonnade extending the whole length of the south side of the building secures the means of exercise in all weathers. The management of the house is the same system of medical care and treatment which has proved so successful in public institutions for the insane. The proprietors reside on the premises, thus affording to the inmates the advantages of constant supervision as well as the associations of home life. As far as possible the patients attend the parish church, and a chaplain being attached to the establishment religious services are regularly performed.

THE CITY AND COUNTY OF BRISTOL LUNATIC ASYLUM, Stapleton, built at the cost of the Corporation, and managed by a committee of the Town Council, of which F. Terrell, J.P., is the chairman, and J. F. Williams the clerk, was opened on the 26th February, 1861, and cost, including 24 acres of land, £30,000, when it was intended to accommodate 200 patients and the necessary officers and servants. The number accommodated at the present time is 430, and the asylum is now full. Plans are being prepared to increase the accommodation to 700. The patients are of the pauper class, but when there is room to spare private patients are admitted. The staff is as follows :—Medical superintendent, George Thompson, M.D. ; assistant medical officer, Harry A. Benham, M.D. ; chaplain, Rev. James Fountaine, M.A. ; clerk and steward, John Thompson. In the grounds of the asylum is a handsome chapel, which was opened on Aug. 14, 1881.

Macadamised Roads

were first made in Bristol. The system was called after its inventor, Mr. John Loudon McAdam, who was, in 1825, the general surveyor of roads in the Bristol district. The system is of making and repairing roads by using stone broken into fragments, and then laid upon the road, to be worked into solidity by the traffic. This system is now adopted all over the country. He was rewarded by a Government grant of £10,000, but declined the honour of knighthood, which was awarded to his son.

Magistrates.

On February 15th, 1836, twenty-four gentlemen were, after great discussion, nominated as magistrates for the city, twelve from each party. The names were submitted to the Government, and twelve Whigs and six Tories were appointed. There was a heated debate in Parliament, objections being raised against certain gentlemen. The magistracy of the city is now administered by about forty-seven acting justices of the peace (including the Mayor for the time being, who is the chief magistrate), and who are appointed by the Lord Chancellor from time to time on the recommendation of persons locally connected. The justices of the Visiting Committee of the Gaol are five in number, and there are seven licensing justices. The following is a list of magistrates:—

The Right Worshipful the Mayor, Mansion house, Clifton down.
Michael Castle, College road South, Clifton.
C. J. Thomas, Drayton lodge, Durdham park.
Sholto Vere Hare, Knole park, Almondsbury.
John Hare, Litfield place, Clifton down.
W. Terrell, Southmead, Westbury-on-Trym.
Thomas Canning, Bristol.
E. S. Robinson, Sneyd park.
G. R. Woodward, Cornwallis grove, Clifton.
Frederick Terrell, Pembroke road, Clifton.
W. H. Harford, Barley wood, Wrington.
W. H. Wills, M.P., Blagdon.
Herbert Thomas, Ivor house, Durdham park.
James Godwin, Stoke Bishop.
Chris. Godwin, Avon house, Stoke Bishop.
George Wills, 3 Worcester villas, Clifton.
William Pethick, Woodside, Stoke Bishop.
Charles Nash, 3 Oakfield road, Clifton.
W. P. Baker, Broomwell house, Brislington.
William Fuidge, 11 Gloucester row, Clifton.
W. Hathway, Chescombe lodge, Durdham down.
W. A. F. Powell, Norland house, Clifton down.
Mark Whitwill, Redland house, Redland.
G. W. Edwards, 2 Sea Wall villas, Sneyd park.
J. A. Jones, Vale house, Pembroke road.
F. F. Fox, Yate house, Chipping Sodbury.
F. J. Fry, Sermione, 104 Pembroke road.
George H. Leonard, 9 Apsley road, Clifton.
J. C. Wall, Redland lodge, Durdham park.
S. Wills, Keewaydin, 28 Victoria square.
Charles Hill, Clevedon hall, Clevedon.
Wm. Smith, Sundon house, Clifton down.
W. H. Budgett, Stoke house, Stoke Bishop.
H. O. Wills, Redland knoll.
Samuel Derham, Henleaze park.
P. F. Sparks Evans, Trinmore, Clifton down.
John Lysaght, Stoke Bishop.
Samuel Day Wills, 11 Upper Belgrave road.
John W. Hall, Callander house, Clifton hill.
C. Townsend, Avenue house, Cotham park.
C. B. Hare, Clarence house, Clifton park.
J. F. Lucas, Summerlands, 111 Pembroke rd.
William Spark, Apsley road.
David Macliver, 67 Pembroke road.
T. Wedmore, Druids house, Stoke Bishop.

Magistrates' Office,

Bridewell street. The façade is of Box stone in the classic Greek type. A carved frieze of red Mansfield stone is introduced with good effect in prominent positions. On the face of the porch the symbolical panellings comprise a torch representing the lamp of truth, with the scales and sword of justice, the city arms above, and surmounted with the gigantic statue of justice (in Portland stone). Entering the vestibule on the right are the magistrates' clerk's offices and ante-room. The general offices, 34 feet by 17 feet, lie immediately on the left. A lobby is placed on the right of the main corridor, which runs through to the back or public entrance in Silver street. This waiting hall is elaborately paved with mosaic tiles, having the city arms on the central circle, while the walls are broken up by a series of arches filled in with wrought iron grille work. Rooms for witnesses, solicitors, &c., lie behind. Opening out of the corridor are the courts proper. The larger of these measures nearly 40 feet by 27 feet, with a height of 28 feet. Light is obtained from three large windows high up in the side walls, and in the ornamental coved and panelled ceiling is a gas sunlight. The justices' bench, raised above the floor, has a high pilastered and panelled dado at the back—the civic arms being carved behind the chairman's seat—continued at a lower level all round the court. Doors at each end of the bench communicate with the magistrates' retiring rooms. The clerk's desk is fixed in front of the chairman, the dock occupies the centre of the court, and the solicitors have a table between those points. The witness box is located on the right of the justices, and on the opposite side are the reporters' seats. Desks for the superintendent of police and other functionaries fill up the body of the court, and the public gallery affords accommodation for more than fifty persons.

The Second Court, planned on similar principles, but reduced dimensions, has an oblong skylight. The principal retiring room for the justices is about 19 feet square, and is lighted by an ornamental glass lantern. The second retiring room has much the same features. The furniture and fittings, designed to correspond with the lines of construction, consist of American walnut in the more important chambers and pitch pine in the subordinate departments. In the basement of the building are large lock-up places of detention capable of holding a couple of hundred prisoners, warders' rooms, and waiting rooms for the friends of prisoners. Prisoners at the divisional police stations or under remand at the Gaol are conveyed by van to the Central police station yard, there being communication from thence to the cells of the magistrates' courts, so that the "rogues' march" through the streets is now a thing of the past. The courts sit daily for the transaction of public business.

Mansion House. The original Mansion house, or the official palace of the city sovereign, was on the north side of Queen square, near the Custom house, but was destroyed by fire during the riots on the 30th October, 1831 (*see* "Riots"), when the rioters forced the wine cellars, in which were 400 dozen of choice wines, threw out into the square the furniture, china, glass, &c., distributed the liquor with unsparing hands, and soon the whole area became a scene of drunken revelry, wherein intoxicants led men hitherto respectable to join the criminal and abandoned classes in arson and robbery. From that period until 1874 the city was without an official residence for its Mayors. In that year Alderman Proctor presented to the city "Elmdale," as a Mansion house for the official residence of the Mayors of Bristol. The property was valued at the time of presentation at upwards of £16,000. It is situated at the junction of Canynges' road with Clifton down, near the western end of Limetree promenade. It has magnificently fitted reception and banqueting rooms for the Judges, the Judges' associates and the Mayor, also a spacious billiard-room, all of good proportions, elegantly furnished and chastely decorated. Shields of the arms of Bristol ancient worthies suitably adorn its entrance hall, Indian and Turkey carpets, silk hangings of the richest dye, easy lounges, &c. The furniture of the banqueting hall is of solid Riga oak, and that of the reception-room of oak and gold inlaid with walnut. Jacobian in style. In one of the rooms is a unique Belgian cabinet filled with rare old Bristol china, the gift of Robert Lang. The expenses in connection with the Mansion house, exclusive of the Mayor's salary (£700), for the year ending the 25th March, 1883, amounted to £842 9s. 9d.

Manufactures.

Amongst the industries carried on in Bristol, the following comprise the principal (*see* "Trades") :—

AGRICULTURAL IMPLEMENTS. Surrounded as the city is by the agricultural districts of Gloucestershire, Somersetshire, Monmouthshire and Wiltshire, the manufacture of farming implements of all descriptions is carried on very extensively. The Bristol Wagon Works Company is the principal firm.

ALKALI. The Netham Chemical Company Limited, St. George's, employ between 400 and 500 men. They manufacture alkali, caustic soda, soda crystals, bleaching powder, sulphuric and muriatic acids, muriate of soda and sal ammoniac.

BED AND MATTRESS. A large home, colonial and export trade is carried on in upholstering in all its branches. The following are the leading firms: Cordeux, Sons and Co., St. James' barton; Johnston and Co., Quay street; Laverton and Co., Maryleport street; Maggs and Co., St. Augustine's parade; Trapnell and Gane, College green.

BEER. The largest and oldest brewery in the city is George and Co.'s old porter brewery, Bath street. There are a number of other houses that can turn out over 4,000 gallons of beer per day. The principal brewers are :—W. J. Rogers, Old Market street; Charles Garton and Co., Lawrence hill; James and Pierce, Bedminster; J. and T. Usher and Co., Horfield road; Sykes and Co., Redcliff street; Bishop and Butt, Redcliff mead; Bowley and Bristow, St. Paul's; Gibbings Brothers, St. Michael's; Hardwick & Co. Limited, Ashton gate; Harvey and Co., Stokes croft; J. H. Lockley and Son, Lewin's mead.

BOOTS AND SHOES. A few years ago these were not deemed worthy of classification, but were included under the head of shoemakers. In 1862 the number of manufactories was only six; this number has now quintupled, and they furnish employment for considerably over 5,000 hands, and it has become one of the staple manufactures of the West. Whilst the speciality of Northampton is for men's, Stafford and Leicester for women's, and Norwich for children's shoes, Bristol combines the whole. Bristol has carried off the medals at most exhibitions for excellence of workmanship. One of the oldest establishments in the city is that of Derham Brothers, which was established at Wrington in 1843, with a branch in this city. The trade having made great headway, they removed entirely to Brunswick square in 1854. The premises soon becoming too small, they removed to those now occupied by Gardiner and Sons, Nelson street, and in 1865 made their final move to the spacious and imposing buildings in Barton street, St. James', which are 150 feet long, 40 feet broad and seven stories high, and where they keep 2,000 persons employed, executing as many as 400 to 500 orders per week, which are exported to all parts of the globe. In 1870 the firm opened a branch at Northampton, where is produced for the most part heavy work, *i.e.*, men's boots, and in the Bristol house the lighter kinds of boots, principally medium and best class, are manufactured. A large number of workpeople are employed outside the factory, who return in due course the boots and shoes in a finished state. In the factory the piecework system almost exclusively prevails, and the most perfect mechanical aids are brought into requisition. Waterman and Co., another large factory, was established about 1800. Upwards of 100,000 pairs of boots and shoes are stored in the warehouse, and from 200 to 300 hands employed. The other principal houses in the trade consist of Brightman Brothers, Lewin's mead west; Cridland and Rose, Dighton street; James Smith and Sons, King's square, established 1859; H. Steadman and Co., Castle green; Whiting, Webb and Co., Portland square.

BOTTLES. Since 1853 all the factories engaged in this branch of industry have merged into one house, that of Messrs. Powell and Ricketts, of the Phœnix works, St. Philip's. Their output equals very nearly that of the whole glass manufactories of the 18th century.

BRASS. Brass was first made in England at Baptist mills, Bristol. The works were afterwards removed to Hanham and Keynsham. There are now three important manufactories in the city, viz., Adlam and Sons, Elbroad street; Llewellins and James, Castle green, established 1800; Bush and De Soyres, Cheese lane.

BRUSH, &c. There is little doubt but that the industry of brushmaking has formed a part of the trade of the city for considerably over a century. The burgesses who followed the occupation and voted at the election in 1734 were only nine in number, but at the contest in 1781 no less than 58 brushmakers exercised the suffrage. There are now several large houses in the city, who are also mop, mat and sieve manufacturers, prominent amongst whom are Greenslade and Co., Thomas street, founded in 1820, where upwards of 200 men are employed and 3,000 brushes of different kinds made daily; E. Brison and Co., Peter street; and W. H. Vowles, Castle street.

CABINET WORKS. There are several houses in the city of high repute, and some of them are the largest in England. Steam power is extensively used for turning, planing, moulding, veneering, mortising, carving, &c. Furniture suited to every grade of domicile from the humble cottage to the stately mansion is made, and these establishments give employment to several thousand hands. The works of many of the houses can be inspected on application. Several firms have carried off the highest awards at various exhibitions. The large import of foreign timbers, particularly those kinds used in the manufacture of household appliances, has been and still is one of the largest in England, and the best description of furniture is produced at a much less cost than in London and many other large manufacturing cities. The consequence is that not only is there a large retail trade done in the city, but a very extensive wholesale trade, considerable quantities being sent to all parts of the United Kingdom, especially the North of England, in addition to which a brisk trade is done with India, Africa and Australia. The largest makers are Uriah Alsop, Broadmead; Laverton and Co., Maryleport street; Smith and Co., St. Augustine's parade; Trapnell and Gane, College green.

CARRIAGES. This trade ranks as an important industry in Bristol, and has for a couple of centuries been noted for the excellence of its workmanship. The principal manufacturers are John Fuller and Co., St. George's road; T. and J. Perry, Stokes croft; J. Barton and Sons, Quay head; Rogers and Co. Limited, College place, established in 1798. These firms turn out annually for home and exportation a large number of handsome and well-built broughams, Victorias, wagonettes, Stanhopes, shooting phætons, dog carts, gigs, Whitechapel carts, Irish cars, &c. Each of the above manufactories have spacious salerooms.

CHINA. The china factory, which was in Castle green, was closed in 1777. The celebrated Bristol china, for which such fabulous prices are now given, was manufactured by Champion and others at the above works.

CIGARS. The manufacture of cigars is carried on extensively in Bristol by three houses, viz., Hudden and Co., Victoria street; W. D. and H. O. Wills, Redcliff street; and D. Glass and Co., Clare street.

CLOTHING, WHOLESALE. Considerable activity is shown in this department of trade in Bristol. Orders flow in from all parts of the world, and the old city has won a good reputation for quality. The following constitute the principal wholesale houses:—Clarke and Co., Colston street; Simpson and Murray, Victoria street; Solomon Brothers, Bridge street; Taylor, Tucker and Co., Broadmead; R. Todd and Co., Tailors' court, Broad street; D. H. Walsh and Co., Quay street; Wathen, Gardiner and Co., Broad street; C. Wills and Co., Victoria street.

COCOA AND CHOCOLATE. The world-renowned business of J. S. Fry and Sons, Union street, was commenced as far back as 1728 by Walter Churchman, in Narrow Wine street. His patents were subsequently purchased by Joseph Fry, who may be strictly regarded as the founder of the firm. He dying in 1787, the business passed into the hands of Mrs. Anna Fry, who carried it on in conjunction with her son, J. S. Fry. This gentleman ultimately became head of the firm, and successfully managed the business for a considerable period with his three sons, Joseph, Francis and Richard, of whom Francis Fry is the only survivor. At the present time the business is in the hands of the sons of Francis and Joseph Fry, who are assisted by several of the junior members of the family. The factory was removed from Narrow Wine street to Union street soon after it came into the possession of Joseph Fry, and here was erected by J. S. Fry one of the earliest steam engines used for manufacturing purposes in Bristol. The chocolate which was made found an extensive and ready sale in London and all the principal towns of the country. About the year 1840 it was found necessary, from the rapid spread of the business, to increase the manufacturing premises. This was done, and all the best appliances of the day provided. Two decades had scarcely passed away when, in 1860, the builder's art was again called into requisition, and further additions were made to meet the growing wants of the business, the latest addition being the splendid factory at the bottom of the Pithay and extending into Nelson street, covering an enormous area of ground. This was built in 1878. The gigantic chimney to this building, 200 feet in height, can be seen from very nearly all parts of the city. The firm have now three main factories, with separate steam power of the most improved description in each. Then there are two auxiliary factories for the manufacture of the boxes and packing cases and of canisters. The factories are connected by bridges. Cocoa in the raw state is obtained principally from South America (North and West). The most noted kinds are produced in Venezuela, the capital of which— Caracas—gives the name to a choice description of cocoa made by Messrs. Fry. Of the West India Islands, Trinidad and Grenada ship the largest quantities, but cocoa is grown also in St. Lucia, Dominica and Jamaica. Very large quantities are grown in Equador and Brazil. An inferior kind is produced in Hayti, and recently the cultivation of the cocoa plant has been introduced with success into Ceylon. Over 1,100 hands are employed, about half being girls and women. The firm endeavour to provide as far as possible for the spiritual and material well-being of their employés; every morning the workpeople assemble to hear the Scriptures read. Prize medals have been awarded to the firm by the Exhibitions of London 1851, New York 1853, Paris 1855, London 1862, Dublin 1865, Paris 1867, Paris 1870, Moscow and Vienna 1873, Paris 1878, Sydney 1880, Melbourne 1881, Christchurch, N.Z., 1882, Diploma of Honour (highest award), Amsterdam, 1883.

CONFECTIONERY. The increase in this trade has of late been rapid in Bristol. The two leading wholesale houses are Sanders and Ludlow, Redcliff street, and Stanton and Champion, Lewin's mead. The latter, in 1869, only employed 20 hands, and now there are over 300, and 20 tons of confectionery are made now to every ton made then. The machinery in use by this firm is very extensive.

MAN   DICTIONARY OF BRISTOL.   **MAN**

CORRUGATED IRON. The works of J. Lysaght and Co. Limited, Silverthorne lane, are the largest in Enland, occupying about 3½ acres of ground. On one side are the Great Western and Midland railways, and on the other is the Feeder, so that there is the advantage of both rail and river communication. Some three or four years ago the chief shareholder of these works acquired the Swan Garden works at Wolverhampton, and the two works are now one concern. All the iron used in St. Philip's is manufactured at Wolverhampton, and brought from thence in barges up to the riverside front of the establishment in St. Philip's. In the course of a year thousands of tons of iron are sent. The galvanising shop is 150 feet long, 120 feet wide and 70 feet high, and the roof is supported by four massive Bath stone pillars. About 400 men are engaged. Working day and night is the rule of this busy hive, and as much as 2,000 yards of netting a day can be turned out. In February, 1883, the firm erected separate works from their galvanising establishment on St. Philip's marsh for the making of spelter. The proprietors may justly be proud of their works and workpeople. Some of the best skilled workmen in the country are employed by them, and a more complete manufactory it would be impossible to imagine. The firm do not forget the comforts of their workpeople, and for their benefit they have provided a large hall, library and kitchen, where a cook is kept. In this kitchen the workpeople can have their meals cooked, special apartments being provided for the women employed in the works. Pattern-shops, drawing offices and clerks' offices (the latter being recently rebuilt) complete the principal features of interest on these large premises. Everything in connection with the business is done under personal supervision, and this fact no doubt is to a large extent the secret of the great success of the firm. The works are lighted by the electric light. There are two other manufactories in the city, also a number of millwrights, boilermakers and general engineers.

CORSETS AND STAYS. This is a branch of industry which, from a small beginning, has risen to the dignity of a staple trade. In 1853 half-a-dozen sewing machines were introduced to the stitching of the heavy makes. These machines were clumsy, and therefore did not find much favour with the trade. Skilled mechanics, however, by the constant improvement of the old and the invention of new machines, have revolutionised the business, so that there are now at least 1,000 machines and some 2,500 hands employed, and Bristol turns out more of this work annually, both for export and home trade, than any other town in the kingdom. The chief houses are:— Young and Neilson, Portland square, and Chappell and Allen, Weare street.

COTTON. The Great Western Cotton Company Limited, Barton hill, are the only works of the kind in the West of England, and were established in 1837. The manufacture is principally for the East India and China markets. The main spinning mill is six stories high, and, with the weaving sheds and outbuildings, covers seven acres of ground. Altogether there are nearly 100,000 spindles and 1,600 looms constantly at work. The building is supposed to be fire-proof. All the doors are of iron, and the floors are either of iron or some other fire-proof material. The metal soon gets warm by the action of the machinery, and we suppose this is the reason why so many of the employés, especially the females, work on their naked feet. Over 1,600 hands are constantly employed, and fully 1,200 of these are women and girls. Nearly all are paid by piecework. In connection with the works are well-appointed shops for the joiners and mechanics, and an efficient staff is kept up in each department. The entire repairs and alterations required in the mill are executed on the premises. The whole of the cotton used by the company is brought from America, shipped at Liverpool, and transmitted by water to Bristol. The cotton is packed in bales compressed by hydraulic power, bound with hoop-iron bands. Each bale weighs about 450℔, and the average consumption is about 200 bales per week. The spinning mill contains 300 windows, and the immense pile of buildings has several powerful steam engines.

CREOSOTED TIMBER. The firm of R. and R. Bayly, Silverthorne lane, have extensive premises, where they cut and pickle timber for Brunel's longitudinal principle on railways.

DISTILLING is carried on somewhat extensively. The Bristol Spirit Distilling Co. Limited, St. Philip's, was established in 1780, and converted into a company in 1863. W. Butler and Co., St. Philip's and Crew's hole, are tar and resin distillers, and they employ a large number of hands.

ENGINE WORKS. The Avonside Engine works, unfortunately for Bristol, are in the market, though still in operation. The works are most advantageously placed, and are intersected with lines of railway, communicating on the one hand with the Midland system, and having access to the Great Western and South Western railways, and on the other hand with a wharf on the Floating harbour, thus affording every facility for the supply and removal of goods by either transit. The buildings are extensive, of good elevation and of a substantial character, and comprise: Iron foundry, smiths' shop, forge and steam hammer shop, boiler-makers' shop, tender and tank shops, boiler-makers' machine shop, marine engine and frame and tender erecting shop, boring mill, with fitting shop over; grinding houses, locomotive erecting and packing shop, brass foundry and brass finishing shop, coppersmiths' shop, carpenters' and pattern-makers' shops and lofts, general stores; works, drawing and general offices, and eleven dwelling-houses. The various shops are fitted with costly tools and machinery, and are capable of turning out 75 locomotives per annum, besides marine engines and the general engineering and iron foundry business.

FLOORCLOTH, &c. The only floor-cloth manufactory in the city is that of John Hare and Co., Temple gate. The original founder of the firm was John Hare, the great grandfather of the present proprietors. John Hare devoted himself to the arts, and made his way to Bristol. When he arrived there, it is said, he lay down in a garden and went to sleep. On awakening he was so struck with the beauty of the place that he remarked, "If ever I live to be a rich man I should like to build myself a house here." He became a rich man, and built a house near, but not a house for himself; he erected Zion chapel, Bedminster, to show his thanks to God for the good fortune that had attended him, and he was buried there in 1839, though his remains were afterwards removed to Arno's vale cemetery. In 1820 the business passed into the hands of his sons, Charles Hare and Sir John Hare. In 1840 these were succeeded by Chas., John and Sholto V. Hare. The first-named partner died in 1855, and in 1866 the other two retired. Many old firms have been merged into the present one. In 1791 Withers and Westcott transferred their business to J. Hare and Co., who in 1848 purchased the extensive white lead works and rolling mills of T. H. and H. Riddle, and in 1862 the firm acquired the floorcloth factory in St. Philip's marsh. Although of late years there have been many inventions which have for certain purposes superseded oilcloth, it is a striking feature, and very creditable to the Bristol make, that large shipments are annually made to America. There are about 15 acres of land now occupied by the firm in carrying on their business, and this includes the space covered by their petroleum cellars in Arno's vale, their Albert floorcloth factory and flax mills, situated in St. Philip's marsh; their commodious white lead works and lead rolling mills in St. Philip's; their oil and colour works, covering over three acres of land at Bath bridge; and next the head office and floorcloth works, immediately facing the Great Western railway station. These various works, which are separated partly on account of the danger of fire, and because it would be extremely difficult to obtain a site in the city of such large acreage as would be required for the whole works, are all essential more or less to the manufacture of floorcloth. It might be interesting to note that some years ago, at the close of the Crimean war, the Sultan of Turkey instructed J. Hare and Co. to prepare for him a series of very large landscape floorcloths, each one containing views of places in Europe of well-known beauty. Two, however, of the most effective of these series contained in the centre a beautiful drawing of the harbour and fortifications of Sebastopol, and the other the Palace of Sweet Waters in the Bosphorus. The proprietors are ever ready to allow persons visiting the city or residing in the neighbourhood to go through the works, and on several occasions have thrown their works open to scientific and other societies which have visited Bristol, who derived considerable pleasure from the run over them. The firm employ between 300 and 400 hands.

FLOUR. The flour trade is carried on extensively. There are three large mills driven by powerful machinery, one of which employs over 150 men, who turn out about 4,000 sacks a week. The following are the principal firms:—William Baker and Sons, Redcliff back; Grace Brothers, Welsh back; A. D. Morton and Son, Temple gate.

HATS. This important industry is a growing one. At present there are about twelve wholesale manufacturers in full operation. The trade has passed through three or four years of great depression, but the year 1882 proved one of steady advancement, and 1883 has exhibited marked signs of further improvement, the home trade showing great elasticity and the export trade much activity. Some houses have never been so full of orders as in 1883. The following are the leading wholesale houses:—Betty Brothers, Victoria street; H. D. Carver and Son, Castle green; T. Glass and Co., Castle green; Howes Brothers, Newfoundland road; Lewis F. Marsh and Co., Castle green; H. Simmons, St. James' barton; Stabbins and Tyler, Castle green.

IRON ROLLING MILLS. At present there are three in Bristol, viz:—Bush and De Soyres, Cheese lane; Joseph Tinn, Ashton Rolling Mills; George Tinn, Silverthorne lane. The Bristol Iron Foundry was established in 1764. Chilled rolls, now so extensively used, were first made here.

JOINERY is brought to a fine pitch of perfection, there being extensive machinery for executing everything in connection therewith. Brock and Bruce's works, Albert road, St. Philip's, are probably the largest, this firm supplying a large portion of the West of England and South Wales with joinery work, together with many specialities of seating and fittings of churches and chapels.

LEAD AND COLOUR. There are five firms in the city for lead smelting and desilvering, viz.:—Charles Hare and Co., Avon street; Panther Lead Company Limited, Avon street, established 1st January, 1857; Capper Pass and Son, Bedminster; Sheldon, Bush and Co., Cheese lane; S. Wills and Co., Castle green, established about 1820. (See "Relics," sub-heading, "Shot Tower.")

LITHOGRAPHY FOR ALMANACS. The demand for coloured almanacs has grown to an enormous extent, and a natural consequence is that as the demand increases so does the competition among producers. Each firm striving to produce the most artistic work, the specimens have now reached perfection as near as possible, and the Bristol houses can hold their own with any others in the kingdom. Some idea of the growth of the trade in almanacs and pictorial advertisements may be gathered from the fact that one Bristol house in 1866 printed 32,000, whilst in 1882 the same firm turned out the enormous number of 685,000 coloured almanacs at an average cost of about 6d. each. The leading firms are:—E. S. and A. Robinson and Co., who employ over 250 hands; J. Lavars, Broad street; W. Bennett, John street; Mardon, Son and Hall, Milk street.

MANURE. The following local houses are noted for their specialities, and command an extensive business:—Avon Manure Company, St. Philip's marsh; Bryant and Co., St. Philip's marsh; Lockyer and Sons, St. Philip's marsh; Norrington, Hingston and Co., Crew's hole, St. George's; H. and T. Proctor, Prewett street, Cathay, established 1812; J. Robinson, Bathurst wharf; J. R. Turner, St. Philip's marsh.

MINERAL WATERS. The manufacture of mineral waters is one of the most prosperous in the city, and as new beverages are continually being introduced to meet the increasing demand for temperance drinks, its growth has been very rapid. The highest awards for mineral waters at the leading exhibitions have been granted to Bristol houses for their productions. The following are the principal manufacturers:—W. Summers and Co., Milk street and Bridge street; Carter and Co., Wilder street; Schweppe and Co., Queen Charlotte street; Brooks and Co., Captain Carey's lane.

OPTICAL WORKS. The year 1762 saw the commencement of the manufacture of optical instruments in this city. For a considerable number of years the manufacture of scientific instruments was carried on in Clare street by J. King, also by his son, T. D. King, who succeeded in obtaining honorable mention and medal at the London Exhibition of 1851. The business was then removed to St. Augustine's parade, and about the year 1853, on his retirement, it was taken on by the two senior hands, H. Husbands and W. Clarke, in whose names it was conducted and steadily increased until 1870, when W. Clarke withdrew. It has since been continued by H. Husbands, who, with the assistance of his sons, has still extended it, and it is still the largest works in the West of England and South Wales. In 1880 the first consignment of goods by the present proprietor was prepared and forwarded to the Melbourne Exhibition, and received the only gold medal awarded to the British court for scientific instruments, and thereupon a branch business was established at Queen street, Melbourne. The firm have also taken another first award for photographic apparatus at the Dundee Exhibition. In the spectacle department the most recent improvements are adopted for ascertaining the defects of vision and correcting imperfect sight, and spectacles are largely manufactured on the premises. M. W. Dunscombe, St. Augustine's parade, has been for several years the successor to J. Braham, as an optician.

ORGAN BUILDING has never developed so much as within the past twenty years. Vowles and Co., St. James' square, are noted for their manufacture, and nearly fifty hands are employed by the firm. Early in the present century the firm of Brice and R. Seede, organ builders, existed in Bristol, and in 1814 J. Smith, the founder of Vowles and Co.'s manufactory, carried on business at 69 Castle street. He was then the only organ builder in Bristol, and in after years reconstructed many of the instruments made by the Seede family. Specimens of the work of the latter still exist in St. Paul's, Portland square, St. Peter's (City),

St. Joseph's hall, Trenchard street, and in the Masonic hall, Park street. This latter organ is about 120 years old. J. Smith built the organs in the chapel of the Countess of Huntingdon, Lodge street, in St. Nicholas' church, in the Moravian chapel, and in the Bath abbey (all since rebuilt in accordance with modern requirements). For several years after the Vowles' family succeeded to the old concern it was continued in Castle street, and twenty years ago removed to St. James' square. The present firm have built or rebuilt nearly all the organs in the city (including that in Redcliff church and that at the Grammar school), have erected instruments in about fifty churches in the vicinity of Bristol, and have done considerable work in all the counties of the kingdom and abroad.

PAPER BAGS. The manufacture of these articles finds employment for a large number of women and girls. The output of machine and hand-made bags from one firm alone (that of E. S. and A. Robinson and Co.) is over one million and three-quarters per week, and for the sake of despatch in the execution of orders over 120 tons of sugar bags and ten millions of thin bags are always kept in stock. The other local makers are :—C. T. Jefferies and Sons, Redcliff street; Mardon, Son and Hall, Milk street; Stephens and Hookins, Narrow Wine street.

PAPER HANGINGS. The manufacture of paper hangings is one of comparatively recent date. In the days of William III. some fair attempts were made to decorate rooms with designs on paper, but the size of the design was limited to the sizes of the sheets of paper then made. Later on this was somewhat improved by the pasting together of the sheets, forming necessary lengths of uniform width, and printing upon these in one or more colours. This cumbrous mode rendered production costly, which was increased by the Government duty which had to be paid upon each sheet, the same being stamped in proof of payment. Under these circumstances it is not surprising that the one or two factories existing in Bristol in the early part of the present century should have languished and ultimately expired. The introduction of papers made in continuous lengths and removal of the stamp duty caused a fresh departure in the trade, and about 1843 Cotterell Brothers (now of Clare street) laid down plant and commenced the manufacture of paper hangings in extensive premises in Broadmead. This firm started the work on the French method of block printing, the pattern intended to be produced being previously carved on square blocks of pear wood, the fine lines, edgings, &c., being formed with copper, a different block with a separate portion of the pattern being required for each different tint placed upon the paper. These artistic productions being supplied at a moderate price, immediately created a demand which has from then to the present time continued to increase, and the trade has so grown from the factory above-mentioned that Bristol is now recognised as one of the chief seats of the paper hanging trade in the kingdom. Of course in these days of steam and electricity block printing by hand has to a large extent been superseded by machinery. The firm of Cotterell Brothers is so widely known that buyers in the Colonies and India receive their patterns and goods with appreciation. Their premises are in Clare street, Baldwin street, and Marsh street. The reputation of the following firms also stands very high :—Hellyar and Crinks, Victoria street, and T. C. Stock, Victoria street.

PLATE AND WINDOW GLASS. The business of John Hall and Sons, Broadmead, was started in the year 1788. They are the originators of brilliant cut glass, and at the present time are second to no other makers. All branches of the trade are carried out with great vigour by the firm. Their showroom is a noble apartment, extending half the width of the premises, and lighted by eight pointed windows, each light filled with stained glass, the idea being that an architect or builder may select at a glance a pattern or design suitable for the work on which he might be engaged. Other windows are filled with ecclesiastical lead work, most effective in appearance. One large window is formed of brilliant cut glass, for which the firm received a gold medal at the London Exhibition in 1851. S. Cashmore and Co., Victoria street, are also large merchants.

POTTERY. The first record of a pottery in Bristol is in the reign of Edward I. Mediæval earthenware vessels of different periods of local manufacture occur down to the reign of Elizabeth, at which time there was a pottery in full work. Towards the middle of the 18th century the pottery of Mr. Champion, Castle green, issued specimens of the plastic art of surpassing beauty and skill, even rivalling the best productions in the East. His patent was sold to a firm in Staffordshire in 1777. About 1738-50 Richard Frank, the Bristol delf potter, had his works on Redcliff back, removing from thence to Temple back in 1777; continued from that date under Ring to 1788, Ring and Carter 1795, Pountney and Allies 1818, Pountney and Gouldney 1837, and J. D. Pountney 1851. The factory is still known by the name of Pountney and Co., and is worked in connection with the Victoria pottery, St. Philip's marsh. There are about 250 hands employed. The yearly consumption of coal is 5,000 tons, and about 3,000 tons of raw material are used. The manufacture is ordinary white and printed ware, which is exported in great quantities. In the counting-house of this firm are preserved four tiles, on which are drawings of the works in 1820 from the pencil of the celebrated china painter, Filfield.

ROPE. In the firm of W. Terrell and Sons Limited, Welsh back and Canon's marsh, Bristol boasts of the largest ropemaking establishment in the West of England. Wire rope for the rigging of ships and steamers, flat ropes for colliery purposes, long hemp and manilla rope and twine for ordinary purposes are largely made. Several patents have been granted to this firm for the packing of cylinders and steam chests of engines, and large quantities are supplied to all the leading railway companies of the United Kingdom. The rope and twine walks of this firm are quite a sight, the length of them being very great, extending from the waterside almost adjoining Green's bridge to the Gas works. These walks are covered and well lighted, so that work is never interrupted by weather. The firm give employment to over 100 workpeople, many of them being young women.

SNUFFS are made at most of the tobacco houses, but it is generally believed that its manufacture does not keep up in proportion to the increase of population.

SOAP AND CANDLES. The principal house is Christopher Thomas and Brothers, Broad plain works. The firm was originally founded in 1825 in the old Red Lion yard in Redcliff street, now occupied by Henry Prichard and Co., oil merchants. In 1833 the concern was united with that of Capper and Sons, Queen street, now occupied by the Castle Sugar Refinery Company, and here the manufacture of candles was first carried on by the firm. In 1841 a further amalgamation was made with Fripp and Co., and then finally settled upon the present site on the Broad plain. In viewing the premises of this manufactory, one is struck with the unique chimney towering high above one of the principal additions to the other buildings. This is said to be an exact copy of the tower of Palazzo Vecchio, the great Town hall of Florence. Near it, and built in the side of the wall, is a carved stone figure of the Winged Bull of Nineveh, the familiar trademark of the firm. Another noted firm which carries on a large business is that of Lawson, Phillips and Billings, Marsh soap works.

STONE WARE. Glazed stone ware, known as Bristol ware, which superseded the old salt glaze, was the invention of, and was first made in 1835 by, the late William Powell, at Temple gate pottery, still carried on under the title of William Powell and Sons. Several ingenious inventions of Septimus Powell have greatly simplified this manufacture. A similar material, known in the trade as the glazed vitrified stoneware, is manufactured by steam power by J. and C. Price Brothers, Victoria street, which firm was established in 1740. Both these wares are warranted to resist the action of acids.

SUGAR. This is perhaps the most ancient and celebrated of Bristol's industries. The first mention of sugar being imported here from the Canaries was in 1526, although it is certain that the trade existed before that date. Of those who have founded great mercantile houses as West India sugar merchants in Bristol and become eminent may be mentioned the names of Daniel, Miles, Gibbs, Bright, Protheroe, Baillie and others. Generations have passed away since their time, but some of their descendants still remain who to some extent maintain the traditional fame and honour of Bristol merchants. Sixty years ago there were ten refineries, but Finzel and Co.'s improved process in the manufacture of their celebrated "Bristol crystals" tended to place the trade in fewer hands, whilst giving employment to largely increased numbers. The glory and fame of this house has, alas, departed. Though attempts have been made to again start those stupendous works at Counterslip, it is argued by many that the great bar against the future prosperity of this concern, as indeed all other refineries, is the foreign system of allowing a bounty on manufactured sugar exported to this country. Whether this be so or not, it is to be hoped that shortly Counterslip will be again the scene of activity, and armed with machinery of a more modern type, so as to compete with rival ports. The local dues on sugar are now on a level with Greenock, Leith, Hull, the Tyne ports and Cardiff. The immense premises of Finzel and Co. were erected in 1846 at an outlay of £250,000. The tall chimney that towers above these works is 20 feet in diameter at the bottom, and tapers gradually to the height of 203 feet, the top diameter being 4 feet 8 inches. The height is one foot superior to that of the London monument, which is 202 feet. The number of bricks it contains is 220,000, and it was finished in 1849. There are now two sugar refineries in operation in Bristol, viz., the Old Market street and the Castle, Queen street.

TANNING. In 1861 there were nine tanneries, and now there are six, viz. :—J. Plenty, Pennywell road; J. Cox and Co., Bedminster; P. and S. Evans and Co., St. Philip's and Bedminster; Hassell and Cogan, Baldwin street and Baptist mills; John Drake and Co., Bedminster; Ware and Sons, Bedminster. The leather made in this locality has always been of an excellent quality. The growth of commerce caused such a demand for leather that it would soon have attained a fabulous price but for the introduction of American tanned leather and Turkish valonia. Bristol is very favourably situated for the importation of hides and valonia. The principal tanning materials used in Bristol are oak bark, valonia, myrobalmus, mimosa, terra japonica, divi-divi, and recently hemlock extract. The quantity of leather tanned in Bristol is sufficient to provide soles for nine million pairs of boots annually. Twelve months are required to make thick leather both pliable and impermeable, and this system has resulted in such a success that Bristol now not only produces the largest quantity of any town, but the quality of its leather may be said to rival that of any other in Great Britain.

TOBACCO. Bristol has won a world-wide reputation for its manufacture of "the weed," and Bristol bird's-eye is the delight of many a veteran smoker. There are six firms in the city engaged in the manufacture of tobacco, and all descriptions are made here. The oldest establishment is that of W. D. and H. O. Wills, which has been considerably over a century and a half in existence, having from time to time absorbed various firms, such as those of Williams, Ricketts, Leonard and Co., James Stansfield and Co., Maurice James and Co., and John Wodehouse and Co. The present partners are W. H. Wills, M.P., H. O. Wills, Edward P. Wills, Frederick Wills and G. A. Wills. The handsome building in Redcliff street was rebuilt in 1869. The private counting-house is adorned with many portraits. These portraits mean much. They are part of the history of the concern, and it is no wonder that the worthy members of the firm look on them and speak of them with pride. There are likenesses of the grandfather and fathers of the present members of the firm; but it is not so much these that attract notice as those of a number of elderly people in homely garb, who are evidently workpeople. And such they are—men and women, who have been, or who are at present, in the employ of the firm, all of them having been in the service for over forty years, and in some instances for more than half a century. Many interesting things, all bearing on the history of the firm or of the trade, are to be seen in this room. There is a view of the quaint old gabled building which formerly occupied the site of the present works. Before it was pulled down it was painted by J. Jackson Curnock. There is also an original letter from George Washington, afterwards President of the United States, who writes as follows:—

"Virginia, 25th November, 1759.—Gentlemen,—Sometime this week I expect to get on board the Cary for your house fifty hogsheads of tobacco of my own and Jno. Parke Curtis's, which please to insure in the usual manner. I shall also by the same ship send you ten or twelve hogsheads more if I can get them on board in time; but this, I believe, will be impracticable if Capt. Tulman uses that dispatch in loading which he now has in his power to do.—I am, gentlemen, your most obedient humble servant, G. WASHINGTON. P.S.—My goods per Capt. Yates are arrived in James River, and I thank you for your diligence in sending them.—Robert Cary, Esq., and Company."

In addition to these works, the firm have a manufactory on Holborn viaduct, London, as well as two supplementary manufactories in Bristol, one of which is carried on under bond, the better to meet the requirements of their foreign trade. The other noted tobacco houses are:— W. O. Bigg and Co., St. John's bridge; Edwards, Ringer and Co., Redcliff street; Franklyn, Morgan and Davey, Welsh back; D. Glass and Co., Clare street; Hudden and Co., Victoria street.

VINEGAR. The manufactories of this article—Panter, Woodward and Co., Holton street, and Purnell, Webb and Co., Redcliff street—give employment to a large number of hands.

WAGONS. The most noted company is that known as the Bristol Wagon Works Company Limited. The works are at Lawrence hill, and there are spacious showrooms in Victoria street. The company was established in 1866. They employ about 700 hands, and their works now cover upwards of twelve acres of land. The work of the company may be divided into two branches—one for the home market and the colonies, consisting of wagons, carts, vans, &c., for ordinary roads and for agricultural purposes, and the other branch is for railway carriages and wagons. The trade of the firm is cosmopolitan. Sweden, Russia, Austria, Italy, Portugal, Spain, the West Indies, China, South Africa, New

153

Zealand, Australia and Egypt are amongst their markets; but England, Ireland, Wales, and especially British India and South America, furnish their largest customers.

Maps. The first attempt to delineate correctly the ichnography of Bristol was in William Wyrcestre's time. Ricart's plan, taken from the *Mayor's Calendar*, is fanciful and of no value. The earliest engraved map of the city that can be traced is called "A Map of the City of Brightstowe, by George Hoefnagle." Hoefnagle's map, published in Braun's *Civitates Orbis Terrarum*, 1573, has been proved to be an inaccurate copy of one "measured and laid down in platforme by me, W. Smith, at my being in Bristow the 30th and 31st of July, Ano. Dmi. 1568." Speed's, Millerd's, Rocque's and Donne's are of more recent date. The map issued with the first number of this *Dictionary* is the most recent published. From a search which has been made in the British Museum for the compilers of this *Dictionary* it appears that "Bristol Channel" is not so described on any map before 1584. It occurs in the *Spieghel der Zeevaardt van de Navigatie* ("Mirror of Navigation"), by L. Z. Waghenaer Leyden, fol. 1584. There is no chart of the channel in question in the vol., but the name occurs on chart 20, just off the Cornish coast, in Dutch, as follows:— "Die Canael van Brostu." In an equally rare English translation of it by Sir Anthony Ashley, 1588, it runs thus:—"The Chanell of Bristol." This serves to show that by our seamen of the Tudor period it was understood to extend to the Land's End, and not to the contracted limit assigned to it by our *Admiralty Pilot*, just published, viz., by a line drawn from St. Ann's Head at the mouth of Milford Haven to Hartland Point on the coast of Devon. In a "Map of Britain in the time of the English Saxons, especially during the Heptarchy," Bristol Channel is marked

"Seavern Flu." In a later French map it is called "Sabrina.".

Marine Board, Local.
The offices for the examination of masters and mates are in Prince street. (*See* "Board of Trade" offices).

Markets.

CATTLE MARKET, Temple meads, facing the New cut, to the east of Bath bridge, stands on about four acres of ground, and was opened on February 4th, 1830. In the centre of the entrance is a neat dwellinghouse for the clerk of the market, and on either side of this structure are large iron gates 18 feet wide. The colonnade commencing from the gate contains 140 pillars of Hanham stone. On the left of the entrance accommodation is provided for 7,000 sheep, 2,000 of which may be placed under cover, 5,000 pigs, 300 horses, five compartments for fat beasts holding 50 each, and ten for lean beasts holding 80 each; total for oxen, 1,050. There is also a trotting course of 140 yards in length and 30 feet in width. Market is held every Thursday. The Bristol Joint Railway Station adjoins the market. This market is managed by a committee of trustees appointed by the Corporation, to whom the market belongs. (*See* "Fairs.")

CHEESE MARKET is held in Union street market every Wednesday and Friday.

CORN AND FLOUR MARKET meets in the Exchange every Tuesday and Thursday.

FISH MARKET, in Nicholas street, is very commodious and completely covered in. It was formerly a meat market. The front has been rebuilt of late years. Market held daily.

HAY, STRAW AND COAL MARKETS are held on Tuesdays and Fridays in that part of St. James' churchyard where the fair was formerly held, which is separated from the burial ground by iron railings. The tolls received from these markets for the year ending March 25th, 1883, were £131 15s. 8d.

HIDE, SKIN, FAT AND WOOL MARKET, 88 Thomas street. The principal sales are on Thursdays and Saturdays. Fat sale, 10.30; hide and skin, 12.45. (See "Fairs.")

HIGH STREET MARKET, opened on April 14th, 1849, consists of three arcades, occupied on Wednesdays and Saturdays by dealers in butter, cheese, eggs, poultry, bacon, &c. The arcade in front of the south of Exchange is termed the Gloucestershire market, and that to the west the Somersetshire market; the other, known as the eastern arcade, is on the left entering from High street. On the site formerly occupied with wooden rows for the sale of butcher's meat, a building of Bath stone in the Italian style of architecture is now used for the same purpose, its main entrance being in Nicholas street. The framing of the roofs is constructed of iron and covered with Welsh slates. The windows are glazed with rough glass, which, whilst preventing the sun's rays, affords plenty of light. The avenue leading from High street, with which the three arcades are connected, is spanned by iron girders and covered in with a glass roof. Fruiterers and market gardeners here dispose of their produce daily in neatly arranged stalls on each side. During 1883 this market underwent renovation. £2,361 13s. 6d. was received on account of rents during the year ending 25th March, 1883.

LEATHER MARKET. A market for tanned leather was established at the Back hall on January 7th, 1790, to be thenceforth continued Thursdays.

UNION STREET MARKET (or St. James' market) was rebuilt in 1858-9. The upper portion is used exclusively as a wholesale meat market, and the lower for the sale of meat, vegetables, fruit, cheese, &c. Market days on Wednesdays and Saturdays. In the front of the market are a few small shops. The rents received on account of these markets for the year ending March 25th, 1883, amounted to £374 16s. 8d.

Marquis of Bristol. The city gives title to a marquisate, which is at present enjoyed by the noble family of Hervey. The title was created in 1622 by James I., and was first conferred upon the ancient family of Digby. The earldom became extinct in 1698, but in 1703 John Hervey was created Baron Hervey, and in 1714 Earl of Bristol. The fifth Earl was created Marquis of Bristol in 1826, in the person of Frederick William Hervey, who is also a Deputy-Lieutenant of Suffolk. His second title is Earl Jermyn. His lordship is Hereditary Steward of Bury St. Edmunds, a patron of 20 livings, and is Liberal-Conservative in politics. His residences are as follow:—6 St. James' square, S.W.; Carlton and White's clubs; Kemptown, Brighton; Putney heath, Surrey; and Ickworth park, Bury St. Edmunds, Suffolk.

Mayor. The Town Council, on the 9th November in each year, elect one of the citizens to be Mayor for the ensuing year. The Mayor is the chief magistrate of the city for the time being, and by virtue of the office is styled the Right Worshipful the Mayor of Bristol, and takes precedence of everyone in the city, being Her Majesty's representative. His Worship has the right to take his seat on the bench of any of the common law courts. An amusing instance of the exercise of this right is on record in the year 1762, when John Noble was Mayor, he, being in London, proceeded to the Court of Admiralty, at Westminster, and claimed the right. The Judge, then sitting, was much surprised, and was about to take harsh measures, until he was informed by one of the Council that the Mayor of Bristol was by charter thus privileged. The Mayor, having been accommodated with a seat by the side of his lordship, rose, bowed, and said that, having asserted

155

the claims of his city, he would at once withdraw. In the year 1826 rules were obtained in the King's Bench in the nature of a *quo warranto* calling upon John Haythorne (Mayor), and Gabriel Goldney and John Savage (Sheriffs), to show by what authority they held their offices. The substantial question raised was whether the right of election was vested in the Mayor, Aldermen and Common Council as a select body, or whether the burgesses at large had not under the charters a voice in the election of their officers. For the rules, custom and the old charters were pleaded, showing that Bristol was an ancient town and not a corporation by prescription. As such the burgesses had a right, which they had constantly exercised, of choosing their Mayor long antecedent to their first Common Council, which was established under the charter of Edward III. (1373), and that the charter of Charles II. was void, consequently elections under it were not valid. Contra it was argued that elections took place under the charter of 9 Anne, by which the power of election was confided in 42 of the more discreet citizens and burgesses, besides the Mayor, to whom the power of election was given. The rules as they related to both the Mayor and Sheriffs were discharged, and thus was established the validity of the elections according to the charter of 9 Anne. In the commission of assize for gaol delivery the Mayor is included with the Judges on circuit. The allowance to the Mayor is £700 per annum and carriage (and £100 the first year he holds office for re-decorating carriage), and he resides at the Mansion house, Clifton down. The Mayor has the use of the city plate (*see* "Council" sub-heading "Plate"). On Sept. 3rd, 1836, it was enacted by a by-law that any gentleman refusing to serve the office of Mayor should be fined £100. The gold chain of office worn by the Mayor is elaborate in ornament and peculiarly handsome. It weighs 26 oz. 4 dwts., and was purchased by the Corporation in 1828 at a cost of £285. By charter the Mayor is made the King's escheator; he has thus the dignity of an earl, and a sword of state is borne before him in his official capacity (*see* "Council" sub-heading "Sword Bearer"). The following is a list of Mayors from 1836 :—

1836 11th January, William Fripp.
1836 9th November, James George.
1837 John Kerle Haberfield.
1838 John Kerle Haberfield.
1839 James Norroway Franklyn.
1840 Robert Phippen.
1841 George Woodroffe Franklyn.
1842 James Gibbs.
1843 William Lewton Clarke.
1844 Richard Poole King.
1845 John Kerle Haberfield.
1846 William Goldney.
1847 John Decimus Pountney.
1848 John Kerle Haberfield.
1849 John Kerle Haberfield.
1850 John Kerle Haberfield.
1851 William Henry Gore-Langton.
1852 Robert Gay Barrow.
1853 John George Shaw.
1854 John George Shaw.
1855 John Vining.
1856 John Vining.
1857 Isaac Allan Cooke.
1858 James Poole.
1859 John Bates.
1860 Odiarne Coates Lane.
1861 John Hare.
1862 Sholto Vere Hare.
1863 Thomas Porter Jose.
1864 William Naish.
1865 Joseph Abraham.
1866 Elisha Smith Robinson.
1867 Francis Adams.
1868 Francis Adams.
1869 William Killigrew Wait.
1870 Thomas Canning.
1871 William Proctor Baker.
1872 William Hathway.
1873 Thomas Barnes.
1874 Christopher James Thomas.
1875 John Averay Jones.
1876 George William Edwards.
1877 George William Edwards.
1878 George William Edwards.
1879 Henry Taylor.
1880 Joseph Dodge Weston.
1881 Joseph Dodge Weston.
1882 Joseph Dodge Weston.
1883 Joseph Dodge Weston.

Medical Provident Institution, formed for the purpose of providing working-men and their families with medical advice and drugs independent of charity. The members have the advantage of choosing from the medical staff a family doctor, who, when necessary, visits the members at their own homes, advising them in all that concerns the prevention as well as the cure of disease, and refers to the Royal Infirmary and General Hospital cases which can there be more suitably treated. The members are required to subscribe at the rate of one penny per week to cover doctors' fees, the cost of medicine and working expenses. An institution formerly in private hands, with dispensaries at Easton, Bedminster, Hotwells, Barton hill and Upper York street, St. Paul's, has now been amalgamated with this institution. Donors and subscribers to the amount of £5 and upwards are entitled to election on the general committee. Dr. Beddoe, president.

Members of Parliament.

The city has returned two members to Parliament since the reign of Edward I. (1283). Although its population has increased some twenty-eight and the value of its property fifty-fold, it has only the same weight to-day in the House of Commons it had six centuries ago. Appended is a list of the Parliamentary representatives of Bristol from 1734 to the present time:—

Date.	Name.	Votes.
1734	Elton, Sir A., Bart.	2,420
	Coster, Thomas	2,071
1739	Southwell, Edward	2,559
1741	Elton, Sir A., Bart.	
	Southwell, Edward	No
1742	Hoblyn, Robert	contest.
1747	Southwell, Edward	
	Hoblyn, Robert	
1754	Nugent, Hon. Robert	2,590
	Beckford, Richard	2,248
1756	Smith, Jarritt	
1761	Nugent, Hon. Robert	No
	Smith, Sir Jarritt	contest.
1768	Clare, Lord (née Nugent)	
	Brickdale, Matthew	
1768	Clare, Lord	
1774	Cruger, H.	3,565
	Burke, Edmund	2,707
1780	Brickdale, Matthew	2,771
	Lippincott, Sir H., Bart.	2,518
1781	Daubeny, George	3,143
1784	Brickdale, Matthew	3,458
	Cruger, H.	3,052
1790	Worcester, Marquis of	544
	Sheffield, Lord	537

Date.	Name.	Votes.
1796	Bragge, Charles	364
	Sheffield, Lord	340
1801	Bragge, Charles	
1802	Bragge, Charles	
	Baillie, Evan	
1803	Bragge, Charles	No
1806	Bathurst, Charles Bragge	contest.
	Baillie, Evan	
1807	Bathurst, Charles Bragge	
	Baillie, Evan	
1812	Davis, Richart Hart	1,907
1812	Davis, Richart Hart	2,895
	Protheroe, Edward	2,435
1818	Davis, Richard Hart	3,377
	Protheroe, Edward	2,250
1820	Bright, Henry	2,997
	Davis, Richard Hart	2,811
1826	Davis, Richard Hart	3,887
	Bright, Henry	2,815
1830	Davis, Richard Hart	5,012
	Baillie, James Evan	3,377
1831	Baillie, James Evan	No
	Protheroe, Edward, jun.	cont'st
1832	Vyvyan, Sir R. R., Bart.	3,695
	Baillie, James Evan	3,160
1835	Miles, Philip John	3,709
	Vyvyan, Sir R. R., Bart.	3,313
1837	Miles, P. W. S.	3,833
	Berkeley, Hon. F. H. F.	3,212
1841	Miles, P. W. S.	4,197
	Berkeley, Hon. F. H. F.	3,743
1847	Berkeley, Hon. F. H. F.	4,381
	Miles, P. W. S.	2,595
1852	Berkeley, Hon. F. H. F.	4,681
	Langton, W. H. G.	4,531
1857	Berkeley, Hon. F. H. F.	No
	Langton, W. H. G.	cont'st
1859	Berkeley, Hon. F. H. F.	4,432
	Langton, W. H. G.	4,285
1865	Berkeley, Hon. F. H. F.	5,296
	Peto, Sir M., Bart.	5,223
1868	Miles, J. W.	5,173
1868	Berkeley, Hon. F. H. F.	8,759
	Morley, Samuel	8,714
1870	Robinson, E. S.	7,832
1870	Hodgson, K. D.	7,815
1874	Hodgson, K. D.	8,888
	Morley, Samuel	8,782
1878	Fry, Lewis	9,342
1880	Morley, Samuel	10,704
	Fry, Lewis	10,070

SAMUEL MORLEY is the youngest son of the late John Morley. He was born at Homerton in 1809, and married, in 1841, Rebekah Maria, daughter of Samuel Hope, of Liverpool. He is a member of the firm of J. and R. Morley, London, wholesale hosiers, and the firm carry on works, which are of great magnitude, at Nottingham; he is a magistrate for Middlesex and a commissioner of lieutenancy for London. In politics he is a Liberal, and voted in 1869 for the disestablishment of the Irish

Church; he is in favour of local control in the granting of licenses. Sat for Nottingham from July, 1865, till May, 1866, when he was unseated on petition. Stood unsuccessfully for this city in May, 1868, but was elected in December following. His addresses are :—34 Grosvenor street, W.; 18 Wood street, Cheapside, E.C.; Hall place, Tunbridge, Kent.

LEWIS FRY is the fourth son of Joseph Fry, and younger brother of the Hon. Justice Fry. He was born in 1832, and married, in 1859, Elizabeth, daughter of Francis Gibson, of Saffron Walden, Essex, who died in 1870. He was admitted a solicitor in 1854, and is head of the firm of Fry, Abbot, Pope and Brown, of this city. He is a Liberal in politics, and is in favour of the granting of licenses being decided by local option. He has sat for Bristol since December, 1878. His local address is :—Goldney house, Clifton hill.

The following represent the counties of Gloucester and Somerset and the cities of Gloucester and Bath :—

Gloucestershire, West	..Col. R. N. F. Kingscote.
" "	..Lord Moreton.
" East	..Right Hon. Sir M. Hicks-Beach.
" "	..J. R. Yorke.
Somersetshire, Mid	..Major R. H. Paget.
" "	..W. S. Gore-Langton.
" West	..E. J. Stanley.
" East	..Sir P. J. W. Miles, Bt.
" "	.Lord Brooke.
Gloucester (City)	..O. J. Monk (vacancy).
Bath	..Sir A. D. Hayter, Bart.
"	..E. R. Wodehouse.

Merchant Shipping Office, Prince street. (See "Board of Trade.").

Merchant Venturers' Society, The, is now the only guild remaining in the city. It was incorporated by Edward VI. December 18th, 1551, and subsequently confirmed by Elizabeth and Charles I., and is now established under the authority of the charter of 1638. The society possess manors and lands to the amount of upwards of £3,000 per annum, in trust for the maintenance and support of certain almshouses in this city, governors of the Colston school and of the Trades and Mining schools (see "Schools" and "Almshouses"), and for other charitable uses. Most of the principal merchants are members of the society, their best energies being continually engaged in promoting the welfare of the city and the interest of its trade and commerce with all parts of the world, in addition to numerous works of philanthropy, education, &c., at home. The master, wardens, assistants and commonalty meet annually on the 10th of November in their hall, and elect one to be master, two of the assistants to be wardens, and ten to be assistants for the following year. The master must be one who has been master, warden or assistant. The present master nominates one candidate, the wardens and assistants one, and the commonalty one, and from these three the election is made by a majority of the whole society present. The ordinary meetings are held monthly. No salaries are paid to the master or any of the officers, nor does any pecuniary benefit accrue to members. The right of admission into the society, according to present regulations, is obtained in three ways, by birth, by apprenticeship, or by purchase. Every son of a Merchant Venturer, born after his father became a member, is entitled by birth, after taking up his own freedom of the city, to be admitted into the Society of Merchants. No necessary qualification exists with respect to the trade or profession actually exercised by him. The only refusal to admit on that ground was on the application of a clergyman. The case was dismissed by the society and finally rejected. One of the present members of the society has taken orders since he entered it without ceasing to be a member. Those who claim to be admitted by apprenticeship must (nominally) have served a Merchant Venturer for seven years in a mercantile capacity. The hall of the society stands at the corner of Marsh street and King street; it was erected in 1701, and newly fronted in 1790. In the front of the building are three niches. In the upper one over the entrance is a figure intended for George III.; in each of the others is a vase, on which are carved the arms of the society. There are a pair of fine wrought iron gates in front, embellished with the coat of arms of the worshipful society, picked out with divers colours. They are known as the "gilded gates." The entrance is by a flight of stone steps. Adjacent to the hall is a suite of offices for the accommodation of the society. The interior contains a capacious reception-room, handsome if somewhat sombre in its wainscot and gold, in which are placed the portraits of deceased Venturers, and an inner large hall, which is decorated in the richest style. Panels contain portraits of the chartering monarchs; the emblazoned arms of distinguished members of the society, amongst them the famous Cabots; and the decoration of the mantlepiece is typical of the local imports. Amongst the portraits may be noticed one of Robert Bright, also one of Queen Anne, by Kneller. The motto of the society is "*Indocilis Pauperiem Pati.*" Cooke Clarencieux granted the society its coat of arms, which consists of Father Time with his scythe and a mermaid with an anchor.

Microscopical Society.

The Bristol Microscopical Society was founded in 1843, and can claim to be one of the oldest provincial microscopical societies in England. As its name would imply, its immediate functions are the furtherance and investigation of microscopy in all its branches. From time to time enrolled on its list of members have been names well known to the scientific world at large. The meetings of the society, with the exception of July, August and September, are held on the third Thursday in each month. C. King Rudge, L.R.C.P., president; H. A. Francis, vice-president; Rev. W. Locock, 13 Alexandra road, Clifton, secretary.

Minerals.

The mineral fields round Bristol are very extensive as well as rich; indeed the city would almost appear to be built upon one vast subterranean area of mineral wealth, the large coal basins being traversed by almost parallel seams of iron clay, whilst limestone of the best description for furnace purposes is quarried in any quantity on the banks of the river. (*See* "Geology.")

Ministers.

In Bristol there are 252 Episcopalian and 89 Dissenting ministers, including Baptist, Bible Christian, Congregational, United Methodist Free Church, Primitive Methodist, Wesleyan, Moravian, Presbyterian, Brethren and Unitarian, and 25 Roman Catholic priests and friars.

Missionary Society,

Bristol. The 71st anniversary of the Bristol branch of the London Missionary Society was held in Sept., 1883, when it was announced that the receipts for the past year amounted to £2,451 1s. 2d., and that there had been remitted to the parent society £2,322 4s. 7d., the travelling, printing, postage, hire of rooms, and other incidental expenses of the local charity having amounted to £128 16s. 7d. In connection with this society it is worthy of note that for the ten years ending 1883 the congregation attending Highbury chapel have contributed the following amounts on the occasion of the annual collection:—

1874	£465	15	7
1875	532	4	2
1876	548	13	0
1877	578	6	7
1878	607	11	8
1879	625	3	0
1880	660	14	2
1881	701	13	1
1882	755	1	1
1883	784	18	9
Total	£6,260	1	1

H. O. Wills, treasurer; Rev. H. Arnold Thomas, M.A., Rev. U. R. Thomas and Frank N. Tribe, secs.

Missions.

ASSOCIATION FOR THE PROPAGATION OF THE GOSPEL IN FOREIGN PARTS. Depôt for the society's publications, 19 College green. Revs. W. Prideaux and H. B. Heberden, secretaries.

BAPTIST MISSIONARY SOCIETY. The officers of the Bristol Auxiliary of this society are:—G. H. Leonard, treasurer; Rev. G. D. Evans and Edward Robinson, secretaries.

BRISTOL BRANCH OF THE UNITED ZENANA AND MEDICAL MISSION. The society is established for elevating the degraded condition of the women of India. This branch contributes £500 per annum to the mission. The first annual meeting of the local branch was held May 24th, 1883, at Worcester lodge, College road. Mrs. E. Williams, hon. sec.

BRISTOL DOMESTIC MISSION, Montague street, for visiting the poor at their habitations and affording them temporal and spiritual aid. Wm. Tucker, Clare street, treasurer; Rev. Wm. Hargrave, 6 Oakland road, secretary; Rev. W. Matthews, Mission house, Montague street, missionary.

BRISTOL SEAMEN AND BOATMEN'S MISSION. This branch was established ten years ago. During 1882 the number of meetings held was 456; attendance, 21,597; visits to the shipping, &c., 7,212; visits to the sick, 657; Scriptures read, 3,532; Scriptures given (English and foreign) 641; Scriptures sold at cost price, 313; prayer books given, 327; hymn books given, 407; tracts, magazines, &c., given, 30,583; hours engaged in the work, 2,142. A mission superintendent conducts the English and Foreign Seamen's Bethel, St. George's road.

CHRISTIAN WOMEN'S UNION. The fourth annual conference of this union was held at the Victoria rooms in September, 1883, when several papers of a missionary character were read and discussed. The purpose of the union is not that each member should conform to each other, but that each member may be better acquainted with one another as a means of forming a bond of christian love and sympathy. Mrs. Meredith, president; Miss Gibbs, King square, secretary.

CHURCH MISSIONARY ASSOCIATION, in aid of the missions in Africa and the East. Rev. W. S. Bruce and E. W. Bird, secretaries.

CITY MISSION, established 56 years ago. The society employs nine missionaries, who, during 1882, paid 25,167 house-to-house visits and conducted 1,902 public services. W. Mack, treasurer. (*See* "City Mission Society.")

CLIFTON COLLEGE MISSION, Newfoundland road, was set on foot in 1875, with the intention of interesting the boys of the college in work for their poorer neighbours. An area in St. Barnabas' parish (now a separate district known as St. Agnes) was selected for the work. A large workshop, with the adjoining premises, was converted into a mission. The mission is in a very healthy condition, and the interest manifested in the movement by the working classes is very encouraging. The mission possesses a library containing nearly 500 volumes of good literature. A men's mutual improvement society meets weekly during the winter months for lectures, discussions, and readings or recitations. Last winter 111 members joined the association. Attached to the mission is a cricket club, a gymnasium for men over 21 years of age, a mothers' meeting, a sewing class, a temperance society, a penny bank, a provident society, a Sunday school with 404 children on the register, viz., 155 infants, 132 girls and 117 boys; also a workman's club (*see* "Clubs"). Rev. T. W. Harvey is the mission curate.

EASTVILLE MISSION consists of a mission church, which was opened 27th September, 1882, by the Bishop. Mothers' meetings in the Freeland buildings' mission-room, an infant school, free night schools for both sexes, a Sunday school and Bible classes are held. Rev. J. G. Norman, M.A., Beaufort house, Eastville, curate in charge.

IRISH CHURCH (Bristol and Clifton Auxiliary). Meetings are held annually, and church collections made on behalf of the objects of the mission. Rev. T. H. Clark, local hon. sec.

LAY PROTESTANT MISSIONARY ASSOCIATION, for the diffusion of Gospel and Protestant truth among the Roman Catholics and Protestants by means of house visiting, discussion classes and tract distribution. L. Clarke, 6 Old Park hill, missionary.

LEWIN'S MEAD DOMESTIC MISSION, Lower Montague street, for visiting the poor at their homes and affording them temporal and spiritual aid. Rev. W. Hargrave, M.A., 8 Oakland road, hon. secretary.

MISSION TO SEAMEN. The object of the society is the spiritual welfare of the seafaring classes at home and abroad, and in pursuance of this the society uses every means consistent with the principles and the received practice of the Church of England. The work was first taken up in Bristol in 1835 by Rev. Dr. Ashley. His plan was to hire boats and visit the ships lying in the roadsteads of the Bristol Channel, for the purpose of holding services, preaching and distributing books and tracts. In 1837 a society was formed under the name of the Bristol Channel Mission, and in 1839 a mission cutter was built fitted up with a chapel capable of accommodating 130 persons. To this cutter the name of *Eirene* (Peace) was given, and she is believed to have been the first vessel ever built for such a purpose. In 1845 the name of the mission was altered to the Bristol Channel Seamen's Mission, and in 1858 it was again altered to the present comprehensive title of "Mission to Seamen." The mission now employs a colporteur and two Scripture readers for the Bristol harbour, and one colporteur and Scripture reader for Kingroad and Avonmouth and Portishead docks, and in the Seamen's Institute lately erected at the latter place. On the 1st January, 1880, the reading-room of the Seamen's Institute, Prince street, was opened, and on the 10th February following the chapel of the institute (*see* "Churches"). F. W. Lavington, 107 Pembroke road, hon. secretary.

MISSION TO THE JEWS (the Bristol and Clifton auxiliary of the London Society for Promoting Christianity amongst the Jews). The 68th anniversary of the auxiliary was celebrated in 1883, when it was reported that the income locally amounted in the previous year to £701 18s. 3d. Rev. W. Saunders, St. Silas', hon. sec.

SOCIETY FOR PROMOTING CHRISTIANITY AMONG THE JEWS. The treasurer of the Bristol Auxiliary is E. J. Bird, and the hon. secretary Rev. D. E. M. Simmonds.

SOCIETY FOR PROMOTING CHRISTIAN KNOWLEDGE. The depository of the District Committee is at Park street viaduct. Rev. J. G. Alford, hon. secretary.

UNITED BRISTOL MISSION, founded in 1857 for the purpose of inviting all orthodox Christians, without denominational distinction, to assist to carry the Gospel to the masses who systematically absent themselves from the public means of grace. The mission at present employs ten missionaries, who by house-to-house visiting, cottage lectures, open air preaching, distribution of Bibles, conversations with working classes, and by every legitimate means, seek out the ignorant, the careless and the depraved. James Inskip, 3 Pembroke road, treasurer.

WESLEYAN MISSIONARY SOCIETY, Bristol Auxiliary, formed in 1813. William H. Budgett, treasurer.

Monuments. The following is a list of the principal monuments, and as the old city churches are lavish in the display of effigies and figures, the following statement as to different stages is given :—(1)

Figures in stone, with plain sloping roofs and without inscription, are the oldest. (2) In 1160 plain prismatic roofs began to be ornamented. (3) In the same century sloping roofs gave place to armorial bearings. (4) In the 13th century flat roofs and figures were carved on the covers. (5) In the next stage an arch was built over the monument to protect it. (6) After this a chapel was annexed to the church. (7) The last stage was the head bound and feet tied, with children at the base or cherubims at the feet. Figures with their hands on their breasts and chalices represent priests. Figures with crozier, mitre and pontificals represent prelates. Figures with armour represent knights. Figures with legs crossed represent either crusaders or married men. Female figures with a mantle and a large ring represent nuns. Those in scale armour are the most ancient (*temp.* Henry II.). Those in chain armour or ring mail come next (*temp.* Richard I. to Henry III.). Those with children or cherubims are between the 14th and 17th centuries. Brasses are for the most part subsequent to the 13th century. Saints lie to the east of the altar, and are elevated above the ground; the higher the elevation, the greater the sanctity. Martyrs are much elevated. Holy men not canonised lie on a level with the pavement. Founders of chapels, &c., lie with their monument built into the wall. Capital letters and Latin inscriptions are of the first twelve centuries; Lombardic capitals and French inscriptions, of the 13th century; German text, of the 14th century; English and Roman print, subsequent to the 14th century. Tablets against the wall came in with the Reformation. The modern idea for monuments is that of stained glass windows.

The churches in which the monuments will be found are printed in italics at the end of each paragraph, and, except where otherwise specified, are city churches.

ALDWORTH, THOMAS, died 1598; JOHN, died 1615; FRANCIS, died 1623. *St. Mark's.*

ALDWORTH, Family of. A sumptuous tomb, with figures of himself and wife, 1634. *St. Peter's.*

ALOY, THOMAS. Bearing a Latin inscription, 1692. *St. Michael's.*

BANGLEY, JOHN, died October 8th. 1836, and was buried in the Cathedral. *St. Matthew's* (Kingsdown).

BARKER, JOHN, an altar tomb, with the figure of a civic dignitary, and an inscription above setting forth that he was Mayor and Alderman. Died 1607 (supposed). *St. Werburgh.*

BARRETT, MARIA, wife of William Barrett, historian. Tablet against a column in the south transept. About 1790. *Cathedral.*

BAYNTON, MARIA, died in 1602. *St. Mark's.*

BENGOUGH, HENRY, Alderman, died 10th April, 1818, aged 80. *St. Mark's.*

BERKELEY. THOMAS II., son of Maurice II., and great grandson of Robert Fitzhardinge, buried beneath an arch between the Berkeley chapel and the south aisle, where an altar is raised to his memory; died 23rd July, 1321. MAURICE, fourth Lord Berkeley, and ELIZABETH, his wife, buried in the large altar tomb lying between the choir and Elder Lady chapel in the fourth bay from the north-east. It formerly bore at the head an inscription, superadded in 1742, stating that it was the "monument of Robert Fitzhardinge, Lord of Berkeley, descended from the Kings of Denmark," who was the founder of the abbey, but it is fully authenticated that the figures represented the above-named; died 18th June, 1368. Sir JAMES, second son of Maurice II., died 13th June, 1404, buried with his father. THOMAS, fifth of his name, is the last of the family buried here. The position of his tomb is uncertain. Died 22nd January, 1532. *Cathedral.*

BERKELEY, Lord RICHARD, of Stoke Gifford, died 1604, aged 71. *S. Mark's.*

BERKELEY, Sir THOMAS DE, Stoke Gifford, and his wife CATHERINE.

An altar tomb on the north side of chancel, upon which, under a carved canopy, are effigies. *St. Mark's.*

BIDDULPH, Rev. T. T., died 19th May, 1838. Incumbent of the parish for 38 years. *St. James'.*

BIRD, EDWARD, R.A., painter, died Nov. 2nd, 1819, aged 45. *Cathedral.*

BIRD, WM., died Oct. 8th, 1590. Mayor of Bristol, 1589. *St. Mark's.*

BIRDE, WILLIAM, died 1590. Elizabethan monument. *St. Stephen's.*

BLANKET, EDWARD. In re-pewing in 1844 a beautiful tomb was discovered, which was supposed to be in honour of the above-named. He was the original manufacturer of the woollen covering, since called by his name, and was Member of Parliament for Bristol in 1362. *St. Stephen's.*

BLECKER, JOHN, brewer. *Redcliff.*

BOOTH, Rev. ROBERT, Dean of Bristol, died 1720. Tablet. *Cathedral.*

BOUCHER, GEORGE. *St. Werburgh.*

BRICKDALE, MATTHEW, died Sept. 8th, 1831, aged 97. Represented the city in Parliament. Tablet. *Temple.*

BRIDGES, Rev. Dr. N., died 17th July, 1834, aged 84. Inscription; also a monument against the wall in the east aisle of the north transept of St. Mary Redcliff. *St. Nicholas.*

BROOK, Sir JOHN, and Lady. He was one of the judges of assize, being also seneschal of the King's palace and of Glastonbury abbey; died in 1522. *St. Mary Redcliff.*

BROUGHTON, Rev. THOMAS, M.A., died 21st Dec., 1774, aged 71; tablet in north aisle of chancel. *Redcliff.*

BUCK, Rev. CHARLES, died Oct. 28th, 1858, rector of the parish for 28 years. Tablet. *St. Stephen's.*

BURY, Rev. S., and Wife. In the churchyard. 1729. *St. James'.*

BUSH, PAUL, first Bishop of Bristol, died 1558, and was interred in the north aisle, where there is a low altar tomb to his memory. *Cathedral.*

BUTLER, Bishop, author of *Analogy*, two memorials. He was twelve years Bishop of this diocese, afterwards became Bishop of Durham. Died at Bath, 6th June, 1752, aged 60. *Cathedral.*

BUTLER, MARGARET, the wife of Nicholas Butler, died on 27th June, 1642, aged 74 years. *Cathedral.*

CARPENTER, Rev. LANT. monument in Lewin's mead (Unitarian) chapel, of which he was pastor. Drowned off the coast of Italy on April 5th, 1840. *Lewin's Mead Chapel.*

CARPENTER, MARY, a medallion. Died June 15th, 1877. *Cathedral.*

CANYNGES, WILLIAM (the second). Under a canopied recess beneath the central window, an altar tomb supporting recumbent effigies of William Canynges and his wife. The inscription is as follows:—

William Cannings, ye richest merchant of ye town of Bristow, afterwards chosen 5 times Mayor of ye said towne, for the good of the comonwealth of the same. He was in the order of the priesthood 7 years, and afterwards Dean of Westbury, and died the 7th Nov., 1474, which said William did build, within ye said town of Westbury, a college (with his Canons), and the said William did maintain by the space of 8 years 800 handy-craftsmen, besides carpenters and masons, every day 100 men. Besides, King Edward the IVth had of ye said William 3,000 marks for his peace to be had in 2,470 tons of shipping.

Then follow the names, &c., of his ships and a metrical tribute to his memory. *St. Mary Redcliff.*

CHAMBER, THOMAS, and his wife ANN, an inscription on a stone near Canynges' tomb. 1620-47. *Redcliff.*

CHATTERTON, THOMAS, "the boy poet." Within the railings that enclose the church, but not upon *consecrated* ground, is the monument of this extraordinary youth. It originally stood under the north porch. It is in the Perpendicular style, with a representation of a Colston school boy as a finial. Chatterton died 24th August, 1770. Nearly opposite the south transept, a little within the lower wall of the graveyard, is a tombstone inscribed with the names of his parents and some relations. Whether the poet was brought from London and interred here is not positively known (*see* "Chatterton"). *S. Mary Redcliff.*

CLARK, THOS., sculptor, died May 16th, 1829, aged 55. *St. Mark's.*

CLARKE, CHARLES STEWART. A memorial window in baptistry. Died Sept. 15th, 1877, aged 69. *Cathedral.*
CLARKE, SAMUEL. *St. Stephen's.*
CODRINGTON, Lord ROBERT, died Feb. 14th, 1618, aged 46. *Cathedral.*
COKE, RICHARD. *St. Mary Redcliff.*
COKE, WILLIAM, servant of Wm. Canynges. *St. Mary Redcliff.*
COOKSON, ELIZABETH. A large tablet in the west wall. Died Dec. 20th, 1852, aged 63. *Cathedral.*
COLAS, WILLIAM, servant to Wm. Canynges. *St. Mary Redcliff.*
COLLINGS, DANIEL STRATTON, Captain in the 82nd Regiment. Military monument. Died at Malta, January 29th, 1855. *Cathedral.*
COLSTON, EDWARD, Bristol's great philanthropist, whose memory is perpetuated every November (*see* "Colston Societies"). A fine marble monument in a recumbent position on an altar-tomb, by Rysbrach, modelled from the original picture by Richardson, and is draped in the costume of the period. It is situated at the eastern end of the north aisle. Every Sunday a bouquet of flowers is placed on the bosom of the statue. On the pedestal is the following:—

EDWARD, THE SON OF WILLIAM COLSTON, ESQ., AND SARAH, HIS WIFE, WAS BORN IN THIS CITY NOVEMBER 2ND, 1636. DY'D AT MORTLAKE, IN SURRY, OCTOBER 11TH, 1721, AND LIES BURIED NEAR THIS MONUMENT.

In the background of the monument is a pedimental canopy headed with the words—

THE PUBLIC CHARITIES AND BENEFACTIONS GIVEN AND FOUNDED BY EDWARD COLSTON, ESQ.

IN BRISTOL.
On St. Michael's Hill.
1691.—An almshouse for 12 men and 12 women, the chief brother to receive 6 sh., the others 3 sh. per week, besides coal, &c. To a chaplain, £10 per annum. The whole to be paid by fee-farm rents on estates in Northumberland, Cumberland and Durham, and by some houses and lands near the house. The charge about £8,500

In King Street.
Six saylors to be maintained in the Merchant almshouse by a farm in Congresbury, Somerset. The charge £600

In Temple Street.
1696.—A school for 40 boys to be cloath'd and taught, endowed with an annuity out of the manor of Tomarhear, Somerset. An house and garden for ye master. Ye charge 8,000
1702.—To ye re-building ye boys' hospital, and for six boys to be cloath'd, maintain'd, instruct'd and apprenticed. A farm of £70 per annum, in Congresbury. Ye charge 1,500

In St. Peter's Parish.
To the Mint workhouse 200
And for placing out poor children.. 290

On St. Augustine's Back.
1708.—A hospital for a master, two ushers and a catechist, and for one hundred boys to be instructed, cloath'd, maintain'd and apprentic'd, the charge about 40,000
£100 per annum, to be given for 12 years after his death, either to those who have been apprentic'd from the hospital of St. Augustine's back, or for the apprenticing of boys from Temple school, by £10 each 1,200

To the several Charity Schools.
Each £10 per an., given for many years while he liv'd, and to be continued for 12 months after his death.

To ye Repairing and Beautifying of Churches.
All Saints' 250
Cathedral 260
Clifton 50
St. James' 100
St. Mary Redcliff 100
St. Michael 50
St. Stephen's 50
Temple 160
St. Thomas' 50
St. Warburgh 160
For reading prayers at All Sts. every Monday and Tuesday morning, £7 per annum 140
For 12 sermons at Newgate, £6 per an. 120
For 14 sermons in Lent, £20 per an. 400

IN LONDON.
To St. Bartholomew's hospital .. 2,500
To Christ church " .. 2,000
To St. Thomas' " .. 500
To Bethlem " .. 500
To the new workhouse without Bishop's gate 200
To the Society for Propagating the Gospel 300
To the Company of Mercers 100

IN SURREY.
At Sheen.
An almahouse for six poor men, built and endowed .. ..

At Mortlake.
For the education and clothing of 12 boys and 12 girls, £45 per an. £900
To 85 poor people at his death, 20s. each 85

· IN DEVONSHIRE.
Towards building a church at Tiverton 20

IN LANCASHIRE.
Towards building a church at Manchester 20
To 18 charity schools, in several parts of England, for many years of his life, and to be continued for 12 years after his death, £90 per annum.
To the augmentation of 60 small livings 6,000

In all £70,695

The inscription concludes :—

THIS GREAT AND PIOUS BENEFACTOR WAS KNOWN TO HAVE DONE MANY OTHER EXCELLENT CHARITIES, AND WHAT HE DID IN SECRET IS BELIEVED TO BE NOT INFERIOR TO WHAT HE DID IN PUBLIC.

Laid in the floor, facing the monument, is a large stone painted black, bearing the Colston arms in gold, and inscribed in gold letters are the words—

In the vault underneath lies the body of Edward Colston, Esq., who died at Mortlake, 11th October, 1721. Also Sarah Colston, daughter of Edward Colston, jun., Esq., and great niece of the above, died 28th January, 1722, aged 15 years.

All Saints'.

COLSTON, WILLIAM, father of Edward Colston, died 21st November, 1681, aged 73. *All Saints'.*

CONYBEARE, JOHN, Bishop of Bristol and Dean of Christchurch, Oxford, an inscribed stone at the foot of the Bishop's throne, also a tablet on the north wall of the choir. Died 13th July, 1755, aged 63. *Cathedral.*

COSTER, THOMAS, Member of Parliament for Bristol. Died September 30th, 1769. *Cathedral.*

COTTLE, AMOS JOHN, and JOSEPH. *Cathedral.*

CRAUFORD, Dr., a monument by Chauntrey. *Cathedral.*

CYSTYNS, WILLIAM, died February 25th, 1586. *St. Werburgh's.*

DAUBENY, GEORGE, Alderman and Member of Parliament for Bristol. Died May 26, 1806, aged 63. *S. James'.*

DAVID, ABBOT, "was buried under a marble, with the figure of a human skull and cross on it," in the north transept. *Cathedral.*

DAY, ELIZABETH, in the chancel. Died 1718. *St. Philip and Jacob.*

DAY, Rev. WILLIAM, A.M., vicar of parish for 22 years. Died Sept. 7th, 1832, aged 66. *St. Philip & Jacob.*

DRAPER, ELIZABETH. An elegant monument. Died August 3rd, 1778, aged 35. *Cathedral.*

DRAPER, MABEL, and RICHARD LE. Two stone coffins, 1311. *St. Nicholas'.*

EAGLES, Rev. JOHN, A.M. (Oxon). Died Nov. 9th, 1855. *Cathedral.*

EASTERBROOK, Rev. JOSEPH, Vicar. Died Jan. 21st, 1791, aged 40. *Temple.*

EDEN, Rev. JOHN, vicar of parish for 41 years. Died 1840, aged 77 years. *St. Nicholas'.*

EDWARDS, WM., Capt. 17th R.I. Died Dec. 18th, 1853. *Cathedral.*

ELBRIDGE, JOHN, philanthropist, original founder of the Infirmary. Died Feb. 22nd, 1738. Also a tablet in the Infirmary. *Christ Church.*

ELTON, ISAAC, and two daughters. Stone inscription. Died Oct. 23rd, 1714, aged 34. *St. Philip's.*

ELTON, JACOB, Capt. R.N. A Latin inscribed monument against the wall of the south aisle, next the Newton chapel. Killed 29th March, 1745, in an engagement between his ship, *Anglesea*, and *L'Apollon*. *Cathedral.*

ELWYN, CŒCILIA, and her daughter, CŒCILIA ELEANOR. Tablet. Died June 3rd and 12th, 1811, respectively. *Temple.*

ELWYN, WILLIAM BRAME, and MARIA. The former died on May 27th, 1841; the latter, March 28th, 1818. *Cathedral.*

ESTERFIELD, JOHN, twice Mayor and an Alderman. A brass was inserted in the stone, but it has now disappeared. *St. Peter's.*

ESTLIN, JOHN BISHOP, surgeon, and founder of the Eye Dispensary, Frogmore street (*see* "Hospitals"). Died on June 10th, 1855, aged 67 years. *Unitarian Burial Ground.*

ESTLIN, Rev. Dr. J. PRIOR, father of the above. Minister at Lewin's mead 46 years. Died Aug. 10th, 1817, aged 90. *Unitarian Burial Ground.*

EVANS, Rev. HUGH CALEB, A.M., pastor of chapel for 23 years. Died March 28th, 1781, aged 64 years. *Broadmead (Baptist) Chapel.*

EVANS, Rev. CALEB, D.D., eldest son of the above, pastor of chapel for 10 years. Died Aug. 9th, 1791, aged 54. *Broadmead (Baptist) Chapel.*

FARMER, THOMAS, Mayor and Alderman. Died Nov., 1624, aged 83. Brass in north aisle. *Christ Church.*

FOOT, Rev. WM., an inscription in Redcross street. Died May 13th, 1782, aged 74. *Baptist Burial Ground.*

FOSKETT, Rev. BARNARD, pastor of chapel 34 years. Died Sept. 17th 1758, aged 73. *Broadmead (Baptist) Chapel.*

FOSTER, NATHANIEL, D.D., Prebendary. South side of choir. Died Oct. 20th, 1757, aged 39. *Cathedral.*

FRAMPTON, W., founder of church and three times Mayor. *St. John's.*

FRANKLAND, Dr. JOHN, Dean of Gloucester and Master of Sidney College, Cambridge. *St. Stephen's.*

FREELING, Sir FRANCIS, Bart., secretary to the General Post Office. Mural tablet. Died on 10th July, 1836. *St. Mary Redcliff.*

FREKE, THOMAS. *St. Stephen's.*

FYDELL, ELIZABETH ANNE. Died 3rd January, 1805. *Cathedral.*

GAUNT, Sir HENRY. A much worn effigy recumbent on a panelled tomb in south aisle, date 1268. *St. Mark's.*

GAUNT, MAURICE DE, and GOURNAY, ROBERT DE. In the south chapel of the south aisle are two cross-legged effigies in chain armour supposed to represent the abovenamed. *S. Mark's.*

GEORGES, Sir ROBERT, died 1619, an inscription, and to ELENA, his wife, died 1607. *St. Mark's.*

GIBBES, HENRY, Mayor and Alderman, and his wife, ANNE, at the east end of the south aisle. *St. James'.*

GIBBS, JAMES, Mayor of Bristol in 1842. Died Feb. 24th, 1853, aged 63 years. *St. Mark's.*

GLOUCESTER, ROBERT, Earl of. A recessed tomb in wall of south aisle supporting a recumbent effigy; above it a brass plate with the inscription:

Within this tomb was interred Robert, son of King Henry I., Earl or Consul of Gloucester, Lord of Bristol and builder of its castle, the pious and munificent founder of this church and of the priory of St. James. He died XXXI. October, A.D. MCXLVII., ætatis suæ lvii. or lviii.
St. James'.

GORE, WILLIAM, Major 33rd Regt. of Foot; Lieut.-Col. Bristol Volunteers in 1797, and again in 1803. Died 5th July, 1814, aged 63. *Cathedral.*

GRAY, ROBERT, D.D., Bishop of Bristol. Against west wall of Newton chapel a marble monument. Died Sept. 28th, 1834, aged 73. *Cathedral.*

GWILLIAM, MORGAN. In north wall of choir an effigy supposed to represent this the last official who presided over the monastery. *Cathedral.*

HABERFIELD, Sir JOHN KERLE, six times Mayor. Marble bust. Died Dec. 27th, 1857. *St. Mark's.*

HALL, Rev. ROBERT, A.M., pastor of chapel five years. Died Feb. 21st, 1831, aged 66. *Broadmead Chapel.*

HALL, WILLIAM, a stained glass window. Died Nov. 22nd, 1857, aged 64. *St. Mary Redcliff.*

HARRINGTON, GEORGE, Mayor and Alderman of the city. Died Jan. 2nd, 1639. *St. Peter's.*

HAWKINS, Sir JOHN, 1723. *Temple.*

HENDERSON, ANTONY AUGUSTUS, and ANTONY, father and son. Inscription on monument (1816). *Cathedral.*

HESKETH, Lady, cousin of the poet Cowper. The inscription over her remains is as follows:—

Dame Harriet Hesketh, the eldest daughter of Ashley Cowper, Esq., clerk of the Parliament, widow of Sir Thomas Hesketh, of Ruthford hall, in Lancashire. Born July 1733. Died 15th January, 1807.
Cathedral

HINDE, JOHN, Mayor of Bristol in 1669. *Temple.*

HOOK, Sir HUMPHREY, of Kingsweston. *St. Stephen's.*

HOOKE, ANDREW. Tablet. Died Feb. 20th, 1687, aged 72. *St. James'.*

HOWELL, Bishop, buried under a plain stone, with one Latin word inscribed thereon, *Expergiscar* ("I shall awake"). 1646. *Cathedral.*

HULETT, SUSANNA, died Oct. 3rd, 1692, aged 44. *St. Thomas'.*

HUNDRED, DAVID. At the entrance to the Elder Lady chapel is a marble slab, with an incised human skull and cross. Chosen abbot in 1216, resigned 1234. *Cathedral.*

JAMES, ELIZABETH, died 1599. *St. Mark's.*

JAMES, THOMAS, Mayor 1605, and "Parliament man" for Bristol in the reigns of Elizabeth and James I. Died in 1613. *St. Mark's.*

JAY, JOHN. In the chancel floor a black marble slab inlaid with brass, with engraved figures of adult male and female, and underneath 14 children. Died 1480. *St. Mary Redcliff.*

JUYN, Sir JOHN, Chief Justice of the King's Bench and Recorder of Bristol. In the Lady chapel. Died March 24th, 1439. *St. Mary Redcliff.*

KATER, JOHN HERMAN, sugar refiner. Died 31st July, 1803, aged 65 years. *St. Thomas'.*

KENTISH, EDWARD, M.D., a senior physician of St. Peter's hospital. A tomb. Died Dec. 5th, 1832, aged 69 years. *Unitarian Burial Ground.*

KITCHEN, ROBERT, Mayor, Sheriff and Alderman. A brass over the vestry door. Died on Sept. 5th, 1594. *St. Stephen's.*

KNIGHT, Sir JOHN, Mayor in 1691, Member of Parliament 1693. On the north wall of the chancel is a long Latin inscription to members of his family. *Temple.*

KNOWLE, EDMUND. The mitred figure of this abbot is in the north wall of the choir. Died June 9th, 1332. *Cathedral.*

LAMB, Very Rev. Dr., and to the memory of FRANCES ANNE, CHARLES and ARTHUR, his children. *Cathedral.*

LAMYNGTON, JOANNES, vicar of this church in 1393. *St. Mary Redcliff.*

LAYARD, Rev. CHARLES PETER, D.D. Tablet. Was Dean of the Cathedral, and in 1812 sold the fine brass eagle, presented in 1683 by the Rev. G. Williamson, which now stands in St. Mary-le-port church. Died 10th April, 1803, aged 55. *Cathedral.*

LITTLE, FORTUNE. Small marble tablet. Died 28th June, 1777, aged 57 years. *St. Mary Redcliff.*

LLOYD, ANNE. Died 1779, aged 52. *St. Augustine's.*

LLOYD, RICHARD. A brass inscribed to himself and his six sons and seven daughters (arms f. ermine, a cross saltire, sable), 1621. *Temple.*

LOUDE, ROBERT. Incised brass, representing a priest in eucharistic vestments bearing a chalice. Died Feb. 23rd, 1461. *St. Peter's.*

LOVE, Rev. SAMUEL, M.A. Tablet. Died Oct. 18, 1773, aged 29. *Cathedral.*

LOWDER, SAMUEL, and LUCY. Date 1793. *St. Michael's.*

LUCAS, SAMUEL. A stained glass window and brass. Died Jan. 13th, 1853, aged 83. *St. Mary Redcliff.*

LYLTIR, JOHN, and MARGARET, his wife. An old English inscription. *St. Philip and Jacob.*

MASON, MARY. Tablet in Elder Lady chapel. The epitaph deserves attention:—

Mary, the daughter of William Shermon, of Kingston-upon-Hull, Esq., and wife of the Rev. William Mason, the poet.

Died March 27th, 1767, aged 28. *Cathedral.*

MAZE, PETER, an eminent merchant. A marble monument. Died 14th June, 1849, aged 80. *Cathedral.*

MEDE, Sir THOMAS, and his wife. East of north aisle a double altar-tomb; in the first compartment are recumbent effigies of these two, and in the second a brass with figures of a man and two women engaged in prayer. Dec. 20th, 1475. *Redcliff.*

NEWBURY, WALTER. "Carved in pontificalia, lying on back with crozier and mitre." Died 1463. *Cathedral.*

NEWLAND, or NAILHEART, JOHN. "Over his grave is his statue in pontificalia graven or carved out from stone, lying on the back with a crozier in his hand and mitre on his head." *Cathedral.*

NEWTON, ATHALIN. A storied monument, having a canopy supported by six fluted pillars; upon the sculptured sarcophagus lies the effigy of a lady, supposed to be the above-named, wife of John Newton, of the Newtons of Barrs court. *St. Peter's.*

NEWTON, RICHARD. A tomb of grey marble is assigned by Mr. Ellacombe to Richard Newton, the time of whose death (1500) would agree with the style of the tomb. An inscription, affixed in 1748, states the tomb to belong to

Sir Richard Newton Cradock, of Barrs court, one of His Majesty's Justices of the Common Pleas, who died December the 13th, 1444.

It has been proved, however, that Judge Cradock and his lady are buried in Yatton church. *Cathedral.*

NOBLE, JOHN, Mayor, Sheriff and Alderman. Tablet against south wall. Died Mar. 11, 1768, aged 58. *S. James.*

NORTHALL, HENRY. Died May 9th, 1673, aged 70. *St. Peter's.*

NORTHALL, J., son of above. Died Feb. 20th, 1669, aged 39. *St. Peter's.*

NORTON, ANDREW. Three brasses to his memory and of his two wives, ELIZABETH & ELLEN. 1527. *S. Peter's.*

O'BRIEN, PAT. COTTER. Over 8ft. 3in. in height. Died Sept. 8th, 1806, aged 45. *Trenchard St. (R.C.) Chapel.*

OWEN, Sir HUGH, Bart. Died Jan. 13th, 1698, aged 53. *St. Augustine's.*

PELOQUIN, DAVID. Marble tablet. Died 21st March, 1766, aged 66 years. *St. Stephen's.*

PENN, Sir WILLIAM. Tablet to the memory of the father of the famous Quaker. Died Sept. 16, 1670. *Redcliff.*

PHILLIPS, HARRIET. Tablet. Died Sept. 24th, 1813, aged 23. *Cathedral.*

PHILLIPS, WILLIAM, subsacrist for 45 years. He was instrumental in saving the Cathedral during the riots of October, 1831. The mob, having burnt the Bishop's palace, proceeded to the Cathedral, but Phillips succeeded in wresting an iron bar from a rioter and routing the mob. Died 2nd April, 1849, aged 79. *Cathedral.*

PINNEY, WILLIAM. Inscribed tablet in north aisle. *St. Augustine's.*

POPHAM, DOROTHY, died 1646. *St. Mark's.*

PORTER, family. Marble tablet on the west wall of the transept, to the memory of the following members of this talented family:—William Ogilvie Porter, M.D., Colonel John Porter, Sir Robert Ker Porter, Jane Porter, Anna Maria Porter and William Porter. 1810-50. *Cathedral.*

POWELL, WILLIAM, the actor. Died 3rd July, 1769. *Cathedral.*

POWELL, WILLIAM. Stained glass window. Died Feb. 23rd, 1854, aged 64. *St. Mary Redcliff.*

PRETTYMAN, HENRY GEORGE. A Latin inscription. Died Oct. 16th, 1807, aged 17 years. *Cathedral.*

PRINGE, MARTIN, merchant. Died 1626, aged 46. *St. Stephen's.*

PYTLEY, THOMAS. Inside the communion rails, and forming part of the stone, with this inscription:—

Here lyeth the body of Thomas Pytley, symtims keper of the Queen's forest, who dyed the last day of October, 1596.

The forest referred to was that of Kingswood, which extended to Lawford's gate. *St. Philip and Jacob.*

ROBERTS, Rev. THOMAS, A.M., pastor of the chapel for 34 years. Tablet. Died Dec. 21st, 1841.

Old King Street (Baptist) Chapel.

ROBERTS, WILLIAM ISAAC. Died Dec. 26th, 1806. *St. Michael's.*

ROGERS, GEORGE, solicitor. Tablet to his memory and that of ELIZABETH, his wife. 1840. *Cathedral.*

ROWLEY, THOMAS. Brasses of a male and female figure, stating that Thomas Rowley died 1478, and his wife, Margaret, 1470. *St. John's.*

RUSSELL, Sir JAMES, Knt. An inscription on the north side of the communion table, beneath a fractured entablature, supported on two Corinthian columns. Died Nov. 15th, 1674, aged 74. *St. James'.*

RYLAND, Rev. JOHN, pastor of the chapel 31 years. Died May 25th, 1825, aged 72. *Broadmead (Baptist) Chapel.*

SALLEY, Bishop. Sculptured recumbent figure. Died 1516. *S. Mark's.*

SAVAGE, RICHARD, poet, who died a debtor in Newgate, Bristol, 1743.

An inscription states his grave to be about six feet from the north wall of the church. *St. Peter's.*
SCHIMMELPENNINCK, MARY ANNE, authoress. Mural monument. Died 29th August, 1856. *Cathedral.*
SEYER, RICHARD TWINE, Lieut.-Colonel Bengal Army. Died 20th April, 1833, aged 48. *St. Michael.*
SHIERCLIFF, EDWARD. Monumental inscription. Died Feb. 1st, 1798. *St. Augustine's.*
SMITH, CLARA ANN, poisoned by by M. A. Burdock, October 26th, 1833. *St. Augustine's.*
SMITH, RICHARD, surgeon to the Bristol Infirmary for 46 years. Inscription upon a gravestone in the churchyard. Died Jan. 24th, 1843, aged 70. *Temple.*
SMITH, THOMAS, died 8th October, 1730. *St. Peter's.*
SNIGGE, Sir GEORGE, Knt., Recorder, from 1592 to 1604. Monument at eastern end of south aisle. Died Nov. 11th, 1617, aged 73. *S. Stephen's.*
SOMERSET, Sir CHARLES. Kneeling figures of the Knight in complete plate armour, and his lady and daughter on a stybolate beneath a Corinthian canopy. 1598. *St. James'.*
SOMERSET, Colonel Lord JOHN THOMAS HENRY, seventh son of Henry, fifth Duke of Beaufort. A handsome marble tablet with inscription. Died Oct. 3rd, 1846. *Cathedral.*
SOMERSET, Right Hon. and Rev. Lord WILLIAM GEORGE HENRY SOMERSET, sixth son of Henry, fifth Duke of Beaufort. *Cathedral.*
SPRY, Rev. BENJAMIN, A.M. A stained glass window. Died October, 1806. *St. Mary Redcliff.*
SOUTHEY, ROBERT, born at No. 11 Wine street, 12th August, 1774. In 1813 became Poet Laureate. Fine white marble bust and inscription. Died March 21st, 1843. *Cathedral.*
STANDFAST, Rev. RICHARD, rector of parish over 51 years. Died August 24th, 1684, aged 78. *Christ Church.*
STANHOPE, ELIZABETH CHARLOTTE, died 13th June, 1816. *Cathedral.*
STEAR, Capt. RICHARD, aged 23, and his brother, EUGENE, aged 16. Drowned near Blacknore, August 20th, 1722. *St. Peter's.*
STOCK, J. EDMONDS, M.D. A tomb. Died Oct. 4th, 1835, aged 61 years. *Unitarian Burial Ground.*
STONE, JOHN, three times Mayor; he married four wives. Monument. Died 24th June, 1575. *Temple.*
SUMMERS, Rev. SAMUEL, pastor of chapel 3 years. Died Dec. 15th, 1836, aged 46. *Broadmead (Baptist) Chapel.*
SURTEES, Rev. JOHN, for 36 years Canon. Monument. Died Dec. 23rd, 1857, aged 73 years. *Cathedral.*
SWIFT, WILLIAM, 1628. *St. Mark's.*
THORNE, NICHOLAS, Chamberlain and Mayor, founder of the Bristol Grammar school in connection with his brother. Died 19th August, 1546, aged 50 years. *St. Werburgh's.*
THORP, Rev. W., pastor of chapel 27 years. Died 7th May, 1833, aged 62. *Castle Green (Independent) Chapel.*
THROGMORTON, MARGARET, died in 1635. *St. Mark's.*
TOWGOOD, Rev. RICHARD, A.M., Prebendary. An inscription. Died Oct. 11th, 1713, aged 59. *Cathedral.*
TYDDESTILLE, or TYDDELEY, WALTER, bailiff in 1377. An altar-tomb, with the effigy of a figure in the costume of a burgess or merchant. Died 20th March, 1380. *St. Stephen's.*
UPTON, GEORGE. An inscription. Died Jan. 25th, 1608. *St. Mark's.*
VASSALL, Colonel. His remains were brought from South America, where he died of a mortal wound received at the storming of Monte Video, Feb. 3rd, 1807. *St. Paul's.*
VAUGHAN, Sir CHARLES. Monumental tomb, with an inscription. Died Feb. 16th, 1630. *Cathedral.*
WALWYN, R. Monument in white marble to three children. *Cathedral.*
WASBOROUGH, RICE, organist. Died 11th April, 1802, aged 54. *Cathedral.*
WASBROUGH, MATTHEW, inventor of the fly-wheel. Brass plate. Died Oct. 21st, 1781, aged 28. *St. Peter's.*
WASTFIELD, ELIZABETH, died Dec. 28th, 1770, aged 60. *Cathedral.*
WEBB, Lieutenant. Marble tablet. Died Dec. 20th, 1796, aged 72. *Portland Street (Wesleyan) Chapel.*

WESTFIELD, THOMAS, D.D. A Latin inscription written by himself. Died June 25th, 1644. *Cathedral.*

WHISH, MARTIN, chairman of the Board of Excise for nearly 40 years. Died Oct. 26th 1826. *Cathedral.*

WHISH, Rev. MARTIN RICHARD, M.A., vicar of Bedminster parish 46 years. A tablet. Died 7th April, 1852, aged 70. *St. Mary Redcliff.*

WHITSON, Alderman, Mayor, and four times Member of Parliament for the city; a princely benefactor to the poor. 1629. *St. Nicholas.*

WRIGHT, JOHN, M.D. A memorial. Died Dec. 23rd, 1794, aged 62 years. *Unitarian Burial Ground.*

WRIGHT, Rev. THOMAS, brother of above. Tablet. He was minister of the Society of Protestant Dissenters in Lewin's mead during the space of 48 years. Died 14th May, 1797, aged 70. *Unitarian Burial Ground.*

WYLD, WM. HOPTON, Alderman. A window. Died on March 29th, 1858. *St. Mary Redcliff.*

YOUNG, Sir JOHN, Knt., and his wife, JOANE. He was knighted by Elizabeth on her visit to the city in 1574. *Cathedral.*

At Arno's Vale Cemetery.

It would be impossible within the compass of this work to give a complete list, or even a summary, of the many handsome monuments that adorn this picturesque and sacred "God's acre"; we simply give a brief list of the most striking mementoes, after a few casual visits, of those honoured and respected citizens, and others who are "gone before."

ABBOT, HENRY, of The Priory, Abbot's Leigh, Alderman, and trustee of the municipal charities. Born March 1st, 1812; died April 3rd, 1874.

ADLAM, ELIZABETH, wife of Geo. Adlam, died 21st July, 1869, aged 60.

ADLAM, JOHN THOMAS. Born Oct. 29th, 1860; died Oct. 21st, 1877.

ALSOP, URIAH, children of.

BALL, family. Three monuments.

BARNES, FRANCIS K., died July 13th, 1876, aged 83.

BARTLETT, JOHN, died August, 1852, aged 55.

BIGWOOD, family.

BREILLAT, JOHN, C.E., died 14th April, 1856, aged 86. He, in 1811, introduced gas into Bristol, and founded the present Gas Light Company, of which he was engineer nearly 40 years. It may be interesting to know that the first interment in the Cemetery was of the wife of the above; it took place 29th July, 1839.

BRITTAN, HENRY, died Dec. 6th, 1881.

BRUNT, ISAAC HARPER, died Sept. 4th, 1883.

BUCK, Rev. CHARLES, for 28 years rector of St. Stephen's. Died Oct. 28th, 1858, aged 63.

BURDER, Rev. JOHN, died May 17th, 1867, aged 82.

BUSH, JAMES, died March 13th, 1864, aged 60.

BUSH, Major, late of H.M. 96th Regt.; also late Lieut.-Col. B.R.V. Corps. Died Aug. 5th, 1877, aged 69.

BUTCHER, JAMES E., Lieut.-Col. Madras Native Infantry. Died Dec. 30th, 1868, aged 67.

BYRNES, wife of Rev. L. H. Byrnes, died Feb. 14th, 1876, aged 51.

CARR, THOMAS, M.I.M.E., sole inventor of the disintegrator. Died March 29th, 1874, aged 50.

CHAPMAN, ALFRED, died Feb. 7th, 1863, aged 37.

CHILCOTT, ALFRED, died Feb. 6th, 1880, aged 62.

CHUTE, JAMES HENRY, died July 23rd, 1878, aged 68.

CLARK, JOHN, died August 4th, 1881, aged 75.

CLARK, HENRY, surgeon. Family vault. October, 1858.

CLARKE, FREDERICK FRYER, drowned in the river Avon, Dec. 25th, 1879, aged 26 years.

COALES, FRED. BEN. Born 27th July, 1826; died Dec. 20th, 1881.

COLE, JOHN, died Sept. 11th, 1869, aged 64.

CORDEUX, THOMAS, died Dec. 31st, 1855, aged 76.

CORNISH, JOHN WILLIAM, and family.

COWLIN, WILLIAM, died March 28th, 1877, aged 68.
CRIPPS, family. Monument.
CROUCH. In memory of twelve of that family.
DANDO, JOSEPH, died 23rd June, 1860, aged 79.
DERHAM, HENRY, died Jan. 26th, 1882.
DITCHETT, SAMUEL DAY. Born Jan. 18th, 1829; died April 18th, 1859.
DODDRELL, T. D. Born June 2nd, 1788; died Sept. 4th, 1840.
DREW, Captain EDWARD.
EDKINS, ROSE E., died 3rd July, 1871, aged 23.
ELLIS, ROBERT WILLIAM. Born March 30th, 1826; died Dec. 19th, 1881.
EVANS, DAVID PARKER, died Nov. 13th, 1880, aged 64.
EVENS, JAMES, wife of. Died Dec. 29th, 1882, aged 62.
FERRIS, SUSANNAH, the wife of Richard Ferris. Died 2nd April, 1850, aged 67.
FISH, JOSEPH, and wife, JANE. The former died Jan. 17th, 1883, aged 74; the latter, Nov. 4th, 1875, aged 69.
FOLLWELL, MARY, wife of Edward Follwell. Died Feb. 17th, 1873, aged 33.
FRANCIS, WILLIAM, and family.
FRAYNE, WILLIAM, wife of. Died April 20th, 1866, aged 61.
GARDNER, JAMES ANTHONY, late of H.M. Royal Fusiliers. Accidentally drowned at Alwaye, in the East Indies. Aged 30 years.
GARDNER, WALTER, died Oct. 23rd, 1880, aged 58.
GIBSON, WILLIAM MIDDLETON. Born August 11th, 1827; died Dec. 11th, 1878.
GLASS, EDWARD, died Oct. 10th, 1876, aged 69.
GLENDENNING, JOHN, late minister of the Tabernacle, Penn street, in this city. Died 25th May, 1871, aged 59.
GWYER. Two to this family.
GWYNNE, A. T. JONES, died July 14th, 1869, aged 78.

ROY, RAM-MOHUN, Rajah. The monument to this Prince is said to be the finest in the Cemetery, and bears the following inscription:—

Beneath this stone rest the remains of Rajah Ram-Mohun Roy, a conscientious and steadfast believer in the unity of the Godhead. He consecrated his life with entire devotion to the worship of the Divine Spirit alone. To great natural talents he united a thorough mastery of many languages, and early distinguished himself as one of the greatest scholars of his day. His universal labours to promote the social, moral and physical condition of the people of India, his earnest endeavours to suppress idolatry and the rite of Suttee, and his constant zealous advocacy of whatever tended to advance the glory of God and the welfare of man, live in the grateful remembrance of his countrymen. This tablet records the sorrow and pride with which his memory is cherished by his descendants. He was born in Radhanajore, in Bengal, in 1774, and died at Bristol, Sept. 27th, 1833.

HALL, Rev. ROBERT, M.A. Born May 2nd, 1764; died Feb. 21st, 1831. (The medallion of this tomb is remarkably fine.)
HARE, BRIDGET, widow of Charles Hare. Born May 8th, 1787; died May 2nd, 1860.
HARE, CHARLES BOWLES, died 3rd August, 1855, aged 45 years.
HARRIS, RICHARD, died 12th July, 1870, aged 76.
HARRIS, WILLIAM, died July 17th, 1879.
HASSELL, ROBERT, wife of. Died Dec. 19th, 1862, aged 31.
HATHERLEY, JOHN EDWARD, died Jan. 13th, 1881, aged 54.
HAWKINS, THOMAS, died April 1st, 1881, aged 73.
HERAPATH, WILLIAM, Sen., J.P., Professor of Chemistry, F.G.S. Died Feb. 13th, 1868, aged 71.
HILL, CHARLES, died 27th June, 1872, aged 77.
HILL, MATTHEW DAVENPORT, died June 7th, 1872, aged 79.
HOLLINS, JAMES, vicar of St. Clement's for 20 years, from its consecration in 1855. Died April 14th, 1875, aged 53.
HOSEGOOD, MARY ANN, wife of Obed Hosegood. Died Nov. 6th, 1877, aged 55.

INSKIP, —, wife of James Inskip. Died 27th August, 1869, aged 31.
JEFFERIES, CHARLES THORNTON, died Feb. 2nd, 1871, aged 60.
JONES, RICHARD, died Jan. 18th, 1867, aged 67.
JOSE, THOMAS PORTER, died Jan. 19th, 1875.
KEDDELL, GEORGE, surgeon, died Dec. 5th, 1865, aged 58.
KEPPLE, wife of S. J. Kepple. Died August 12th, 1876, aged 53.
KING, CHRISTOPHER JOHN, died 15th April, 1882, aged 55.
KINTON, WILLIAM, died 23rd June, 1819, aged 68.
LANGTON, HENRY GORE, M.P. for Bristol from 1852 to 1865. Died 16th May, 1875, aged 73.
LEWIS, THOMAS, died April 18th, 1859.
LINDREA, WILLIAM, died Jan. 20th, 1859.
LOGAN, JAMES, M.D., died Dec. 16th, 1881.
LOWTHER, ELIZA, wife of Captain James Lowther. Died 20th June, 1874, aged 37.
LUCAS, EDWARD, died Feb. 20th, 1879.
LUCAS, JOHN, and family.
LUCAS, THOMAS, Alderman, and other members of the family.
LYON, GILBERT, M.D., practised for 45 years as a doctor. Died Oct. 5th, 1873, aged 70.
MATTHEWS, ROBERT LEONARD, died 1st May, 1869, aged 27.
MATTHEWS, THOMAS GADD, died 23rd June, 1860, aged 58.
MEDWAY, wife of H. A. Medway. Died August 17th, 1876, aged 49.
MELSOM, HENRY, died March 22nd, 1866, aged 53.
MILLER, JOSEPH, died March 1st, 1869, aged 64.
MORGAN, RICHARD, R.N., died 5th June, 1867, aged 74.
MUNDY, THOMAS C., wife of. Died Oct. 6th, 1875.
NASH, EZEKIEL, died Jan. 2nd, 1845. Family vault.
NEAT, WILLIAM, pugilist. Died March 22nd, 1858, aged 69.
"His end was peace."

NIBLETT, ISAAC, died Dec. 11th, 1860.
NORRIS, ROBERT, died Dec. 8th, 1850, aged 34.
OGDEN, FRANCIS BARBER, late Consul of the United States of America at this port. Born March 3rd, 1783; died July 4th, 1857, aged 74, having served his country during a period of 28 years.
OLIVE, L. J., died 17th June, 1865, aged 60.
OUTERBRIDGE, WILLIAM, Captain. Died July 24th, 1876, aged 65.
PALMER, JAMES, late banker of this city, died Feb. 27th, 1880, aged 87 years.
PHILLIPS, MARY, and BESSIE B., wives of Augustus Phillips. The former died Nov. 7th, 1860, aged 45; the latter, Nov. 19th, 1865, aged 26.
PILLERS, A. W., died Oct. 5th, 1882, aged 46.
PRATT, Rev. J. ADEY, 16 years pastor of Kingsland chapel. Died Jan. 4th, 1867, aged 56.

The monument erected by the Sunday schools of Bristol and neighbourhood as a tribute of affection.

PRICE, CHARLES, died Jan. 22nd, 1869, aged 70.
PROCTOR, THOMAS, Alderman and Magistrate, died May 15th, 1876, aged 64. Also MARY, wife of the above, died Jan. 4th, 1883, aged 67.
REED, WILLIAM BATEMAN. Born 20th April, 1813; died 28th June, 1880.
REYNOLDS, THOMAS, died Sept. 28th, 1867, aged 88.
RICHARDSON, URIAH, professor of music, and many years bandmaster of the Bristol Volunteer Rifles. Died Nov. 30th, 1872, aged 55.
ROBINSON, ELIZABETH, and LOUISA, wives of E. S. Robinson. The former died Jan. 18th, 1871, aged 50; the latter, April 10th, 1875, aged 34.
ROGERS, Rev. AARON, a faithful pastor of St. Peter's for 30 years. Died Sept. 4th, 1872, aged 68.
ROPER, Rev. HENRY I., 35 years pastor of Congregational church, Bridge street, afterwards at Clifton down. Died April 6th, 1874.

ROSSITER, THOMAS LEONARD B. (and other members of the family). Died Jan. 7th, 1862, aged 25.
ROUGHSEDGE, WILLIAM, died 5th March, 1866, aged 77.
ROWE, RICHARD, died Sept. 15th, 1877.
SANDERS, WILLIAM, F.R.S., F.G.S. Died Nov. 12th, 1875.
SMART, THOMAS TONEY, L.A.C., L.R.C.P., for 42 years medical officer of the Bedminster Union. Died 26th August, 1882, aged 68.
SMITH, GEORGE JAMES, died Jan. 17th, 1876.
SMITH, JAMES, died Sept. 10th, 1871.
SMITH, JOSEPH, died Dec. 3rd, 1854, aged 77.
SNOW, JOHN, died April 5th, 1883, aged 59.
SOMERTON, WILLIAM HENRY, died Sept. 24th, 1870, aged 74.
SPARK, WILLIAM, wife of. Born Dec. 18th, 1815; died Dec. 26th, 1867.
STOCK, Lieut.-Col., late of the 10th Regt. of Foot. Died March 9th, 1877, aged 68. (Also a tablet in the chapel.)

From his unassuming demeanour few people knew that they had in their midst a soldier who had so gallantly served his country. To record his worth and her irreparable loss, this tablet is erected by his sorrowing widow.

STONE, ALFRED, died Jan. 3rd, 1878, aged 37. The inscription on the monument is to this effect:—

As a gifted musician he was widely known, and as a genial friend greatly beloved. The members of the Bristol Musical Festival Society raised the monument in affectionate remembrance of their first conductor.

STROUD, JOHN, died June 18th, 1881, aged 87.
SUMMERS, WILLIAM, died April 23rd, 1876.
SWAYNE, CHAMPENY, surgeon (and other members of the family). Died 8th August, 1852, aged 66.
SYMONDS, Dr. J. A., died Feb. 25th, 1871.
TAYLOR, JOHN, former proprietor of the *Times and Mirror*, died April 11th, 1857.

TAYLOR, THOMAS TERRETT, family.
TEMPLE, JAMES, died June 24th, 1881, aged 76.
TERRELL, WILLIAM, and family.
THOMAS, Rev. DAVID, B.A., 40 years Independent minister in Bristol, first at Zion, Bedminster, and 31 years at Highbury, Cotham. Died Nov. 7th, 1875, aged 64.
TRAPNELL, WILLIAM, Nov. 11th, 1876, aged 47.
TRULL, JAMES, died Nov. 9th, 1874, aged 67.
TYNDALL, THOMAS O., and his wife. Died Sept. 14th, 1869, aged 55.
ULLATHORNE, JOHN, died Feb. 18th, 1882, aged 53.

A tribute to the memory of his valuable services as Secretary to the Bristol Licensed Victuallers' Association.

WALSH, DAVID HENRY, died Oct. 7th, 1877.
WARRY, JOHN, died Jan. 5th, 1868, aged 83.
WATHEN, MARY S., wife of Chas. Wathen. Died April 4th, 1881, aged 46.
WESTON, THOMAS, and family.
WETHERMAN, JOHN, died Oct. 14th, 1877, aged 71.
WHITLEY, L. MARIA, died Nov. 23rd, 1881, aged 24.
WHITTALL, JAMES (and others of the family). Died Oct. 10th, 1856, aged 24.
WILLIAMS, JOSEPH, surgeon, died of cholera, Sept. 8th, 1849, aged 26. The best testimony to his character is the brief but heroic narrative of his death. When the pestilence which had been raging in Bristol broke out in the crowded wards of Stapleton workhouse he was amongst the first to volunteer on a service fraught with peril. Impelled by an ardent sense of duty and the philanthropic intrepidity which braves all danger to aid the distressed, he laboured day and night—heedless of friendly remonstrance—amid the sick and dying, until, strength and nature being overwrought, he was seized by the fatal malady, from which he was the means of rescuing others, and fell with the calmness of a Christian

in one of the noblest causes in which life can be laid down. The Corporation of the Poor of the city of Bristol have caused this tomb and inscription to be placed above his remains to mark their grateful esteem for the memory of a man to whose skill, courage and devotion the public were much indebted at a season of great gloom and suffering.

WILLS, WILLIAM DAY, died May 12th, 1866, aged 69.

WOOD, JOHN, died March 8th, 1868, aged 54.

The principal monuments in the Episcopalian Chapel at the Cemetery:—

CLAXTON, WILLIAM, and family. Merchant of the city of Bristol. Died on the Feast of St. John the Baptist, 1873, aged 75.

HABERFIELD, Sir JOHN KERLE, Knt. Born Oct. 23rd, 1785; died Dec. 27th, 1857.

He served the office of Mayor of the city of Bristol six times, and was seven times governor of the Incorporation of the Poor. The generous hospitality and bountiful charity which distinguished his life will long be remembered in the city, the interests of which he was always the first to promote. He was ever ready to assist those struggling with pecuniary difficulties and to relieve the poor. He died universally beloved and lamented, and in affectionate regard for his memory his friends have erected a monument in the Mayor's chapel in Bristol to perpetuate his worth and their loss. His widow pays this last tribute of deep affection to her husband in the place where his remains are interred.

Also in remembrance of Sarah, widow of the above, who died at her residence, 41 Royal York crescent, Clifton, 8th December, 1874. 76 years.

HILL, S. 1874.

HILL, THOMAS WILLIAM, formerly an oil merchant of this city. He founded and largely endowed the almshouses for poor women at Berkeley place, Clifton, which bears his name, and the "Hill ward" at the Bristol Royal Infirmary, and was also a munificent contributor to the building and endowment of the church and schools of St. Silas, and of the schools and soup kitchen of St. Luke, Bedminster. Died Jan. 21st, 1874, aged 85.

Mortality, Rate of in Bristol per 1,000. The city stands very low in this respect. The following is the return of the Registrar-General for the past seven years:—

1876 .. .. .. 22·6 per 1,000
1877 .. .. .. 22·5 "
1878 .. .. .. 22·2 "
1879 .. .. .. 21·9 "
1880 .. .. .. 21·0 "
1881 .. .. .. 19·6 "
1882 .. .. .. 19·2 "

It will be observed that the rate per thousand has been steadily decreasing in each of the above years. Out of the 28 largest towns in England Bristol occupies the second place, as may be seen by reference to the Registrar-General's annual returns.

Mortuaries. There are three for the reception of dead bodies found in the city by the police, viz.: In St. Paul's, Meadow street; St. Philip's, near the Marsh bridge; Bedminster, Police station.

Municipal Elections. Ordinary municipal elections take place on the 1st November in each year. Those inhabitants whose names have been placed on a published list called the burgess roll are entitled under the Municipal Corporations Reform Act 1835 to elect from themselves a certain number of persons to constitute a corporate body called a Town Council. (*See* "Aldermen" and "Council.")

Municipal Reform Act 1835. This Act, though opposed by the Corporation in the House of Lords, was passed September 9th, 1835. (*See* "Wards.")

Murders. The following is a list of executions for murder and other crimes, from 1741 to the present date, that have taken place —except those of Bailey and Barry, who were executed at Gloucester; the record being here given as the crime was committed at Horfield— within the city's precincts.

GOODYERE, SAMUEL, Captain. Murdering his brother. March 30th, 1741.

M'HONEY, MICHAEL, and WHITE, C. Murdering Goodyere's brother. March 30th, 1741.

WILLIAMS, JANE. Murdering her child. April 30th, 1741.

NICHOLAS, WILLIAM, a boy. For poisoning his mother. April 23rd, 1748.

JONES and JACKSON. Highway robbery. April 23rd, 1752.

SCUDAMORE, —. Returning from transportation. April 23rd, 1752.

ARNOLD and CRITCHLEY. Felony. May 7th, 1753.

HOBBS, —. Murder. Aug. 24th, 1758.

SHEPPARD, WILLIAM DELAN. Felony. May 24th, 1761.

WARD, PATRICK. Shooting a warder. October 16th, 1761.

DAWSON, WILLIAM. Robbery. April 16th, 1764.

SLACK, —. Horse stealing. April 16th, 1768.

FULKNER, JOHN, drummer. Shot on Brandon hill. Dec. 10th, 1771.

BRITTAN, JONATHAN. Forgery. May 15th, 1772.

DANNETT, ISAAC. Forgery. April 2nd, 1774.

HAYNES, DANIEL. Housebreaking. Sept. 22nd, 1775.

CREWYS, THOMAS. Forgery. May 15th, 1778.

LOVEDAY, B., and BURKE, J. Felony. October 12th, 1781.

PROTHEROE, SHENKIN. Gibbeted on Durdham down. March 31st, 1783.

GAME, GEORGE. Hung on Bedminster down. March 31st, 1783.

SHUTTLER, WILLIAM. Housebreaking. May 23rd, 1783.

WILLIAMS, WILLIAM, alias Motley. Forgery. May 23rd, 1783.

RANDALL, —. Hung at Totterdown. May 23rd, 1784.

COLLINS, JOHN. Murder. April 8th, 1785.

COOK, AMBROSE. Robbery. Oct. 6th, 1786.

MACNAMARA, EDWARD. Forgery. May 7th, 1790.

HUNGERFORD, WILLIAM. Housebreaking. July 9th, 1790.

HAMBLINGTON, ROBERT. Housebreaking. May 3rd, 1793.

SMITH, BENJAMIN. Forgery. April 24th, 1795.

POWELL, DUGGAN and BABER. Forgery. April 26th, 1799.

HAYNES, R., alias Dick Boy. Shooting at the officers. April 25th, 1800.

MAYNARD, ROBERT. Housebreaking. May 1st, 1801.

M'LEOCHLAM, DUNCAN. Forgery. May 1st, 1801.

HOWIE, Captain W. Sinking a vessel. May 8th, 1801.

BOBBETT, CHARLOTTE, and DAVIES, MARIA. Murdering Davies' child. April 2nd, 1802.

BADGER, WILLIAM. Forgery. April 30th, 1802.

MINNETT, JESSE. Horse stealing. April 22nd, 1803.

M'QUIRE, HUGH. Forging a seaman's order. April 22nd, 1803.

TYSO, JOSEPH. Forgery. April 26th, 1805.

CARTER, WILLIAM. Forgery. April 26th, 1816.

HARWOOD, JOHN. Murder. April 13th, 1821. The first criminal executed at the Drop, Bristol New Gaol.

MILLARD, RICHARD. Forgery. May 2nd, 1828.

WALKER, WILLIAM. Housebreaking. April 29th, 1831.

DAVIS, CHRISTOPHER; CLARKE, WILLIAM; GREGORY, THOMAS; and KEYES, JOSEPH. Rioting. Jan. 27th, 1832.

BURDOCK, MARY ANN. Murder (by poison). April 15th, 1835.

THOMAS, SARAH HARRIET. Murder. April 20th, 1849.

BAILEY and BARRY. Executed at Gloucester for the Horfield child poisoning. January 12th, 1874.

HOLE, WILLIAM. Murder. April 26th, 1875.

DEACON, —. Murder. April 24th, 1876.

DISTIN, W. J. Murder. Nov. 22nd, 1880.

Museum and Library,

Queen's road, top of Park street, is in the Gothic style of architecture, commanding a prominent position on a broad platform with a flight of steps, and is built from the joint designs of Foster and Ponton, architects. It contains two spacious library rooms, two large museum rooms, lecture theatre, laboratory, committee room, and some smaller apartments. The building, capacious as it appears, is not sufficiently large to meet the requirements of the subscribers, and the exterior is still incomplete. The association was formed in 1871 by the union of two societies, the Bristol Institution for the advancement of Science, Literature, and the Fine Arts (founded in 1823), and the Bristol Library Society. The former of these had for about fifty years occupied the building at the bottom of Park street (see "Freemason's Hall"). The Bristol Library Society, which was established in 1772, was for many years in occupation of the building in King street, now the Free Lending Library. The cost of the present building was raised by the sale of the Park street building, and by donations amounting to between £8,000 and £9,000, a gift of £1,000 from the late J. N. Sanders, of Clifton, being a special endowment for the museum. The total cost exceeded £20,000. The proprietary body consists of shareholders, including those possessing shares in the two other societies and donors of £10 and upwards to the building fund. The society is maintained by annual subscriptions, according to the following scale:—

	Shareholders. Gs.	Non-Shareholders. Gs.
For use of the whole building	2½	3
" Library & Newsroom	2¼	2½
" Newsroom & Museum	2	2
" Library and Museum	2	2
" Museum	1	1
" Library	1¼	1¼

The museum is open to visitors at merely a nominal charge, and is especailly rich in objects illustrative of geology, palæontology, zoology, anthropology and mineralogy. The collection of fossil saurians is a very complete one; there is a good series of minerals, a collection of plastercasts from the antique, including a complete set of casts of the Elgin marbles; stuffed mammalia, birds, reptiles and fishes, and a series of skeletons and skulls said to be the finest out of London. It also contains a fine collection of modern Indian textile fabrics. The library contains over 50,000 volumes, many of them very rare and valuable. Under the arcade at the front entrance are two stone urns, which formerly surmounted the side pillars of the Temple gate at the south entrance to the city. In the outer hall is the original statue of "Eve at the Fountain," by the late E. H. Baily, R.A., a Bristolian; also fine casts of the Belvedere Apollo, Laocöon, Dying Gladiator, Venus de Medici, Capri Diana, Thalia, Canova's Hebe and his Dancing Girls. A cast of the bust of Hermes, the only authentic work of Praxiteles, the Greek sculptor, which was lately discovered at Olympia, and is now in Berlin, has been recently presented by F. F. Tuckett. Here is also a portrait, by H. P. Briggs, R.A., of the Rajah Ram-Mohun Roy, the first Hindu reformer. The building is the head-quarters of many scientific societies. The number of visitors admitted by payment at the doors during 1882 was 14,385, as against 15,275 in 1881. Of these, 12,791 paid 2d., 220 paid 3d., and 1,374 paid 6d. The number admitted by subscribers' orders was 258. The museum is open to the public daily (except Sundays) from 10 a.m. to 6 p.m. in summer, and sunset in winter, at a small charge. The library is open to subscribers only from 9.30 a.m. to 9 p.m., but books cannot be taken out after 6 p.m. The newsroom is open from 9.30 a.m. to 9.30 p.m.

Music. Music is by no means a newly developed art in Bristol. For several generations past musical societies have sprung into life and died out, and upon their ashes new associations have been reared. More recently music has assumed a different phase in our old city; but to the minds of amateurs who have passed the zenith of life, and who are acquainted with the musical history of the past, doubts will arise as to whether Bristol has made strides in musical affairs proportionate to the growth of her population. *Curas cithara tollit* ("music is a specific for care"), the inscription over the entrance to the old Assembly rooms, in Prince street, is sufficient to show to what extent our forefathers appreciated the divine art, and what effect its sweet sounds had upon them when gathered in that hall, away from scenes of activity and care, to hear the performance of an oratorio, a symphony, or to listen to sweet voices singing those charming compositions of our madrigal writers. In this sketch it is not intended to speak minutely of the state of music in the past, but briefly to touch upon it and lead up to the present. In bygone days existed the Bristol Catch Club and the Cecilian Society, ably conducted by Robert Broderip, organist of the Mayor's chapel at the close of last century. Amongst other prominent societies of a later age were the Bristol Vocal Society, the Choral Society, the Harmonic Society, the Sacred Harmonic Society, the Philharmonic Society, and the Classical Harmonists' Society, with which many eminent professionals and amateurs were connected. College green, Park street, and the old Gloucester hotel at the Hotwells were then places where the members of these societies met to practise, and concerts were given in Prince street and at the Hotwells before the erection of the Victoria rooms, which, when that was built, became the most popular concert hall. The last of these old associations was the Classical Harmonists' Society, conducted for some time by the late J. D. Corfe, and later by Philip John Smith. It was this society that first gave in Bristol the *Elijah* soon after its production at Birmingham, and performed other choral works (many of which have not since been heard here). Amongst them were Rossini's *Stabat Mater*, Spohr's *Fall of Babylon* and *Last Judgment*, Haydn's *Seasons* and *Creation*, Beethoven's *Mount of Olives*, Handel's *Messiah*, *Israel in Egypt*, *Judas Maccabæus, Samson, Dettingen Te Deum*, and *Acis and Galatea*, Gounod's *Messe Solennelle*, Mendelssohn's *Christus, Walpurgis Night, Hymn of Praise, St. Paul* and *Antigone*, Costa's *Naaman* and *Eli*, and, we believe, selections from Handel's *Jephtha, Saul, Deborah* and *Solomon*. These were given with a complete and highly efficient band (including many first-class musicians), and at the operatic concerts many of the finest orchestral symphonies and overtures, including Mendelssohn's *Reformation Symphony*, were performed. Mdlle. Titiens, Madame Grisi, Madame Lablache, Madame Dolby, Miss Martha Williams, Miss Catharine Hayes, Mrs. P. J. Smith, Madame Weiss, Miss Birch, Madame Clara Novello, Madame Rudersdorff, Madame Sherrington, Miss Poole, Mr. Sims Reeves, Signor Mario, Mr. Tom Hohler, Mr. W. H. Cummings, Mr. Santley, Mr. Thomas, Herr Formes, Mr. J. Lockey, Mr. H. Phillips, Herr Staudigl and Mr. Weiss were amongst the names of the principals who contributed their services during the period of existence of the society. The new Colston hall was opened by a concert under the direction of Philip J. Smith, the name of whose body of 500 vocalists being then changed to that of the Colston hall Philharmonic Society. A small organ was placed there by the conductor, and George Riseley gave his first organ recitals upon it. The society did not live long after this. Some misunderstanding arose when the present organ was built in the Colston hall by H. Willis. Philip J. Smith retired, and the organisation which he had been principally instrumental in keeping together collapsed. So much for defunct societies. As regards existing ones, the Madrigal Society, established 1837, stands preëminent. The Orpheus Glee Society was started seven years after, and eleven years ago the Bristol Musical Festival Society was organised. These and other musical bodies will be dealt with more extensively under their respective heads.

Musical Societies.

BRISTOL CHOIRS ASSOCIATION was formed in 1881, and consists of members of the choirs of the Congregational and Baptist churches of the city, who meet weekly for combined practise under the choirmaster (W. J. Kidner). In accordance with the chief object of the association, special attention is given to such methods as tend to a general improvement in psalmody, and the committee continue to be much encouraged by the results so far attained. The general committee consists of the organist and a representative from the choir of each associated chapel.

BRISTOL MUSICAL ASSOCIATION. Established in 1881 for the special purpose of providing concerts for the working classes, on Saturday evenings, in Colston hall. There are 2,000 tickets at 3d. issued for each concert; also a limited number at 1/-, the president's gallery being reserved for subscribers and guarantors. The choir and band consists of 150 members. The concerts are of a miscellaneous character. Among the works already performed are *The Messiah, Creation, May Queen. Lauda Sion, Stabat Mater, Acis and Galatea,* &c. Rev. J. M. Wilson, M.A., president; A. Krauss, treasurer; G. Riseley, organist; and G. Gordon, conductor.

BRISTOL MUSICAL FESTIVAL SOCIETY. Several gentlemen, whose musical tastes are great, conceived the idea of founding in Bristol a Musical Festival Society on the lines of the great Birmingham institution. Being persons of influence, and having the will and the means, they put their ideas into practical shape early in 1872. In an almost incredibly short space of time an excellent choir was gathered under Alfred Stone, several oratorios were put in rehearsal, and in October of the following year the first festival was held. Alderman Barnes (then Mayor) presided at a public meeting held in January, 1874, when the society was consolidated. Two resolutions were passed—one "That a society be formed, to be called the Bristol Musical Society, the main objects of which will be :—(1) The establishment of triennial musical festivals ; (2) To give in intermediate periods a series of performances at popular prices, not exceeding four in any one year, of which one is intended to be with a complete band ; (3) The maintenance of an efficient chorus ; and (4) The acquisition and maintenance of a musical library." The second resolution was :—"That the society shall consist of not more than 300 members, and the liabilities of each member shall be limited to £25." Upon these lines the society has gone. The choir has grown considerably—to nearly double its original size, and there are now on the register nearly 400 members. A further development took place during the winter months of 1880-1-2-3. Vocal training classes were formed in connection with the society, and a small fee of 3d. per lesson was charged. The result was highly satisfactory: 1,140 attended the classes, of whom 350 passed a successful examination and were awarded certificates for efficiency in singing at sight, in time, and for theoretical knowledge. At the present time arrangements are announced for an instrumental class in addition to the continuation of the vocal training classes. After the festival in 1879 the liability of the guarantors was reduced to £10, and the number was increased from 300 to 500. Her Most Gracious Majesty the Queen is patron of the society, H.R.H. the Duke of Edinburgh is the president, and there are 150 vice-presidents. The Executive Committee consists of 26 gentlemen residing in Bristol. William Smith is the chairman, C. B. Hare vice-chairman, G. W. Edwards the treasurer, and Henry Cooke the hon. secretary. The late Alfred Stone was the original choirmaster, and on his death, in 1878, D. W. Rootham was appointed to the post, which he still efficiently fills. Walter J. Kidner is the secretary.

Triennial Festivals. In October, 1873, the first musical festival was given in Bristol. The event was ushered in with a flourish of trumpets, metaphorically and musically speaking, and triennially the festival has been repeated. Although comparatively short time was afforded the late Alfred Stone, the first conductor, to collect a choir and prepare them for the arduous work, the inaugural gathering was a success. Haydn's *Creation*, Mendelssohn's *Elijah*, Macfarren's *St. John the Baptist* (performed for the first time), Mendelssohn's *Hymn of Praise*, Rossini's *Stabat Mater* and Handel's *Messiah* were the oratorios rendered, besides miscellaneous selections. The principal *artistes* were Mesdames Lemmens Sherrington, Otto Alvsleben, Patey, Miss Enriquez and Miss Julia Wigan ; Messrs. Sims Reeves, Edwd. Lloyd, Vernon Rigby, Charles Santley and Lewis Thomas. The receipts amounted to £5,842, as many as 11,548 persons paid for admission, and the balance being made up to £200 was divided between the Bristol Royal Infirmary and the Bristol General Hospital. In October, 1876, the second festival took place, when the chief works rendered were Mendelssohn's *Elijah*, Verdi's *Requiem Mass*, Handel's *Israel in Egypt*, Spohr's *Fall of Babylon*, Beethoven's *Engedi*, Mendelssohn's *Hymn of Praise*, and Handel's *Messiah*. Mdlle. Titiens, Madame Edith Wynne, Mdlle. Albani, Mesdames Patey and Trebelli-Bettini, Messrs. Edward Lloyd, Harper Kearton, W. H. Cummings, Maybrick, H. Pope and Herr Behrens were the principals. So great were the expenses of this festival that there was a balance against the society, necessitating a call on the guarantors of one guinea each. This is the only call made on the guarantors during a period of ten years. The receipts were £6,687, and 12,978 persons paid for admission. The collections after the morning performances amounted to £210, and it was divided between the Infirmary and Hospital. The third festival was held in October, 1879, when Handel's *Samson*, Mendelssohn's *First Walpurgis Night*, *Elijah* and *Hear my Prayer*, Brahm's *Rinaldo*, Mozart's *Requiem*, Beethoven's *Choral Symphony* and Handel's *Messiah* were given. On this occasion Mesdames Albani, Patey, Trebelli, Miss Emma Thursby, Messrs. E. Lloyd, Barton McGuckin, R. Hilton and Charles Santley were engaged. The receipts were £6,158 17s. 4d., and 11,963 persons secured tickets. After the morning performances collections were taken for the two chief medical charities, and the donations reached £207 19s. 6d. The Infirmary and Hospital received £250 each, and £110 6s. 8d. was reserved for contingencies. The fourth festival was held in October, 1882. The works then rendered were Mendelssohn's *Elijah*, Beethoven's *Mass in D*, Gounod's new sacred trilogy, *The Redemption*, Haydn's *Spring*, Rossini's *Moses in Egypt*, Mackenzie's *Jason* (written expressly for the festival) and Handel's *Messiah*. The principals were Mesdames Albani, Patey, Trebelli, Miss Anna Williams, Messrs. Edward Lloyd, Joseph Maas, Harper Kearton, Robert Hilton, Montague Worlock and Charles Santley. The receipts amounted to £6,263 2s., and 11,209 tickets were sold. The collections at the morning-concerts reached the sum of £214 15s. 2d., which was divided between the Infirmary and Hospital. Charles Hallé conducted, and also furnished the band for each of the festivals, and G. Riseley presided at the organ. One special event marked this festival: the Duke and Duchess of Edinburgh were present at the performance of *Moses in Egypt*. The streets through which the royal personages passed to and from the railway station were gaily decorated, and a most fitting reception was given to the distinguished visitors. The guard of honour consisted of city volunteers. On taking his leave of the Festival Committee, His Royal Highness expressed his gratification at the performance, and consented to be president of the next festival. The committee have definitely decided to hold another festival in 1885. The choir has been re-formed and works are in rehearsal.

BRISTOL OPERATIC SOCIETY. In 1881 this society was started, and although its beginning was small it has increased in numbers, influence and proficiency. The idea of the promoters was to develop a taste for, and an increased knowledge of, operatic singing. There are now 40 acting members. Besides giving operatic concerts, *Pinafore* and *The Pirates of Penzance* have been produced. Other operas are in preparation. Richelieu Jones is the honorary conductor.

CATHEDRAL CHOIR. When the new nave of the Cathedral was completed greater scope was afforded for grand musical services. A design was matured to give special services during the Advent season, the musical portion of which should be the feature, and thereupon a voluntary choir was formed for the purpose of assisting the lay clerks on these occasions. In December, 1878, the first of these services was held, at the last of which Mendelssohn's *Hymn of Praise* was rendered by the combined choir, consisting of about 250 voices, accompanied by full orchestral band. At the third Advent service, in 1879, Spohr's *Last Judgment* was given; in 1880, Mendelssohn's *St. Paul;* in 1881, Handel's *Dettingen Te Deum* and Mendelssohn's *Lauda Sion* were rendered; and in 1882 Spohr's *Last Judgment* was repeated. On each occasion a full orchestral band accompanied, and whilst the offertory was being taken at the last special services in 1881 and 1882 the band played Beethoven's *Symphony (No. 5) in C minor*. George Riseley prepared the choir and conducted in the Cathedral, in the nave of which the choir and band sat. The choir meet for rehearsal in the Blind Asylum.

CHURCH CHORAL UNION. This association was established four years ago for the object of improving the rendering of the musical portion of the Church service, and in this the promoters have been successful, for there has been a marked improvement in the singing of the choirs attached to the association, and the members have also considerably increased. Much time and attention are spent in preparing the various parish choirs for the event which is annually celebrated in the Cathedral. Nearly 600 choristers took part in the fourth festival in 1883, being an increase of about 200 during the four years. The churches represented and the numbers of the respective choirs were as under:—

Cathedral (organist, Riseley)	31
St. Saviour (Tittle)	25
St. Paul, Clifton (Cook)	32
St. Mary, Tyndall's park (Smith)	43
St. John, Redland (Hill)	28
All Saints' (Bucknall)	34
St. Andrew (Jones)	31
Christ church, Clifton (Barrett)	41
Frenchay (Cole)	22
Fishponds (Yalland)	23
Redcliff (Lawson)	55
St. Paul, Bedminster (Nurse)	27
St. Nicholas (Dyer)	27
St. Stephen (Cook)	30
St. Michael, Bishopston (Coster)	35
Temple (Edwards)	22
St. Mark, Easton (Fothergill)	28
St. Barnabas (Matthews)	31
St. Augustine (Simpson)	29
Total	589

The trainers of the choir are J. Barrett, Cedric Bucknall (Mus. Bac.), E. Cook, W. F. Dyer, W. J. Lawson and F. W. Smith, who conduct sectional rehearsals.

CLIFTON AMATEUR PHILHARMONIC SOCIETY is a private body of ladies and gentlemen, who, for the enjoyment of singing, meet together during a portion of the year on alternate Fridays at the Drill hall, Queen's road, and for charitable purposes give concerts occasionally. The society was established by Miss Kirby in 1878, and now there are about 80 members. D. W. Rootham is the conductor, and Dr. Highett the president and secretary.

CLIFTON COLLEGE MUSICAL SOCIETY was established by W. F. Trimnell, the present music master of the college. There are about 100 members, consisting of masters and students, who meet weekly during term time. An orchestral society, under J. O. Brooke, is also connected with the college. Concerts are given at intervals, with band accompaniment, without extraneous aid, and every Christmas the chief musical gathering of the year takes place.

FRANK W. SMITH'S CHOIR has been in existence about eight years, and is composed of 18 men and 20 boys, members of the choir of St. Mary the Virgin, Tyndall's park, of which F. W. Smith is organist and choirmaster. The services of members are voluntary. At the annual concert, generally given for some object connected with the church, German glees, part songs, and other compositions for male voices are sung. The choir has always maintained a high state of efficiency.

JOHN BARRETT'S CHOIR (formed in October, 1880, for the express purpose of performing, as far as possible, works entirely new to the Bristol public) comprises about 90 well-selected voices, male and female, all well trained, and a concert is given annually. Rehearsals take place on Saturday evenings in the arch room of Colston hall, from 7 to 8.30. The choir have performed some classical works as well as miscellaneous compositions. Amongst the former may be mentioned Bach's *Magnificat in D*, Schubert's *Mass in E flat*, and *Miriam's Song of Triumph*; Schuman's *New Year's Song* and *Paradise and the Peri*; Mendelssohn's *Lauda Sion* and Gade's *Spring Message*. J. F. Nash, hon. secretary.

MONDAY POPULAR CONCERTS. During the winter months a high-class orchestral concert is given fortnightly at the Colston hall by a band of nearly 70 performers, under the conductorship of George Riseley, who formed the orchestra in 1877. Although special attention is paid to instrumental pieces, variety is afforded at the entertainments by one or two vocalists. From 1877 to the end of the season of 1882 313 works were performed, including 31 symphonies, 25 concertos and compositions with orchestral accompaniments, 87 overtures, 106 miscellaneous works, 34 dance pieces, 22 instrumental solos, and 8 choral works. The last concert given under George Riseley as sole director took place on December 18th, 1882. At that time there was an intention on his part to resume the concerts in October, 1883; but finding that under his unaided management, and in consequence of the great expense attached to them, they were not financially successful, he intimated his determination to abandon them entirely. Many musical gentlemen, feeling that such a loss would be a stigma on the city, combined together for the purpose of reorganising the excellent concerts. Two meetings were held at the Councilhouse in December, 1883, and resolutions were passed deciding that the musical gatherings should be re-started under the direction of a committee should a sufficient sum in the shape of donations be contributed, each contributor of a guinea and upwards being enrolled as a member. Cordial support has been given the new scheme, and George Riseley having offered his services gratuitously for three years, the concerts were recommenced in February, 1884, on almost precisely the same plan as formerly. Charles Miller, Albion chambers, and the Rev. H. J. Wiseman, Clifton college, hon. secs.

MADRIGAL SOCIETY. In the year 1837 the late Edward Taylor, the Gresham Professor, gave a series of lectures of a most interesting character on madrigal music at the Philosophical Institution, Park street. So great was the enthusiasm engendered by the lectures that a few gentlemen met at the residence of the late Alfred Bleeck and established the Bristol Madrigal Society, electing that gentlemen as first president. Originally the members numbered 30, but now they have increased to 103, of whom 30 are trebles. From the commencement until, 1865 the late J. D. Corfe conducted, and in the latter year the *bâton* passed into the hands of D. W. Rootham, who still retains it. G. W. Edwards is now president; C. Tovey, G. Barrett and W. Williams are the vice-presidents, and E. A. Harvey is the honorary secretary. At the annual "ladies' night," given in January in each year, the company that gather is always large, fashionable, and really picturesque. The tuneful compositions of Pearsall, Wilbye, Morley, and other old writers, interspersed with works from the pens of more modern musicians, are presented, and give pleasure to those who are favoured with the artistic admission tickets to the large *salon* of the Victoria rooms, where the delightful *réunions* are held.

ORGAN RECITALS. The organ in the Colston hall is the finest in the West of England; indeed, there are few to surpass it in the country. It has four manuals, about 60 stops, and the pneumatic action and pistons are attached. Since its erection by Henry Willis, the maker, recitals have been given upon it at rather irregular intervals by George Riseley. Cedric Bucknall (Mus. Bac.) gives recitals occasionally on the large organ at the Victoria rooms.

ORPHEUS GLEE SOCIETY. From small beginnings this excellent society has grown up, and it now stands unrivalled in the country. When T. H. Crook (who was born in Bristol, and was a pupil of the late well-known D. Hodges, organist of St. James') was a young man, he gathered round him a few musical amateurs—about eight in number—who met for practise at the old Talbot hotel. The pieces rehearsed were glees and part songs. The number continued to grow for a few years, and in 1844 a scheme was devised for establishing a society. Accordingly an association sprang into existence, and to it was given the name of the Bristol Orpheus Glee Society, males only being admitted to membership. From 1844 T. H. Crook was the director, and on "ladies' nights" year after year he was to be seen in his accustomed position on the orchestra until 1875, when he conducted his last concert at the Victoria rooms. On his resignation the late Alfred Stone succeeded him, and his first appearance as director was at an intermediate concert given in 1875, when the members of the British Association, then visiting Bristol, were entertained at a *soirée* in Colston hall. Everyone regretted the untimely death of Alfred Stone in 1878, and as a tribute of respect, and also with a view of assisting his widow and orphans, a memorial concert was given in Colston hall. George Riseley kindly offered to act as conductor; his services were accepted, and the entertainment was instrumental in obtaining about £160. A few months after this the Orpheus Glee Society elected George Riseley as conductor, and he has held the post up to the present time. The society has been growing in numbers and popularity since its establishment, and now there are about 70 names on the register. The members meet to practise every alternate Monday during the winter months, and the society annually gives its "ladies' night" in February. T. Usher, hon. secretary.

PEOPLE'S CONCERT SOCIETY is really a re-establishment under another name of the Handel Society. As the latter it was formed in 1877 by A. Whittaker, but owing to the bad weather which prevailed on so many occasions the receipts were not sufficient to pay expenses, and it collapsed in 1881. In the latter year, however, A. Whittaker resuscitated it under the name of the People's Concert Society. The special objects of the society, under both names, was and is to give oratorios, chiefly the compositions of Handel, at prices within the means of the working classes, 2,000 tickets at 3d. being issued for each concert. Handel's *Messiah* (three times), *Samson*, *Judas Maccabæus* and *Ode on St. Cecilia's Day*, Haydn's *Spring* and *Creation*, Sullivan's *Martyr of Antioch* and Mendelssohn's *Elijah* have been performed. There are 150 members in the choir, and at the concerts a band of about 40 instrumentalists, principally amateurs, are engaged. A. Whittaker is the conductor.

POMEROY CHAMBER CONCERTS are given about four times each season in the small Victoria rooms, when the highest form of classical music is given by some of the finest performers in the country.

ST. MARY REDCLIFF MUSICAL SOCIETY consists of about 60 members, ladies and gentlemen. It was established three years ago by J. W. Lawson, organist of St. Mary Redcliff church, who is the conductor. Concerts are given occasionally in the School, Ship lane, Redcliff. Amongst the works that have been rendered by the society are Mendelssohn's *Athalie*, Stainer's *Daughter of Jairus*, Mendelssohn's *Hear my Prayer*, Mozart's *Splendente Te Deus*, and Dr. Bridges' *Boadicea*. The vicar of Redcliff church is the president, Alderman Cope-Proctor

the treasurer, and F. T. B. Logan hon. secretary.

THE GRAMMAR SCHOOL CHOIR is composed of the boys attending the school (with additional help kindly rendered by a few of the old boys), and numbers about 80 voices. The annual concert is given at the close of the Midsummer term. Since the appointment of the present choirmaster the following works have been creditably rendered:—Selections from Mendelssohn's *Hymn of Praise* and *Elijah*; Lahee's cantata, *Building of the Ship*; Stainer's *Daughter of Jairus*; anthems, glees, &c. The choirmaster is the Rev. H. O. Powell-Jones, B.A. (Cantab).

National Benevolent Institution. Founded by the late Peter Harve, and established in this city in 1810 for the relief of distressed persons in the middle ranks of life of whatever country or creed. The institution gives annuities of £10, £12 and £16, and is supported by subscriptions. J. Lewis, 24 Berkeley square, hon. sec.

Natural History.

ETHNOLOGY. The various races of man who inhabited the West of England in early and prehistoric times have left numerous signs of their presence in the Bristol neighbourhood, though the city itself is said not to have been a place of importance until late in the Saxon period. Among the earliest of these may be mentioned the fine megalithic remains at Stanton Drew, about five miles south of Bristol, which consist of more or less perfect circles of upright stones with an avenue connecting them, and are considered the third in importance of these monuments remaining in Britain, the other two being those at Stonehenge and Avebury, in Wilts. So-called "Druidic stones" remain also at Stoke Druid, a mile west of Durdham down, and near Bitton, on the opposite side of Bristol. All these were probably erected by the early Celtic inhabitants, who are also supposed to have originally constructed many of the camps and earthworks on the hills surrounding the city, and the sunken trackways, some of which may be distinctly traced, which connected these camps. The earlier *prehistoric* races have left few remains in our neighbourhood. In the Leigh woods and near Worle are remains of ancient circles supposed by some antiquaries to have been "pit-dwellings," and a few flint and stone implements, both of the earlier, rough description, and of the later polished, or neolithic period, have been met with within a few miles of Bristol. The encampments at Worle and Dolberry are fine early works, and, like the two in Leigh woods and the Clifton camp, were probably of British origin, though the latter were no doubt much altered when they were occupied by the Romans. There are a few round barrows beyond Dyrham and Sodbury, but these ancient sepulchral remains are much more abundant further north, on the hills near Stroud. The earthwork known as "the Wansdyke," which terminates at Maes Knoll, the huge mound visible three miles south of Bristol on the eastern end of the Dundry range, is said to have formed the boundary in this part of the country between the Dobuni, who inhabited Gloucestershire, and the Belgæ, a more powerful tribe, who, about B.C. 300, drove the earlier race northward and constructed this dyke as the boundary of their territory. The Romans, though they occupied several camps in the vicinity and built a few villas and temples, do not appear to have discovered the natural advantages of the site now covered by our city; many coins and other Roman remains have, however, been found in the neighbourhood, and the road may be still traced across Durdham down which is supposed to have led to the station of Abona and the passage across the Severn. After the departure of the Roman legions the houses and cities they had built in this part of England were probably occupied by the Celts and Romanised Britons, until Ceawlin, King of the West Saxons, in 571, gained his great victory at Dyrham, about six miles north-east of Bristol, when Bath, Cirencester, Gloucester, and all this part of the country fell into the hands of the victorious invaders. One of the first results of the capture of these towns by the Saxons was the destruction of the beautiful palaces and temples built by their more civilised predecessors, for which these roving savages had no further use. Soon after this Bristol is first heard of in history, and rapidly under the Saxons, Danes and Normans became one of the chief towns of the kingdom.

According to Dr. Beddoe, a great authority on such subjects, considerable ethnological differences may be noticed in the inhabitants of the country surrounding our city. The smooth features and fair hair so frequent in North Wilts and on the Gloucestershire hills indicate Saxon origin; further west, in the Avon valley, dark-haired people are more numerous, indicating a greater admixture of Celtic or British blood; in the low country south and west of Bristol the fair Frisian type is common, while on the higher ground the British element is stronger. Across the Severn a race with dark hair and eyes are said to be descended from the Silures. In Bristol itself people of Welsh descent are very numerous, while Irishmen are comparatively rare.

ZOOLOGY.

It has already been stated in the article on the Flora of the district that the neighbourhood of Bristol offers a rich field for those who take an interest in the works of nature. For the geologist there are the celebrated bone-beds at Aust containing remains of huge fishes and saurians, the oolitic quarries at Dundry, and the interesting Avon section; while the zoologist, the entomologist and the botanist will find a great variety of species in the woods, fields, and marshes, and on the hills and downs around Bristol.

The MAMMALIA are now represented by a much smaller number of species than once were living in a wild state in the district. In the deposits of the Avon, in peat-bogs and in limestone caverns on the hillsides, bones, teeth, and other remains have been found, not only of some twenty kinds of animals still met with in a wild state in England, but also of species now only found wild on the continents of Europe, Asia, Africa, or North America, and even of some few which are no longer living in any part of the world. Among these may be mentioned the cave-lion, panther, hyæna, wild cat, bear, glutton, wolf, wild horse, elk, reindeer, aurochs, wild boar, beaver, marmot, lemming, and some species of voles and rats. The musk-sheep is only found at the present time in Arctic North America, but as remains of that animal have been discovered near the river Avon associated with those of the reindeer, it is probable that at the time they lived in these parts the climate was an arctic one. Remains have also been found of two species of elephants, two of rhinoceros, the hippopotamus, and other equally tropical species. The list of animals still found wild in the Bristol neighbourhood, though not very extensive, contains some interesting species. Three or four kinds of bats represent the *Chiroptera*. Of the *Insectivora*, the hedgehog, mole, and two or three species of shrew are common. The *Carnivora* are represented by the badger, fox, marten, polecat, stoat, weasel and otter; of these one of the rarest is the badger, the last English representative of the bear family, of which species a fine pair, male and female, was recently killed in the Leigh woods; the otter is also gradually getting scarcer. Of the *Rodentia*, or gnawing animals, we have the squirrel, dormouse (rare), three kinds of mice, two rats, three voles or water-rats, the hare and rabbit; the second species of rat, the old English black rat, is now very scarce, having here, as elsewhere, had to give place to its larger, brown Norwegian rival, but specimens of the old native species are still occasionally caught here. Two kinds of seals and several of the *Cetacea* have been captured in the Bristol Channel, including two species of whales, two porpoises, the dolphin and the grampus.

BIRDS.—Of the 400 species of British birds 168 have been recorded from the Bristol district. The white-tailed eagle, the peregrine falcon, and eight species of hawks, including the rare merlin and honey-buzzard, have been shot in the neighbourhood; four species of owls, the ring-ousel, the rare pied-flycatcher, the rock-pipit, shore-lark, snow-bunting, cross-bill, rose-pastor, raven, hoopoe, bee-eater, quail, great northern diver, cormorant, and the stormy-petrel may be named as amongst the more noteworthy of the Bristol birds, a complete list of which has been published by E. Wheeler in the *Proceedings of the Bristol Naturalists' Society*, where particulars of dates and localities may be found. Nightingales seem to be getting more plentiful than formerly, and may be heard nearly every spring in the woods at Leigh, Henbury, and other places in the immediate vicinity of the city.

REPTILES. A single specimen of the hawk's-bill turtle, taken in the Severn, was recorded in Bell's *British Reptiles*, p. 9, where only two other instances of its occurrence off the coasts of Britain are mentioned. The viper and common snake are both rather plentiful in some localities in the neighbourhood, the former being quite sufficiently common in the woods at Leigh, Westbury, Brockley combe, &c. The common lizard and the blind or slow worm— commonly mistaken for the viper by the unlearned in natural history—

are also frequent, both being still occasionally seen amongst heather on Durdham down, where a few years ago they were common. Of the *Amphibia*, the common toad, the frog, and two species of newts are our only native representatives, though specimens of the green or tree-frog have more than once been noticed at Clifton and near Stapleton, having probably escaped from confinement, or been let loose in the vain hope of their being able to acclimatise themselves.

FISHES. Though hardly to be considered a satisfactory hunting ground for disciples of Isaac Walton, the neighbourhood of Bristol still has a few streams where those who know how to catch them may secure such dainties as trout, perch and pike. Very fine eels are found in the Avon, Frome, and other streams, and roach, dace, carp, chub, tench and loach, with other smaller fry, are also to be caught in the clearer waters. Most of the commoner salt-water fish are found in the Bristol Channel, though few are caught above Weston-super-Mare. Sharks and other monsters of the deep are sometimes seen off Clevedon and Portishead; while salmon, though abundant in the Severn, seldom make the mistake of exploring our Bristol river. One fine specimen which made the venture in the spring of 1883 did not find the experiment successful, being captured in a half-dying state on the surface of the water nearly under the Clifton Suspension bridge.

MOLLUSCA. Of the marine forms only a few of the commoner species are to be found on the shore of the Bristol Channel and at Avonmouth. The land and fresh-water species are extremely well represented in the district, only one genus being absent. In the *Proceedings of the Bristol Naturalists' Society* will be found a catalogue of the 105 local species, with their various habitats, &c. The carnivorous slug *(Testacella)* is sometimes rather common in gardens at Clifton, though scarce elsewhere.

CRUSTACEA. A few of the smaller species of crabs, &c., may be found on the alluvial flats at Avonmouth and on the coast of the Bristol Channel; shrimps are caught in considerable quantities in the same localities. The streams in this neighbourhood are not sufficiently clear for cray fish, which are rather common in the northern and eastern portions of the county. Fresh-water shrimps may sometimes be studied alive in the water supplied by the Bristol Waterworks Company.

ARACHNIDA. About 63 species of spiders were recorded by the late W. W. Stoddart from the immediate neighbourhood of Bristol, and probably many more will be added to the list when the district is more carefully worked, all W. W. Stoddart's captures having been made within a few years.

INSECTS. Some idea of the great variety of the representatives of this class in the Bristol district may be formed when it is stated that one local collector captured upwards of 250 species (excluding the numerous *brachelytra* which he did not collect) within a few miles of the city during one season.

Coleoptera. Among the rarer of the local species may be mentioned the pretty *Lebia chlorocephala*, found under stones on Durdham down; *Sphodrus leucopthalmus*, rather scarce in cellars, &c.; *Elater balteatus*, *Hypulus quercinus* and *Eros minutus*, among old trees in Leigh woods; the very rare *Bolbocerus mobillicornis*, a few specimens of which have been found in meadows near Baptist mills; and the fine longicorn, *Lamia textor*, which should be looked for at dusk amongst old willows at Bedminster.

Orthoptera. This order has been quite neglected by local collectors, but some interesting species have been observed. Many species of grasshoppers may be found on the downs and hill-sides, including the great green *Gryllus viridissimus*. True locusts are sometimes found, one having been captured on St.

Michael's hill last year. The large American cockroach, *Blatta Americana*, is sometimes found on board ships and in outhouses near the quays, but fortunately it has not established itself as a permanent addition to our insect pests. The mole-cricket is scarce, but the shrill-voiced field-cricket is abundant in some localities, as is also the domestic species, so difficult to dislodge from houses where it has once effected a settlement.

Neuroptera. Numerous species of dragon-flies, caddis-flies, and other insects of this order may be captured on the banks of the Avon, Frome, and other streams. Very few species from this district have been recorded.

Hymenoptera. Two cases containing a small collection of Bristol bees may be seen in the Bristol Museum, to which institution they were presented by the late W. L. Walcott, who possessed a large collection of the *hymenoptera* of the district, including most of the known British species of bees, wasps, ants and saw-flies.

Lepidoptera. This is the most popular of the orders of insects with English collectors, and in this neighbourhood many rare and interesting species have been captured. Four-fifths of the British butterflies have been recorded from the district, including the rare "Bath white," the "Queen of Spain," the "Camberwell beauty," and the very local blue *Lycœna Acis*. Among the moths the scarce sphinges *D. lineata* and *galii* and *C. celerio* have more than once been recorded, and the " Death's-head " (*A. Atropos*) is sometimes rather common in the larval state in potato grounds. Single specimens of the very rare *Sesia andreniformis* and of the beautiful *Deiopeia pulchella* have been taken near Clifton; *Acidaria holosericata* is sometimes abundant near Durdham down, though elsewhere it is found only in one or two places in England; the rare hook-tip (*D. sicula*) is still sometimes captured in its only British habitat, the Leigh woods; the unique British specimen of *Miselia bimaculosa* was taken on Durdham down, and is now in the British Museum collection; many other scarce *noctuœ*, about 40 species of *Pyrales* and a similar number of *Crambites* have been recorded, and the *Micro-lepidoptera* (*Tortrices, Tineina* and *Pterophori*) are well represented. A complete catalogue of the *Lepidoptera of the Bristol Coalfield* is in course of publication by the Naturalists' Society, and is expected to be finished in their volume for the year 1884.

Rhynchota. This order has received little attention from local entomologists, but a few rare and interesting species were recorded by E. Wheeler in a paper published a few years since. The marshy ground at Stapleton and Avonmouth, and the many other favourable collecting grounds round Bristol, would no doubt, if properly worked, produce as good results in this order as they have in the more popular divisions of insects.

Diptera. Little, is known of the two-winged flies of the district. One of the most venomous species, the mosquito, is frequently reported from the lower parts of the city in hot summers, but it is probable that its English cousin, the common gnat (*Culex pipiens*), is mistaken for it.

VERMES. The most interesting species of this division are the *Rotifera* and other minute creatures, of which microscopists will find a great variety, including some not yet noticed elsewhere, in the ponds and ditches near Stapleton, Clifton and Leigh.

SPONGIIDA. Fresh-water sponges are occasionally found in the Frome and other local streams.

Naturalists' Society, The, attained its majority in April, 1883. Its object is to concentrate and stimulate scientific life. During its existence 220 papers have been contributed by 74 members. There are botanical, entomological, geological, chemical and physical sections, each having a separate president and secretary. The aggregate number of members and associates is 185. Subscription, 10/- per annum. The method of publication of the society's proceedings is in annual parts, of which three constitute a volume. *Rerum cognoscere causas* is the motto of the society. John Beddoe, M.D., F.R.S., president; Adolph Leipner, F.Z.S., 47 Hampton park, and James W. White, 51 Royal York crescent, hon. secs.

Neptune, Victoria street. This figure has been the subject of special enactments. It formerly stood very near the approaches to Bristol bridge, which, being about to be widened, and the site occupied by the statue required, a clause was introduced into the Act for Neptune to be removed to another place in Temple street, on the passing of which it was subsequently done, the new situation being very near to where Dr. White's almshouse now stands. Some years after, the trustees of that charity being about to rebuild the front of that establishment, the statue was found to be in the way, and they endeavoured to obtain its removal, but this was declined by the authorities, unless the trustees found a site for it, which they did. A piece of glebe land belonging to the vicar of Temple parish being available, the statue was removed, the trustees of Dr. White's charity paying £3 per annum for its use. In this remote spot, at the termination of a narrow lane skirting the churchyard of Temple, the statue remained until 1872, when by the exertions of the vicar of the parish it was finally removed to its present site at the junction of Temple street with Victoria street, being restored to its pristine use as an ornament to a drinking fountain (*see* "Drinking Fountains"). The monument is of lead, and consists of the figure of Neptune holding a dolphin and trident, and tradition asserts that it was the gift of a plumber to commemorate the destruction of the Spanish Armada in 1588.

New Cut, running from Netham to the Avon at Rownham, together with the connecting floating harbour, was commenced in May, 1804, and completed in May, 1809. During the excavation a large quantity of trees was discovered about 20 feet below the surface embedded in the clay; they were lying mostly in one direction, and appeared as though they were swept suddenly down by a hurricane. To celebrate the successful conclusion of the undertaking, about 1,000 workmen who had been employed were regaled with a dinner in a neighbouring field.

Newgate stood in the angle between Fairfax street and Castle Mill street. It was famous as the prison of the early Quakers, the Nonconformists and the poet Savage. Mention is made of prisoners in this gaol as early as 1148. It was rebuilt in 1691 by a rate of sixpence in the £ upon the inhabitants. John Howard visited this prison in 1775. He then described it "white without and foul within; the dungeon or pit, down 18 steps, is 17 feet diameter and 8½ high. It is close and offensive, only a small window." "Felons," he says, "were allowed a pennyworth of bread a day before trial, two pennyworth of bread after conviction." The prisoners were allowed to hang out a basket, into which passers-by dropped their doles; there was also a contribution box for the same purpose. The following are a few characteristic examples of the local mode of formerly punishing:— In 1615, one Phelps, a fellmonger, was pressed to death. In 1705, Thos. Davis was whipped at a cart tail till he bled to death; Maria Prichard was whipped, stripped to the waist; Mary Ketchmay was whipped till she died. In 1736, Joshua Harding and John Newnham were hanged, but when cut down and placed in coffins both came to life; the latter a few hours after died, but Harding was taken care of in a charity house. This prison was abandoned in 1820 for the Gaol on the New cut (see "Gaols").

Newspapers. As long as the "Act for preventing abuses in printing seditious, treasonable and unlicensed books and pamphlets, and for regulating printing and printing presses," was in force, there was not a single newspaper published in the West of England. This Act, known as the "Licensing Act," expired in 1695, when, remarks Lord Macaulay, "English literature was emancipated, and emancipated for ever, from the control of the Government." Printing presses were soon after established in the chief provincial centres of population and trade, and, before the end of the century, were at work in Bristol, Plymouth, Exeter, Shrewsbury, &c. William Bonny, who had been in business in London, set up his press in Bristol in 1695. Seven years after was issued "*The Bristol Post-Boy*, giving an account of the most material news, both foreign and domestick. Printed by Wm. Bonny, Corn street, Bristol." The above is copied from "No. 91," containing the news "from Saturday, August 5, to Saturday, August 12, 1704." From this it appears that the first number of the first Bristol newspaper, of which we have any authentic record, must have been published near the end of 1702, being the same year that Queen Anne ascended the Throne, and in which London produced the *Daily Courant*, the first daily newspaper published in this country. *The Bristol Post-Boy* was printed on a small folio leaf, and on coarse whity-brown paper. The quantity of news it contained in a year would not be more than is often found in two numbers of some of our present daily papers. No published price is named on Bonny's paper, but on one published at Norwich, in 1708, the public were informed that the price was "a penny, but a halfpenny not refused." How long *The Bristol Post-Boy* existed we do not know; the last number we have any note of was issued in May, 1712.

In 1713 appeared Sam Farley's *Bristol Postman;* or "weekly intelligence from Holland, France, Spain, &c., with general occurrences, foreign and domestick." "No. 24" is dated "Saturday, July 25th, 1713." It forms 12 pages, small quarto, and is much better turned out than Bonny's paper. Pictorial initial letters are on every page, and a woodcut on each side of the title—a postman full gallop on the left, and a ship in full sail on the right. It was printed "at the house in St. Nicholas street, near the church." The price, "deliver'd to any public or private house in this city," was "three-halfpence," and "deliver'd for the county, twopence."

Farley's *Bristol Newspaper* appeared in 1725, four pages, small folio, price "twopence." "Printed at my house below the Dolphin, in Wine street." Under the above heading is a woodcut, being a bird's-eye view of Bristol, in which the old bridge, with houses on it, figures.

Subsequently Samuel and Felix Farley were in partnership, and printed the *Bristol Journal* in Castle green. The partnership was dissolved in 1752, and Felix then started *Felix Farley's Bristol Journal*. On the death of Samuel Farley, his niece, Sarah Farley, carried on the old paper. We copy the title of the number issued January 13th, 1770: "*The Bristol Journal*. Printed by Sarah Farley, in Castle green. 2,804 weeks since this *Journal* was published." About 1808 Sarah Farley's paper appears to have been merged into the *Bristol Mirror*. In 1853 *Felix Farley's Journal* was incorporated with the *Bristol Times*, which was founded in 1839, and in 1865 there was a further amalgamation with the *Bristol Mirror*, which was first published in 1773. The *Bristol Times and Mirror* is published five days a week at one penny, and on the Saturday at twopence. The present style of the firm is T. D. Taylor, J. H. Goodenough Taylor and W. Hawkins.

In October, 1715—that is, in less than three years after Sam Farley issued the first number of *The Bristol Postman*—appeared "*The Bristol Weekly Mercury*, from Holland, France, Spain, &c." "Bristol: Printed by Henry Green," who modestly informs the reading public that his paper was "far excelling all other newspapers." The only number of this paper we have ever seen is "No. 61," dated "Saturday, December the 1st, 1716," from which its present possessors have permitted us to copy the title. If any record of the existence of *The Bristol Weekly Mercury* has appeared in print before it has escaped our notice.

In January, 1742, appeared *The Bristol Oracle and County Advertiser*, "by Andrew Hooke, Esqre." Printed by J. Watts, for the "author." Folio, four pages. "Esquire" Hooke also, about the same date, published *The Oracle; or Bristol Weekly Miscellany*. Printed by B. Hickey, Nicholas street. In 1745 *The Oracle County Advertiser* was published by "A. Hooke, at his printing offices in Shannon court, Corn street."

On January 26th, 1790, Bulgin and Rosser, printers, 3 Wine street, advertised their intention to issue a new and impartial weekly paper, to be entitled the *Bristol Mercury and Universal Intelligencer*. On August 13th, 1818, this was purchased of Wm. Pine by Browne and Manchee for a joint-stock company, copyright £600, material to be taken at a valuation : the number then printed was 300 weekly.

The *Bristol Mercury* was published weekly by W. H. Somerton on Nov. 17th, 1829, and passed to his sons (G. and C. Somerton) in 1859, and in January, 1860, they started in conjunction with it the *Bristol Daily Post*, published on the remaining five days of the week, and in January, 1878, the two papers were incorporated under the title of the *Bristol Mercury and Daily Post*. This is issued at one penny daily throughout the week ; on Saturday a supplement of eight pages is published, containing all the news of the week, which can be had for an additional penny. In July, 1883, it was purchased by Wiliam Lewis and Sons, proprietors of the *Bath Herald*.

The *Clifton Chronicle* is published on Wednesdays, and was established 1850; Austin and Son, proprietors.

On June 1st, 1858, the *Western Daily Press* (first daily newspaper in the West of England), on Feb. 12th, 1859, the *Bristol Observer* (Saturday penny paper with original tales), and on May 29th, 1877, the *Bristol Evening News*, were founded by Peter Stewart Macliver.

At the end of the last century the following weekly newspapers were published in Bristol :—*Sarah Farley's Bristol Journal*, *Felix Farley's Bristol Journal*, *Bonner and Middleton's Bristol Journal* (afterwards *The Mirror*), *The Bristol Gazette* (established 1767) and *The Bristol Mercury*. The stamp duty on each of these papers was "threepence-halfpenny."

During the present century several newspapers have been started in Bristol, such as *The Bristolian* (1827), *The Bristol Liberal* (1831-2), *Bristol Advertiser* (1856), *Bristol Police Chronicle*, *Bristol Standard* (discontinued January 23rd, 1842), *Bristol Evening Star*, *Western Telegraph* (1870), &c., but they had only a brief existence.

Nightingale Valley,

in Leigh woods, was a road ere the Christian era dawned, being a means of communication between the three forts that crowned the heights, two on the Somersetshire side and one on the Gloucestershire. It is a beautiful combe or glen. On each side abutting on the river the rocks rise nearly as high as those of St. Vincent, and almost as precipitously.

Nurses' Society. The Bristol District Nurses' Society has been established twelve months. Its object is to provide a body of trained nurses to attend the sick poor in their own homes. For carrying on the work the city is divided into seven districts, viz.: St. Paul's, Bedminster, St. Jude's, St. Agnes', St. Philip and Jacob, and Holy Trinity. During the year 1882 the following work was done by the society:—In St. Paul's district there were 99 cases on the nurse's book, and the total number of visits paid 1,468. In the district of St. Jude's the number of nurses' visits average 45 a week. In St. Philip and Jacob the total visits paid in nine months was 2,228. The total of visits in St. Agnes' district was 1,436. Rev. T. G. Luckock, vicar of Emanuel, Clifton, hon. sec.

Nurses' Training Institution and Home, 24 Richmond terrace, Clifton. The 20th annual report of this institution was presented on February 9th, 1883, from which it appeared that the earnings of the nurses in the previous year amounted to £1,184, and that 260 cases had been nursed during that period; also that there were 25 nurses working and 4 pupils training. Miss O'Brien, hon. sec.

Observatory, erected on the summit of St. Vincent's rock in 1828. The excellent camera obscura embraces the whole of the surrounding scenery from the gallery rails to the horizon. It was opened in 1829. (See "Ghyston's Cave.")

Occupations. The following is a list of occupations of males and females in Bristol according to the last census:—

Occupations.	Males.	Females.
Persons engaged in general or local government—		
National government	458	33
Local government	404	10
East India and Colonial service	1	—
In defence of the country—		
Army, at home	260	—
Navy, ashore or in port	136	4
Professional occupations—		
Clerical profession	411	105
Legal profession	391	—
Medical profession	291	504
Teachers	411	1,313
Literary and scientific persons	64	2
Engineers and surveyors	130	—
Artists	447	253
Exhibitions, shows, &c.	47	3
Domestic offices or services—		
Domestic service	1,439	12,319
Other services	67	3,741
Commercial occupations—		
Merchants and agents	3,691	73
Dealers in money	162	—
Engaged in insurance	182	2
Conveyance of men, goods and messages—		
On railways	1,065	5
On roads	1,691	9
On canals, rivers and seas	2,060	12
In storage	356	10
Conveying messages, porterage, &c.	2,252	57
Agriculture—		
In fields and pastures	138	7
In woods	2	—
In gardens	252	14
Engaged about animals	447	1
Working & dealing in books, prints and maps—		
Books	1,008	220
Prints and maps	171	2
Working and dealing in machines and implements—		
Machines	1,087	5
Tools and implements	71	2
Clocks, watches and scientific instruments	257	5
Surgical instruments	8	8
Army and ordnance	27	—
Musical instruments	98	3
Type, dies, medals, coins	7	1
Tackle for sports and games	9	12
Engaged about houses, furniture and decorations—		
Houses	5,990	26
Furniture and fittings	1,234	168
House decorations	223	20
Working and dealing in carriages and harness—		
Carriages	556	5
Harness	226	16
Working and dealing in ships and boats—		
Hull	339	1
Masts, rigging, &c.	90	1
Working and dealing in chemicals and compounds—		
Colouring matter	45	14
Explosives	3	4
Drugs and other chemicals	290	35
Working and dealing in tobacco and pipes	190	414
Working and dealing in food and lodging—		
Board and lodging	600	613
Spirituous drinks	789	82
Food	3,821	1,002

Occupations.	Males.	Females.
Working and dealing in textile fabrics—		
Work and worsted	37	21
Silk	8	2
Cotton and flax	173	598
Hemp and other fibrous material	134	37
Mixed or unspecified material	660	832
Working and dealing in dress	4,969	10,196
Working and dealing in various animal substances—		
Grease, gut, bone, horn, ivory, whalebone	259	18
Skins	682	29
Hair and feathers	198	90
Working and dealing in various vegetable substances.		
Oils, gums and resins	272	10
Cane, rush, straw	129	23
Wood and bark	947	80
Paper	226	542
Working and dealing in various mineral substances—		
Miners	605	4
Coal, coal gas, &c.	471	14
Stone, clay & road-making	608	3
Earthenware and glass	508	123
Salt	4	—
Water	21	—
Precious metals and jewellery	147	15
Iron and steel	1,918	20
Copper	42	—
Tin and zinc	150	4
Lead	50	1
In other mixed or unmixed metals	385	12
Vaguely described—		
Makers and dealers	838	749
Mechanics and labourers	6,341	109
Dealing in refuse matter	140	85
Without specified occupations	38,406	78,381

Offences, Public. The number of persons proceeded against summarily before the justices during 1883 was 6,354, as compared with 6,300 the previous year. Of these, 3,374 were apprehended, and 2,980 proceeded against by summons. In drunk and disorderly cases there was a decrease of 44, and in simple larceny a decrease of 47, whilst larceny from the person shows an increase of 13 cases. Begging has been largely on the increase during the year; the number of persons apprehended was 316, against 106 in the previous year. There are 38 convicts at large on license in the city, many of whom are reported to be doing their best to obtain honest employment. During the year 19 publicans and 41 beerhouse keepers were reported, resulting in 10 convictions against the former and 34 against the latter. The nature of crimes during 1882 and 1883 was as follows:—

	1882.	1883.
Murder	—	2
Manslaughter	1	—
Wounding with intent to do bodily harm	5	4
Rape	—	1
Concealing the birth of infants	2	—
Indecent assaults	—	1
Assaults and inflicting bodily harm	3	—
Sacrilege	1	3
Burglary and housebreaking	15	27
Breaking into shops, warehouses, &c.	15	29
Cattle stealing	—	1
Horse stealing	1	1
Sheep stealing	—	1
Larceny in dwelling-houses	6	6
Larceny from the person	9	18
Larceny by servants	3	4
Larceny simple	151	226
Larceny on the river	17	12
Stealing pictures	10	7
Embezzlement	2	2
Larceny by servants in the Post-office	1	1
Receiving stolen goods	3	1
Fraud	16	25
Malicious injuries to property	1	—
Forgery	4	1
Uttering counterfeit coin	1	—
Perjury	—	2
Attempting to commit suicide	22	9
Conspiracy	1	1
Incorrigible rogues	—	1
Totals	290	386

Office of Works, Corn street (London and South-Western Bank buildings). The office has for its head the Right Hon. G. J. Shaw-Lefevre, M.P., who is called the First Commissioner of Works. His office is at 12 Whitehall place, London, and there are branch offices in Bristol, Edinburgh and Leeds. The office is charged with the supervision of all Crown buildings throughout the kingdom. The head of the Bristol department is E. G. Rivers, surveyor, and J. Wager, assistant surveyor.

Official Receiver in Bankruptcy. This office was created on the passing of the Bankruptcy Act 1883; and the local appointment, after confirmation by the Chamber of Commerce, was made by the Board of Trade, in November, 1883, in the person of Edward Gustavus Clarke, chartered accountant. The district over which that gentleman has jurisdiction embraces Bristol, Bath, Frome, and Wells. The appointment is worth £1,000 per annum. The duties of the Official Receiver are set forth in part iv. clauses 66 to 71 of the Bankruptcy Act 1883. Offices of the local Receiver: Bank chambers, Corn st.

Omnibuses. Since the introduction of the tramway system into the city, the number of omnibuses plying has been greatly reduced. One or two 'buses run to the Hotwells from the Exchange at frequent intervals in the day, one to Hanham, and another to St. George's and Kingswood. There are also one or two 'buses that run from the Grand, the Talbot, and the Royal hotels to the Joint Railway station, Temple meads. (*See* "Cab Regulations" and "Carriers.")

Open Spaces, Parks, Places, Terraces, &c. Bristol does not abound in public parks and open spaces like some large centres of industry, but, in addition to its magnificent Downs, Brandon hill and College green (*see* those headings), it possesses the following:—

BEDMINSTER PLEASURE GROUND. This resort was liberally presented to the city by Sir Greville Smyth, Bart., Ashton court, on June 15th, 1882. The land, which comprises 21½ acres, is situated on the Long Ashton side of Clift house, and is nearly triangular in shape. In offering the site to the committee of the Sanitary Authority, Sir Greville expressed a wish that the use of the most suitable part might be granted to the Bedminster Cricket Club on the same footing as a portion of Durdham down is granted to the Clifton Cricket Club. Seats have been placed in the ground, and when it has been suitably laid out and enclosed, it will form an admirable spot for recreation, being close to the thickly populated district of Bedminster, and accessible from the Hotwells by means of the Rownham ferry. The land is beautifully situated, undulating and finely wooded.

BERKELEY SQUARE, north-east of Brandon-hill and top of Park street, is formed of well-built houses on three sides, the south-east being left open. There is a large planted area in the centre, which is open to residents in the square; it was erected on the site of Bullock's park in 1786. The square is on a gentle slope, and is enclosed from the carriage ways by a wall and iron palisades.

BRIGHTON PARK, Clifton, near the South parade, erected in 1849, is situated midway between the Victoria rooms and Clifton down station.

BRUNSWICK SQUARE, St. Paul's, was built in 1788. It is one of the green spots of Bristol open to the public. Its area is 1 acre 36 perches. Brunswick Congregational chapel (*see* "Chapels") and the Unitarian burial ground (*see* "Cemeteries") are situated on one side of the square, which also contains some spacious residences. The paths through the square are asphalted.

BYRON PLACE (Upper), a noble and elevated range of buildings at the back of Berkeley square, pleasantly situated on the north-west slope of Brandon hill.

CALEDONIA PLACE, Clifton, a range of 31 spacious houses opposite the West mall, commanding a view of Leigh woods, &c., from the western end.

CLIFTON PARK, near Christ church, a delightful and fashionable part of Clifton, including some of the most magnificent houses and villas in the neighbourhood, being surrounded with fine shrubs, exotic plants, gravel walks, &c., with a railed-in plantation in the centre.

COLONNADE, THE, Hotwells, is a range of semi-circular built houses, in one of which the celebrated poetical milkwoman, Ann Yearsley, kept a circulating library for some years.

CORNWALLIS (or Lower) CRESCENT, Clifton, is a range of 40 very fine houses below the Royal York crescent, and much sheltered from the north-west wind. The back has extensive views from a south aspect.

COTHAM PARK possesses several fine residences, chiefly designed in the Grecian style. Perhaps the most notable building is the lofty round tower, or look-out, in the grounds of Francis Fry, which is 70 ft. high; from its summit a delightful view of the scenery for many miles round is obtained.

COTHAM PLEASURE GROUND, Cotham grove, opened July 29th, 1881, is between two and three acres in extent, and lies immediately to the right of Lovers' walk. There are two entrances, one at the upper and the other at the lower end of the walk. Entering at the upper gate, the ground has a gradual slope towards the west, but on the north side there is a considerable space nearly level. There are terraces with winding paths, and at the most suitable spots thirty recesses have been drawn for ornamental seats. A few yards inside the upper entrance is a mound six feet above the level of the path, and here has been fixed a circular seat, with a flagpole in the centre. The seat is approached by gravel paths, and in front of it is a border of ornamental trees and evergreens with surroundings of ornamental rock-work. On the north side of this rock-work is a terrace 12 feet wide, a second lower down is 10 feet wide, and a similar walk on the south side of the rockwork of the same width. The other walks are 8 feet wide. Dispersed about the ground are nearly 2,000 evergreen and deciduous shrubs and conifers and 30 standard ornamental trees of different varieties, amongst them being the scarlet chesnut *(pavia rubra)*, the double-blossom thorn *(cratægus oxycantha pleno)*, limes *(tilia Europæa)*, silver weeping birch *(betula alba, laciniata* and *pendula)*, maples, &c. Amongst the ornamental coniferæ are *pinus sylvestris*, with its pretty silvery tint and light green foliage ; *abies douglasii*, *biota orientalis* and *pyramidalis*, several varieties of the *pinus*, also the *retinospora ericoides*, *pisifera*, and *plumosa*. Specimens of the English yew *(taxus baccata)* and the Irish variety *(taxus baccata fastigiata)* are also to be found, as well as representatives of the *arborvitæ* family *(thuja compacta, falcata, tartarica, occidentalis, gigantea, thujopsis)*, &c. There is a good collection of deciduous and flowering shrubs, nearly every variety worthy of cultivation being represented. The old Scotch fir *(pinus sylvestris)* still remains, and at equal distances three young trees of the same variety. The natural slope of the ground adds greatly to its attractiveness.

COTHAM TERRACE, a neat row of residences near Highbury chapel, behind which formerly stood the city gallows, and opposite to which stood Bewell's cross.

DOWRY SQUARE, Hotwells, was formerly a garden or plantation, with a walk around it enclosed with rails.

HAYMARKET (or HORSEFAIR), a large open space where the hay market is held weekly (*see* "Markets"). On this spot were buried those who fell during the raging of the great plague in the city.

HOPE SQUARE, Hotwells, is called after Lady Hope, who founded a chapel which stands on the eastern side. (*See* "Chapels.")

KING SQUARE, St. James', was commenced in 1755. In February, 1838, the cross rows of lime trees were cut down, and the iron railing erected. Its area is 1a. 0r. 22p. Substantial brick houses flank either side of this green spot. A paved walk up its centre leads to Spring hill, Kingsdown. The square is maintained in good order, and the shrubs and green sward make it attractive.

LITFIELD PLACE, Clifton down, so-called from this part of the downs having been once known as Leadfield, there being lead mines which were formerly worked. In front of the houses is a fine plantation.

PARAGON, THE, a semi-circular range of 15 handsome houses; a delightful spot, with a plantation back and front. From the south-west end, over an immense precipice, a fine view is obtained.

PORTLAND SQUARE, St. Paul's, so named in honour of the Duke of Portland, who, when it was formed, was High Steward of Bristol. The houses in the square are entirely built of freestone, a noticeable feature being that the corners and centres of the fronts of the northern and southern sides are elevated by attic stories as well as the corner houses of the other sides. In the centre of the eastern side stands St. Paul's church (*see* "Churches"), with its lofty tower. Most of the fine dwelling-houses here are now converted into shoe and corset manufactories. The centre of the square is laid down with grass, surrounded with elms and shrubs. It is railed off from the general public, the right of admission being reserved to the occupants of houses in the square. The area is 2 acres 1 rood.

PROCTOR'S BOULEVARD. On the south side of the New cut (Coronation road), from Bath bridge to Avon Clift tannery, the late Alderman Proctor converted the bank into a beautiful boulevard, having at his own expense planted it with some thousands of trees and placed seats at suitable intervals.

QUEEN SQUARE, in the centre of the city, encloses an area of 7½ acres (said to be just that of the great Pyramid), bordered with young elm trees, and railed in from the carriage way with intersecting gravel and asphalted walks (the paths are eight in number radiating from the monument) across and round the green between the trees. The ground it now occupies was in former days called the Marsh—a name still preserved in the locality by the nomenclature of Marsh street. It originally served not only as a public promenade and for military exercises and athletic sports, but for bear-baiting and other popular diversions of a like barbarous kind. On these occasions elevated seats were erected for the use of the Aldermen and other civic dignitaries. The erection of houses round the square commenced in 1698, and occupied 23 years in process, being finished in 1726. On the 18th May, 1702, Queen Ann and Prince George, her husband, visited the city, which occasioned the name of Queen square to be attached to this extensive quadrangle. In 1734 David Hume, then in his 23rd year, was located in a merchant's office on the south side of this square. On the same side once resided Capt. Woodes Rogers, who discovered Alexander Selkirk, the original Robinson Crusoe, at the uninhabited island of Juan Fernandez. The trees were first planted in 1705, and in 1749 there were as many as 287, but in 1765 they were reduced to 57. The excessive high winds of 1881–82 blew down many of these fine old trees, and those that remained were so decayed as to become dangerous, and the city authorities, in November, 1882, had the old ones removed and young ones planted in their stead. In the centre, upon a high pedestal, is an equestrian statue of William III., habited as Cæsar; his right arm is extended, holding a truncheon. It is wholly cast of brass after a model presented by Rysbrach, and executed by Van Oost, a teacher of flower painting. It is universally allowed by connoisseurs to be one of the finest equestrian statues in the United Kingdom. It was set up in 1735. Towards its erection, which cost £1,800, the Corporation contributed £1,000, the Society of Merchants £500, and the remainder was defrayed by voluntary subscriptions. The old Custom and Mansion houses and other residences were burnt down during the riots in 1831 (*see* "Riots"). The square is the rallying point of political and temperance processions.

REGENT PLACE, fronting the north-east end of the Royal York crescent. Here is the Clifton post-office, and here were erected the first handsome shops in Clifton.

RICHMOND PARK, Clifton, extending from opposite Arlington place, Victoria park, is built on the grounds of Curtin's nursery gardens.

ROPEWALK, an asphalted pleasure ground opposite St. Mathias' church, was opened in 1882. This playground for children was formed after the river Frome had been arched over.

ROYAL YORK CRESCENT, Clifton, is a magnificent range of 52 handsome houses having a south aspect. At No. 3 the Empress Eugénie was once a schoolgirl. The scenery from here is delightful.

ST. JAMES' CHURCHYARD was, on June 30th, 1882, opened as a public pleasure and recreation ground. Asphalt paths wind through the ground, and iron seats are placed at suitable intervals. The green sward is well rolled, and there are ornamental shrubs, flower-beds, and pretty little arrangements of rockery. The ground occupies 1a. 1r. 13p., and is central and close to the doors of thousands of the industrial classes, for whose welfare more particularly the churchyard has been devoted to its new use. Facing the Horsefair a fountain and cross has, at the expense of a lady, been erected. It is an imposing erection of freestone, the head being of red Mansfield stone, and in two niches at the top are placed figures of St. James and St. Paul. The basin of the fountain is of red granite. There are certain legal difficulties in the way of the Corporation taking over the pleasure ground from the vicar and churchwardens of St. James'; it was therefore opened without formal transfer to the city.

ST. JAMES' SQUARE, St. James, is a quiet and retired situation. The area of the square is pitched and paved. On the western side is the Young Men's Christian Association.

ST. PHILIP AND JACOB CHURCHYARD. Like the disused burial grounds of St. James' and Temple churches, this one is being transformed and made to appear more attractive, and, when completed, will be a very welcome promenade to the inhabitants of the surrounding courts and alleys.

SOMERSET SQUARE, Cathay. This square was formerly an open meadow of about three acres, with a brook running through it, but of the latter there is now no trace. In 1756 the present houses on the north and west sides were erected. The square is to be kept open for the free use of the occupiers of the houses. Some years ago there was a fountain in the centre; it has now ceased to play, but the structural masonry still remains.

TEMPLE CHURCHYARD having been levelled and the enclosure set in order, was opened July 20th, 1880; but it is not so free of access as the churchyard of St. James'.

TYNDALL'S PARK. Pryce says that the first mention of this park is in 1797, and that the house was then standing, it having three good fronts towards the park, and was then, as now, in the occupation of the Tyndall family. The Royal fort, erected in 1644, stood in the park. The fort is now demolished, and is replaced by houses still bearing its original name.

VICTORIA SQUARE, Clifton. The area of this square is laid out very tastefully and richly stocked with shrubs. The centre is divided by a public walk called Birdcage walk. The enclosure is only accessible to the residents of the square. On each side the houses are of magnificent proportions and design. On the south side is St. James' church or Hensman's Memorial church (*see* "Churches"). In the centre of the north-west wing, carved in freestone, and placed in a semi-circular arch over the cornice, the Royal arms, finely sculptured, are displayed; and although appearing so small, its weight is two tons.

VYVIAN TERRACE, near Christchurch, Clifton, which was erected in 1847-8, has a neat plantation in front.

WINDSOR TERRACE, Clifton, below and under the Paragon, is well situated, and commands some of the most delightful and picturesque scenery in Clifton. It is erected on foundations laid by Watt, the inventor of patent shot (*see* "Shot House Tower"). At No. 4 resided Hannah More.

WORCESTER TERRACE, Clifton, at the northern side of Clifton park; erected in 1850.

Ordnance Survey Offices.
The local offices are at 28 and 29 Richmond terrace, 27 and 28 Berkeley square, and 59 Pembroke road.

Organs.
The following are specifications of the principal organs in Bristol, but there are also excellent instruments in most of the churches and chapels, the largest being in the churches of St. James', Bristol, and All Saints' and Christchurch, Clifton. The instruments at All Saints' church and Tyndale (Baptist) chapel are the only ones (in addition to Colston hall and Victoria rooms) which are blown by mechanical means. (*See* also "Organ Building" under the heading of "Manufactories.")

The BRISTOL CATHEDRAL organ has 39 draw stops and 2,008 pipes. Its compass is from GG to G. In the great organ the stops are—Open diapason (large), open diapason (small), claribella, stopped diapason (each 8 feet), principal (4 feet), twelfth (3 feet), fifteenth (2 feet), sesquialtera (four ranks), mixture (two ranks), trumpet (8 feet), clarion, principal (each 4 feet). Swell organ: Double diapason (16 feet), open diapason, stopped diapason (each 8 feet), harmonic flute, principal (each 4 feet), twelfth (3 feet), fifteenth (2 feet), mixture (two ranks), cornopean, trumpet, hautboy (each 8 feet). Choir organ: Gamba, dulciana, stopped diapason (each 8 feet), principal, flute (each 4 feet), piccolo (2 feet), clarinet (8 feet). Pedal organ (compass from CCC to F): Open diapason, bourdon (each 16 feet), principal (8 feet). Couplers: Swell to great, swell to great in octaves, swell to pedals, great to pedals, choir to pedals, pedal octaves. Accessory movements, &c.—There are eight composition pedals, and the pneumatic leverage has recently been applied to the great organ. The instrument was originally built by Renatus Harris about the year 1700. Improvements and additions have from time to time been made, the last being effected two years ago, when it was renovated by W. G. Vowles, of this city.

The COLSTON HALL organ, built by H. Willis, of London, cost £3,000. The compass of the instrument is from CC to C (61 notes). In the great organ the stops are—Double diapason (16 feet), open diapason (large), open diapason (small), violoncello, claribel flute (each 8 feet), octave or principal (4 feet), quint (3 feet), super octave or fifteenth (2 feet), furniture (five ranks), trombone (16 feet), tromba (8 feet), clarion (4 feet). Choir organ: Violoncello, dulciana, claribel flute, lieblich gedact (each 8 feet), flute octaviante (4 feet), flageolet (2 feet), bassoon, posaune, corni di bassetto (each 8 feet). Swell organ: Contra gamba (16 feet), open diapason, lieblich gedact, salcionel, vox angelica (each 8 feet), principal (4 feet), fifteenth (2 feet), echo cornet (three ranks, various), contra posaune (16 feet), hautboy, corni di bassetto, vox humana, cornopean (each 8 feet), clarion (4 feet). Solo organ: Concert flute, viola di gamba, flute harmonique (each 8 feet), violin (4 feet), tuba major, clarinet, oboe (each 8 feet), tuba clarion (4 feet). Pedal organ: Double diapason (32 feet), open diapason, violone, bourdon (each 16 feet), octave or pedal principal (8 feet), mixture (three ranks), bombard (16 feet). The total number of stops is 62, and speaking pipes 3,245. Couplers: Choir to great, choir to pedal, solo to great, great to pedal, swell to great, swell to pedal, swell sub-octave, swell super-octave, solo to pedal. Accessory movements, &c.—Nine composition pedals, pedal for tremulant, 16 pneumatic pistons for changing the stops, four to each manual. Pneumatic leverage is applied to the great, swell, and pedal organs. The instrument is blown by three double cylinder hydraulic engines, the pressure being derived from the mains of the Waterworks Company.

The GRAMMAR SCHOOL organ (the compass of which instrument is from CC to G) contains 41 draw stops and 1,756 pipes. It was built by W. G. Vowles, of St. James square. The great organ stops are—Double diapason (16 feet), open diapason, gamba, clarabella flute (each 8 feet), principal (4 feet), twelfth (3 feet), fifteenth (2 feet), sesquialtera (three ranks), posaune (8 feet), clarion (4 feet). Choir organ: Viola di gamba, dulciana, lieblich gedact (each 8 feet), wald flute, flute harmonique (each 4 feet), cornb di bassetto (8 feet). Swell organ: Double diapason (16 feet), open diapason, salicional, vox angelica, lieblich gedact (each 8 feet), principal (4 feet), fifteenth (2 feet), contra fagotto (16 feet), cornopean, oboe (each 8 feet), clarion (4 feet). Pedal organ: Open diapason, bourdon, bombard (each 16 feet), violoncello (8 feet). Couplers: Swell to great, swell to great super-octave, swell to great sub-octave, swell to choir, choir to great, swell to pedals, choir to pedals, great to pedals, pedal octave with extra octave of pipes on two stops. Accessory movements, &c.—There are seven combination pedals, and a tremulant is also attached to the organ.

ST. MARY REDCLIFF organ has 41 stops, 2,198 pipes and 6 composition pedals. The pneumatic lever is applied to the great organ keys and couplers. There is every reason to believe that this organ must have been the first in England that had pedals, and at the date of its original erection (1728-9) over the west end of the church was pronounced to be unapproached even by any in London. Harris and Byfield were the original builders, the father of the former having settled in Bristol towards the latter part of his career, and dying here about the year 1715. In 1866 the old organ was taken down and reconstructed by W. G. Vowles, and erected on the north and south sides of the chancel. It was re-opened August 1st, 1867, by John Stainer, M. A., Mus. Bac. (Oxon.) The instrument now contains—in the great organ: Double open diapason (16 feet), open diapason (large), open diapason (small), stopped diapason (each 8 feet), principal, flute (each 4 feet), twelfth (3 feet), fifteenth (2 feet), sesquialtera (five ranks), mixture (three ranks), trumpet (8 feet), clarion (4 feet). Choir organ: Open diapason, bell gamba, stopped diapason (each 8 feet), flute à cheminée, harmonic flute (each 4 feet), piccolo (2 feet), cremona (8 feet). Swell organ: Bourdon (16 feet), open diapason, stopped diapason, dulciana, vox angelica (each 8 feet), principal (4 feet), mixture (various), double bassoon (16 feet), trumpet, hautboy (each 8 feet), clarion (4 feet). Pedal organ: Open diapason, violone, bourdon, trombone (each 16 feet), principal (8 feet). Couplers: Swell to great, swell to choir, choir to great, great to pedals, choir to pedals, swell to pedals. Accessory movements, &c.—Three combination pedals to the swell and great organs, and the pneumatic leverage is applied to both these manuals.

The VICTORIA ROOMS organ has a compass from CC to G (56 notes). The stops in the great organ are—

Double diapason (16 feet), open diapason (large), open diapason (small), stopped diapason (each 8 feet), quint (6 feet), octave or principal, waldflute (each 4 feet), octave quint (3 feet), super-octave or fifteenth (2 feet), sesquialtera (three ranks), mixture (three ranks), furniture (three ranks), trumpet (16 feet), posaune, trumpet (each 8 feet), clarion (4 feet). Choir organ: Double diapason (16 feet), gamba, dulciana, stopped diapason gemshorn (each 8 feet), octave quint (3 feet), super-octave or fifteenth (2 feet), cymbal (two ranks), stopped flute (4 feet), piccolo (2 feet), bassoon, bass clarionet, treble trumpet (each 8 feet). Solo organ: Grand tuba mirabilis (8 feet), grand tuba clarion, claribel (8 feet), harmonic flute and flageolet (each 4 feet), doublette (2 feet), vox angelica (two ranks), krum horn and vox humana (each 8 feet). Swell organ: Double diapason (16 feet), open diapason, salcionel and stopped diapason (each 8 feet), octave or principal (4 feet), octave quint (3 feet), super-octave or fifteenth (2 feet), sesquialtera (five and four ranks), suabe flute (4 feet), cornopean, trumpet, hautboy (each 8 feet), clarion (4 feet). Pedal organ: Double open diapason (32 feet), open diapason (metal), open diapason (wood), bourdon (each 16 feet), octave or principal (8 feet), octave quint (6 feet), super-octave (4 feet), sesquialtera (five ranks), trombone (16 feet), octave trombone (8 feet). There are altogether 68 stops and 4,004 speaking pipes in the organ. Couplers: Swell to great, choir to great, solo to great, pedal to great, pedal to choir, pedal to swell, pedal to solo. Accessory movements, &c.—There are nine composition pedals, four pneumatic combination pistons to each manual, two tremulants, and the pneumatic leverage is attached to the great, swell, and solo organs. The instrument is blown by three single cylinder hydraulic engines, formerly driven by pressure from the mains of the Waterworks Company, but now the power is generated by a gas engine. Hill originally built the organ for the Panopticon (now the Alhambra theatre), London. When that institution failed it was taken away and subsequently placed in the south transept of St. Paul's cathedral, whence it was ultimately removed to its present position by Bryceson and Son.

Orphanages.

ASYLUM FOR POOR ORPHAN GIRLS, situated at the bottom of Ashley hill, instituted January 1st, 1795. The object of this institution is to rescue poor orphan girls (who have lost both parents) from idleness and vice, to instil into their minds the principles of religion and morality, and to accustom them to habits of industry by employing them in household work in order that they may be qualified for domestic service, and to board, clothe and educate them until situations can be provided. The institution, which is supported by voluntary contributions, provides for about 60 inmates. It was commenced in the buildings of the old Magdalen charity at Hook's mills, the foundation stone of which was laid 22nd August, 1827, at a cost of £3,050. The church attached was formerly a private one for the use of the inmates; it is now open to the public. Henry Cooke, hon. sec.

THE NEW ORPHAN HOUSES, Ashley down, consist of five large buildings, with accommodation for 2,050 children, besides officials. Mr. George Müller, who was born at Kroppurstardt, in Prussia, in 1805, and is still living, commenced this laudable work in November, 1835. In April, 1836, a house in Wilson street was opened for female orphan children, and within the year an orphanage for infants was added. This was followed in November, 1837, by one for boys; and in July, 1843, a fourth was opened. These houses were not built or specially adapted for the purpose thus applied, and in June, 1849, they were removed to their present situation.

The first building was erected in that year, the second in 1857, the third in 1862, the fourth in 1868, and the fifth in 1870, the total cost of the five houses being about £115,000. The buildings are solid, well built, destitute of ornament, roomy, lofty, light, well drained, and efficiently ventilated. Though varying somewhat, they have a great resemblance, and are of Pennant stone, dressed with plain freestone. The ground floor of each building contains playrooms, schoolrooms, dining hall and other offices. The first floor comprises dormitories, teachers' bedrooms, offices, &c., and the second floor dormitories, teachers' bedrooms, sick ward, &c. The annual expense of clothing and maintenance of each orphan was, in 1883, £13 12s. 10d.; this includes every expense without exception. There is no capitation grant, grant in aid, or part payment. The sole conditions of admittance are that a child be a legitimate orphan, destitute and bereaved of both parents by death. Over £900,000 have been received in the form of voluntary contributions for the institution and its cognate agencies since the work was begun in 1836. No debt has been contracted; no personal application for aid has been made by any connected with the work; their trust is in God, and their only invested fund a living faith in Him who says "Feed my lambs." That faith has at times been severely tried: the inmates have risen in the morning penniless and without food for the day, but the little ones have never hungered, the Father of the Fatherless has sent them "day by day their daily bread" and always in time. The visiting days are as follows:—House No. 1, Wednesdays, 2.30, 3.0, and 3.30 p.m.; No. 2, Tuesdays, 2.30, 3.0, and 3.30 p.m.; No. 3, Thursdays, 2.30, 3.0, and 3.30 p.m.; Nos. 4 and 5, Fridays and Saturdays, 2.30, 3.0, and 3.30 p.m.; from November to March, 2.30 and 3.0 only. No. 1 contains boys, girls and infants, storerooms, bakery, &c.; No. 2, girls only; No. 3, girls only; No. 4, boys only; No. 5, girls only. On Sunday mornings one fourth of the children attend (in rotation) Bethesda chapel, Charlotte street, Park street, the procession to which place is a spectacle never to be forgotten. For those whose turn it is to remain at home services are held in the dining halls of the institution. George Müller, director; James Wright, co-director.

Parliamentary Papers. The annual Government returns of the trade and navigation of the United Kingdom with foreign countries and British possessions, reports of Her Majesty's Consuls and Secretaries of Legation in foreign countries, statistical abstracts and records, and other books of reference affecting trade and commerce, and the city and country generally, are to be seen at the offices of the Chamber of Commerce, Guildhall, Small street, on the introduction of a member.

Patent Office, The, is situated in Bristol Bank buildings, Corn street. The office is established under the Designs and Trade Marks Acts, for inventors and others seeking protection to their inventions, designs, or trade marks, at home or abroad. Information and instructions as to procedure are afforded, and a handbook of particulars, with table of fees, are to be obtained gratis. Nicholas Watts, Assoc. Mem. Inst. of Civil Engineers, agent.

Pauperism. The subjoined tables show the distribution of pauperism between local unions (*see* "Rates"):—

RATABLE VALUE, POPULATION, PAUPERISM, &c., OF EXISTING LOCAL UNIONS IN JANUARY, 1882.

Unions.	Ratable value.	Population.	No. of Paupers.
Bristol Union	£343,641	56,964	3,594
Barton Regis	682,664	165,871	5,393
Bedminster	291,539	67,703	3,420

During the year ending Lady-day, 1882, there was an average of 3,533 paupers relieved in the Bristol Union at a cost of £36,641 7s. 10¾d., being at the rate of £10 7s. 5¼d. per head. The poor rate in the Bristol Union for half-year 1882 was 1/11 in the £.

Pawnbrokers. There are 49 pawnbrokers' establishments in the city. The "three golden balls," usually seen over pawnbrokers' establishments, is frequently a question of speculation. They are derived from the Medici family, whose arms were "three gilded pills," in allusion to their profession of medicine. They were the richest merchants in Florence and the greatest money lenders. The Lombards were the first money lenders in England, and those who borrowed money of them deposited some security or pawn.

Pawnbrokers' Provident and Benevolent Association has been established 20 years. Since its formation over £82 has been paid to sick and unemployed members and to the widows of deceased members. H. C. Dawe, president.

Pharmaceutical Society, in connection with the National Union. Most of the leading chemists of the city are members. They meet occasionally at the Museum and Library, Queen's road, for the advancement of pharmacy and other matters in connection with that branch of science. Algernon Warren, 24 Redcliff street, hon. sec.

Photographic Association, Bristol and West of England Amateur. The objects are the communication of new and interesting information connected with photography, and the mutual improvement, benefit and recreation of its members. The meetings are held on the fourth Wednesday in each month, at 8 p.m. There are eight evening meetings and four or more excursion meetings in the year, the annual and first evening meeting being held in October. Officers are elected or re-elected annually. The Council arrange for the reading of papers, and make a point of using their utmost endeavours to make the meetings and everything connected with the association interesting, enjoyable and instructive. A monthly journal of their transactions is issued. The association held its first international exhibition at the Fine Arts Academy, Queen's road, in December, 1880, and another at the same place on December 17th, 1883, which remained open for four weeks. Gold, silver and bronze medals were then awarded for the best specimens of workmanship. Entrance fee, 10/6; annual subscription, 10/6; corresponding members' annual subscription, 5/-. H. A. H. Daniel, hon. sec.

Physicians. Of physicians, surgeons and accoucheurs in the city there are about 188; two aural surgeons, five opthalmic surgeons, 30 dental surgeons and dentists, and one surgeon chiropodist.

Pie Poudre Court. This relic of a Saxon age is now incorporated with the Tolzey court. Until some ten years ago, under the porch of the ancient hostelry known as the "Stag and Hounds," Old Market street, a solemn farce was performed annually, on the 30th September, by the formal opening of this court. It is said to have originated in the reign of Alfred; at any rate, it is famous for its antiquity, "since a time whereof the memory of man runneth not to the contrary," and was originally established for the settlement of disputes which arose during the Bristol fair, and was looked upon as a sure and speedy way in which "justice is done." The term "Pie Poudre" has many derivations assigned to it. Some say it meant that justice might be obtained before those departing could shake the dust from their feet; and others, that it was a court for the "dusty-footed"— that is, for people without the city walls—to settle their disputes. The phrase is one of those old Norman-French ones so common in English law, and is very likely to have some reference to the "pedlars" who frequented the fairs in all parts of the country, so that judgment could be given instanter before the thief could bolt or the debtor abscond. The opening ceremony was as follows: A procession walked from the Councilhouse to Old Market street, consisting of the sheriffs, a seneschal, sergeant-at-mace, and other officers; on arrival at the "Stag and Hounds" toasted cheese, cider and metheglin —a Saxon wine peculiar to western counties—were distributed amongst the parties doing business at the court. This latter custom was abolished some years before the extinction of the court, because the people used to tilt the bowl and upset the liquor over one another, consequently fees were substituted for refreshments. The portico of the "Stag and Hounds" was generally decorated on court day with a covering of sand, and drapery of old carpet suspended at one end, a table and a few deal chairs. The court having been duly opened, the business was conducted at the Tolzey court office from Sept. 30th to Oct. 15th inclusive. One peculiarity was the reading of a list of names, the owners of which were ordered to "come forth and do your free suit and services," which, considering they had been dead for centuries, was rather an unreasonable request. With jocose solemnity, the Registrar would then ask his clerk if these people had been duly summoned; and, with a keen sense of the fun of the thing, the clerk would answer in the negative, adding, "They could not be found." The Judge was then asked if he would fine them for non-attendance, and, with great and becoming gravity, he replied that he would not "under the circumstances." The Recorder of Bristol was, by virtue of his office, Judge of this court.

Pilots. There are 38 licensed pilot skiffs for this port, the owners of which chiefly reside at Pill. In Arrowsmith's (late Bunt's) *Tide Tables* will be found the rates and regulations for pilotage, as prescribed by 47 George III., cap. 33, and the by-laws of the Town Council, January 1st, 1853.

Pilots' Union, established for the purpose of resisting the attempts to curtail pilotage limits and sundry other subjects affecting the ancient rights and privileges of those who daily expose their lives in pursuit of a pilot's avocation. Nearly the whole of the pilots in the Bristol Channel are members of the union.

Police. On Saturday, 25th June, 1836, the Bristol police commenced their perambulation of the city. Some time previously preparations had been made for the new city guard, and the full complement of men having been engaged, they were drilled at the Exchange the day before entering upon their novel duties. The drilling over, they were divided into sections and marched to the respective stations, which were as follow :—City station, Guardhouse, Wine street; Bedminster station, Bedminster Causeway; Clifton station, Brandon hill; St. Philip's station, near Trinity church. At the period of establishment the force numbered 227—namely, one superintendent (Joseph Bishop), four inspectors (Gardner, Stephens, Jarrard and Atwood), 24 sergeants, 197 constables, and one clerk. Each man was attired in uniform, and carried a lamp, a rattle, a cutlass and a staff. At each station there was also a set of hand-bells, which, in case of fire, was carried into the streets and rung. (This practice was discontinued in 1851.) In 1844 the Central policestation was built, and the year following the force was increased by 20, and by 50 in 1857. Various reforms have been made since then, until now the city may be said to have a tolerably perfect force constituted thus :—One chief constable (E. A. Coathupe), four superintendents, 16 inspectors, one inspector of public carriages, one detective-inspector, 25 sergeants, 303 constables, seven detectives, and one chief clerk. The River police, established in June, 1872, is composed of two sergeants and 13 men, and their floating station is adjacent to Prince street bridge. The grand total of the force is 374. Amongst the improvements made in connection with the force are the lettering of each division—A B C D, which was done in 1876; the formation of a police fire brigade (see "Fire Brigade") in 1877; the introduction of a van for the conveyance of prisoners in 1880, and the appointment of mounted police, some of whom patrol the Downs during winter evenings. Many, if not all, of these changes have been effected by the present chief constable. Four horses are kept at the Central or A division station for fire brigade work and general purposes. At a meeting of the Town Council, February 12th, 1884, it was resolved that a floating fire engine should be procured at a cost of £2,500, to be worked by the water police. The B division is Bedminster. A new station on the site of the old one was erected in 1882. The C division is Clifton. The station here was built in 1836, but has been considerably altered and enlarged since. The D division is St. Philip's. A new station was opened here in 1869. At Redland there is a reserve station, which is but temporary. In time a new station will be built in the neighbourhood of Elgin park, and when it is established certain districts will be re-arranged. As before stated, J. Bishop was the first superintendent, the next being Capt. Fisher, R.N., and the third J. Sims Hancock, who was succeeded by the present chief. A. N. Ruddock was the first surgeon, R. Bernard the second, R. W. Tibbits the third, and Richardson Cross the present one. Every morning the prisoners are brought in the van from the divisional stations to the magistrates' court (see "Magistrates' Office"), and those committed are taken to the New gaol (see "Gaols"), Horfield. There is an efficient brass band in connection with the force (T. Glover being bandmaster), and a superannuation fund, to which each officer contributes. The total cost of the force for the year ending 25th March, 1883, was £32,688 5s. 4d., towards which Her Majesty's Treasury and the Prison Commissioners contributed £16,026 16s. 8d. Formerly, in case of an accident happening, the unfortunate sufferer had to be conveyed to a hospital or to his house either on a police stretcher, or on a shutter, or in a cab—a most unsuitable vehicle for a person with a broken limb; but now there is no necessity for any of those modes of conveyance, as a member of the Watch Committee has procured from New York an ambulance of the kind so extensively used in that city, which is placed at the Central police-station, Bridewell street, and is horsed and worked by the Fire Brigade, so that when the news of an accident is received the ambulance is immediately despatched to the sufferer; the United Telephone Company offer the use of their apparatus at the Central and Clifton stations and at the cab rests, and renters of telephones throughout the city allow summonses for the ambulance to be sent through their instruments when any accidents occur in their neighbourhood. With the exception perhaps of Clifton, all the stations are admirably adapted. The Bedminster station has been reconstructed, and was re-opened in July, 1882. It is a a massive and imposing structure. The architectural character is that of a military mediæval castle, adapted to its present purpose. It is erected upon the ground occupied by the old station, and the Corporation were fortunate in having in hand so valuable and spacious a site, for if it had been necessary to have acquired a similar plot of land so well situated it would probably have cost the city £2,000. The central tower, rising to a height of 50 ft., and surmounted by an open battlemented parapet, imparts a pleasing and substantial air to the whole structure. The right and left wings being recessed 8 ft. from the line of street front give furthei prominence to the tower, whilst the vaulted archway extending through the principal block of buildings to the spacious yard in the rear forms a fine entrance. In the north-east corner of the yard, and near to the entrance from New Charlotte street, have been erected a mortuary, an inquest-room, a waiting-room for witnesses, and a private apartment for the coroner. Upon the south side are buildings for the fire engine, hose reel, stretcher, whilst the yard itself presents a spacious area of 200 square yards. The clock, which forms a conspicuous feature in the tower, is the gift of E. S. Robinson, and was manufactured by T. Gath, of Small street. It is an eight-day clock, with two illuminated dials, one over the main entrance and the other in the rear, and is fitted with an automatic lighting apparatus.

Political Associations,

&c. There are two political registration societies, the Conservative and the Liberal. Both attend to the registration of voters of their respective parties on the Parliamentary register and the municipal ward lists, and both promote the adoption of those principles consistent with their views relating to Imperial and local politics. The offices of the former association are at 56 Queen square—J. J. Justice, secretary ; and those of the latter at 15 Bridge street—T. Adams, sec.

There are other societies of a political nature for disseminating opinions affecting their respective parties, such as—

THE BRISTOL JUNIOR CONSERVATIVE ASSOCIATION, which meets every month at 56 Queen square. A. H. Patterson, hon. sec.

THE BRISTOL JUNIOR LIBERAL ASSOCIATION meet at 15 Bridge street. F. N. Tribe, Westfield park, hon. sec.

THE BRISTOL OPERATIVE LIBERAL ASSOCIATION has various branches in the city, viz., at Bedminster, Barton hill, &c., and meetings of the association are held at the Star coffee-house, Old Market street. Annual soirées jn connection with the association are held at the Colston hall, in November, when the Members of Parliament for the city give an account of their stewardship and other political passing events. J. Pembery, Willway street, St. Philip's, hon. sec.

THE RADICAL REFORM ASSOCIATION meet at the Castle coffee palace, Castle street. J. W. White, hon. sec.

THE BRISTOL WOMEN'S LIBERAL ASSOCIATION, for the promotion of Liberal principles and the diffusion of knowledge on political questions of general and local interest among the women of Bristol, and this object is carried out by meetings, lectures, discussions, social gatherings, &c. Each member pays an annual subscription of 1s. The association was founded December 19th, 1881. Miss Helen M. Sturge, Chilliswood, Tyndall's park, and Miss Tribe, 7 Westfield park, Redland, hon. secs.

THE BRISTOL WORKING MEN'S CONSERVATIVE ASSOCIATION has over twelve branches in the various districts of the city. Office : St. Philip's Conservative Club, 59 Old Market st.

Since 1858 there have been nine elections, all contested, the results being as follow :—

1859—Hon. F. H. F. Berkeley	(L)	4,432
(April) W. H. G. Langton	(L)	4,285
F. W. Slade	..(C)	4,205
1865—Hon. F. H. F. Berkeley	(L)	5,296
(July) Sir Samuel M. Peto	..(L)	5,228
Thomas F. Fremantle..	..(C)	4,269
1868—John William Miles	..(C)	5,173
(April) Samuel Morley ..	..(L)	4,977
1868—Francis H. F. Berkeley	(L)	8,759
(Nov.) Samuel Morley ..	..(L)	8,714
John William Miles	..(C)	6,694
1870—Elisha Smith Robinson	(L)	7,832
(March) Sholto Vere Hare..	..(C)	7,062
1870—Kirkman D. Hodgson..	(L)	7,816
(June) Sholto Vere Hare..	..(C)	7,238
1874—K. D. Hodgson ..	..(L)	8,888
(Feb.) S. Morley	..(L)	8,732
S. V. Hare	..(C)	8,522
G. H. Chambers ..	..(C)	7,626
1878—Lewis Fry	..(L)	9,342
(Dec.) Sir Ivor Guest ..	..(C)	7,795
1880—S. Morley	..(L)	10,704
(April) Lewis Fry	..(L)	10,070
Sir Ivor Guest ..	..(C)	9,395
E. S. Robinson	(Indep.)	4,100

The number of electors on the register in 1858 was 12,833, and the following are the comparative figures in the Parliamentary register for the several local wards for 1883-4:—

Wards.	For 1884.	For 1883.
Bedminster	5,298	5,255
Central	1,948	2,024
Clifton	2,877	2,831
The District	2,475	2,546
St. Mary Redcliff	1,363	1,451
St. Augustine	1,038	1,091
St. James	888	959
St. Michael	615	602
St. Paul	1,856	1,796
St. Philip and Jacob	6,080	6,159
Westbury-on-Trym	1,925	1,924
Freemen outside the city	139	141
	26,502	26,779

Poor Law Management.

The city is under three distinct authorities, viz.:—The Incorporation of the Poor for the ancient city; Barton Regis Union, for the parishes of Clifton, St. Philip and Jacob (Out), the district of St. James' and St. Paul, and the parish of Westbury; Bedminster Union, for the parish of Bedminster.

Population, &c.

According to the census of 1881, the population was 206,503; the number of inhabited houses, 32,147; and the ratable value, £884,630 17s. 6d. The estimated population up to the present time is 213,000. These figures refer to the population within the borough boundary, but it is well known that a large number of persons engaged in business reside just outside the boundary. If the parishes immediately surrounding the city were included, according to the last census the population would amount to 290,898.

The population of Bristol within its municipal boundaries for this century is as follows:—

	Ancient City.	Added Districts.	Total.
1801	40,814	20,339	61,153
1811	46,592	24,891	71,483
1821	52,889	32,219	85,108
1831	59,074	45,334	104,408
1841	64,266	60,880	125,146
1851	65,716	71,612	137,328
1861	66,027	88,066	154,093
1871	62,662	119,890	182,552
1881	56,964	149,539	206,503

The foregoing does not include the population of the suburban districts. The three Unions in 1881 numbered:—

Bristol	57,499
Barton Regis	166,068
Bedminster	67,331
Total	290,898

AGES OF MALES AND FEMALES 1881 CENSUS.

Ages.	Males.	Females.
Under 5	13,500	13,923
" 5*	11,973	12,210
" 10	11,182	11,633
" 15	9,572	11,346
" 20	7,880	11,274
" 25	7,464	9,455
" 30	6,370	7,844
" 35	5,659	6,844
" 40	4,849	6,124
" 45	4,001	5,148
" 50	3,257	4,484
" 55	2,543	3,386
" 60	2,273	3,219
" 65	1,455	2,399
" 70	944	1,678
" 75	500	986
" 80	209	481
" 85	64	164
" 90	11	53
" 95	5	11
100 upwards	—	1

* This column should be read thus:—5 and under 10, 10 and under 15, and so on.

CONDITION AS TO MARRIAGE AND AGES OF MALES AND FEMALES IN BRISTOL.

Ages.	Unmarried.		Married.		Widowed.	
Under	M.	F.	M.	F.	M.	F.
15	36,655	37,766	—	—	—	—
18	9,496	11,576	—	75	269	—	1	1
20	5,615	7,725	2,240	3,492	25	57
25	3,452	5,465	10,185	11,304	197	538
35	1,021	2,300	9,124	9,437	363	1,231
45	448	1,465	6,339	6,280	471	1,887
55	257	1,002	3,959	3,292	600	2,311
65 and upwards	150	918	2,075	1,464	963	3,394
Total	57,094	68,216	33,997	35,538	2,620	9,409

Port and River Improvement Plans.

To give anything like a fair and adequate account of each would occupy a volume of itself; it is simply, therefore, intended here to record, briefly, in chronological order, the principal schemes that have from time to time been propounded.

The original dock works were completed in 1809, and comprised the damming-up of that portion of the old river running through the city and extending from Rownham to Hanham, the construction of the present Floating harbour and basins, and the formation of a New cut for the tideway (*see* "New Cut" and "Docks"). These improvements yielded accommodation sufficient for the shipping frequenting the port up to about the time of the transfer of the old docks (*see* "Docks Transfer") from the Old Dock Company to the Corporation. To meet the wants of increased shipping, and that Bristol might maintain her position as a port, various schemes were brought forward.

In 1830 — Milne, C.E., suggested the erection of a pier, 800 feet, at Portishead, making due provision for three landing stages.

In December, 1839, I. K. Brunel, C.E., proposed the following schemes: 1st, a lock of entrance to Cumberland basin of sufficient dimensions to admit large vessels into the Floating harbour and cutting off the most dangerous points in the river; 2nd, the construction of distinct locks at Sea mills; 3rd, the construction of a pier at Portishead, and a railway from thence to Bristol.

In 1841 John (afterwards Sir John) Macneil proposed a pier at Portishead.

In November, 1852, J. M. Rendel, C.E., proposed an important and perfectly arranged design for a dock at the actual mouth of the Avon, 80 acres in area, the erection of two piers there, and other works in connection.

In 1853 C. F. Thomas proposed the conversion of Wood Hill bay, Portishead, into an outer harbour and docks, by cutting a channel through Portishead hill. In the same year W. R. Neale, C.E., proposed the construction of a dock in Portishead pill (where it is now situated).

In 1859 T. Howard, C.E., simultaneously with G. Thornton, C.E., proposed an elaborate plan for the dockisation of the river Avon from its mouth. Prior to this the latter gentleman suggested an abridgment of J. M. Rendel's scheme, and in 1860 he proposed the construction of a small dock, &c., at Avonmouth for ocean-going steamships (*see* "Docks Transfer"). Several other minor schemes were put forward about this time, amongst which there may be mentioned one for the formation of a landing stage and dock at Dunball island. The Town Council, the Chamber of Commerce, and the citizens generally were actively engaged in discussing the question of docks, and Messrs. Parkes and Green published their respective ideas on the capability of port improvement. The former suggested a widening, and in some places a deepening, of the existing channels of the river, including the diversion of the tidal currents at the mouth of the river into the old narrow channel north of Dunball island. The latter proposed, as far as possible, the restoration of the entrance of the river to its original course, by running out embankments from the mainlands on the Somersetshire and Gloucestershire shores, and the general widening and deepening of the river. T. Howard expressed his opinion of the practicability of turning the whole of the river into a floating harbour. In the same year the Town Council referred the subject to Sir William Cubitt, C.E., and T. Page, C.E., with a request that they would report generally as to the claims of T. Howard's plans and others. John (now Sir John) Hawkshaw was afterwards substituted for Sir William Cubitt. J. Hawkshaw gave the preference to J. M. Rendel's as being of good general arrangement, though too large and costly. J. Hawkshaw spoke in high terms of praise of T. Howard's scheme for dockising the river, as also did T. Page, but he did not coincide in the opinion that the Avon ought to be turned into a floating harbour, and suggested as an alternative the construction of a dock at Avonmouth.

Shortly after this the Chamber of Commerce passed a resolution asking the Town Council to construct a dock at the mouth of the river, with a railway to connect it with Bristol, and during 1860 and 1861 the Town Council held several meetings on the subject, and in February, 1861, they resolved, by a majority of 32 to 17, "that it is not expedient to incur any further liability on the fixed property of the city for the purpose of making dock accommodation for ocean steamers at the mouth of the river."

In 1861 the Corporation went to Parliament with a scheme for widening and improving the river, and an independent company, known as the Port Railway and Pier Company, sought powers to construct a railway from Hotwells to Avonmouth, with a pier at the latter place. Both were unsuccessful that year, but in 1862 the company's bill passed, and a short pier was constructed running out into the passage of the Old, or North, channel of the river, which at that time existed between the Gloucestershire side and Dunball island. This passage has been for some years closed and the pier useless.

In 1864 the Bristol Port and Channel Dock Company was formed, and constructed the present Avonmouth dock (see "Docks"). Side by side with the Avonmouth scheme grew the dock at Portishead (see "Docks"), promoted by the Bristol and Portishead Pier and Railway Company.

In 1871, in accordance with clauses contained in both companies' Acts, the Board of Trade nominated D. Stevenson, C.E., and J. Ball to investigate the position and prospects of both undertakings. Their joint report was that both schemes were fitted to effect the object in view, viz., the reception, accommodation, and the loading and unloading of ocean-going steamers and sailing vessels of large dimensions; and that, as they were indispensable to the interests of the port of Bristol, it was recommended that the Corporation should subscribe to the share capital of both.

On June 18th and July 1st, 1872, this important question came before the Council, when it was resolved, by 33 votes to 22, not to contribute to the Avonmouth docks, and by 36 votes to 19 to subscribe £100,000 to the capital of the Portishead Docks Company. In addition to this, the Council resolved to spend a considerable sum in improving the existing harbour; and, in accordance with plans of T. Howard, C.E., the new works at Cumberland basin (see "Docks") were proceeded with in 1872-3.

On the opening of the docks at the mouth of the river severe competition was soon felt, and in November, 1877, the Chamber of Commerce memorialised the Town Council to give the question of dockisation of the river prompt and effective attention; and at the Council meeting on the 1st January, 1878, a committee was appointed to report on the subject. In that year suggestions were made with reference to the purchase of the new docks by the city.

The Dockising Committee of the Town Council having referred the subject to the docks engineer (T. Howard), that gentleman reported in 1879, wherein he reiterated his opinion that the scheme of dockisation which he recommended in 1859 was thoroughly practicable. The Town Council, however, on the 1st July, 1879, passed the following resolution:—"That, in the opinion of this Council, the creation of large docks at the mouth of the river has rendered it inexpedient at the present time to adopt any scheme for dockising the river."

In 1880-1 the dockising question was again revived, also that of the city purchasing one or both docks at the mouth of the river; and bills promoted by the Corporation and the Docks Companies were this year introduced into Parliament for that purpose, but were lost. A Corporation Act was obtained in 1881, enabling the city to meet more effectively the competition with the Avonmouth and Portishead docks, and to consolidate their capital and loans and to convert them into perpetual debenture stock, which was availed of by the Corporation.

The Chamber of Commerce again approached the Town Council in September, 1880, urging that body to reconsider the question of dockisation, and a committee for the purpose was appointed on October 19th, 1880. On the 26th January, 1881, a report on the flood question was presented by T. Howard, R. Rawlinson, H. J. Marten, and C. J. Symons; and on April 30th, 1883, the report of the Dockising Committee was issued, which was a most elaborate document for dockising at a cost of £1,736,875, and which, after reiterating the opinion of the docks engineer (T. Howard) and Sir John Coode's proposals, stated that "the reports and memoranda go far to prove the practicability and desirability of dockising the river, and they recommend the Council to authorise the further expenditure for a new survey and a thorough and complete investigation of all the physical conditions requisite for an exhaustive consideration of the question in all its bearings at a cost of about £3,000." The chairman of the Committee (C. Townsend) moved a resolution in the Council on the 25th May, 1883, to that effect, but it was lost in favour of an amendment, moved by W. Pethick, to the effect that the report be received, but that until some arrangement be made for placing all the docks of the port under one management, and the Council have decided whether it is desirable to undertake the expenditure estimated for dockising the river, it is not expedient to incur the expense of any further engineering investigation. This amendment was carried by 34 votes to 8.

The question of forming a Harbour Trust, and thus uniting the three concerns, was agitated in 1881 and 1882, and bills entitled the Bristol Docks and Harbour Board Bill, and the Bristol Port and Docks Commission Bill, were introduced, but both failed to obtain the sanction of the Committee of the House of Lords. In 1883 the latter bill was again introduced in an amended form, but was withdrawn.

On February 12th, 1884, the Corporation resolved to provide a gridiron at Cumberland basin at a cost of £6,500.

On February 19th, 1884, at a special meeting of the Council, it was unanimously resolved that the Avonmouth and Portishead docks be purchased upon the following terms:—

"*Avonmouth.* The undertakings of the Bristol Port and Channel Dock Company and the Bristol Port and Channel Dock Warehouse Company Limited for £525,000 Bristol Corporation 3½ per cent. debenture stock, of which £450,000 is to bear interest from the day aforesaid and £75,000 from the expiration of five years from that day; and if within six months after the passing of the Act the Council shall be satisfied that the companies have accurately estimated the amount recoverable in future from the railway companies for services to be rendered at the dock at the rate of £1,750 per annum calculated on the traffic for the year 1883, a further sum of £25,000 like stock, to bear interest from the expiration of seven years from the day aforesaid—provided that if the Council shall not be so satisfied they shall be entitled to call on a valuer, to be named in the Act or appointed by the Board of Trade, to determine whether the companies have overestimated such amount, and if so, to what extent; and such £25,000 stock shall be reduced proportionately to the deficiency, and the value of the loose plant and stores of the companies on the day aforesaid to be ascertained by valuation between the parties, and paid in cash within two months therefrom.

"*Portishead.* The dock undertaking of the Bristol and Portishead Pier and Railway Company, and the undertaking of the Portishead Warehouse Company Limited, for £250,000 Bristol Corporation 3½ per cent. debenture stock, of which £225,000 is to bear interest from the day aforesaid and £25,000 from the expiration of five years from that day; and the value of the loose plant and stores of the companies on that day to be ascertained by valuation between the parties, and paid in cash within two months therefrom. The purchase to include not only the existing warehouses and machinery, but also the granaries, warehouses, and complete machinery and appliances arranged or provided for by the companies, and the Corporation to participate with the other shareholders in the dock undertaking in the proceeds of the sale in respect of the shares it holds therein."

Post Office. The first mention of a post-office in this city is in 1670, but the site is unknown. In 1700 Henry Pine, or Pyne, is spoken of as postmaster, and members of his family held the office till 1777. He was a party to an agreement to lease a piece of land, "with liberty to build on the same, for the conveniency of a post-office." The building was to have a second story extended by a truss of 18 inches. This site is not known. Subsequently the business of the office was removed to Small street, and was carried on in a house formerly occupied by the *Bristol Mirror*, now the Assize courts. In 1748 a new office was opened in Corn street, in premises now occupied by the Lancashire Life Assurance Company and a tea dealer's warehouse. On March 25th, 1868, the business of the office was again removed to Small street. The present buildings are Crown property, and the style of architecture is the Palladian.

To show the immense multiplication of letter traffic since the introduction of the penny post, and of the rapid growth of the Post-office in other departments, the following figures are appended:—

LETTERS, &C.

Clerks.	Letter Carriers.	Letters weekly.	Newspapers.	Books.
1820..	4	13	—	—	—
1841..	—	—	46,000	—	—
1851..	25	35	109,000	—	—
1871..	—	—	200,000	17,000	17,000
1875..	50	101	230,000	51,000	22,000
1882..	191*	152	387,791	—	—

* Twenty-six are females.

MONEY ORDERS.

	Issued.	Paid.
1834	300	—
1851	20,000	—
1875	44,000	140,000
1881	31,851	115,434
" Postal orders (1st year)	11,579	27,937

SAVINGS BANK.

	Deposits and Withdrawals.
1875	15,228
1881	15,561

TELEGRAMS.

Year ending March 31st.	Forwarded.	Delivered.	Totals.
1872..	85,386	214,426	299,812
1882.	276,406	391,891	668,297

It appears from the report of the Postmaster-General that during the year ending March 31st, 1883, the number of letters received in the returned letter office of Bristol was 333,519, against 333,128 in 1881. The number of letters re-issued to corrected addresses was 2,193, against 2,107 in the previous year; 282,250 letters were returned to the senders, against 279,948; 15,111 letters were returned unopened from foreign countries, against 14,495; 33,965 letters could neither be delivered nor returned to the senders, as against 36,578. The number of post-cards received was 14,850, against 15,766; 358,064 books were received, against 358,247; and 15,278 newspapers, as against 16,209 in the previous year. It will thus be seen that there was an increase of 391 letters received at the office; but in the number of letters which could neither be delivered nor returned there was a decrease of 2,613. The number of newspapers dealt with was 931 fewer; whilst there was an increase of 2,302 in the number of letters returned to the senders.

In 1858 there were seven offices, including the head office, and 17 pillars and boxes, whereas in 1883 there were 29 offices and 75 pillars and boxes. In the year that the business was transferred from Corn street the postal packages in one week for this city and its delivery in the neighbourhood amounted to 210,817; a week's return in 1883 gave a total of 413,465.

In 1864 the Post-office staff comprehended the postmaster, 35 clerks, 41 letter carriers, one inspector, making a total of 77; in 1883, with the telegragh officials, the following is the return:—

Postmaster	1
Chief clerk	1
Superintendents	2
Assistant-superintendents	7
Clerks	8
1st class sorting clerks and telegraphists	41
2nd class sorting clerks and telegraphists	96
2nd class sorting clerks and telegraphists (female)	26
Inspector of town postmen	1
Assistant-inspectors of town postmen	3
1st class town postmen	83
2nd class town postmen	15
Suburban postmen	5
Auxiliary sorters	17
Auxiliary stampers	5
Auxiliary postmen	60
Rural postmen	3
Inspectors of telegraph messengers	2
Messengers	67
Total	443

In 1854 the Clifton branch office in Regent place had two clerks and five postmen; it now employs nine clerks and 32 postmen. In 1854 the letters were 21,400 per week, and in 1882 64,192 per week. The staff is included in that of the head office.

Telegraphs.—Prior to the Government taking over the telegraphs, there were three telegraph offices in Bristol, viz.:—The Electric and International, on the Exchange; the Magnetic in Exchange avenue, where W. R. Stock's office is situated; and the United Kingdom Telegraph Company, with a station in Corn street in a building since occupied by Barber and Co. At present the telegraph stations in the city number 17, and are—the head office in Small street, and branch offices at Clifton, North street, Redcliff, Queen square, the Royal hotel, Queen's road, West street, Cotham, Redland, Horfield, Hotwells, Bedminster, Stapleton road, Totterdown, Temple gate, and the Cattle market.

Parcels Post.—In order to facilitate the reception and despatch of parcels by parcels post (which came into operation on August 1st, 1883), a spacious building, entirely devoted to this new branch of the postal system, and known as the parcel depôt, was erected on the open space immediately outside the down platform of the Joint station at Temple meads. It is 80 feet by 35 feet, has been constructed of corrugated iron, and has been specially fitted up for parcels post work. The arrangements of the interior, with a view to expediting the reception and sorting of the parcels as they come to hand, are of the most complete character, simple in design and effective in working, while the building has been constructed upon a site which admits of its being extended at any time that increase of work might render necessary. Edward C. Sampson, head postmaster.

Protestant League, The, established for the prevention of Romanism, Ritualism and Rationalism. The league is open to members of the Church of England and Evangelical Nonconformist bodies, and has several branches in the city belonging to working men. S. Bradfield, secretary.

Provident Society, The, has been in operation for 50 years. Thousands of poor persons have derived benefit by it, and been enabled to provide suitable clothing, &c., by their own self-denial and forethought without recourse to charity. The depositors receive the amount of their year's savings, with a premium of a penny on the shilling, partly in money and partly in warm, comfortable clothing or bedding.

Public-houses. The number of public-houses, including hotels and ale and porter stores, in Bristol, is 1,280. (*See* "Licensed Houses").

Public-house Signs.

Much of the city's history, and more of its manners, may be gleaned from public-house signs. A large number are selected out of compliment to the Lord of the Manor, or some wealthy man in the neighbourhood, or because the proprietor of the inn is or was some servant whom "it delighted the lord to honour." When the name and titles of the lord became exhausted, his cognizance or his favourite pursuit was adopted. As the object of the sign is to speak to the feelings and attract attention, another fruitful source is either some national hero or great battle. The proverbial loyalty of our city has naturally shown itself in tavern signs, such as the "Victoria," the "Prince of Wales," the "Crown," and so on. In the vicinity of the shipping, houses will be found to accord with some peculiarity associated therewith. Some signs indicate a past or present speciality of the house or locality, some a political bias, some an attempt at wit and some purely fanciful, whilst others are in commemoration of some great event at about the time of the establishment of the inn. The following list may exemplify the subject :—

THE ANGEL, in allusion to the angel that saluted the Virgin Mary.

THE BEAR, from the popular sport of bear-baiting.

THE BELL, in allusion to races, a silver bell having (up to the time of Charles II.) been given to winners.

THE CAT AND WHEEL (see "Inns, Old ").

THE CHEQUERS intimates that a room is, or was, set apart for merchants and accountants, where they can be private, make up their accounts, or use their "chequers" undisturbed. The "Chequers" inn formerly stood in the Horsefair, but was pulled down on the construction of New Union street, and was, in the days of St. James' fair, extensively patronised for the purposes implied above.

THE COACH AND HORSES signifies that it is, or was, a posting house, a stage coach house, or both.

THE GLOBE is the cognizance of the King of Portugal, and intimates that Portuguese wines may or might be therein obtained.

THE HOLE-IN-THE-WALL, Upper Maudlin street, so-called because it is approached by a passage or hole in the wall.

THE PLUME OF FEATHERS, a loyal sign in honour of the Prince of Wales.

THE SPREAD EAGLE is the coat of arms of Germany. The sign therefore indicates that German wines could or may be obtained within.

THE WHITE HART, the cognizance of Richard II.

THE WHITE SWAN, the cognizance of Henry IV. and Edward III.

Pugsley's Field.

On the site known as Mother Pugsley's field and well now stands Fremantle square and the adjoining buildings. This property belonged to a young man named Pugsley, who held a command in Prince Rupert's army, and received his death from a shot at the corner of Nugent hill and Somerset street, on his own land. Just below the spot, and about 40 feet from the top of the hill, a double spring issued from the daisied turf, the lesser fountain being specially famed for its healing qualities. Hither came daily, when peace was restored, the hero's young and beautiful widow to mourn her lost one, and by deeds of Christian kindness and words of wisdom to benefit many a young beginner in life. Rejecting repeated offers of marriage, she lived on thus for 55 years, dying in August, 1700, and leaving in her will money to buy bread for ever for 16 poor women inmates of St. Nicholas' almshouse in King street, a sixpenny and a ninepenny loaf each at Easter, and a twopenny loaf on Twelfth day. Her wedding garment was to be her shroud, her wedding sheet she had kept for her winding sheet; and thus borne on a bier, coffinless and covered with flowers, with two young girls strewing herbs and flowers on her path, and a musician preceding the procession playing upon the violin, whilst old St. Nicholas rang out a merry wedding peal, she was carried through the streets of the city to the field which bore her name, and there, in the presence of tens of thousands of spectators, was laid in her husband's grave.

"St. Nicholas' bells are ringing to-day,
Some great folks or other are wed, I dare say."
Merrily, merrily, do they ring,
It isn't the birthday of Queen or of King.
I wonder whatever on earth it can be,
Look! how the people are running to see,
Some wonderful sight
Must surely invite
Their attention, and cause such excessive delight
And hey diddle, diddle,
Do hark! There's a fiddle!
The thing is an incomprehensible riddle.
But here comes a crowd, and oh! what upon earth
Can that corpse, on that bier, have to do with such mirth?
And as true as I live, on each side there's a maiden,
Dressed all in white, with the sweetest herbs laden,
Which they strew as they go,
What a singular show!
Whose funeral is it? I should like to know,
Who is it wound up in that white sheet so snugly,
Without coffin, or pall, or the like?
GAMMER PUGSLEY.—"DIX."

On rebuilding the wall under which the hapless pair were buried, the skull of the husband was found with a bullet hole in one side of his forehead.

Pumps, City.

ST. PETER'S. At the south-west corner of Peter street is St. Peter's pump, over the well of St. Edith. The well was sunk and surmounted by an open work cross in 1474 by W. Spencer, Mayor in 1473. The cross was rebuilt in 1633, and is now in neighbourship with the old Civic High cross at Stourhead. In the accounts of St. Peter's church is a charge, in 1662, of 1/6 for "pullinge down of a May pole put up at St. Peter's plump."

WINE STREET PUMP has long been a nuisance, and many attempts have been made to remove it. In 1773 the inhabitants of the street petitioned the Corporation to have it removed into the Corn market, as the railings round the pump caused an obstruction to the traffic. The Corporation ordered "the railings around the pump to be taken down and four large stones to be erected, in order to prevent carriages running against the pump." This gave a width of 22 feet on each side of the structure. The Corporation took further steps to comply with the petition, but was defeated in a lawsuit by Peter Muggleworth, who maintained that the pump was serviceable in case of fire, &c. The pump still stands in its original position, but in the opinion of many it has been an eyesore for years. A notice has recently been affixed to it that unless the water is boiled it is unfit for domestic purposes.

Quakers.

The history of the Bristol Quakers is one of peculiar interest. During the earlier days of their existence they suffered great persecutions, and the severity of the measures enforced against them is illustrated by the fact that in the year 1683 they were fined £16,440 for not attending the Establishment church. The fact that their place of meeting has been founded on the ruins of an old Dominican monastery is an intelligent explanation of the otherwise ambiguous designation of "Quakers' friars," bestowed upon the locality between Broadmead and Rosemary street. (See "Chapels," sub-heading "Society of Friends.")

Quarter Days.

In this city there is a peculiar diversity of opinion as to the correct date for the concluding quarter-day of the year, and some years ago the late Judge Fisher, of the local County court, endeavoured, but failed, to settle the vexed question. Some are in favour of December 21st, others the 24th, and again the 25th is contended for as the correct day; the latter is the recognised date in other parts of the kingdom. The other quarter-days recognised in Bristol as in other parts of England are Lady-day (25th March), Midsummer-day (24th June), and Michaelmas-day (29th September).

Quays. (*See* "Docks.")

Queen Square. (*See* "Open Spaces.")

Ragged Schools. (*See* "Schools.")

Railways.
In 1858 there was but one railway station in the city, viz., that at Temple meads. There are now ten, viz., the Joint station, St. Philip's, Clifton (Port and Pier), Clifton bridge (Portishead line), Clifton down (Clifton Extension), Montpelier, Stapleton road, Lawrence hill, Bedminster and Ashley hill.

The BRISTOL JOINT PASSENGER STATION, in Temple meads, is a structure in the Tudor Gothic style, erected in 1871-8, and its façade presents a rather imposing appearance. The general plan of the station is in the form of the letter V, the through traffic passing along one side and the Midland departure and the local Great Western traffic starting from the other. The central portion of the station is used for booking offices, refreshment rooms, &c. There is a clock tower about 100 feet in height. The up main passenger station is 500 feet long, with a roof in a single span of 125 feet. The passenger stations and platforms for the Midland and local Great Western trains are about 1,000 feet long, covered with a roof of 77 feet span. Its total cost, including the reconstruction of the adjoining cattle market and the cost of additional property, was over £200,000.

The BRISTOL AND EXETER RAILWAY was incorporated by Act of Parliament 6 William IV., cap. 36 (19th May, 1836), for making a broad guage line from Bristol to Exeter. Subsequent Acts were obtained for the construction of branches to Weston-super-Mare, Clevedon, Cheddar, &c. The main line (length 75½ miles) was opened in the following sections: 1st, from Bristol to Bridgwater, on 14th June, 1841; 2nd, from Bridgwater to Taunton, on 1st July, 1842; 3rd, from Taunton to Beam bridge, on 1st May, 1843; 4th, from Beam bridge to Exeter, on 1st May, 1844. By an Act of Parliament dated 27th June, 1876, this line was sold to the Great Western Railway Company, the terms being 6 per cent. for six years from 1st January, 1876, and afterwards 6½ per cent. in perpetuity.

The BRISTOL AND NORTH SOMERSET, incorporated by Act of Parliament 21st July, 1863, connects Bristol with Radstock, where it joins the Frome branch of the Great Western Railway, and thus forms a continuous line between Bristol and Frome. Its length is 15¼ miles. Opened 3rd Sept., 1873. Capital, 30th June, 1883:— Received : Ordinary stock, £410,072; debenture stock, £124,500; total, £534,572. Expended on lines and works, £636,807 ; debit balance, £102,235, covered by available powers for the issue of shares and loan capital to the extent of £98,228 nominal value. An agreement with the Great Western Railway Company provided, amongst other things, that the latter company should guarantee the interest on this company's debenture stock to the extent of £5,500 per annum for the first five years after the opening of the line, and thenceforth such interest to be a first charge on the gross receipts before any division of profits with the Great Western be made. A bill is now before Parliament for the disposal of this company's line to the Great Western Railway Company upon the following terms :— For the six months ending the 31st December, 1884, £4,818 ; for the year 1885, £9,910 ; 1886, £11,280 ; 1887, £11,280 ; 1888 and thereafter, £11,555.

The BRISTOL AND PORTISHEAD RAILWAY, 10 miles in length, belonging to the Bristol and Portishead Pier and Railway Company, was opened 16th April, 1867, and was worked under agreement with the Bristol and Exeter Railway, and afterwards by the Great Western Railway (in consequence of the amalgamation of the former company with the latter). The Great Western Railway work it at 40 per cent. of the receipts. It was formerly broad guage, but is now converted to narrow. The line from Portishead junction to Clifton bridge was doubled in June, 1883. The stations on the line are Clifton bridge, Pill, Portbury, Portishead, and Portishead pier. By an Act of Parliament, 13th July, 1871, the company was authorised to construct docks at Portishead and other works. (See "Docks.")

BRISTOL AND SOUTH WALES UNION RAILWAY. This company was incorporated by 20th and 21st Vic., cap. 54 (27th July, 1857), to construct railways between Bristol and South Wales, joining the latter at Portskewet, in the county of Monmouth, with a steam ferry across the river Severn in connection therewith at the New Passage. The length on the Gloucestershire side of the Severn to New Passage is 11½ miles. The original capital was £300,000,.in £25 shares; loans, £98,000. The line was opened 9th September, 1863. The Great Western Railway worked the traffic from the commencement, and by the Great Western Act of 1868 it was merged into and amalgamated with that company, the latter taking upon it the following liabilities :—(1) The debenture debt of the Union, bearing interest not exceeding 5 per cent., £98,000. (2) The preference share capital of the Union bearing interest in perpetuity at 5 per cent. on and from the 1st February, 1870. These shares are converted into Great Western (South Wales Union) guaranteed 5 per cent. preference stock, £120,450. (3) The ordinary share capital of the Union on and from the 1st February, 1870, converted into and rank with Great Western ordinary stock, £168,225. The broad guage was first adopted, but since the amalgamation the whole of it has been converted into narrow. Christopher James Thomas was the chairman, and Leonard Bruton the secretary, of the Bristol and South Wales Union Railway Company.

The BRISTOL HARBOUR JUNCTION RAILWAY connects the Great Western Railway with the Floating harbour at Wapping, where there is a wharf and depôt. The original capital was £165,000, of which £50,000 was provided by the Bristol Municipal Corporation for making the wharf and depôt, the company undertaking to pay £2,000 a year, or 4 per cent. upon that amount, leaving £115,000 for the share capital raised by the Great Western and Bristol and Exeter Railway Companies, with power to borrow one-third the amount. Other capital has since been raised by the companies, viz. :—In 1869, £50,000; and in 1874, £109,000; total capital received to 30th June, 1875, £324,000. The line was opened, only for goods traffic, on the 11th March, 1872.

The BRISTOL PORT RAILWAY AND PIER was incorporated by Act of Parliament 17th July, 1862. The line, which is single, runs from Hotwells (under the Clifton Suspension bridge) to Avonmouth, with stations at Sea mills and Shirehampton. Its length is 5¾ miles. Capital, £125,000 in £10 shares, and £41,000 on loan. Commenced February 19th, 1863; opened for traffic March 6th, 1865. The Clifton Extension Railway joins this line at Sneyd park junction. The company's affairs are at present in Chancery.

The CLIFTON EXTENSION RAILWAY is a short loop line connecting Clifton with the termini of the main lines at the Joint station, Temple meads. It was opened for traffic on the 1st October, 1874. The route is connected with the Stapleton road junction, on the Bristol and South Wales Union Railway, whence it cuts through Ashley vale and by a tunnel to Montpelier, where there is a station, and from thence, over Horfield road, through the lower part of Cotham and Redland, passing under Whiteladies' road to Clifton down station. At Ashley hill junction there is a loop line to Fishponds, on the Midland Railway. The line is worked jointly by the Great Western and Midland Companies, the former company having running powers from Bristol to Clifton and *vice versa*, and the latter from Clifton to Fishponds, there joining the main line. The platforms of the Clifton station, 500 feet in length, are covered in with a glass roof. The booking hall and all other offices are fitted up with great taste and every convenience for travellers. A small footbridge connects the up and down platforms. There is a large coal depôt at the station. From Clifton station the line runs under Durdham down in a tunnel, 1,740 yards in length and 160 feet in its maximum depth from the surface of the Down, cut through solid limestone rock. The railway then unites with the Port and Pier Railway at Sneyd park. At the time of writing, this portion of the line from Clifton is not opened for passenger traffic, though it was completed in 1875. Strenuous efforts have been made by the Town Council and Chamber of Commerce, urging upon the companies the importance of opening this branch. A large goods traffic is carried over the line by both the above-mentioned companies from the Avonmouth dock to Bristol, the Midlands and Western counties.

The GREAT WESTERN RAILWAY presents the greatest public work ever constructed in this or any other country, and offers an unrivalled instance of the enterprise of capitalists. The company was originally incorporated by Act of Parliament on August 31st, 1835, 5th and 6th William IV., cap. 107, entitled, "An Act for making a railway from Bristol to join the London and Birmingham Railway, near London, to be called 'The Great Western Railway,' with branches therefrom to the towns of Bradford and Trowbridge, in the county of Wilts."

After the passing of the Act difficulties arose in the matter of the proposed junction with the London and Birmingham Railway, and in 1836 it was decided to build a separate terminus at Paddington, in which year also the determination of the directors to adopt a guage of 7 feet instead of the ordinary guage of 4 feet 8½ inches was officially announced.

On January 3rd, 1825, the first railroad between Bristol and Bath was projected; Sheriff Gardiner took the chair at the "White Lion" tavern, Broad street, Bristol, for the purpose of receiving the report of J. M. Tucker, the surveyor. The capital was to be £100,000 in 4,000 shares of £25 each. On the 2nd February following a meeting of the London and Bristol Railroad Company, the capital of which was to be £1,500,000 in shares of £100 each, was held at the "London" tavern to receive the report of John Loudon McAdam, who advised the construction of a turnpike road in connection with the railway *viâ* Wallingford, at an estimated cost of £130,000. Richard Hart Davis, M.P., was the chairman.

On 30th July, 1831, a public meeting was held in the Guildhall for the purpose of forming a railroad to London; estimated cost, £2,808,330. The bill was read a second time in the House of Commons March 6th, 1834, but was rejected by the Lords on July 25th.

On October 8th, 1834, a meeting was held in the hall of the Society of Merchant Venturers, when it was determined to apply afresh for an Act to complete the whole line of the Great Western Railway; and in November the Corporation of Bristol and the Merchant Venturers agreed to take each of them 100 shares. The allotment of shares in Bristol was well taken up.

The first length of the Great Western system opened was from Paddington to Maidenhead in June, 1838, to and from which place passengers were conveyed in the now obsolete coaches of the day; and it may be mentioned that for some months nothing but passengers and a few parcels were carried on the railway.

In 1839 the line was opened to

Twyford, and in the same year the company first commenced to carry goods traffic, and in the following year first conveyed Her Majesty's mails over that portion of the line then opened. In the latter year the line was opened to Reading, and subsequently as far as Steventon. At this period passengers were conveyed at very cheap fares by goods trains, which at that period acted as an equivalent to the Parliamentary trains of the present day.

Later on in 1840 the line was extended to Farringdon road (the present Uffington station), and the line between Bristol and Bath was first used for public traffic on 31st August, 1840. The following is a statement of the receipts that day:—Bristol, £223 17s. 1½d.; Keynsham, £21 14s.; Bath, £230 19s.; total, £476 10s. 1½d. The number of passengers conveyed was 5,880. The 17 miles between Farringdon road and Hay lane, near Wootton Bassett, were opened in December, 1840, the length of line then in working being 92 miles.

June, 1841, saw the opening between Wootton Bassett and Chippenham, and on the last day of the same month the whole main line was completed and opened throughout, and the construction of a railway between the great cities of London and Bristol was accomplished. The building of the noted Box tunnel had considerably retarded the opening of the length between Chippenham and Bath. The tunnel, with one or two exceptions, is the longest railway tunnel in England, being 9,680 feet, or more than a mile and three-quarters in length. The permanent shafts of this tunnel (28 feet in diameter and averaging 240 feet in depth) were let in September, 1836; but no portion of the tunnel was contracted for until September, 1837, and the larger part of it not until February, 1838; it was completed in 1841, and stands unrivalled for magnitude, &c., amongst works of its kind. The area of its section is about 900 square feet, and the tunnel is perfectly straight; the light is visible through it from end to end, so much so indeed that in the summer months the sun may be seen to rise at one end and set at the other. It took about three years to complete, and upwards of 20 millions of bricks were used in the arching, besides a great extent of freestone walling. It cost upwards of £500,000.

In the first half of 1841 the dividend of the Great Western Company was at the rate of 3 per cent., but in the second half of the same year it rose to 6 per cent., the latter being on the complete line.

In the following year Her Majesty made her first journey by railway, the Great Western having the honour of carrying her on the occasion. In the same year the second excursion organised by the company was run from Bristol to London, and carried about 700 passengers, who were conveyed at what was then considered the low fare of 21/- for the double journey.

In 1843 powers were obtained to construct a line from Didcot to Oxford, and in 1844 the Oxford, Worcester and Wolverhampton Railway was proposed, and the Bristol and Exeter line was completed and opened throughout to Exeter, as was also the branch to Oxford.

In 1845 the directors were authorised to apply for powers to make railways between Bath and Salisbury, with branches to the towns of Bradford, Frome and Radstock; Reading to Newbury and Hungerford; Reading to Basingstoke; Wilts and Somerset to Dorchester and Weymouth; Taunton to Yeovil, and others.

In 1854 the Shrewsbury lines, *i.e.*, the Shrewsbury and Chester and Shrewsbury and Birmingham, were leased to the Great Western, which at that time did not extend beyond Banbury; but in the next year it was continued to Birmingham, and soon afterwards the connection between the systems was complete.

The same year saw the Wilts, Somerset and Weymouth lines partially opened, besides the opening of the Wycombe and Radstock branches.

The year 1863 witnessed the amalgamation of the West Midland and South Wales lines with the Great Western.

In 1872 the guage of the line between Swindon and New Milford was altered from broad to narrow, and about the same time the Wilts, Somerset and Weymouth branch was similarly altered.

As already stated, the Bristol and Exeter Railway was absorbed into the Great Western in 1876, the South Devon in 1878, and the Monmouthshire in 1880.

The shareholders of the Bristol and Exeter, South Devon and Great Western Railway Companies met in Bristol, Plymouth and Paddington, and agreed upon their amalgamation scheme on December 17th, 1875.

The Great Western Railway have also a branch from Yatton to Cheddar, called "The Cheddar Valley line," which was opened August 3rd, 1869.

Bristol claims to be the centre of the vast system of the Great Western Railway. Its total mileage at the end of 1883 was 2,268, and it extends to the north, south, east and west of England and Wales, with direct steam communication to France and Ireland. The number of train miles run during 1883 was:—Passenger, 14,298,157; goods, 16,047,939; and the revenue during the year was £7,868,321.

MIDLAND RAILWAY. In 1838 a tramway was constructed extending a few miles to the north-east of Bristol to a point now known as the Westerleigh junction; here it turned away to the left and threw off several branches, one of which continued to Coalpit heath. The Bristol and Gloucester line was flanked on the east and south by the broad guage system. In this arrangement there were important advantages, one of which was, that a junction could be effected at Bristol with the Bristol and Exeter system, and negotiations were at one time entertained by which the Great Western Company should work the Bristol and Gloucester line.

The Bristol and Gloucester Company agreed to subscribe £50,000 towards the purchase of shares in the capital of a projected extension of the Bristol and Exeter line to Plymouth.

The first half-yearly meeting of the Bristol and Gloucester Company was held in Bristol on September 29th, 1842, and on July 8th, 1844, the new line was opened for passenger traffic. A large number of persons assembled at Gloucester to welcome the arrival of the first train, but unfortunately it did not approach with the dignity of demeanour befitting so august an occasion. On rounding a rather sharp curve, within half a mile of its destination, in consequence of a defect in bolting one of the sleepers, on which the rails rested, the engine went off the rails and dragged several carriages after it. The train was proceeding slowly; the passengers alighted uninjured, and reached the terminus on foot.

In the year 1845 the negotiations for a union of the Birmingham and Gloucester and Bristol and Gloucester lines, which had previously been unsuccessful, were resumed. It had been found that the meeting of the two independent lines with different guages had involved serious disadvantages, and losses to both companies, and, with a view of introducing uniformity of system and of guage, it was resolved that there ought to be identity of interest. At present, however, it was undecided whether the broad guage should be carried through to Birmingham or the narrow guage be continued to Bristol, an issue which might appear of secondary moment, but which really involved the question whether the Great Western system was to surround the midland counties of England, and whether it was to perpe-

RAI DICTIONARY OF BRISTOL. **RAT**

tuate a conflict of guage between the north and the west. This was a rivalry, too, in which, though the Midland and the Great Western Companies were the chief competitors, all existing railways were concerned. Thus it came to pass, that the two western lines which had been struggling for existence found that they were engaging national attention and were the objects of national interest—a prize to be contended for by eager rivals. The rivalry was close and keen. The endowment offered by the Great Western was in share capital; that of the Midland was in cash—a guaranteed 6 per cent. dividend. The terms of both companies were submitted on the same day, but the Midland carried off the palm, and thus was brought about the union of the Bristol and Gloucester with the Midland system at Bristol, and the chain of railway communication was completed between the north and west of England.

This company also run to Bath viâ the Bath and Mangotsfield Extension line, which was opened August 4th, 1869, and the station on St. Philip's batch on the 2nd May, 1870.

The London and South-Western, the London and North-Western and the Somerset and Dorset Railway Companies have local agents and offices in Bristol.

PROJECTED NEW LINE TO LONDON. In 1882-3 Parliamentary notices appeared in the newspapers for a new line, intituled, the Bristol and London and South Western Junction Railway, commencing by a junction with the London and South Western Railway, at Grateley, running to Westbury and Radstock, and then joining the Bristol and North Somerset Railway, branching off from that line just before its entrance into Bristol, crossing the Feeder and the Great Western line, passing to Old Market street, where there was to be a station, thence to the Horsefair, and on to Lewin's mead and the Drawbridge, with a goods station at the former and a passenger station at the latter site. The scheme was very generally approved by all classes of the citizens. Whilst the bill was proceeding through its various stages, and after a mass of local evidence had been given, it underwent several modifications, the result being that on the 24th April, 1883, whilst in Committee of the House of Commons, it was decided that the preamble of the bill had not been proved, and consequently the bill was thrown out and the scheme abandoned.

Rainfall. The following table shows the mean and extreme quantities of rain in the several months and in the year, as derived from thirty years' observations at Clifton :—

	Greatest Fall. Depth.	Date.	Least Fall. Depth.	Date.	Mean Rainfall of 30 years.
	Inches.		Inches.		Inches.
January	6·416	1872	0·311	1855	3·251
February	4·871	1876	0·413	1862	2·318
March	4·865	1867	0·544	1853	2·216
April	4·068	1882	0·092	1854	2·144
May	6·304	1869	0·227	1676	2·362
June	7·104	1860	0·619	1870	2·623
July	6·180	1882	0·509	1868	2·959
August	8·608	1865	0·409	1880	3·595
September	7·404	1866	0·022	1865	3·355
October	7·135	1882	1·276	1879	3·799
November	6·085	1875	0·541	1855	2·866
December	6·962	1876	0·607	1853	2·841
Year	48·280	1882	22·746	1864	34·813

Ratable Value of the City. The following figures show the growth of net ratable value of fixed property within the municipal boundaries of the city and borough :

Ancient City.	Added Districts (see "Boundaries").	Total.
1841..£212,318	.. £193,888	.. £406,206
1851.. —	.. —	.. 437,726
1861.. 237,168	.. 271,820	.. 508,98
1871.. 301,214	.. 418,769	.. 719,98
1881.. 344,481	.. 562,385	.. 906,86

218

Ratepayers' Protection Association. A non-political organisation, formed in 1881, for the purpose of checking extravagant expenditure of public bodies and the promotion of candidates for municipal elections. Henry Collins, sec.

Rates. These consist of the Sanitary, Poor, Harbour, Borough (if required), Sewer and Borough Dock rates (once a year), all of which, with the exception of the two latter, are assessed half-yearly.

The BOROUGH RATE is levied to meet the deficiency in the city's income. The rate is apportioned and assessed by the Town Council on the several districts, and is collected by the Incorporation of the Poor (see that heading) and the overseers of the five parishes or districts of the enlarged city boundaries, and paid over by them to the city treasurer. The gross sum raised by the rate varies considerably. For the years ending 31st March, 1882-3, the following were the amounts:—

	1882.	1883.
Corporation of the Poor	£12,463 15 4	£12,695 2 0
Parish of Clifton	7,627 4 0	6,397 11 ..
" Bedminster	3,333 13 0	3,274 5 5
" Westbury	3,143 12 10	2,997 0 3
" St. Philip & Jacob (out)	2,445 1 4	2,173 18 7
District of St. James and St. Paul	6,409 6 6	5,063 8 7
Total	£35,419 13 0	£32,601 5 10

The subjoined figures show the total of the rates levied for 1882, as compared with 1881, in the several parishes of Bristol for municipal, sanitary, poor law, school board and dock purposes:—

	1882. s. d.	1881. s. d.
Ancient City Parishes	5 11	6 3
Bedminster	5 11	6 5
St. Philip and Jacob	5 5	5 11
Clifton	5 1	5 5
Westbury (city part)	5 1	5 4
The District	5 2	5 3

SANITARY RATE. The ordinary expenses for sanitary purposes, as well as the sums required to repay by annual instalments the monies, with interest, borrowed by the Authority for street improvements, or for the exercise of the various powers conferred by Acts of Parliament as a Board of Health, are defrayed by taxes levied by the Town Council as a Sanitary Authority twice in each year.

SEWER RATE. The whole area of the city is divided into six sewer districts, on each of which a separate annual rate is assessed, to pay off annually a twentieth or thirtieth part of the money borrowed for the construction of the main sewer of the district, with interest thereon. The amount of these rates is £10,000 per annum at the present time.

Reading Rooms. For the principal, see the headings of "Athenæum," "Clubs," "Commercial Rooms," "Libraries" (Free Lending), and "Young Men's Christian Association."

Recorders of Bristol. The first on record is in 1344, when William de Coleford held the office; he is also noted for having drawn up an account of the customs of the city, and for having preserved the forms of the oaths to be administered to the members and officers of the Corporation. Many of the Recorders were men most highly distinguished in their profession, who rose to the highest legal offices in the country. Since the passing of the Municipal Reform Act the following have held the office of Recorder to the city:—

Appointed by the old Corporation.
1827. July 26th. Sir Charles Wetherell. Died August 17th, 1846.

Appointed by the Crown.
1846. September. Richard Budden Crowder (appointed a Judge of the Court of Common Pleas in 1854).
1854. April 10th. Sir Alexander James Edmund Cockburn (appointed Lord Chief Justice of the Common Pleas in 1856).
1856. December. John Alexander Kinglake. Died July 8th, 1870.
1870. July. Sir Robert Porrett Collier. Resigned in 1870.
1870. September 13th. Montague Bere (appointed a County Court Judge in 1872).
1872. August 26th. Thomas Kingdon Kingdon. Died December 2nd, 1879.
1879. December 11th. Charles Grevile Prideaux.

The latter gentleman at present holds the office of Recorder and Steward of the Tolzey court; his salary for the year ending March 25th, 1883, was £549 6s. 3d. In 1554 it was ordained "that from henceforth none shall be elected and chosen to be Recorder of this city under the degree of a Bencher."

Recruiting Depots. The recruiting offices in Bristol are as follow : Head office, Barracks, Horfield ; district office, Glo'ster house, Hotwells ; Royal Marine office, 45 Broad quay ; and Artillery Reserve Forces, 17 Elliston road, Redland.

Redland (Rubea terra) lies to the north-east of Clifton, and is included in the parish of Westbury-on-Trym. It formerly belonged to the Abbot of Tewkesbury, who, in the year 1129, granted to one William of Kent 2½ acres of land here for a pound of wax, to be paid at the vigil of St. James, at the church of that name in the city.

Reformatories. (*See* "Schools.")

Registration of Births, Deaths and Marriages. A person having to register a birth or death must attend at the proper registrar's office at one of the appointed times for registration ; or the registrar will, if requested, attend at the person's residence, on payment of a fee of one shilling.

Births and Deaths.

BIRTHS must be registered within 42 days. Penalty for neglect, £2. After three months a birth cannot be registered except in the presence of the superintendent registrar, and on payment of fees to him and the registrar. After twelve months a birth can be registered only on the Registrar-General's authority, and on payment of further fees.

DEATHS must be registered within five days, or a written notice sent to the registrar within that time, which notice must be accompanied by a certificate of the cause of death, signed by a registered medical practitioner. The death will then have to be registered within 14 days by some proper person, who must attend at the registrar's office for that purpose. Penalty for neglect in either case, £2. After twelve months a death can be registered only on the Registrar-General's express authority, and on payment of fees.

For registering births and deaths the city is divided into the following districts :—1st District, comprising the parishes of St. Thomas, Temple and St. Mary Redcliff. 2nd District, comprising the ward of Castle Precincts and the parishes of St. Ewen, All Saints, St. Leonard, St. Maryle-port, St. Werburgh, St. Peter, Christ Church, St. John, St. Nicholas and St. Stephen. 3rd District, comprising the parishes of St. Paul and St. Philip and Jacob within the city. 4th District, comprising the parish of St. James within the city. 5th District, comprising the parishes of St. Michael and St. Augustine (with St. George, Brandon hill).

The Barton Regis district is as follows :—(1) Clifton district, comprising the parish of Clifton. (2) The Ashley district, comprising the district of the united parishes of St. James and St. Paul and the parish of Horfield. (3) St. George district, comprising the parish of St. George. (4) St. Philip and Jacob district, comprising the district of St. Philip and Jacob, without. (5) Westbury district, comprising the parishes of Henbury, Compton-Greenfield, and Westbury-upon-Trym. (6) The Stapleton district, comprising the parishes of Winterbourne, Stoke Gifford, Filton and Stapleton.

The Bedminster district is distinct from the above.

Marriages.

The expense of a marriage at a register office, altogether, is 7/-, viz., 5/- to the registrar and 2/- to the superintendent registrar, and 2/7 additional for the certificate of marriage, if required. The superintendent registrar for the district is H. T. M. C. Gwynn, All Saints' court.

Relics of Old Bristol.

Many of the interesting and historic relics of "ye olden tymes" have been demolished by fire or to make room for street and other improvements. The following is, however, a list of relics (see "Inns, Old," "Council House," "Assize Courts," "Castle," &c.) :—

ASSIZE COURTS' HOTEL, Small street, contains a highly enriched apartment of the 16th century, with a sumptuously carved fireplace and a cross-ribbed deep moulded ceiling, with bosses and pendants at the intersections. The frontage of the building is modern, having been rebuilt in 1881.

At J. WINTLE AND SONS, Clare street, Edward Bodwick, the Ashantee traveller, was born in 1793.

At 48 COLLEGE GREEN Robert Southey and S. T. Coleridge lodged in 1794.

At 25 COLLEGE STREET Coleridge lived in 1795, and at 58 resided Mrs. Marther Fricker, Sarah Coleridge's aunt.

At 16 (formerly 15) QUEEN SQUARE the famous David Hume served a brief clerkship.

At 20 (formerly 19) QUEEN SQUARE (south side) once resided Captain Woodes Rogers, who discovered Alexander Selkirk, the original Robinson Crusoe, at Juan Fernandez. Burke lodged here in 1774. On the east side Sir Nathaniel Wraxall was born in 1751.

CANYNGES' HOUSE, Redcliff street, now occupied by C. T. Jefferies and Sons. It was built about the middle of the 15th century by the second William Canynges, and was doubtless a residence with a chapel incorporated. The chief remains are a Perpendicular hall, with a high pitched ornamental roof and a louvre in the centre. Behind the hall is, or was, an apartment with a highly enriched Renaissance fireplace and other carved decorations. The original floor of encaustic tiles is yet preserved. This interesting relic suffered much from the disastrous fire in October, 1881.

FRANKLYN, MORGAN AND DAVEY, tobacco merchants, Welsh back. These premises have a very unpretending exterior, but the interior contains one of the finest Jacobian apartments in the West. The carved door, chimney piece, ceiling and staircase are exquisite. The building pertained to the Langton family.

GREAT HOUSE. This building formerly stood where the Colston hall is now. Here Sir John Young resided, and received Queen Elizabeth and her Court. In 1642 the house was inhabited by Sir Ferdinando Gorges. The Prince of Wales (Charles II.) slept here in 1645; also on one occasion his mother, Henrietta Maria; and, in 1687, James II. and his Queen were guests in the same mansion. The old house was then converted into Colston school, and ultimately sold to the Colston Hall Company (see "Colston Hall"), who took it down for the purpose of erecting their present spacious hall.

GUARD HOUSE PASSAGE, Wine street, divides Jones and Co.'s premises. It is so called from being the city station of the ancient watchmen. Until 1881, at the entrance to this passage, stood a fine Decorated gateway, formerly belonging to the residence of William Yate, who was Mayor in 1596. The carved device of a gate, with the initials W. and C. B. on the brackets of the bow window over the arch, is a rebus of his name. The gateway is now removed to Bishopston.

HAYWARD'S, J., corner of High street and Corn street, is a classical spot, for here stood the shop of Jos. Cottle, the once famous publisher, who, in 1796, issued from his press the earliest edition of Coleridge's and Southey's poems in two separate volumes. In Cottle's parlour Wordsworth first committed to paper his poem on Tintern abbey, and Coleridge wrote part of his *Religious Musings* in the same room.

HOLLAND HOUSE, corner of High street and Wine street. This curious old pargetted house was constructed in Amsterdam, and brought to Bristol in pieces and re-set up in its present position—date 1676. There is a very grotesquely carved bracket within the shop window.

No. 34 HIGH STREET bears date 1686. Here is a good specimen of a leaden snow box and shoot attached to the front of the house.

NORMAN GATEWAY, College green, was the entrance to the abbey. A difference of opinion exists amongst authorities as to whether it is original Norman work or Perpendicular restoration of the old work. The superstructure of the arch is assigned to Abbots Newland, or Nailheart, and Ellyot (1481-1526), whose statues occupy two of the niches on the southern side, with their coats of arms beneath. On the northern side are statues of Henry II. and Robert Fitzharding. The Latin inscription over the crown of the arch on this side is as follows :—" Rex Henricus secundns et Dominus Robertus filius Hardinge filii Regis Daciæ hujus monasterii primi fundatores extiterunt " (King Henry the Second and Robert, son of Harding, who was son of the King of Denmark, were the first founders of this monastery). The picturesque character of this fine gateway has been greatly impaired by the removal of the ancient bay windows and the substitution of the present sashes.

SHOT TOWER, Redcliff hill, is celebrated as being the first tower erected for the purpose of making patent shot. The letters patent are dated Dec. 10th, 1782, and were granted to one William Watts, a plumber of this city. The discovery is said to have arisen from a dream by his wife. She told her husband that she had been engaged whilst asleep in making those diminutive globes by dropping melted lead into a well of water beneath. The experiment was first tried through a kitchen colander ; hence the method afterwards adopted of causing the molten lead to descend through a perforated frame from a great height into water, where, having suddenly congealed, the particles assume a spherical shape. For the smallest shot the frame must be at least 10 feet above the water, and for the largest shot 150 feet or more above the water, and so on in proportion to the size of the shot intended. Watts sold his patent to Messrs. George for £10,000, and spent the money in building the foundation of Windsor terrace, Clifton, which project, thus far having absorbed all his funds, he was unable to proceed with the superstructure of houses. He afterwards kept a hosier's shop at 26 High street. The shot works are still carried on by Messrs. Sheldon Bush and the Patent Shot Company on Redcliff hill and Cheese lane (*see* "Manufactories ").

SLATER'S, J. and A., Lewin's mead. At the entrance will be found the ponderous doors that formerly served as gates to one of the entrances of the city.

SPYCER'S DOOR, Welsh back. Of the picturesque Decorated style employed in the earlier mansions there are but few specimens left; the most notable, if not the very earliest, is this handsome door.

SYKES AND Co., Redcliff street brewery. The gateposts of this establishment are portions of the ancient gallows from St. Michael's hill.

Religious Census. The spirited proprietors of the *Western Daily Press*, on October 30th, 1881, made a census of all the religious denominations, when the results recited under the heading of "Churches and Chapels" were ascertained.

Religious Denominations are given under the headings of "Chapels" and "Churches."

Religious Societies will be found under their respective headings.

Rents from City Estates. For the year ending 31st March, 1883, the city exchequer received in the shape of gross rents and tolls from various Corporation property the following:—

Estates at Portishead	£2,066	17 7
" Hinton	786	4 2
" Woodmancott ..	147	7 10
" in the city (various)	,678	2 6
" at Chew Magna ..	54	0 0
" Filton	170	0 0
Exchange and St. Nicholas' markets	2,361	13 6
St. James' market	374	16 8
Hay and Coal markets ..	131	15 8
	£22,770	17 11

Reservoirs. (*See* "Water Works.")

Rifle Corps. (*See* "Volunteers.")

Rifle Drill Hall. (*See* "Halls, Public.")

Ringers, St. Stephen's. (*See* "St. Stephen's Ringers.")

Riots, Bristol. By this term is usually understood the frenzied outburst of a lawless section of the populace, chiefly of the lowest class, in ostensible relation to the Reform Bill of 1831. This, however, was not the first riotous insurrection which occurred in the city, and we may go back to the days of Edward II., and find one of even more fatal results. This we may call the BRISTOL CASTLE RIOT, which endured for several years. In 1312 William Randolph, who had been four times Mayor of Bristol, took upon him, in company with 13 of the principal burgesses, the control of the revenues of the town, a procedure that was opposed by the townspeople in general. The levy of a custom on the shipping for the King's use, and the imposing of certain tolls in the market, still further aggravated the malcontents, whose active resistance to the measures induced the King to take the government and revenues of the town into his own hands, and appoint an officer whose authority was to overrule the regular administration. This was Bartholomew de Badlesmere, the constable of the Castle, who was granted the town at the annual rent of £210, the rents, profits and customs of the place to be his own. The Mayor (William Hore) and the bailiffs so fiercely resented this outrage on their prerogatives, and were so well supported by the townsmen, that Badlesmere forebore to enter the town to assert his pretensions. This opposition again caused the interference of the King, who appointed Thomas de Berkeley, with certain of the royal justices, to put an end to the disturbance. They met in the Guildhall, where the more numerous party were against Badlesmere's usurpation, passion so overcoming debate on the question that the factions came to blows, 20 men being killed within the building and many injured. As in the Reform riots, the Judges were in extreme danger, but the Mayor (J. Taverner) so far restrained the popular madness that he was allowed to escape. The King's officers were driven out of the town to the protection of the Castle, the garrison of which was also defied by the malcontents. These, to prevent a surprise, built a fortified wall in the line of the present Dolphin street, from whence they maintained warfare against the stronghold. This state of things more or less continued till 1316, when Badlesmere and other of the royal barons brought an army against the walls of the town, which, after four days' siege, surrendered. The King's pardon for the insurrection was finally granted by the payment of a fine on the part of the townsmen of 4,000 marks.

BRISTOL BRIDGE RIOTS. In the latter part of September, 1793, occurred serious outrages on account of the customary toll on Bristol bridge not having been withdrawn,

223

it being the popular opinion that such tax should cease by the 29th of that month. On the ground that the expenditure was not yet met, £2,000 being wanted, the commissioners leased out the tolls for another year. The populace thereupon assembled in refractory mood, broke down the gates and sacked the toll-houses. A regiment of militia under Lord Bateman was called on the scene, and drew up in two lines, extending from High street to the north-west toll-house and across the end of Bridge street. After an ineffectual attempt to effect a quiet dispersion, the soldiers, with the sanction of the magistrates, fired, but mostly with raised musketry, or the slaughter would have been frightful. As it was 12 persons were killed on the spot and 33 were carried wounded to the Infirmary, besides many to their own houses. It is considered that on the whole not fewer than 40 were slain.

BRISTOL MARKET RIOT. On the 23rd March, 1811, there was a riotous outbreak in the Market in consequence of fresh butter being raised to half-a-crown a pound (a price that it nearly reached also in 1871).

The BRISTOL REVOLUTION of 1831, as it has been magniloquently termed, unlike the previous disturbances, which were a mere local accident arising from temporary circumstances, had undoubtedly the broader basis of a political principle in its origin. The strong feeling against the Tories for their opposition to the Reform Bill while passing through the Legislature acted as the first incentive to the outbreak; but the whole movement resolved into a tumultuous gathering of the dregs of the people, to whom a political cry was only a pretext for letting slip the dogs of war upon the rights of property, and for burning and wasting in their frenzy the homes of peaceful citizens who had done nothing to provoke their violence. On Saturday morning, October 29th, the Recorder and Judges, attended by a cavalcade of Sheriff's officers, came into the city to open the assize commission. This was the signal for riot and pillage, which began with hooting, yelling, and pelting with stones and other missiles, and continued till the Recorder (Sir Charles Wetherell) came to the Guildhall; as he was to dine the same evening with the civic dignitaries at the Mansion-house he was not lost sight of by the crowd, who followed him thither, and when a squadron of the 14th Light Dragoons and a troop of the 3rd Dragoon Guards, who, under Colonel Brereton, had been summoned to Queen square, arrived at that spot, they found a licentious rabble attacking the Mansion-house, the whole of the windows of which they had broken. The Riot Act was read, but the mob increased to such an extent that it was deemed expedient for Wetherell to leave the Mansion-house, which he did at six o'clock, making his escape over the roofs of the adjoining houses, and finally in the course of the night he left the city. During this scene the military stood looking on, waiting from their commander orders to interfere. Colonel Brereton, who was a man of humane disposition, hoped to quell the tumult by persuasive measures. Upon Capt. Gage applying to him for orders he was told to move his men about, and by kind words endeavour to disperse the rioters, but without drawing swords. The outrages and violences of the mob, however, increasing from impunity, about eleven o'clock the Colonel ordered Capt. Gage to clear the streets, but not to hurt the people. The Colonel reported to the magistrates that the riot was slackening, that the mob were in good humour, and that he had been shaking hands with them till his arm ached. But the insolence of the rascality increased, and at twelve o'clock at night the military were ordered to draw swords, which had the effect of scattering the rabble, who were pursued through the streets.

At the top of the Pithay a dragoon shot a man (who had wounded him) dead, and there were many injured. This decisive mode of action prevented the reassembling of the mob during the night. Until ten o'clock on Sunday morning the streets were patrolled by only a few detached parties, when the whole troop was marched to Queen square. Instead of the 14th there attacking the mob, the mob attacked the military, who were obliged to charge in their own defence and to use their pistols, or they would have been torn from their horses. Still disinclined to extreme measures, Colonel Brereton, to conciliate the mob, ordered Capt. Gage to march the whole squadron out of the city, saying that they would be all murdered. The soldiers were then withdrawn to Keynsham, leaving the town and the lives and property of the inhabitants at the mercy of a mass of infuriated ruffians. A thundering attack was made upon the Mansion house by the mob, who, forcing their way in, took possession of the wine cellar, and further inflamed their wild passions by the choice liquors they therein found. In no long time the Mansion house and two sides of Queen square were in flames, 41 spacious houses being ultimately consumed. With a faint gleam of consideration for those they were injuring, which stands out in grim relief in the midst of surrounding horrors, they would knock at a house door and give the inmates half-an-hour's warning to save what they could, at the expiration of which brief notice they would begin their work of destruction. Soon after this the mob proceeded to the old Bridewell, St. James' back, and released the prisoners that were to have been tried by the Recorder; the whole of this prison was then burnt except two cells. The Gaol on the New cut was afterwards attacked, and 175 prisoners freed; but the buildings, except the governor's house, which was destroyed, resisted the flames. At Lawford's gate prison the like work of demolition and liberation was also accomplished. At 8 o'clock on Sunday evening the Bishop's palace, adjacent to the Cathedral, was fired and destroyed. The Chapter library was wasted and the Cathedral archives burnt. One precious document, the *Cartulary* of the Chapter property, with the margin singed, was lately restored to the Cathedral by John Taylor, afterwards chief city librarian, who accidentally came into possession of the volume. The Cathedral itself was saved from the incendiaries by the spirited conduct of the sacristan and a few other persons, who met the first of them with a bar of iron (yet preserved).

In Queen square the fury of the mob again increased, and the Mansion house was set on fire, the Custom house also being shortly after in conflagration. Here some of the incendiaries sat down to a meal in an upper apartment, when suddenly the flames burst in upon them. Some threw themselves from the windows, others from the housetop, and were dashed to pieces, others fell back into the flames. One woman who jumped from the window died next morning. The Excise office in King street afforded plenty of liquid fuel in about 50 puncheons of rum, which became ignited, the fires of ruin now kindled being such as might have afforded a picture for a local Milton —"the millions of flaming swords," whose blaze far round illumined the walls of the bottomless abyss, as told in the mighty language of the original poet, finding an illustration in the Sodom and Gomorrah-like scene presented. The reflection of fires on the horizon was seen at a distance of 40 miles round. One fellow was heard to say (we mention it as an instance of coarse humour):— "I'm curs'd if this bean't very funny. Charley com'd down here to try the prisoners; but Charley funk'd, and so he cut and run'd away. Well, we turn'd judges, and so we found all the pris'ners not guilty; and I'm d———d if we arn't made a reg'lar gaol deliv'ry!" The delirium of destruction having lasted from Saturday to 3 o'clock on Monday morning, there was a cry of "Hold, enough!" on the part of the authorities, the Mayor sending a peremptory request to the chief officer of the soldiers to quell the riots at any cost. The 14th Dragoons thereupon spread across Queen square, the focus of the devilish revels, and picked out the most active marauders, about ten or twelve of whom were cut down round the statue of William III. The troops followed the flying mob over the town. In Marsh street a man who attempted to seize the bridle of one of the Dragoons had his head cut off for his temerity; and in Castle street, likewise, a powerful man who had been actively cheering on the rioters was singled out by a private, who, with a backhanded stroke, left him headless. Those who had still heads to keep endeavoured to save them by shrinking into the lanes and passages where their houses stood. There was no further temporising on the part of the military or the magistrates, and the "Bristol Revolution" ceased.

It is impossible to say how many perished in all during the riots. The official list showed 12 killed and 96 wounded, but these numbers included only those who were taken to the hospitals, those killed and burnt while engaged in plundering the houses being unascertained. From time to time heads without bodies, trunks without members, and fragments of limbs were successively exposed to public gaze. Four of the rioters were hanged, and the unfortunate Colonel Brereton, who when brought to trial was unable to stand the sneers of the ladies in court, committed suicide. The amount of compensation for damages charged by the Parliamentary commissioners on the citizens was £68,208 1s. 6d.

Rivers. (*See* "Avon," "Frome," and "Severn.")

Rowing Clubs. The two recognised clubs practising on the Floating harbour are the Ariel and the Redcliff. Both have spacious dressing barges near Bristol bridge. Ariel: Entrance fee, £1 1s.; subscription, £1 11s. 6d. W. Gange, captain; G. E. Davies and R. W. Horne, hon. secs. Redcliff: E. J. Kiddle, captain; F. Giband, hon. sec.

CLIFTON ROWING CLUB. Practice at Salford; 82 hon. and active members; entrance fee, 10/6; annual subscription, 21/-. G. Leonard, Apsley road, hon. sec.

Rownham (or Ruan-ham) means in Cornish the "roundabout river town." Probably a ferry existed here in the days of the coracles, when Ashton vale and Rownham meadows were swampy morasses. Certain it is that about the time of the foundation of the monastery in Bristol, in 1148, it became the property of the abbot thereof, and was the readiest way of access to his country house at Abbot's Leigh. The site of the ferry has of late years been changed, owing to the alterations at the entrance to Cumberland basin; it was originally about 100 yards lower down the river. At low water the Avon was fordable at this spot by horsemen.

Royal Visits. The following is a list of the principal to this ancient and loyal city:—King John visited Bristol 19 times. Henry II. was four years at school in Baldwin street. Henry III. held his first Council in this city. Edward I. twice spent Christmas in the city. Edward II. was here in 1308, 1321 and 1326. Richard II. arrived here in 1387 and 1399; Henry VI., in 1446; Queen Margaret, in 1456; Edward IV., in 1461 and 1474; Prince Edward, son of Henry VI., in 1471; Henry VII., in 1486; Henry VIII., in 1534; Elizabeth, on August 13th, 1574, accompanied by a large retinue; Anne of Denmark (James' Queen), June 4th, 1613; Duke of Lennox, uncle of James I., in 1609; Charles I., accompanied by the Princes Charles and James, Duke of York, in 1643; Prince Charles, in February, 1645; the Lord-Lieutenant of Ireland, Oliver Cromwell, July 17th, 1649, and he appears to have stayed for about a fortnight. After the Restoration, on September 5th, 1663, the King and Queen, with James, Duke of York, and Prince Rupert, and several other noblemen, were received here. Queen Catherine liked her visit so well that she came again on July 11th, 1677. James II. visited Bristol in August, 1686, and with his Queen in 1687, and again September 12th in the following year; Queen Anne, youngest daughter of James I., with Prince George of Denmark, her husband, September 1st, 1702; Princess Amelia, in 1728, on the opening of the water communication between this city and Bath; Prince of Orange, February 21st, 1734; Prince and Princess of Wales, November 10th, 1738; Duke of York, second son of George III., 27th December, 1761, and also in 1795; Prince of Wales and the Duke of Sussex, in October, 1807; Queen Charlotte, wife of George III., with Princess Elizabeth and the Duke of Clarence, afterwards William IV., December 7th. 1817; the Prince and Princess of Denmark visited some of the manufactories in this city and Clifton on July 13th, 1822; the Duchess of Kent, Princess Victoria, Baroness de Letzen, and Lady Catherine Jenkinson and party, October 19th, 1830; two Persian princes, the Prince of Orange with his two sons, and the Prince of Oldenburgh, nephew of the Czar of Russia, in June and July, 1836 (they and their suites were entertained by the Mayor); the Duke of Cambridge, to attend the meeting of the Royal Agricultural Society, on July 12th, 1842; H.R.H. Prince Albert visited Bristol to be present at the launch of the *Great Britain*, July 19th, 1843; the King of Saxony and the Prince of Prussia inspected this vessel at this port in 1844; the Queen Dowager, with suite, visited Clifton in August, 1845; the Grand Duke Constantine of Russia visited the city and neighbourhood on June 18th, 1847; Princess Oldenburgh of Russia and suite and the ex-Queen of France, consort of Louis Philippe, in August, 1852; the Duke and Duchess of Brabant, cousins of the Queen, arrived in Clifton November 16th, 1853; H.R.H. the Prince of Wales visited Bristol *incognito* 12th October, 1856, on his tour through the West of England; the Prince of Orange visited the city February 13th, 1860; H.R.H. the Prince of Wales opened Knowle race-course in March, 1873, and again visited the city July 9th, 1878, on the occasion of the Royal Agricultural Show on Durdham down—the streets were decorated on a large scale; H.R.H. the Duke of Edinburgh, on the 9th November, 1881, inspected the Naval Reserve, and made a detour to examine the Sailors' institute and church, Prince street, and in October, 1882, His Royal Highness, in company with the Duchess, again visited the city, on the occasion of the Fourth Musical Festival—a very cordial reception was then given; and on January 28th, 1884, H.R.H. the Prince of Wales paid a visit to Sir Philip and Lady Miles at Leigh court, and attended a concert at the Colston hall in aid of the Royal Infirmary and General Hospital.

Sailors' Home. (*See* "Homes.")

Samaritan Society. The greater part of the funds of this society are applied to the relief of the family bread-winner during temporary inability to work through illness. Each case is personally investigated by some member of the committee, and it is believed that fraud and imposture on the one hand, and thoughtless harshness on the other, are rendered well nigh impossible under their system. They also aim at assisting the large class of domestic servants. The society on the recommendation of the medical men at the Royal Infirmary and General Hospital, provides for convalescent servants' maintenance at the Servants' home on Montague hill for four weeks, if so long a time is required for them to regain strength before re-entering service. The society also contributes towards the outfit of those young persons who enter domestic service for the first time. Under the first of these heads 91 persons during 1882 were relieved in sums varying from 3s. to 6s. for various periods; 24 convalescent servants assisted, and 4 young persons entering service provided with clothing. Rev. J. Hart Davies, M.A., St. James' vicarage, hon. sec.

Sanitary Inspection is effected by a medical officer (Dr. Davies) and a superintendent inspector of nuisances, assisted by three assistant district inspectors. Each has under his control skilled labourers to perform menial work, such as the immediate removal of minor nuisances not requiring constructive work, white-liming courts and alleys in the summer, and disinfecting houses and clothing. Two new inspectors were appointed in January, 1884, under the Factory and Workshop Act, 1883, viz., an inspector of bakehouses and an inspector of meat and fish, to assist the medical officer in carrying out the provisions of the Act, which are now actively enforced.

The whole city is divided into three districts and apportioned between the district inspectors, who are held responsible for their respective districts. The whole of the inspecting staff meet daily, at 11 o'clock, at the offices, Prince street, where the district inspectors report to the medical officer and to the inspector of nuisances on the condition of the districts and prevalence or absence of infectious diseases, and other matters within their province, and receive instructions on every case reported.

The system of inspection carried on here differs from that of most, if not all, other places, in the removal of minor nuisances, the liming of courts and alleys, and other work properly within the duties of a landlord, by the officers and at the cost of the Sanitary Authority. Everyone practically acquainted with the difficulty of having such nuisances remedied by the landlords or occupiers of poor tenements will readily understand why the system is adopted, viz., to avoid delay and prevent the spread of disease. Each district inspector has on an average a population of about 70,000 under his supervision.

Every ship in the port, or in Bristol waters, is subject to the inspection of the Port Sanitary Authority in the same manner as a house within the district. The Port Sanitary Authority and the District Sanitary Authority in this case are one and the same body, viz., the Mayor and Corporation of Bristol.

When a house is known to be infected, and no means have been adopted by the owner or occupier to disinfect it, the responsible parties are required by the Sanitary Authority (under the provisions of the Sanitary Act, 1866) to have this done. The Authority disinfect houses and clothing gratuitously for the poor and people of only moderate means. A small charge is made for doing this for the wealthier classes. In all cases after disinfection the owner or occupier is required to cleanse and purify the premises at his or her own expense.

The mode of disinfection generally adopted for a room is :—(a) To fill it with pure chlorine gas, evolved from a mixture of common salt, binoxide of manganese and sulphuric acid, after first closing the windows, the fireplace and every crevice in the walls. The door is then shut and the room kept close for 24 hours. (b) To fill the room with sulphurous acid gas by burning sulphur (1lb. to 2lb. according to size) in the room closed, as before described. This is the plan now generally adopted both for the disinfection of rooms, hospital wards, or infected cabs. The bedding and other articles of clothing are afterwards removed by the officers of the Sanitary Authority for further disinfection in a hot-air apparatus. The room is then cleansed.

Another effective method of disinfecting houses adopted is to force into a room, by means of an ingenious apparatus called the "Asphyxiator," a large quantity of sulphurous acid gas. When this is adopted the quantity of gas thrown into the room acted upon should be such as to render the atmosphere of it fatal to any organic life within it. The room should be kept closed for 24 hours, and afterwards cautiously opened and ventilated. To disinfect a large room by this process requires the consumption of several pounds of sulphur, and a man to be employed for several hours working the bellows of the apparatus.

For the disinfection of clothes, bedding, and other such articles by hot air, two large hot air disinfecting chambers, heated by gas, have been set up by the Sanitary Authority; in these the infected articles are exposed for an hour or more to a heat of 250° Fah. The temperature of the chambers can be raised to 300°, but it having been found by experiment that some fabrics scorch at this heat it is considered unsafe to raise the temperature above 250°.

In addition to the above means of disinfection, the men under the district surveyors visit the courts, alleys and poorer parts of the city regularly, and apply antiseptics and disinfectants to closets, drains, gullies and other places, if anywise offensive or supposed to contain infection. For this purpose Calvert's carbolic acid powder, containing 15 per cent. of pure carbolic acid and coarse sulphate of iron is extensively used. These disinfectants are supplied to the poor gratuitously when required.

In case of typhoid fever or cholera being reported in any house, the whole of the communicating drains in the locality are disinfected with sulphate of iron and carbolic acid. At the present time the district inspectors are largely engaged in a complete and systematic house-to-house inspection of the poorer districts. Records of defects found are kept, and the owners required to remedy them.

To obviate the necessity of using public conveyances for persons suffering from infectious diseases, the Sanitary Authority have set up a large and convenient carriage, and placed it at the command of every qualified medical practitioner free of charge. This externally, for obvious reasons, cannot be distinguished from a private carriage; the interior is lined with American leather, which can be washed without injury to the material. After each time of using the carriage is cleaned and disinfected with sulphurous acid gas. Persons using the ambulance are required to find a horse and driver.

The hospitals for smallpox and fever, situate in St. Philip's marsh, are open under certain regulations. Pauper patients are provided for by the several unions.

All the principal streets are well and carefully watered during dry weather from the 1st April to the 30th September. This is done by contract taken for three years. The water is supplied at a rate agreed upon from the mains of the Bristol Waterworks company.

The sanitary arrangements of this city, whatever their good points or shortcomings may be, are the outgrowth of necessity, each step having been taken or extended as some urgent want has required it. New discoveries in medicine and of the nature of diseases, and further experience in the use of preventive measures, will doubtless render the sanitary arrangements of the future superior to those of the present, as those of the present surpass those of the past. (*See* "Sewerage" and "Scavenging.")

Savings Banks. (*See* "Banks.")

Scavenging. This is done by contract, generally let for three years; the conditions of the contract are minute and stringent. The principal thoroughfares are swept and cleansed daily; the others twice or three times a week, or as the case may require, according to the state of the weather. The scavengers' carts go their rounds regularly to remove all house ashes and refuse. The public are required to put these in places convenient for removal by the scavengers at their periodical calls. As a matter of convenience to the residents of the poorer parts of the city, who are frequently without any utensils in which to keep their ashes, the Sanitary Authority have placed large iron boxes as receptacles for such, in convenient places, near populous courts and alleys.

School Boards. In the autumn following the passing of the Elementary Education Act, 1870, the Town Council unanimously passed a resolution for the formation of a School Board in this city. The first Board was elected January 27th, 1871, and consisted of the following members:— Lewis Fry (chairman), M. Whitwill (vice-chairman), Archdeacon Randall, Dr. S. D. Waddy, Dr. F. W. Gotch, Dr. Percival, Dr. Caldicott, S. V. Hare, T. Turner, W. H. Budgett, Herbert Thomas, H. F. Lawes, J. Ford, U. Alsop and W. P. Baker. The first business that claimed the attention of the Board, after it was duly constituted, was a communication from the Education Department, asking for precise information as to the requirements of the district in respect of public school accommodation, as to the amount and character of the existing school provision, and as to the manner in which any ascertained deficiency should be met. The Board at once resolved to obtain by a strict house-to-house visitation a return or census of the names, residence and ages of all children between 3 and 13 years of age, and of the schools, if any, at which they were attending. This inquiry was first made by way of experiment in the ward of St. James, and was afterwards extended to the whole city. The report of the census committee presented to the Board on the 8th of August, 1871, showed that the number of children requiring elementary education was 27,554, and that the total accommodation in elementary schools (exclusive of industrial schools, workhouse schools and private adventure schools) was 23,337. The number of children between 5 and 13 stated upon the returns not to be in attendance at school was 5,318. The Board proceeded to verify the results of the census by actual inquiry at the several schools, and this investigation showed that to the 5,318 children referred to as not being at school there must be added 4,074 who were not known at the schools they were said to attend, or whose attendance had been so irregular that they had been struck off the school registers. It thus appeared that the number of children whose education was entirely neglected or was not satisfactorily accounted for was upwards of 9,000. A code of by-laws was prepared for enforcing the attendance of children at school in accordance with the provisions of the Education Act, and with a view of putting the powers obtained under the Act into as speedy operation as possible the city was divided into four districts, viz.:—District No. 1, comprising the wards of Bristol, St. James, St. Paul and the District; No. 2, St. Philip and Jacob; No. 3, Bedminster and Redcliff; No. 4, St. Augustine, Clifton and St. Michael. To each of these districts an officer was appointed for the purpose of enforcing the by-laws and encouraging school attendance, and the work proving too heavy for one person a second was, in July, 1872, appointed to each district.

In October, 1871, the Board divided itself into four standing district committees, each taking the oversight and work of the officers in one district, and holding frequent meetings for the purpose of receiving the explanations of parents upon whom notices had been served. In the first two years that the district committee and officers were at work no less than 51,534 visits were paid to the homes of the children, 4,967 notices were served upon parents, and 3,100 parents appeared before the district committees. In those cases in which the efforts of the officer failed to bring about the attendance of the child, resort was had to proceedings before the magistrates. During the time referred to 850 summonses were issued, and of these 31 were dismissed or withdrawn, and in the remaining 819 cases a conviction for a breach of the by-laws was obtained. Apart from that the officers brought before the magistrates 58 children who were committed to industrial schools. The Board drew up and issued addresses to employers of labour and to those engaged in various religious and benevolent efforts among the poor classes upon the means of promoting and encouraging the attendance of children at school, and several conferences were held with school managers with a like object in view. The Board is not in possession of any return of the number on the school registers in March, 1871, but the average attendance at that date was 13,385, whereas in October, 1873, it had increased to 16,970, the number on the registers at the latter date being 23,654, in addition to which it was ascertained that 4,000 children were in more or less regular attendance at non-efficient schools. With respect to the wards in which the accommodation was deficient the Board reported as follows:—"That the deficiency in the District ward was sufficiently met by the available accommodation in the contiguous wards of St. James and St. Paul; that the deficiency in Bedminster and Redcliff wards was not large enough to necessitate immediate additional provision; that as regarded St. Augustine's ward there was sufficient available accommodation in the adjacent wards of Clifton and St. Michael's; and that the deficiency in the ward of St. Philip and Jacob should be met by the establishment of three groups of schools, giving together accommodation for 1,500 children."

The schools transferred to the Board during the first three years were:—In district No. 1, Blackfriars' school and the St. James's back day industrial school; district No. 2, Kingsland road schools, Thrissell street schools and the River street school; district No. 4, Clifton schools. The following table shows the number of children on the registers and the average attendance in these schools after they had been taken over by the Board:—

School.	No. on Register.	Average Attendance.
Kingsland—Boys	217	167
Girls	164	112
Clifton—Boys	141	102
Girls	92	61
Thrissell street—Girls	123	90
Infants	132	103
River street—Boys	161	103
Blackfriars'—Boys	62	49
Girls	76	47
Industrial—Mixed day	87	52
	1,255	886

The Board drew up with much care a code of regulations for the management of its schools, and the regulations as to religious instruction and observances were framed as follow:—"The Bible shall be read in the schools, and there shall be given such instruction therefrom and such explanations as are suitable to the capacities of the children; provided always—(a) That in such instruction and explanations the provisions of sections 7 and 14 of the Act of 1870 be strictly observed both in letter and in spirit, and that no attempt be made to give the teaching a denominational character. (b) That in the event of an application by managers, parents or ratepayers of the districts, showing special cause for the exception of any particular school from the operation of this regulation — in whole or in part—the Board shall consider such application and determine thereupon. Arrangements may be made for offering prayer and using hymns at the time or times when (according to section 7, subsection 2, of the Elementary Education Act, 1870) religious observances may be practised. Subject to the approval of the Board the arrangements for such religious observances shall be left to the discretion of the managers and the teacher of each school, with the right of appeal to the Board by any manager, teacher, or parent, or by any ratepayer of the district; provided always that in the offering of prayer and in the use of hymns the provisions of the Act of 1870 in sections 7 and 14 be strictly adhered to both in letter and in spirit, and that no attempt be made to give to such religious observances a denominational character. During the time or times when any religious observance is practised or instruction in religious subjects is given, any children withdrawn from such observances or instruction shall receive instruction in secular subjects in a separate room."

The first triennial election took place on the 22nd January, 1874, and the Board was composed of the following:—W. P. Baker, W. H. Budgett, R. W. Butterworth, Dr. Caldicott, Canon Clarke, T. Coomber, L. Fry, Dr. Gotch, A. Hall, H. F. Lawes, Rev. T. C. Price, H. B. O. Savile, Rev. U. R. Thomas, Rev. S. A. Walker and Mark Whitwill. Lewis Fry and Mark Whitwill were unanimously re-elected chairman and vice-chairman of the new Board. The work of the Board was continued in the most systematic manner, and the total cases considered and adjudicated upon by the district committees during the year 1874 was 3,118, while during the same year 613 summonses were issued at the instance of the Board, and the fact that out of this number only 26 were dismissed or withdrawn afforded satisfactory evidence of the care and judgment exercised in sending cases before the magistrates. In 1874 the officers of the Board were instrumental in bringing before the magistrates 24 children who were committed to industrial schools. The number of children on the registers of efficient elementary schools in December, 1874, was 24,737, as against 23,046 in the same month of 1873, or an increase of 1,691 children.

The schools in Freestone road, St. Philip's, were the first built by the Board. They were erected at a cost of £4,500, and were opened in August, 1874; and those in Kingsland road, which had been occupied temporarily, were then given up. During the same year the Counterslip British school was offered to the Board, and arrangements were made for opening it as a Board school at the commencement of 1875. The new schools projected or in course of erection were Barton hill schools, to accommodate 750 children; Ashton gate, 450; and Hotwells, 500; the former being intended to supersede the Thrissell street schools, and the latter the Clifton Board schools. It was determined to relinquish the day industrial school in consequence of part of the premises being taken for street improvements, but towards the end of the year the alteration and addition to the premises at Carlton house, undertaken by the Board to fit them for an industrial school for girls, were completed; the school was duly certified by the Secretary of State, and a body of managers, consisting of five members of the Board and four ladies, a matron, and other officers were elected, and the institution was started on its useful career.

At the second triennial election, in January, 1877, the previous members were elected with the exception of H. F. Lawes, A. Hall and R. W. Butterworth, in whose places J. Inskip, J. F. Norris and Miss H. Richardson were elected. According to statistics compiled at the end of the year there was school accommodation in the city for 28,638 children, and a new school for infants in Bedminster, and a Board school for boys and girls and infants in Mina road, St. Philip's, were in course of erection, which when completed would give additional accommodation for 1,250 children. The average number on the register for the year was 27,179, and the average attendances 19,074, or 70·2 per cent. The fact that the increase in the average attendances had been smaller than usual was attributed in a great measure to the increased scarcity of regular employment among the working classes, and to the consequent inability of a large number of parents not only to pay school fees, but to provide sufficient clothing for their children; and these difficulties in the way of school attendance had not, it is considered, been lessened by the transference, under the Act of 1876, of the power to pay school fees for non-pauper children from the School Board to the Board of Guardians. The percentage of children who had made 250 attendances had increased from 13,331 in 1875 to 15,509 in 1877. The total accommodation provided in the eight Board schools, not including the two industrial schools, was 3,338, while the number on the register was 3,660, and the average attendance 2,362.

The next triennial election took place on the 22nd June, 1880, when the following were elected:— Dr. Caldicott, Monsignor Clarke, G. W. Edwards, F. F. Sparke Evans, A. Hall, J. Inskip, G. F. Jones, J. F. Norris, W. Kearsey, Rev. T. C. Price, Miss E. Sturge, Rev. U. R. Thomas, M. Whitwill, Rev. C. Witherby and J. H. Woodward.

M. Whitwill was elected chairman, and Dr. Caldicott vice-chairman of the Board. Jos. Gould, H. C. Perry, Rev. W. S. Bruce and W. Smith were afterwards elected co-optatively to take the place vacated by A. Hall, deceased, and W. Kearsey, Rev. C. Witherby and J. F. Norris resigned. During the existence of the Board 166 places for infants were added to the Ashton gate school, and the Friends' boys' school, Merchant street, and the Highbury British school, Anglesea place, were taken over, while the rebuilding of the Sussex street school, and extensive alterations at the Anglesea place school for giving enlarged accommodation, were commenced. The accommodation provided in Board schools stood at the close of the three years ended 1882 at 5,191 places, with 5,656 names on the registers, and an average attendance of 3,634. The following table shows the cost of maintenance in the nine Board schools during the last school year:

School.	Average Attendance.	Total Cost.	Cost per Child.
Ashton gate*	532	£940 6 4	£1 15 4
Barton hill*	733	1184 16 8	1 12 4
Blackfriars	165	432 10 0	2 12 8
Clifton*	448	847 17 7	1 18 0
Merchant street	228	656 10 3	2 17 7
Mina road*	489	920 18 9	1 17 8
River street	243	597 7 2	2 8 0
St. Philip's*	589	1010 8 1	1 14 3
Sussex street	207	263 4 9	1 5 4
	3634	£6853 19 7	£1 17 8¼

* These schools were built by the Board.

For the purpose of comparison it may be stated that the cost of maintenance per child in average attendance in Board schools throughout England and Wales was for the year 1881-2 £2 1s. 6d., so that the cost per head in the Bristol Board schools was 3s. 9½d. less than the average. The total expenditure was met as follows: Government grants, £2,506 1s. 11d.; school fees, £1,209 14s. 10d.; rates, £3,029 5s. 3d.; rent, &c., for hire of rooms, £106 17s. 7d. The cost of the Carlton house industrial school for the three years was £2,793 2s. 6d. The number of children admitted from the commencement up to the end of the last school year was 93. Nine of these died, and 35 left after completion of training, of whom 50 were doing well and 5 were not satisfactory. The number then in the school was 53. Towards the total cost of the school the Treasury had contributed £1,421 4s. 7d. in the three years, or £473 14s. 11d. per annum. Besides the maintenance of the Southwell street school the Board was contributing at the end of 1882 to the maintenance of 372 Bristol children committed by Bristol magistrates to various industrial schools, and the amount so contributed during the three years was £3,663 11s. 8d. Previous to the formation of the Board the contribution to industrial schools was made by the Town Council, and this should be borne in mind when criticising School Board expenditure. With regard to the day industrial school the number admitted during the three years under review was 311, of whom 244 had left and 146 were at the close of the period on the school registers. Of these, 20 had left Bristol, 45 had been licensed to public elementary schools, their condition and character having improved, 12 had gone into the workhouse, 75 had left school, having passed age, 91 had been sent to certified industrial schools, and 1 had died. The average attendance in 1880 was 50; in 1881, 55; and in 1882, 70. The cost for the three years, after deducting school fees and proceeds of sale of firewood chopped by the boys, had been £1,565 18s. 7d. Towards this the Treasury had contributed £341 6s. 9d., and the balance of £1,224 11s. 10d. had been borne by the rates. The school accommodation provided by efficient schools at the close of 1882 was 30,817 children, viz.:—In No. 1 district (part of Bristol, St. James, part of St. Paul, and the District), 6,935; No. 2 (St. Philip, North and South, part of Bristol and part of St. Paul), 8,167; No. 3 (Bedminster, East and West, and Redcliff), 8,704; and No. 4 (St. Augustine, Clifton, St. Michael and Westbury), 7,011. During the three years the district committees considered 14,094 cases, and the visits paid by the officers numbered 385,998. In the same period 3,562 summonses were issued, with the following results:—Fined, 2,280; attendance and detention orders, 808; sent to industrial schools, 85; withdrawn after adjournment, 309; dismissed or not served, 80. Besides this the officers were instrumental in taking before the magistrates 112 children who were subsequently sent to certified industrial schools. With regard to the school attendance the average on the registers in efficient schools in 1882 was 29,996, and the average attendance 22,170, or 73·9 per cent., and the progress of the work which the Board has in hand might be further judged by the fact that the number of children who had qualified themselves for examination, by making not less than 250 attendances in the school year, had increased from 13,331 in 1871 to 19,281 in 1882.

We come now to the finances of the Board for the three years ending with 1882. The total income, including a balance of £458 from the previous period, was £40,200 11s. 7d., and the items included the following: Grants from the Committee of Council on Education and grants from the Science and Art Department, £7,324 17s. 2d.; contributions in aid of industrial schools, £1,732 15s. 4d.; payments by rating authorities at 2½d. in the pound, £26,500; school fees, £3,447 15s. Under expenditure, the expenses of administration were £6,639 15s. 3d.; maintenance, £18,460 14s.; contributions towards industrial schools, £8,022 12s. 9d.; capital charges, £1,391; loans, £3,835 11s. 8d.; cookery school, £397 18s. 10d. At the close of the year there was a balance in hand of about £1,450. During the three years 189 teachers and 6,040 scholars presented

SCH DICTIONARY OF BRISTOL. **SCH**

themselves for examination under the Scripture prize scheme, and of these 116 teachers and 755 scholars obtained prizes. The question of temperance teaching in the schools engaged the attention of the Board soon after the election, and after full consideration of the subject it was resolved that the teachers should be requested to avail themselves of every suitable opportunity supplied by the Scripture lesson of teaching the evils of drunkenness by warnings, cautions, admonitions and examples; and that the reading and copy books should be rendered helpful in that direction, and if suitable picture cards and diagrams bearing on the subject could be obtained, they should form some part of the furniture of the schools, and that the use of the schoolroom should be granted free of charge for approved lectures on the subject.

At the triennial election in Jan., 1883, the following were elected members of the Board :—M. Whitwill, Rev. U. R. Thomas, Rev. E. G. Gange, Rev. W. S. Bruce, Rev. T. C. Price, Monsignor Clarke, Miss Sturge, Mrs. Grenfell, Miss Douglas, J. Inskip, G. F. Jones, J. H. Woodward, J. Gould, H. C. Perry and A. Froud. Since that time a new truant school has been built by the Board, and increased accommodation has been provided for about 200 children at the Sussex street school. The Anglesea place schools were opened 10th September, 1883, after extensive alterations and additions, giving accommodation to 160 boys, 162 girls and 162 infants; and the new schools in Newfoundland road will accommodate 252 boys, 252 girls and 287 infants.

Mark Whitwill is the chairman of the present Board, and the Rev. U. R. Thomas vice-chairman. Monsignor Clarke is chairman of the Finance Committee, and M. Whitwill, the Rev. U. R. Thomas, Rev. T. C. Price and J. Gould are the chairmen of the respective district committees. B. Wilson has filled the office of clerk since 1871; B. B. Wilson, assistant clerk. Offices: Guildhall, Broad st.

BEDMINSTER. Offices: Totterdown. The ordinary Board meetings are held on the second Monday in each month; committee meetings the last Friday in every calendar month. W. A. Pitt, 35 Nicholas street, clerk to the Board.

ST. GEORGE'S. Monthly meetings of this body are held at the Parochial offices, Cloud's hill. The monthly attendance at schools in this district is as appended :—

	On Books.	Average.	Per Centage.	On Books.	Average.
	1883.			1884.	
Board Schools ..	2339	1640	70.1	2507	1796
Voluntary ditto	1692	1199	70.8	1751	1317.3
Totals	4031	2839	70.4	4258	3115.3

Rev. J. Tyrrell Baylee, chairman; A. T. Philpott, clerk.

Schoolmasters' and Schoolmistresses' Benevolent Association. The annual subscriptions of this society for 1881-2-3 were as follow :—General fund: 1881, £51 4s.; 1882, £56 1s. 6d.; 1883, £60 10s. Orphan fund: 1881, £6 15s.; 1882, £7 2s.; 1883, £7 15s. 6d. H. J. Walker, Temple Colston school, secretary.

School of Science and Art, in Queen's road, is in connection with the Science and Art Department of the Committee of the Council on Education, and was established in 1853. The course of instruction is that appointed by the Department of Science and Art, and is adapted to the requirements of the locality and includes the following :—(1) Elementary, (2) Advanced, (3) Painting, (4) Technical. The work of the school is divided into two grades, called 2nd and 3rd grades (the 1st grade applies to the elementary instruction given to children in national and other day schools). The 2nd grade consists of instruction in freehand drawing, geometry, prospective and model drawing. The 3rd grade comprehends all the work executed in the school during each year. The following are the terms:—For amateurs, on Tuesdays and Thursdays, from 11 to 1 o'clock, day classes, elementary, 12/- per month; 26/- per quarter of ten weeks; day classes, advanced, 18/- per month; £2 per quarter of ten weeks. For general students, on Mondays and Fridays, from 11 to 1 o'clock, or Tuesdays and Thursdays, from 11 to 1 or 2 to 4 o'clock, 9/- per month; 21/- per quarter of ten weeks. Entrance fees, 5/-. There are also evening classes on Mondays, Wednesdays and Fridays, from 7 to 9.30 o'clock. Terms:—To artizans and their children, 2/- per month; to tradesmen and others, 3/- per month. Entrance fee, 2/-. Evening classes for ladies are held on Mondays, Wednesdays and Fridays, from 7 to 9 o'clock. Terms, 3/- per month; entrance fee, 2/-. Queen's prizes and local prizes are distributed annually amongst the students. Fred. Wills, hon. sec.; J. Nicol Smith, head master. (*See* also "Fine Arts Academy.")

Schools.
British Schools.

There are about 18 schools under this heading in connection with the various Nonconformist bodies, and Lewin's Mead United, and Redcross Street are the oldest schools.

LEWIN'S MEAD UNITED SCHOOLS, THE, are institutions of considerable local interest, not only on account of their comparative antiquity, but more especially because of the singular completeness of design with which their promoters in the early part of the present century sought to benefit the young of both sexes and of all conditions in life. When it is remembered that so eminent an advocate of education as Dr. Lant Carpenter (the father of the late Mary Carpenter) was minister of Lewin's mead chapel from 1817 to 1840, it will not be deemed surprising that around such a centre there gradually arose during that period a cluster of institutions, supported by the members of his congregation, which to the present day attest his high appreciation of the benefits of instruction for all classes, and his clear conception of the peculiar needs of the times in which he lived.

The earliest of the educational institutions included under the name of "The Lewin's Mead United schools" was founded in 1787 by Dr. Wright, then minister of the chapel. This was the "Charity School for Girls" (known subsequently as the Girls' Daily or Industrial school), which was intended as a fitting counterpart to the Stokes' Croft School for Boys, an institution founded and endowed by members of the Lewin's mead congregation in 1722. Twenty-one girls between the ages of 9 and 14 years, the daughters of respectable members of the congregation, were received as day-pupils in a house in Lewin's mead, opposite the chapel gates; they were clothed, had free dinners every Sunday, were instructed in reading, household work, washing, needlework, &c., and during the last two years of their stay in the school, in writing and arithmetic. In 1826 the new school premises at the rear of the chapel, with entrance into Johnny Ball lane, were built by the congregation, and the Charity school found there a larger and more commodious home, where it still remains. The scholars have always been in the habit of attending one or both of the Sunday services at Lewin's mead chapel.

In 1818 a spacious lecture room was erected over the stables on the chapel premises, and here the minister held every Sunday a private class for religious instruction. This class, which was continued for many years, seems to have been instrumental in supplying teachers to the Boys' and Girls' Sunday schools, which were first established as separate but co-ordinate institutions in 1821, the girls meeting in the lecture room, and the boys in the eastern gallery of the chapel. In 1826 the new school premises, already mentioned, afforded a comfortable home to both these schools. The Girls' Sunday school is still conducted there. In 1856 the Boys' Sunday school was transferred to the commodious room in Maudlin street. The following paragraph from the printed report for 1831 has some historical interest:—"On the never-to-be-forgotten Sunday of the riots (October 30th) all the children in the schools who were present in the chapel were collected into the lower schoolroom at the close of the service; they were warned of the state of the city, and charged to keep at home during the rest of the day out of the way of the evils which might occur, and also to tell their parents what was said to them; and the warning may have contributed to that freedom of the children and their parents from the dreadful evils that ensued, which has excited the devout thankfulness of many."

Another reference to the printed report for 1831 will not be without interest: "During the late alarming riots the masters and mistresses of the Infant and Intermediate schools very properly felt it their duty to remain quietly at their posts, and they requested the parents to leave their children with them during the whole of the Monday, and engaged to devote their time entirely to them. Some parents thankfully accepted the kind offer, but others were too much alarmed to trust their little ones from under their own protection. It is gratifying to learn that only two instances have occurred of the parents of any of these children being implicated in the late disgraceful transactions."

The special purpose which the congregation had in view in erecting the buildings in the rear of the chapel in 1826 was the accommodation of the Charity school (when, in 1825, the house in Lewin's mead became no longer available) and of the two Sunday schools; but the larger premises admitted of further use, and hence the establishment of an Infants' school, an institution then almost entirely unknown out of London. This was from the first very successful and largely attended. It is a very noteworthy fact that from the foundation of this school all the children attending it, as well as those of the other and kindred institutions, have had the benefit of gratuitous medical supervision. This has been at times most efficacious in the arrest of cholera and other epidemic diseases. A dispensary, under the care of Dr. Eliza W. Dunbar, is still maintained, the children paying only the cost price of medicines used. This school was transferred in 1878 to the new premises in Maudlin street.

In 1829, in the lecture room, an Intermediate or mixed British school was commenced; boys and girls, at a charge of threepence per week, were taught together with the greatest success by a master and mistress till 1837, when various causes led to a separation of the two constituent parts. The girls, then limited to 40 in number, were removed to the other premises, and united as one school to the Charity school so far as regarded the regular routine of elementary instruction. The Boys' British school continued to occupy the lecture room till the opening of the new Boys' school in Maudlin street in 1856. It was at length discontinued in 1878, owing to the completion of School Board schools for boys in the neighbourhood.

The average attendance of scholars attending the Lewin's Mead United schools for the quarter ending February 29th, 1884, was as follows:—

Girls' Charity or Industrial school   12
Girls' Sunday school   48
Boys' Sunday school   100
Infant school (British)   97
Girls' school (British)   68

The United schools were placed under Government inspection in 1847. The Lewin's mead congregation raised in 1825 for the erection of the new school premises, £991, exclusive of annual subscriptions, and for the Boys' school in Maudlin street, in 1856, £1,022, exclusive of Government grant for this purpose of £350.

REDCROSS STREET SCHOOLS. The Bristol Royal Lancastrian school was the *first* school established in this city for the education of the children of the poorer classes. At the outset a room was rented in Nicholas street for the training of boys only, John Picton being the first master. After three years' work the committee in their first printed report, dated December 31st, 1810, stated that the total number of boys admitted since the commencement in 1808 had been 800, with an average attendance in 1810 of 230.

In 1812, four years after the establishment of this school, a report refers to the *new* Church of England schools, and it says:—"With these new schools the committee are desirous of joining heart and hand for the general success of education." The year 1813 was marked by the establishment of a girls' school, called the "Lancastrian school for the education of females."

In 1815, at a "very numerous and respectable" meeting of subscribers held in the Guildhall, with Edward Protheroe, M.P., in the chair, it was decided to unite with the parent society in London, and the following resolution was passed:—"That this society do adopt the title of 'The Bristol Auxiliary British and Foreign School Society,' and that in future its surplus annual income be remitted to the society in London, after defraying the necessary expenditure of the schools for the time being in this city, excepting the sums subscribed to the building fund." In the balance sheet for the following year practical effect seems to have been given to the resolution, for a sum of £250 was remitted to the parent society in London.

In 1817 a vigorous effort was made to secure the necessary funds for the erection of the new schoolroom in Redcross street, and the annual meeting felt it "to be its duty to recommend sermons to be preached in aid of the building in all places of public worship in the city." The report for 1817 says:—"A few weeks only have elapsed since the friends of the education of the poor had to witness an interesting spectacle. After a most impressive and liberal discourse, delivered in St. Philip's church by the Rev. Wm. Day, the foundation of a building capable of accommodating about 500 boys and 400 girls was laid by our liberal friend and benefactor, Michael Castle, in the presence of a vast number of spectators." The first annual meeting held in the school house, Redcross street, was on March 26th, 1818, and the report records that "under circumstances and prospects thus pleasing this ample and eligible building has been erected in which we are now assembled." 302 boys and 235 girls were in attendance this year, and upwards of 3,000 boys and 800 girls had passed through the schools since their foundation. Since this time the school has had an uninterrupted course of prosperity. Its growth has necessitated the addition of two classrooms for senior boys and one for juniors. The boys' school can now accommodate nearly 600 scholars. The latest statistics show that the large number of 42,804 children have been educated in the schools since their foundation. In 1883 there were 1,046 names on the register, with an average attendance of 809. The course of instruction is somewhat advanced for an elementary school, including, in addition to the usual subjects taught, lessons in drawing from nature, shorthand and French. The present head master, J. H. Reed, was appointed in 1862, and the head mistress, Miss A. Crossman, in 1864. The girls' school, in 1883, was transferred to the Bristol School Board.

Certified Industrial Schools and Reformatories.

ARNO'S VALE REFORMATORY, Brislington, is managed by the trustees of the Roman Catholic convent of the Good Shepherd. There are about 300 inmates.

CLIFTON WOOD SCHOOL, established in 1849. The average age of boys on admission is ten years; they are subject to detention until they have completed their sixteenth year, but they are in most cases, if their conduct has been good, sent out on license soon after they have attained the age of fifteen. The average number of boys in the school during the year 1883 was 210. The number finally discharged during the year was 68, whose average detention had been 3¼ years. The number admitted was 47, of whom 18 came from Bristol, 2 from Gloucestershire, and 27 from other counties. Every boy of proper age, and not physically disqualified, is employed one half of the day (not exceeding 3½ hours) in the workshop. Brushmaking, tailoring, shoemaking and laundry work are carried on, and are sources of income to the institution. The cost per head, after deducting the cost of the boys' labour, for the year 1883 was £13 1s. 3d. A number of the boys on their discharge emigrate to Canada, where they are at once provided with situations. W. R. Garrett, secretary; W. Hibbins, supt.

KINGSWOOD REFORMATORY, about four miles from Bristol, founded upwards of 30 years ago, mainly through the exertions of Mary Carpenter and Russell Scott; the house was built by Rev. John Wesley, and was at that time occupied as a Wesleyan school. Several trades are taught, such as carpentering, shoemaking, tailoring and farming, but the chief work is that of brick-making, and in this respect the committee have been in conflict with the different Secretaries of State, as it was considered by many to be utterly unfit for reformatory work. The committee, in spite of the opposition, continued the work, which was in former years a great financial success, over £1,000 profit per year having been made; but of late the manufacture has resulted in a loss. There are nearly 150 boys in the school, and many of those who have left are known to be leading honest and respectable lives. The income of the institution is derived from sums paid by the Treasury, by counties and boroughs for the maintenance of children, and from the profits on the industrial work of the boys. Rev. Canon Ellacombe, hon. sec.; Lieut.-Col. N. Lowis, superintendent.

PARK ROW ASYLUM was founded in February, 1855, by Mrs. George Anthony Sawyer, for hopeful discharged female prisoners. The shelter is extended over a period often of two years, according to circumstances, as none whose conduct is good leave without being provided with a situation, unless returning to their friends by their own desire. The rules of the institution provide that no penitentiary case and no cases of pickpockets are admissible. No candidate can be admitted who has been to prison more than once, and no candidate is admissible under the age of 16 years. On entering the asylum the candidate undergoes a short period of probation in her dormitory, associating gradually during this time with the other inmates, first at prayer in the chapel, then at lessons, and lastly at meal times. If, after the time of probation, she is still willing to remain in the asylum, she is then fully admitted and receives the clothes of the house. Much benefit is derived from this mode of semi-seclusion, as the candidate is daily visited by the lady superintendent and by the ladies of the committee, and great moral influence is thus obtained before any free intercourse takes place with the other inmates.

The employment of the young women consists of all sorts of household work—washing, cooking, baking, needlework, knitting stockings and socks; and in this way, when work is plentiful, the inmates are enabled to earn a considerable sum. A few hours are daily devoted to religious instruction, reading and writing, and singing of hymns and psalms is daily practised. The inmates are also instructed in the first elements of arithmetic and geography. Divine service is held in the little chapel connected with the institution every Sunday, and during the week there are Bible classes, and classes for spelling, needlework and singing, conducted by lady friends of the asylum, the ladies associated with the management frequently visiting it and taking the greatest interest in the inmates.

At the beginning of 1883 there were 13 young women in the house, and 11 were admitted during the year, making a total of 24. The institution is supported by voluntary subscriptions and donations, and is under the direction of a sub-committee of ladies taken from the general committee. On Thursdays, from 10 to 4 o'clock, the asylum is open to the public. Miss Ware, Pen Avon house, Clifton, hon. sec.

PARK ROW CERTIFIED INDUSTRIAL SCHOOL was started by Mary Carpenter in April, 1858, and was almost the first (if not the first) in England. It will accommodate 80 boys. The total number sent to the school from 1859 to December, 1883, was 457. It is supported by voluntary contributions, with Government and School Board allowances for boys sent under the Act, and contributions enforced from their parents. The school is open to visitors Tuesdays and Thursdays. J. Langabeer, superintendent.

RED LODGE REFORMATORY FOR GIRLS, Park row. This school was commenced at Kingswood before the Reformatory Schools Act was passed. It was mainly through Mary Carpenter that this Act was obtained in August, 1854, and this school was the first established in Great Britain for the reception of convicted girls under the Act. The premises known as the Red lodge were purchased by the late Lady Noel Byron, widow of the poet, in 1854. A few girls entered the institution as voluntaries in the following month, and, in accordance with the desire of Lady Byron, the late Mary Carpenter undertook the sole management of the institution. The school was certified on the 9th December, 1854 (the certificate being signed by Lord Palmerston), and from that time girls have been received under magisterial sentence.

Before proceeding further with the history of the institution, a word or two in reference to the building may prove of interest. The Red lodge is supposed to have been in ancient times one of two lodges standing near the entrances which led through the ornamental grounds to the monastery of St. Augustine. On the site of the monastery Sir John Young, a Bristol merchant, built the Great house in the time of Elizabeth, and the Queen was entertained by Sir John Young at the Red lodge during one of her progresses through Bristol. In the course of time the Great house and the Red lodge got separated, and the latter, previous to being bought for its present purpose, was in the possession of the late Dr. Prichard, the learned author. What is now called the "oak room" is a remarkably handsome apartment of the Elizabethan period, and contains some of the finest examples of panelling and carving to be met with anywhere. In this interesting apartment the inmates are now assembled for morning and evening prayers, and for evening service on Sundays. In the morning of that day they attend at Lodge street chapel for worship. In the superintendent's room is a tablet to the memory of the lady who purchased the house, bearing the following inscription:—
"Sacred to the memory of Anne Isabella Noel, Dowager Lady Byron, who, ever devoting the many talents entrusted to her to the service of her Master, purchased these premises

September, 1854, for the purpose of rescuing young girls from sin and misery and bringing them back to the paths of holiness. She was born May 17, 1792, and departed this life May 16, 1860. Faithful unto death." The school accommodates 54 girls. Taking the three years ending 1881, there were 42 discharges, and of these 24 were doing well, 1 had died, 8 were returned as doubtful, 4 had been convicted of crime, and 5 were unknown. Taking the year 1882, the total cost of the institution was £1,067 1s. 7d., the whole being met by grants from the Treasury, contributions from county and borough rates, and the industrial profits of the institute. The reformatory is now managed by a committee, under the chairmanship of Herbert Thomas. The reports of the Government inspector are of a most gratifying character. Laundry work forms an important item, twelve girls being regularly employed, contributing a considerable amount to the expenses of the institution. Miss Langabeer, matron.

STANHOPE HOUSE, Cotham road (South). Established in 1866, and is intended for the reception of destitute and vagrant girls of the Protestant persuasion sentenced to an industrial school under the Industrial Schools Act of 29th and 30th Vic. (1866), chap. cxxiii. It is supported by voluntary contributions, with Government allowance for girls sent under the Act. The school is about to move this year to Ashley house, Somerset street. No girl is admitted above the age of 14 years. The course of instruction consists of reading, spelling, writing and ciphering, such knowledge of geography and history as enable the girls to read with intelligence ordinary books of an instructive and interesting character, and such general information as make them more able to discharge well the duties likely to devolve on them in life. This secular instruction is given for three hours daily. The religious instruction is from Holy Scripture, and comprises the doctrines and precepts of Christianity, and is given daily. The industrial education consists of washing, cooking, baking, needlework and house work. The clothing provided for the girls is a simple and neat uniform. The average number of girls in the school is 50. Mrs. E. Croggan, Beaufort road, hon. sec.

ST. JAMES' BACK SCHOOL owes its origin to Mary Carpenter, and was originally a day feeding school; that is to say, children were induced to attend and remain at school throughout the day by means of meals provided for them, and a portion of the school hours were devoted to industrial work. On the death of Mary Carpenter, the school was, in October, 1877, converted into a day industrial board school. During the year 1883 103 boys and 14 girls had been sent to school by the magistrates under orders of detention, 139 had left, and at the close of the year there were 127 attending. The children are admitted to the school as early as six o'clock in the morning, and some of them remain engaged in various duties until seven in the evening. They are provided with breakfast at half-past eight, dinner at half-past twelve, and tea at half-past five o'clock, and the intervals are fully occupied with scholastic and industrial work, according to a time-table approved by the Board. The girls do needlework, and take part in turns in the work of the kitchen and washhouse; and the boys, besides assisting in the household work, in the way of scrubbing and cleaning, devote a portion of their time to chopping sticks, the institution supplying all the Board schools with firewood. The school is supported by the rates and contributions from the Treasury. Mrs. Cross, matron.

TRUANT SCHOOL, Southville street, was established by the School Board, and to which boys who are confirmed truants are committed and detained for such time as the Board consider necessary to cure them of their truant habits. The system has been found to work extremely well, the boys who have been sent to it often afterwards making the best attendances at the day elementary schools. There is a truant School Board officer whose duty it is to look after these children. (See "Training Ships.")

Collegiate Schools.

CATHEDRAL SCHOOL, Lower College green, founded 36th of Henry VIII., was reorganised under a scheme approved by the Queen in Council in May, 1882. The aim of the school is to provide education, higher than elementary, for the choristers of the Cathedral and other boys being day scholars. All scholars pay a tuition fee of £2 a term for the ordinary school course. Boys are required to pass an examination for admission, and unless they are choristers or probation choristers must be not less than eight years of age. Two foundation scholarships are tenable in this school, exempting the holders from payment of the ordinary school fee. Each scholarship is tenable for two years, and is open to boys whose names have been at least twelve months on the books and who are under twelve years of age. The average number of boys at present attending the school is 115. Rev. Henry W. Pate, M.A., is the head master, and there are three assistant masters.

CLERGY DAUGHTERS' SCHOOL, St. George's street, Park street, was originally founded in Gloucester. About ten years ago Rev. A. Peache bought and presented to the committee the present buildings. The school receives 68 pupils, who are prepared for the Cambridge and other examinations. The object of this school is to provide for the daughters of clergymen of the Church of England in straightened circumstances an appropriate education according to the principles of the Church of England. The pupils all appear in the same dress, and are received from all parts of the United Kingdom. Miss Lawton, head mistress.

GRAMMAR SCHOOL. The date and the manner of the foundation of this school are involved in considerable doubt. It is, however, the oldest and most important of the public schools in this city, and is a classical school of the first grade with a modern department. Evans ascribes 1528 as the date when Nicholas and John Thorne were sheriffs of this city; others have, however, adopted 1532 as the more probable, this being the date of Robt. Thorne's will. There is no specific bequest of money for the foundation of the school, simply a devise of £1,000 to be distributed and ordered as his executors should deem best for his soul. A deed poll of Nicholas Thorne, dated July 1st, 1561, after reciting the laudable purposes of these executors in the foundation of a free school of grammar, declares that certain lands and property are given to the mayor, burgesses and commonalty of the city of Bristol and their successors for ever, for the purpose of founding a free Grammar school within the house called the "Bartilmews." St. Bartholomew's priory and hospital, which became the first Bristol Grammar school, goes back a long way in history, for its foundation has been ascribed to the beginning of the 13th century. It stood close to the bottom of what is now Christmas steps, and there the work of education was begun and carried on. Nicholas Thorne lived till 1546, and was buried in St. Werburgh's church. An inscription to his memory in old English characters was removed from the church on its demolition, and was subsequently fixed in the great hall of the new Grammar school in Tyndall's park. This inscription speaks of his enriching Bristol "with a noble school at his own and his brother's expense," and the tablet is probably correct in attributing to him a large share in the actual establishment of the school. The Thorne connection with the school continued after the death of Robert and Nicholas Thorne, and in a document dated later in the century the broad objects of the school were set out as follow: "And for the establishment of a free school and one schoolmaster, and one or two ushers as need or occasion hereafter shall be, to teach and bring up youth in learning and virtue, and especially in grammar and other good literature, and the better education and bringing up of children and others who may resort thither for learning and understanding of the tongues, to the glory of God and for the advancement of the said city." About 1769 the school was transferred to Unity street—the hospital school founded by John Carr. (See "City School.")

The school continued under the management of the Mayor and Corporation till 1842, when it was handed over to the Municipal Charity Trustees. At this time the school had fallen into decay, and the then head master, though still residing in the master's house, had for some years received no pupils.

On the 24th January, 1848, the school was re-opened, Dr. Evans, formerly Fellow of Jesus college, Oxford, being selected out of 200 gentlemen who applied for the position of head master. The school had been partly re-built to make it more equal to modern requirements, and on the opening day between 200 and 300 boys were admitted. Dr. Evans died in 1854, and T. C. Hudson, M.A., was head master in his place till 1860. Dr. Caldicott was the next to take charge of the responsible duties, and for 23 years maintained an honoured connection with the institution.

The history of the school since 1848 has been one of unbroken prosperity. On the appointment of the Endowed Schools' Commissioners a long controversy arose on the question of government, management and studies of endowed schools.

Eventually in 1875 a scheme was framed, and, having been approved by Her Majesty the Queen in Council, was established, under which the school has attained greater eminence. This scheme provided that "the governing body of the school shall consist of the municipal trustees for the time being and six other persons, to be appointed as follows, viz.: Two by the Bristol School Board, two by the Bristol Town Council, one by the masters on the permanent staff of the Grammar school, one by the masters and mistresses on the permanent staff of the Red Maids' school, Queen Elizabeth's hospital, and the day schools attached to those foundations in Bristol respectively. Every governor, other than the municipal trustees, shall be appointed to hold office for six years and then retire. No master or mistress of any school shall be governor. Religious opinions, or attendance or non-attendance at any particular form of religious worship, shall not in any way affect the qualification of any person to be a governor."

On April 18th, 1876, the ground in Tyndall's park was taken for the new school, and on June 11th, 1877, the foundation-stone of the building was laid by Herbert Thomas, chairman of the governing body. School work commenced in the new place on February 15th, 1879; but the formal opening ceremony was not till May 17th of that year, when the Right Hon. W. E. Forster, M.P., gave an interesting address, and a presentation was made by the "old boys" to the then head master, Dr. Caldicott. The school was built from designs by Foster and Wood, and blending structural solidity and strength with elegance of design, it is well worthy of the exceptionally fine site it occupies, on six acres of the most eligible portion of Tyndall's park. The great hall is a magnificent apartment, 140 feet long, 50 feet broad, and 50 feet high from the floor to the collar-beam of the roof. There are two transepts; the one on the east side is reserved as the head master's place, and the other forms the entrance lobby. There are nine class rooms for teaching. In the gallery of the great hall is a fine organ, the munificent gift of W. H. Wills, M.P. (see "Organs"). On April 14th, 1880, the formal opening of the organ took place at the annual school concert. The clock and bells in the tower were the gift of Messrs. Wills. The school is capable of accommodating 400 boys, and has at present 300 pupils.

At Midsummer, 1883, Dr. Caldicott, having accepted a living at Shipton-on-Stour, vacated the head mastership, and R. Leighton Leighton, M.A., head master of Wakefield Grammar school, was elected in his place. Minor alterations have taken place in the school routine from time to time. Divinity is taught throughout the school, including (in the classical division of the upper school) the Greek of the New Testament. But from this teaching a parent (or guardian) may claim exemption for any boy by written application to the head master. In the preparatory department, which is intended for boys under 12 years of age, the course of instruction includes Latin, French, English grammar, geography, English history, arithmetic, drawing, writing, spelling, and vocal music. The school proper has three divisions, viz. :—
(i.) The lower school, which continues the grounding begun in the preparatory department, with the addition of either Greek or German, at the parents' option. The course of instruction is designed to lay a solid foundation of elementary knowledge on which to base the special studies of the upper school, and which at the same time will serve as a sound business education for those boys who cannot spare time for more advanced study. On promotion from the lower school, a boy enters either (ii.) the classical division or (iii.) the modern division of the upper school. In the classical division the work is chiefly literary, i.e., Greek, Latin, French, history, and English composition, with the addition of mathematics, drawing, and vocal music. This division will give the most suitable preparation for the legal or medical professions, and for those various branches of business which require general ability rather than a knowledge of chemistry or physics or advanced mathematics. In the modern division the work consists principally of mathematics, science, including chemistry (theoretical and practical), electricity and magnetism, and French, with the addition of German (or Greek), Latin, English composition, history, drawing, and vocal music. This division will prepare for London Matriculation, the Military and Home Civil Service examinations, and those branches of business in which science and mathematics are specially required. Both divisions of the upper school will prepare boys to enter the older universities. The terms for tuition are now £4 per term, or £12 per annum for boys over 14 years of age, and £3 per term, or £9 per annum, for those under 14. Arrangements are made for boarders with some of the masters.

Four scholarships are offered every year, of £9 per annum each, tenable for two years, for boys under 13 years of age; two of £12 per annum each, tenable for three years, for boys under 15 years of age; and one of £6, tenable for one year, with no restriction of age. These scholarships are preferentially given as entrance scholarships to boys who have been for at least one year pupils of certain local schools; failing properly qualified candidates from such schools, they are open for general competition. For boys who shall have been at least two years in the school there will be offered every year a "Sanders' scholarship" of £15, tenable for one year, by boys of 17 years of age; a "Members' scholarship" of £15 per annum, tenable for two years, by boys of 15 years of age; and a "Wills' scholarship" of £20 per annum, tenable for two years, by boys between 16 and 17 years of age. For boys who, having been pupils of the school for at least six consecutive terms, are proceeding from the school to the university, there is offered for competition every year a scholarship of £50 per annum, tenable for four years, at any college of Oxford or Cambridge. The "Burges' scholarship" of the like value, tenable for the like time, is offered every fourth year. There are also two scholarships of £100 per annum each, tenable for five years at St. John's college, Oxford.

THEOLOGICAL INSTITUTE, Upper Byron place, was founded in 1863, for training young men as pastors and evangelists for Congregational churches. There are 21 students in residence. It is supported entirely by voluntary contributions. Candidates for admission should apply to Rev. S. W. McAll, M.A., Upper Sydenham road. The principal of the institute is Rev. J. P. Allen, M.A.

TRADE AND MINING SCHOOL, Nelson street, was established in 1856. The object of the school is to provide an education in the applied sciences, and was one of the first in England to undertake such systematic teaching. Boys are received at the age of nine years, and are first passed through the elementary course, which constitutes the common groundwork of all branches of higher education. They are then offered the choice of a thorough commercial training or of a preparation on its scientific side for pursuits connected with manufactures and the constructive arts. Its mining department deals with the sciences required in mining and engineering, and it has a chemical laboratory for the study of practical chemistry, analysis and assaying, which is open to others besides members of the school. Among the most important features of the institution are the evening classes, where courses of instruction for pupils of all ages in high mathematics, applied science, classics, modern languages, and other subjects of equal utility are provided. The present accommodation being somewhat meagre, the number of pupils is greatly limited, but nevertheless the school has within the last dozen years carried off a very fair proportion of the Royal scholarships which the Science and Art Department of the Committee of Council on Education has during the period mentioned offered for open competition throughout the United Kingdom. In addition to these honours it has won several scholarships and exhibitions at Oxford and elsewhere.

The distinguished career of the school has suggested to the Society of Merchant Venturers the idea of developing it further, and this ancient guild are, as these pages pass through the press, erecting upon the ground formerly occupied by the old Bristol Grammar school, at the corner of Unity street and Denmark street, a building which will be known as

THE MERCHANT VENTURERS' SCHOOL. This stupendous pile of handsome buildings is four stories in height and covers an area of about 26,000 feet. It is in the 14th century Gothic style of architecture, the exterior being faced with the Cattybrook company's red pressed bricks, with best Box ground dressings and green slating. There are two front elevations, one facing Unity street and the other Denmark street, and the total height of that in the last-named street from the footings is 104 feet, whilst that in Unity street is 80 feet high. Upon the basement, which (owing to the situation of the building on the slope of the hill in Unity street, connecting College green with Denmark street) is level with Denmark street at the east end and two-thirds below the level of Unity street at the west end, there are three engineering workshops and testing rooms, a gymnasium, a dining hall 74 feet by 22 feet, kitchen offices complete, engine and hot water apparatus rooms, and coal and fuel cellars. There is a long corridor separating the dining hall from the ten cloak rooms on the basement, and also covered and open playgrounds, 126 feet long by 56 feet wide. The ground floor is reached from the basement by a flight of steps, and here are four classrooms, each 25 feet by 22 feet and 15 feet high, committee, reception and waiting rooms, and a library and museum 44 feet square, several retiring rooms and conveniences. The great hall, the finest feature in the building, is situated on the same floor, but at the rear of the Unity street front, facing the Mayor's chapel, and from that side it obtains its light. The hall is 30 feet by 45 feet and 28 feet high. The classrooms are entered from the great hall aisle or open corridor. The great hall is attractively fitted and adorned. Its style is of a later period than that of the building generally, and lined with oak panelling 18 feet high at the east end, where the platform is, whilst along the remaining sides it is 7 feet high. Gas is laid on to the hall, but in all probability it will be lighted, as will other parts of the building, by electricity. There is a fan traceried ceiling of oak, designed to overcome the otherwise flat service thereof. The open corridor arcade is of Portland stone, the pillars being 22 feet high. The library and museum are decorated in keeping with the hall—an 8 feet 6 inch pitch pine dado fixed around the interior, whilst the other portions of the wall are plastered, and the ceiling is of pitch pine to match the dado; the corridors are faced with waterfaced red bricks and Corsham stone dressings. The porter's and caretaker's quarters are also on this floor.

The entrances to the school are from Unity street, the boys entering from the western end of the block, whilst the principal entrance is in the centre of the Unity street front. The most important and elaborate staircase runs up from the main or central entrance, the stairs being of hard Massa Carrara marble, and effectively arcaded. There are six flights, the steps numbering 74. The second staircase—that for the boys—consists of the same number of flights, but instead of marble, pennant stone is adopted. On the first floor there are four general classrooms similar in size to those on the floor below; the artificers' drawing school, 59 feet by 22 feet, obtaining light from both Unity and Denmark streets; the engineering lecture room, 32 feet by 30 feet; the diagram room; an art drawing school, 34 feet by 23 feet; library, cloak rooms, &c. The upper portion of the great hall passes into this floor, and the classrooms all open into the gallery of this hall. On the second or topmost floor are situated the chemical lecture room, 43 feet by 28 feet; the physical science lecture room, 42 feet by 37 feet; and the chemical laboratory, 53 feet by 31 feet. Each room is lighted from the sides and by a skylight, and is about 17 feet high. On this floor are the physical science and metallurgical laboratories, each about 32 feet by 22 feet. The latter laboratory contains a series of furnaces for the experiments carried on there. This is about the first building in which metallurgical laboratories have been placed upon the topmost floor. Previously they have been erected in the basement, and much inconvenience experienced from the fumes ascending to the other parts of the schools. The advantage, then, in having these laboratories on the upper floor is obvious. This floor also contains the combustion, balance, special operation, class and masters' rooms. A lift is provided from the basement to the uppermost floor, and this proves of great convenience in bringing the various ores, fuel, &c., to the several flats. The ceilings of the majority of the rooms are panelled with pitch pine, and the internal facings of the walls of the principal rooms consist of Cattybrook red brick with Corsham stone dressings.

The building cost considerably over £30,000, exclusive of the site, upon which several thousand pounds were expended. The Society of Merchant Venturers deserve well of the city for providing not only a splendid and well appointed building which is an ornament to the city, but for forwarding the nucleus of a great school of scientific and technical education for those who by-and-by will be engaged in the various commercial, mining, engineering, and manufacturing industries of this city.

Endowed Schools.

There are nine endowed schools in the city, and appended hereto is a description of each:—

CITY SCHOOL, or QUEEN ELIZABETH'S HOSPITAL, was founded by the will of John Carr, the probate of which is dated April 10th, 1586. The will devises certain property for the purpose of providing an "hospital or place for bringing up of poor children and orphans, being men children," such as shall be born in certain places named, and whose parents are deceased or fallen into decay and not able to relieve them. The will directs that the hospital shall be conducted after the manner of Christ's hospital, London, and makes the Mayor and Commonalty of Bristol "patrons, guiders and governors of the said hospital for ever." The school was accordingly formed "in the mansion house of the late hospital or house of Billesweeke, otherwise called the Gaunts" (Unity street). From that site it was removed by exchange, about 1769, to the house of St. Bartholomew's (bottom of Christmas steps), at that time occupied by the Grammar school. In 1847 the school, having come under the management of the Charity Trustees, was removed to its present healthy and pleasant site on a slope of Brandon hill, occupying four acres, and having a frontage of 400 feet. It partly stands on what was, 600 years ago, a cemetery of the Jews, whose gravestones having been used in the base of the building, it has been wittily observed "that the boys educated at the school will always have a good Hebrew foundation."

A scheme for the government of the school received the approval of Her Majesty in Council on May 13th, 1875, and by such it will develop itself into three schools when the income will suffice, viz., Queen Elizabeth's hospital, which is a boarding school, Queen Elizabeth's day school, and Carr's day school.

In Queen Elizabeth's hospital 160 boys are maintained and educated as foundation boarders. Of this number 60 are poor orphan boys of Bristol and Congresbury, aged between eight and ten years, and 100 are boys from the elementary schools of Bristol and Congresbury, who are eligible for admission between the age of ten and twelve years, inclusive of one boy of either class (the former to be preferred) from the parish of Netherbury.

When the day schools are established 50 will be poor orphans who have lost one or both parents, or boys whose parents from mental or physical incapacity are unable to maintain or educate them, such boys having been born or resident for three years in certain localities and being between the age of eight and ten; 50 must have attended for at least one year some public elementary school in the city, and be between the age of ten and twelve, and have been born or resident for three years within the boundaries of the city borough; the remaining 50 must have attended, at least one year, Queen Elizabeth's day school or Carr's day school, subject to the same limitations of age and place of birth or residence as in the case of the second 50. The subjects of instruction are the ordinary subjects of a second grade school. No definite regulations are laid down in the scheme for the two day schools of the foundation. The trustees of the school are the lords of the manor of Congresbury and Wick St. Lawrence, the advowson of the vicarage of which is also their property. They are also owners of land in Winterbourne, Siston, Henbury and Almondsbury, in the county of Gloucester, and of considerable house property in the city of Bristol. Under the Endowed School Commissioners' scheme the governors of the Grammar school are *ex officio* the governors of this school, and the net income, about £6,000, is annually paid over by the municipal trustees to this body. There is an exhibition fund of £200 per annum to be appropriated in carrying boys of merit to some place of higher instruction. The present head master is Robert Jackson, who is assisted by a staff of six resident masters.

COLSTON'S BOARDING SCHOOL, or HOSPITAL, was founded and endowed in 1708 by Edward Colston (*see* "Monuments"), at the Great house in St. Augustine's place, its object being "to educate in the principles of the Church of England and to maintain and clothe 100 poor boys, and to place them out to apprentice." It was necessary that boys should be either sons of freemen or born within the city of Bristol, with the exception of one-fifth of the total number, who might be chosen from any other place; but from eight to ten of the town boys were always to be from Temple parish, "that being the place of the founder's nativity." The settlements also directed that "any boys of kin to the founder, or bearing the name of Colston, should have a right to be preferred before any others." No boy could be admitted before the age of seven years, nor after ten years, nor could he remain in the school longer than seven years. By the founder's directions the Society of Merchant Venturers were constituted sole managers of the estates of the charity and governors of the hospital, and twelve gentlemen, chosen by Colston himself (with power to fill up any vacancies afterwards occurring in the body), were called his "nominees," and were by him appointed visitors. In the event of certain contingencies, defined in the settlements, the governors of Christ's hospital, London, were empowered to discharge the functions of either or both of the above bodies. All vacancies in the school were filled up in moieties by these two bodies, the nominees in their half including all the "country" boys. Further regulations for the management and government of "his hospital" were made by Colston in 1712, 1715, and finally in 1718.

In 1858, owing to the improved value of the property and to its judicious management, the trustees considered that they were in a position to add 20 boys to the foundation; but the Great house in St. Augustine's not affording sufficient accommodation, and the surrounding buildings precluding the possibility of its enlargement, it became a question whether the school should be removed. As, however, great difference of opinion prevailed upon the subject, the matter was brought before the Master of the Rolls, who eventually approved of the proposal. The trustees thereupon purchased the former palace of the Bishop of Gloucester and Bristol for £12,000; and a new wing having been added to the building, the school was formally removed in 1861 to its present locality in Stapleton, where, with its grounds and a bathing-place, it occupies a space of about seven acres.

The hospital is a boarding school; its object, not being merely elementary, is to supply a sound, practical and liberal education in accordance with the principles of the Church of England. The management of the trust is still vested in the hands of the Society of Merchant Venturers (*see* "Merchant Venturers"); but a new governing body is appointed for the schools consisting of 23 members, viz., the Bishop of the Diocese and the rector of Stapleton *ex officio*, 13 from the Society of Merchant Venturers, two appointed by the magistrates of Gloucestershire and Somersetshire, three by the Bristol School Board, and three co-optative.

The school now comprises two elements:—

(1) *Foundationers*, of whom 80 are chosen from within the Parliamentary borough of Bristol, and 20 from the counties of Gloucester, Somerset and Wilts. They must have attended an elementary school for a year preceding their application. They are elected in order of merit, as tested by a competitive examination in the subjects of Standard IV.(Code 1875)for boys between the years of 10 and 11, and in those of Standard V. for boys between 11 and 12 years of age; they must also satisfy the examiner of their knowledge of the Church catechism. The foundationers receive board and tuition gratuitously, and, if necessary, an allowance towards clothing.

(2) *Paying Scholars*. The number of these is limited only by the extent of accommodation; but, if necessary, the governors are empowered to enlarge the building. These boys pass an entrance examination, one standard lower for corresponding ages than that fixed for foundationers, and enjoy all the advantages of the school upon payment of about £30 per annum. No boy can be admitted under 10 or over 12 years of age, nor can any remain beyond the school term in which he attains the age of 15 years.

By direction of the scheme, the governors apply a sum of not less than £100 per annum in maintaining exhibitions competed for by boys who have attended the boarding for not less than two years immediately preceding the award thereof, tenable at any grammar school, or other place of liberal or professional education approved by the governors. Rev. J. Hancock, M.A., head master.

COLSTON SCHOOL, Victoria street. Founded by Edward Colston in 1710 for the clothing and instruction of 40 boys. By consent of Colston's trustees and the Education Department, the school was in 1864 amalgamated with a public elementary one, and the scholars on the endowment are taught in classes with the ordinary pupils. The ·foundation stone of the present building was laid by C. O. Lane, Master of the Society of Merchant Venturers, 16th December, 1864, on the site of the old Temple church schools, and was opened on 21st February, 1866. It is in the Italian style of architecture. Boys 260, girls 180. Master, H. J. Walker. Mistress, Miss Barnes.

ELBRIDGE'S CHARITY SCHOOL, Fort lane, St. Michael's hill, was built by John Elbridge (*see* "Hospitals,"subheading "Infirmary") in a part of his garden in 1738. By his will he endowed it with £3,000. It was erected for 24 girls, who were to be taught reading, writing, arithmetic and sewing, and a suit of clothes was to be given each once a year. The dwelling-house for the master and mistress was erected in 1748. The school is not now regarded as a charity one, being St. Michael's National Girls' school, and the endowment is now shared by boys' and infants' schools. Patron, Rev. W. Heywood.

REDCLIFF BLUE GIRLS' SCHOOL, Redcliff hill, was formerly in Temple street and commenced about 1720, and was supported by voluntary contributions till 16th May, 1798, when, from legacies and donations, further subscriptions were not required. The school was amalgamated with the National school in 1869. Fifty girls are now on the endowment, who are educated, and clothed in blue. Mistress, Mrs. Green.

REDCLIFF ENDOWED BOYS'SCHOOL, Redcliff Parade. Lower department founded 1856; upper department, September, 1879. This latter is for children whose parents can afford to send them for a longer period than is usual in elementary schools, and are taught by certificated masters. Accommodation for 490. Master, J. T. Francombe.

RED MAIDS' SCHOOL, Denmark street, founded by Alderman Whitson, who by a will dated March 27th, 1627, bequeathed certain property to the Mayor, burgesses and commonalty of Bristol to provide for 40 poor women children, daughters of freemen or burgesses, dead or decayed in estate. These children were to be taught to read English, to sew and to do other laudable work towards their maintenance. The mayoress, or the "ancientest alderman's wife," was to appoint the work to be done by the children, and the school was to be carried on in some convenient room in the new mansion house of the Gaunts in Queen Elizabeth's hospital. The present buildings were erected in 1840 on part of the site of the house of the Gaunts.

The government of this school and of Queen Elizabeth's hospital is under the management of the governors of the Grammar school, together with four ladies appointed by the governors.

Formerly the school accommodated 120 girls, but under the new scheme not more than 80 are to be boarded, and it is to be removed from its present site. A new day school is to be formed for girls on the present site for as many as can be accommodated, and in course of time another day school will be founded in some other part of the city.

In the Red Maids' school proper, 50 girls of the 80 foundationers are orphans or girls whose parents, from mental or physical incapacity, are unable to maintain or educate them; are also born or resident for three years within the boundaries of the borough, and between 8 and 10 years of age. Fifteen are to have attended for at least one year some public elementary school in Bristol between the age of 10 and 12, and born or resident for three years within the borough boundaries; and the remaining 15 to have attended for at least one year one of the proposed schools of the foundation, subject to the same limitations of age and place of birth and residence as in the case of the second 15.

The subjects of instruction are similar to those in Queen Elizabeth's hospital, with the addition of domestic economy, the laws of health, needlework and (if the governors shall so decide) telegraphy, or some other skilled industry suitable for women. The children, dressed in their red gowns, white aprons and tippets, plain straw bonnets trimmed with blue ribbon, attend divine service Sundays at the Mayor's chapel (St. Mark's), College green. Miss Roberts, mistress.

STOKES' CROFT ENDOWED SCHOOL. This is one of the oldest endowed schools in Bristol, having been founded in 1722 by Abraham Hooke, merchant, who had filled the office of Sheriff in the year 1706, together with others of the Society of Protestant Dissenters worshipping in Lewin's mead. For upwards of a century the boys were clothed in a dress similar to that at present worn by the boys of the City school, and 30 were boarded as well as educated. It was, however, subsequently resolved no longer to board and clothe them, but rather to increase their number to 40, to be educated only, save that on Sundays 30 were to dine at the school upon their return from the morning service at Lewin's mead meeting. As late as the year 1851 it was resolved to abolish the Sunday dinners and confine the work of the school to education only. In regard to the admission of boys to the school preference is given to those whose parents attend Lewin's mead meeting, but should there not be a sufficient number of such candidates the most eligible of those whose parents may attend other places of worship are appointed. Boys are required to pass a preliminary examination before they are admitted, which is from about the age of eight years, and they are expected to remain until they are fourteen. The management consists of a body of feoffees selected from among the worshippers at Lewin's mead meeting, who are appointed for life, a treasurer and governor being elected from that number. David Churchill, master.

Infant Schools.

Many of the British and National schools have infant classes attached to them; but the two oldest distinct infant schools are that in the Old Park, St. Michael's, which was built in 1837 by the late Mrs. Hayes (accommodation for 150), and Temple Church Infant school, in Victoria street, founded early in the present century in a room given by John Hare. It is now used as a mission room, and the school was removed in 1870 to its present location. It has been under Government inspection since 1860. Average attendance, 196.

Miscellaneous Schools.

MARINE SCHOOL, in Prince street, is an establishment for instructing lads apprenticed to the sea in nautical astronomy, navigation and mathematics, thus qualifying them for receiving certificates as masters and mates.

MEDICAL SCHOOL, Tyndall's park. Founded in 1853. This is now affiliated to the University college. (*See* "University.")

PILE STREET MIXED SCHOOL, Redcliff, was opened in 1880. The premises were formerly occupied by the boys of the Redcliff Blue Coat school. Accommodation for 60.

SCHOOL OF CHEMISTRY, Kingsdown parade; opened in 1847. The laboratory is open daily for research or instruction, and courses of lectures are given at intervals in the classroom. Dr. Griffin, conductor.

National Schools.

There are over 40 belonging to the Established Church (*see* "Churches"). Those having any historical pretensions are mentioned.

CHRIST CHURCH SCHOOL, Lower Nelson place, Clifton, was founded in 1852, enlarged in 1861, rebuilt in 1877, and re-opened Jan. 5th, 1878. Accommodation for 150 girls, 114 infants, and 172 boys.

CLIFTON NATIONAL SCHOOL, Park place. Established in 1850, and the present premises built in 1876. Accommodation for 200 boys, 120 girls and 60 infants.

ST. PETER'S, Castle Mill street. Founded in 1855, and is built on part of the old Castle wall. Boys, 100; girls and infants, 180.

ST. PHILIP AND JACOB, Mary Bush lane. Built on the precincts of the Bristol castle, and was opened 11th June, 1862, by the Rev. S. E. Day. The buildings accommodate 200 boys, 250 girls and 150 infants. In 1878, by the advice of Her Majesty's inspector, the boys' and girls' schools were amalgamated.

Night Schools.

At many of the National and British schools evening classes are held during the winter months for the education of young men who have, for some reason or another, neglected their education.

Private Schools.

There are considerably over 150 private boarding and day schools in Bristol for boys and girls, but it would be beyond the compass of this work to enumerate them.

Ragged Schools,

Ash lodge, Temple, and Brightbow, Bedminster. A Ragged School Society was formed in 1847 by Lord Teignmouth, Sergt. Stephens, Messrs. Tritton and Ramsden, and a committee composed of several gentlemen, the present High Sheriff (Lieut.-Col. H. B. O. Savile, R.A.) forming one of the number. The work done by these schools in the past has been very much appreciated. They are entirely dependent upon voluntary contributions. The committee meet on the first Wednesday in each quarter, at 19 College green. Commander Roberts, secretary.

There are also ragged schools in connection with St. James' parish on Marlborough hill, St. Philip and Jacob in Bread street, and St. Luke's in William street, Whitehouse street, Bedminster.

Sunday Schools
were opened in this city at the close of the last century. Amongst the oldest may be mentioned that of Lodge street, which was founded in 1796, the Tabernacle school in 1800, West street Baptist in 1801, St. George's road Free Methodists in 1809. Nearly all the British and National schools have Sunday schools associated with them.

SUNDAY SCHOOL TEACHERS' ASSOCIATION, in connection with the Church of England, whose object is to promote the general efficiency of Sunday schools, was founded ten years ago. Lectures and training lessons are given during the winter months in the various schoolrooms, and a teachers' competitive examination takes place annually. Rev. W. T. Hollins, M.A., 2 Portland square, and N. Strickland, Cotham road, hon. secs.

SUNDAY SCHOOL UNION. The principal schools in connection with the Nonconformists belong to this Union, which was established in 1813. Depôt, 4 St. James' square. Secretaries, J. L. Bradshaw, F. D. Ashmead.

(*See* "Clifton College," "Baptist College," "University," "Orphanages," "Homes," &c.)

Scripture Readers' Army Friend Society (Bristol and Clifton Auxiliary). The sole object of this society is to spread the knowledge of Christianity among soldiers. Colonel Biggs, secretary and treasurer; Mrs. Newbolt, secretary and treasurer of Ladies' Committee.

Scripture Readers' Association, instituted in 1845, for the purpose of providing for the parishes in Bristol and its vicinity laymen, members of the Church of England, whose duty it is to read the Scriptures from house to house, and also by means of Bible classes, cottage and schoolroom lectures, &c., endeavour to bring to the hearts and homes of our people the saving knowledge of God's Word. The society has at present 19 of these agents employed under the supervision of the parochial clergy, and the population actually visited by them in Bristol and suburbs is upwards of 80,000. It is supported wholly by voluntary contributions. Edward Slaughter, Clifton, treasurer; Rev. Thomas C. Price, 8 Charlotte street, Park street, hon. sec.

Severn River, The, is navigable throughout, and for large ships up to Gloucester. It is connected with the Thames by the Thames and Severn canal. Adjacent to the river is the Gloucester and Berkeley canal, which runs to Birmingham and South Staffordshire. A bridge of 1,387 yards in length spans the river near Sharpness, and here also is a spacious dock. At the New Passage ferry are two piers of the Bristol and South Wales Union Railway, where the steamers convey passengers to and fro daily. The river here is about 2½ miles wide, but at low water the rocky shore is bare on the Gloucestershire side to within 480 yards of Monmouthshire. Through a narrow channel here called the Shoots, 15 fathoms deep, the river flows with great velocity. The low light sandstone cliff on the Monmouthshire side is the Lady beach; opposite lie the English stones. It was on these rocks that 60 of Cromwell's troopers, in chase of Charles, were upset by the treacherous ferrymen, when they were all swept away by the tide. In consequence of this the Protector abolished the ferry, and it was transferred to Aust, but when the railway was opened it was replaced on the original site. Above Portskewet pier is the Charston island, with a light (green) for the navigation of the ferry steamers. In this locality a tunnel is being constructed by the Great Western Railway under the Severn, so as to establish unbroken railway communication between the West of England and South Wales. The river Wye flows into the Severn at Beachley, where there are extensive earthworks supposed to be British. The rise and fall of the tide in this river are greater than any other in the world. The mouth of the Severn is at Kingroad, where it unites with the Bristol channel.

Sewerage. Bristol has adopted that of water carriage by close tubes or drains, constructed of bricks and cement or burnt stone ware. Owing to the difference of level and the different inclinations of the ground, the system of sewers in the borough is very extensive, consisting in fact of six different sets of main sewers and communicating drains. The sewers as they now exist were commenced by the old Commissioners of Paving and Lighting. Since the application of the Public Health Act to the borough, in 1851, they have been carried on under the direction of the Town Council, acting as the Sanitary Authority. The aggregate length of the main sewers is about 150 miles, constructed at an expense of about £161,000. At present they discharge their contents into the tidal river Avon at two different points, situated below the city, one on the north side and one on the south side of the river.

Sheds for foreign cattle were opened at Cumberland basin on May 27th, 1879. Several spacious sheds for the accommodation of vessels discharging cargoes have been constructed by the Docks Committee during the past few years on the quays of the Floating harbour, which prove of great convenience to shippers. (*See* "Maps.")

Shells. The Bristol district is particularly rich in its land and freshwater mollusca, for of the 127 British species no less than 104 have been recorded as occurring in the vicinity. Of these it is probable that 9 have been incorrectly included in the list, as it is unlikely that such shells as, for instance, *Clausilia biplicata, Succinea oblonga, Limnæa involuta* and *glutinosa*, and *Vertigo alpestris* have actually been obtained here. This reduces the list to 95, all of which are well authenticated, and among them are many of our rarer forms; indeed Bristol is frequently mentioned in works on Conchology as a locality for some of the scarce species. The Downs and St. Vincent's rocks, Leigh woods, the alluvial plain extending from Shirehampton to the Aust cliffs, the valley of the Frome, and, farther away, Brockley combe and Kenn moor, offer the greatest attraction to and best repay the conchologist. Leigh woods will yield most of the woodland species, among the most noticeable being *Helix arbustorum, Helix aculeata, Helix fusca* and *Helix sericea, Zonites fulvus* and *radiatulus*, and *Pupa marginata*. On the Downs and St. Vincent's rocks the pretty *Cyclostoma elegans* is abundant, together with the curiously named *Helix lapicida*, the minute *Vertigo pygmæa*, and a number of the commoner sorts. In the gardens of Redland the carnivorous slugs *Testacella haliotidea* and *Maugei* are not unfrequent, the latter, which is by far the most common of the two, having been originally imported into this city about the year 1830, being brought here probably in the egg state among the mould attached to the roots of foreign plants. It has become naturalised in several parts of the country. At Brockley combe may be found the local *Cochlicopa tridens*, of which there is a numerous colony, *Achatina acicula, Vitrina pellucida*, and very

253

many more will here reward the diligent seeker, last, not least, among them being the little *Acme lineata*, a rare shell that has also been obtained from among the rejectamenta of the Avon, where Dr. Jeffreys also secured its almost unique variety *sinistrorsa*, a monstrosity that as yet has only been procured in one other locality in Britain. At Kenn moor the numerous ditches contain a large quantity of freshwater shells, among others *Planorbis corneus* and *contortus, Limnœa stagnalis* and *palustris, Bithinia Leachii, Valvata piscinalis* and *cristata* may be mentioned. From the somewhat similar ditches in the vicinity of Avonmouth, specimens of the *Pisidia* and *Planorbes* are especially plentiful, and in addition there are *Limnœa truncatula, Physa hypnorum*, and the uncommon little bivalve *Sphærium lacustris.* The river Frome, too, offers a considerable variety. In it the large freshwater mussels *Anodonta cygnea* and *Unio tumidus* are numerous, and among the others *Neritina fluviatilis, Ancylus fluviatilis* and *Limnœa auricularia* are conspicuous. At Ashley hill there is a colony of *Helix cantiana*. *Balia perversa* is to be had with seeking from an old wall near, and the Boiling wells and the adjoining railway embankment also are worthy of investigation. About 70 varieties of species have hitherto been reported, but the list is very incomplete and receives frequent additions.

The marine shells cannot be said to be numerous. On the banks of the Avon, at just about high water mark, *Conovulus denticulatus* and *myosotis*, particularly the latter, may be seen in myriads, while from the brackish pools at Avonmouth *Hydrobia ventrosa* and *Rissoa ulva* can be readily procured. *Littorina rudis* is plentiful among the loose stones at the water's edge, where also dead shells of the bivalve *Tellina solidula* strew the ground. It is recorded that the beautiful violet shell of the ocean-loving *Ianthina communis* has been taken on the shore after strong westerly gales.

Sheriffs.

(*See* also "Corporation Officers.") The appended is a list of those who have held the office since the passing of the Municipal Reform Act :—

1836	Daniel Cave—George Bengough.
"	Thomas Kington—Michael H. Castle.
1837	Thomas K. Bayly—Michael H. Castle.
1838	Francis Savage.
1839	Richard Vaughan.
1840	Hugh Vaughan.
1841	Thomas Jones.
1842	Jeremiah Hill.
1843	Thomas Wadham.
1844	John Harding.
1845	Thomas Hill.
1846	Abraham G. Harford Battersby.
1847	Edward Sampson, jun.
1848	Peter Maze, jun.
1849	John Jasper Leigh Bayly.
1850	Joseph Walters Daubeny.
1851	John Battersby Harford.
1852	Robert Bright.
1853	Philip John William Miles.
1854	Robert Phippen.
1855	Albany Bourchier Savile.
1856	George Oldham Edwards.
1857-8	J. G. Smyth (not sworn in) declined to serve ; his predecessor performed the duties during the year.
1858-9	W. H. Harford.
1859-60	W. Montague Baillie.
1860-1	Joshua Saunders.
1861-2	G. R. Woodward.
1862-3	C. D. Cave.
1863-4	William Wright.
1864-5	H. Cruger Miles.
1865-6	J. C. Hurle.
1866-7	W. H. Miles.
1867-8	W. G. Coles.
1868-9	Robert Phippen, died July 5th, 1869.
1869-70	Thomas Proctor.
1870-1	John Fisher.
1871-2	W. P. King.
1872-3	T. Todd Walton.
1873-4	T. Todd Walton.
1874-5	Charles Hill.
1875-6	George Bright.
1876-7	William Smith.
1877-8	W. H. Wills, M.P.
1878-9	C. B. Hare.
1879-80	R. L. G. Vassall.
1880-1	F. F. Fox.
1881-2	W. E. George.
1882-3	J. Lysaght.
1883-4	Lieut.-Colonel H. B. O. Savile.

Shipping.

SAILING. Bristol has from time immemorial played an important part in maritime affairs, and to attempt to trace the history of the shipping of the city and port of

Bristol would take us back far into the regions of tradition; but at present it is not our intention to revert to the remote period of uncertainty, but to that of certainty.

The natural position of the port offered such obvious advantages—situated upon the river Avon, and in close proximity with the Severn estuary and the Bristol channel, thus having direct and uninterrupted navigable communication with the sea, and its central occupation and means of access to all parts of the United Kingdom by land, must have been the reasons for the earliest Britons and the Romans selecting Bristol as one of their important military, commercial and shipping stations, in proof of which we have only to look at Sea mills, where was the Roman station Abona, and the defensive works found on the heights of Clifton down and neighbourhood.

A writer ("Gesta Stephani") in 1141 regarded Bristol as "forming a port fit and safe for a thousand vessels. It binds the circuit of the city so nearly and so closely that the whole city seemed to swim on the water, and wholly to be set on the river banks."

Amongst the earliest authentic details of the shipping trade of the port is that of the extensive traffic in slaves, which was carried on for many years, resulting in very large fortunes being made therefrom. In these times the shipping intelligence was very meagre; we, however, find that the port was a resort of ships from Ireland, Norway, and other countries, bringing leather, corn, wine, wool, &c.

Bristol ships and Bristol men were well represented at the siege of Calais, the city having supplied to Edward III. no less than 23 ships and 608 men, the largest of any port with the exception of London, which supplied 25 ships and 662 men.

Henry VI.'s time introduces us to the greatest English merchant of the 15th century—William Canynges, who gave special lustre to Bristol's history. He was the owner of a fleet of vessels amounting to about 3,000 tons, and traded with great enterprise to many foreign ports. Amongst the most prominent adventurers of Bristol were John and Sebastian Cabot, who set sail in the *Matthew* with Bristol sailors in May, 1497, and who discovered America and landed there on the 24th June that year, for which service Henry VII. granted the intrepid explorer the munificent sum of £10 from his privy purse. The Cabots were the instruments of Thorne and Eliot, the Bristol merchants, who fitted out the ship which led to the discovery of the "New isle"—names which are too often obscured by those of the navigators. It therefore redounds to the credit of Bristol that Bristol adventurers actually anticipated Columbus; it is undoubted that they were the first English navigators to successfully make the trans-Atlantic passage, and the first navigators within historic periods who landed on and explored Newfoundland, New England and Nova Scotia. It was no mere chance that threw this good fortune to Bristol, for it was then and for long after the second seaport of the kingdom, and Sebastian Cabot was one of its worthiest citizens. He made expeditions not only to North but to South America and to Russia, was appointed Grand Pilot of England, and became, in 1552, at the age of 80, first governor of the Society of Merchant Venturers, which still exists to dispense over £3,000 per annum in charity (*see* "Merchant Venturers"). From Bristol sailed Martin Frobisher, and hence, too, in 1603 set out the first expedition, under Matthew Pringe, for the discovery of the North-west passage.

Pepys, in his praises of the mixture of Spanish wine known as "Bristol milk," says the luxury was supported by a thriving trade with the North American plantations and with West Indies, and that the passion for colonial traffic was so strong (about 1685) that there was scarcely a shopkeeper in Bristol who had not a venture on board of some ship bound for Virginia or the Antilles. And Macaulay, speaking of Bristol towards the close of the 17th century, describes it as the first seaport.

One of the most striking points in local history, in comparison with modern times, is the frequent recurrence of announcements of ship launches for the navy and the merchant service, amongst which may be mentioned the following :—

In 1627, ship *Charles*,	30 guns.
" 1665, frigate *Islip*,	30 "
" 1666, " *Nantwich*,	44 "
" " " *St. Patrick*,	52 "
" 1668, " *Edgar*,	72 "
" 1679, " *Northumberland*,	70 "
" " " *Oxford*,	54 "

This sketch would be incomplete without mention of the name of Edward Colston, the West India merchant and the Bristol philanthropist, who imported sugar and other produce, and is reported to have only lost one vessel out of the fleet which had brought him his immense profits, and his name must ever stand in local annals side by side with that of Canynge, as a merchant prince, who combined a vigorous capacity in the shipping trade with a genuine desire to devote to the best interests of his country the wealth thus obtained. (*See* "Monuments," sub-heading "Colston.")

Privateering was carried on somewhat extensively about 1745, when several prizes were brought into the port, and the slave trade formed a prominent feature in the history of the port in the 18th century. In the latter part of that period an active North American and West Indian trade was carried on. It is recorded that 70 large ships were employed in the West India trade in sugar, rum, mahogany, &c. The Guinea trade was also "very flourishing," and in the Mediterranean, to Norway, Hamburg, &c. Ships were also employed to export manufactured goods to Florida, Carolina, Maryland, New York, Philadelphia, Newfoundland, and Quebec, returning with tobacco, rice, tar, deer skins, timber, fur, indigo, logwood, &c.

Goods were also brought by water from Birmingham and the North of England in trows, and no less than 100 were employed in bringing goods to and from Bristol *viâ* the Severn. The trade to Africa for ivory, gold dust, &c., was cultivated with great spirit and success. Ships were also sent to Greenland in the whale fishery exploits.

STEAM. But to pass over many notable intervening events, it was from the port of Bristol that the *Great Western* steamship made her maiden trip across the Atlantic. The *Great Western* was not literally the first steam vessel that crossed, for, *inter alia*, the American *Savannah* steamed and sailed from New York to Liverpool in 31 days in 1819; but the former was the first to start as a regular trader on commercial principles, and may fairly claim the honour of being the pioneer of the trans-Atlantic steam service. The *Great Western* was built by Wm. Patterson, cost £63,000, was 1,340 tons register, with engines of 440 horse power, and was launched July 19th, 1837. She started on her first trip with seven passengers April 8th, 1838, and returned with 66 passengers May 22nd, having occupied only 15 days 10 hours on the outward and 14 days on the homeward trip, and consumed on the double journey 450 tons of coal. From April, 1838, to November, 1844, she made 70 passages and conveyed 5,774 passengers, averaging 13 days on her homeward passages.

It will be interesting to state that it was with regard to this vessel that Dr. Lardner, at the meeting of the British Association in this city in 1836, remarked that such a voyage was no more practicable than a voyage to the moon, and made some legendary statement about swallowing the boiler. Thus the credit of proving that steam could be successfully applied to the requirements of commerce in trans-Atlantic voyages indisputably belongs to Bristol, and unquestionably the first steamer constructed for the Atlantic trade was the *Great Western*.

Her celebrated coadjutor, the *Great Britain*, was commenced in 1839, its cost was £97,000, and was floated out of dock, in the presence of H.R.H. Prince Albert, July 19th, 1843. She was propelled with a screw and built with a view to speed, and in her first trip to London in 1845 she beat the fastest steamer. Her length was, over all, 318 feet; breadth of beam, 50 feet; depth of hold, 32·6 feet; register tons, 3,500; horse-power, 500. She is still afloat, and in February, 1884, discharged a cargo of grain in the Mersey.

The reasons of the failure of these vessels could not be placed more lucidly or more cogently than they were put many years ago by that far-seeing marine engineer, the late Scott Russell, in a lecture on "Very large Ships," delivered at the Athenæum on April 15th, 1863. His conclusions and advice are as fresh now as when first uttered, and as worthy of careful consideration. We make no excuse for reproducing them *in extenso*.

"The history of the *Great Western* is, to my mind, the history of one of the most prudent and well-conducted enterprises in the history of great ships. In 1835 the inhabitants of Bristol undertook the construction of that vessel. It was determined by the Great Western Steamship company that, for the purpose of carrying cargo as well as passengers, the most speedy and certain passage, the greatest economy of power, and the full assurance of a profitable return, they would require a vessel of the very large size of 1,200 tons; and it was hoped that with 400 horse-power such a vessel would make the passage out in less than 20 days and return in 13, whereas in sailing packets the time occupied was 36 and 24 days. The *Great Western* was well designed, well executed, and well managed, was most creditable to Bristol, and yet failed to secure the permanence of the American trade which they had wanted. What were the causes of this failure?—for unquestionably the success of the *Great Western* was the foundation upon which plans were formed to rob Bristol of the fruits of its labour.

"The mistake which the undertakers committed at the outset is one on which undertakings in any degree novel are more likely to be shipwrecked than any other. I strongly advise you never to begin any new line of steam navigation with a single ship. If you have not confidence in a new line, do not begin it; but if you do, let it be with ships, otherwise you run two risks. First, the risk of total failure, by some accident or mistake that has nothing to do with the undertaking; and second, that if you succeed with one ship only, it will not suffice to maintain a trade with regularity, and your rival, on seeing your success, will be able to start a rival undertaking as quickly as you can build another ship, so that he has every chance of stepping in and reaping the fruit of your labour. The last of these consequences is exactly what followed the undertaking of the *Great Western*. The moment Mr. Cunard saw that she had succeeded he rushed in and built FOUR *Great Westerns*. These he built all alike, all copies of one another, with the machinery of all identical, and the result was the triumphant success with which we are all acquainted. If he had built one vessel only, his failure would have been certain. Such was the misfortune or cause of ultimate failure of the *Great Western*. She was one, and she ought to have been at least two. Two *Great Westerns* early and promptly put upon that line would have made Bristol the great trans-Atlantic steamship harbour of England.

"I now come to the second Bristol ship—the one that ought to have been the second *Great Western*—and in this second ship I regret to say that all the good sense and practical wisdom which had caused the success of the *Great Western* seemed to have abandoned them in the undertaking of the *Great Britain*. What was wanted was a sister to the *Great Western*. What was built was as unlike her as it was possible to conceive. Thus, then, while other people were copying the wisdom of the original Bristol shipowners, they themselves forgot all their wisdom and took to quite another course. What they did was as follows:—

"1. Instead of building a second *Great Western* they built a single ship of a new sort, as different from her as possible, so that they had all the disadvantages of two experimental vessels instead of having a couple of one sort.

"2. The second mistake was one of a still more fatal kind. They determined to make their second ship a museum of inventions. The old model and proportions of the *Great Western* were utterly abandoned, so that there were no two things in common between her and her companion. She was to be 300 feet instead of 236 feet long, 50 feet beam instead of 35; her tonnage, 3,443, instead of 1,340; her horsepower was to be raised to 1,000. Next, in regard to shape. That was entirely revolutionised, and turned into an imitation of Sir W. Symonds' new and empirical form of ship. Next, she was to be made of iron, which was wise for a ship of that magnitude. In regard to her novelties there was no limit, and the whole ship and her machinery was a congregation of experiments. In the middle of her progress she was altered from a paddle-wheel to a screw propeller ship; and that experiment was not enough, for the propeller must needs be propelled by a kind of chain gearing for communicating the power of the engine to the screw. Now the result is well known to you. Nevertheless, it is easy to see that if she had been a simple companion to the *Great Western*, Bristol might have retained the advantages she had achieved; instead of that, she built a ship which had to be sold as a disastrous bargain to ply in the trade of a rival port, where her ingenious engines had to be taken out, her new screw gear got rid of, and the destiny and arrangements of the vessel so changed that she became a new ship, of slow speed and auxiliary power."

From 1844 to 1871 Bristol not only abdicated her pride of place, but made no attempt to utilise the natural advantages she possessed as a seaport. The success which attended the venture of the two steamships above referred to placed an immense power within the reach of Bristol, sufficient to make it the central port for ocean-going steamers, instead of allowing other rival ports to snatch the supremacy which legitimately belonged to her.

In July, 1871, the present Great Western Steamship company was established. The pioneer steamer was the *Arragon*, 1,317 tons gross and 837 net. She arrived in Bristol June 23rd, 1871. Her cost amounted to only half that of the *Great Western*, though nearly of the same dimensions, viz., 245 feet long and 1,317 registered tonnage, and on her first voyage she carried 44 passengers, with a freight of 1,000 tons. This steamer, which commenced her voyage from Bristol to New York on July 1st, 1871, was unfortunately lost in a fog on November 1st, 1882, by going aground in Fox bay, Anticosti island, Gulf of St. Lawrence; but under the able and judicious managers of the line the company has so far developed itself as to have led to the purchase of other steamers, with the engagement of a number of others, and arrangements have been made for a considerable extension of the undertaking, which will give a further material impetus to direct intercourse with the Colonies and the United States.

The following is a list of the company's steamers, with their tonnage:

	Gross.	Net.
Devon	1,856	1,186
Cornwall	1,871	1,205
Somerset	1,923	1,240
Bristol	1,983	1,274
Gloucester	2,004	1,304
Warwick	2,526	1,648
Dorset	2,637	1,716

In addition to the above company, the City line of steamers was established in 1880 by Charles Hill and Son, whose skilful and experienced administration is rendering this second effort a very successful venture. This line has been singularly unfortunate with their steamers. Though established so recently, they have lost no less than three of their vessels, all of them new boats, built to Messrs. Hill's order for the Atlantic trade. The first loss was the *Bristol City*, the first steamer of the line, and she left New York for Bristol in December, 1880, with a crew of 28 hands, and was never afterwards heard of. The *Bath City*, after encountering terrific weather in the Atlantic, foundered off the banks of Newfoundland in 1881, and a portion of her crew was drowned, whilst others died from frost-bite and exposure in an open boat, the survivors being rescued by an American barque. The *Gloucester City* left Bristol on the 8th February, 1883, for New York, and foundered at sea off the banks of Newfoundland on the 23rd February, after having been in collision with ice. The crew of about 28 hands were rescued by the steamer *Freja* and landed at Havre.

The following is a list of the company's steamers:—

	Net Tonnage.
Brooklyn City	1,123
Jersey City	1,261
Llandaff City	1,259
New York City	1,131

During the summer of 1868 the Portishead Pier and Railway Company commenced running a daily service of packets to Lynmouth and Ilfracombe, and have since that date, during the summer, continued to do so. They have a fine steamer called the *Lyn* that performs the journey on an average in five hours.

The Bristol General Steam Navigation Company also, not content to remain limited to the smaller class of vessels for the home and European trade, have entered upon the East India trade, which we may hope is but the precursor of more to follow. This company has communication with Amsterdam and Rotterdam, by their steamers *Sappho* and *Constance*, about every fortnight; with Bordeaux, by the *Calypso*, about every three weeks; with Cork, Wexford, Dublin, and ports in the Bristol channel weekly, by steamers *Briton*, *Argo*, *Juno* and *Xema* every Friday.

The Fell line of steamers run to Antwerp about every fortnight.

The steamers *Avon*, *Princess Alexandra*, *Severn* and *Solway* run to Belfast, Glasgow and Greenock twice a week.

Steamers run at frequent intervals to Hamburg, Nantes, Paris and Rouen, and there is also continuous communication with Cardiff, Liverpool, London, Milford, Neath, Newport, Padstow, Swansea and Wadebridge by well-appointed steamers for passengers and goods.

There are also a number of small steamers and traders, which take goods only, that ply weekly between Bristol and Aberayron, Aberystwith, Boscastle, Bude, Cadiz, Cardigan, Carmarthen, Charente, Chepstow, Gloucester, Langharne, St. Clear's, Llanelly, Lydney, Lynmouth, Lynton, Haverfordwest, Newnham, Oporto, &c.

Although these records of local progress may not show such imposing signs of strength and development as are to be found in many other centres, and even in ports of the Bristol channel, yet they are vigorous steps in the right direction, and Bristolians may fairly congratulate themselves that local maritime interests are so steadily and surely unfolding. The openings, however, are not yet all occupied, and there is still room for a much larger extension of local ocean steamship proprietorship; but Bristol may yet pleasantly dwell on the fact that the increase has been of no mean character, and is still in the full vigour of its development.

(*See* also "Docks," "Imports," "Exports," "Manufactures," "Port Improvements," and "Trades.")

Shows.

BEDMINSTER WORKMEN'S FLOWER SHOW AND HOME ENCOURAGEMENT SOCIETY. Established in 1878. At the sixth annual show, held in a field at Southville on the 18th and 19th July, 1883, there were 563 distinct entries, against 326 competitors the previous year. The subscription list then reached £83, against £47 in 1882, and admittances to the show produced £50 against £30. The prizes awarded amounted to £67 16s. 6d. Edward Parsons and J. R. Tennear, hon. secs.

BIRDS. The Bristol Canary and British and Foreign Cage Birds' Society have now held seven annual exhibitions at the Athenæum, Corn street. It is open to the counties of Gloucester and Somerset.

BRISTOL, CLIFTON, AND WEST OF ENGLAND DOG SHOW. Six annual exhibitions of sporting and other dogs have now been held in the Rifle Drill hall, Queen's road, under Kennel Club rules. The exhibits include St. Bernards (rough and smooth coated), Newfoundlands, bloodhounds, mastiffs, greyhounds, retrievers (wavy and smooth), sheep dogs, pointers (large and small), English setters (other than black and tan), spaniels, bull dogs, bull terriers, fox terriers (champion class), fox terriers, skye terriers, Dandie Dinmonts, Bedlington terriers, Irish terriers, Dacshunds, pugs, toy terriers (rough and smooth), sporting and non-sporting dogs and puppies, and foreign dogs.

FLOWER SHOWS. The Chrysanthemum and Spring Show Society hold two shows annually at the Victoria rooms; established 14 years. George Webley, hon. sec. (*See* "Horticultural Shows.")

REDLAND AND KINGSDOWN WORKMEN'S FLOWER SHOW AND HOME ENCOURAGEMENT SOCIETY. The 11th annual show was held on the 8th and 9th March, 1883, in an iron building adjoining St. Saviour's church, Woolcott park, and comprised spring flowers, window boxes, cases of ferns, models, articles for use and ornament in a cottage home, needlework, cookery, and wheatmeal bread. Joseph H. Perry, 15 Clyde road, hon. sec.

Sieges of Bristol.

The appearance of Bristol in history is very gradual. Of the Roman occupation of the place (if indeed under the Empire it was not an unreclaimed swamp) there is little traceable evidence, and it is not till the time of the Danes that we find any signs of social life at the spot. Of the Danish conquest of Bristol there is no record, but that it was a Danish settlement is clear from the fact that there are yet many Danish coins extant of local mintage, and that Edmund Ironside in 1016 marched upon the garrison of the Danes here stationed and put them to flight. This is the first historical siege of Bristol, if siege it can be called, for the place immediately surrendered.

SAXON SIEGE. In 1068 three sons of Harold—Godwin, Edmund and Magnus—resolving to re-conquer the kingdom of their fallen sire, came at the head of fifty-two ships from Ireland up the Bristol Channel, and finally to Bristol. How strong the place must have been even at that time may be inferred from the fact that the Saxon princes with their fifty-two ships were unable to capture the town, but reversed their prows and made off with judicious speed, leaving it still under the Norman banner.

260

Siege under Edward II. In 1312 there was a rebellion of the townspeople on account of their objection to certain royal imposts payable to the constable of the Castle of Bristol. The place was in a state of anarchy, an irregular warfare being maintained between tower and town for several years. In the spring of 1314 the sheriffs of the counties of Gloucester, Somerset and Wilts collected upwards of 20,000 men, of which army the Earl of Gloucester took the command, in order to reduce the townsmen to obedience; but by the encouragement of John le Taverner, the Mayor, so stout a resistance was made to the King's forces that the siege for the present was raised. In 1316, however, Maurice de Berkeley was ordered to cut off all communication by sea, whilst Badlesmere, the constable of the Castle, carried on the siege by land. Bulwarks were raised against the walls, and battering rams were brought against them from the Castle. For four days the townsmen resisted, but when they found the walls and houses shaken by the engines of the besiegers they surrendered themselves to the royal clemency. The besiegers entered the town and the principal burgesses were thrown into prison, a fine of 4,000 marks being afterwards accepted by the King as indemnity for the insurrection.

Siege by Bolingbroke in 1399. In Shakespeare's *Richard II*. (Act III., Scene 1) is a passage headed "Bolingbroke's Camp at Bristol," where that noble, together with the Dukes of York and Northumberland and other leaders of the people, are represented as presiding at the condemnation of Scrope, Earl of Wiltshire, Sir John Bushey and Sir Henry Green, three of the creatures of Richard II., whose sun had now gone down. Previously to this Bolingbroke, Earl of Lancaster, had descended upon Bristol with his huge northern army, which place surrendered without delay; and after four days' siege of the Castle the governor, Sir William Courtenay, consented to treat with the Duke of York.

Siege of 1642. In preparation for the part soon to be enacted, the great tower of the Castle was restored to its original strength and ordnance planted on the top, the walls of the city were repaired and strengthened, and the gates and portcullises made ready for defence. A fort was erected on the southern skirt of Brandon hill, near the river, thence called the Water fort. This communicated with the fort on the summit of that hill itself, where considerable remains of the redoubt are still to be seen. Brandon fort, trended by a wall to the south-east corner of (now) Berkeley square, passed the top of Park street, and proceeded upwards to the Windmill fort, afterwards called the Royal fort, on St. Michael's hill. The curtain then sloped easterly to Colston's fort, near the "Montague" tavern, and thence onward to the fort at Prior's hill, near the west end of St. James' place and Somerset street, Kingsdown. Hence it pursued its course by Stokes' croft gate, across the river Frome to Lawford's gate. Then, after reaching the Avon, the end of Temple back, it completed its circuit by taking in Temple and Redcliff gates, and meeting the Avon again beyond the latter point. The whole compass of the outworks was five miles. The height of the curtain was in no place more than 6 feet, and the graff, or ditch, did not exceed 7 feet wide and 5 feet deep.

The Mayor (Richard Aldworth) was a Royalist, but his wife belonged in feeling to the aliens. In keeping with his loyalty, he refused the admission of Lord Poulet with the Parliamentary troops into the city; but Mrs. Mayoress and some other women addressed a petition to the Corporation that the Parliamentary forces, with Colonel Thomas Essex at their head, might be received. The request was soon realised (Dec. 5th), Essex, after an affray at Frome gate, finding an entrance at another point, Newgate, when he immediately took upon himself the governorship of the city and castle. He was soon (February 16th, 1643) followed by Colonel Fiennes (son of Lord Say and Sala), with ten troops of horse and foot. Some suspicion of the fidelity of Essex being excited, Colonel Fiennes caused him to be arrested while visiting at the house of his friend, Captain Hill, by Redland green, Fiennes himself then assuming the military command of Bristol.

On March 6th Prince Rupert and his brother Maurice, with 10,000 horse and foot, having marched from Basingstoke, arrived on Durdham down, in the hope that a secret plot of some Royalists within the walls, headed by Alderman Yeomans, of Wine street, and George Boucher, a wealthy merchant of Christmas street, to admit the King's troops into the city, would find a successful issue. The plot failed, the two leaders were hanged, and Prince Rupert for a time withdrew from the place.

On Tuesday, July 18th, Rupert marched from Oxford, and on the following Sunday quartered at Westbury college, two miles north of Bristol, intending to win Bristol once more for the King. On Monday morning the Prince assembled all his horse and foot on Durdham down, sending thence his trumpeter to demand the surrender of the city. On refusal by the governor, batteries were erected to play upon Windmill and Prior's hill forts. Colonel Wentworth was sent to relieve Colonel Washington, who had been stationed at Clifton church, and to cast up a battery against the fort on Brandon hill, and the fire commenced on the side of both factions. No impression being made by the batteries of the besiegers, the next morning a council of war was called, and it was determined to storm the city from all points at once, the time to be daybreak on Wednesday. Accordingly, at three o'clock, the assault began by the firing of the Cornishmen on the other side of the town. A desperate endeavour was made to win the works and line of Prior's hill fort, which was under the command of Robert Blake, afterwards the distinguished Admiral; but after long fighting and the loss of Captain Nowell, with 19 men, no entrance could be effected, the assault on Windmill fort also failing through want of ladders. Meanwhile operations had been more successful elsewhere in the line. Colonel Washington finding a weak place in the curtain running between Brandon and St. Michael's hills, at the point corresponding with the present entrance to Park row, there condensed his attack, and breaking through made passage for horse and foot. Rupert, with a thousand Cornish foot, now arrived to second Washington, and by mid-day the assailants had won their way to the Cathedral, which they invested, together with the adjoining churches of St. Mark and St. Augustine. At two o'clock the governor, who had boasted that a flag of truce should be his winding sheet, made signs for parley, and before ten at night a treaty was concluded, by which it was agreed to surrender the city on condition that the inhabitants should not be plundered. Lord Clarendon estimates that about 500 foot soldiers, besides officers, were killed on the King's side in the several assaults, the loss of the victors being believed to have exceeded that of the vanquished. Besides a contribution from the citizens to save the city from being sacked, as much as £100,000 was seized in the Castle.

The reduction of Bristol by Prince Rupert was followed by other successes on the King's part, and the royal cause was for a while in the ascendant, but the gathering might of Cromwell was destined to undo all that these victories had accomplished. Sherborne having fallen into the power of the Parliament, Sir Thomas Fairfax concluded that a great moral effect would be gained by the capture of Bristol. Accordingly, on Friday, 22nd August, 1645, he arrived at Clifton, and began operations for a siege or storming of the city. On September 4th he sent a summons for the surrender by the Royalist garrison, demanding an answer the same evening. At first Rupert seemed inclined to treat, but the conditions being too exacting and peremptory, negotiations were broken off and the enemy prepared to storm. On the Gloucestershire side everything succeeded. The lines were carried and 22 cannon and many prisoners were taken, and all the forts except Prior's hill fort, which was so high that a ladder of 30 rounds scarcely reached the top. Beneath this place Colonel Ramsborough fought nearly three hours. At length some of the soldiers, entering through the embrasures, helped others up, in spite of the shot from four pieces of cannon, and the colours were captured; the defenders yielded, and the fort was won. The infuriated assailants "immediately," says Cromwell, "put almost all the men in it to the sword." Next day, while Fairfax and Cromwell were sitting within the captured entrenchment discussing their successes, a ball, aimed by a cannon from the Castle, whistled within two handbreadths of them. A little more accuracy of aim might have had the effect of rolling back the tide of war, and been the means of diverting the current of many succeeding years' history.

On the Somersetshire side the attack failed through the shortness of the ladders. But the place was lost to the King, the Prince sending his trumpeter to Sir Thomas Fairfax to desire a treaty for the surrender of the town. This was conceded on less favourable terms than had before been demanded.

"We had not killed of ours in the storm," says Cromwell, "nor in all this siege 200 men. He who runs may read that all this is none other than the work of God. He must be a very Atheist that doth not acknowledge it."

On Thursday the garrison marched out with Prince Rupert at their head. The number of the Prince's foot was about 2,000, of horsemen, including his lifeguards, noblemen and gentlemen, 700. Cromwell waited his coming out, and Fairfax convoyed him over Durdham down to Westbury, where the Prince quartered for the night and departed for Oxford the following day.

The King was at Ragland when the news came of the loss of Bristol. The blow was one of the heaviest he had received, but he made it heavier by dismissing Rupert from his service.

Signs. A peculiarity of the city during the 18th century was the number and oddity of the signs that hung over the shops, and which were engraven on billheads and cards, such as the "golden leg" to represent a hosier, the "wheatsheaf" a corn merchant, &c. As trades multiplied, the ingenuity of younger shopkeepers was taxed to invent new and striking emblems to distinguish their shops; some placed their late master's with their own—hence grew up such badges as the "Eagle and Child," others struck out such grotesque combinations as the "Cock and Bottle," others were perverted by the populace until the "Swan and the Lyre" became the "Goose and the Gridiron." Besides the overhanging and the wall signs, the mercers, hatters, shoemakers, &c., used also to thrust out poles like that of the barber chirurgeon with its spiral tape, upon which they hung samples of their goods. In 1792 a local Act of Parliament was obtained, which compelled the removal of all projecting or overhanging signs, but it has evidently fallen into disuetude by the appearance of Wine, High, Castle, and Old Market streets, &c. (*See* "Public-house Signs.")

Society of Artists. The fourth exhibition of water-colour sketches and paintings from the easels of the members of this society was opened in May, 1883, at the society's rooms, 10 Park street. The exhibits numbered about 120, were confined to local subjects, and included many interesting bits of old Bristol, the opportunities for sketching which become every year more rare. (See "Fine Arts Academy.")

Solicitors. In Bristol there are over 140 certificated individuals and firms practising as solicitors.

Steam Roller, The, was first used in this city in October, 1878.

Stock and Share Brokers. There are 13 firms and individuals, 10 of whom are members of the Stock Exchange. Strict privacy is maintained on the Exchange, and visitors are not admitted. The members of the Exchange meet daily at 12 and 2 o'clock for the transaction of business at St. Stephen's street buildings (Messrs. Bryant, Perry and Lowe's premises). The Exchange was for some time in the Royal Insurance buildings, then transferred to Small street court, and in November, 1882, removed to St. Stephen's street.

Stocks. The last exhibition of paying penalty in the stocks in this city was on Redcliff hill in August, 1826, by two men for three hours, who refused to pay a fine for unseemly behaviour during a funeral in Redcliff church.

Strangers' Friend Society, founded by John Wesley. The recipients of the charity do not chiefly belong to what are called the degraded class. Many of those who are helped are hardworking men and women temporarily overtaken by sudden illness, misfortune or want of work. Visitors faithfully adhere to their principle, never in any case to render material help until after visiting at the homes. This rule not only enables the visitors to render the best possible assistance in all cases where help is really needed, but it also prevents any waste of the society's funds upon professional paupers. Though the name of the society seems to indicate a limited sphere of operation, as a matter of fact there is no other claim to help recognised but that of sore distress. The blind, the lame, the halt, the hungry and the half-clad, the widow and the fatherless, all who are in need and seek the help of the society, find always true sympathy and assistance so far as the funds of the society will permit. The means for the carrying on of this work, for now nearly a century, have never failed, but the claims upon it are increasing year by year. During 1882 the visitors dealt with 3,367 cases and relieved 3,315. Offices, Broad street.

Street Pavements. The Sanitary Authority have placed on many of the public lamps in the principal thoroughfares the notice, "Keep to the right," which, when adhered to, greatly facilitates locomotion in the crowded business thoroughfares.

Streets, Lanes, &c. Within the last quarter of a century large districts in the borough, formerly fields and nursery gardens, have been laid out for building, and operations of an extensive character have been carried on in the suburbs. From 1858 to 1870 many main roads were formed, and since then these have been intersected by streets, and almost every available spot is covered with houses; Bedminster, Totterdown, Knowle, Easton, Stapleton, Ashley, Montpelier, Woolcot park, Clifton wood, the nursery ground from Clifton down station to Apsley and Pembroke roads and Redland bearing witness to the number of new thoroughfares.

The following is a brief description of some of the thoroughfares of the city :—

BALDWIN STREET was once the outer ditch of the city. It was originally called Balderwynne street, supposed to be named in honour to the Queen of William I., whose father was Baldwin, Earl of Flanders. It is said that Henry II. received his education at one of the houses in this street. In 1881 a new thoroughfare was cut through from the Drawbridge, which unites with the original street and now forms one. It contains many handsome buildings.

BARRS LANE is mentioned in 1129, beside which was a "pound" and two great barns.

BARTON, THE, St. James'. The Barton farm is mentioned as early as 1086.

BATH STREET was opened in 1792, its site being provided by the curtailment of Thomas and Temple streets and by the sacrifice of the greater part of Tucker street. Previous to this the only entrance viâ Temple street was through Tucker st.

BELL LANE, at the bottom of Broad street, was the scene of the fires that "Jack the Painter" lit up in Bristol (for incendiarism, in Portsmouth dockyard, he was afterwards hanged).

BRIDGE STREET is built upon the spot occupied by the ancient shambles, or flesh market. It was of some importance in the middle ages and was called Worship street, as it was one of honour and dignity, on account of the merchandise of wool landed there.

BROADMEAD. In the time of William Wyrcestre this thoroughfare was a spacious meadow, from whence it is supposed by some to have derived its name; others again assert that it received its nomenclature from the appellation given to the cloth (brodmedes) made upon this spot in the middle ages.

BROAD STREET, though one of the original thoroughfares of the city, has gradually assumed a totally modern aspect, there being only the gateway and church of St. John. The branch of the Bank of England, the Grand hotel, the Guildhall, and other public buildings are to be found here.

BROAD WEIR. When the second wall of the city was built the Jews built themselves houses here.

CALLOWHILL STREET was named after Thomas Callowhill, a Bristol merchant.

CASTLE MILL STREET, so named because here stood the Castle mill, driven by water which passed from the adjacent mill pond on Broad weir into the river Frome.

CASTLE PRECINCTS embrace the space which lies between the parishes of St. Philip and Jacob on the east and that of St. Peter on the west. the river Frome on the north, and the waters of the Avon on the south. Within these boundaries once stood (as its name implies) the Castle of Bristol.

CASTLE STREET is built upon the site and with the ruins of the Castle immediately upon its demolition in 1654–1666. Before it was made the citizens had to pass down Lower Castle street, along Castle ditch and up Newgate hill in order to get from the east into the city.

CHRISTMAS STREET was so called by William Wyrcestre, who says it was otherwise named Knife or Knightsmiths' street, of course from being inhabited by the cutlers and armourers. The joined thoroughfares of Christ's Mass street and Host street, however accidental in name and juxtaposition, inevitably recall old memories of the sacramental days, and its association with St. Bartholomew's and St. Augustine's does not help to dispel the mediæval atmosphere of the locality. The name of Knightsmiths' street was obtained in 1248. In 1490 it was pitched and paved. The arched entrance to the old religious hospital of St. Bartholomew is the chief object of ancient interest remaining in the street. (See "Schools," sub-heading "City School.")

CLARE STREET was opened in 1770, and was so named from Nugent, Lord Clare, who represented the city in Parliament at the period the street was built. At No. 9 once lived

Richard Priest, woollen draper, who was killed in a duel with pistols between himself and Henry Smith, an attorney at Bristol.

COLLEGE STREET. In 1771 the Bishop's park, where this street now stands, was obtained from the Dean and Chapter by Samuel Worral on a lease of 90 years, at £60 per annum. The ground, before the erection of the present houses, was a paddock, where citizens resorted for the sport of snipe shooting, which bird was to be found there in abundance. A glance down the dull red lines of uniform tenements reveals the fact that they have gone down in the social scale. At No. 48 lodged, in 1794, Robert Southey and S. T. Coleridge, with their common friend George Burnet. In 1795 Coleridge lodged at 25 College street, one pair of stairs room.

CORN STREET appears to have obtained its appellation, not from the wheat field, but from the proper name of one of its chief inhabitants, John Corn, who was of a Shropshire family, but by a deed of 1402 styles himself of Bristol. The street was spoken of as Old Corn street as early as 1200. In this street are to be found the principal banks, insurance offices, Council house, Exchange, &c. (*See* those headings.)

COUNTERSLIP, near Bath street, is a corruption of "Countess's slip."

CULVER STREET occupies the site of the "culver," or pigeon-house, belonging to Gaunt's hospital.

DIGHTON STREET and others in the neighbourhood of King square were commenced in 1755. The street was so called in compliment to the Dighton family, several of whom were interred in St. James' churchyard.

DOLPHIN STREET, formerly Defence lane, takes its name from the Dolphin inn which once stood here. In the large room of this inn the early Bristol Baptists held their meetings.

DUKE STREET, King square, was formerly known as Brick-kiln lane.

ELLBROAD STREET receives its name from Elle bridge.

GREAT GARDENS, Temple street, once bore the name of "Bristol's military gardens." They were in the 18th century a choice resort, and were laid out in the stiff antique style. St. Paul's fair was removed from Temple street to the Great gardens in 1825.

HAYMARKET, THE, was established by the Corporation on October 1st, 1784. The clerk then being furnished only with beams and scales, the magistrates determined to erect a weighing machine, which was opened for public use on the 15th February, 1785.

HORSEFAIR, fronting St. James' churchyard. The meaning and the origin of the place speaks for itself. It presents a few old gabled houses.

HOST STREET, so called because the Host was carried in procession through it. Edward IV., Henry VII., Queen Elizabeth and Charles I. are among the distinguished visitors to Bristol who passed with more or less ceremony and pageantry through the street. In 1490 the street was paved. It is fast being demolished; at the present moment it retains a few old gabled houses that show it to have been once a handsome thoroughfare, but the houses are grimy and squalid, and inhabited by a poor class of people.

JACOB'S WELLS is very ancient; it probably dates back to the time when the Jews buried their dead on the spur of Brandon hill, nearly opposite to this famous spring. The well rises in Clifton hill.

JOHNNY BALL LANE (Maudlin street) is so named from the owner of the property outside the Franciscan convent.

JOHN STREET. The arch at the end of this street, on which a house is built, was a gateway belonging to the old city wall.

KING STREET, Queen square, was constructed in the 17th century. It is a street of many gables, with some fair specimens of modern architecture. The Theatre, Coopers' hall,

Library, and other buildings are worthy of note. (*See* those headings.)

LEWIN'S MEAD, named after Leofyn, youngest brother of Sweyn, Earl of Bristol, 1049. In deeds of the 14th century is named Lowan's mead. There are a few quaint and curious houses left.

LIMEKILN LANE was called Cow Lane down to the time of the Commonwealth.

MARSH STREET. William Wyrcestre describes this street as "a large and long way, where dwelt many merchants and also mariners." In the riots of 1831 this street supplied its quota towards the tumult. In the summer of 1603 a pestilence broke out in Pepper alley in this street, and during a year's devastating progress through the city, it destroyed 2,600 lives. The low public-houses supplied Clarkson, the slave abolitionist, with fertile evidence of the kind required to demonstrate the iniquities of the traffic.

MAUDLIN STREET was formerly styled Magdalen lane.

MERCHANT STREET is called by William Wyrcestre Marshal street. It was a military way from the Castle to Kingsdown, which was the arena for military exercises and tournays.

NARROW WINE STREET. At No. 3 in this thoroughfare was born Matthew Wansborough, the rival of Jas. Watt in the invention, or rather the application, of the crank and flywheel to the steam engine.

NELSON STREET, from St. John's gate to Bridewell street, was formerly called Haulier's lane. In the time of Edward III. it was called Grope lane.

NICHOLAS STREET was a part of the inner pomerium of the city.

NINETREE HILL, at the north end of Stokes' croft, is so called from nine elms that stood upon the knoll. Here, also, was situated Prior's hill fort, Prior's hill being the proper name of the steep.

ORCHARD STREET occupies a portion of the site of the orchard attached to Gaunt's hospital.

PARK STREET. The building of this thoroughfare in Bullock park began in 1775. The viaduct at the bottom was opened 4th April, 1871. At No. 10 resided Hannah More.

PERRY ROAD, a new thoroughfare connecting Park row with Upper Maudlin street, was opened on the 20th August, 1868. The road is called after J. Perry, who was chairman of the Streets Committee.

PETER STREET was formerly called Castle street, as leading to the Castle.

PHILADELPHIA, PENN and HOLLISTER STREETS. In 1697 William Penn, the founder of the colony of Pennsylvania, resided in Bristol, during which period he arranged the building of these streets. Penn's wife was a daughter of Dennis Hollister, from whom was purchased the ground on which these streets are erected.

PHIPPEN STREET, leading from Redcliff hill to Pile street, a thoroughfare of modern construction, was named after the late Robert Phippen.

PIPE LANE is so named from the Carmelites having conveyed water from Brandon hill along this lane to their house on St. Augustine's back.

PITHAY, THE, formerly known as Aylward street, after Aylward, warder of Bristol castle in 930, branches off from the north side of Wine street. Its name implies a sinuous declivity, so called from the Norman *pint*, a well, and *hai* or *hey*, a hedge or inclosure of stone. It stands upon the fortifications of the second wall that surrounded the city. In 1820 some portions of this wall were uncovered, and it was found to be 6 feet in thickness. The city gate that once stood at the end of this avenue was demolished in 1764.

PRINCE STREET was named as a compliment to Prince George of Denmark. John Wesley frequently preached here.

QUAY STREET was known originally as "Old Jewry," or "Jewrie lane," the Jews having probably dwelt in this part. They certainly had

267

a synagogue near here, which is said to have been in a vault beneath what was afterwards St. Giles' church.

REDCLIFF STREET contains a number of massive buildings, the most capacious, perhaps, being that of W. D. and H. O. Wills, tobacconists. Its architecture is a sort of semi-Theban style.

REDCROSS STREET is celebrated as the birthplace of Sir Thomas Lawrence, portrait painter, in 1769. The house, No. 6, still stands.

ROSEMARY STREET was formerly Rosemary lane. In Wm. Wycestre's time it was Rush lane, and at a still earlier date it was called Irish mead.

RUPERT STREET, leading from St. Augustine's back to Lewin's mead, is formed by the covering in of the river Frome, and was opened in January, 1859. The street is so named because the troops of Prince Rupert entered the city in this locality.

SMALL STREET is interesting from having formerly given lodging to many illustrious visitors to the city, amongst whom may be mentioned the Earl of Leicester, the Earl of Warwick (1587), Charles I. (1643), Prince Charles and the Duke of York, Oliver Cromwell (1649), Queen Catherine (1697), James II. (1686), and others. The General Post Office is to be found here.

STEEP STREET, formerly called "Stype street," is now demolished, and has given way to Colston street.

ST. JAMES' BACK. This locality in William Wyrcestre's time was almost wholly occupied as open garden ground, belonging to the few houses of the opulent who were located in that neighbourhood. Wm. Botoner, or Wyrcestre, the great antiquary, was born here in 1415.

ST. MARY-LE-PORT STREET is of very narrow proportions throughout, particularly at the west end, where the houses almost meet at top and nearly overhang the entire thoroughfare beneath. The street was first pitched or paved in 1490. Some of the houses once belonged to the Company of Brewers, whose arms appear on their plastered fronts.

ST. STEPHEN STREET was opened for traffic in 1771. Previous to the building of Clare street it was called Fisher lane, the fish market having been held there.

TEMPLE MEADS. The Joint Railway station and neighbouring buildings now stand where formerly were meads or fields.

TEMPLE STREET and GATE. The present unattractive aspect of this street is in strong contrast to the picture recalled to the imagination by the associations of its name. The extraordinary powers and privileges accorded to the Templars lingered in their district here till the time of Henry VIII., one of these privileges being that of sanctuary within the circuit of their demesnes. As the chief entrance to the town, old Temple gate witnessed some rare pageantry on the approach of the several illustrious visitors to Bristol who passed beneath its arch. The gate stood near the east end of Pile street, which still bears the name. The small portion of Temple street now remaining has a very sorry, grimy and mutilated aspect, but it preserves some quaint gabled houses of the 16th century.

THOMAS STREET. In this street are several old inns identical with those licensed in 1606. Of these are the "White Lion" and "Three Kings."

TOWER LANE derives its name from one of the mural towers of the ancient city being here situated.

TRINITY STREET, behind the Royal hotel, is built on an ancient garden of St. Augustine's monastery.

TUCKER STREET, a narrow thoroughfare adjoining Bath street, so called from being formerly entirely inhabited by clothiers or drugget makers, one of the ancient manufactures of the city. The weaving of cloth was brought from Normandy, and clothmakers were called *tonkers*, from the German *tuch*—cloth; hence *tucking* mill, common in Somerset.

UNION STREET was constructed in 1775. It is celebrated for having Fry's cocoa warehouse in its midst.

VICTORIA STREET, Temple, is a handsome thoroughfare of recent construction, formed out of Temple and Thomas streets. It contains many elaborate buildings, and is the main artery from the city to the Joint Railway station.

WELSH BACK, probably so called from the Welsh coasting vessels being berthed here during their stay in this city. The principal corn warehouses are here situated.

WHITELADIES' ROAD, so termed from a cottage named the Whiteladies', which stood on the site now occupied by the South parade. The road is facetiously known as the *Via Sacra*, from the number of places of worship it contains.

WINE STREET, instead of deriving its name from some connection with the fruitage of the vine, is a misnomer for *Wynch* street, that being the name of the pillory that once stood near the west end of the thoroughfare. *Wynch* means a tourniquet or windlass, as a "wynchwell," and the instrument of punishment was so named from being placed on a turning beam. The street has several historical associations connected with it. Amongst them may be mentioned that Robert Southey, the poet, was born at No. 9 on the 12th August, 1774; Thomas Cadell, the eminent bookseller, was also born in this street. It is now noted for its extensive drapery establishments.

ZION ROAD, Clifton, was begun in 1784.

(*See* "Bridges," "Open Spaces.")

St. Stephen's Ringers.

There is nothing to show when, where, or under what circumstances "The Antient Society of St. Stephen's Ringers" was first established. That it is the oldest of all the existing guilds or societies of Bristol is a matter beyond doubt. It is also clear that it existed in and probably long before the time of good Queen Bess, as the virgin queen has always been greatly honoured in the traditions of the society. The annual meeting is held upon the anniversary of her birth, November 17th; and that, upon the occasion of her visit to Bristol, she was so charmed by the tintinabulatory efforts of the society that she promised to grant it a charter is a matter as firmly established as anything can be established by tradition.

The earliest documentary evidence possessed by the society is a copy of certain "ordinances," dated 1620, which the members bound themselves to observe. The wording is very quaint, and the penalties for infringement of rules quainter still. Some of the provisions tend to show that from its earliest days the society was to a certain extent of a convivial nature. We print here some of the most characteristic clauses of the ordinances :—

Imprimis. For the choosing of every Master you shall put three honest men into the Election, and he that hath most voices to pass on his side shall be Master of the Company of Ringers for the year ensuing.

Item. You shall have four quarter days every year—(that is to say), the 1st, Saint Stephen the Martyr; the 2nd, the Annunciation of the Blessed Virgin Mary; the 3rd, Saint John the Baptist; and the 4th, Saint Michael the Archangel.

Item. Upon every one of the said quarter days every one that is a Freeman of the said Company shall pay to the Master for the time being, for his quarteridge, one penny. And if he doth or shall deny or neglect to pay the same he shall pay, for such his offence, three pence—one penny thereof to the Sexton, and the other two pence to the Company.

Item. There shall be none made free of the said Company unless he give the Company a breakfast, or pay the sum of three shillings and four pence in money.

Item. If any one of the said Company, after the time that he shall come into the Church to ring, shall curse or swear, or make any noise or disturbance, either in scoffing or unseemly jesting, that the party so offending shall pay for his offence three pence, to be divided as aforesaid.

Item. If any one of the said Company, after the time that he shall come into the Church to ring, shall be so saucy as to take the rope to ring before the Master for the time being and the eldest of the said Company who have been Masters shall be settled where they please to ring, the party so offending shall pay, for such his offence, two pence—one penny thereof to the Sexton, and the other penny to the Company.

Item. If any of the said Company shall take a rope out of his fellow's hand when the Bells [are] doing well, and do make a fault, to fly off or come too near, he shall pay for his offence one penny to the Company.

Item. It is agreed that every one that shall be chosen Master of the said Company shall spend, of his own proper money, the sum of two shillings towards a breakfast, and the rest of the Company to pay the rest of the reckoning.

Item. If any one of the said Company shall be so rude as to run into the Belfry before he do kneel down and pray, as every christian ought to do, he shall pay, for the first offence, six pence, and for the second he shall be cast out of the Company.

It will be seen from the above that the society was originally one of bell-ringers pure and simple; but sometime after, the date of these ordinances its nature must have entirely changed, and at least from 1732, from which date the record of its meetings has been kept, has been composed of much the same constituents as at present—gentlemen to whom campanology is a mystery, but who are fond of good fellowship and pleasant gatherings.

For some 150 years subsequent to the abovementioned date the society seems to have had no object save that of meeting once a year, dining mainly, and observing certain old customs which are even now religiously adhered to. Among these may be mentioned a kind of procession which takes place during the annual gathering. A number of the members conduct round the room a person dressed to represent a Spanish Don—a custom which probably is some relic of the Spanish Armada. The ordinances, or—as they are improperly called—the charter, is then read with mock solemnity.

A curious topical version of the old song "The golden days of good Queen Bess" is also sung, each verse being allotted to a different member or honoured visitor, who, unless he wishes to incur certain penalties, must sing. We transcribe the song in full :—

THE GOLDEN DAYS OF GOOD QUEEN BESS.

To my muse give attention, and deem it not a mystery,
If we jumble together music, poetry and history,
The times for to display in the days of good Queen Bess, sir,
Whose name and royal memory posterity may bless, sir.
   Oh! the golden days of good Queen Bess!
   Merry be the memory of good Queen Bess!

Then we laugh'd at the bugbears of Dons and their Armadas,
With their gunpowder puffs and most blustering bravadoes;
For we know how to manage both the musket and bow, sir,
And could bring down a Spaniard just as easy as a crow, sir.
   Oh! the golden days, &c.

Then our streets were unpav'd and our houses were all thatched, sir,
Our windows were all laticed and our doors were only latch'd, sir;
Yet so few were the folks who would plunder or would rob, sir,
That the hangman was starving for want of a job, sir.
   Oh! the golden days, &c.

Then our ladies with large ruffs tied round about their necks fast,
Would gobble up a pound of beefsteaks so fat for breakfast;
While a snugly quill'd up coif their sweet noddles just did fit, sir,
And truss'd they were up tight as rabbits for the spit, sir.
   Oh! the golden days, &c.

Then jerkins of doublets and yellow worsted hose, sir,
With a huge pair of whiskers, form'd the dress of all our beaux, sir;
Strong beer they did prefer to claret, port, or hock, sir,
And no poultry they priz'd like the wing of an ox, sir.
   Oh! the golden days, &c.

Good neighbourhood then was plenty too as beef, sir,
And the poor from the rich never wanted kind relief, sir;
While merry went the mill clack, the shuttle, and the plough, sir,
And honest men could live by the sweat of their brow, sir.
   Oh! the golden days, &c.

Then the folks every Sunday went twice at least to church, sir,
And never left the parson or his sermon in the lurch, sir;
For they judged that the Sabbath was for people to be good in, sir,
And thought it Sabbath-breaking if they dined without a pudding, sir.
   Oh! the golden days, &c.

Then football and wrestling, and pitching of the bar, sir,
Were preferr'd to a flute, a fiddle, or guitar, sir,
And for jaunting and junketting, the favourite regale, sir,
Was a walk to Mother Day's, there to feast on cakes and ale, sir.
   Oh! the golden days, &c.

To greet a royal visit paid to Bristol's loyal town, sir,
St. Stephen's sons, with cheerful peal, their various cares did drown, sir;
When good Queen Bess a code of laws to give did condescend, sir,
Which in her royal *belle*-ship's name we'll manfully defend, sir.
   Oh! the wholesome ringing-laws, &c.

Bristol maids, aye, and widows, too, by royal decree, sir,
From that time made their spouses of this ancient city free, sir;
With privilege beside, which they all inherit still, sir
Of hanging out their smikets white to dry on Brandon hill, sir.
 Oh! the golden days, &c.

Then our great men were good, and our good men were great, sir,·
And the props of the nation were the pillars of the State, sir;
For the Sovereign and the subject both one interest supported,
And our powerful alliance by all Powers then was courted.
 Oh! the golden days, &c.

Thus renowned they liv'd all the days of their lives, sir,
Bright examples of glory to those who survive, sir;
May we, their descendants, pursue the same good way, sir,
And Victoria, like Queen Bess, have her golden days, sir;
And may a longer reign of glory and success
Make her name eclipse the fame of good Queen Bess.
 Oh! the golden days of good Queen Bess!
 Merry be the memory of good Queen Bess!

In 1874 a feeling grew up among the members that a society so closely allied to one of the finest churches in Bristol needed more than the fact of its antiquity and its pleasant annual dinner in order to justify its existence. The rector (Rev. Field Wayet) suggested that it should take for its object the restoration of the grand old church. His proposal was cordially received, and since then the society has devoted itself to restoring and beautifying its parish church. Since 1874, by the exertions of its members, nearly £2,000 has been collected and expended on St. Stephen's church. The cumbrous mahogany Corinthian reredos was removed and replaced by one of stone, designed by C. T. Hansom, F.S.A. The great east window was entirely renovated, the stained glass being by Hardman. New carved oak choir stalls were substituted for the old mahogany structures. The chancel was handsomely tiled, and marble altar steps laid down. During the present year the restoration of the baptistery has been completed, and a handsome font has been placed there. The work of restoration undertaken by the society is by no means finished, its object being to make St. Stephen's church second in beauty only to St. Mary Redcliff.

The treasurer to the Restoration committee is the rector.

The first master of this ancient society whose name has been recorded was Stephen Bangle, in 1732. The present master is A. J. W. Bennett. The chair between these two dates has been filled by many gentlemen whose names are also well known in connection with the commerce of Bristol. There is a small fund (£50) in connection with the society. This was bequeathed in various sums, at various times, by persons who wished a knell to be rung on a certain day. The treasurer is F. J. Fargus.

Suppression of State Regulated Vice. The first public agitation for the repeal of the C.D. Acts took place at the Social Science Congress in this city in 1869. In Bristol there are now a Gentlemen's Committee, a Working Men's Association, and three branches of the Ladies' National Association. J. L. Daniell, secretary of the South Western Counties for the Abolition of State Regulation of Vice.

Suspension Bridge. (*See* "Bridges.")

Swimming.

THE LEANDER CLUB, who meet at Popham's Baths, Kingsdown, numbered, in 1883, 120 members. It was established in 1879. Entrance fee, 2/-; subscription, 2/6. W. Ridler, 47 St. Michael's hill, hon. sec.

Sword Bearer. (*See* also "Corporation Officers.") In 1836, under the old Corporation, John Foy Edgar held this office; he died on November 5th, 1850, aged 83. On November 25th, 1850, Francis Grevile Prideaux was appointed, and he died October 27th, 1865, aged 75. On November 9th, 1865, William Spry Stock succeeded to the office, and he died July 17th, 1877, aged 68. On August 14th, 1877, Edward Stock was elected to the office. In 1883 that gentleman resigned, and J. A. Bush was elected.

Tailors' Hall, Tailors' court, Broad street, is built on the ground granted to the Fraternity of Tailors of St. Ewen's, wherein they met on festival days in their gowns to wait on the Mayor, and where they transacted the business of their society. The hall is now principally used for temperance gatherings. (*See* "Halls, Public.")

Taxation, Imperial. According to the return for 1881, the property and profits assessed to income tax in the city of Bristol amounted to £3,503,629, and the property and income tax total charged was £62,732. The duty charged on inhabited houses was £19,322. For the collection of the land tax, income tax, and inhabited house duty collectors are appointed in the various parishes. The tax surveyor's office is at 63 Queen square; open from 10 a.m. to 4 p.m. daily, and Saturdays from 10 a.m. to 1 p.m.

Teachers. *Pupil Prize Scheme.* The chief object of this scheme is to increase the efficiency of the elementary schools by improving the training and instruction of pupil teachers. This scheme confines its examinations to the subjects that are contained in the Government syllabus, and by so doing it secures pupil teachers from schools of every denomination. The work for each year is divided into three parts, and at the end of three months there is an examination in each part, while the fourth examination embraces the work of the whole year. The benefits of the scheme are acknowledged by all who have given it a fair trial, and these are a large majority of the teachers of Bristol. In no case in which a pupil teacher has done really well have there been withdrawals from the examinations, and in other cases the withdrawals have been so few that in the tenth year the number of departments in connection with the scheme is larger than at any previous time. In other parts of the country there are like schemes, while in several large towns, such as London, Liverpool, and Birmingham, large sums are spent on the teaching and examination of pupil teachers, but in none of these at so small cost as at Bristol. During the year 1883 the four examinations were attended by 278, 282, 294, and 268 pupil teachers, or an average number at each examination of 280. The number of teachers who have obtained 75 per cent. of the maximum marks, and thus gained prizes, is 40. J. D. Griffiths, hon. sec. (*See* "Schools.")

Telegraph. Bristol was connected by telegraph with London and other large towns in March, 1852. (*See* "Post Office.")

Temperance Associations. It will be interesting to record that the first mention of temperance in Bristol is in the form of a challenge from one named William Bulpin, a chimney sweep of Steep street, in *Felix Farley's Bristol Journal,* August 27th, 1836, to discuss the subject; he proposed to adopt the moderate system.

Space will not permit entering into a detailed account of all the temperance organisations now existing. The following rank as the principal ones :—

BAND OF HOPE UNION, established in 1862. Its object is the general supervision of the various bands, without interfering with the local arrangements or internal regulations of any. On the 29th October, 1863, the first anniversary was held at the Athenæum, and for 15 years the annual festival had been held in that hall early in the month of May. In 1873 the report showed that there were 50 bands, with a membership of 8,539; in 1883, the number of bands was 66, and the number of members was about 10,000. J. T. Grace, treasurer.

BLACK RIBBON ARMY, THE, does not go so far as some of the armies in the path of abstinence, yet strictly exacts from all its members industry, temperance, and thrift. Practically the head-quarters are at the Coffee tavern, Cumberland road, and at Avonmouth, where meetings are held every Monday in the dinner hour. The chief objects are, to provide pay in time of sickness, and assistance either to the widow of a member on the death of her husband, or *vice versa*. If a member comes to work or to the lodge meeting in a state of intoxication he is fined; should the offence be repeated he is mulcted in a sum double the first penalty, and the third offence means instant deprivation of membership. The subscription is very low, seeing how quickly a member becomes entitled to all the privileges of the army. Sixpence a week is paid, and in four weeks the subscriber becomes a full member, and, should he fall ill, is entitled to 10/- a week for the first ten weeks, and 6/- for the next ten weeks. The sick are visited at least three times a week by two "black princes," especially appointed for the purpose. At the end of the year the accounts are officially balanced, and the sum remaining in hand after all demands have been satisfied is equally divided amongst the members. This division comes at a season when it is likely to be most useful to a member and his family. For the enjoyment of the army, Messrs. King have provided an excellent and full band. Occasionally there is a grand parade, and on these high festivals everyone appears in the uniform of the army, which is a very effective one, consisting of a dark grey suit with black trappings. The commander-in-chief rides at the head of the column, mounted on a fine black horse. He wears a sword, and his head-gear is similar to that worn by the doctors of the regular army, the feathers being jet-black. The physique of such men as deal-runners, corn porters, and general dock labourers is pretty well known, and to see these all attired in well-fitting tunics and overalls when marching out is a very gratifying and pleasing sight. The army has now been established nearly two years, during which time Messrs. King have kindly held themselves responsible for all the liabilities incurred in case the subscriptions of the members were not sufficient to meet the demands made.

INDEPENDENT ORDER OF GOOD TEMPLARS, a non-beneficiary temperance brotherhood, admitting both sexes. Principles: Abstinence from the use of, or giving to others, anything that will intoxicate; also aim at entire prohibition of the public sale of intoxicating beverages. E. Hodge, Brighton street, City road, district deputy.

SONS OF TEMPERANCE. Registered under the Friendly Societies Acts 1875-6. A sick and burial society, having six branches in Bristol. Fund amalgamated, and having a graduated scale of payments and benefits. Ages from 18 to 45. Registered office, 1 Temple street. E. Grey and F. C. J. Stone, secretaries.

TEMPERANCE SOCIETY AND GOSPEL TEMPERANCE UNION. The former was founded in 1835, and both amalgamated in January, 1883. The secretaries are J. G. Thornton and Rev. T. B. Knight.

WESTERN TEMPERANCE LEAGUE. This organisation publishes a journal entitled *The Western Temperance Herald*. J. G. Thornton, 3 Woodland terrace, Hampton road, sec.

WHITE RIBBON ARMY. The headquarters are at Prince street, Bedminster. The organisation was founded by Mrs Terrett.

YOUNG MEN ABSTAINERS' UNION. The object of this union is to promote total abstinence from all intoxicants, and the diffusion of temperance sentiments amongst young men. Meetings are held every Wednesday evening at the Young Men's Christian Association, St. James' square. The subscription is 1/- per annum. Thos. McCall and William Nott, hon. secs.

There are also societies known as the Western Temperance League, the Blue Ribbon Army, the Bristol Red, White and Blue Ribbon Army, a branch of the United Kingdom Alliance, the White Cord Army, the Friends' Total Abstinence Society, and the Church of England Temperance Association.

Telephone. The Telephone Exchange was commenced in this city in November, 1879, and the following statistics show the growth of the institution :—

Week ending.	No. of Subscribers.	No. of Calls.	Average per Subscriber.
Feb. 27, 1880	20	340	17 per week. 2·43 per day.
Feb. 26, 1881	88	1,915	21·76 per week. 3·62 per day.
Feb. 25, 1882	154	3,261	21·17 per week. 3·51 per day.
Feb. 24, 1883	235	6,669	28·84 per week. 4·72 per day.

The Exchange is open day and night, with the exception of from 9 a.m. Sunday to 9 a.m. Monday, and the subscription is £15 a year, if within one mile of the telephone exchange at Bristol or Clifton (a branch exchange having been recently opened there). The rates in New York are £30, in Paris £25, and in London, Manchester, and Liverpool £20. The cabstands at Bristol bridge, Drawbridge, Blackboy hill, and Whiteladies' gate are connected with the Exchange, and further facilities are promised to subscribers by a communication with the railway stations, and by extending the wires to Stoke Bishop, Sneyd park, &c.

The Bristol Exchange is at present owned and managed by the United Telephone Company Limited. The offices of the Exchange are in the Queen Victoria buildings, High street. In the building is an apartment known as the "switch room;" all the wires are here brought together, and a number of females are engaged throughout the day in listening for the calls of the subscribers and putting them into communication with others. So far as the conversation between the subscribers is concerned, the whole thing is to these young lady operators nothing more than a dumb show, and absolute secrecy, often so essential in communications upon commercial transactions, is ensured. H. F. Lewis, manager for the company in the West of England.

Theatres. The earliest mention of a building used regularly for theatrical purposes in Bristol is contained in an old account-book of Queen Elizabeth's hospital, in the possession of the Charity Trustees. All that is known of this first Bristol theatre is that, under date 1617 and following years the receipt is entered of sums of £1 10s., "rent of the Play-house in Wyne street." Before this time mystery-plays, moralities, and masques had probably been acted in Bristol, in the precincts of the great monasteries, and courtyards of inns and large houses. The "St. Katherine's players," mentioned by Ricart in his *Calendar*, written about 1532, are supposed by the late William Tyson, F.S.A., to have been connected with the Hospital of St. Catherine, at Bedminster. Ricart's audit also mentions sums of 6/8, 10/-, 13/4, &c., as paid in 1532 and following years to various noblemen's players for performing before the Mayor and Corporation in the Guildhall. John Taylor thinks it probable that Shakespeare himself appeared in Bristol, as the company to which he belonged is known to have been here in 1597.

In 1613 theatrical performances were forbidden at St. James' fair, on account of the plague in Wales, from which it appears that they usually formed part of the amusements at these great gatherings. As before stated, nothing is now known of the theatre in Wine street, except the above-named entries of rent receipts, and for nearly a hundred years after this local historians have nothing to tell us of the history of the stage in Bristol.

In 1704 the Puritan element was

so powerful in the city that, on a petition from the grand jury, the acting of stage plays in Bristol was prohibited. It is not known for certain where the theatre was situated in which these plays had been given, but it is supposed to have been in Tucker street (now Bath street), in a house afterwards used as an Independent chapel, of which — Gough was minister in 1714; this building was destroyed when Bath street was made, in 1786. The prohibition of 1704 does not seem to have been quite effectual, as two years later, in 1706, another grand jury brought the subject before the Quarter Sessions, when "Mr. Power and his company" were prohibited from acting stage plays within the liberties of the city. According to the late city librarian (J. F. Nicholls), Power and his company had been performing in the theatre on St. Augustine's back (afterwards Lady Huntingdon's chapel), now Salem chapel, and on this second decision against them they took refuge in the theatre at Jacob's wells. This is probably a mistake. Power's company most likely removed *outside the city* to a building in Stokes' croft, the site of which was nearly opposite the Baptist college. This was used as a theatre for some years, advertisements of performances there in 1743 and 1745 being still in existence.

About 1726 the "new theatre" at Jacob's wells was built by John Hippisley, the original "Peachum" of Gay's *Beggar's Opera*, which was first played in London in 1728, and had the unprecedented run of 63 successive nights. "The Liston of his day," as Hippisley has been called, managed this little theatre successfully for many years, bringing down for his summer seasons in Bristol many actors and actresses from London, where at that time performances were not given during the hot weather. In a little book called *Memorials of the Bristol Stage*, written by Richard Jenkins in 1826, some interesting details are given of Hippisley and other Bristol actors of this period, and the arrangements and incidents connected with the Jacob's wells' theatre are most amusingly described. It was not, apparently, a very complete or attractive structure, for Chatterton lampoons it in a poem called "The Exhibition," wherein he says:—

Lost to all learning, elegance and sense,
Long had this famous city told her pence ;
Avarice sat brooding in a whitewash'd cell,
And pleasure had *but* a Jacob's well.

Two MS. volumes were given by the late Richard Smith to the Bristol Museum and Library, which contain numerous notes on the early history of the stage in Bristol, and copies of advertisements and play-bills from the year 1747 (Jacob's wells' theatre) to 1810 (King street).

The Theatre Royal, in King street, was opened 30th May, 1766, the prologue being written by Garrick, and he also pronounced it to be the most complete of its dimensions in Europe. There was great opposition to its erection, especially by the Quakers. The first performance consisted of a concert of music and a specimen of rhetoric; the latter was a comedy entitled *The Conscious Lovers*. The proceeds of this performance (£63) were given to the Infirmary. It was not till 1778 that a special license was obtained from the King to settle the theatre on a firm basis by overruling the by-laws of the city, under which players in unlicensed houses were liable to be punished as rogues and vagabonds. This theatre is now one of the oldest in the kingdom, and probably the only one in which during its early days such histrionic stars as Shuter, Young, Quick, Siddons, the Kembles, Macready and Powell have appeared. In more recent times its boards have been graced by Marie Wilton (now Mrs. Bancroft), Madge Robertson (now Mrs. Kendal), Henrietta Hodson, Kate and Ellen Terry, Arthur Stirling, Arthur Wood, the Rignolds, and many others, whose successes on the London stage after they left

Bristol caused our little King street theatre to be reckoned as amongst the best schools for actors in England. The original proprietors of this theatre numbered 48, and their shares were £50 each. The shareholders are entitled to a silver ticket, which gives free admission to every performance. The theatre has been under the management of Andrew Melville since the 4th Dec., 1881, when it was re-opened after extensive alterations and renovation.

The latest addition to our local list of theatres is the one in Park row, which was opened October 14th, 1867, Shakespeare's beautiful play *The Tempest* having been selected for the opening performance. The architect was C. J. Phipps, F.S.A., who, in this design, has closely followed the treatment he adopted in the Queen's theatre, Long Acre. The Italian frontage, rather severe, calls for no special mention, but the interior presents many features of note. The design of the auditorium is strikingly original. Each tier recedes, so that two balconies are formed. The plan of the lower box tier may be said to resemble three-quarters of an oval; the upper tier is the same shape, but considerably larger; while the gallery line forms a perfect circle, running round the proscenium and forming a cornice. The dimensions of the house are as follow:—Length from curtain to front of lower boxes, 44 ft. 6 in.; width between lower boxes, 38 ft.; width of proscenium 30 ft., height 28 ft. 6 in.; height from pit to centre of ceiling, 50 feet; depth of stage from curtain line, 60 ft.; width of stage between walls, 64 ft.; width between walls of stage, including scene docks, 107 ft. The decorations, which are Greco-Italian, are all on the flat, and the frieze over the proscenium is embellished with a fine classical representation of Apollo and the Muses. The theatre will accommodate over 2,200 persons. In 1869 the pantomime was *Robinson Crusoe*, and on Boxing Night that year the pit and gallery entrance was the scene of a terrible catastrophe, 18 persons being trampled to death. George M. and James M. Chute are the present managers.

Thorne Society, The, formed of old Grammar school boys. The first dinner of the society was held January 17th, 1872.

Tides in the Bristol Channel and the Avon. The Bristol Channel and the Bay of Fundy are the most remarkable estuaries in the world for the rise of tides. The crest of the free tidal wave of the ocean, which in the deep waters of the Atlantic rolls forward with great force, and while the rate of progress of the crest of the wave onwards towards Kingroad is much diminished, the actual set or run of the tide in flood and ebb, owing to the greater rise and fall, becomes more rapid. There is, as it were, a gradual heaping up of the water, due to the acquired momentum converting a wide wave with small vertical depth into a narrower but deeper wedge-shaped mass. The highest spring tides are from 45 to 47 feet.

As regards the Avon, its course lies at right angles to that of the Severn, and its tide may be considered to be generated from the passing tide of the Severn rather than directly due to the momentum of the original tide wave. As the tide rises in Kingroad it flows into the Avon, and a current is established there which soon acquires a momentum of its own. Owing to the resistances encountered, the high-water mark at Cumberland basin rises on an average about 7 inches higher than it does at the mouth of the river. (*See* "Avon," "Frome," and "Severn.")

Tokens. The Bristol coins of Charles I. are very numerous, although they were all minted in the period between the 27th July,

1643, and the 10th September, 1645, and are distinguished by the mint mark B.R. for Bristol in monogram. All have on the reverse the declaration which Charles made, that he would presérve "the Protestant religion, the laws and liberties of his subjects, and the privileges of Parliament." It is in an abbreviated Latin form, RELIG. PROT. LEG. ANG. LIBER. PAR., and occurs together with this motto from the 68th Psalm, EXURGAT DEUS DISSIPENTUR INIMICI ("Let God arise, let his enemies be scattered.") The gold pieces are sovereigns and half-sovereigns, 140½ grains and 70½ grains weight respectively. The silver coins are half-crowns, shillings, and sixpences.

Besides the legal money, it appears that counterfeit tokens were made at Bristol during the occupation of the city by the Royalist troops. These coins are of two sizes—one about the diameter of a threepenny-piece, the other rather less. They bear on the obverse a rose crowned; on the reverse, a crown, or below it on the exergue. These worthless coins were abolished by Cromwell, and a fresh coinage of Bristol farthings was substituted; these bear the initial "R" under the date.

The Bristol farthing of 1652 is one of the earliest dated town pieces. There are two types. The first of these is circular, eight-tenths of an inch in diameter, and made of copper. Obverse, a ship issuing from a castle (the arms of Bristol); reverse, the letters C.B. (for Civitas Bristol), and in the centre, surrounded by the legend, "A BRISTOL FARTHING." No inner circle on either side. There are several specimens in the British Museum, some differing slightly in their execution. The second type is of copper; diameter, eight-tenths of an inch. Obverse, a ship issuing from a castle, surrounded by a corded inner circle. Legend, "THE ARMS OF BRISTOLL." Reverse, two large letters, C.B., the date below them, all within a corded inner circle.

Some farthings, bearing date 1662, have a small "R" under the date.

In 1811 so great was the deficiency of specie that it was almost impossible to obtain change in silver for a guinea, which would then readily fetch 26/-. Bank notes for £1 formed the chief circulating medium. Shopkeepers gave a premium of 1/- in the pound to obtain silver from those who had hoarded it. To counteract this evil, several Bristol tradesmen issued, with the tacit consent of the Government, sundry silver and copper tokens, which were available for the purchase of small articles and the payment of wages. The shilling tokens were worth intrinsically eightpence, and the sixpenny fourpence. Some copper tokens had been issued during the scarcity of coin in 1793–5.

Tolls or Turnpikes.

Totterdown and Underfall toll gates were ordered to be abolished by the Town Council on June 30th, 1863. Turnpikes were abolished entirely throughout the Bristol district during the year 1867.

Tolzey Court, The,

is the most ancient Court of Record by prescription, which has existed from time immemorial, and, as understood traditionally, from the time of the Saxons. It is certain the court existed long prior to the creation of a sheriff of Bristol, which was not till the year 1373, by charter 47 Edward III.

When the Castle of Bristol became a royal residence, the appendages and appointments of a regal palace became, of course, annexed to it; and accordingly mention is made in the charters and other authentic documents of the King's marshal, constable of the Castle, seneschal, or steward of the household, who were judges of the Palace court, justices of the forest of Kingswood, &c. When this establishment took place the old court of the Hundred became united to the Palace court, in which the King's seneschal was assisted by the bailiff. The court was held at the Tolzey, a place where the King's tolls and duties were collected, and it was called the Court of the Tolzey. The word Tolzey is derived from the Saxon word *Toll*, and denotes a payment. In this Court of the Tolzey all actions of debt, assumpsit, covenant, trespass, trover, and other civil actions arising within the city could be prosecuted by action or by foreign attachment, and its jurisdiction extended to the whole of the county of the city on land, and by water to the Flat and Steep Holms. The trial of the court is by jury, and a plaintiff's costs in a defended action do not in ordinary and usual cases exceed £13, including brief, counsel's fees, trial, verdict, and judgment. A defendant's costs in cases where he is successful are not so much. Charles Greville Prideaux, Q.C., Judge; Arthur H. Wansey, Deputy Judge and Registrar.

Tontine Warehouses, on the Quay, were erected in 1698, and are said to be the first brick buildings in the city.

Town Clerks. The following are the Town Clerks since 1836 :—Feb. 23rd, Daniel Burges (*vice* Ebenezer Ludlow, resigned); died April 16th, 1864, aged 88. March 29th, 1849, Daniel Burges, jun. (*vice* Burges, resigned); died Nov. 10th, 1874, aged 64. Nov. 20th, 1874, Wm. Brice (*vice* Burges, deceased). Sept. 28th, 1880, Daniel Travers Burges (*vice* Brice, resigned). (*See* also "Corporation Officers.").

Town Council. (*See* "Council" and "Aldermen.")

Tract Society, The, is an auxiliary of the parent society, London. Grants of books, tracts, cards, and illustrated papers are made for mission-rooms, Sunday-school libraries, mothers' meetings, hospitals, &c. Jos. Bartlett, hon. sec.

Trade League, Fair, is a branch of the National Fair Trade League Association. It was formed in this city on the 17th November, 1881, and during the winter of that year 22 ward meetings were held under the auspices of the league. The objects the society seeks are the removal of the unequal and unjust conditions under which the country is placed by the absence of free and reciprocal interchange of commerce between this and foreign nations, and advocates the principle that it is the highest policy of any State to develop its internal sources of production. President, Henry Gregory.

Trades. In addition to the "manufactories" (*see* that heading, also "Imports" and "Exports"), there are a number of extensive trades that have hundreds of employés, and large business connections throughout the United Kingdom, in addition to foreign transactions. Prominently amongst the trades of Bristol is that of grain, the principal warehouses being on the Welsh back. During the year ending Dec. 31st, 1883, 2,199,190 qrs. were imported into Bristol, Avonmouth, and Portishead, being an increase of 220,706 qrs. over the previous year. No port in the United Kingdom is better situated to receive and distribute grain to all centres in the midland and western counties of England than Bristol, and there is every prospect during future years that the grain, flour, seed, and oil-cake trade will continue to develop and enlarge. The timber trade is also an important one, nearly the whole of the premises in Canon's marsh and the lower portion of Cumberland road being devoted to this branch of trade. During 1883, 6,333,033 cubic feet of timber were imported into Bristol, and the previous year 6,189,392 feet. Another staple trade of the city is that of oils and petroleum. In this respect it ranks as third in the kingdom.

The resumption of the ocean steam trade with America and other places has given a great impetus to the provision trade in Bristol, bringing to the front several houses of enterprise and opening up new branches of business for firms of established reputation. Freights to Bristol are as low as those to Liverpool, and provisions can be bought as cheaply in the former as in the latter port; in fact, many buyers who formerly were supplied at Liverpool have been attracted to the Bristol market.

Trade Protection Societies. The following are the principal:—
BREWERS' MUTUAL PROTECTION ASSOCIATION. J. S. Pitt, John street, secretary.
BRISTOL AND WEST OF ENGLAND MERCHANTS' ASSOCIATION. E. T. Collins, secretary, 39 Broad street.
BRISTOL PROVISION TRADE ASSOCIATION. Chas. Gardner, president.
BRISTOL, WEST OF ENGLAND, AND SOUTH WALES PROTECTION SOCIETY, 4 Nicholas street.
KEMP'S MERCANTILE OFFICE. S. Sprod, 13 John street, agent.
MASTER BUILDERS' ASSOCIATION. W. H. Phillips, Small street, sec.
MERCANTILE AGENCY. H. W. Barber, 11 Small street, secretary.
STUBBS' MERCANTILE OFFICE. L. Hockridge, Nicholas street, manager.

Trades' Associations, Workmen's. The following are the principal in this city, most of which meet at the Star coffee-house, Old Market street:—Boilermakers' Society, Boot-top Cutters' Union, Brushmakers' Trade Society, Builders' Labourers' Society, Carpenters' and Joiners' Society, Clickers' Trade Society, Coopers' Association, Engineers' Society, Operatives' Trade and Provident Society, Painters' Society, Printers' Society, Shipwrights' Society, and Stonemasons' Society. A congress in connection with trades' unions was held at the Athenæum on September 9th, 1878.

Trades' Council, The, meet at the Star coffee-house. It was established in 1873, and revised in 1877 and 1883. The Council is composed of representatives of duly organised trade societies, and secures for them a permanent centre of communication, with ready means of rendering mutual advice and assistance in times of difficulty or distress. John W. H. Wall, 38 Croydon street, Easton road, secretary.

Training Ships.
DÆDALUS. On the Floating harbour, at Mardyke, is an old man-of-war frigate called the *Dædalus*, now used as a training ship for the Naval Reserve. An incident in this ship's history has made her name familiar. In August, 1848, the great sea serpent, 100 feet long, with head 16 in. wide, and jaws that when open would hold a good-sized man upright, came swimming at the rate of 15 miles an hour, and paid a passing visit to this good ship, the *Dædalus*, in the South Atlantic Ocean. Perhaps he thought her "very like a whale" (some people thought he was); however, the ship carried too many guns, so his ophidian majesty politely made his bow, passed under the ship's beam, and went about his business. The Bristol Royal Naval Artillery Volunteers drill on this ship.
FORMIDABLE. This vessel, with its tender, the *Polly*, is stationed at Kingroad, off Portishead pier. It is called the Bristol training ship, and is for homeless and destitute boys. The ship is certified under the Industrial Schools Act for the reception, maintenance, and education of such of the above class as have not been convicted of felony. Boys may be received without a magistrate's order, on a guarantee of a weekly sum equivalent to the State allowance of 6/-. No boy who has been sent to prison can be admitted. The *Formidable* is 2,289 tons burthen, pierced for 84 guns, and carries a crew of between 800 and 900 officers and men when in

commission. The vessel was lent by the Admiralty for an industrial ship in 1869, and arrived at Kingroad in September that year. She is associated with and perpetuates the name of the grand old English *Formidable*, Sir George Rodney's flagship, which broke the line of battle of the French fleet in April, 1782, and settled the victory of that eventful day. Anchored 400 yards off the pier, she can be visited at any time except Sundays, and she is well worth a visit. She is admirably adapted for the work, and has accommodation for 350 boys, very nearly that number being now on board. Since the institution was established no less than 1,102 boys have been trained and passed out: 757 of these have gone to sea, the remainder into the army, to employment ashore, or have emigrated. The boys, in addition to a large gymnasium on board, have a fine swimming bath launched every summer in the dock. The *Polly* tender, in which 30 boys at a time are taken for practical training during her summer cruising, proves a valuable addition to the ship's good work. Capt. Nicholetts, R.N., superintendent. (*See* "Schools," sub-heading "Industrial Schools.")

Tramways. The system of tramways between the Drawbridge and Redland was laid down by the Corporation in 1873. The first car tried on the line was on July 30th, 1875, though not opened for traffic till taken over and worked by the Bristol Tramways Company Limited, in conjunction with the following routes, which it has developed and is still working:—Redland section, from Perry road to Redland, opened August 9th, 1875; section from Perry road to Old Market, opened September 30th, 1876; Victoria street section, as far as Bath bridge, opened April 12th, 1879; from Bath bridge to the Three Lamps, Totterdown, November 8th, 1879; Hotwells section opened June 24th, 1880; Bedminster section opened November 17th, 1880; steam tramway to Horfield opened November 18th, 1890 (steam-engines ceased running November 4th, 1881); Baldwin street and Bath street and Tower hill line opened April 30th, 1881; double line, from Park street to Redland, opened November 23rd, 1882. The company has expended a sum of about £175,000 in establishing a complete system for the city and suburbs, and carry over 5¼ millions of passengers annually. Rails were laid in 1882 in conjunction with the Horsefair and the Drawbridge, but up to the present time this section has not been opened for traffic. The company has 40 cars running daily over the various sections of their line at intervals of a few minutes from 8 a.m. to 11 p.m., and the average distance each car covers is 54 miles daily, so that the mileage covered by all the cars daily is equal to a journey of 2,160 miles. The horses work 3½ hours per day, during which period they each traverse about 14 miles. On Sundays the cars commence running at 2 p.m. to 10 p.m. G. White, secretary; C. Challenger, Bristol bridge, traffic manager.

Tyndall's Park. (*See* "Open Spaces.")

Unions or Workhouses. There are three within the province of the city:—

THE BARTON REGIS, formerly the Clifton Union, is at Eastville. It was founded in 1837, and is constructed to accommodate 1,180 inmates. Meetings of the Union are held at the Workhouse every Friday at 10.30 a.m. John Yalland, chairman; C. H. Hunt, clerk.

THE BEDMINSTER WORKHOUSE is at Long Ashton, three miles from the city. Meetings are held every Tuesday, at 10.30 a.m. H. L. A. Weatherley, chairman; H. O'B. O'Donoghue, clerk.

THE BRISTOL WORKHOUSE is at Stapleton. Its site occupies about twelve acres of ground, and was purchased by the Government at the commencement of the present century on which to build a prison, well known in the locality as the French prison. When peace with America and France was restored, the place was neglected and fell almost into a state of decay. In 1838 the Bristol Incorporation of the Poor purchased the property, to convert it into a supplementary workhouse to St. Peter's hospital. As the number of inmates increased it was found impossible to carry out that classification so essential to a well-regulated house. In 1860 the Incorporation of the Poor decided to build a workhouse, and on the 13th April, 1860, Thomas Brooks, builder, of this city, signed a contract to complete the new building for £19,000. James Medland and Alfred Wm. Maberly, of Gloucester and London, were the architects. John Perry was then the governor of the Incorporation. The building by the time it was finished cost about £23,000. In addition to this there is a hospital for infectious diseases, built for £3,000, which is said to be the best in the West of England. There is also an infirmary containing 150 beds. The boys' and girls' schools are the only portions remaining of the French prison. All the buildings will together accommodate about 1,590 inmates. R. T. Hughes, master. (See "Incorporation of the Poor.")

University College was founded in 1876, to supply a need felt for years in the city. Various circumstances led to its establishment, although the scheme took practical shape through an appeal made to the citizens by the faculty of the Bristol Medical school for assistance, that additional accommodation might be provided for its students. The instruction in science and other subjects which University college now so admirably affords was formerly given through the Cambridge extension lectures, and evening classes under the auspices of the South Kensington Art Department. Sufficient funds were received to enable the college to be started, and towards the cost of maintaining the institution Balliol college and New college, Oxford, each promised £300 a year for the first five years; the Clothworkers' company gave an assurance of aid to the extent of £500 per annum, on condition that instruction should be given in clothworking, scouring, bleaching and dyeing, and that lectures in the same should be delivered at Stroud; and £1,300 a year was guaranteed by various citizens. With these assurances, and about £22,000 having been subscribed, preparations were made to launch the college. A council was elected, the Rev. Dr. Elliot, Dean of Bristol, being president, and E. Stock secretary. In May, 1876, two professors and four lecturers were advertised for, and on October 10th of the same year the college commenced its operations in the building in Park row formerly used as an institution for the deaf and dumb, the objects of the college being to supply for persons of either sex above the ordinary school age the means of continuing their studies in science, languages, history, and literature, and particularly to afford appropriate instruction in those branches of applied science which are more nearly connected with the arts and manufactures. In the same year the seal of the college was affixed to an agreement between the college and the Bristol Medical school, whereby it became affiliated with the college, in accordance with the articles of association. The start was encouraging, although the want of room in the temporary premises was a considerable drawback. The college progressed, and widened the scope of its teaching, subjects and professors being added as it went on, and scholarships as they were granted were open to competition, and afforded an encouragement for earnest work on the part of students. Professor Marshall was appointed principal in July, 1877, and continued to hold that office until 1881, when he resigned, owing to ill-health, and Professor Ramsay succeeded to the post. For several years the inconvenience arising from instruction being obliged to be given at different buildings had to be borne with; but early in the year 1880 the council, who had before the starting of the college secured a piece of ground in Tyndall's park, adopted the plan of C. F. Hansom to place on it a permanent building. The first wing of the college was opened in October, 1880; but as it did not afford sufficient space for all the classes several departments had still to remain in Park row. Additional funds having been secured, a second wing was built; and when it was completed, in January, 1883, the long looked-for desideratum was secured—namely, having all the departments practically under one roof; for although the structure used by the medical school is at present detached from the main building, it will ultimately be incorporated in the college when the scheme is complete. This is the present state of the college. Though the space is very limited, the two wings are fitted up on the best possible principles for teaching the various subjects. From time to time progress will be made towards completing the college as funds come to hand, but the greatest difficulty now is that of finance, as has been the case throughout.

A botanical garden has been arranged in front of the building for the benefit of students.

The college is open to men and women, and lectures and classes are held every day and evening through the session. The scholarships in connection with the college are:— Three Gilchrist scholarships, each of the value of £50 per annum and tenable for three years. Three general scholarships—1st, value £25; 2nd, value £15; 3rd, value £10. One Chemical scholarship, value £25. Two Catherine Winkworth scholarships—1st, value £15; 2nd, value £15. Open to women only. All except the Catherine Winkworth scholarships are open to men and women. As to the support of the college, comparatively great results have accrued from very small resources. The annual subscriptions amount to about £1,200. The average total receipts from students has been about £1,850, but during the session 1883-4 it increased to £2,200. The annual expenses of the college are about £4,600. In 1876, when the college was opened, 423 students were enrolled. During the succeeding sessions the number of students fluctuated. In the day and evening classes of the session 1883-84 539 students were enrolled. Although this number was exceeded in 1878-79, when 577 students were in attendance, the session of 1883-84 was the most successful in regard to entries to the various classes, they being 908 against 850 entries in 1878-79. The engineering department especially has grown considerably. District classes are held at Redcross street and Bedminster in connection with the college. At the class in Redcross street in 1882-83, when it was first opened, there were 49 students, and in 1883-84 they had increased to 96. At the Bedminster class, opened in 1883-84, 25 students were enrolled.

Little or nothing relating to the Medical school has been said in the above short sketch. The date 1828 is given as that when the Medical school was founded. Long before that time lectures on chemistry and medicine were given, and regular courses of lectures on anatomy by two of the surgeons to the Infirmary. Dissecting rooms were also opened, under the direction of Dr. Riley, in Lower College green, and another at the rear of 25 King street, the then residence of H. Clark. Those were times when difficulties were experienced by everyone who wished to pursue medical and surgical studies, as the Legislature threw obstacles in the way of the most necessary branch of training—namely, dissecting. Much interest was taken in the lectures given by Dr. Riley, and so greatly did they become appreciated and their value recognised, that he and Hy. Clark were induced to prepare and issue a prospectus of a medical school, to be opened at premises in Old park. During the first twenty years of its existence no support or encouragement was accorded the school by the public or the profession; but gradually the claims of the school came to be recognised, and for many years now it has been in a prosperous condition, especially since its affiliation with the University college. Of the pupils who have passed through the school, many have attained high distinction. The statistics given above do not at all relate to the students of the Medical school; for, although affiliated with the University college, it is carried on as a separate department. With its fame has the number of its pupils grown, and with the extension of researches in medicine and surgery have more perfect appliances for teaching been secured. During the session 1883-84 97 students attended the school.

Students at the school have the privilege of continuing their practical studies in medicine and surgery at the Infirmary and Hospital, in connection with which institutions are valuable scholarships and prizes. The Medical school, together with the Infirmary and Hospital, provide for every detail of the professional curriculum required by the University of London, and students can complete at these institutions the entire course of study required for the diplomas of the Royal College of Physicians of London, the Royal College of Surgeons of England, the Apothecaries' Society of London, and the Army and Navy Boards. The prizes connected with the Infirmary are Suple's Medical Prize, consisting of a gold medal, value five guineas, and about seven guineas in money; Suple's Surgical Prize, similar in character; Clarke's Prize, consisting of the interest of £500, given to the most successful student on the completion of his third year's study; Tibbits' Memorial Prize, being the interest of £315, awarded the student who shows the greatest proficiency in practical surgery; Crosby Leonard's Prize, being the interest of £300, a surgical prize; the Pathological Prizes, value three guineas each. The scholarships and prizes connected with the Hospital are: The Martyn Memorial Entrance Scholarship, value £20, awarded to the most successful competitor in the competitive examination in subjects of general education; Clarke Scholarship, a surgical prize of £15; Sanders' Scholarship, being the interest of £500, offered for proficiency in medicine, surgery, and diseases of women; Lady Haberfield Prize, the interest of £1,000, also awarded for proficiency in medicine, surgery, and diseases of women. All the scholarships and prizes at both institutions are given annually. The Medical school has a governing body of fifteen members, five of whom are elected by the council of University college, one member by the committee of the Infirmary, one by the committee of the Hospital, three members by the staff of the Infirmary, three by the staff of the Hospital, and two by the faculty of the Medical school. William Proctor Baker is the chairman, and Dr. E. Markham Skerritt dean of the faculty. The council of University college consists of twenty-two members. Eleven are elected by the governors of the college; one member each is nominated by the Vice-Chancellor of the University of Oxford, the Vice-Chancellor of the University of Cambridge, the Vice-Chancellor of the University of London, the Lord President of the Privy Council, by Balliol college,

Oxford, by New college, Oxford, by the principal and professors of the college, by the Worshipful the Clothworkers' company, and two members by the Bristol Medical school. The Rev. Gilbert Elliot, D.D., Dean of Bristol, is president and *ex-officio* member of the council; Albert Fry is chairman; Wm. Killigrew Wait, vice-chairman; Wm. Proctor Baker, treasurer; and Alfred E. Stock, secretary. Governors of the college are:—(1) All donors of £50 and upwards for life, and all annual subscribers of £5 and upwards during subscription; (2) nominees of corporate bodies or associations, who are donors of £250 or upwards in perpetuity, or annual subscribers of £10 or upwards during subscription; (3) certain official and representative persons. Governors are entitled to vote according to the amount of donation or subscription.

When the University buildings are completed they will form a handsome addition to the present scientific and educational establishments in Bristol. It will be Gothic in style. There will be four sides and a central open quadrangle, and the section devoted to medical teaching will unite it with the Museum buildings. The front of the college, to face the Museum road, will be highly ornamented, and a tower will occupy the centre. The main buildings will be built of Hanham stone with freestone dressings, similar to the two sections already erected, and the front will be of freestone. The estimated cost of the structure when completed will be £50,000. Upon the two portions now finished and in use between £12,000 and £15,000 have been spent.

Vaccination. All persons may avail themselves of the services of the medical gentlemen appointed to the district in which they reside *free of charge*, the Act requiring in all such cases that the expenses be defrayed by the Guardians or Corporation of the Poor. Children must be vaccinated under three months old, under a penalty of 20/-.

Victoria Rooms, Queen's road, occupies the finest site in Clifton. The spacious and noble portico of this fine façade is supported by a cluster of massive Corinthian columns, which bear a rich entablature and pediment, with classic carvings in high relief representing the "Advent of Morning." A broad flight of steps leads up to the building, flanked by colossal sphinx on either hand. The building was commenced in 1840, and cost £20,000. It was opened on the 24th May, 1842, the occasion being celebrated by a public dinner presided over by the Mayor, G. W. Franklyn, and at which about 300 guests were present. The saloon, which is 118 feet long and 55 feet wide, and will accommodate 1,700 people, contains a grand organ, which formerly stood in the nave of St. Paul's cathedral, but which was originally built for the Panopticon, Leicester square. There is also a small room in the building which will hold about 400. (*See* "Halls, Public," for hiring, &c.)

Volunteer Corps.

THE OLD BRISTOL VOLUNTEERS were enrolled in the year 1797, and on the 19th May that year the regiment, consisting of ten companies, was reviewed for the first time on Durdham down, by Lieut.-General Rooke. In 1804 they were employed in active garrison and prison duty, having to mount guard over 500 French prisoners who were lodged in a building at Stapleton, afterwards known as the French prison. Colonel Gore was the Lieut.-Colonel of the Royal Bristol Volunteers, and, according to the inscription on the monument raised to his memory in Bristol cathedral by the whole regiment — officers, non-commissioned officers and privates—"in public and unanimous testimony of esteem for his character as a soldier and a gentleman." His spirit and military knowledge eminently contributed to the high reputation of the regiment for skill and discipline, and preserved it in harmony and order until it was finally disbanded in 1814.

FIRST (CITY OF BRISTOL) VOLUNTEER BATTALION GLOUCESTERSHIRE REGIMENT was the earliest battalion in this city under the Volunteer Act. On May 18th, 1859, the first meeting was held in furtherance of the volunteer movement, and at a committee meeting held three days afterwards we find that rifle green (to which the corps still adhere) was determined upon as the colour of the uniform. The motto of the old Bristol Volunteers, "In danger ready," was adopted, and the arms of the corps have been from the first the city arms, surmounted with cross rifles as crest. The equipment then cost about £9 per man, and had to be defrayed either by subscription or by individual members. Offices and orderly room were first obtained for the corps in the basement of the Exchange, the quadrangle of which, then not roofed in, formed a suitable place in summer for recruit and setting-up drill; and the Society of Merchant Venturers placed at the service of the corps an open space in the rear of their hall in King street, in which the members learnt the "goose step" and squad drill. Queen square, too, was frequently resorted to for company drill and for occasional parades, and the Observatory hill long remained a favourite place for morning drills. The carriage drive alongside the Great Western hotel in College green (now the Turkish baths) and a large enclosed space in the rear were rented for drill purposes, and were used until the erection of the Drill hall, at the top of Park street. The first public parade of the corps was on the 24th of September, 1859, and took place in Queen square. Nearly 600 members had by this time been enrolled, but only about 300 had passed into the ranks, or been provided with their uniforms.

In the spring of 1860 the volunteer officers of the country were presented at court, and on the 23rd of June in that year came the memorable review of volunteers before the Queen in Hyde park. The Rifle corps went up in strong force, and won the highest praise for the state of efficiency they had acquired in so short a period. The first inspection was to have taken place on August 25th, 1860, and there was a muster of 619 of all ranks in the Exchange; but the rain descended in torrents, and it was deemed inadvisable to march the regiment to Durdham down, and it was therefore inspected on the following Saturday, September 1st.

In 1883 the Rifle corps became more intimately connected with the regular army by being constituted the 1st (City of Bristol) Volunteer Battalion of the Gloucestershire Regiment. The Bristol Rifle corps has taken part in all the great reviews of volunteers held in the south-western or midland districts. The first was the Gloucester review, held on September 18th, 1860, at which there were 6,000 volunteers under arms, and the Bristol Rifles numbered one-twelfth of the whole, viz., 500. The Warwick review was on July 24th, 1881, and the Bristol Rifle corps then numbered 550. The review on Durdham down took place on June 18th, 1862. The Oxford volunteer review was on June 24th, 1863, and was attended by the Bristol Rifles; and at the Windsor review, on July 9th, 1881, the Bristol Rifle corps numbered 779.

The first rifle range which the corps possessed was situated at Sneyd park; but on the construction of the Port and Pier railway, which ran through the centre of it, a removal was necessary, and ground was taken at Bedminster. Subsequently an extensive range was secured on the banks of the Severn at Avonmouth. From its foundation to the present time, the corps has enjoyed an enviable reputation for the number of skilled marksmen it has produced and the high standard of excellence it has maintained in musketry practice. Many of the chief honours obtainable at Wimbledon have from time to time been won by Bristol riflemen, and again and again has the regiment met picked teams from crack corps in various parts of England in friendly shooting matches, and invariably have they been successful.

Honorary members are admitted to the corps, without being subject to military drill, but entitled to wear the uniform, attend practice, and enjoy all the other priviliges of the corps, on paying an entrance fee of £5 5s. and an annual subscription of £3 3s. Since the formation of the corps nearly 6,000 men have passed through its ranks. Arthur Mowbray Jones, colonel; W. R. Worsley and E. M. Harwood, majors.

ARTILLERY CORPS. At a meeting, presided over by the Mayor, on the 12th November, 1859, Colonel (then Major) Savile was requested to raise a corps, and the proposition having received the sanction of the Secretary of State for War, on the 21st December that year Major Savile was gazetted Major Commandant of the First Gloucestershire (Bristol) Artillery Corps. On the marriage of his Royal Highness the Prince of Wales, on March 10th, 1863, the guns of the corps fired a royal salute on Durdham down; and on August 22nd in the same year two Whitworth guns, purchased by private subscription, were presented to the corps. The drill hall erected in the parade ground was opened March 20th, 1865.

Drills are held daily at 7.30 a.m. and 7.30 p.m. from Easter to Whitsuntide. The corps, too, has been familiarised with active military duty by frequent encampment at Portishead, Clevedon, and Brean down. The first camp at Portishead battery was formed in May, 1871, and in the summers of 1873, of 1876, and of 1880 the regiment was under canvas at Portishead, on two of these occasions for nearly a month. On June 15th, 1874, the corps went into camp on Brean down; on July 17th, 1878, a camp was formed at Clevedon; and on July 12th, 1879, a portion of the brigade attended a camp formed at Staddon heights. The corps was present at the great review in Hyde park in 1860, at Gloucester in the same year, at Warwick in 1861, on Durdham down in 1882, at Oxford in 1863, at Hyde park in 1863 and 1864, at Wells in 1865, on Lansdown in 1866, at Portsmouth in 1868, and at Windsor in 1881, at which review it was estimated there were 53,500 volunteers present, and the Bristol Artillery corps numbered 420 of all ranks. Besides these the corps took part in a sham fight at Cadbury camp in August, 1867, and at Almondsbury in June, 1869; attended the demonstration and fired a salute at the opening of the Clifton Suspension bridge on December 9th, 1864, and has shared in many other public demonstrations. In March, 1880, an order was promulgated by the Secretary of State for War directing that the First Administrative Brigade of Gloucestershire Artillery Volunteers should be consolidated into a single corps, with headquarters at Bristol, to be known as the 1st Gloucestershire Artillery Volunteers, and its establishment to consist of 720 of all ranks, divided into nine batteries. The Clevedon, Newnham, and Gloucester corps, which orginally formed an administrative brigade to the Bristol corps, therefore ceased to exist as separate corps, and became batteries 7, 8, and 9 of the consolidated corps. The strength of the Bristol corps at the end of the volunteer year, 1860, was 312, and of the headquarter batteries of the consolidated corps, in 1883, 450. In 1880 a cadet corps was formed, consisting of boys attending the Bristol Grammar school. Both in carbine and heavy-gun prize competitions the Bristol artillerymen have won considerable renown, and have established the reputation of the corps year by year at the National Artillery Association meetings at Shoeburyness. H. B. O. Savile, R.A., hon. colonel; A. H. Versturme, colonel; W. F. Nelson, major.

BRISTOL ENGINEER VOLUNTEER CORPS was originally formed in April, 1861, amongst the employés of the Bristol and Exeter Railway Company, in their locomotive sheds in Bath road. In 1866 the headquarters were removed to the offices in the basement of the Exchange, formerly used by the Rifle corps, and the recruiting of the regiment was not restricted to men in the employ of the railway company. In 1867 the Bristol corps and the Gloucester corps were formed into an administrative battalion. In 1880 the War Office reorganised the administrative battalions and formed them into a consolidated body; the Bristol Engineer corps was the only case in which a separate battalion was formed from an existing administrative corps, and that was done in recognition of the vitality shown by the Bristol Engineers, and the thoroughness of the work done by them. When the headquarters were removed to the Exchange the corps suffered under the disadvantage of having no yard for engineering practice. A removal of the headquarters was made to Avon street in 1873, where they remained established for ten years, until, in 1883, the permanent headquarters were secured for the regiment in Trinity street, and for the past two years the engineering work has been carried on in a yard in Canons' marsh. The possession of the spacious drill shed and the convenient offices is producing its effect, not only in an improved tone, but in increased strength, the present number of members enrolled being within 20 of the authorised establishment, 700. Since the corps was established 2,540 have passed through the ranks. Detachments from the Bristol Engineers have attended the Royal Engineers' camp of instruction at Chatham since 1874, and have earned distinction by the knowledge they have shown of practical engineering. The field officers and all the captains hold certificates of proficiency for having passed through an advanced class of instruction at the School of Military Engineering at Chatham; and of 22 such certificates held by the whole of the Volunteer Engineer officers of the kingdom the Bristol corps enjoys the distinction of holding the large proportion of nine. The battalion attended the local reviews at Lansdown and at Cadbury camp, and at the Windsor review, in 1881, the strength of the regiment was 570 of all ranks. Though the Engineers naturally devote their best energies to engineering, they nevertheless find time to make good practice at the rifle range, and some of the best prizes at Wimbledon have been won by its members. The rifle range at Bedminster is admitted to be one of the best in the country. From the earliest establishment of the regiment it has had an excellent brass band, consisting, even to the instructors, solely of volunteers. There is also a drum and fife band and a bugle band in connection with the corps. E. C. Plant, lieutenant-colonel; H. Wiltshire, major.

CLIFTON COLLEGE CADET CORPS. This, the first Engineer Cadet corps in the country, and the only one connected with a first grade public school, was established February 1st, 1876, with 80 members. From the year 1878 the Clifton College Cadets have been represented in the public schools (Ashburton Shield) and the cadet corps' trophy competitions at Wimbledon. The present strength of the corps is 111, and 520 have passed through its ranks, a large percentage of whom are now holding commissions in the army. Many of the boys on leaving Clifton go to Woolwich or Sandhurst, and the military training they receive in the Cadet corps they find of great service to them in pursuing their studies in preparation for examination for commissions, and the various cadet corps of the different public schools have furnished very many excellent officers to the volunteer service. In addition to the ordinary drill, engineering work is done very thoroughly by the cadets at Clifton college, and they are exercised in spar bridging, barrel pier bridging, modelling, knotting, and lashing. It forms a recognised part of the recreation of the college, and it is managed by the school officers, who are students in the sixth form. A strong representative company of cadets was attached to the battalion at the Windsor review. The present officers are Capt. R. S. Giles, Lieut. H. R. Jupp, Lieut. E. G. Burr, and Lieut. Adair.

ROYAL GLOUCESTERSHIRE HUSSARS (BRISTOL TROOP). This troop was formed in 1883, and numbers nearly 50. It is attached to the Royal Gloucestershire Hussars, a regiment of yeomanry cavalry long associated with the ducal house of Beaufort. T. Butt Miller, captain.

ROYAL NAVAL ARTILLERY VOLUNTEERS. When the Naval Volunteer Act passed in 1873 there were several gentlemen in this city—at the head of whom was Milton Lewis—who felt a desire to establish a Naval Volunteer corps here. They petitioned the Admiralty, who not only granted their prayer, but gave them permission to drill on board the *Dædalus*, the headquarters of the Naval Reserve. The corps commenced with the modest number of 24 men, but was soon placed on a recognised footing by the appointment on the 19th January, 1874, of Commander Roberts as officer instructor. For some reason, however, which was not quite apparent, the corps did not succeed, and it had very nearly come to a premature end when Admiral, then Captain, Dunn, R.N., undertook the command, and that gave a fresh impetus to the corps, and on the 6th of August, 1874, the Lords of the Admiralty met the Mayor and citizens in the Guildhall, and elicited their approval of the establishment of the corps. The support then promised by the Mayor, C. J. Thomas, on behalf of the citizens, and by W. A. F. Powell, the Master, on behalf of the Merchant Venturers, has been ever since accorded the corps, which has enjoyed the confidence and support of the citizens. On the 9th of Oct., 1875, two cutters were given to the corps by the Government, which added much to the interest the members took in the training. On the 24th of March, 1876, the Admiral-Superintendent of Naval Reserve inspected the corps for the first time, and expressed himself well pleased with the progress made. For some years past, members of the corps have gone to sea in one of her Majesty's gunboats for a week's cruise and gun practice. The present strength is 225. The Swansea corps, numbering about 200, is attached to the Bristol brigade, making a total of 425. The average number of drills for each man during the past year was 56, in addition to the gunboat cruising. On the 21st of June, 1884, Lady Brassey presented the corps with new colours. R. Betton Sayce, R.N., commander.

Wards. (*See* "Council," "Aldermen," "Municipal Elections.")

Water Supply. Bristol is now chiefly supplied with water from Chewton Mendip, East Harptree, Barrow and Chelvey, in Somerset, by the Bristol Water Works Company, which was incorporated in 1846. The chief source of supply is 16 miles distant from the city. The storage reservoirs at Barrow are 66½ acres in extent, with a depth of from 20 to 25 feet. The capacity of the reservoirs is 53,300,000 cubic feet, or 332,000,000 gallons. The water is conveyed by means of aqueducts and tunnels as far as

Barrow, whence it flows in pipes, nearly 100 miles in length, to all parts of the city. There are branch reservoirs in Oakfield road and on Durdham down, into which the water is pumped for the use of the high level districts. The company has of late extended its operations and increased its supply by the purchase of other springs. The supply is ample and excellent in quality, as the following analysis by the city analyst shows:—

	Grains.
Carbonate of lime	14·55
Sulphate of lime	3·60
Chloride of calcium	0·63
Chloride of sodium	0·06
Chloride of magnesium	a trace
Peroxide of iron	0·18
Silica	0·06
Organic matter	0·12
Total contents per gallon	19·20

Hardness, as estimated by Clarke's test, 18·3 deg.

The hardness of the water, which is moderate, being chiefly due to the carbonate of lime, which deposits on boiling, is well adapted for domestic purposes; but its chief point of commendation, in a sanitary sense, is the fact of its being derived from sources above the reach of human contamination, and having thus the seeds of disease contained in human excreta excluded from it. No case of enteric fever has ever been traced to this water, and the rate of mortality from diarrhœa in the city has for some years been the lowest in England. (See "Mortality, Rate of.")

The revenue from water rates for the year 1883 was £70,946 4s. 6d., being an increase of £1,932 5s. 5d. over that of the previous year.

The company have in progress works for bringing from the Mendip hills the waters of the Sherborne springs. This supply, which is of excellent quality, will be collected at its source and conveyed by iron pipes of 21 inches diameter, partly laid in tunnel, a distance of 13 miles direct into the heart of the city. During the great drought of 1864 the minimum daily yield of the Sherborne springs was one million gallons. The aqueducts, tunnels, and iron pipes by which the water is conveyed, and the reservoirs, are monuments of engineering skill, and well worthy of a visit. Before the company was formed the citizens obtained their water from various local springs, and it was customary in many parishes to trace the supply to its source once a year.

Weights & Measures. The office for stamping and adjusting weights and measures is in Bridewell street. The fees received for the year ending 25th March, 1883, as per the city treasurer's accounts, were as follow:—Fees on stamping, £247 5s. 7d.; fees on adjusting, £464 10s. 2d.; total, £711 15s. 9d. Thomas Crew, inspector.

Whitson, John. (See "Monuments;" also "Schools," sub-heading "Red Maids' School.")

William III. Statue. (See "Open Spaces," sub-heading "Queen Square.")

Women's Suffrage. The Bristol committee is the chief centre in the West of England of this society, which has for its object to obtain the extension of the Parliamentary franchise to women who possess the qualifications which entitle men to vote, and was formed very early in the progress of the movement. The Bristol committee originated in a meeting at the house of Recorder Hill. Professor F. W. Newman was its first secretary, and he both wrote and lectured on behalf of the movement. Most of those whose names were connected with the committee still continue to work for the movement, but are now aided by a larger committee, a body of correspondents, and subscribers in many places of the West of England and South Wales. On the death of Lady Amberley, Lady Anna Gore Langton became president. Many will remember the speeches she gave both in Bristol and London on behalf of a cause of which she used to say, "I feel the demand is *just*, and that is why I am its advocate." Since her death the society has not elected another president, but amongst its vice-presidents are many leading citizens of Bristol and Members of Parliament for the West of England. The first large meetings of the Bristol society were held in 1871, when Mrs. Fawcett gave a lecture in the Large Colston hall, Professor Newman presiding, and in 1873, when Lady Amberley presided at a meeting in the Broadmead rooms. Since then many meetings have been held, the largest being a meeting of women only, held in the Colston hall, November 3rd, 1880, Mrs. Beddoe in the chair, when it was calculated that 3,000 women were present. The movement is now under the Parliamentary leadership of Hugh Mason, member for Ashton-under-Lyne. The organ of the society is the *Women's Suffrage Journal*, edited by Miss Becker in Manchester, and may be obtained at any of the society's offices. The office of the Bristol branch is at 20 Park street. The following are its officers: Rev. Urijah R. Thomas, chairman of committee; Mrs. Ashworth Hallett and Miss Sturge, hon. secs.; Mrs. Grenfell, treasurer; Miss Helen Blackburn, secretary; Miss Maria Colby, assistant secretary.

Working Women's Association,

formed for the consideration and discussion of the social position of women. Social gatherings take place occasionally at Hamilton's rooms, Park street. Alan Greenwell, president.

Workmen's Clubs.

In several of the poor and thickly populated parishes are clubs of this description. (*See* "Clubs.")

Young Men's Christian Association,

St. James' square, was formed January 17th, 1853. The total area of ground on which the building and gymnasium stand is about 1,500 square yards. The front is protected by a palisade. The rooms approached by the entrance on the left are chiefly occupied by the Sunday School Union (*see* "Schools"); the entrance on the right is the main one to the building, and opens into a spacious hall, on the left of which is the secretary's office and library, and immediately opposite on entering is a staircase leading to the reading-room, coffee-room, and reference library on the first floor. The lecture-room and class-rooms are on the second landing. The home is situated on the right of the institute. Amongst the religious agencies of the institute may be mentioned the Sunday afternoon Bible-class, mission work, daily mid-day meeting for prayer, Saturday evening young men's evangelistic meeting, and the weekly meetings for employés. Of the intellectual resources of the association, the libraries, both circulating and reference, the reading-rooms and lectures, during the winter months, form the principal. The social aspects of the association consist of the home, soirées, &c., and the recreation of a rambling club, gymnasium (*see* "Gymnasiums"), geology class, cricket club, swimming, boating, &c. The institute is open from 9 a.m. to 10.30 p.m. Terms of subscription: Over 20 years of age, 10/6 per annum; under 20 years, 5/-; gymnasium, 5/- extra. Subscribers of one guinea are entitled to all the privileges of the institution.

William Day Wills was the first president, and was succeeded at his decease, in 1865, by George Thomas. The adjoining portion of the premises, No. 4 St. James' square, was rented; and, after an outlay of £300 for furnishing and repairs, was opened on June 14th, 1853, a large meeting being afterwards held in the Broadmead rooms. In the year 1863 those premises were purchased for the sum of £700, including the redemption of the land-tax and purchase of ground-rent. Increased accommodation became needful, and in 1872 the addition of the adjoining premises, No. 5 St. James' square, was made, and alterations and improvements were effected at an expenditure of £2,500 during the presidency of R. Charlton, who was succeeded in that office by Wm. Terrell. The want of an association hall had long been felt; but the way for its erection did not open until the visit of D. L. Moody and Ira D. Sankey, of the United States of America, to this city in October, 1882, when an appeal was made, and the sum of £3,000 contributed for the purpose. The memorial stone was laid on the 4th July, 1883, by Joseph Storrs Fry, president of the association, and it was formally opened on June 30th, 1884.

The new hall measures 97 feet in length by 45 feet in breadth, with a height of 35 feet. Sitting accommodation is provided for about 1,400 persons, while 2,000 can find standing room at a mass meeting. The structure is designed in the Italian style, and the material employed for the walling is best red Cattybrook moulded brick with terra cotta enrichments, including an ornamental frieze. The roof is covered with patent lock-jaw tiles, and the coved ceiling is of plaster panelling. The ventilation is carefully arranged for. In the central turret a large pneumatic ventilator is capable of extracting sufficient air without admitting any downward draught. Flues built along both sides of the hall on the principle of Tobin's pipes supply abundance of fresh air. The flooring is of pitch-pine block parqueterie, and the hall seated with chairs. There are windows at the ends and sides of the hall; but as the light is somewhat obstructed by adjacent premises, the roof is freely pierced with skylights. Gas stars give the hall artificial illumination. The hall was opened on the 30th of June, 1884. T. Jameson, secretary.

In addition to the foregoing association, there are several denominational societies in connection with the various churches and chapels of the city. One of the oldest and strongest is that belonging to Arley chapel, which was established in 1876, and numbers about 50 members. Rev. J. C. Gray, president; W. R. Chapman, secretary.

Young Women's Christian Association and Home, founded in 1861. Its objects are to provide a comfortable and christian home for young women engaged in business or in tuition, and it supplies a place of resort, especially in the evenings, for a large number of young women. On Sundays a Bible-class is held at three o'clock. Classes during the winter session for singing, French, and other branches of study are arranged for as required by the members. The rooms of the association are opened all day, and closed at 10.30 p.m. A subscription of 2/- per quarter admits to the library, reading-room, use of piano, and all other meetings held in connection with the association, except the secular classes, for which the terms are very moderate. The lodgings are 2/6 per week, including attendance, gas, and coal; also entire or partial board on reasonable terms, if required. The work of the institution was formerly carried on at 3 King square, but now at 18 Royal promenade (see "Homes"). Miss Savill, treasurer and secretary.

Zigzag is a steep, winding footpath cut in the St. Vincent's rocks, a short distance from the Suspension bridge, and leads from the Hotwells to the summit of Clifton down.

Zoological Gardens, Clifton, are situated in the most delightful and frequented part of Clifton. The first report of the society was published in 1836, and stated that "in the summer of 1835 it was resolved that a society be formed, which shall consist of such persons as shall become members thereof by the payment of the sum of £25, and that the person so paying shall be considered the proprietor of one share in the property and effects of the society, and that the whole number of shares shall not exceed 500. For the furtherance of the purposes of the society, a provisional committee was appointed, which proceeded to purchase a piece of land in the neighbourhood of Clifton, to obtain plans for its adaptation to the purposes of a zoological garden, and to execute those plans with as much dispatch as was consistent with the season of the year and a careful regard to the economy which the existing extent of their immediately available funds rendered advisable. How far they have succeeded in their labours will best be seen by an inspection of the garden and examination of their accounts."

The committee purchased 12 acres of land from Francis Adams for the sum of £3,456 10s., and desired to form not only a zoological society, but also a botanical garden. The first balance-sheet was issued on the 7th May, 1836. In its early days the gardens do not appear to have been able to meet its current expenses without the aid of *fêtes*, for as early as 1846-7 this plan of obtaining "gate money" was adopted. The first horticultural *fêtes* were held in 1855, and were "marked by universal approbation." These were continued yearly till 1864, when, in consequence of the visit of the Bath and West of England Agricultural Show to Bristol, it did not take place. In 1865 they were resumed, but ceased altogether in 1867. In 1868 the Rajah of Mysore presented to the committee an elephant, which, notwithstanding it was a gift to the society, cost in transit to the gardens £163 10s. In July, 1876, an unfortunate accident occurred during a display of fireworks by the falling of a rocket-stick into the eye of a man standing outside the gates. He eventually lost the sight of both eyes, and the committee in some degree compensated him by the payment of £500.

The principal, or northern, entrance to the gardens is from the verge of the Downs, and immediately leads to the Great terrace, which forms an exceedingly pleasant promenade, the borders and adjacent plateau being studded with choice trees and shrubs from various climes, as also with some of Nature's gayest flowers, which give to the *tout ensemble* a charming appearance; while arbours and seats are judiciously placed in various parts, forming pleasant and cool retreats for the exercises required for health and for pleasure. There is also an entrance from the south in College road.

The feeding hours of the carnivora vary from 3 to 7.30 p.m., according to the season and weather, of which notice is given at the entrance gates.

An agreeable feature to the gardens is the artistically and tastefully laid out lake, the borders here and there being adorned with choice shrubs. In the centre is placed a fountain, which, when in full play, has a very pleasing effect. Round the margin of the lake has been formed a walk, which not only improves its appearance, but also very materially adds to the comfort of those who enjoy a promenade round the water and take an interest in the various fowls which disport themselves on its surface. The gardens also have a refreshment pavilion, which is open daily, an orchestra for music, giant strides for children, ladies' cloak-room, &c. The terms of subscription are:—A whole family residing in one house, £1 1s. per annum; the whole family of a shareholder, 10/6 per annum; one person per annum, 10/6. Special rates for schools, &c. J. T. Jackson, secretary.